Les Invalides. *See p156.*

Time Out Guides Limited
Universal House
251 Tottenham Court Road
London W1T 7AB
Tel + 44 (0)20 7813 3000
Fax + 44 (0)20 7813 6001
Email guides@timeout.com
www.timeout.com

Contributors

Introduction Simon Cropper. **History** Peterjon Cresswell, Simon Cropper (*Love hurts* Rebecca Hirschfield; *No more heroes* Peterjon Cresswell; *The heir apparent?* John Shandy Watson). **Paris Today** Richard Woodruff (*So wrong, Marianne?* Peterjon Cresswell). **Paris Tomorrow** Richard Woodruff. **Where to Stay** Tina Isaac (*Reet boutique* Heather Stimmler-Hall). **Sightseeing** Simon Cropper, Alison Culliford, Natasha Edwards (*Scandale!* Peterjon Cresswell; *Tours* Oliver Brock; *House man* Natasha Edwards; *Cemetery greats* Simon Cropper, Natalie Whittle; *Writer way* Alison Culliford; *Chirac's grand projet* David Nowell-Smith; *Paris against the clock* Natalie Whittle). **The Louvre** Alison Culliford, Natasha Edwards. **Restaurants** Rosa Jackson. **Cafés & Bars** Peterjon Cresswell. **Shops & Services** Rosa Jackson, Kate van den Boogert (*Forward marché!* Rosa Jackson). **Festivals & Events** Simon Cropper. **Cabaret, Circus & Comedy** Anna Brooke. **Children** Ricardo Bloch. **Dance** Marie-Laure Ferreyra. **Film** Simon Cropper. **Galleries** Natasha Edwards. **Gay & Lesbian** Toby Rose. **Music** Chris Moore, Stephen Mudge (*The next big sing?* David McKenna). **Nightlife** Lucia Scazzocchio. **Sport & Fitness** Peterjon Cresswell, Heather Stimmler-Hall, Patrick Welch, Richard Woodruff (*Rolling, rolling, rolling...* Dora Whitaker; *One cool pool* Simon Cropper). **Theatre** Catherine Bredeson. **Trips Out of Town** Peterjon Cresswell, Simon Cropper, John Shandy Watson. **Directory** Simon Cropper, David Nowell-Smith (*Wi-Fi, where find?* Patrick Welch; *The anglo frequency* Richard Woodruff).

Maps JS Graphics (john@jsgraphics.co.uk), except pages 415, 416.

Photography by Héloise Bergman, except: page 10 Giraudon/Bridgeman Art Library; page 15 The Art Archive/National Gallery London; page 18 The Art Archive/Dagli Orti; pages 20, 22 akg-images; page 21 Hulton-Deutsch Collection/Corbis; page 23 Bettmann/Corbis; page 25 AFP/Getty Images; page 55 Grégoire Gardette; page 152 Musée du Quai Branly, Paris/Nicolas Borel and Hugues Dubois; page 168 Will Fulford-Jones; pages 181, 182, 198, 199, 201, 204, 210 Britta Jaschinski; pages 187, 223, 226, 227, 230, 231, 256, 321, 333, 346, 347, 352 Karl Blackwell; page 190 Barry J Holmes; page 213 Tony Gibson; pages 288, 290 Agathe Poupeney; page 294 Alain Goustard, EMOC; page 314 Steve Brown; page 327 Pierre-Yves Brunaud; page 349 Art Directors & Trip; pages 354, 355 (c) Parc Astérix 2005. The following images were provided by the featured establishments/artists: pages 26, 37.

The Editor would like to thank Karen Albrecht, Yuko Aso, Nicole de Fouchécour, Michel Dietz, Jan Fuscoe, Sarah Guy, Jiayi Huang, Sam Le Quesne, Poppy McPherson, Catherine Ruggieri, Claudia Schall, Thierry Sayegh, Denys Viollet, Helen Whyle and all contributors to previous editions of *Time Out Paris*, whose work forms the basis for parts of this book.

Contents

Introduction

'Paris sera toujours Paris', warbled Maurice Chevalier, whereas Rick did his hard-boiled best to comfort Ilsa with the notion that they would 'always have Paris'; and Oscar Wilde reckoned Paris was the place good Americans go to when they die. Mention the French capital, it seems, and forever-ness – 'always', 'toujours' – is never far behind.

Well, it's hardly surprising. When was a city so often filmed, photographed, fêted, painted, hymned, sung about, written up, talked up, dreamed of, reported, coveted? Its museums and monuments are household names all over the world, its way of life – something to do with long lunches, red wine, café terraces, cigarette smoke, illicit liaisons – a byword. Paris? It's been around forever.

And yet familiarity poses a challenge: to see the eternal clichés for what they are – nice things, but far less than the whole picture. In our view, you should take Paris as you might a detective novel, riddled with all-too-obvious clues. In other words, look again, and look harder. Even on your first visit, you'll have a strong mental picture of the place; try, if at all possible, to erase it. Try to stop thinking of Paris as a tourist destination. And if you don't get to see Sacré Coeur at close quarters on this trip, don't worry: it will still be there next time.

Instead, stand still and look about you. Shove the map to the bottom of your bag and follow your nose. Venture out from the monument-heavy centre to the outer districts – the villagey parts of the 13th arrondissement, say, or buzzing Belleville at the junction of the 10th, 11th, 19th and 20th. And another piece of advice: if at all possible, even haltingly, even in pidgin French, *talk to the locals*. In most cases, especially in the already-convivial setting of bars and cafés, Parisians are much friendlier than their reputation for aloofness suggests. Do all this, and you'll take home memories and knowledge that your friends and colleagues will never have.

Most of the writers of this guide have lived in Paris for years, and each will tell you that new finds and surprises are a weekly, if not daily occurrence. 'J'ai deux amours', sang Josephine Baker, born in Missouri and resident for most of her life in the French capital: 'mon pays et Paris'. Two loves – home and Paris. You won't have to spend much time in this city before you see what she meant.

ABOUT TIME OUT CITY GUIDES

This is the 14th edition of *Time Out Paris*, one of an expanding series of Time Out guides produced by the people behind the successful listings magazines in London, New York and Chicago. Our guides are written by resident experts who have striven to provide you with the most up-to-date information you'll need to explore the city or read up on its background, whether you're a local or a first-time visitor.

THE LIE OF THE LAND

To make both book and city easier to navigate, we've divided Paris into areas. They are: the Islands; Right Bank (The Louvre, Palais-Royal and Les Halles; Opéra & Grands Boulevards; the Champs-Elysées & western Paris; Montmartre & Pigalle; Beaubourg & the Marais; Bastille & eastern Paris; North-east Paris) and Left Bank (The Latin Quarter & the 13th; St-Germain-des-Prés & Odéon; Montparnasse & beyond; The 7th & the 15th). These are our breakdowns, and are not the official *arrondissements* you will see signposted around town – although every address listed here gives its arrondissment number. We've also included map references that point to our street maps at the back of the guide. For further information on getting around, *see p364*.

ESSENTIAL INFORMATION

For all the practical information you might need for visiting the city, including visa and customs information, advice on disabled facilities and access, emergency telephone numbers, a list of useful websites and the lowdown on the local transport network, turn to the Directory at the back of this guide. It starts on p364.

THE LOWDOWN ON THE LISTINGS

We've tried to make this book as easy to use as possible. Addresses, phone numbers, bus information, opening times and admission prices are all included in the listings. However, businesses can change their arrangements at any time. Before you go out of your way, we'd strongly advise you to phone ahead to check opening times and other particulars. While every effort and care has been made to ensure

The **Louvre**. *See p80.*

the accuracy of the information contained in this guide, the publishers cannot accept responsibility for any errors it may contain.

PRICES AND PAYMENT

Prices are given in euros, and have been verified with each venue or business. We've noted whether shops, hotels, restaurants and other establishments accept credit cards or not, but have only listed the major cards – American Express (AmEx), Diners Club (DC), MasterCard (MC) and Visa (V). Many businesses will also accept other cards. Note that the Visa card is referred to locally as *la Carte Bleue*.

The prices we've listed in this guide should be treated as guidelines, not gospel. If prices vary wildly from those we've quoted, ask whether there's a good reason. If not, go elsewhere – then please let us know. We aim to give the best and most up-to-date advice, so we want to know if you've been badly treated or overcharged.

Advertisers

We would like to stress that no establishment has been included in this guide because it has advertised in any of our publications and no payment of any kind has influenced any review. The opinions given in this book are those of Time Out writers and entirely independent.

TELEPHONE NUMBERS

The country code for France is 33. All Paris telephone numbers begin with 01. If dialling Paris from abroad, drop the initial 0. If calling within France, dial all ten digits. A handful of numbers listed begin with 08 – these can be free, at low rate or high rate. For details, check www.agence.francetelecom.com. For more information on telephones and codes, *see p383.*

MAPS

We've included a series of indexed colour street maps to the city at the back of this guide – they start on p402 – and, where possible, a grid reference for each address given in the guide. The maps now also pinpoint specific locations of hotels (❶), restaurants and cafés (❶) and bars (❶). There's an overview map on p398 and a Métro map on p416.

LET US KNOW WHAT YOU THINK

We hope you enjoy *Time Out Paris*, and we'd like to know what you think of it. We welcome tips for places that you consider we should include in future editions and take notice of your criticism of our choices. You can email us at guides@timeout.com.

There is an online version of this book, along with guides to over 45 other international cities, at **www.timeout.com**.

In Context

The Louvre. *See p80.*

The execution of **St Denis**. *See p11.*

History

From the Romans to the 'Raffarindum', Paris has seen it all.

The earliest settlers seem to have arrived in Paris around 120,000 years ago. One of them lost a flint spear-tip on the hill we now call Montmartre, and the still dangerous-looking weapon is to be seen today in the Stone Age collection at the **Musée des Antiquités Nationales** (*see p176*). There was a Stone Age weapons factory under present-day Châtelet, and the redevelopment of Bercy in the 1990s managed to unearth ten Neolithic canoes, five of which are now high and dry in the **Musée Carnavalet** (*see p110*). The fluctuating level of the river probably forced people to dwell on one of the area's many hills.

By 250 BC, a Celtic tribe known as the Parisii had put the place on the map, and given the modern capital its name. The Parisii were river traders, wealthy enough to mint gold coins. The **Musée de la Monnaie** (*see p149*) has an extensive collection of their small change. Their most important *oppidum*, a primitive fortified town, was located on an island in the Seine, which is generally thought to have been what its today's Ile de la Cité.

ROMAN PARIS

A superb strategic location and the capacity to generate hard cash were guaranteed to attract the attention of the Romans. Julius Caesar arrived in southern Gaul as proconsul in 58 BC and soon used the pretext of dealing with invading barbarians to stick his Roman nose into the affairs of northern Gaul. The Gauls didn't appreciate the attention, and in 54 BC the Eburones from the Meuse valley rebelled against the Romans. Other tribes joined in: in 52 BC the Parisii rose up with the rest of Gaul.

Caesar had his hands full dealing with the great Gaul marauder Vercingetorix, so he sent his general Labienus with four legions and part of the cavalry to secure the passage of the Seine at Lutetia, as they called Paris. The Gauls were massacred, although a contingent of Parisii escaped to be defeated later with Vercingetorix at the Battle of Alesia. The subsequent surrender of Vercingetorix left the Paris region and the rest of Gaul in Roman hands. Roman Lutetia was a prosperous town of around 8,000 inhabitants. Apart from centrally heated villas and a temple to Jupiter on the main island (remains of both are visible in the **Crypte Archéologique**; *see p77*), there were the sumptuous baths (now the **Musée National du Moyen Age**; *see p138*) and the 15,000-seater **Arènes de Lutèce** (*see p145*).

CHRISTIANITY

Christianity arrived in around 250 AD in the shape of Denis of Athens, who went on to become the first Bishop of Paris. Legend has it that when he was decapitated by Valerian on Mons Martis, the mount of the martyrs (today better known as Montmartre), Denis picked up his head and walked with it to what is now St-Denis, to be buried there. The event is depicted in Henri Bellechose's glorious *Retable de Saint-Denis*, to be found exhibited in the **Louvre** (*see pp80-87*).

Gaul was still a tempting prize. Waves of barbarian invaders – Alamans, Francs and others – began crossing the Rhine from 275 onwards. They sacked more than 60 cities in Gaul, including Lutetia, where the population was decimated and the buildings on the Montagne Ste-Geneviève were pillaged and burned. The bedraggled survivors used the rubble to build a rampart around the Ile de la Cité and to fortify the forum, although few citizens remained in the shadow of its walls.

It was at this time that the city was renamed Paris. Protected by the Seine and the new fortifications, its main role now was as a rear base for the Roman armies defending Gaul, and it was here in 360 that Julian was proclaimed emperor by his troops. In the same year, the first Catholic council of Paris was held, condemning the Arian branch of Christianity as heresy. The city's inhabitants, however, had concerns more pressing than theology.

Around 450, with the arrival of the Huns in the region, the people of Paris prepared once again to flee. They were dissuaded by a feisty woman named Geneviève, who was famed in the Christian community for her piety. Seeing the walls of the city defended against him, no less a pillager than Attila the Hun turned back and was defeated soon afterwards.

CLOVIS

In 464 Paris managed to resist another siege, this time by the Francs under Childeric. However, by 486, after a further blockade

lasting ten years, Geneviève had no option but to surrender the city to Childeric's successor, Clovis, who went on to conquer most of Gaul and founded the Merovingian dynasty. He chose Paris as capital of his new kingdom, and it stayed that way until the seventh century, in spite of various conflicts among his successors.

Under the influence of his wife, Clotilde, Clovis converted to Christianity. He founded and was buried in the basilica of the Saints Apôtres, later rededicated to Ste Geneviève when the saviour and future patron saint of Paris was interred there in 512. All that remains of the basilica today is a single pillar in the grounds of the modern Lycée Henri IV; but there's a shrine dedicated to Ste Geneviève and some relics in the fine Gothic church of **St-Etienne-du-Mont** (*see p143*) next door.

Geneviève and Clovis had set a trend. The Ile de la Cité was still the heart of the city, but, under the Merovingians, the Left Bank was the up-and-coming area for fashion-conscious Christians, with 11 churches built here in the period (against only four on the Right Bank and one on the Ile de la Cité). Not everyone was sold on the joys of city living, though. From 614 onwards, the Merovingian kings preferred the *banlieue* at Clichy, or wandered the kingdom trying to keep rebellious nobles in check. By the time one of the rebels, Pippin 'the Short', decided to do away with the last Merovingian in 751, Paris was starting to look passé.

Pippin's son, Charlemagne, built his capital at Aix-la-Chapelle, while his successors, known as the Carolingian dynasty, moved from palace to palace, consuming the local production.

> **'The Norsemen sacked the city, and Charles II had to cough up 7,000 pounds of silver to get them to leave.'**

Paris, meanwhile, was doing quite nicely for itself as a centre for Christian learning, and the city had grown to house a population of 20,000 by the beginning of the ninth century. This was the high point in the popularity and political power of the great abbeys like St-Germain-des-Prés, where transcription of the Latin classics was helping to preserve much of Europe's Roman cultural heritage. Power in the Paris region was exercised by the Counts of Paris.

THE VIKINGS

In 845 the Vikings appeared before the walls. Unopposed, the Norsemen sacked the city, and King Charles II, 'the Bald', had to cough up 7,000 pounds of silver to get them to leave. Recognising a soft touch when they saw one, the Vikings returned to sack the city repeatedly between 856 and 869, burning churches with heathen abandon. Better late than never, Charles organised the defence of the city. Fortified bridges were built – the Grand Pont over the northern branch of the Seine and the Petit Pont over the southern, blocking the passage of the Viking ships further upstream.

In 885, Gozlin, Bishop of Paris, had just finished repairing the Roman walls when the Vikings showed up once again; this time they found the city defended against them. After a siege lasting a year, King Charles III, 'the Fat', arrived at the head of an army but, deciding that discretion is indeed the better part of valour, handed over 700 pounds of silver and politely invited the Norsemen to pillage some other part of his kingdom. The Count of Paris, Eudes, having performed valiantly in the siege of 885-86, was offered the royal crown when Charles was deposed in 888. Although the Carolingians recovered the throne after his death in 898, Eudes' great-nephew, Hugues Capet, was elected King of France in 987, adding what remained of the Carolingian dominions to his territories around Paris.

PARIS FINDS ITS FEET

Under the Capetian dynasty, although Paris was now at the heart of the royal domains, the city did not yet dominate the kingdom. Robert 'the Pious', king from 996 to 1031, stayed more often in Paris than his father, restoring the royal palace on the Ile de la Cité, while Henri I (1031-60) issued more of his charters in Paris than in Orléans. In 1112 the abbey of **St-Denis** (*see p172*) replaced St-Benoît-sur-Loire as principal monastery, so confirming the pre-eminence of Paris over Orléans.

Paris itself still consisted of little more than the Ile de la Cité and small settlements under the protection of the abbeys on each bank. On the Left Bank, royal largesse helped to rebuild the abbeys of St-Germain-des-Prés, St-Marcel and Ste-Geneviève, although it took more than 150 years for the destruction wrought there by the Vikings to be fully repaired. The Right Bank, where mooring was easier, prospered from river commerce, and three boroughs grew up around the abbeys of St-Germain-l'Auxerrois, St-Martin-des-Champs and St-Gervais. Bishop Sully of Paris began building the cathedral of Notre-Dame in 1163.

The growing complexity of government during the 12th century, and the departure of kings on crusade, meant that the administration tended to stay in the Palais de la Cité and the royal treasure in the fortress of the Temple (built by the newly founded order of the Templars). The wisdom of this approach was confirmed by the disaster of Fréteval in 1194, where King Philippe-Auguste was defeated by Richard the Lionheart, losing much of his treasure and his archives in the process.

This minor hiccup aside, the reign of Philippe-Auguste (1180-1223) was a turning point in the history of Paris. Before, the city was a confused patchwork of royal, ecclesiastical and feudal authorities, exercising various powers, rights and privileges. Keen to raise revenues, Philippe favoured the growth of the guilds, especially the butchers, drapers, furriers, haberdashers and merchants: so began the rise of the bourgeoisie.

He also ordered the building of the first permanent market buildings at Les Halles, and a new city wall, first on the Right Bank to protect the commercial heart of Paris, and later on the Left Bank. At the western end, Philippe built a castle, the Louvre, to defend the road from the ever-menacing Normandy, whose duke was also King of England.

A GOLDEN AGE

Paris was now the principal residence of the king and the uncontested capital of France. No longer threatened by foreign invasion, the city found itself overrun by a new and altogether deadlier menace that exists to this day: lawyers. And barristers, bailiffs, prosecutors, sergeants, accountants, judges, clerks and all the bureaucratic trappings of royal government.

> **'Masters and students of the Sorbonne were already gaining a reputation for rowdiness.'**

To accommodate the rapidly growing royal administration, the Palais de la Cité, site and symbol of power for the previous thousand years, was remodelled and enlarged. Work was begun by Louis IX (later St Louis) in the 1240s, and later continued under Philippe IV ('le Bel'). This architectural complex, of which the **Ste-Chapelle** and the **Conciergerie** (for both, *see p77*) can still be seen today, was inaugurated with great pomp at Pentecost 1313. Philippe invited Edward II of England and his queen, Isabelle of France. The English were impressed: they soon came back for a long stay.

The palace was quickly filled with functionaries, so the king spent as much of his time as he could outside Paris at the royal castles of **Fontainebleau** (*see p347*) and, especially, **Vincennes** (*see p174*). The needs of the plenipotentiaries left behind to run the kingdom were met by a rapidly growing city population, piled into rather less chic buildings.

Paris was also reinforcing its identity as a major religious centre: as well as the local clergy and dozens of religious orders, the city was home to the masters and students of the university of the **Sorbonne** (established in 1253; *see p144*), who were already gaining a reputation for rowdiness. An influx of scholars from all over Europe gave the city a cultural and intellectual cachet it was never to lose.

By 1328 Paris was home to approximately 200,000 inhabitants, making it the most populous city in Europe. However, that year was also notable for being the last of the medieval golden age: the dynasty of Capetian kings spluttered to an inglorious halt when Charles IV died without an heir. The English quickly claimed the throne for the young Edward III, the son of Philippe IV's daughter. Refusing to recognise his descent through the female line, the late king's cousin, Philippe de Valois, claimed the French crown as Philippe VI. So began the Hundred Years War between France and England – a war which in fact would go on for 116 years.

Love hurts

Forbidden sex, separation, castration and undying lust give the story of the most famous star-crossed lovers of the Middle Ages all the ingredients of a damn good modern potboiler. On top of that, the tale offers a window on the intellectual pursuits and social mores of the time.

Abélard (a nickname meaning 'honeyed-mouth', given for his smooth dialectical skills) was a minor Breton noble, whose wandering brought him in 1100 to Paris. Here, at the embryonic University of Paris – then primitive schools that met in the Notre-Dame cloister – debate raged over the nature of universal ideas. Realism, drawing on Aristotle, proclaimed the actual existence of general ideas like 'man'; nominalism claimed that general ideas are just verbal abstractions. Abélard found fame with conceptualism, his synthesis of the two. He left his former master, William of Champeaux, a realist, and set up a rival school at the autonomous abbey of Ste-Geneviève.

Fame brought arrogance, as Abélard explains: 'I began to think myself the only philosopher in the world, with nothing to fear from anyone, and so I yielded to the lusts of the flesh'. He met 18-year-old Héloïse, the precocious niece of Canon Fulbert, and a rare medieval woman of letters. Abélard persuaded her uncle to accommodate him (marked by a plaque at 9 quai aux Fleurs). Thus: 'We were united, first under one roof, then in heart; and so with our lessons as a pretext we abandoned ourselves entirely to love.' Even his love poems, sung by his students, did not tip Fulbert off, until Héloïse became pregnant and her lover secretly removed her to Brittany. Then tragedy struck.

Abélard promised Fulbert to marry her in secret (the Church was only just beginning to forbid marriage within its higher orders, but a publicised marriage would ruin his career). Héloïse maintained that marriage would not subdue her uncle's rage, and argued that matrimony would not only dishonour Abélard but hinder his studies. Citing classical philosophy, she declared that she would rather be his mistress, bound to him by true love, but was unable to persuade Abélard. After the lovers' son, Astrolabe, was born and entrusted to Abélard's sister, Fulbert spread word of the secret marriage. Abélard spirited his wife away to a convent at Argenteuil. Fulbert, suspecting Abélard was ridding himself of Héloïse for good, immediately had the philosopher castrated.

Abélard, 'readier to perform whatever can be honourably done by setting me wholly free from the heavy yoke of carnal desire', pursued a distinguished career as a philosopher and abbot. Héloïse took vows out of love for him and ultimately became a renowned abbess, but their correspondence reveals the depth of her torment: 'Remember, I implore you, what I have done, and think how much you owe me. While I enjoyed with you the pleasures of the flesh, many were uncertain whether I was prompted by love or lust; but now the end is proof of the beginning. I have finally denied myself every pleasure in obedience to your will, kept nothing for myself in order to prove that now, even more, I am yours.'

Separated in body but never entirely in spirit, Abélard and Héloïse were reunited in death, at the Paraclete, the oratory-cum-convent that Abélard had established and given to Héloïse and her fellow nuns.

In 1817, after a circuitous route, their remains came to rest in a neo-Gothic tomb at Père-Lachaise cemetery (*see p130* **Cemetery Greats**), in peaceful communal repose by the south-east corner adjoining rue du Repos.

TROUBLES AND STRIFE

To make matters worse, the Black Death (bubonic plague) ravaged Europe from the 1340s. Those not zapped by the plague had to contend with food shortages, ever-increasing taxes, riots, repression, currency devaluations and marauding mercenaries. Meanwhile, in Paris, the honeymoon period for the king and the bourgeoisie was coming to an end. Rich and populous, Paris was expected to bear the brunt of the war burden; and as defeat followed defeat (notably the disaster at Crécy in August 1346) the bourgeoisie and people of the city were increasingly exasperated by the futility of the sacrifices they were making for the hideously expensive war. To fund the conflict, King Jean II tried to introduce new tax laws – without success. When the king was captured by the English at Poitiers in 1356, his problems passed to his 18-year-old son, Charles.

The Etats Généraux, consultant body to the throne, was summoned to the royal palace on the Ile de la Cité to discuss the country's woes. The teenage king was besieged with angry demands for reform from the bourgeoisie, particularly from Etienne Marcel, then provost of the local merchants. Marcel seized control of Paris and began a bitter power struggle with the crown; in 1357, fearing widespread revolt, Charles fled to Compiègne. But as he ran, he had Paris blockaded.

Marcel called on the peasants, who were also raging against taxes, but they were quickly crushed. He then called on Charles 'the Bad' of Navarre, ally to the English, but his arrival in Paris made many of Marcel's supporters nervous. On 31 July 1358, Marcel was murdered and the revolution was over. As a safeguard, the returning Charles built a new stronghold to protect Paris: the Bastille.

By 1420, following the French defeat at Agincourt, Paris was in English hands; in 1431 Henry VI of England was crowned King of France in Notre-Dame. He didn't last. Five years later, Henry and his army had been driven back to Calais by the Valois king, Charles VII. Charles owed his grasp on power to Jeanne d'Arc, who led the victorious French in the Battle of Orléans, only to be betrayed by her compatriots, who decided she was getting too big for her boots. She was captured and sold to the English, who had her burnt as a witch.

By 1436 Paris was once again the capital of France. But the nation had been nearly bled dry by war, and was still divided politically, with powerful regional rulers across France continuing to threaten the monarchy. Outside of the French borders, the ambitions of the Austrian Habsburg dynasty represented a serious threat. In this general atmosphere of instability, disputes over trade, religion and taxation were all simmering dangerously in the political background.

RENAISSANCE AND REFORMATION

In the closing decades of the 15th century, the restored Valois monarchs sought to reassert their position. A wave of building projects was the public sign of this effort, giving us such masterpieces as St-Etienne-du-Mont, **St-Eustache** (*see p104*) and private homes like the Hôtel de Cluny (which now houses the Musée National du Moyen Age) and the **Hôtel de Sens** (*see p112*), which today houses the **Bibliothèque de Forney** (*see p113*). The Renaissance in France peaked under François I. As well as being involved in the construction of magnificent châteaux at Fontainebleau, **Blois** and **Chambord** (for both, *see p360*), François was responsible for transforming the Louvre from a fortress into a royal palace. He held open house for such luminaries as Leonardo Da Vinci and Benvenuto Cellini. He also established the Collège de France to encourage humanist learning outside the control of the clergy-dominated universities.

Despite burning heretics by the dozen, François was unable to stop the spread of Protestantism, launched in Germany by Martin Luther in 1517. Resolutely Catholic, Paris was the scene of some horrific violence against the Huguenots, as supporters of the new faith were called. The picture was complicated by the political conflict between the Huguenot Prince de Condé and the Catholic Duc de Guise.

By the 1560s the situation had degenerated into open warfare. Catherine de Médicis, the scheming Italian widow of Henri II, was the real force in court politics. It was she who connived to murder prominent Protestants gathered in Paris for the marriage of the king's sister on St Bartholomew's Day (23 August 1572). Catherine's main aim was to dispose of her powerful rival, Gaspard de Coligny, but the situation got out of hand, and as many as 3,000 people were butchered. Henri III attempted to reconcile the religious factions and eradicate the powerful families directing the conflict, but the people of Paris turned against him and he was forced to flee. His assassination in 1589 brought the Valois line to an end.

THE BOURBONS

The throne of France being up for grabs, Henri of Navarre declared himself King Henri IV, launching the Bourbon dynasty. Paris was not impressed. The city closed its gates against the Huguenot king and the inhabitants endured a four-year siege by supporters of the new ruler. Henri managed to break the impasse by having

Cardinal Richelieu.

himself converted to Catholicism (and was later heard to quip, *'Paris vaut bien une messe'* – Paris is well worth a mass).

Henri set about rebuilding his ravaged capital. He completed the **Pont Neuf** (*see p72*), the first bridge to span the whole of the Seine. He commissioned place Dauphine and the city's first enclosed residential square – the place Royale – now **place des Vosges** (*see p112*). The square was the merry scene of jousting competitions and countless duels.

> ### 'François Ravaillac fatally stabbed the king while he was stuck in traffic.'

Henri also tried to reconcile his Catholic and Protestant subjects, issuing the Edict of Nantes in 1598, effectively giving each religion equal status. The Catholics hated the deal, and the Huguenots were suspicious. Henri was the subject of at least 23 attempted assassinations by fanatics of both persuasions. Finally, in 1610, a Catholic by the name of François Ravaillac fatally stabbed the king while he was stuck in traffic on rue de la Ferronnerie.

TWO CARDINALS

Since Henri's son, Louis XIII, was only eight at the time of his father's death, the widow, Marie de Médicis, took up the reins of power. We can thank her for the **Palais du Luxembourg** (*see p153*) and the 24 paintings she commissioned from Rubens, now part of the Louvre collection.

Louis took up his royal duties in 1617, but Cardinal Richelieu, chief minister from 1624, was the man who ran France. Something of a schemer, he outwitted the king's mother, his wife (Anne of Austria), and a host of princes and place-seekers. Richelieu helped to strengthen the power of the monarch, and he did much to limit the independence of the aristocracy. The cardinal was also a great architectural patron. He commissioned Jacques Lemercier to build what is now the **Palais-Royal** (*see p93*), and ordered the rebuilding of the Sorbonne.

The Counter-Reformation was at its height, and lavish churches such as the baroque **Val-de-Grâce** (*see p143*) were an important reassertion of Catholic supremacy. The 16th century was 'Le Grand Siècle', a time of patronage of art and artists, even if censorship forced the brilliant mathematician and philosopher René Descartes into exile.

The first national newspaper, *La Gazette*, hit the streets in 1631; Richelieu used it as a propaganda tool. The cardinal founded the **Académie Française** (*see p149*), a sort of literary think-tank, which is still working, slowly, on the dictionary of the French language that Richelieu commissioned from them in 1634. Richelieu died in 1642; Louis XIII followed suit a few months later. The new king, Louis XIV, was five years old. Anne of Austria became regent, with the Italian Cardinal Mazarin, a Richelieu protégé, as chief minister. Rumour has it that Anne and Mazarin may have been married. Mazarin's townhouse is now home to the **Bibliothèque Nationale de France – Richelieu** (*see p171*).

Endless wars against Austria and Spain had depleted the royal coffers and left the nation drained by exorbitant taxation. In 1648 the royal family was chased out of Paris by a popular uprising, 'la Fronde', named after the catapults used by some of the rioters. Parisians soon tired of the anarchy that followed. When Mazarin's army retook the city in 1653, the boy-king was warmly welcomed. Mazarin died in 1661 and Louis XIV, now 24 years old, decided he would rule France without the assistance of any chief minister.

SHINE ON, SUN KING
The 'Roi Soleil', or Sun King, was an absolute monarch. 'L'état, c'est moi' (I am the State) was his vision of power. To prove his grandeur, the king embarked on wars against England, Holland and Austria. He also refurbished and extended the Louvre, commissioned **place Vendôme** (*see p94*) and **place des Victoires** (*see p95*), constructed the Observatory and laid out the *grands boulevards* along the lines of the old city walls. The triumphal arches at **Porte St-Denis** and **Porte St-Martin** (for both, *see p99*) date from this time too. His major project was the palace at **Versailles** (*see p351*), a massive complex that drew on the age's finest architectural, artistic and landscape-design talents. Louis moved his court there in 1682.

Louis XIV owed much of his brilliant success to the work of Jean-Baptiste Colbert, nominally in charge of state finances, but eventually taking control of all the important levers of the state machine. Colbert was the force behind the Sun King's redevelopment of Paris. The **Hôtel des Invalides** (*see p156*) was built to accommodate the crippled survivors of Louis' wars, the **Salpêtrière** (*see p170*) to shelter fallen women. In 1702 Paris was divided into 20 *quartiers* (not until the Revolution was it re-mapped into arrondissements). **Le Procope** (*see p149*), the city's first café, opened in 1686. Although its original proprietor, Francesco

Procopio dei Coltelli, would no longer recognise it since a 1989 facelift, the place is still in business. Colbert died in 1683, and Louis' luck on the battlefield ran out. Hopelessly embroiled in the War of the Spanish Succession, the country was devastated by famine in 1692.

The Sun King died in 1715, leaving no direct heir. His five-year-old great-grandson, Louis XV, was named king, with Philippe d'Orléans as regent. The court moved back to Paris. Installed in the Palais-Royal, the regent set about enjoying his few years of power, hosting lavish dinners that degenerated into orgies. The state, meanwhile, remained chronically in debt.

THE ENLIGHTENMENT
Some of the city's more sober residents were making Paris the intellectual capital of Europe. Enlightenment thinkers such as Diderot, Montesquieu, Voltaire and Rousseau were all active during the reign of Louis XV. Literacy rates were increasing – 50 per cent of French men could read, 25 per cent of women – and the publishing industry was booming.

The king's mistress, Madame de Pompadour, encouraged him to finance the building of the **Ecole Militaire** (*see p159*) and the laying out of place Louis XV, known to us as **place de la Concorde** (*see p94*). The massive church of **St-Sulpice** (*see p153*) was completed in 1776. Many of the great houses in the area bounded by rue de Lille, rue de Varenne and rue de Grenelle date from the first half of the 18th century. The private homes of aristocrats and wealthy bourgeois, these would become the venues for numerous salons, the informal discussion sessions often devoted to topics raised by Enlightenment questioning.

The Enlightenment spirit of rational humanism finally took the venom out of the Catholic–Protestant power struggle, and the increase in public debate helped to change views about the nature of the state and the place and authority of the monarchy. As Jacques Necker, Louis XVI's finance minister on the eve of the Revolution, put it, popular opinion was 'an invisible power that, without treasury, guard or army, gives its laws to the city, the court and even the palaces of kings.' Thanks to the Enlightenment, and an ever-growing burden of taxation on the poorest strata of society to prop up the wealthiest, that power would overturn the status quo for good.

THE FRENCH REVOLUTION
Louis XVI had poor control of his country's swelling problems, and French intervention in the Seven Years War and the American War of Independence had left the country practically bankrupt. Subsequent attempts to introduce

new taxes met with strong opposition from the bourgeoisie. After a ruined harvest and a harsh winter, bread prices soared, as did discontent. Springtime in 1789 brought riots on the rue du Faubourg-St-Antoine, where factory workers' wages had been cut. The *parlements*, or high courts, urged Louis to call a meeting of the Etats Généraux – the representative body for the First Estate (the clergy), the Second Estate (the nobility) and the Third Estate (the bourgeoisie and commoners).

On 5 May 1789, the king reluctantly faced the Etats at Versailles. The Third Estate, which had as many members as the other two combined, demanded that the three merge into a single assembly, with one vote per member. Louis refused. On 20 June the Third Estate reconvened on the playing courts at the Jeu de Paumes at Versailles and swore to establish a national constitution. The embattled Louis eventually conceded and allowed the Etats to form the Assemblée Nationale. But behind the scenes, the king was gathering troops to disband the assembly; and on 12 July he publicly, and foolishly, dismissed the commoner's ally, finance minister Jacques Necker, prompting a violent counter-coup. On 13 July Camille Desmoulins, a young unemployed lawyer, empassioned an angry crowd gathered in the Palais-Royal garden to take action. The next day, the crowd pillaged Les Invalides for arms, marched on the Bastille prison and proceeded to tear it down. Only seven prisoners were imprisoned there, but the symbolic victory was immense (and enduring, as the annual *quatorze juillet* celebrations show; *see p275*). A chastened Louis came to Paris on 17 July to acknowledge the crowds at the Hôtel de Ville.

The establishment of the constitution forged ahead, and sparked furious debate. Tax breaks for the nobility and clergy were abolished, the country was divided into local governments and Roman Catholic Church property was seized. Two Parisian convents hosted two newly formed political clubs. On the Left Bank, at a 13th-century Franciscan convent (some parts of which are still standing at 15 rue de l'Ecole de Médicine), the Cordeliers club charged its members, mostly the poor *sans-culottes* (so called because they couldn't afford breeches), a few cents to hear monarchy-bashing speeches by its leading lights. These included the figures of Desmoulins and Marat. On the Right Bank, the more radical Jacobins, who included the likes of Mirabeau, Danton and Robespierre, took up residency in a Dominican convent on rue St-Honoré, later knocked down by Napoléon.

One of Louis' original problems, the price of bread, had not budged. In October a mob of starving women marched the 12 miles (19 kilometres) to Versailles and demanded that the king come to Paris. He promised to send the women grain, an offer they rejected by decapitating some of his guards. Louis wisely transferred to the Tuileries. In the months that followed, the Jacobins roused powerful Republican feeling. Fearing greater danger at home and hoping to gain support abroad, the king and his family attempted to flee Paris on 20 June 1791. With Louis disguised as a valet, they got as far as Varennes, where a commoner recognised Louis' face from his portrait on a coin. Louis, Marie-Antoinette and family were brought back to Paris in disgrace, crowds throwing things at their coach, and poking their heads through the window and spitting.

On 14 September Louis accepted the new constitution, and the Revolution appeared to be over. But other monarchies were plotting to reinstate the king. In 1792 Austrian and Prussian troops invaded France, gaining rapidly on Paris with easy victories against a weak French army. The Republicans, rightly, suspected Louis of conspiring with the enemy, and scrabbled together their own army to capture him, ringing out the cannons on Pont Neuf to enrol the public. On the morning of 10 August, the Tuileries palace rang with gunfire. Swiss guards enlisted to defend the king put up a staunch fight, but were hacked to death along with all the palace staff. Two bloody days later, the royal family was incarcerated in the Temple prison by the radical Commune de Paris, headed by Danton, Marat and Robespierre.

Rampant suspicion about possible traitors led the Revolutionaries to the gates of the city's prisons. They invaded, and murdered 2,000 so-called traitors, including the Princess of Lamballe, whose head was stuck on a spike and paraded past the royal family at the Temple. The monarchy was abolished on 22 September; the king was executed on 21 January. A trial, Robespierre claimed, was out of the question, since it would put 'the Revolution itself in the dock.' The guillotine, a symbol of the Revolution's brutality (in fact, invented by Dr Guillotin as a humane method of execution) stood at the place de la Révolution and took thousands of heads, including that of Louis' widow, Marie-Antoinette, almost a year later. She awaited her fate in a wallpapered prison cell at the Conciergerie.

There was precious little dignity to this particular period of the Revolution. Within the Revolutionary Convention, which had replaced the Assemblée Nationale, the Jacobins had expelled the monarchist Girondins (a young

Girondist, Charlotte Corday, retaliated by stabbing Marat to death at his home) and were gathering dictatorial momentum. Headed by 'l'incorruptible' Robespierre, the Jacobins in September 1793 vowed to wage terror against all rebels, Girondins and dissidents. In the Great Terror of 1794, the guillotine was transferred to place du Trône Renversé ('Overturned Throne', now place de la Nation), and sliced through 1,300 necks in six weeks. The bodies were dumped in the Picpus garden (now the **Cimetière de Picpus;** *see p116*). The tumbrils, or two-wheeled carts, which carried the dead, were painted green to disguise their bloody load.

Almost everybody wanted the Terror to end. The French army had successfully beaten off foreign forces, and the incessant killing began to look unnecessary. Robespierre and his cohorts attempted some democratic reform, but most people wanted them gone. On 28 July 1794, he was executed and the reign of terror collapsed. The biggest and bloodiest revolution was over.

NAPOLEON

Amid the post-Revolutionary chaos, power was divided between a two-housed Assembly and a Directory of five men. The French public reacted badly to hearing of England's unsuccessful attempts to promote more popular rebellion; when a royalist rising in Paris needed to be put down, a young officer from Corsica was the man to do it: Napoléon Bonaparte. Napoléon quickly became the Directory's right-hand man. When they needed someone to lead an Italian campaign against Austria, Napoléon was the man. Victory saw France – and Napoléon – glorified. After a further, aborted, campaign to Egypt in 1799, Napoléon returned home to put down another royalist plot, made himself the chief of the newly governing three-man Consul – and by 1804 was emperor.

After failing to squeeze out the English by setting up the Continental System to block trade across the Channel, Napoléon waged wars of massive scope against Britain, Russia and Austria. On his way to the disaster of Moscow, Napoléon gave France the *lycée* educational system, the Napoleonic Code of civil law, the Legion of Honour, the Banque de France, the **Pont des Arts** (*see p72*), the **Arc de Triomphe** (*see p119*), the **Madeleine** church (he re-established Catholicism as the state religion; *see p97*), the **Bourse** (*see p95*) and the **rue de Rivoli**. He was also responsible for the centralised bureaucracy that still manages to drive the French mad.

As Russian troops – who had chased Napoléon's once-mighty army all the way from Moscow and Leipzig – invaded France, Paris

itself came under threat. Montmartre, then named Montnapoléon, had a telegraph machine at its summit, one that had given so many of the emperor's orders and transmitted news of so many victories. The hill fell to Russian troops. Napoléon gave the order to blow up the city's main powder stores, and thus Paris itself. The officer refused. Paris accommodated carousing Russian, Prussian and English soldiers while Napoléon was sent to exile in Elba.

A hundred days later, he was back, leading an army against Wellington and Blücher's troops in the midsummer mud of Waterloo, near Brussels. A further defeat saw the end of him. Paris survived further foreign occupation. The diminutive Corsican died on the South Atlantic prison island of St Helena in 1821.

ANOTHER ROUND OF BOURBONS

Having sampled revolution and military dictatorship, the French were now ready to give monarchy a second chance. The Bourbons got back in business, briefly, in 1815 in the person of Louis XVIII, Louis XVI's elderly brother. Several efforts were made to adapt the monarchy to the new political realities, though the new king's Charter of Liberties was not a

Napoléon.

wholly sincere expression of how he meant to rule. Liberal intellectual activity flourished nevertheless, with figures such as the caricaturist Daumier regularly poking satirical fun at the bourgeoisie.

When another brother of Louis XVI, Charles X, became king in 1824, he decided that enough royal energy had been wasted trying to reconcile the nation's myriad factions. It was time for a spot of old-fashioned absolutism. But the forces unleashed during the Revolution, and the divisions that had opened in French society as a result, were not to be ignored – the people were happy to respond with some old-fashioned rebellion.

In the 1830 elections, the liberals won a hefty majority in the Chamber of Deputies, the legislative body. Charles's unpopular minister Prince Polignac, a returned émigré, promptly dissolved the Chamber, announced a date for new elections and curtailed the number of voters. Polishing off this collection of bad decisions was the 26 July decree abolishing the freedom of the press. The day after its issue, 5,000 print workers and journalists filled the streets and three newspapers went to press. When police tried to confiscate copies, they sparked a three-day riot, 'les Trois Glorieuses', with members of the disbanded National Guard manning the barricades. On 30 July Charles dismissed Polignac, but it was too late. He had little choice but to abdicate, and fled to England. As French revolutions go, it was a neat, brief affair.

Another leftover from the *ancien régime* was now winched on to the throne – Louis-Philippe, Duc d'Orléans, who had some Bourbon blood in his veins. A father of eight who never went out without his umbrella, he was eminently acceptable to the newly powerful bourgeoisie. But the poor who had risked their lives in two attempts to change French society were unimpressed by the new king's promise to embrace a moderate and liberal version of the Revolutionary heritage.

THE NINETEENTH CENTURY

Philosopher Walter Benjamin declared Paris 'the capital of the 19th century', and he had a point. For sure, it was smaller in dimension than its global rival of London, but in intellectual and cultural spheres it reigned supreme. On the demographic front, its population doubled to one million between 1800 and 1850. Most of the new arrivals were rural labourers from across France who had come to find work on the ever-expanding city's building sites. Meanwhile, the middle classes were doing well, thanks to the relatively late arrival of the industrial revolution in France, and the solid

administrative structures inherited from Napoléon. The poor were as badly off as ever, only there were more of them.

The back-breaking hours worked in the factories would not be curbed by legislation: 'Whatever the lot of the workers is, it is not the manufacturer's responsibility to improve it,' said one trade minister. In Left Bank cafés, a new bohemian tribe of students derided the materialistic government. Workers' pamphlets and newspapers, such as *La Ruche Populaire*, gave voice to the starving, crippled poor. A wave of ill-feeling was gradually building up against Louis-Philippe.

On 23 February 1848, hundreds of Parisians – men, women and students – moved along the boulevards towards a public banquet at La Madeleine. The king's minister, François Guizot, had forbidden direct campaigning by opposition parties in the forthcoming election; as a way around this, the parties held banquets instead of meetings. One diarist of the time noted that some of the crowd had stuffed swords and daggers underneath their shirts, but the demonstration was largely peaceful – until the troops on the boulevard des Capucines opened fire, igniting a riot.

As barricades sprang up all over the city, a trembling Louis-Philippe abdicated and a liberal provisional government declared a republic. The virtual epidemic of poverty and unemployment was stemmed by creating national *ateliers*, or workshops, but such 'radical' reforms made the right extremely nervous. A conservative government took power in May 1848, and shut down the *ateliers*. A month later, the poor were back in the streets. Some 50,000 took part in these 'June Days' protests, but they were quite comprehensively crushed by the troops of General Cavaignac. In total, about 1,500 Parisians died and some 5,000 were deported.

As the pamphleteer Alphonse Karr said of the revolution's aftermath, 'plus ça change, plus c'est la même chose' (the more things change, the more they stay the same). In December 1848 Louis Bonaparte – nephew of Napoléon – was elected president. By 1852 he had moved into the Tuileries palace and declared himself Emperor Napoléon III. Hugo called him Little Napoléon, but the diminutive Bonaparte held on to power for 22 years – significantly longer than his 'bigger' diminutive forebear.

THE SECOND EMPIRE

The emperor appointed a lawyer as *préfet* to mastermind the reconstruction of Paris. In less than two decades, prefect Georges-Eugène Haussmann had created the most magnificent city in Europe. His goals included better access

Controversial **Captain Dreyfus**. See p22.

expression of Haussmann's vision, while the rich mix of styles in Charles Garnier's **Opéra** (*see p97*) is often seen as typical of Second Empire self-indulgence.

Not everyone was happy. Haussmann's works destroyed thousands of buildings, including beautiful Middle Ages monuments; on the whole of Ile de la Cité only Notre-Dame survived. Entire residential areas were wiped off the map, and only the owners of the buildings themselves were compensated; tenants were merely booted out and left to fend for themselves. Writers and artists lamented the loss of the more quirky Paris they used to know, and criticised the unfriendly grandeur of the new city. But there was no going back.

The emperor's meddling foreign policy would be his downfall. After the relatively successful Crimean War of the mid 1850s, he tried in vain to impose the Catholic Maximilian as ruler of Mexico. Maximilian's execution was the subject of Edouard Manet's famous painting. Manet would be the precursor of the burgeoning Impressionist movement, which would include Monet, Renoir, Degas and Cézanne. Napoléon's next misadventure, the Franco-Prussian War of 1870, divided the figureheads of this artistic movement. They either fought or fled. Monet's stay in London marked him: he discovered the light techniques used by Turner. After the war, Manet, Monet and Renoir would move to bucolic, riverside locations, to experiment with the contrasting use of colours and light. Artists flocked to Paris to emulate them. Impressionism begat Fauvism and Matisse, Cubism and Picasso. Paris was the mecca of the art world.

At home, the city's rapid industrialisation saw the rise of Socialism and Communism amid the disgruntled working classes. Napoléon III gave limited rights to trades unions. Abroad, though, the now constitutional monarch was a disaster. A sick man, dominated by his wife Eugénie, he allowed himself to be drawn into a war with Prussia. France was soon defeated. At Sedan, in September 1870, 100,000 French troops were forced to surrender to Bismarck's Prussians; Napoléon III himself was captured, never to return.

The war continued, and back in Paris, a provisional government hastily took power. Elections gave conservative monarchists the majority, though the Paris vote was firmly Republican. Former prime minister Adolphe Thiers assumed executive power. Meanwhile, Prussian forces marched on Paris and laid siege to the city. Paris held out, starving, for four brave months, its citizens picking rats from the gutter for food. Léon Gambetta, a young politician, escaped in style (by hot-air balloon) but failed to raise an army in the south.

to railway stations, better water supplies, an extended sewer system and a long list of new hospitals, barracks, theatres and *mairies*. It was a colossal, revolutionary project and it transformed the capital. Haussmann created a network of wide, arrow-straight avenues that were better ventilated and more hygienic than the narrow streets they replaced – particularly in the old quarters on the islands and just off the Seine, whose rapid improvement would see the largest slum clearance ever accomplished in Europe. Now, with their unobstacled vistas, these streets were far more aesthetic. Their dimensions also had political advantages: the streets would be harder to barricade, and troops would be able to reach the scene of any future insurrection faster and in greater numbers. (Boulevard de Sébastopol, in particular, was conceived as a military fast track to the centre.)

So synonymous is Haussmann with the recasting of the city, and with a certain architectural style, that he's sometimes believed to have designed the buildings himself. He was indeed a formidable administrator, but no civil engineer: architectural detail he left to others. Shrewdly, he refused to employ the official architects of the day and hired instead more modest practitioners – people like Gabriel Davioud – who were much easier to command. The tree-lined streets radiating out from **place Charles-de-Gaulle** (*see p119*) are the classic

In January 1871 the provisional government signed a bitter armistice that relinquished the industrial heartlands of Alsace and Lorraine and agreed to pay a five-million franc indemnity. German troops would stay on French soil until the bill was paid.

But with occupying army camps stationed around their city, Parisians considered the treaty a dishonour and remained defiant. Thiers ordered his soldiers to enter the city and strip it of its cannons, but the insurgents cut them short. The new government scuttled off to the haven of Versailles, while on 26 March Paris elected its own municipal body, the Commune, so called in memory of the spirit of 1792. The 92 members of the Commune hailed from the left and working classes; their agenda was liberal (schools would be secularised, debts suspended) but war-like (Germany must be defeated). Paris itself was given a little makeover: the column projecting Napoleonic glory into place Vendôme was pulled down, and statues of the great emperor were smashed all over town.

Thiers would not stand by and watch. Artillery fire picked at the Communards' sandbag barricades on the edges of Paris. The suburbs fell by 11 April. In the sixth week of fighting, troops broke in through the Porte de St-Cloud and covered the springtime city in blood. The ill-equipped Communards faced a massacre: 25,000 were killed in days. In revenge, hostages were taken and shot, including the Archbishop of Paris. The infamous *pétroleuses*, women wielding petrol bombs, burnt off their anger, torching the Tuileries and the Hôtel de Ville. On the ultimate day of *la semaine sanglante*, 28 May, 147 Communards were trapped and shot in **Père-Lachaise cemetery** (*see p136*), against the 'Mur des Fédérés', still an icon of the Commune struggle. The dead were buried in the streets, the prisons crammed with 40,000 Communards; thousands of others were deported.

THE THIRD REPUBLIC

Out of the ruins of the Second Empire rose the Third Republic, a hasty compromise given little chance of survival even by those who supported it. In fact, its makeshift constitution was to survive until 1940, thus becoming the most enduring – so far – in modern French history.

Thanks mainly to the huge economic boost provided by colonial expansion in Africa and Indo-China, the horrors of the Commune were soon forgotten in the self-indulgent materialism of the turn of the century. The **Eiffel Tower** (*see p160*) was built as the centrepiece of the 1889 Exposition Universelle. In 1891 the first line of the métro opened, linking Porte Maillot and Vincennes in 25 minutes. For the next Exposition Universelle, in 1900, the **Grand Palais** (*see p120*) and **Petit Palais**, the **Pont Alexandre III** (*see p72*) and the Gare d'Orsay (now the **Musée d'Orsay**; *see p159*) were built to affirm France's position as a world power. The first cinema had opened (1895), and

Frenchmen sign up for near-certain death in the **Great War**. *See p22.*

clubs like the **Moulin Rouge** (*see p278*) were buzzing. The lurid life of Montmartre, depicted by Toulouse-Lautrec – and its cheap rents – would attract the world's artistic community.

In 1894 a Jewish army officer, Captain Alfred Dreyfus (*see p142* **Scandale!**), had been dismissed in disgrace from the army and deported to Devil's Island, convicted of selling secrets to the Prussians. The affair rocked the French establishment to its self-satisfied roots. Emile Zola famously championed the Jewish officer's cause in *J'Accuse!*, an open letter to President Faure, as did statesmen such as Georges Clemenceau and Jean Jaurès. The Catholic right wing sided with the army, and lost heavily when Dreyfus was proven innocent.

THE GREAT WAR

Against the backdrop of the major European powers attempting to outdo each other to industrialise and carve up the atlas, France and England came to a political understanding in 1904: the Entente Cordiale. With the inclusion of Russia, this became the Triple Entente, which was slowly stacking up against the Triple Alliance of Germany, Italy and Austro-Hungary. Nationalist tensions rose as European empires crumbled. On 3 August 1914 Germany declared war on France.

Although the Germans never made it to Paris in World War I – German troops were stopped 20 kilometres (12 miles) short of the city by the French victory in the Battle of the Marne – the artillery was audible. Paris, and French society, suffered terribly in the war, despite ultimate victory.

The nations gathered at Versailles to make the peace and established new European states. The League of Nations was formed. Artists responded to the horrors and absurdity of the

conflict with Surrealism, a movement founded in Paris by André Breton, a doctor who had treated troops in the trenches and embraced Freud's theories of the unconscious. In 1924 it had a manifesto, a year later its first exhibition. Again, artists (and photographers) – Dali, Man Ray – flocked to Paris. By now Montmartre was too dear, and Montparnasse became the hub of artistic life. The inter-war years were a whirl of activity in artistic and political circles. Paris became the avant-garde capital of the world, recorded by Hemingway, F Scott Fitzgerald and Gertrude Stein, who had made the city their home and source of inspiration.

> **'The Vichy government was so eager to please the Germans, it organised anti-Semitic measures without prompting.'**

Meanwhile, the Depression unleashed a wave of political violence, Fascists fighting Socialists and Communists for control. The election in 1936 of Léon Blum's Front Populaire saw the introduction of such social benefits as paid holidays for workers. At the same time, many writers were leaving Paris for Spain to cover – and, indeed, to take part in – the Civil War. Across the German border, the contentious territories of Alsace-Lorraine – and the burden of the World War I peace agreements signed in Paris – became one of many bugbears held by the new chancellor, Hitler. As war broke out, France believed that its Maginot line would hold strong against the German threat. The Nazis simply bypassed it through Belgium.

Fighting for the **Liberation of Paris**, 1944. *See p23.*

No more heroes

'And the winner is... le Général de Gaulle!'
Even reading the results in traditional reverse order could do little to wring any suspense from the situation: the nation's war hero won the TV history poll hands down. France 2 viewers voted de Gaulle 'Greatest Frenchman of all Time', sitting proudly atop a top ten of bobbled-hatted undersea explorers, anarchic comics, benevolent priests and chemists, and a top 100 dominated by cheesy and controversial figures from the nefarious world of French showbiz.

Inspired by the BBC series *Great Britons* (won by de Gaulle's counterpart across the Channel, Winston Churchill), France 2 asked a 'representative sample' (in fact, only 1,038 people) to pick their favourite French person. They arrived at a mixed bag of 100, only 32 of whom were still alive. Edith Piaf polled more votes than Napoléon, moustache-wielding anti-globalisation protester José Bové beat out Jean-Paul Sartre, and France 2's own smarmy presenters Michel Drucker and Thierry Ardisson were pipped by Louis XIV in a photo finish.

Not surprisingly, the broadsheets had a field day, panning the show as another lowbrow import from across *La Manche* and arguing over populist choices from the world of stage and screen outvoting some of the world's greatest literary heavyweights. While cultural debates raged, a whisper could be heard from a humble grave in the cemetery of the modest parish church of Colombey-les-Deux-Eglises: 'I told you so'.

THE SECOND WORLD WAR

Paris was in German hands within weeks of the start of hostilities. The city fell without a fight. A pro-German government was set up in Vichy, a spa resort with enough hotels to accommodate the number of administrators. It was headed by the ageing World War I hero Marshall Pétain, popularly known as the 'Victor of Verdun', while a young army officer, Charles de Gaulle, went to London to organise the Free French opposition. For those happy to get along with the German army, the period of the Occupation presented few hardships and, indeed, some good business opportunities. Food was rationed and tobacco and coffee went out of circulation, but the black market thrived. In other ways, life went on much as before: each month during the winter of 1939-40, 800,000 Parisians still managed to go to the cinema.

For those who resisted, there were the Gestapo torture chambers at avenue Foch or rue Lauriston. The Germans further discouraged uncooperative behaviour with executions: one victim, whose name now adorns a métro station, was Jacques Bonsergent, a student caught fly-posting and shot because he refused to reveal the names of his friends who escaped.

Paris was also a bad place in which to be Jewish. The Vichy government was so eager to please the Germans, it organised anti-Semitic measures without prompting from the occupier. As of the spring of 1941, the French authorities deported Jews to the death camps, frequently via the internment camp at Drancy. Prime Minister Pierre Laval claimed it was a necessary concession to his Third Reich masters. (Laval would later flee to Spain, be refused political asylum by Franco and be handed to the Americans. After a failed attempt at poisoning himself, he was shot in 1945.)

In July 1942, 12,000 Jewish French citizens were rounded up in the Vélodrome d'Hiver, a sports complex on quai de Grenelle, and then dispatched to Auschwitz. (In July 1994 a memorial to the victims was finally erected near the site of the long-demolished sports arena.)

THE LIBERATION

Paris survived the war practically unscathed, ultimately due to the bravery of one of its captors. On 23 August 1944, as the Allied armies of liberation approached the city, Hitler ordered his commander, Dietrich Von Choltitz, to detonate the explosives that had been set all over town in anticipation of a retreat. Von

Choltitz refused. On 25 August 1944, French troops, tactfully placed at the head of the US forces, entered the city, and General de Gaulle led the parade down the Champs-Elysées.
Writers and artists swept back into Paris to celebrate and seek out old haunts. Hemingway held court at the Ritz and Scribe hotels with the great journalists of the day, clinking glasses with veterans of the Spanish Civil War such as photographer Robert Capa and George Orwell. Picasso's studio was besieged by well-wishers.

However, the Liberation was not the end of France's troubles. De Gaulle was the hero of the hour, but relations between the interim government he commanded and the Resistance – largely Communist – were still tricky. Orders issued to *maquis* leaders in the provinces were often ignored. The Communists wanted a revolution, and de Gaulle suspected them of hatching plans to seize Paris prior to August 1944. Meanwhile, de Gaulle knew he had to commit every available French soldier to the march on Germany, or risk being sidelined by the other allies after the war. With no military forces to spare for domestic law and order, he had to leave homeland security to the very people – the 'patriotic militias' – who were most likely to be at least sympathetic to the Communist cause; or, even more dubiously, gendarmes who had previously worked with the occupying power.

When it came to rebuilding the country, the uncomfortable compromises multiplied – even to the point of injustice. Companies that had worked with the Germans were the best equipped, and thus the most useful; and while a handful of collaborating industrialists, including the motor vehicle baron Louis Renault, were imprisoned, many got off scot-free. In any case, recovery was slow to come. There were shortages of everything. Food was as hard to come by as it had been during the war; indeed, many complained they had been better off under the Germans. Medical supplies were inadequate, as were basic necessities. Even in the ministries, paper was so scarce that correspondence had to be sent out on Vichy letterhead with the sender crossing out 'Etat Français' at the top and writing 'République Française' instead. It was a poor state of affairs.

THE FOURTH REPUBLIC

On 8 May 1945, de Gaulle made a broadcast to the nation to announce Germany's surrender. Paris went wild. Cars hooted their horns, church bells rang, sirens wailed, artillery boomed and low-flying aircraft zoomed overhead. Crowds packed out the Champs-Elysées and the city's fountains were switched back on. It was the party to end all parties.

The euphoria didn't last. There were strikes. And more strikes. Liberation had proved to be a restoration, not the revolution the Communists, now the most powerful political force in the land, had hoped for. The Communist Party was, in at least one respect, as pragmatic as everyone else: it did its utmost to turn parliamentary democracy to its advantage, to wit, getting as many of the top jobs as it could. (It even lobbied to get members into the Académie Française.) The pragmatism stopped, however, at its tendency to see Fascists and fifth columnists in every shadow; the French Communist leader, Maurice Thorez, would travel around town only in an armoured limousine with bodyguards in tow, for fear of assassination attempts.

> **'A vote was passed maintaining de Gaulle in his position as head of state – but he remained an antagonistic leader.'**

A general election was held on 21 October 1945. The Communists secured 159 seats, the Socialists got 146 and the Catholic Mouvement Républicain Populaire got 152. At the Assemblée Nationale's first session a fortnight later, a unanimous vote was passed maintaining de Gaulle in his position as head of state – but he remained an antagonistic leader. His reluctance to take a firm grip on the disastrous economic situation alienated many intellectuals and industrialists who had once been loyal to him, and his characteristic aloofness only made the misgivings of the general populace worse. He, on the other hand, was disgusted by all the political chicanery – what he called its *pourriture*, or rot. On 20 January 1946, he abruptly resigned.

France, meanwhile, looked to swift industrial modernisation under an ambitious plan put forward by internationalist politician Jean Monnet. While the economy and daily life remained grim, brash new fashion designer Christian Dior put together a stunning collection of strikingly simple clothes: the New Look. Such extravagance horrified many locals, but the fashion industry boomed. Meanwhile, the divisions in Paris between its fashionable and its run-down working-class areas became more pronounced. The northern and eastern edges – areas only revived in the late 20th century by a taste for retro, industrial decor and cheap rent – were forgotten about.

Félix Gouin, the new Socialist premier, quickly nationalised the bigger banks and the coal industry. But the right wing was growing, and there was even a rise of royalist hopes. A referendum was held in May 1946 to determine the crucial tenet of the Fourth Republic's constitution: should the Assemblée Nationale have absolute or restricted power? The results were a narrow victory for those who, like de Gaulle, had insisted the Assemblée's power should be qualified. De Gaulle's prestige increased, but it was to be another 12 years, and a whole new constitution – the Fifth Republic – before he got his hands back on the levers of power. He spent much of his *'passage du désert'* writing his memoirs.

THE ALGERIAN WAR AND MAY 1968

The post-war years were marked by the rapid disintegration of France's overseas interests – and her rapprochement with Germany to create what would become the European Community.

When revolt broke out in Algeria in 1956, almost 500,000 troops were sent in to protect national interests. A protest by Algerians in Paris on 17 October 1961 led to the deaths of hundreds of people at the hands of the city's police. The extent of the violence was officially concealed for decades, as was the use of torture against Algerians by French troops. Algeria became independent in 1962.

Meanwhile, the slow, painful discoveries of collaboration in World War II, often overlooked in the rush to put the country back on its feet, were being faced. The younger generation began to question the motives of the older one. De Gaulle's Fifth Republic was felt by many to be grimly authoritarian. There are certainly those who believe that he designed it to be an elected monarchy, which is interesting when you consider that it's the constitution still in use to this day.

In the spring of 1968, students unhappy with overcrowded university conditions took to the streets of Paris at the same time as striking Renault workers. These *soixante-huitards* sprang the greatest public revolt in French living memory. For that, and for the left, at least, the revolutionaries of 1968 are still revered as heroes. At the time, they were students crammed into universities that had been somewhat cheaply expanded in order to accommodate them. The talk of politics grew across the campuses, turning against the government's stranglehold on the media and President de Gaulle's poor grasp of the economy. Ministers did indeed at the time have a sinister habit of leaning on the leading newspaper editors of the day, and television was dubbed to be 'the government in your dining room'. Inflation was high, and the gap between the working classes and the bourgeoisie was becoming a chasm.

Waving, drowning? **Jacques Chirac**. *See p27.*

But still, de Gaulle echoed many when he said the events of May 1968 were simply 'incompréhensible'. The touchpaper was lit at overcrowded Nanterre university, on the outskirts of Paris, where students had been protesting against the war in Vietnam and the tatty state of the campus.

On 2 May, exhausted by the protests, the authorities closed the university down and threatened to expel some of the students. The next day, a sit-in was held in sympathy at the Sorbonne. Police were called to intervene, but made things worse, charging into the crowd with truncheons, tear gas and a comprehensive lack of judgement. The city's streets were soon flooded with thousands of incensed student demonstrators, now officially on strike. The trades unions followed, as did the *lycées*. By mid May nine million people were on strike, and not just in Paris: factories all over the country were occupied by workers.

On 24 May, de Gaulle intervened – naturally via the nation's television sets. His speech warned of civil war and pleaded for people's support. It didn't go down too well: riots quickly broke out, with students storming the Bourse, only to be thwarted by more police tear gas. Barricades sprang up all over the Latin Quarter, which had become something of a

The heir apparent?

It has enough French farce that Molière could have written it, though the backstabbing is more redolent of Dumas. It even has an American storyline of marrying the boss' daughter for a shot at romancing the company. In any event, the high drama at the top of French politics is an intriguing tale.

President Jacques Chirac is set on having anyone other than young(ish) pretender Nicolas Sarkozy (*pictured*) succeed him. And while there's a certain amount of hubris in Chirac choosing his successor to preserve his legacy, he has a more pressing reason to ensure the man at the top is friend not foe. Once he loses office, Chirac also loses his immunity from prosecution (or even answering the questions magistrates have said they'd like to ask him). It's rather ironic, then, that Chirac's potential saviour, Alain Juppé, took a tumble for charges of corruption during Chirac's mayoralty, receiving a suspended sentence and a ten-year ban on public office. Though this was later reduced to a year, the political damage had been done: Chirac needed a new heir.

It could all have turned out so differently. Chirac first met Sarkozy when the fresh-faced 'Sarko' gave a barnstormer of a speech – his first – at a party congress in Nice in 1975. An impressed Prime Minister Chirac then took him under his wing. Their relationship went beyond work – Sarkozy was welcomed into the Chirac household and struck up a friendship with Chirac's daughter, Claude. Rumours circulated that a romance took place – though Claude insisted to Béatrice Gurrey, *Le Monde* journalist and author of *Le Rebelle et le Roi*, that she had never been his mistress. (Why, also, would Sarkozy have been a witness at her wedding in 1992?)

If this put a frost on Sarkozy's relationship with Chirac *père*, it was nothing to the deep freeze that ensued after Sarko betrayed him. Having his place in the inner circle, and post of budget minister under Prime Minister Edouard Balladur, Sarkozy gambled on black and threw his support behind Balladur's 1995 presidential campaign. Chirac didn't speak to Sarkozy for years. Having backed the loser, Sarko spent time in the political wilderness.

It wasn't until 2002 that Sarkozy made his comeback: though he hadn't forgiven him, Chirac sought to harness Sarko's steadily rising popularity as a can-do interior minister. But presidential ambition was never far from the surface. Shunted to the unenviable post of finance minister in 2004, Sarkozy bid for Juppé's old job as chairman of the UMP – the party Chirac had founded, and considered a stepping-stone on the path to ultimate power. Despite having been mayor of Paris and prime minister at the same time, Chirac insisted that Sarkozy couldn't hold two jobs – he must choose between his ministerial role and the chairmanship. He relented after defeat in the European constitutional referendum. Chirac's latest 'dauphin', Prime Minister Dominique de Villepin, not only gave Sarko his Interior Ministry post back but also made him deputy PM, in the vain hope that he'd quieten down.

Sarko just kept on sniping. He held a rival garden party to Chirac's traditional Bastille Day shindig, and even likened him in the media to the oblivious Louis XVI.

Attacking the presidency isn't really a good idea. A dressing-down from upstairs, leaks that his marriage was on the rocks and hints of a media backlash all suggested that the brash Sarkozy shouldn't count his chickens just yet. But then a health scare in September 2005 seemed to put Chirac's hopes for a third term in 2007 to rest: for now, it looks likely that de Villepin will be the anointed successor. Interesting times lie ahead.

battleground, with the Odéon theatre and the amphitheatre of the Sorbonne packed every night with activists and students.

Five days later, as the street violence reached its peak, de Gaulle fled briefly to Germany and Prime Minister Pompidou sent tanks to the edges of Paris. But the crisis did not quite come to such extremes. Pompidou conceded pay rises of between seven and ten per cent and an increase in the minimum wage; the country went back to work. A general election was called prematurely for 23 June, by which time the right had gathered enough red-fearing momentum to gain a safe majority.

MITTERRAND

Following the largely anonymous presidencies of Georges Pompidou and Valéry Giscard d'Estaing, the Socialist François Mitterrand took up the task in 1981. The verdict on Mitterrand is still not in: the early part of his presidency saw him introducing some radical political and economic reforms, but the necessities of pragmatism and compromise led to their reversal, and he left the Socialist Party in some disarray. At any rate, Mitterrand made a big difference to Paris – visitors to the city can thank him for his *Grands Projets* without worrying about suggestions that they might represent a most unrepublican form of self-aggrandisement. Mitterrand was responsible for IM Pei's Louvre **pyramid** (*see p80*), the **Grande Arche de la Défense** (*see p117*), the **Opéra Bastille** (*see p312*) and the more recent **Bibliothèque Nationale de France – François Mitterrand** (*see p171*).

CHIRAC, BUSH AND IRAQ

France may still boast the world's fourth-largest economy, the nuclear deterrent and a permanent seat on the UN Security Council, but her influence on the world stage had been waning for years until President Chirac, flushed from re-election and well aware he was on to a PR winner, stood up late in early 2003 to oppose the US-led invasion of Iraq. France's official disapproval of George Bush culminated in the threat to use its Security Council veto against any resolution authorising the use of force without UN say-so, a move inspired by Chirac's hunger for an international role, his fear of the consequences among France's five million Muslims of an attack on Iraq, traditional Gallic anti-Americanism, and a genuine belief that this particular war at this particular time in this particular place was wrong.

Whatever the reason, it did Chirac no harm at all. His personal approval ratings soared at home, at one stage breaking the 80 per cent barrier, and abroad he became the darling of the Islamic world, Africa, Asia and large swathes of continental Europe. He also acquired a most-hated-man status in America rivalled only by Osama Bin Laden and Saddam Hussein, but that was a small price to pay.

Chirac's domestic popularity couldn't last. His prime minister, Jean-Pierre Raffarin, and the centre-right government began attacking some of France's more prized national institutions with a programme of long-overdue reforms, starting with the state pension system. The obvious fact that a steadily greying population coupled with fewer people in work equals serious pension shortfall did not prevent some of the largest nationwide protests France has seen since 1995, with striking métro staff, hospital workers, postmen, teachers and rubbish collectors bringing the capital to a virtual standstill.

Planned restrictions on the uniquely Gallic, exceptionally generous (and thus heavily indebted) system of unemployment benefit for out-of-work performing-arts professionals like actors, musicians and backstage staff led to a further round of protests, as well as the cancellation of France's equivalents of Edinburgh and Glyndebourne, the Avignon and Aix summer cultural festivals. Then came the official mismanagement and aloofness that characterised the two-week heatwave of August 2003, during which as many as 14,000 elderly people died. Government ministers put their heads in the sands, and Chirac did not deign to open his mouth, still less cut short his holiday in Canada. The popularity of president and prime minister plummeted to all-time lows, from which they have barely recovered.

The national mood stayed gloomy through 2004, and the clouds darkened further in 2005, as Paris surprisingly lost its Olympic bid, French voters said No in the referendum on the European Constitution, a poll found only 32 per cent of respondents willing to express confidence in their president, and commentators and analysts warned that France could be about to enter its worst period of social unrest for more than a decade. Even Jean-Pierre Raffarin's inevitable resignation after the referendum (or 'Raffarindum', as newspapers punningly called it) and replacement by former foreign minister and Chirac loyalist Dominique de Villepin brought no immediate improvements. According to Pascal Perrineau, a professor at the prestigious Fondation Nationale des Sciences Politiques, known colloquially to all as Sciences-Po: 'The French model is no longer accepted as universal because it doesn't work.' And, more ominously, he concluded: 'The French do not change things by consensus, they change things by conflict.'

Key events

EARLY HISTORY

250 BC Lutetia founded on the Ile de la Cité by a Celtic tribe, the Parisii.
52 BC Paris conquered by the Romans.
AD 260 St Denis executed on Mount Mercury.
360 Julian, Governor of Lutetia, is proclaimed Roman Emperor by his troops.
451 Attila the Hun nearly attacks Paris.
496 Frankish king Clovis baptised at Reims.
508 Clovis makes Paris his capital.
543 Enormous Benedictine Monastery of St-Germain-des-Prés founded.
635 King Dagobert establishes international Fair of St-Denis.
800 Charlemagne becomes first Holy Roman Emperor. Moves his capital from Paris to Aix-la-Chapelle (Aachen).
845-880 Paris sacked by the Vikings.
987 Hugues Capet, Count of Paris, becomes King of France.

THE CITY TAKES SHAPE

1136 Abbot Suger begins the construction of the Basilica of St-Denis.
1163 Building of Notre-Dame begins.
1181 Philippe-Auguste establishes a new market at Les Halles.
1190-1202 Philippe-Auguste constructs a protective city wall.
1215 University of Paris is recognised by Rome with the Papal Charter.
1246-48 Louis IX (later St Louis) constructs Sainte-Chapelle.
1253 Sorbonne founded.
1340 Hundred Years War with England begins – lasting 116 years.
1357 Revolt by Etienne Marcel.
1364 Charles V moves royal court to the Louvre and builds Bastille and Vincennes fortresses.
1420-36 Paris under English rule.
1422 Henry V of England dies at the Château de Vincennes.
1463 First printing press in Paris.

THE WARS OF RELIGION AND AFTER

1528 François I, the Renaissance King, begins rebuilding the Louvre.
1572 23 August: the brutal massacre of Protestants on St Bartholemew's Day.
1589 Henri III assassinated.
1593 Henri IV converts to Catholicism, ending Wars of Religion.
1605 The construction of place des Vosges and Pont Neuf.

1610 Henri IV assassinated.
1635 Académie Française founded.
1643 Cardinal Mazarin becomes regent.
1648-53 Paris under continual threat by the 'Fronde' rebellion.
1661 Louis XIV begins personal rule – and the transformation of Versailles; the fall of Fouquet.
1667 Paris given its first street lighting.
1671 Building of Les Invalides.
1672 Creation of the Grands Boulevards on line of Charles V's city wall. Portes St-Denis and St-Martin built.
1680 Comédie Française founded.
1682 Louis XIV transfers court to Versailles.

ROYALTY TO REPUBLICANISM

1700 Beginning of the 15-year War of the Spanish Succession.
1715 Death of Louis XIV; Philippe d'Orléans becomes regent.
1753 Place Louis XV (later place de la Concorde) begun.
1785 Fermiers Généraux Tax Wall built.
1789 The first meeting of Etats Généraux since 1614.
1789 14 July: Paris mob takes the Bastille. Oct: Louis XVI forced by protesters to leave Versailles for Paris.
1791 21 June: Louis XVI attempts to escape Paris – unsuccessfully.
1792 September Massacres. 22 Sept: Republic declared. Royal statues removed.
1793 Execution of Louis XVI and Marie-Antoinette. Louvre museum opens to the public.
1794 The Terror – 1,300 heads fall in six weeks. July: Jacobins overthrown; Directoire takes over. A young officer from Corsica, Napoléon Bonaparte, is their right-hand man.
1799 Napoléon returns from Egypt to stage a military coup – becomes First Consul.
1804 Napoléon crowns himself emperor at a grand ceremony at Notre-Dame.
1806 Napoléon commissions the building of the Arc de Triomphe.
1814 Napoléon defeated; Russian army occupies Paris; Louis XVIII grants the Charter of Liberties.
1815 Napoléon regains power (the 'Hundred Days'), before defeat at Waterloo. Bourbon monarchy restored, with Louis XVIII.
1830 July: Charles X overthrown; Louis-Philippe of Orléans becomes king.
1836 Completion of Arc de Triomphe.

1838 Daguerre creates first daguerreotype photos. Paris gradually becomes a global mecca for visual arts.
1848 Louis-Philippe overthrown, replaced by Second Republic. Most men get the vote. Louis-Napoléon Bonaparte elected President.

CULTURAL EVOLUTION
1852 Louis-Napoléon declares himself Emperor Napoléon III: Second Empire. Bon Marché, first department store, opens.
1853 Haussmann made Préfet de Paris.
1862 Construction of Palais Garnier begins. Hugo's *Les Misérables* published.
1866 *Le Figaro* daily newspaper founded.
1870 Prussian victory at Sedan; siege of Paris. Napoléon III abdicates.
1871 Commune takes over Paris; May: *la semaine sanglante.*
1874 First Impressionist exhibition in Nadar's *atelier* on bd des Capucines.
1875 Bizet's *Carmen* at Opéra Comique.
1889 Exposition Universelle on the centenary of Revolution: Eiffel Tower built. Moulin Rouge opens. Montmartre becomes the artistic hub.
1894-1900 Dreyfus case polarises opinion.
1895 Dec: world's first public film screening by the Lumière brothers at the Jockey Club, now the Hôtel Scribe.
1900 Exposition Universelle: Grand Palais, Petit Palais, Pont Alexandre III built. First métro line opened.

THE WORLD WAR YEARS
1914 As World War I begins, Germans beaten back from Paris at the Marne.
1918 11 Nov: Armistice signed in the forest of Compiègne.
1919 Peace conference held at Versailles.
1927 La Coupole opens in Montparnasse. Paris again the cultural and literary mecca as writers and artists flock here in the inter-war years. Surrealism flourishes.
1934 Fascist demonstrations.
1936-37 France elects Popular Front under Léon Blum; first paid workers' holidays.
1940 Germans occupy Paris. 18 May: de Gaulle's call to arms from London. Life in occupied Paris goes on.
1941-42 Mass deportations of Paris Jews.
1944 Aug: Paris liberated.
1946 Fourth Republic established. Women given the vote.
1947 Christian Dior launches the New Look. Marshall Plan gives post-war aid to France.

1949 Simone de Beauvoir's *The Second Sex* published.
1955-56 Revolt begins in Algeria; demonstrations on the streets in Paris.
1957 Opening of CNIT in new La Défense business district.
1958 De Gaulle President: Fifth Republic.

EUROPEAN UNION AND NEW WORLD ORDER
1958 France founder member of what would become the European Economic Community – today's European Union.
1962 Algerian War ends.
1968 May: student riots and workers' strikes in Paris and across France.
1969 De Gaulle resigns, Georges Pompidou becomes President.
1973 Boulevard Périphérique inaugurated.
1977 Centre Pompidou opens. Jacques Chirac wins first mayoral elections.
1981 François Mitterrand elected President; abolition of the death penalty.
1989 Bicentenary of the Revolution: Louvre Pyramid and Opéra Bastille completed.
1995 Jacques Chirac elected President.
1997 General election: Socialist government elected under Lionel Jospin.
2001 Socialist Bertrand Delanoë elected Mayor of Paris. He begins the gradual transformation of Paris by introducing a series of crowd-pleasing civic projects.
2002 The success of National Front leader Jean-Marie Le Pen in the first round of the presidential elections paves the way for Jacques Chirac's landslide re-election. Jean-Pierre Raffarin becomes Prime Minister as France becomes governed by the centre-right.
2003 Jacques Chirac threatens to veto any US-led attempt to authorise military action against Iraq. France offers no material contribution to the subsequent invasion. Parliament approves powers to France's regions and *départements*, perhaps signalling a move away from highly centralised government. Jean-Pierre Raffarin's proposals to reform state pension and unemployment benefit cause widespread strikes. Some 15,000 people die in the August heat wave.
2004 Muslim headscarves and other symbols banned from French schools. Massive gains for the Socialists in regional elections.
2005 French voters reject the proposed new EU constitution. Raffarin replaced by former foreign minister Dominique de Villepin.

Paris Today

Interesting times.

First of all, there was the people's *non* to the European Constitution. Then there was the *non* to Paris 2012 from the International Olympic Committee. As if that wasn't enough, billionaire businessman François Pinault, frustrated by bureaucratic delays, decided to abandon the French capital and take his major new contemporary art museum to Venice.

In the last year or so, things just have not gone the right way for Paris – or, indeed, for President Jacques Chirac. The French electorate's rejection of the EU Constitution last June was seen, above all, as a protest vote against the inaction of Chirac. (Although Parisians signalled their difference from the national majority – not for the first time – by voting 66 per cent in favour of the constitution.)

In the lead-up to the June referendum, Chirac's government had failed to deliver. Unemployment stubbornly remained among the highest in Western Europe (around ten per cent), while a hefty public deficit (which still breaches European Union limits) had forced the partial – and highly unpopular – privatisation of aero

engine firm Snecma, with France Télécom and Gaz de France to follow. In addition, the loi Fillon, a new education law aimed at reforming the *baccalauréat*, had triggered month-long demonstrations and occupations of *lycées*, with many of the Paris protests ending in violence.

After 55 per cent of his electorate had voted against the European Constitution, Chirac was left with little option but to take action. Unsurprisingly, the chief scapegoat was Prime Minister Jean-Pierre Raffarin, who duly resigned. Just the month before, Raffarin's suppression of the Pentecost bank holiday (a measure aimed at raising funds for the elderly) had been met by widespread strikes. Chirac replaced the unpopular Raffarin with his loyal henchman, Dominique de Villepin, previously best known as the foreign minister who said 'non' to the Iraq war. Never elected to office, Villepin is a career diplomat and published poet whose appointment had been initially met with justifiable doubt. Yet the polls show he has since managed to gain considerable popularity, and his promise to make employment the national priority has been backed up by action, notably in the shape of the *contrat nouvelle embauche* (CNE). This new employment contract relaxes France's famously rigid labour laws, letting companies of fewer than 20 employees fire workers without notice during their first two years.

Villepin's new-found credibility makes him a strong candidate for taking over from Chirac at the 2007 general election (assuming the current president decides to step down). Recent polls, however, clearly indicate that Nicolas Sarkozy (*see p26* **The heir apparent?**) is the man most likely to win a third term for Chirac's centre-right UMP party. Viewed with some suspicion by Chirac, 51-year-old Sarkozy has made no secret at all of his presidential ambitions, nor of his disdain for rival Villepin.

While Sarkozy may have been snubbed for the prime ministerial job, he nonetheless had reason to be satisfied with the post-referendum cabinet shuffle. At the end of 2004, the energetic Sarkozy was elected UMP party leader, and told the position was incompatible with his role as finance minister. Forced to stand down from government, Sarkozy only had to wait until June to have his cake and eat it. Chirac appointed him both interior minister and *ministre d'Etat* (roughly equivalent to deputy prime minister), while allowing him to continue as party leader. In his role as interior minister, Sarkozy has promised to clamp down on immigration: he didn't hesitate to repatriate a number of radical Islamist leaders in the wake of the London bombings.

'If the *non* to the Olympic Games was a knock for Chirac, it was a devastating blow for Delanoë.'

An even larger – though related – challenge arose in November 2005, just as this guide was going to press. Major riots spread across the country over several consecutive nights, as warehouses, restaurants and thousands of cars were set ablaze. Sarkozy reacted in his characteristic hard-line manner, sending in police squads by the bus-load (some were shot at); but his inflammatory comments that the rioters were 'riff-raff' who should be 'pressure-cleaned' from the *banlieue* estates where the violence took place were widely criticised.

It's not only the usually popular Sarkozy who has been criticised; politicians in general have lost favour. Last year, both Chirac and left-wing Paris mayor Bertrand Delanoë lost their place among the nation's 50 favourite French

personalities. The biannual Ifop survey placed tennis- turned rock-star Yannick Noah at the head of the list, while *Libération* journalist and released Iraqi hostage Florence Aubenas turned up in 12th place. During her 157-day captivity from January 2005, Aubenas and her guide Hussein Hanoun were constantly evoked in the press amid regular public campaigning for their release.

Bertrand Delanoë's fall from the best-loved national figures list is a slight to the Paris mayor with presidential ambitions. If the *non* to the Olympic Games was a knock for Chirac, it was a devastating blow for Delanoë, who put much of his ample energy behind the Paris 2012 campaign. In keeping with his fun-loving image, Delanoë decided to wow the Olympic Committee by transforming the Champs-Elysées – for just 24 hours – into a showcase for sport, complete with a 700-metre (2,300-foot) athletic track, tennis courts, a swimming pool and an equestrian arena. Alas, the spectacle was not enough to win over the IOC and, despite its favourite status, Paris lost out in the final voting process for the third time in 20 years. The French media accused winner London of underhand lobbying tactics, and bemoaned a decision that seemed to be made on political rather than sporting grounds.

Despite this setback, Delanoë remains a well-regarded figure, whose latest populist cultural innovation, the Nuit des Musées (a night of free entry to Paris museums), was as great a success as his now well-established Nuits Blanches and Paris Plage events. Meanwhile, Delanoë's extensive array of urban development projects are flourishing. A major regeneration of the previously abandoned site east of the Gare d'Austerlitz continues to go from strength to strength. By the end of 2006 this up-and-coming area around the Bibliothèque Nationale de France François Mitterrand will be home to four universities, a floating open-air swimming pool on the Seine, and a footbridge linking the Bibliothèque to the Parc de Bercy. The mayor's next big project is to be a major facelift of the much-maligned Les Halles gardens and subterranean shopping centre, with Paris-born David Mangin on board as architect.

Delanoë has also made a priority of traffic and public transport, creating multiple bus and cycle lanes, while this year heralds the opening of a new Parisian tramway. Eventually destined to cover the perimeter of the city (just inside the Périphérique), the line initially opens in the south (around Les Maréchaux), and will be bordered by acres of lawns and more than a thousand trees. Further projects envisage the creation of more green spaces, and the extension of several existing métro lines to link up with a new tram network due to be built in the *banlieue*.

While Delanoë recognises the necessity for urban growth, he also knows that Paris depends on its heritage – and a new urban planning doctrine announced last year introduces a number of regulations aimed at protecting the capital's historical cityscape. Preservation is at the heart of the Plan local d'urbanisme (PLU), with an additional 4,000 buildings and 1,500 parks, gardens and cemeteries falling under state protection. The PLU also confounds Delanoë's desire to reintroduce skyscrapers to the Paris skyline, stipulating that any new towers must not climb any higher than 37 metres (120 feet).

The price of such rigid protectionism is arguably a lack of dynamism. In this light, the loss of François Pinault's major new contemporary art museum was a significant blow for the city. In 30 years of art collecting, 70-year-old Pinault had assembled a 2,500-strong 'who's who' collection of late 20th-century works. Having found a prime spot on the Ile Séguin, in the middle of the Seine just south-west of the city, Pinault commissioned Japanese architect Tadao Ando to design a strikingly futuristic museum. Scheduled for completion in 2005, the project was hobbled by

recurrent bureaucratic obstacles and endless delays in obtaining planning permission. By early 2005 construction had not even begun. Not unreasonably, Pinault wanted to see the project realised within his lifetime – so he simply bought the Palazzo Grassi in Venice and took his collection to Italy.

'Many observers believe that *The Da Vinci Code*'s popularity is at least partly responsible for the return of American tourists.'

Pinault's experience is far from unique. While Paris is universally renowned for its museums, new cultural projects are often subject to a long gestation period. 2005 should finally see the opening of the new Musée des Arts Premiers, Chirac's pet project that was originally scheduled for a 2004 opening, while the long-awaited Cité de l'Architecture et du Patrimoine should also open its doors in the Palais de Chaillot at Trocadéro. And the Musée de l'Orangerie, home to Monet's grandiose *Water Lilies*, has seen its 2001 reopening date put back indefinitely following the discovery of a 15th-century mural during renovations.

The biggest cultural opening of 2005 was the new headquarters of the Cinémathèque Française (*see p294* **'thèque five**) in a long-abandoned Frank Gehry building at the edge of the Parc de Bercy. France's national film institute now boasts four screens, temporary exhibition space, and, for the first time in nearly a decade, a *musée du cinéma* – allowing the cinephile public to finally appreciate one of the world's most prolific collections of film props, costumes and photographs. Cinema attendance continues to rise in Paris (29.1 million entries in 2003), although the trend is ever more towards multiplexes (compared with ten years ago, Paris has fewer establishments, but more screens). Indeed, the success of the multiplexes poses an ever-greater threat to smaller cinemas, with the three-screen Gaumont Grand Ecran at place d'Italie facing closure, and the future of the historic Grand Rex still uncertain. Fortunately, the Ville de Paris has established a fund to help renovate the city's numerous independent cinemas. Such support is ever more essential, given the explosion of TV channels and internet providers. Last year, the launch of the *télévision numérique terrestre* (TNT) made 14 channels available for the price of a digital adapter, while Pink TV became France's first gay channel.

Perhaps the biggest surprise on the media front was the unprecedented welcoming

So wrong, Marianne?

Look into any of the 20 town halls proudly representing each Paris arrondissement – or, indeed, the palatial municipal hub of the Hôtel de Ville itself (*see p107*) – and you'll see what French intellectuals are gloomily referring to as the 'Mariannisation' of France's once heavyweight culture.

There, centrepiecing a table in the lobby or doubling up as an ornate paperweight on the mayor's desk, will be a bust of Marianne, the very symbol of France, the *Liberté, Egalité* and *Fraternité* of 1789 personified. Even visitors who have the most casual acquaintance with French iconography will recall her face from coins, postage stamps or the old 100 franc note; and, of course, she's there as the bare-bosomed *patriote* storming the barricades, rifle and tricolore in hand, in Delacroix's 1830 painting *Liberty Leading the People*.

But ask any Frenchman – and certainly any *française* – and he or she will tell you that the current Marianne has the features not of an idealised figurehead of republican virtue, but of French housewives' favourite afternoon TV presenter, Evelyne Thomas. The idea of making Marianne in the likeness of a French celebrity isn't new: it began as a

joke by sculptor Alain Gourdon (aka Aslan) in 1970, when the national icon bore an entirely deliberate resemblance to Brigitte Bardot. Since then, at irregular intervals, Marianne's Phrygian cap has graced the likenesses of Mireille Mathieu, Inès de la Fressange and Catherine Deneuve – all clearly several notches above trash-telly talk-show hosts. Thomas at least holds a degree in Political Science and International Law, and has moved up from gruesome human-interest show *C'est mon choix* (It's My Choice) on France 3 to *Combien ça coute?* (How Much Does That Cost?) on TF1. And the sitter for the previous bust, 2000's millennial Marianne Laetitia Casta, best known for her work in lingerie catalogues, allegedly legged it to London to escape the French taxman: not – if true – exactly patriotic behaviour.

But perhaps the biggest difference between Deneuve and the populist Thomas or 36D-cup Casta is that the latter two were selected by the 36,000 vote-seeking mayors of France. There's no longer a Bardot to personify both French values and womanhood – instead, a nation of shoppers gets its mayors to vote in someone off the telly. Symbolic, eh?

of Hollywood crews to the capital's most celebrated monuments. Culture Minister Renaud Donnedieu de Vabres had noted that 62 per cent of tourists claim to visit France after seeing it on the big screen. He thus set up a commission to promote the country's castles, parks and museums in the cinema. Among the beneficiaries was Sofia Coppola, who filmed her forthcoming *Marie Antoinette* at Versailles, while Ron Howard spent several nights in the Louvre, directing Tom Hanks and Audrey Tautou in *The Da Vinci Code*.

Paris will not have to await the opening of Howard's movie to benefit from the popularity of *The Da Vinci Code*, however. Dan Brown's bestselling novel, much of which takes place in Paris, has already given birth to at least three companies offering *Da Vinci Code* tours of the capital. Tired of answering questions about the book's fictional details, the Eglise St-Sulpice has mounted a sign repudiating the book's content. Still, many observers believe the novel's popularity is at least partly responsible for the return of American tourists (an increase of 7.1 per cent in 2004 relative to the previous year) following the post-Iraq downturn. While the tourist industry is still not as buoyant as it

was back in 2002, France nonetheless led the world in tourist arrivals (75 million) in 2004.

One sector that shows no signs of fragility is the Paris property market. In the first quarter of 2005, the annual price rise for flats in the capital reached 14.5 per cent. The *bo-bos* (bohemian bourgeois) have consequently taken their search for affordable flats to more working-class quarters like the Goutte d'Or and Sainte-Marthe in the north, and have inflicted the capital's highest property price inflation on these areas (22.8 per cent in the 10th arrondissement). Paris is becoming so expensive that Parisians, and especially those with children, are moving out to the *banlieue*. The number of three- and four-bedroom flats sold in the capital fell by two per cent in 2004, while it increased by around the same amount in the outer suburbs.

But if 2005 was the year of *non* for Paris, at least one man said *oui*. After a year of self-imposed absence from the national football team, Zinedine Zidane's return was heralded as the end of a (relative) crisis in French football. The press prattled happily about 'l'effet Zidane' and its impact beyond the realm of sport. It just goes to show that anyone can have a year off and still come back to renewed success.

The **RER entrance** at Gare St-Lazare.

Paris Tomorrow

Ch-ch-ch-*changements.*

Shortly after you leave the plane at Orly airport, you flash your biometric ID card at the scanner. Another electronic card – the multipurpose Navigo pass – has already served as your air ticket, and it now lets you into the line 14 Métro station at Orly. The whole journey was pre-paid on the internet, *naturellement.* The driverless train speeds its way to central Paris in a matter of minutes – the time to make a quick subterranean phone call. On emerging at Châtelet, you buy a drink by swiping your Navigo across a vending machine. A short stroll through the traffic-free centre brings you to Les Halles gardens, which were extensively redeveloped 15 years ago. Sitting on a bench, you read the latest news on your PDA, courtesy of the free, city-wide Wi-Fi service.

This is Paris circa 2026, as envisioned by the current planners and shapers of the future – notably in the form of Mayor Bertrand Delanoë. In 2004 the left-wing mayor (who hopes to be elected President sometime between 2006 and 2026) commissioned a major poll to find out

how Parisians would like to see their city develop. Happily, the results neatly reflected his own plans and policies to protect historical Paris while creating a more user-friendly city with fewer cars, better public transport and less pollution. Paris may have a reputation as the city that never changes, but Delanoë does not see preserving its heritage as an obstacle to progress.

Public transport has a prime place in Delanoë's vision of the future, and the Paris transport authority (RATP) has obliged the mayor with a catalogue of projects in the offing. Over the next 15 years, several Métro lines are to be extended to improve transit between Paris and its suburbs, while the high-tech line 14 could eventually reach as far as Gennevilliers in the north and Orly airport in the south. Thanks to its anti-suicide platform doors and driverless, high-speed trains, line 14 has already set the blueprint for the future – and the RATP is studying the possibility of automating other lines.

The eco-friendly tramway will become a big force in Paris by 2026, with a major new tram network skirting the city's perimeter just inside the Périphérique. The first part of the line opens this year in the south, with a second section scheduled for 2011. Again, the project aims to strengthen links between Paris and its suburbs by connecting with a number of métro and RER stations. The tram also points the way to Delanoë's vision of a greener Paris; the initial eight-kilometre (five-mile) stretch of track will be bordered by 36,000 square metres (390,000 square feet) of lawns and over 1,000 trees.

Ever the innovator, the RATP has also been working on a high-tech service for its fleet of buses. Most irresistible are the plans to fulfil every urban motorist's dream by making the traffic lights automatically turn green. Needless to say, the system will be reserved for bus drivers, who will benefit from the co-ordination between the traffic lights and the existing GPS equipment aboard the city's buses. GPS technology is also behind plans to offer a localised information service on plasma screens. Bus passengers will be able to watch aerial 3D views of the surrounding streets, along with expected arrival times. Most innovatively, the screens will broadcast regularly updated mini-documentaries, cultural reports, and weather and news bulletins about the different areas en route. The RATP plans to test both projects this year.

If travel around Paris promises to be easier in 2026, so, too, does getting away from the city. With its high-speed TGV train already able to hit over 300 kilometres per hour (186 miles per hour), the SNCF simply has to lay down compatible track to radically cut journey times in France – and beyond. By 2010 Parisians will be able to reach Strasbourg in just one hour 50 minutes (compared with nearly four hours today), while Rennes will be less than an hour and a half away come 2017, and journeys to the city of Toulouse will be cut by two hours.

If these multiple public-transport initiatives are to succeed, Parisians will have to abandon their beloved cars – and Delanoë is not afraid to make doing so easier. Since coming to power in 2001, Delanoë (who drives an electric car) has managed to achieve a 13 per cent reduction in traffic thanks to a policy of multiplying bus lanes, decreasing residential parking fees, and widening pavements. Between 2001 and 2004 pollution was cut by 19 per cent on the city's main east–west thoroughfare, the rue de Rivoli.

With some 82 per cent of Parisians polled declaring their support for his far-sighted transport policies, Delanoë has become even more ambitious. His avowed aim is to reduce traffic in central Paris by 25 per cent within

the next five years. The first stage of his three-step plan will see the speed limit reduced to 30 kilometres per hour (19 miles per hour) in the first four arrondissements, and current parking fines tripled. Some 90 kilometres (56 miles) of bike lanes have been set up since 2001 (with a 32 per cent increase in bicycle travel), and the policy will continue, with new cycle lanes to be built along the Seine. From 2007, cars will be banned from Seine-side embankments and from the centre of Paris at weekends, while the roads around Les Halles will be pedestrianised. The final phase of his ambitious plan sees the first four arrondissements (the area immediately north of the Seine between place de la Concorde and place de la Bastille) closed to all non-residential private vehicles by 2012.

'The ultimate fantasy is of a wholly subterranean Périphérique, and a city entirely bordered by green spaces.'

Another environmentally sound project for the near future consists of covering sections of the city's ringroad. Over 100,000 Parisians live alongside the 35-kilometre (22-mile) Périphérique, enduring noise levels of up to 70 decibels, as well as the city's highest pollution levels. The first of three areas to be relieved of such pollutants will be the north-eastern Porte des Lilas at the end of 2006. With eight lanes of moody motorists shut away beneath their feet, residents will be able to enjoy a new 17,300-square-metre (186,000-square-foot) area landscaped with a large garden and sports fields. The ultimate fantasy is of a wholly subterranean Périphérique, and so a city entirely bordered by green spaces.

One effect of hiding parts of the Périphérique is to bring Paris closer to its suburbs. Unlike many major cities, Paris has rigidly defined limits. Since 1860 the city has comprised the same 20 arrondissements that cover the same 105 square kilometres (41 square miles). Completed in 1973, the Périphérique only served to deepen the geographical and administrative division between Paris and its expanding suburbs. In 2004 just over two million people lived in Paris, while the *agglomération de Paris* ('Greater Paris') numbered almost ten million. In the future, Parisians may have to bin their notorious condescension towards the suburbs as inflated housing prices force them out of the centre. (Such a migratory trend is already well established among couples with children.)

At the same time, Delanoë's transport policies are designed to improve links to the suburbs, with an additional 70-kilometre (44-mile) tram line intended to encircle the city way beyond the Périphérique by 2015. All these signs point towards a 'Grand Paris', where the traditional Paris/*banlieue* gap is less forcefully expressed than has been the case.

Of course, Paris is unlikely to be trumped by its suburbs in the near future, and a number of urban development projects can guarantee its place in the limelight for a while to come. The most significant of these is the regeneration of the Seine-side strip in the south-eastern 13th arrondissement. This year, the area will gain a footbridge linking the Bibliothèque François

Leaning towards the future: Arquitectonica's 15-storey **Exaltis Tower** at La Défense.

Mitterrand to the Parc de Bercy, and a floating open-air swimming pool filled with filtered water from the Seine. By 2015, four universities will be up and running, a new park will cover the area's rail tracks, and the warehouses between the Gare d'Austerlitz and Bibliothèque will have been converted into the city's docks and home to the French Fashion Institute.

Meanwhile, the 1970s architectural disaster that is the Les Halles gardens and subterranean shopping centre will undergo a much-needed facelift. Formerly the old market district, Les Halles has more recently acquired a reputation as a hangout for petty criminals and drug dealers. Paris-born architect David Mangin has been entrusted with overseeing the transformation, envisaging a broad avenue through landscaped gardens. The most optimistic completion date is 2012. Elsewhere, the northern Batignolles area that was to host the Olympic village will be reborn as a large park surrounded by offices, shops and housing. Other projects remain undecided. The *petite ceinture*, the long-abandoned train network around the outskirts of Paris, has alternatively been considered for use as a new public transport network, a freight service or a landscaped public walkway.

> ### 'Delanoë has, for the moment at least, lost his battle to resurrect the long-taboo debate about building skyscrapers.'

For the city that never changes, such projects sound uncharacteristically bold. However, the fabric of Paris lies in its historical monuments and buildings – and a new urban-planning doctrine adopted last year introduces a number of regulations aimed at protecting the city's patrimony. Three years in the making, the Plan local d'urbanisme (PLU) defines the shape of__ the Paris cityscape for the next 15 to 20 years. Preservation is at the heart of the doctrine, with an additional 4,000 buildings joining the 1,900 already under state protection. Some 1,500 green spaces (parks, gardens, cemeteries) have been designated protected areas, while a vast area of ground floor space is reserved exclusively for shops. The PLU also aims to improve the balance throughout the various arrondissements between social housing and office/residential property. Hence, any new housing development in the bourgeois centre or west must contain at least 25 per cent social housing, compared with just 20 per cent in the rest of Paris. New constructions must also be limited to 37 metres (121 feet) in height, meaning that Delanoë has, for the moment at least, lost his campaign to resurrect the long-taboo debate about building skyscrapers within the city.

Many observers argue that such restrictive measures result in the 'muséfication' of Paris, whereby the Grands Projets of the Mitterrand era have been eschewed in favour of cosmetic retouching (the renovation of the east around the Bibliothèque, of the Beaugrenelle area in the 15th arrondissement, or of Les Halles). In the face of such ultra-conservatism, Delanoë's relatively ambitious projects have enjoyed quite remarkable success.

Even if the cityscape of central Paris is not likely to change significantly, the technological landscape is set to revolutionise life. Transport tickets will be electronic, with the RATP's Navigo smart card set to become the norm. By swiping the chip-based Navigo card over a scanner, passengers can currently gain access to the city's Métro and buses. In the long term, Navigo could allow travellers to connect with other forms of transport – and the same card could eventually serve as an electronic purse, used for low-value purchases in *boulangeries*, newsagents and *tabacs*. From 2007, French residents will also be equipped with an electronic identity card containing a digitised photo and fingerprints of the holder.

The internet bug continues to grip France. During 2006, French households are set to become the second most connected in Europe, and France Télécom recently announced plans to develop a 1GB-per-second connection in 20 French cities. The future of Wi-Fi in Paris also looks rosy, with ever more 'hotspots' (wireless access points) installed in cafés, airports and train stations. The ultimate vision is of a wireless city – where anyone can surf the net anywhere. To this end, the 3rd arrondissement has been used as a trial ground for free-access hotspots, where five key public locations have been Wi-Fi-enabled. The RATP, meanwhile, has already experimented with hotspots in 12 métro stations and on its No.38 bus route (*see p367* **Wi-Fi, where find?**). In the long term, the plan is to equip all 373 métro stations. As hotspots can emit a signal that fans out to a distance of 100 metres (328 feet), this would give vast areas of the city Wi-Fi connectivity.

In 2026 Paris will undoubtedly still be Paris – the city that Baron Haussmann so radically reshaped in the 19th century. At the same time, quality of life looks set to improve, thanks to a number of environmentally friendly projects and technological innovations. Visiting tourists can only hope that the Parisians' love of new technology will extend to robot dogs that are incapable of fouling the pavement.

Where to Stay

Where to Stay   **40**

Features

Where to Stay

From marble-clad palaces to budget bedrooms – Paris has hotels for everybody.

For some, a hotel is a base at which to sleep and scrub up before stepping out to explore the city. For others, it's a feature in its own right. Whatever your take, there's a Paris hotel to fit the bill. We've found the best in each category, from marble-clad palaces fit for a Sun King to cramped yet cosy hotels with bare-stone breakfast rooms, via sleek boutique hotels with daring colour schemes. We've also got budget addresses where you needn't stay any longer than it takes for a shower and some shut-eye.

CLASSIFICATION AND FACILITIES

Hotels are graded according to an official star rating system designed to sort palace from pit stop – but we haven't followed it in this guide. Said star ratings usually reflect room size and mere presence of a lift (rather than decor, staff or atmosphere), and we don't think the system is of much practical value when making your choice. Instead, we've divided the hotels into four categories, according to the price for one night in a double room with shower/bath facilities: Deluxe €300+; Expensive €200-€300; Moderate €100-€200; Budget up to €100.

Deluxe means air-conditioning, double-glazed windows, a bar and restaurant (except in the smaller boutique hotels), with babysitting and airport shuttle services; in-room extras often include modem connection and room service, plus other extras depending on the hotel. Expensive ones offer similar amenities and services. Moderate means an in-room phone, modem connection and breakfast service; at the budget hotels you can normally be assured of a TV and in-room phone. We provide a list of the key services below the description of each hotel. For gay hotels, see p306.

NEED TO KNOW

Note that all hotels in France charge an additional room tax (taxe de séjour) of around €1 per person, sometimes included in the posted rate. Hotels are often booked solid during the major trade fairs (January, May, September), and it's hard to find a quality pillow on which to lay your head during fashion weeks (January

and early July for haute couture, March and October for prêt-à-porter). However, at quieter times, including July and August, hotels often offer reasonable special deals at short notice; phone ahead or check their websites to find out. Same-day reservations can be arranged in person for a nominal commission fee at the Office de Tourisme de Paris (see chapter **Resources A-Z: Tourist information**).

Several websites offer discount booking: www.parishotels.com guarantees the lowest prices online, which can be up to 70 per cent off the rack rate; and www.ratestogo.com offers big discounts on four-star hotels for last-minute reservations (up to two weeks in advance).

The Islands

Expensive

Hôtel du Jeu de Paume

54 rue St-Louis-en-l'Ile, 4th (01.43.26.14.18/fax 01.40.46.02.76/www.jeudepaumehotel.com). M° Pont Marie. **Rates** €165-€230 single; €250-€395 double; €495 suite; €18 breakfast. **Credit** AmEx, DC, MC, V. **Map** p411 K7 ❶
With an oh-so-discreet courtyard entrance, original 17th-century beams, private garden and a unique timbered breakfast room that was once a real tennis court built under Louis XIII, this is a charming hotel. It's now filled with a nicely slung-together array of modern and classical art. A dramatic glass lift and catwalks lead to the rooms, which are simple and tasteful, and have Pierre Frey fabric walls.
Bar. Gym. Internet (web TV). Room service.

Moderate

Hôtel des Deux-Iles

59 rue St-Louis-en-l'Ile, 4th (01.43.26.13.35/fax 01.43.29.60.25/www.deuxiles-paris-hotel.com). M° Pont Marie. **Rates** €145 single; €130-€164 double; €11 breakfast. **Credit** AmEx, MC, V. **Map** p411 K7 ❷
This peaceful 17th-century townhouse offers 17 soundproofed, air-conditioned rooms done out in faintly colonial style. Attractive features include a tiny courtyard off the lobby, and a vaulted stone breakfast room with fireplace (which helps it feel less like a cellar than many such breakfast rooms). The equally pleasant Hôtel Lutèce, at nearby No.65 (01.43.26.23.52), is run by the same management. *Concierge. Internet. TV.*

Green '❶' numbers given in this chapter give the location of each hotel as marked on the street maps. See pp402-411.

Five generations of craftsmanship – **Hôtel Edouard VII**. *See p46*.

Budget

Hospitel Hôtel Dieu

1 pl du Parvis-Notre-Dame, 4th (01.44.32.01.00/fax 01.44.32.01.16/www.hotel-hospitel.com). M° Cité or Hôtel de Ville. **Rates** €91 single; €102 double; €7.70 breakfast. **Credit** MC, V. **Map** p410 J7 ❸
Hospitel has 14 spotless rooms with colourful contemporary decor and a limited view of the spires of Notre-Dame. It's used by families of the Hôtel Dieu hospital's in-patients and staff; they usually take up about half the hotel's capacity. A medical smell is present but not strong, bathrooms are quite large, and you couldn't ask for a better sightseeing base in all of Paris.
No smoking. Room service.

The Louvre, Palais-Royal & Les Halles

Deluxe

Hôtel Costes

239 rue St-Honoré, 1st (01.42.44.50.00/fax 01.42.44.50.01/www.hotelcostes.com). M° Tuileries. **Rates** €350 single; €500-€600 double; €700-€1,400 suite; €30 breakfast. **Credit** AmEx, DC, MC, V. **Map** p403 G5 ❹
If attitude is more important than service, then this temple of stylish notoriety is for you. And don't even think of whipping out your autograph book, no matter how many A-listers you might find at the low-lit bar (*see p213* **Overnight sensations**). The Costes boasts one of the best pools in Paris, a sybaritic Eastern-inspired affair with its own underwater music system. The same management is also responsible for the sleek Hôtel Costes K in the 16th, with a fabulous spa and all.
Bar. Concierge. Gym. Parking (€30). Pool (indoor). Restaurant. Room service. Spa. TV.
Other locations: Hôtel Costes K, 81 av Kléber, 16th (01.44.05.75.75).

Hôtel de Crillon

10 pl de la Concorde, 8th (01.44.71.15.00/fax 01.44.71.15.02/www.crillon.com). M° Concorde. **Rates** €510-€605 single; €630-€890 double; €995-€8,200 suite; €32-€47 breakfast. **Credit** AmEx, DC, MC, V. **Map** p403 F4 ❺
The height of neo-classical European magnificence, the Crillon lives up to its *palais* reputation with decor strong on marble, mirrors and gold leaf. The Michelin-starred Les Ambassadeurs (*see p187*) has an acclaimed chef, and the Winter Garden tearoom has a gorgeous terrace and live harp music. And at classes given here by the city's top floral designers you can even learn how to recreate those trendy flower arrangements seen throughout the hotel.
Bar. Business centre. Concierge. Gym. Internet. No-smoking room(s). Parking (free). Restaurants (2). Room service. TV.

The best Hotels

For budget with beauty

Familia Hôtel (*see p58*); Grand Hôtel Lévêque (*see p62*); Hôtel Chopin and Hôtel Paris France (*see p47* **Budget beds**).

For Marais hipsters

Hôtel Axial Beaubourg (*see p54*); Hôtel Bourg Tibourg (*see p54*).

For cyber luxury

Hôtel le A (*see p50*); Murano Urban Resort (*see p53*); Park Hyatt Paris-Vendôme (*see p46*).

For that fashion feel

Hôtel des Tuileries (*see p45*); Hôtel du Petit Moulin (*see p54*); Hôtel Plaza Athénée (*see p50*).

For spa indulgence

Four Seasons George V (*see p49*); Le Grand InterContinental (*see p46*); Hôtel Costes K (*see left*); Hôtel Meurice (*see below*).

For history

Hôtel de la Bretonnerie (*see p54*); Hôtel du Jeu de Paume (*see p40*); Hôtel St-Merry (*see p54*).

For views

Hôtel Brighton (*see p45*); Hôtel Meurice (*see below*); Terrass Hôtel (*see p53*); Timhotel Montmartre (*see p53*).

Hôtel Meurice

228 rue de Rivoli, 1st (01.44.58.10.10/fax 01.44.58.10.15/www.meuricehotel.com). M° Tuileries. **Rates** €510-€600 single; €650-€760 double; €1,050-€10,000 suite; €33-€45 breakfast. **Credit** AmEx, DC, MC, V. **Map** p403 G6 ❻
Having spruced up its extravagant Louis XVI decor and intricate mosaic tiled floors in a lengthy facelift, Le Meurice is looking absolutely splendid. All of its 160 rooms are done out in distinct historical styles; among the 36 suites (25 full and 11 junior), the Belle Etoile on the seventh floor provides 360-degree panoramic views of Paris from its terrace. You can relax by the Winter Garden to the strains of regular live jazz performances; for more intensive intervention head over to the lavishly appointed spa with its *vinothérapie* treatments – or get grape products directly into your bloodstream at the gorgeous, high-ceilinged Bar Fontainebleau.
Bar. Business centre. Concierge. Gym. Hairdryer. Internet. No-smoking room(s). Restaurants (2). Room service. Spa. TV.

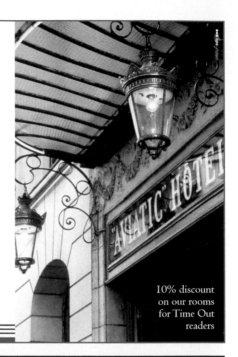

Hôtel Ritz

15 pl Vendôme, 1st (01.43.16.30.30/fax 01.43.16.31.78/www.ritzparis.com). M° Concorde or Opéra. **Rates** €680-€770 single or double; €1,180-€8,500 suite; €35-€43 breakfast. **Credit** AmEx, DC, MC, V. **Map** p403 G4 ❼

This, the grande dame of Paris hotels, has proffered hospitality to Coco Chanel, the Duke of Windsor, Proust, and Dodi and Di. Today's guests have the choice of 162 bedrooms, of which 56 are suites, from the romantic Frédéric Chopin to the glitzy Impérial. There are plenty of corners in which to strike poses or quench a thirst, from Hemingway's elegant cigar bar and the plush Victorian champagne bar to the poolside one inspired by Ancient Greece. *See also p213* **Overnight sensations.**
Bars (2). Business centre. Concierge. Gym. Hairdryer. Internet. Parking (€44). Pool (indoor). Restaurant. Room service. Spa. TV.

Hôtel Sofitel le Faubourg

15 rue Boissy-d'Anglas, 8th (01.44.94.14.00/fax 01.44.94.14.28/www.sofitel.com). M° Concorde. **Rates** €365 single; €435-€495 double; €575-€995 suite; €2,000 apartment; €23-€28 breakfast. **Credit** AmEx, DC, MC, V. **Map** p403 G4 ❽

This hotel is close to the major couture boutiques – unsurprisingly, as it used to be the *Marie Claire* offices. The rooms have Louis XVI armchairs, large balconies, walk-in wardrobes and Roger & Gallet smellies in the bathrooms; for shopping widowers, there's a small gym and a hammam. It's quiet, too: the street has been closed to traffic since 2001 because the American Embassy is on the corner.
Bar. Business centre. Concierge. Gym. Internet. No-smoking room(s). Parking (€26). Restaurant. Room service. TV.

Moderate

Hôtel Brighton

218 rue de Rivoli, 1st (01.47.03.61.61/fax 01.42.60.41.78/www.esprit-de-france.com). M° Tuileries. **Rates** €163-€170 single or double; €238-€275 suite; €8-€14 breakfast. **Credit** AmEx, DC, MC, V. **Map** p403 G5 ❾

With several rooms overlooking the Tuileries garden, this hotel is very good value. The Brighton, all faux-marble and mosaic decor, was opened at the start of the 20th century as the Entente Cordiale got under way, and has recently been restored. Rooms are spacious; for a good view, book well in advance.
Concierge. Internet. TV.

Hôtel Louvre Ste-Anne

32 rue Ste-Anne, 1st (01.40.20.02.35/fax 01.40.15.91.13/www.louvre-ste-anne.fr). M° Pyramides. **Rates** €96-€122 single; €111-€184 double; €10 breakfast. **Credit** AmEx, DC, MC, V. **Map** p403 H5 ❿

The friendly staff at this centrally located hotel do everything to make visitors feel at home. The 20 fine air-conditioned rooms are done with a Provençal

peach and ivy theme; for extra space and balcony views of the Sacré-Coeur, book one of the top-floor rooms: they're dearer, but worth the outlay.
Concierge. Internet (wireless). TV.

Hôtel Mansart

5 rue des Capucines, 1st (01.42.61.50.28/fax 01.49.27.97.44/www.esprit-de-france.com). M° Opéra. **Rates** €120-€305 double; €17 extra bed; €11 breakfast. **Credit** AmEx, DC, MC, V. **Map** p403 G4 ⓫

Stay near the ritzy place Vendôme without the ritzy prices. This welcoming, spacious hotel has real style, with a light, roomy lobby decorated in murals inspired by formal gardens. The 57 bedrooms in assorted colour schemes feature pleasant fabrics, period furniture and paintings; five rooms, including the lovely Vendôme duplex, have an excellent view of the square – ideal for planning a jewel heist.
Bar. Concierge. Internet. Room service. TV.

Hôtel des Tuileries

10 rue St-Hyacinthe, 1st (01.42.61.04.17/fax 01.49.27.91.56/www.hotel-des-tuileries.com). M° Tuileries. **Rates** €125-€195 single; €140-€230 double; €220-€250 triple; €13 breakfast. **Credit** AmEx, DC, MC, V. **Map** p403 G5 ⓬

The fashion pack adores this 18th-century hotel (a property of Marie-Antoinette's lady-in-waiting) located in prime shopping territory. The current style purveys a comfy *Ab Fab* feel, with ethnic rugs and the odd smattering of animal prints and bright art, combined with antique furniture, exposed beams and a listed staircase.
Concierge. Internet. Room service (mornings only). TV.

Le Relais Saint-Honoré

308 rue St-Honoré, 1st (01.42.96.06.06/fax 01.42.96.17.50). M° Tuileries. **Rates** €190 double; €280-€320 suite; €12 breakfast. **Credit** AmEx, DC, MC, V. **Map** p403 G5 ⓭

This entirely renovated 17th-century hotel offers 13 rooms and two suites with elegant, traditional decor. The attention to detail is immaculate – although lack of customer care sometimes lets the side down.
Concierge. Internet. No-smoking room(s). Room service. TV.

Budget

Hôtel du Cygne

3 rue du Cygne, 1st (01.42.60.14.16/fax 01.42.21.37.02/www.hotelducygne.fr). M° Etienne Marcel or Châtelet/RER Châtelet Les Halles. **Rates** €60-€90 single; €105 double; €116 twin; €130 triple; €8 breakfast. **Credit** AmEx, MC, V. **Map** p404 J5 ⓮

This traditional hotel in a 17th-century building offers 20 compact, cosy and simple rooms embellished with thoughtful, distinctive touches such as antiques and home-made furnishings. It's set on a pedestrian street in the bustling Les Halles district, so light sleepers might prefer one of the rooms that look over the courtyard; No.35 is the most spacious.
TV.

Opéra & Grands Boulevards

Deluxe

Le Grand InterContinental

*2 rue Scribe, 2nd (01.40.07.32.32/fax 01.42.66.12.51/
www.paris-le-grand.intercontinental.com). Mº Opéra.*
Rates €610-€1,500 double; €2,500-€3,500 suite;
€31 breakfast. **Credit** AmEx, DC, MC, V.
Map p403 G4 ⑮
This 1862 landmark hotel is the chain's European
flagship – but, given its sheer size, perhaps 'mother
ship' would be more apt: it's an enormous palace that
occupies the entire block (three wings, almost 500
rooms) next to the Garnier opera house. In addition
to a stylish allure and technical convenience bestowed
by a recent multi-million-euro refit – the work of illustrious decorator Pierre-Yves Rochon, who also did up
the George V (*see p49*)– the space under the vast *ver-
rière* is one of the best oases in town. Have lunch here
during the week, or, for a break, head to the I-spa and
its seawater treatments.
*Bar. Business centre. Concierge. Gym. Internet. No-
smoking room(s). Parking (€30). Restaurants (2).
Room service. Spa. TV.*

Hôtel Concorde St-Lazare

*108 rue St-Lazare, 8th (01.40.08.44.44/fax
01.40.08.44.69/www.concordestlazare-paris.com).
Mº St-Lazare.* **Rates** €360-€450 double; €685-
€1,580 suite; €24 breakfast. **Credit** AmEx, DC,
MC, V. **Map** p403 G3 ⑯
Guests here are cocooned in soundproofed luxury –
a boon after the bustling crowds of the nearby
grands magasins department stores and St-Lazare
railway station. The hotel's 19th-century Eiffel-
inspired lobby is a historic landmark: the high ceilings, marble pillars and sculptures look much as
they have done for over a century. Rooms are spacious, with double entrance doors and exclusive
Annick Goutal toiletries; the belle-époque brasserie,
Café Terminus, and sexy Golden Black Bar were
styled by Sonia Rykiel. Guests have access to a fitness centre a short distance away.
*Bar. Business centre. Concierge. Internet (wireless).
No-smoking room(s). Restaurant. Room service. TV.*

Expensive

Hôtel Ambassador

*16 bd Haussmann, 9th (01.44.83.40.40/fax
01.53.24.66.96/www.hotelambassador-paris.com).
Mº Richelieu Drouot or Chaussée d'Antin.* **Rates**
€360-€450 double; €545-€990 suite; €63 extra bed;
€11-€12 breakfast. **Credit** AmEx, DC, MC, V.
Map p403 H4 ⑰
If you're looking for vintage style but can't face
another gilded hotel à la Louis XIV, check into this
historic, Haussmann-era hotel, which mixes traditional furniture with contemporary decor. The low-
lit Lindbergh Bar is named after the pilot who
dropped in for a celebratory drink and cigar after

his solo transatlantic flight in 1927. It's ideally situated for shopping at the *grands magasins* or clubbing around the Grands Boulevards, and its summer
rates are excellent value.
*Bar. Business centre. Concierge. Gym. Internet. No-
smoking room(s). Restaurant. Room service. TV.*

Hôtel Edouard VII

*39 av de l'Opéra, 2nd (01.42.61.56.90/fax
01.42.61.47.73/www.edouard7hotel.com). Mº Opéra.*
Rates €295-€390 single; €390-€485 double; €525-
€1,100 suite; €23 breakfast. **Credit** AmEx, DC, MC,
V. **Map** 403 G4 ⑱
Owned by the same family for five generations, this
refined hotel includes artful touches such as Murano
glass lights, smooth wooden features and contemporary sculptures in the entrance hall. The stylish bar
and restaurant Angl'Opéra (with resident star chef
Gilles Choukroun) is decked out in dark mahogany
and comfortable stripes (*see also p186*). Some of the
individually decorated bedrooms offer wonderful balcony views of the Garnier opera house. **Photo** *p41.*
*Bar. Concierge. Internet. No-smoking room(s).
Restaurant. Room service. TV.*

Hôtel Westminster

*13 rue de la Paix, 2nd (01.42.61.57.46/fax
01.42.60.30.66/www.warwickhotels.com). Mº Opéra.*
Rates €420-€570 single or double; €700-€1,300
suite; €23-€28 breakfast. **Credit** AmEx, DC, MC, V.
Map p403 G4 ⑲
This luxury hotel near place Vendôme has more
than a touch of British warmth about it, no doubt
owing to the influence of its favourite 19th-century
guest, the Duke of Westminster (after whom the
hotel was named; the current Duke reportedly still
stays here). The hotel fitness centre has a top-floor
location, with a beautiful tiled steam room and views
over the city, while the cosy bar features deep leather
chairs, a fireplace and live jazz at weekends.
*Bar. Concierge. Gym. Internet (wireless). No-smoking
room(s). Parking (€21). Restaurant. Room service.
TV.*

Park Hyatt Paris-Vendôme

*5 rue de la Paix, 2nd (01.58.71.12.34/fax
01.58.71.12.35/www.paris.vendome.hyatt.com).
Mº Opéra.* **Rates** €580-€670 single or double; €770-
€4,090 suite; €32-€42 breakfast. **Credit** AmEx, DC,
MC, V. **Map** p403 G4 ⑳
A luxurious mix of mahogany, pale limestone, matte
gold and neutral fabrics under high ceilings – set off
by liberal use of rough bronze sculptures serving as
light sconces and doorknobs – makes this hotel a
favourite among fashion editors. Rooms have the latest Bang & Olufsen TVs, and the spa-like bathrooms
– split into huge dressing area and artful shower/
bath zone – have underfloor heating. There's a circular gourmet restaurant, Le Grill, where guests can
watch chefs prepare food in the open kitchen, and a
Med-style courtyard for dining in summer.
*Bar. Business centre. Concierge. Gym. Internet
(wireless). No-smoking room(s). Parking (free).
Restaurants (2). Room service. Spa. TV.*

Budget beds

In addition to the great budget deals listed in this chapter, we've chosen the following hotels for their superb value and quirky style. Every one of the addresses below can supply a good night's sleep for under €85.

Hôtel Chopin
46 passage Jouffroy or 10 bd Montmartre, 9th (01.47.70.58.10/fax 01.42.47.00.70). M° Grands Boulevards. **Rates** €66-€74 single; €77-€88 double; €7 breakfast. **Credit** AmEx, MC, V. **Map** p404 J4
Set in a historic, glass-roofed arcade, the Chopin's original 1846 façade adds to the old-fashioned appeal (*pictured right*). The 36 quiet and functional rooms have salmon-coloured walls and green carpet.

Hôtel Eldorado
18 rue des Dames, 17th (01.45.22.35.21/ fax 01.43.87.25.97/www.eldoradohotel.fr). M° Place de Clichy. **Rates** €25-€45 single; €45-€65 double; €50-€80 triple; €6 breakfast. **Credit** MC, V. **Map** p403 F2 ⑥
This eccentric hotel is decorated with funky flea market finds. The Hôtel Eldorado's winning features include a wine bar, one of the best garden patios in town and a loyal local fashionista following.

Hôtel de Lille
8 rue du Pélican, 1st (01.42.33.33.42). M° Palais Royal Musée du Louvre. **Rates** €38-€46 single; €55-€60 double; no breakfast. **No credit cards. Map** p404 H5 ⑨
Tiny hotel with 14 clean, spacious rooms in belle-époque style. The affiliated Hôtel du Petit Trianon (01.43.54.94.64) in the 6th offers similar rates.

Hôtel de Nesle
7 rue de Nesle, 6th (01.43.54.62.41). M° Odéon. **Rates** €55-€65 single; €75-€100 double; no breakfast. **Credit** MC, V. **Map** p408 H6 ⑨
Minimal hotel services and only nine of the 20 rooms are en suite; but all are decorated with colourful murals and many overlook a charming garden courtyard.

Hôtel Paris France
72 rue de Turbigo, 3rd (01.42.78.00.04/ fax 01.42.71.99.43/www.paris-france-hotel.com). M° Temple. **Rates** €62-€72 single; €76-€112 double; €109-€137 triple. **Credit** AmEx, MC, V. **Map** p404 L4 ⑨

With a great central location, sweet lift, spruce staff and clean, pleasant – although plain – rooms, this is a very useful place to know. The attic has a view of Montmartre and (if you lean out far enough) the Eiffel Tower.

Hôtel Résidence Gobelins
9 rue des Gobelins, 13th (01.47.07.26.90/ fax 01.43.31.44.05/www.hotelgobelins.com). M° Les Gobelins. **Rates** €57 & €63 single; €76 double; €89 triple; €99 quad; €7 breakfast. **Credit** AmEx, MC, V. **Map** p408 K10 ⑥
A tiny lift leads to the colourful rooms equipped with satellite TV and telephone. The breakfast room overlooks a private garden, and there's free internet at reception. Friendly service.

Moderate

Résidence Hôtel des Trois Poussins

15 rue Clauzel, 9th (01.53.32.81.81/fax 01.53.32.81.82/www.les3poussins.com). M° St-Georges. **Rates** €135 single; €150 double; €168 triple; €220 quad; €165-€235 studios with kitchenette; €10 breakfast. **Credit** AmEx, DC, MC, V. **Map** p403 H2 ❷

Just off the beaten track in a pleasant *quartier*, and within uphill walking distance of Montmartre, the Résidence offers hotel accommodation in the traditional manner, but also rare self-catering studios for people who'd rather cook than eat out. Decor is traditional, with a preference for yellow. Mention *Time Out Paris* on reservation for a 15% discount.
Concierge. Internet. Room service (daytime only). TV.

Budget

Hôtel Langlois

63 rue St-Lazare, 9th (01.48.74.78.24/fax 01.49.95.04.43/www.hotel-langlois.com). M° Trinité. **Rates** €89-€104 single; €104-€120 double; €120 twin; €160 suite; €20 extra bed; €10 breakfast. **Credit** AmEx, DC, MC, V. **Map** p403 G3 ❷

Built as a bank in 1870, this belle-époque building became the Hôtel des Croisés in 1896. In 2001, after featuring in the Jonathan Demme film *Charade*, it changed its name to Langlois in honour of the founder of the Cinémathèque Française (*see p294* '**thèque five**). Its 27 spacious bedrooms are all individually decorated in art nouveau style; look out for the delightful hidden bathrooms in the larger ones.
Internet. Room service. TV.

Hôtel Madeleine Opéra

12 rue Greffulhe, 8th (01.47.42.26.26/fax 01.47.42.89.76/www.hotel-madeleine-opera.com). M° Madeleine. **Rates** €79-€85 single; €80-€89 double; €100 triple; €7 breakfast. **Credit** AmEx, DC, MC, V. **Map** p404 J4 ❷

This bargain hotel is just north of the Eglise Madeleine, in the heart of the city's theatre and *grands magasins* districts. Its sunny lobby sits behind a 200-year-old façade that was once a shopfront. The 24 rooms are perhaps a touch basic, but are still nice enough, and breakfast is brought to your room every morning.
Internet. Room service (morning). TV.

Champs-Elysées & western Paris

Deluxe

Four Seasons George V

31 av George-V, 8th (01.49.52.70.00/fax 01.49.52.70.10/www.fourseasons.com/paris/index.html). M° George V or Alma Marceau. **Rates** €695-€900 double or twin; €1,250-€9,000 suite; €35-€46 breakfast. **Credit** AmEx, DC, MC, V. **Map** p402 D4 ❷

There's no denying that the George V is serious about luxury: chandeliers, marble and tapestries; almost over-attentive staff; glorious flower arrangements; divine bathrooms; and ludicrously comfortable beds in some of the largest guestrooms in Paris. The Versailles-inspired spa includes whirlpools, saunas and an impressive menu of treatments for an unabashedly metrosexual clientele; non-guests may now reserve appointments throughout the week, and it's worth every euro.
Bar. Business centre. Concierge. Gym. Internet (high-speed). No-smoking room(s). Pool (indoor). Restaurants (2). Room service. Spa. TV.

Conceptual art at **Hôtel le A**. *See p50.*

Marble galore, a Michelin-starred restaurant and luxurious spa – the **Hôtel Royal Monceau**.

Hôtel le A

4 rue d'Artois, 8th (01.42.56.99.99/fax 01.42.56.99.90/www.paris-hotel-a.com). Mº St-Philippe-du-Roule or Franklin D.Roosevelt. **Rates** €329-€399 double; €450 suite; €590 apartment; €15-€21 breakfast. **Credit** AmEx, DC, MC, V. **Map** p403 E4 ⑳

The black-and-white decor of this designer boutique hotel provides a fine backdrop for the models, artists and media types hanging out in the lounge bar area; the only splashes of colour come from the graffiti-like artworks by conceptual artist Fabrice Hybert. The 26 rooms all have granite bathrooms, and the starched white furniture slipcovers, changed after each guest, make the smallish spaces seem larger than they are. The dimmer switches are a nice touch – as are the lift lights changing colour at each floor. **Photo** *p49*. *Bar. Concierge. Internet (wireless). No-smoking room(s). Room service. TV.*

Hôtel Plaza Athénée

25 av Montaigne, 8th (01.53.67.66.67/fax 01.53.67.66.66/www.plaza-athenee-paris.com). Mº Alma Marceau. **Rates** €565 single; €695-€770 double; €940-€6,600 suite; €14,000 Royal Suite; €35-€46 breakfast. **Credit** AmEx, DC, MC, V. **Map** p402 D5 ⑳

This palace is ideally placed for power shopping at Chanel, Vuitton, Dior and other avenue Montaigne boutiques. Material girls and boys will enjoy the

high-tech room amenities such as remote-controlled air-con, internet and video game access on the TV via infra-red keyboard, and mini hi-fi. The stylish bar full of rock stars and hotshots has modern decor matched by a cool cocktail list (*see p213* **Overnight sensations**) and staff who know what service is. *Bar. Business centre. Concierge. Gym. Internet (high-speed). No-smoking room(s). Restaurants (2; 4 in summer). Room service. TV.*

Hôtel Royal Monceau

37 av Hoche, 8th (01.42.99.88.00/fax 01.42.99.89.90/www.royalmonceau.com). Mº Charles de Gaulle Etoile. **Rates** €550-€750 double; €1,050-€6,800 suite; €30-€42 breakfast. **Credit** AmEx, DC, MC, V. **Map** p402 H5 ㉗

As if the acres of marble and tapestries, a romantic, Michelin-starred garden restaurant and posh health spa with pool weren't luxury enough, the historic Royal Monceau palace has upped the ante with a renovation by Costes' darling Jacques Garcia. **Photos** *above*. *Bar. Business centre. Concierge. Gym. Internet (high-speed). No-smoking room(s). Parking (€29). Pool (indoor). Restaurants (2). Room service. Spa. TV.*

Hôtel de Vigny

9-11 rue Balzac, 8th (01.42.99.80.80/fax 01.42.99.80.40/www.hoteldevigny.com). Mº George V. **Rates** €365-€395 single; €450-€495 double; €500-€725 suite; €21-€32 breakfast. **Credit** AmEx, DC, MC, V. **Map** p403 H5 ㉘

Expensive

Hôtel Pergolèse
3 rue Pergolèse, 16th (01.53.64.04.04/fax 01.53.64.04.40/www.hotelpergolese.com). M° Argentine. **Rates** €195-€350 single; €220-€380 double; €18 breakfast. **Credit** AmEx, DC, MC, V. **Map** p402 B3 ⓷⓪
The Pergolèse was one of the first designer boutique hotels in town, but still looks contemporary a decade or more after being decorated by Rena Dumas-Hermès with Philippe Starck furniture and Hilton McConnico rugs. Rooms are done out in pastel tones with pale wood furniture, and come with Bang & Olufsen TVs and cool, white-tiled bathrooms.
Bar. Concierge. Internet (wireless). No-smoking room(s). Room service. TV.

Hôtel Square
3 rue de Boulainvilliers, 16th (01.44.14.91.90/fax 01.44.14.91.99/www.hotelsquare.com). M° Passy/ RER Avenue du Pdt Kennedy. **Rates** €260-€340 single or double; €410-€520 suite; €8-€20 breakfast. **Credit** AmEx, DC, MC, V. **Map** p406 A7 ⓷⓵
Located in the upmarket 16th hard by the Maison de Radio-France, this courageously modern hotel has a dramatic yet welcoming interior, and attentive service that comes from having to look after only 22 rooms. These are decorated in amber, brick or slate colours, with exotic woods, quality fabrics and bathrooms seemingly cut from one huge chunk of Carrara marble. View the exhibitions in the atrium gallery or mingle with the media types at the hip Zebra Square restaurant and DJ lounge bar.
Bar. Business centre. Concierge. Internet (wireless). No-smoking room(s). Parking (€20). Restaurant. Room service. TV.

Moderate

Hôtel Elysées Ceramic
34 av de Wagram, 8th (01.42.27.20.30/fax 01.46.22.95.83/www.elysees-ceramic.com). M° Charles de Gaulle Etoile. **Rates** €175 single; €200 double; €223 triple; €10 breakfast. **Credit** AmEx, DC, MC, V. **Map** p402 C3 ⓷⓶
A comfortable hotel situated between the Arc de Triomphe and place des Ternes, this has a listed art nouveau ceramic façade dating from its foundation in 1904; the theme continues inside, with a ceramic cornice around the reception. The 57 rooms are clean and modern, with stencilled patterns. Outside is a terrace garden for taking afternoon tea or evening cocktails in fine weather.
Bar. Concierge. Internet (wireless). Room service (breakfast only). TV.

Hôtel Regent's Garden
6 rue Pierre-Demours, 17th (01.45.74.07.30/fax 01.40.55.01.42/www.hotel-regents-garden.com). M° Charles de Gaulle Etoile or Ternes. **Rates** €142-€235 single; €155-€235 double; €13 breakfast. **Credit** AmEx, DC, MC, V. **Map** p402 C3 ⓷⓷

The capital's only Relais & Château hotel has the feel of a private, plush townhouse. Although it's just off the Champs-Elysées, the Vigny is a discreet hotel that pulls in a discerning, low-key clientele. Its 37 rooms and suites have marble bathrooms and individual decor in tasteful striped or floral fabrics. Enjoy dinner in the art deco Baretto restaurant, or a cup of tea in front of the library fireplace.
Bar. Concierge. Internet (wireless). No-smoking room(s). Parking (€23). Restaurant. Room service. TV.

Pershing Hall
49 rue Pierre-Charron, 8th (01.58.36.58.00/ fax 01.58.36.58.01/www.pershinghall.com). M° George V. **Rates** €351-€500 double; €720-€1,000 suite; €26 breakfast. **Credit** AmEx, DC, MC, V. **Map** p402 D4 ⓷⓸
The refreshing mix of 19th-century grandeur and contemporary comfort make the Pershing Hall feel quite large, but this luxury establishment is really a cleverly disguised boutique hotel with just 26 rooms. Fashionable locals frequent the stylish bar and restaurant terrace, nicely set off by a dramatic vertical garden. Designed by Andrée Putman, the neat white-on-white bedrooms emphasise natural materials, with stained grey oak floors, and particularly fine mosaic-tiled bathrooms with geometric styling and copious towels.
Bar. Concierge. Gym. Internet (wireless). No-smoking room(s). Restaurant. Room service. Spa. TV.

This elegant hotel – built for Napoléon III's physician – features appropriately Second Empire high ceilings and plush upholstery, and a lounge looking over a lovely walled garden. There are 39 large bedrooms, some with gilt mirrors and fireplaces. An oasis of calm ten minutes from the Champs-Elysées. *Concierge. Internet (wireless). No-smoking room(s). Parking (€13). Room service (daytime only). TV.*

Budget

Hôtel Keppler

12 rue Keppler, 16th (01.47.20.65.05/fax 01.47.23.02.29/www.hotelkeppler.com). M° Kléber or George V. **Rates** €90-€100 single; €105-€115 double; €120-€135 triple; €7 breakfast. **Credit** AmEx, MC, V. **Map** p402 C4 ③
It's a surprise to find value this good so close to the upmarket shopping and entertainment district of the Champs-Elysées. The Keppler is a pleasing budget hotel with the high ceilings and spacious rooms typical of the area, done in simple, old-fashioned style. *Bar. Concierge. Internet (dataport). Room service. TV.*

Montmartre & Pigalle

Expensive

Terrass Hôtel

12-14 rue Joseph-de-Maistre, 18th (01.46.06.72.85/ fax 01.42.52.29.11/www.terrass-hotel.com). M° Place de Clichy. **Rates** €208 single; €248 double; €336 suite; €18 breakfast. **Credit** AmEx, DC, MC, V. **Map** p403 G1 ③
There's nothing particularly spectacular about this classic hotel, but for those willing to pay top euro for the best views in town, Terrass fits the bill. Ask for room 704 and you can lie in the bath and look out at the Eiffel Tower (and people on the Eiffel Tower can – possibly – see you in the bath). The so-called 'semi-gastronomic' restaurant Diapason on the ground floor opened in September 2005. *Bar. Concierge. Internet (wireless). No-smoking room(s). Restaurant. Room service. TV.*

Moderate

Hôtel Roma Sacré-Coeur

101 rue Caulaincourt, 18th (01.42.62.02.02/fax 01.42.54.34.92/www.hotelroma.fr). M° Lamarck Caulaincourt. **Rates** €60-€130 single; €70-€145 double; €7.50 breakfast. **Credit** AmEx, DC, MC, V. **Map** p403 H1 ③
This hotel is located on the trendier, north side of Montmartre, far from the postcard shops and coach parties, but still within walking distance (uphill) of Sacré-Coeur. From the tiny lobby, a whimsical, Astroturf-covered staircase leads to the 57 rooms, simply decorated in pastels; the priciest enjoy views of the basilica. Air-conditioned rooms are available on floors five to seven for an extra €10 per day. *Concierge. Internet (wireless). TV.*

Timhotel Montmartre

11 rue Ravignan, 18th (01.42.55.74.79/fax 01.42.55.71.01/www.timhotel.fr). M° Abbesses. **Rates** €115-€130 single; €115-€200 double; €150-€180 triple; €8.50 breakfast. **Credit** AmEx, DC, MC, V. **Map** p403 H1 ③
The location on picturesque place Emile-Goudeau makes this one of the most popular hotels in the Timhotel chain. It has 59 nice rooms, comfortable without being plush; try to bag one on the fourth or fifth floor for stunning views over Montmartre. *Concierge. Internet (high-speed). No-smoking room(s). TV.*

Budget

Blanche Hôtel

69 rue Blanche, 9th (01.48.74.16.94/fax 01.49.95.95.98). M° Blanche. **Rates** €32-€65 single; €35-€83 double; €65-€83 triple; €65-€102 quad; €6 breakfast. **Credit** AmEx, MC, V. **Map** p403 G2 ③
If you're prepared to forgo frills and don't mind the rather racy aspect of the neighbourhood, this is a good-value bet. The interior is less than palatial and features less-than-luxurious 1970s furniture, but the rooms are a good size and there's a bar in the lobby. *Bar. Concierge. Room service (morning only). TV.*

Hôtel Ermitage

24 rue Lamarck, 18th (01.42.64.79.22/fax 01.42.64.10.33/www.hermitagesacrecoeur.fr). M° Lamarck Caulaincourt. **Rates** €80 single; €90 double; €116 triple; €138 quad. **No credit cards. Map** p403 H1 ③
This 12-room hotel stands on the calm, non-touristy north side of Montmartre, only five minutes from Sacré-Coeur. Rooms are large and endearingly over-decorated; some higher ones have fine views. *Internet (wireless). No-smoking room(s). Room service (morning only).*

Royal Fromentin

11 rue Fromentin, 9th (01.48.74.85.93/fax 01.42.81.02.33/www.hotelroyalfromentin.com). M° Pigalle. **Rates** (incl breakfast) €69-€130 single; €79-€155 double; €114-€193 triple; €134-€231 quad. **Credit** AmEx, DC, MC, V. **Map** p403 H2 ④
Wood panelling, art deco windows and a vintage glass lift echo the hotel's origins as a 1930s cabaret hall; its theatrical feel attracted Blondie and Nirvana. The 47 rooms, many overlooking Sacré-Coeur, have been renovated in French style, with bright fabrics. *Bar. Concierge. Internet. Room service (breakfast only). TV.*

Beaubourg & the Marais

Deluxe

Murano Urban Resort

13 bd du Temple, 3rd (01.42.71.20.00/fax 01.42.71.21.01/www.muranoresort.com). M° Filles du Calvaire or Oberkampf. **Rates** €350 single; €400-*

€650 double; €750-€2,500 suite; €20-€28 breakfast; €38 brunch (Sun). **Credit** AmEx, DC, MC, V.
Map p411 L5 ④

Behind this unremarkable façade is a super-cool and luxurious hotel that's popular with the fashion set for its slick lounge-style design and high-tech flourishes – like Bang & Olufsen sound systems and clever coloured-light co-ordinators that allow you to change the mood of your room at the press of a button. The bar has 140 varieties of vodka, which can bring the op-art fabrics in the lift to life and make the fingerprint access to the 43 rooms and nine suites (two with private pools) a godsend.
Bar. Concierge. Gym. Internet (high-speed). No-smoking room(s). Parking (€30). Pool (from spring 2006). Restaurant. Room service. Spa (from spring 2006). TV.

Pavillon de la Reine
28 pl des Vosges, 3rd (01.40.29.19.19/fax 01.40.29.19.20/www.pavillon-de-la-reine.com). M° Bastille or St-Paul. **Rates** €345-€420 double; €495-€620 duplex; €545-€790 suite; €20-€25 breakfast. **Credit** AmEx, DC, MC, V. **Map** p411 L6 ④

The owner of this cosy hotel, set back from place des Vosges, makes guests feel they're being welcomed into her own home. The warm fabrics and exposed beams ooze traditional Paris style, but smatterings of modernity are reflected in the newer duplex suites decked out in taffeta and plush purple velvets.
Bar. Concierge. Internet (wireless). No-smoking room(s). Parking. Room service. TV.

Expensive

Hôtel Bourg Tibourg
19 rue du Bourg-Tibourg, 4th (01.42.78.47.39/ fax 01.40.29.07.00/www.hotelbourgtibourg.com). M° Hôtel de Ville. **Rates** €160 single; €220-€250 double; €350 suite; €14 breakfast. **Credit** AmEx, DC, MC, V. **Map** p408 K6 ④

Same owners as Hôtel Costes (*see p43*), the same interior decorator – but don't expect this jewel box of a boutique hotel to look like a miniature replica. Aside from its enviable location in the heart of the Marais and its fashion-pack fans, this tiny hotel is about Jacques Garcia's neo-Gothic-cum-Byzantine decor. Exotic, scented candles, mosaic-tiled bathrooms, luxurious fabrics in rich colours and the cool contrast of crisp white linens create the perfect escape from the outside world. There's no restaurant or bar – posing is done in the neighbourhood bars.
Concierge. Internet (wireless). Room service. TV.

Hôtel du Petit Moulin
29 rue de Poitou, 3rd (01.42.74.10.10/fax 01.42.74.10.97/www.hoteldupetitmoulin.com). M° St-Sébastien Froissart. **Rates** €180-€250 double; €280- €350 suite; €15 breakfast. **Credit** AmEx, MC, V. **Map** p411 L5 ④

Within striking distance of the Musée Picasso and the hip shops on and around rue Charlot, this listed, turn-of-the-century façade masks what was once the

oldest *boulangerie* in Paris, now lovingly restored as a boutique hotel by Nadia Murano and Denis Nourry. The couple recruited fashion designer Christian Lacroix for the decor, and the result is a riot of colour, trompe l'oeil effects and a savvy mix of old and new. Each of its 17 exquisitely appointed rooms is unique, and the walls in rooms 202, 204 and 205 feature drawings from Lacroix's sketchbook.
Bar. Internet (wireless). Parking (free).

Moderate

Hôtel Axial Beaubourg
11 rue du Temple, 4th (01.42.72.72.22/fax 01.42.72.03.53/www.axialbeaubourg.com). M° Hôtel de Ville. **Rates** €112-€130 single; €160-€210 double; €11 breakfast. **Credit** AmEx, DC, MC, V. **Map** p408 K6 ④

This stylish boutique hotel, decorated with white marble floors, mud-coloured walls, crushed-velvet sofas and exposed beams, is just a few yards from the Centre Pompidou. The great-value rooms are not large, but exude refinement and comfort. In 2006 the owners are set to open a slightly more upmarket offshoot, Le Duo, next door.
Concierge. Internet. Room service. TV.

Hôtel de la Bretonnerie
22 rue Ste-Croix-de-la-Bretonnerie, 4th (01.48.87.77.63/fax 01.42.77.26.78/www. bretonnerie.com). M° Hôtel de Ville. **Rates** €116-€149 double; €180 suite; €9.50 breakfast. **Credit** MC, V. **Map** p411 K6 ④

With its combination of wrought ironwork, exposed stone and wooden beams, the labyrinth of corridors and passages in this 17th-century *hôtel particulier* is full of historic atmosphere. Tapestries, rich colours and the odd four-poster bed give a sense of individuality to the 29 suites and bedrooms. There's no air-conditioning, but each room has a fan.
Concierge. Internet (shared terminal). TV.

Hôtel St-Louis Marais
1 rue Charles V, 4th (01.48.87.87.04/fax 01.48.87.33.26/www.saintlouismarais.com). M° Sully Morland or Bastille. **Rates** €79-€99 single; €115-€140 double, twin or triple; €160 suite (quad); €8 breakfast. **Credit** AmEx, MC, V. **Map** p411 L7 ④

Built as part of a 17th-century Célestin convent, this peaceful hotel between Ile St-Louis and place des Vosges has had its bathrooms redone and wireless access installed in the past year. Rooms are compact and cosy, with characteristic wooden beams and traditional decor; book one of the more expensive rooms if you're claustrophobic.
Concierge. Internet (wireless). No-smoking room(s). Parking (€18). Room service (breakfast only). TV.

Hôtel St-Merry
78 rue de la Verrerie, 4th (01.42.78.14.15/fax 01.40.29.06.82/www.hotelmarais.com). M° Hôtel de Ville. **Rates** €160-€230 double; €205-€275 triple; €335 suite; €11 breakfast. **Credit** AmEx, MC, V. **Map** p408 K6 ④

Reet boutique

Fast on the heels of the übertrendy **Murano
Urban Resort** (*see p53*), the latest Paris
designer hotels embrace daring architects,
contemporary interiors, historic inspirations –
and even a return to low-key luxury and
comfort. First to open was the **Hilton Arc de
Triomphe** (51-57 rue de Courcelles, 8th,
01.58.36.67.00, www.hilton.com), a massive
American-style business hotel with original
architecture and decor inspired by the ocean
liners of the art deco era. Then the dowdy
Hotel Queen Elizabeth was completely gutted
and reopened in December 2004 as the
Hôtel de Sers (41 av Pierre-1er-de-Serbie,
8th, 01.53.23.75.75, www.hoteldesers.com;
pictured), with a highly ambitious mix of
minimalist contemporary furnishings, a few
pop art accessories and leftover 19th-century
architectural details such as the grand
staircase. In January 2005 the luxurious
Hôtel Daniel (8 rue Frédéric-Bastiat, 8th,
01.42.56.17.00, www.hoteldanielparis.com)
eschewed the trend of clean lines and
neutrals with an opulent Franco-Chinois
interior full of North African antiques,
Toiles de Jouy fabrics and overstuffed sofas
with jewel-toned satin pillows. And, located
in the upscale 16th, sexy boutique hotel
Le Sezz (6 av Frémiet, 16th, 01.55.31.60.00,
www.hotelsezz.com) opened its doors
the following month with 27 suites all
meticulously designed by sought-after
French furniture designer Christophe Pillet.
The daring decor includes black parquet
flooring, rough-hewn stone walls, camp-style
beds placed in the centre of each suite,
and one-way glass walls in the bathrooms.

The Gothic decor of this former presbytery attached
to the Eglise St-Merry is ideal for a Dracula set, with
wooden beams, stone walls and plenty of iron.
Behind the door of room No.9, a flying buttress even
straddles the bed. On the downside, the historic
building has no lift and only the suite has a TV.
*Concierge. No-smoking room(s). Room service
(daytime only). TV (suite only).*
Other locations Hôtel Saintonge Marais,
16 rue de Saintonge, 3rd (01.42.77.91.13).

Budget

Grand Hôtel Jeanne d'Arc

*3 rue de Jarente, 4th (01.48.87.62.11/fax
01.48.87.37.31/www.hoteljeannedarc.com).
M° St-Paul or Chemin Vert.* **Rates** €58-€70 single;
€82 double; €96 twin; €115 triple; €145 quad;
€6 breakfast. **Credit** AmEx, MC, V.
Map p411 L6 ㊾
This hotel's strong point is its location on a quiet
road round the corner from pretty place du Marché-
Ste-Catherine. Recent refurbishment has made the
reception area striking, and the huge mirror on the
wall adds wow value and the illusion of extra space.
Rooms are colourful (you like orange, right?) and, for
the price, are well sized, comfortable and clean.
Concierge. Room service (morning only). TV.

Hôtel de Roubaix

*6 rue Greneta, 3rd (01.42.72.89.91/fax
01.42.72.58.79/www.hotel-de-roubaix.com). M°
Réaumur Sébastopol or Arts et Métiers.* **Rates** (incl
breakfast) €56-€61 single; €66-€69 double; €70-€85
triple; €92 quad. **Credit** MC, V. **Map** p404 K5 ㊿

You're two blocks from the Centre Pompidou, the Marais and the trendy shops of rue Etienne-Marcel. You've got an immaculately clean bathroom, TV, telephone and a lift to take you to your room. So why are the rates so low? Could be the granny-friendly decor or the squishy mattresses; but since the hotel's 53 rooms are invariably booked solid, it seems that no one is too discouraged.
Concierge. Internet. TV.

Hôtel du Septième Art
20 rue St-Paul, 4th (01.44.54.85.00/fax 01.42.77.69.10). M° St-Paul. **Rates** €59-€80 single; €80-€135 double; €7 breakfast. **Credit** AmEx, DC, MC, V. **Map** p411 L6 ⑤
Cinema aficionados will adore this black-and-white hotel, styled in homage to the 'seventh art': vintage posters and signed photos of stars compete for every inch of wall space. Rooms are basic but some overlook a courtyard. There's a fitness room in the cellar if you want to work towards a Hollywood bod.
Bar. Concierge. Gym. TV.

Bastille & eastern Paris

Moderate

Hôtel Beaumarchais
3 rue Oberkampf, 11th (01.53.36.86.86/fax 01.43.38.32.86/www.hotelbeaumarchais.com). M° Filles du Calvaire or Oberkampf. **Rates** €75-€90 single; €110-€150 double; €170 triple; €10 breakfast. **Credit** AmEx, MC, V. **Map** p411 L5 ⑤
This contemporary hotel in the edgy, happening Oberkampf area is within walking distance of the Marais and Bastille districts. Its 31 rooms are all brightly decorated (colourful walls, mosaics in the bathrooms, wavy headboards and Milan glass bedside lamps); breakfast is served on the tiny garden patio or in your room.
Concierge. Internet (wireless). Room service. TV.

Mercure Terminus Est
5 rue du Huit-Mai 1945, 10th (01.55.26.05.05/fax 01.55.26.05.00/www.mercure.com). M° Gare de l'Est. **Rates** €165 single; €175-€215 double; €260-€350 suite; €31 extra bed; €14 breakfast. **Credit** AmEx, DC, MC, V. **Map** p404 K3 ⑤
Conveniently located right opposite the Gare de l'Est, this great railway hotel combines modern interior design with elements that evoke the classic age of steam: leather luggage handles on the wardrobes, retro bathroom fittings and a library in the lobby. The 200 rooms and public areas all offer wireless internet capacity.
Bar. Concierge. Gym. Internet (wireless). No-smoking room(s). Room service. TV.

Le Pavillon Bastille
65 rue de Lyon, 12th (01.43.43.65.65/fax 01.43.43.96.52/www.paris-hotel-pavillonbastille.com). M° Bastille. **Rates** €130 single; €130 double; €213 suite; €12 breakfast. **Credit** AmEx, DC, MC, V. **Map** p409 M7 ⑤

The best thing about this hotel is its location between the Bastille opera house and the Gare de Lyon. The 25 rooms follow a strict, contemporary yellow-and-blue scheme and are clean and fresh, if a little on the small side.
Bar. Concierge. Internet (wireless). No-smoking room(s). Room service. TV.

The Latin Quarter & the 13th

Moderate

Les Degrés de Notre-Dame
10 rue des Grands-Degrés, 5th (01.55.42.88.88/fax 01.40.46.95.34/www.lesdegreshotel.com). M° St-Michel. **Rates** (incl breakfast) €100-€160 double. **Credit** MC, V. **Map** p408 J7 ⑤
On a tiny street across the river from Notre-Dame, this vintage hotel is a gem. Its ten rooms are full of character, with original paintings, antique furniture and exposed wooden beams (Nos.47 and 501 have views of the cathedral). It has an adorable restaurant and, a few streets away, two studio apartments that the owner rents to preferred customers only.
Bar. Concierge. Restaurant. Room service. TV.

Hôtel la Demeure
51 bd St-Marcel, 13th (01.43.37.81.25/fax 01.45.87.05.03/www.hotel-paris-lademeure.com). M° Les Gobelins. **Rates** €145-€175 double; €230 suite; €13 breakfast. **Credit** AmEx, DC, MC, V. **Map** p408 K10 ⑤
This comfortable, modern hotel on the edge of the Latin Quarter is run by a friendly father and son. It has 43 air-conditioned rooms with internet access, plus suites with sliding doors to separate sleeping and living space. The wrap-around balustrades of the corner rooms offer lovely views of the city, and bathrooms feature either luxurious tubs or shower heads with elaborate massage possibilities.
Bar. Concierge. Internet (high-speed). No smoking. Parking (€17). Room service (breakfast only). TV.

Hôtel des Grandes Ecoles
75 rue du Cardinal-Lemoine, 5th (01.43.26.79.23/fax 01.43.25.28.15/www.hotel-grandes-ecoles.com). M° Cardinal Lemoine. **Rates** €105-€130 single or double; €20 extra bed; €8 breakfast. **Credit** MC, V. **Map** p408 K8 ⑤
A breath of fresh air in the heart of the Latin Quarter, this country-style hotel has 51 old-fashioned rooms set around a leafy garden where breakfast is served in summer. The largest of the three buildings houses the reception area and a stylish breakfast room with a gilt mirror and piano.
Concierge. Internet (dataport). Parking (€30). Room service (breakfast only).

Hôtel du Panthéon
19 pl du Panthéon, 5th (01.43.54.32.95/fax 01.43.26.64.65/www.hoteldupantheon.com). M° Cluny La Sorbonne/RER Luxembourg. **Rates** €168-€245 single or double; €265 triple; €12 breakfast. **Credit** AmEx, DC, MC, V. **Map** p410 J8 ⑤

The 36 rooms of this elegant hotel are beautifully decorated with classic French Toile de Jouy fabrics, antique furniture and painted woodwork. Some enjoy impressive views of the Panthéon; others squint out on to a hardly-less-romantic courtyard, complete with chestnut tree.
Concierge. Internet (wireless). TV.

Hôtel Résidence Henri IV
50 rue des Bernardins, 5th (01.44.41.31.81/fax 01.46.33.93.22/www.residencehenri4.com). M° Maubert Mutualité. **Rates** €87-€185 single or double; €220-€310 apartment; €6-€10 breakfast. **Credit** AmEx, DC, MC, V. **Map** p408 K7 🚳
This belle-époque-style hotel has a mere eight rooms and five apartments, so all guests can be assured of the staff's full attention. It's well situated on a quiet cul-de-sac next to leafy square Paul-Langevin, just a few minutes' walk from Notre-Dame. The four-person apartment rooms come with a handy mini-kitchen, with a hob, fridge and microwave – although you may be reduced to eating on the beds in the smaller ones.
Concierge. Internet (wireless). No smoking. TV.

Select Hôtel
1 pl de la Sorbonne, 5th (01.46.34.14.80/fax 01.46.34.51.79/www.selecthotel.fr). M° Cluny La Sorbonne. **Rates** (incl breakfast) €149-€189 double; €189-€212 triple. **Credit** AmEx, DC, MC, V. **Map** p410 J7 🚳
Located at the foot of the Sorbonne, this 68-room hotel contains an appealing blend of modern art deco features and traditional exposed-stone walls and wooden beams. The winter garden and common areas have recently been redone in a contemporary style with plenty of greenery.
Bar. Concierge. Internet (wireless). Room service (until 10pm). TV.

Budget

Familia Hôtel
11 rue des Ecoles, 5th (01.43.54.55.27/fax 01.43.29.61.77/www.hotel-paris-familia.com). M° Maubert Mutualité or Jussieu. **Rates** (incl breakfast) €78 single; €95-€125 double; €128-€149 triple; €169 quad. **Credit** AmEx, DC, MC, V. **Map** p408 J7 🚳
Set on a bustling street in the Latin Quarter, this old-fashioned hotel has balconies hung with tumbling plants and walls draped with French tapestry replicas, and owner Eric Gaucheron offers a warm and enthusiastic welcome. The 30 rooms have personalised touches such as sepia murals, cherry-wood furniture and stone walls; the communal areas were refurbished in 2005. The Gaucherons also own the Minerve next door, which offers the same splendid package. Both hotels are in demand: book well ahead.
Concierge. Internet (wireless). Parking (€20). Room service (daytime only). TV.
Other locations: Hôtel Minerve, 13 rue des Ecoles, 5th (01.43.26.81.89).

Hôtel Esmeralda
4 rue St-Julien-le-Pauvre, 5th (01.43.54.19.20/fax 01.40.51.00.68). M° St-Michel or Maubert Mutualité. **Rates** €35 single; €65-€95 double; €110 triple; €120 quad; €7 breakfast. **Credit** AmEx, MC, V. **Map** p410 J7 🚳
An offbeat piece of historic Paris, the Esmeralda has 19 floral rooms with antique furnishings and aged wallpaper, as well as the uneven floors and wonky staircase you'd expect in a building that was built in 1640. The eight rooms overlooking Notre-Dame are popular with honeymooners. Book ahead.
Concierge. Room service.

Hôtel de la Sorbonne
6 rue Victor-Cousin, 5th (01.43.54.58.08/fax 01.40.51.05.18/www.hotelsorbonne.com). M° Cluny La Sorbonne/RER Luxembourg. **Rates** €60-€140 single or double; €8 breakfast. **Credit** AmEx, DC, MC, V. **Map** p410 J8 🚳
This cosy hotel between the Luxembourg gardens and the Panthéon features wooden floors, beams and a fire in the salon. The 39 rooms are pale green or lavender, with cheerful geranium-filled window boxes. Bathrooms are tiny but new; choose one with a shower rather than one with a gnome-sized tub.
Concierge. Internet (wireless). Room service (breakfast only). TV.

St-Germain-des-Prés & Odéon

Deluxe

Hôtel Lutetia
45 bd Raspail, 6th (01.49.54.46.46/fax 01.49.54.46.00/www.lutetia-paris.com). M° Sèvres Babylone. **Rates** €400-€550 double; €750-€2,500 suite; €10-€22 breakfast. **Credit** AmEx, DC, MC, V. **Map** p407 G7 🚳
This historic Left Bank hotel is a masterpiece of art nouveau and early art deco architecture that dates from 1910. It has a plush jazz bar and lively brasserie with views of the chic Bon Marché store across the street. Its 250 rooms, revamped in purple, gold and pearl grey, maintain a 1930s feel – slip out of those damp clothes and into a dry Martini.
Bar. Business centre. Concierge. Gym. Internet (high-speed; wireless). No-smoking room(s). Restaurants (2). Room service. TV.

Expensive

L'Hôtel
13 rue des Beaux-Arts, 6th (01.44.41.99.00/fax 01.43.25.64.81/www.l-hotel.com). M° St-Germain-des-Prés. **Rates** €280-€640 double; €740 suite; €17 breakfast. **Credit** AmEx, DC, MC, V. **Map** p410 H6 🚳
Guests at the luxuriously decorated L'Hôtel are more likely to be models and film stars than the starving writers who frequented the place during Oscar Wilde's final days. Under Jacques Garcia's careful restoration, each room has its own special theme:

Mistinguett's *chambre* retains its art deco mirror bed, and Oscar's deathbed room has, appropriately, been decorated with green peacock murals. Don't miss the cellar swimming pool and *fumoir*.
Bar. Concierge. Internet (wireless). Pool (indoor). Restaurant. Room service (daytime only). TV.

Hôtel de l'Abbaye

10 rue Cassette, 6th (01.45.44.38.11/fax 01.45.48.07.86/www.hotel-abbaye.com). M° St-Sulpice or Rennes. **Rates** (incl breakfast) €199-€319 single or double; €370-€458 suite. **Credit** AmEx, MC, V. **Map** p407 G7 ⑥⑥
A monumental entrance leads the way through a courtyard into this tranquil hotel, originally part of a convent. Wood panelling, well-stuffed sofas and an open fireplace in the drawing room make for a relaxed atmosphere, but, best of all, there's a surprisingly large garden where breakfast is served in the warmer months. The 44 rooms are tasteful and luxurious, and the suites have rooftop terraces.
Bar. Concierge. Internet (wireless). Room service. TV.

La Villa

29 rue Jacob, 6th (01.43.26.60.00/fax 01.46.34.63.63/www.villa-saintgermain.com). M° St-Germain-des-Prés. **Rates** €260-€335 double; €440 suite; €40 extra bed; €15 breakfast. **Credit** AmEx, DC, MC, V. **Map** p410 H6 ⑥⑦
Refreshingly modern and stylish, the charismatic La Villa has cool faux-crocodile skin on the bedheads and crinkly taffeta on the taupe-coloured walls. Wonderfully, your room number is projected on to the floor outside your door; useful for drunken homecomings. Keep a look out for excellent offers on last-minute bookings.
Bar. Concierge. Internet (wireless). Room service (until midnight). TV.

Moderate

Le Clos Médicis

56 rue Monsieur-le-Prince, 6th (01.43.29.10.80/fax 01.43.54.26.90/www.closmedicis.com). M° Odéon/ RER Luxembourg. **Rates** €127-€225 single; €157-€225 double; €270 triple; €470 suite; €12 breakfast. **Credit** AmEx, DC, MC, V. **Map** p410 H7 ⑥⑧
Designed more like a stylish, private townhouse than a hotel, Le Clos Médicis is located by the Luxembourg gardens: perfect if you fancy starting every morning with a stroll among the trees. The hotel's decor is refreshingly modern and eminently chic, with rooms done out in taffeta curtains and chenille bedcoverings, and antique floor tiles in the bathrooms. The cosy lounge has a working fireplace.
Bar. Concierge. Internet (wireless). No-smoking room(s). TV.

Grand Hôtel de l'Univers

6 rue Grégoire-de-Tours, 6th (01.43.29.37.00/ fax 01.40.51.06.45/www.hotel-paris-univers.com). M° Odéon. **Rates** €130-€170 single; €150-€215 double; €10 breakfast. **Credit** AmEx, DC, MC, V. **Map** p410 H7 ⑥⑨

Making the most of its 15th-century origins, this hotel features exposed wooden beams, high ceilings, antique furnishings and toile-covered walls. Manuel Canovas fabrics lend a posh touch, but there are also practical features such as a laptop for rent. The same helpful team runs the nearby Hôtel St-Germain-des-Prés, which has a medieval-themed room and the sweetest attic in Paris.
Bar. Concierge. Internet (wireless). No-smoking room(s). Room service (breakfast only). TV.
Other locations: Hôtel St-Germain-des-Prés, 36 rue Bonaparte, 6th (01.43.26.00.19/www.hotel-st-ger.com).

Hôtel des Marronniers

21 rue Jacob, 6th (01.43.25.30.60/fax 01.40.46.83.56/www.paris-hotel-marronniers.com). M° St-Germain-des-Prés. **Rates** €110 single; €153-€168 double; €208 triple; €248 quad; €10-€12 breakfast. **Credit** MC, V. **Map** p410 H6 ⑦⓪
Hidden smack in the centre of the lively St-Germain district through a leafy courtyard, this hotel offers welcome peace and quiet. Afternoon tea is served in the lovely conservatory overlooking a garden at the back, where you'll find the chestnut trees that give the hotel its name. The 37 rooms are mostly reasonably sized, with pretty canopies and fabrics.
Internet (pay terminal). Room service (breakfast only). TV.

Hôtel des Saints-Pères

65 rue des Sts-Pères, 6th (01.45.44.50.00/fax 01.45.44.90.83). M° St-Germain-des-Prés. **Rates** €110 single; €125-€195 double; €295 suite; €12.50 breakfast. **Credit** AmEx, MC, V. **Map** p407 G7 ⑦①
Built in 1658 by one of the architects of Louis XIV, this discreet hotel now occupies an enviable place near St-Germain-des-Prés' designer boutiques. It boasts a charming garden and a sophisticated if small bar. The most coveted room is No.100 (€325), with its fine 17th-century ceiling by painters from the Versailles School; it also has an open bathroom, so you can gaze at scenes from the myth of Leda and the Swan while you scrub.
Bar. Concierge. Internet (wireless). Room service (until 8pm). TV.

Budget

Hôtel du Globe

15 rue des Quatre-Vents, 6th (01.43.26.35.50/fax 01.46.33.62.69/www.hotel-du-globe.fr). M° Odéon. **Rates** €95 single; €105-€120 double; €10 breakfast. **Credit** MC, V. **Map** p410 H7 ⑦②
The Globe has retained much of its 17th-century character – and very pleasant it is, too. Gothic wrought-iron doors lead into florid corridors, and an unexplained suit of armour supervises guests from a post in the tiny salon. The rooms with baths are a bit bigger than those with showers and there are a four-poster bed to be had as well. All 14 rooms were completely renovated in 2004. Take care on the small, winding staircase.
Internet (wireless). TV.

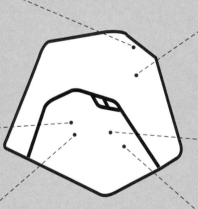

Regents Hôtel

44 rue Madame, 6th (01.45.48.02.81/fax 01.45.44.85.73). M° St-Sulpice. **Rates** €80 single; €80-€110 double; €110 triple; €125 quad; €7 breakfast. **Credit** AmEx, MC, V. **Map** p407 G7
In Paris, it's rare to find a budget option with style, but this discreet hotel located in a quiet street is a lovely surprise, its courtyard garden used for breakfast in the warmer months. The reception rooms are a sunny Provençal blue and yellow, and the bedrooms are comfortable with new bathrooms. Some have small balconies.
Concierge. Internet (dataport). Room service (breakfast only). TV.

Montparnasse

Moderate

Hôtel Aviatic

105 rue de Vaugirard, 6th (01.53.63.25.50/fax 01.53.63.25.55/www.aviatic.fr). M° Montparnasse Bienvenüe, St-Placide or Duroc. **Rates** €139-€175 double; €164-€175 twin; €280 suite; €12 breakfast. **Credit** AmEx, DC, MC, V. **Map** p407 H7
This historic hotel has tons of character, from the Empire-style lounge and garden atrium to the bistro-style breakfast room. The polished floor in the lobby (watch your feet) and the hints of marble and brass lend impressive touches of glamour. The pricier Supérieure rooms have such extras as bathrobes and a modem connection. **Photo** *right.*
Concierge. Internet (pay terminal). Parking (€23). Room service (breakfast only). TV.

Budget

Hôtel Delambre

35 rue Delambre, 14th (01.43.20.66.31/fax 01.45.38.91.76/www.hoteldelambre.com). M° Edgar Quinet or Vavin. **Rates** €85-€115 single or double; €150 suite; €9 breakfast. **Credit** AmEx, MC, V. **Map** p407 G9
Occupying a slot in a small street between Montparnasse and St-Germain, this hotel was home to Surrealist André Breton in the 1920s. Today it's modern and friendly, with cast-iron details in the 30 rooms and newly installed air-conditioning. The mini suite in the attic is particularly pleasing, if not really suitable for the more generously framed.
Concierge. Internet (wireless). Room service (breakfast only). TV.

Hôtel Istria-Montparnasse

29 rue Campagne-Première, 14th (01.43.20.91.82/ fax 01.43.22.48.45). M° Raspail. **Rates** €96-€129 single; €149 double; €10 breakfast. **Credit** AmEx, DC, MC, V. **Map** p410 G9
Behind this unassuming façade is the place where the artistic royalty of Montparnasse's heyday – Man Ray, Marcel Duchamp, Louis Aragon – once lived. The Istria has been modernised since then, but it still has lots of charm with 26 simply furnished rooms,

Empire-style polish at the **Hôtel Aviatic**.

a cosy cellar breakfast room and comfortable living area. Film fans take note: the tiled artists' studios next door featured in Godard's *A Bout de Souffle*.
Concierge. Internet (wireless). No-smoking room(s). Room service (breakfast only). TV.

The 7th & the 15th

Deluxe

Hôtel Duc de Saint-Simon

14 rue de St-Simon, 7th (01.44.39.20.20/fax 01.45.48.68.25/www.hotelducdesaintsimon.com). M° Rue du Bac. **Rates** €245-€265 double; €350-€375 suite; €15 breakfast. **Credit** AmEx, DC, MC, V. **Map** p407 F6 77

A lovely courtyard leads the way into this popular hotel situated on the edge of St-Germain-des-Prés. Of the 34 romantic bedrooms, four have terraces over a closed-off leafy garden. It's perfect for lovers, though if you can do without a four-poster bed, there are more spacious rooms than the Honeymoon Suite.
Concierge. Internet. Room service. TV.

Le Montalembert

3 rue de Montalembert, 7th (01.45.49.68.68/fax 01.45.49.69.49/www.montalembert.com). M° Rue du Bac or Solférino. **Rates** €340-€430 double; €560-€750 suite; €20-€28 breakfast. **Credit** AmEx, DC, MC, V. **Map** p407 G6 78

Grace Leo-Andrieu's impeccable boutique hotel opened in 1989 and is a benchmark of quality and service. It has everything *mode* maniacs (who flock here for Fashion Week) could want: bathrooms stuffed with Contemporel toiletries, a set of digital scales and 360° mirrors to check that silhouette. Decorated in pale lilac, cinnamon and olive tones, the entire hotel has wireless access, and the clattery two-person staircase lifts are a nice nod to old fashionability in a hotel that is otherwise *tout moderne*.
Bar. Concierge. Internet (wireless). Restaurant. Room service. TV.

Expensive

Le Walt

37 av de La Motte-Picquet, 7th (01.45.51.55.83/fax 01.47.05.77.59/www.inwoodhotel.com). M° Ecole Militaire. **Rates** €250-€300 single; €270-€320 double; €12 breakfast. **Credit** AmEx, DC, MC, V. **Map** p406 D7 79

Feel like a star as you walk the spotlit red carpet to your room at this well-appointed boutique hotel. Each of the 25 rooms is decorated in warm milk-chocolate tones, with wooden floors, modern walnut furniture and, above the bed, a giant painting. Many on the sixth floor have views of the Eiffel Tower. The hotel restaurant, decorated in burgundy velour and caramel, with purple gossamer curtains, spills out into the chic little courtyard on warmer days. **Photo** *right*.
Bar. Concierge. Internet (high-speed). No-smoking room(s). Room service (daytime). TV.

Moderate

Hôtel de La Bourdonnais

111 av de La Bourdonnais, 7th (01.47.05.45.42/fax 01.45.55.75.54/www.hotellabourdonnais.com). M° Ecole Militaire. **Rates** €125 single; €150 double or twin; €175 triple; €195 quad; €220 suite; €10 breakfast. **Credit** AmEx, DC, MC, V. **Map** p406 D6 80

The family-owned La Bourdonnais feels more like a traditional French bourgeois townhouse than a hotel, with 56 bedrooms decorated in rich colours, antiques and Persian rugs. The main lobby opens on to a jungle-like winter garden and patio, where guests take breakfast, and an intimate lounge ideal for reading the papers over coffee.
Concierge. Internet (pay terminal). Parking (€15). Room service. TV.

Hôtel Lenox

9 rue de l'Université, 7th (01.42.96.10.95/fax 01.42.61.52.83/www.lenoxsaintgermain.com). M° St-Germain-des-Prés. **Rates** €120-€275 double; €260-€275 duplex; €290-€305 triple; €11-€14 breakfast. **Credit** AmEx, DC, MC, V. **Map** p407 G6 81

The location may be the 7th, but this venerable literary and artistic haunt is unmistakeably part of St-Germain-des-Prés. The art deco-style Lenox Club Bar, open to the public, features comfortable leather club chairs and jazz instruments on the walls. Bedrooms, reached by an astonishing glass lift, have more traditional decor and city views.
Bar. Concierge. Internet (wireless). No-smoking room(s). Room service (until 1am). TV.

Budget

Grand Hôtel Lévêque

29 rue Cler, 7th (01.47.05.49.15/fax 01.45.50.49.36/www.hotel-leveque.com). M° Ecole Militaire. **Rates** €57 single; €87-€93 double; €87-€110 twin; €125 triple; €8 breakfast. **Credit** AmEx, MC, V. **Map** p406 D6 82

Recently renovated with new air-conditioning, the Lévêque is great value for its location on the market street of rue Cler. A charming tiled entrance leads to 50 well-equipped rooms, with sparkling bathrooms in all except the basin-only singles.
Concierge. Internet (dataport). TV.

Hôtel Eiffel Rive Gauche

6 rue du Gros-Caillou, 7th (01.45.51.24.56/fax 01.45.51.11.77/www.hotel-eiffel.com). M° Ecole Militaire. **Rates** €55-€95 single; €65-€105 double; €95-€125 triple; €125-€155 quad; €9 breakfast. **Credit** MC, V. **Map** p406 D6 83

The Provençal decor and warm welcome make this a nice retreat. For the quintessential Paris view at a bargain price, ask for one of the upper floors: you can see the Eiffel Tower from nine of the 29 rooms. All feature Empire-style bedheads and modern bathrooms. There's a tiny, tiled courtyard with a bridge.
Concierge. Internet (pay terminal). TV.

A vast canvas over every bed at well-appointed **Le Walt**. *See p62.*

Youth accommodation

Auberge Internationale des Jeunes
*10 rue Trousseau, 11th (01.47.00.62.00/fax
01.47.00.33.16/www.aijparis.com). Mº Ledru-Rollin.*
Rates (incl breakfast, per person) *Mar-June, Sept-
Oct* €15. *July-Aug* €17. *Nov-Feb* €13. **Credit** AmEx,
MC, V. **Map** p409 N7 ❸❹
Cleanliness is a high priority at this large (120 beds)
hostel close to Bastille and within easy distance of
the Marais. Rooms accommodate between two and
four people, and the larger ones have their own
shower and toilet. With the lowest hostel rates in
central Paris, the place tends to fill up fast in summer, but reservations can be made. Although the
hostel is open all hours with no late-night curfew,
the rooms are closed for cleaning every day between
10am and 3pm.
Internet. Microwave.

Auberge Jules Ferry
*8 bd Jules-Ferry, 11th (01.43.57.55.60/fax
01.43.14.82.09/www.fuaj.fr). Mº République or
Goncourt.* **Rates** (incl breakfast & linens) €20 per
person. **Credit** MC, V. **Map** p405 M4 ❸❺

This friendly IYHF hostel has 100 beds in rooms for
two to six. There's no need – indeed, no way – to
make advance bookings. No curfew, though rooms
are closed between 10am and 2pm.
Internet.

BVJ Paris/Quartier Latin
*44 rue des Bernardins, 5th (01.43.29.34.80/fax
01.53.00.90.91/www.bvjhotel.com). Mº Maubert
Mutualité.* **Rates** (incl breakfast, per person) €26
dorm; €35 single; €28 double. **No credit cards.**
Map p408 K7 ❸❻
The BVJ hostel has 121 beds with homely tartan
quilts in clean but bare modern dorms (for up to ten)
and rooms with showers. There's also a TV lounge
and a work room in which to write up your journal.
Internet.
Other locations: BVJ Paris/Louvre, 20 rue Jean-
Jacques-Rousseau, 1st (01.53.00.90.90).

MIJE
*6 rue de Fourcy, 4th (01.42.74.23.45/fax
01.40.27.81.64/www.mije.com). Mº St-Paul.*
Rates (incl breakfast, per person) €2.50 obligatory
membership) €27 dorm (18-30s); €42 single; €32
double; €28 triple. **No credit cards. Map** p411 L6 ❸❼

MIJE runs three 17th-century Marais residences –
one is a former convent – that provide the most
attractive hostel sleeps in Paris. Its plain, clean
rooms have snow-white sheets and sleep up to eight;
all have a shower and basin. The Fourcy address
has its own restaurant. Curfew is 1am unless you
arrange otherwise with reception. **Photos** *right.*
Internet.
Other locations (same phone): 11 rue du
Fauconnier, 4th; 12 rue des Barres, 4th.

Bed & breakfast

Alcove & Agapes

Le Bed & Breakfast à Paris, 8bis rue Coysevox, 18th
(01.44.85.06.05/fax 01.44.85.06.14/www.bed-and-
breakfast-in-paris.com).
This B&B service offers over 100 *chambres d'hôte*
(€70-€160 for a double, including breakfast) with
hosts who range from artists to grannies. Extras can
include dinner, cooking classes or tours of Paris. The
multilingual website provides good descriptions and
photos of each property.

Good Morning Paris

43 rue Lacépède, 5th (01.47.07.28.29/fax
01.47.07.44.45/www.goodmorningparis.fr).
This company has 100 rooms in the city. Prices
range from €54 for one person to €96 for three. It
also has apartments for two to four people from €75
to €122. Minimum stay is two nights.

Apart-hotels & flat rental

A deposit is usually payable on arrival. Small
ads for private short-term lets run in the
fortnightly anglophone *FUSAC* (www.fusac.fr).

Citadines Apart'hotel

Central reservations 01.41.05.79.79/fax
01.41.05.78.87/www.citadines.com. **Rates** €90-€450.
Credit AmEx, DC, MC, V.
The 17 modern Citadines complexes across Paris
(including around the Louvre and Opéra) tend to
attract a mainly business clientele. Room sizes vary
from slightly cramped studios to two-bedroom
apartments, all with a kitchenette and dining table
suitable for those with children. Rates depend on
neighbourhood, size of apartment and length of stay;
there are discounts for longer stays.

Paris Appartements Services

20 rue Bachaumont, 2nd (01.40.28.01.28/fax
01.40.28.92.01/www.paris-apts.com). Mº Sentier.
Open 9am-6pm Mon-Fri. *Key pick-up* 24hrs. **Rates**
(5-night minimum stay) €83-€150 studio; €135-€214
2-room apartment. Monthly prices on request.
Credit AmEx, MC, V.
This organisation provides furnished studios and
one-bedroom flats in the 1st to 4th districts, with a
weekly maid service, and a 24-hour helpline manned
by bilingual staff. A daily breakfast service and
cleaning can also be arranged.

Historical hostel comfort at **MIJE.** *See p63.*

Sightseeing

Features

Fontaine Stravinsky. *See p105.*

Introduction

You ain't seen nothing yet.

Wheel love: a **Segway tour** stops by the Arc du Carrousel. *See p71.*

Paris is the tourist's perfect city. It's not just that there's such a long roster of things worth sampling – so much history, so many monuments, all those museums, all that *food*; but, what's more, the bag that holds this dizzying number of goodies is one of reassuringly manageable dimensions. You can get a good feel for Paris even just on a day's sightseeing trip, something you can't say of many capital cities; and while its famed beauty certainly doesn't extend to every last nook and cranny, there are few streets here that are not worth walking along.

Walking: that's the secret. The Paris métro is a world champion among public transport networks and merits a ride in its own right; the local buses are clean, frequent and cheap; and there are plenty of **guided tours** (*see p70*) to show you around. By all means, time permitting, try them all. But your best chance of hearing this city's heartbeat lies in putting one foot in front of the other, above ground, among the people who live and work here; only then will you be able to see the 'museum city' clichés for what they are. Paris is alive, thriving: joyous

proof that a city can love the trappings of the contemporary world without forgetting – or fossilising – its past.

Its 20 districts spiral out, clockwise and in ascending order, from the Louvre. These are the *arrondissements*, the pieces that together make a jigsaw puzzle compared by novelist Julien Green to medical models of the human brain, and each piece has its connotations. 5th: *intello*. 6th: chic. 16th: affluent and stuffy. 18th, 19th, 20th: lively and multicultural. Rightly or wrongly, residents are often assessed, at least at first encounter, by their postcodes – and many will tell you that Paris is not a city but, in fact, a coagulation of distinct villages.

We've divided the **Sightseeing** chapter into five sections: the Seine & Islands; Right Bank; Left Bank; the Louvre; and Beyond the Périphérique. The Right Bank and Left Bank sections are also sub-divided by areas which, roughly, follow district guidelines, starting from the centre and working out. If you want to cut to the chase, follow our simple recipe for a potted Paris weekend (*see pp124-125* **Paris against the clock**).

The best Sights

Sightseeing

For literary associations
Cimetière du Père-Lachaise (*see p130 Paris promenade*); Maison de Balzac (*see p126*); Maison de Victor Hugo (*see p110*); Le Panthéon (*see p144*).

For views
Arc de Triomphe (*see p119*); Eiffel Tower (*see p160*); Notre-Dame (*see p74*); Sacré-Coeur (pictured; *see p129*); Tour Montparnasse (*see p167*); Grande Arche de La Défense (*see p177*).

For flâneurs
Boulevard St-Michel (*see p138*); Jardin du Luxembourg (*see p153*); Jardin des Tuileries (*see p92*); Place des Vosges (*see p112*).

For palatial splendour
Assemblée Nationale (*see p155*); the Louvre (*see pp80-88*); Palais du Luxembourg (*see p153*); Palais-Royal (*see p93*); Place des Vosges (*see p112*).

For homely pleasures
Maison de Victor Hugo (*see p111*); Musée des Arts Décoratifs (*see p93*); Musée Carnavalet (*see p111*).

For world-famous art
Centre Pompidou (*see p107*); the Louvre (*see pp80-88*); Musée d'Orsay (*see p159*); Musée Marmottan – Claude Monet (*see p127*); Musée National Picasso (*see p111*); Musée Rodin (*see p157*).

For blood and gore
Les Catacombes (*see p168*); Musée de l'Assistance Publique (*see p138*); Musée d'Histoire de la Médecine (*see p153*).

For sporting heroes
Parc des Princes (*see p329*); Hippodrome de Longchamp (*see p330*); Stade de France (*see p329*).

For dead heroes
Arc de Triomphe (*see p119*); Cimetière du Père-Lachaise (*see p130 Paris promenade*); Cimetière Montparnasse (*see p166*); Les Invalides (*see p156*); Mémorial du Maréchal Leclerc de Hauteclocque et de la Libération de Paris & Musée Jean Moulin (*see p166*); Musée de la Résistance Nationale (*see p174*).

For marvellous mechanisms
La Cité des Sciences et de l'Industrie (*see p134*); Musée de l'Air et de l'Espace (*see p173*); Musée des Arts et Métiers (*see p109*); Musée des Arts Forains (*see p117*); Musée de la Magie (*see p112*); Palais de la Découverte (*see p119*);

For modern architecture
Bibliothèque Nationale de France François Mitterrand (*see p171*); Centre Pompidou (*see p107*); La Défense (*see p177*); Institut du Monde Arabe (*see p145*); Musée du Quai Branly (*see p152 Chirac's grand projet*).

Museums

The Louvre (*see pp80-88* **The Louvre**) is
so vast that it tends to overshadow the
city's hundred-plus museums. The **Centre
Pompidou**, **Musée d'Orsay** and **Musée
Marmottan** are almost as famous, and you
shouldn't miss the world-class ethnic art on
show at **Musées Guimet** and **Dapper** and
the **Institut du Monde Arabe**; nor the
many science museums, from the **Musée des
Arts et Métiers** to the high-tech **Cité des
Sciences et de l'Industrie** at La Villette. For
lovers of the avant-garde, there are the **Palais
de Tokyo Site de Création Contemporain**
and the ARC wing of the **Musée d'Art
Moderne de la Ville de Paris**.

The reason for the rich trove is tied up with
French history. After the Revolution, the huge
royal collections became the property of the
state; then came the 19th-century zeal for *grand
tourisme* – although the ownership of foreign
plunder is a matter of current debate. Both the
French state and the city put large sums into
the upkeep and expansion of collections, while
tiny, unique private museums, like the **Musée
Edith Piaf** or **Musée de l'Eventail**, struggle.

The **Musée du Quai Branly**, the new
museum of primitive and tribal art beside the
Eiffel Tower, opens in 2006 – as does the **Cité
de l'Architecture et du Patrimoine** at the
Palais de Trocadéro. Back in action in 2006 –
if all goes to plan – after closure for various
reasons are the **Musée de l'Orangerie**, the
Musée des Arts Décoratifs, the **Musée
de la Chasse et de la Nature** and the
Pinacothèque de Paris. The themes of
big exhibitions in 2006 include Magritte at
the **Musée Maillol**, Yves Klein at the
Centre Pompidou, Dora Maar at the **Musée
National Picasso**, the Italian avant-garde at
the **Galeries Nationales du Grand Palais**,
Cézanne and Pisarro at the **Musée d'Orsay**.

MUSEUM TICKETS AND PASSES

The most economical way to visit a large
number of museums is the **Carte Musées
et Monuments** (www.parismuseumpass.fr).
Coming in one-day (€18), three-day (€36) or
five-day (€54) formats, it lets you into 70
museums and monuments in Paris (though you
have to pay extra for special exhibitions) and
also jump queues. The card is sold at museums,
tourist offices, branches of **Fnac** (*see p244*)
and major métro stations. In our listings, **CM**
indicates venues where the card is accepted.

The Galeries Nationales du Grand
Palais also now operate an annual pass,
Sésame (www.rmn.fr), which grants handy

A **Batobus** stops by Notre-Dame. *See p78.*

queue-jumping rights, unlimited entry and
various other discounts (€74 couples; €39 solo;
€22 concessions).

Museums often offer reduced admission
for students, children and the over-60s; bring
identification to prove your status. In any case,
all permanent collections at municipal-run
museums are free, and a reduced rate is usually
applicable on Sundays. All national museums
are completely free of charge on the first
Sunday of the month, and most museums
also throw open their doors on one Sunday
in April for the **Printemps des Musées**
(01.40.15.36.00, www.culture.gouv.fr; *see p273*).

MUSEUM OPENING HOURS

Most national museums close on Tuesdays;
most municipal museums close on Mondays.

To avoid the crowds, visit on weekdays, or
to take advantage of the late-night opening
that most of the big museums offer. Pre-
booking is essential before 1pm at the Grand
Palais, and it's also possible to pre-book
the Louvre, the Luxembourg and major
exhibitions. Most ticket counters will close 30
to 45 minutes before the official closing time.

Thousands turn out for the annual **Journées
du Patrimoine** (*see p276*) in September to see
behind the normally closed doors of some of the
capital's oldest and most beautiful buildings.

Paris districts at a glance

Bastille

No so much revolutionary, these days, as creative; the area around iconic place de la Bastille is well stocked with wacky record shops, music venues (starting with the most visible, the eyesore opera house) and some *chouette* bars.

Belleville

One of the city's most multicultural areas: Chinese shops rub up against halal and kosher grocers, and there's a busy street market on Tuesday and Friday mornings.

Bercy

One of the 'it' quarters right now – in spite of a distinct shortage of historic character. Entertainment is a strong point, especially cinema: the new home for the Cinémathèque Française, designed by Frank Gehry, is particularly striking.

Grands Boulevards

Less a distinct quarter than a curving east-west stripe across several others. At the western end it's all large-scale consumerism in the grands magasins; to the east, seediness, buzz and exotic food shops.

Ile de la Cité

The bullseye of the capital, where its history begins – now home to the law courts, Notre-Dame cathedral, the Sainte-Chapelle and a dinky little flower market.

Ile St-Louis

You'd need a huge pile of euros to buy a property on this island of calm, but it costs nothing to explore its charming streets and small, characterful shops.

Les Halles

Once the city's wholesale food market, now home to one of its unloveliest architectural landmarks, the Forum des Halles shopping mall. The streets around it are jammed with small clothes shops – and people.

Madeleine

Monied but lacking in character, this is where the higher class of street-walker plies her trade – appropriately enough in an area named after the church of Mary Magdalene. There are some fab food shops, too.

The Marais

With ancient buildings and a street plan largely unmolested by Haussmann, this is great pedestrian territory. The Marais is the heartland of Jewish and gay Paris, and chock-full of sweet boutiques, art galleries and bars.

Ménilmontant

Hymned in a famous Charles Trenet song ('C'est là que j'ai laissé mon coeur', he

---

TEMPORARY EXHIBITION VENUES
Non-museum exhibition centres include the blockbusting Grand Palais and Palais du Luxembourg, and a host of smaller foundations, libraries and buildings of architectural interest that offer well priced or free exhibitions. Most are open only for exhibitions, so check *L'Officiel des spectacles* before dropping in. Cultural centres include: **Centre Culturel Calouste Gulbenkian** (Portugal; 51 av d'Iéna, 16th, 01.53.23.93.93); **Centre Culturel Irlandais** (Ireland; 5 rue des Irlandais, 5th, 01.58.52.10.30); **Centre Culturel Suisse** (Switzerland; 32-38 rue des Francs-Bourgeois, 3rd, 01.42.71.38.38); **Centre Wallonie-Bruxelles** (Belgium; 127 rue St-Martin, 4th, 01.53.01.96.96); **Goethe Institut** (Germany; Galerie Condé, 31 rue de Condé, 6th, 01.40.46.69.60; 8 av Raymond-Poincaré, 16th, 01.44.43.92.30); **Institut Finlandais** (Finland; 60 rue des Ecoles, 5th, 01.40.51.89.09); **Institut Néerlandais** (Netherlands; 121 rue de Lille, 7th,

01.53.59.12.40); **Maison de l'Amérique Latine** (Latin America; 217 bd St-Germain, 7th, 01.49.54.75.00).

Guided tours

For boat tours, *see p78*.

Coach tours

Les Cars Rouges

01.53.95.39.53/www.carsrouges.com. **Departs** (from Trocadéro) every 10-20mins 9.30am-6.30pm daily. **Tickets** €22; €11 4s-12s. **No credit cards**. Red buses follow a set tour of the major monuments. Hop on at any of nine stops. Recorded commentary.

Cityrama

4 pl des Pyramides, 1st (01.44.55.61.00/www. graylineparis.com). M° *Palais Royal Musée du Louvre.* **Departs** *Winter* 10am, 11.30am, 2pm. *Summer* 10am, 11.30am, 2pm, 3.30pm. **Tickets** €15; €7.50 concessions. **Credit** AmEx, DC, MC, V.

warbles), this is a thriving centre of alternative Paris, awash with artists studios and trendy cafés.

Montmartre

The highest point in the city also has one of its densest concentrations of tourists. The views and Sacré-Coeur should be seen, of course – but then strike out from the crowds and explore the unabashedly romantic side-streets and stairways.

Montparnasse

There's still enough of a good-time feel here – especially after dark – to recall the area's artistic heyday in the 1920s and 1930s. Bars, restaurants and cinemas are abundant.

Pigalle

Sex shops and neon: that's the popular image of Pigalle. There's a lot of both, indeed – but the area has been cleaning up its act in recent years, with the relandscaping of boulevard de Clichy and boulevard de Rochechouart.

St-Germain-des-Prés

World-famous intellectual heritage and some of the most expensive cups of coffee in the city. The district is now best known for fashion houses and luxury brands, though a few publishers remain.

Another double-decker outfit with multi-lingual recorded commentary. Also organises walking tours.

Paris L'OpenTour

13 rue Auber, 9th (01.42.66.56.56/www.paris-opentour.com). M° Havre-Caumartin. **Departs** *Apr-Oct every 10-30mins 9.30am-6pm daily. Nov-Mar every 25-30mins 9.30am-5.15pm daily.* **Tickets** *1 day* €25; €12 concessions. *2 days* €28; €12 concessions. **Credit** AmEx, DC, MC, V.
Green, open-top buses run along four routes past the attractions, with recorded headphone commentary in English and French. Hop on at any of 50 stops.

Paris Vision

214 rue de Rivoli, 1st (01.42.60.30.01/ www.parisvision.fr). M° Tuileries. **Departs** times vary. **Tickets** €19-€92; €9.50-€92 4-11s. **Credit** AmEx, DC, MC, V.
Large air-conditioned coaches take you round the sights. The commentary is basic, and you should make sure you get a top-deck seat. Tours last between two hours and a full day; the longer ones include lunch or a river cruise.

Two-wheeled tours

City-bird

08.26.10.01.00/www.city-bird.com. **Tickets** €70-€100. **Credit** AmEx, DC, MC, V.
For the money-rich and time-poor, a new sightseeing tool: the motorbike. A friendly, knowledgeable driver comes to pick you up, then weaves you through the traffic, supplying banter and history over an intercom, while Paris sights whirl around you. A simple 'taxi-scooter' service is also offered.

Fat Tire Bike Tours

01.56.58.10.54/www.fattirebiketoursparis. com. Meet at Pilier Sud, Tour Eiffel, Champs de Mars, 7th. M° Bir-Hakeim. **Departs** *Bike day tour* mid Feb-May & mid Sept-mid Dec 11am daily; June-mid Sept 11am, 3pm daily. *Bike night tour* Mar & first 2wks Nov 7pm Tue, Thur, Sat, Sun; Apr-Oct 7pm daily. *Segway day tour* mid Feb-mid Dec 10.30am daily. *Segway night tour* Apr-Oct 6.30pm daily. **Tickets** *Day* €24; €22 students. *Night* €28; €26 students. *Both* €48; €44 students. *Segway* €70. **No credit cards.**
Day and night tours in English around the sights, by chunky bike or on a sole-saving but ostentatious Segway. Wet-weather gear is provided. Book for Segway, as well as for bike tours of Giverny and Versailles. Walking tours and bike hire available.

Paris à vélo, c'est sympa!

28 rue Baudin, 11th (01.48.87.60.01/ www.parisvelosympa.com). M° Richard Lenoir. **Departs** *Apr-Oct* 10am Mon, Fri; 3pm Wed; 10am, 3pm Sat, Sun. *Nov-Mar* 10am, 2pm Sat, Sun. **Tickets** €32.50; €28 13s-26s; €18 under-12s. **Credit** MC, V.
Multilingual guided cycle tours with a variety of themes, including nocturnal Paris and Paris at dawn (May-Sept 8.30pm Sat and 6am Sun). Reservations required. Bike hire also available.

Walking tours

See above for **Cityrama** and **Fat Bike Tours**.

Paris Walking Tours

01.48.09.21.40/www.paris-walks.com. **Departs** daily, times vary. **Tickets** €10. **Credit** MC, V.
Informative and enjoyable daily walks given by long-term resident expatriates. Neighbourhoods covered include the Marais, Montmartre and Hemingway's old Left Bank.

► Launched by the Office de Tourisme (*see p385*) in 2005, the **Passeport Paris** is a 48-page directory of museums, shops, restaurants and tour companies, with a money-off coupon for use at each. Valid for a year, it costs €5 and is sold across the city: see www.parisinfo.com for details.

The Seine & Islands

Between the Left and Right banks lies the historic heart of Paris.

Sightseeing

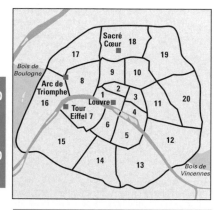

The Seine

The Seine is at once a divide, transport route and tourist attraction. On the first score, the division is as much psychological as physical, between a Left Bank still popularly perceived as chic and intellectual and a Right Bank seen as mercantile. In the second, the Seine is still used to transport building materials; and in the third, as all the boat tours attest (see p76 **Boat tours**), it's a must-see feature.

It hasn't always been so. For much of the 19th and 20th centuries, the Seine was barely given a second thought by anyone who didn't work on it or roar along its quay roads. Then, in the 1980s, the banks along the stretch now known as quai François-Mitterrand became a popular gay cruising area (dubbed Tata Beach), and in 1990 UNESCO added 12 kilometres of Paris riverbank to its World Heritage register. The Parc Tino-Rossi was created on the Left Bank, where riverside tango became a regular event. Then the floating venues – **Batofar** (see p323) and its ilk – became super-trendy; and in the last ten years, it's been one Seineside cultural attraction after another. Stretches of riverside roads are closed on Sundays to give free rein to cyclists and rollerskaters, the Port de Javel becomes an open-air dancehall in the summer and, of course, there's the summer riverside jamboree of **Paris-Plage** (see p275), Mayor Delanoë's inspired idea to bring a bit of the south of France to the embankments – sand, palm trees, loungers, beach huts and all.

The bridges

From the recently cleaned, honey-coloured arches of ancient Pont Neuf to Pont Charles-de-Gaulle, with its smooth lines of aerodynamic magic, the 36 bridges within Paris afford some of the most seductive reasons to visit the city – and some of the best views. The date of the very first construction traversing the Seine is lost in the fog, but there was already a bridge at the position of today's Petit Pont when the Parisii Celts (see p10) had their river trade and toll-bridge operations going in the first century BC. The Romans quickly put up a cross-island thoroughfare in the guise of a reinforced bridge to the south of Ile St-Louis, and another one north of it (where Pont de Notre-Dame now stands), thus creating a straight route from Orléans to Belgium.

The city's *ponts* have been bombed, bashed to bits by buses, boats and barges, weather-beaten to destruction and even trampled to the toppling point: in 1634 Pont St-Louis collapsed under the weight of a religious procession. During the Middle Ages, the handful of bridges linking the islands to the riverbanks were lined with shops and houses, but the flimsy wooden constructs regularly caught fire or got washed away. The Petit Pont, for example, sank 11 times before councillors decided it would be a good idea to ban building on top of bridges.

Pont Neuf was inaugurated in 1607 and has been standing sturdy, gargoyles a-goggle, ever since. This was the first bridge to be built with no houses to obstruct the view of the river. It had a raised stretch of road at the edge to keep walkers separate from traffic and horse dung (the new-fangled 'pavement' soon caught on); the semicircular alcoves that now make handy smooching pit-stops were once filled with teeth pullers, peddlers and *bouquinistes* (see p242).

The 19th century saw a bridge boom – 21 of them in all, including the city's first steel, iron and suspension bridges. Pont de la Concorde used up what was left of the Bastille after the storming of 1789; the romantic Pont des Arts (*pictured p71*) was the first solely pedestrian crossing (built in 1803, rebuilt in the 1980s). The most glitteringly exuberant is the Pont Alexandre III, with its finely wrought lamps, garlanding and gilded embellishments. The most pleasingly practical is the Pont de l'Alma,

The Pont Neuf provides a scenic backdrop for a picnic on the **Pont des Arts**. *See p70.*

with its Zouave statue. This has long been a popular flood-level measure: when his toes get wet the state raises the flood alert and starts to close the quayside roads; when he's up to his ankles in Seine, it's no longer possible to navigate the river by boat. This offers some indication of how devastating the great 1910 flood must have been, when the plucky Zouave disappeared up to his neck – as did large areas of central Paris.

The 20th century also produced some fab additions to the line-up. Pont Charles-de-Gaulle, for example, stretches resplendent like a huge aeroplane's wing, and iron Viaduc d'Austerlitz (1905) is striking yet elegant in the way that it cradles métro line 5. Planned for 2006, and set to be called the Passerelle Bercy-Tolbiac, the city's 37th bridge has a lot to live up to. Plans show a low-lying, cabled construction without any ground supports between the banks, and a walkway that stretches 180 metres, linking the Bibliothèque Nationale to the Parc de Bercy.

Ile de la Cité

In the 1st & 4th arrondissements.
The Ile de la Cité is where Paris began around 250 BC, when the Parisii, a tribe of Celtic Gauls, moved to this convenient bridging point of the Seine and founded a settlement (*see p10*). Romans, Merovingians and Capetians followed, in what went on to be a centre of political and religious power right into the Middle Ages: royal authority concentrated at one end, around the Capetian palace; and the church at the other end, around Notre-Dame.

When Victor Hugo wrote his *Notre-Dame de Paris* in 1831, the Ile de la Cité was still a bustling quarter of narrow medieval streets and tall houses: 'the head, heart and very marrow of Paris'. Assuming the metaphor was apt, Baron Haussmann performed a marrow extraction when he supervised the expulsion of 25,000 people from the island, razed tenements and some 20 churches and left behind large, official buildings – the law courts, the **Conciergerie**, Hôtel-Dieu hospital, the police headquarters and the cathedral. The lines of the old streets are traced into the parvis in front of **Notre-Dame**.

Perhaps the most charming spot on the island is the western tip, where the Pont Neuf spans the Seine. Despite its name, it is in fact the oldest remaining bridge in Paris, begun under the reign of Henri III and Catherine de Médicis in 1578 and taking 30 years in all to complete. The arches of the Pont Neuf are lined with grimacing faces, supposedly modelled on some of the courtiers of Henri III.

Down the steps is a leafy triangular garden, square du Vert-Galant, an ideal spot for picnics. You can also take to the water on the **Vedettes du Pont Neuf** moored on the quay (*see p76* **Boat tours**). In the centre of the bridge is an equestrian statue of Henri IV; the original went up in 1635, was melted down to make cannons during the Revolution, and replaced in 1818. On the bridge's eastern side, triangular place Dauphine, home to restaurants, wine bars and the ramshackle Hôtel Henri IV, was built in 1607, on what was then a sandy bar that flooded every winter. It was commissioned by Henri IV, who named it in honour of his son, the future King Louis XIII. The red-brick and stone houses, similar to place des Vosges (though subsequently much altered in the interest of sun terraces), look out on to the quays and square. The third, eastern side was demolished in the 1860s, when the new Préfecture de Police was built, known by its address, quai des Orfèvres, and immortalised on screen by Clouzot's film and Simenon's Maigret novels. It's a tranquil, secluded spot, though you may not agree with André Breton, for whom 'the sight of its triangular formation with slightly curved lines, and of the slit which bisects its two wooded spaces' made him think of it as 'the sex of Paris'.

The towers of the **Conciergerie** dominate the island's north bank. Along with the Palais de Justice, it was originally part of the Palais de la Cité, residential and administration complex of the Capetian kings. It occupies the site of an earlier Merovingian fortress and, before that, the Roman governor's house. Etienne Marcel's uprising prompted Charles V to move the royal retinue to the Louvre in 1358, and the Conciergerie was assigned a more sinister role as a prison for those awaiting execution. The interior is worth a visit for its prison cells and the vaulted Gothic halls. On the corner of boulevard du Palais, the Tour de l'Horloge, built in 1370, was the first public clock in Paris.

Sainte-Chapelle, Pierre de Montreuil's masterpiece of stained glass and slender Gothic columns, nestles amid the nearby law courts. Enveloping the chapel, the Palais de Justice was built alongside the Conciergerie. Behind elaborate wrought-iron railings, most of the present buildings around the fine neo-classical entrance courtyard date from the 1780s reconstruction by Desmaisons and Antoine. After passing through security, you can visit the Salle des Pas Perdus, busy with plaintiffs and barristers, and sit in on cases in the civil and criminal courts. The Palais is still the centre of the French legal system, though it's been rumoured that the law courts will one day be moved to the 13th or 15th arrondissement.

Across boulevard du Palais, behind the Tribunal du Commerce, place Louis-Lépine is occupied by the green pavilions of the Marché aux Fleurs, where horticultural suppliers sell flowers, cacti and exotic trees. On Sundays, they are joined by twittering caged birds and small animals in the Marché aux Oiseaux. The Hôtel-Dieu, east of the marketplace, was founded in the seventh century. During the Middle Ages your chances of survival here were, at best, slim; today the odds are much improved. The hospital originally stood on the other side of the island facing the Latin Quarter, but after a series of fires in the 18th century was rebuilt here in the 1860s.

Notre-Dame cathedral dominates the eastern half of the island. On the parvis in front of the cathedral, the bronze 'Kilomètre Zéro' marker is the point from which distances to Paris from the rest of France are measured. The **Crypte Archéologique** hidden under the parvis gives a sense of the island's multi-layered past, when it was a tangle of alleys, houses, churches and cabarets. Despite all the tourists, Notre-Dame is still a place of worship, and has its **Assumption Day procession** (*see p276*), **Christmas Mass** (*see p277*) and Nativity scene on the parvis.

Walk through the garden by the cathedral to appreciate its flying buttresses. To the north-east, a medieval feel persists in the few streets untouched by Haussmann, such as rue Chanoinesse, rue de la Colombe and rue des Ursins, though the crenellated medieval remnant on the corner of rue des Ursins and rue des Chantres was redone in the 1950s for the Aga Khan. The capital's oldest love story (*see p13* **Love hurts**) unfolded in the 12th century at 9 quai aux Fleurs, where Héloïse lived with her uncle Canon Fulbert, who had her tutor and lover, the scholar Abélard, castrated. Héloïse was sent to a nunnery. Behind the cathedral, in a small garden at the eastern end of the island, is the **Mémorial des Martyrs de la Déportation**, commemorating those sent to concentration camps.

Cathédrale Notre-Dame de Paris

pl du Parvis-Notre-Dame, 4th (01.42.34.56.10/ www.cathedraledeparis.com). M° Cité/RER St-Michel. **Open** 7.45am-6.45pm daily. *Towers Apr-Sept* 9am-6.45pm daily. *Oct-Mar* 10am-4.45pm daily. **Admission** free. *Towers* €7.10; €5.10 18s-25s; free under-18s. **Credit** MC, V. **Map** p408 J7.
One of the masterpieces of Gothic architecture, Notre-Dame was commissioned in 1160 by Bishop Maurice de Sully, who wanted to rival the smart new abbey that had just gone up in St-Denis. It replaced the earlier St-Etienne basilica built in the sixth century by Childebert I on the site of a Gallo-Roman temple to Jupiter. It was constructed between 1163 and 1334, and the amount of time and money spent on it reflected the city's growing prestige. Pope Alexander III may have laid the foundation stone; the choir was completed in 1182, the nave in 1208;

The view from
Notre-Dame.
See p72.

A high point of Gothic architecture: the **Cathédrale Notre-Dame de Paris**. *See p74.*

the west front and twin towers went up between 1225 and 1250. Chapels were added to the nave between 1235 and 1250 and to the apse between 1296 and 1330. The cathedral was plundered during the French Revolution, and then rededicated to the cult of Reason. The original statues of the Kings of Judah from the west front were torn down by the mob (who believed them to represent the kings of France) and rediscovered only during the construction of a car park in 1977 (they're now on view in the Musée National du Moyen-Age; *see p138*). By the 19th century the cathedral was looking pretty shabby.

Victor Hugo, whose novel *Notre-Dame de Paris* had been a great success, led the campaign for its restoration. Gothic revivalist Viollet-le-Duc restored Notre-Dame to her former glory in the mid 19th century, although work has been going on ever since, with the replacement and cleaning of damaged and eroded finials and sculptures. Although Reims (*see p356*) was the coronation church of the French kings, that didn't stop others with monarchical pretensions: in 1430 Henry VI of England was crowned here; Napoléon made himself Emperor here in 1804; and in 1909 it hosted the beatification of Joan of Arc (you'll find a statue of her inside).

Despite its heavy restoration, the west front remains a high point of Gothic art for the balanced proportions of its twin towers and rose window, and the three doorways with their rows of saints and sculpted tympanums: the Last Judgement (centre), Life of the Virgin (left) and Life of St Anne (right). Inside, stop a moment to admire the long nave with its solid foliate capitals and high altar with a marble *Pietà* by Coustou; the choir was rebuilt in the 18th century by Robert le Cotte but it is surrounded by medieval painted stone reliefs depicting the Resurrection (south) and Nativity (north). Religious paintings, known as the Mays because they were donated by the guilds on 1 May every year, hang in many of the side chapels. Off to the south of the choir, the Treasury contains ornate bishops' copes, church plate and reliquaries designed to hold the Crown of Thorns (which long sat in Sainte-Chapelle; *see p75*). To truly appreciate the masonry, climb up the towers (only a limited number can ascend at one time). The route begins up the north tower and descends down the south. Between the two towers you get a close-up view of the gallery of chimeras – the fantastic birds and leering hybrid beasts designed by Viollet-le-Duc along the balustrade, including the pensive Stryga, who looks down on the capital from the first corner. After a detour to see the Bourdon, the big bell, a tight spiral staircase leads to the top of the south tower from where you can look down on the spire and and have a view of pretty much every monument in Paris. **Photo** *above.*

La Conciergerie

2 bd du Palais, 1st (01.53.40.60.97). M° Cité/RER St-Michel Notre-Dame. **Open** *Mar-Oct* 9.30am-6pm daily. *Nov-Feb* 9am-4.30pm daily. **Admission** €6.10; €4.10 18s-25s, students; free under-18s (accompanied by an adult). *With Sainte-Chapelle* €9; €6.50 concessions. **Credit** MC, V. **Map** p410 J6.

Marie-Antoinette was imprisoned here during the Revolution, as were Danton and Robespierre before their executions. The Conciergerie looks every inch the forbidding medieval fortress, yet much of the pseudo-medieval façade was added in the 1850s. The 13th-century Bonbec tower, built during the reign of St Louis, the 14th-century twin towers, César and Argent, and the Tour de l'Horloge, all survive from the Capetian palace. The visit takes you through the Salle des Gardes, the medieval kitchens with their four huge chimneys, and the Salle des Gens d'Armes, an impressive vaulted Gothic hall built between 1301 and 1315 for Philippe le Bel. After the royals moved to the Louvre, the fortress became a prison under the watch of the Concierge. The wealthy had private cells with their own furniture, which they paid for; others crowded together on beds of straw. A list of Revolutionary prisoners, including a hairdresser, shows that far from all of the victims were nobles. In Marie-Antoinette's cell, the Chapelle des Girondins, are her crucifix, some portraits and a guillotine blade.

La Crypte Archéologique

pl du Parvis-Notre-Dame, 4th (01.55.42.50.10). M° Cité/RER St-Michel Notre-Dame. **Open** 10am-6pm Tue-Sun. **Admission** €3.30; €2.20 over-60s; €1.60 13s-26s; free under-13s. **Credit** (€15 minimum) MC, V. **Map** p408 J7.

Hidden under the parvis in front of the cathedral is a surprisingly large void that reveals bits and pieces of Roman quaysides, ramparts and hypocausts, medieval cellars, shops and pavements, the foundations of the Eglise Ste-Geneviève-des-Ardens (the church where Geneviève's remains were stored during the Norman invasions), an 18th-century foundling hospital and a 19th-century sewer, all excavated since the 1960s. It's not always easy to work out exactly which wall, column or staircase is which but you do get a vivid sense of the sheer layers of history piled one atop another during 16 centuries. There are plans to extend the crypt to uncover part of the foundations of the Merovingian cathedral, slightly further west of the present one.

Mémorial des Martyrs de la Déportation

square de l'Ile de France, 4th (01.46.33.87.56). M° Cité/RER St-Michel Notre-Dame. **Open** *Winter* 10am-noon, 2-5pm Tue-Sun. *Summer* 10am-noon, 2-7pm Tue-Sun. **Admission** free. **Map** p408 J7.

This sober tribute to the 200,000 Jews, Communists, homosexuals and Resistants deported to concentration camps from France during World War II was opened in 1962 on the eastern tip of the island. A blind staircase descends to river level, where simple chambers are lined with tiny lights and the walls are inscribed with poetry. A barred window looks out on to the Seine.

Sainte-Chapelle

4 bd du Palais, 1st (01.53.40.60.80). M° Cité/RER St-Michel Notre-Dame. **Open** *Mar-Oct* 9.30am-5.30pm daily. *Nov-Feb* 9am-4.30pm daily. **Admission** €6.10; €4.10 18s-25s, students; free under-18s (accompanied by an adult). *With Conciergerie* €9; €6.50 concessions. **Credit** MC, V. **Map** p410 J6.

Devout King Louis IX (St Louis, 1226-70) had a hobby of accumulating holy relics (and children: he fathered 11). In the 1240s he bought what was advertised as the Crown of Thorns, and ordered Pierre de Montreuil to design a suitable shrine. The result was the exquisite Flamboyant Gothic Sainte-Chapelle. With its 15m-high windows, the upper level, intended for the royal family and the canons, appears to consist almost entirely of stained glass. The windows depict hundreds of scenes from the Old and New Testaments, culminating with the Apocalypse in the rose window; on sunny days, coloured light dapples the stone. The lower chapel, with its star-painted vaulting, was for the use of palace servants.

Ile St-Louis

In the 4th arrondissement.

The Ile St-Louis is one of the most exclusive residential addresses in the city. Delightfully unspoiled, it offers fine architecture, narrow streets and pretty views from the tree-lined quays, and still retains the air of a tranquil backwater, curiously removed from city life.

For hundreds of years the island was a swampy pasture belonging to Notre-Dame and a retreat for fishermen, swimmers and courting couples; then it was known as Ile Notre-Dame. In the 14th century Charles V built a fortified canal through the middle, thus creating the Ile aux Vaches ('Island of Cows'). Its real-estate potential wasn't realised until 1614, though, when speculator Christophe Marie persuaded Louis XIII to fill in the canal (present-day rue Poulletier) and plan streets, bridges and houses. The island was renamed in honour of the king's pious predecessor and the venture proved a huge success, thanks to society architect Louis Le Vau, who from the 1630s built fashionable new residences along the quai d'Anjou, quai de Bourbon and quai de Béthune (including 3 quai d'Anjou for himself), as well as the **Eglise St-Louis-en-l'Ile**. By the 1660s the island was full up; its smart reception rooms were set at the front of courtyards to give their residents riverside views (unlike the Marais, whose reception rooms were at the rear).

Rue St-Louis-en-l'Ile – lined with fine historic buildings that now contain quirky gift shops and gourmet food stores (many of them open

Tours by boat

Most boats depart from the quays in the 7th and 8th arrondissements, at the foot of the Eiffel Tower, and go on a circuit around the islands, first along the Left Bank and past the Latin Quarter and Notre-Dame, then along the Right Bank, past the Marais and the Louvre.

Bateaux-Mouches

Pont de l'Alma, 8th (01.42.25.96.10/ information 01.40.76.99.99/www.bateaux-mouches.fr). M° Alma-Marceau. **Departs** *Summer every 45mins 10am-2.30pm, every 30mins 2.30pm-11pm daily. Winter 11am, 2.30pm, 4pm, 6pm, 9pm daily.* **Admission** €7; €4 concessions; free under-4s. **Credit** AmEx, MC, V.

If you are after a whirlwind tour of all the essential sites and don't mind crowds of schoolchildren and tourists, this, the oldest cruise operation on the Seine, is the one to choose. Still, the four languages that are crammed into the canned commentary and the high speed of the boat mean that you get only the basic facts. By the way, the origins of the 'Mouches' part of the name is cloaked in mystery – sadly, there was no founder called Monsieur Mouche.

Bateaux Parisiens

Tour Eiffel, port de la Bourdonnais, 7th (01.44.11.33.55/www.bateauxparisiens. com). RER Champ de Mars. **Departs** *Apr-Oct every 30mins 10am-11pm daily. Nov-Mar every hr 10am-10pm daily.* **Admission** €9.50; €4.50 concessions; free under-3s. **Credit** AmEx, MC, V.

BP's trimarans are smarter boats than most, and jaunty Parisian music flavours your cruise. Competent staff provide a live commentary in French, and good English and Spanish. The glass-topped boats should be avoided on hot days as they turn into floating greenhouses.

Batobus Tour Eiffel

08.25.05.05.01/www.batobus.com. Boats stop at Tour Eiffel (Port de la Bourdonnais), Musée d'Orsay, St-Germain-des-Prés (quai Malaquais), Notre-Dame, Jardin des Plantes, Hôtel de Ville, Louvre and Champs-Elysées (Pont Alexandre III). **Departs** *(every 15-25mins) Apr-Sept 10am-10pm daily. Oct-Dec, Feb, Mar 10am-9pm daily. Closed Jan.* **Admission** *Day pass* €11; €5-€7 concessions. *2-day pass*

€13; €6-€8 concessions. *5-day pass* €16; €8-€10 concessions. *Annual pass* €50; €30 concessions.

A public transport and sightseeing hybrid, this is a pleasurable way to cruise through the city, with eight hop-on, hop-off stops between the Eiffel Tower and the Jardin des Plantes. The polite staff, who give tourist information on request, and the presence of some Parisians, make this a classier choice. It can be combined with L'Open Tour (*see p69*) on a two-day ticket that gives you unlimited access to the 50 bus-stops and eight boat-stops.

Canauxrama

13 quai de la Loire, 19th (01.42.39.15.00/ www.canauxrama.fr). **Departs** *Apr-Sept Port de l'Arsenal (50 bd de la Bastille, 12th, M° Bastille) 9.45am, 2.30pm daily; Bassin de la Villette (13 quai de la Loire, 19th, M° Jaurès) 9.45am, 2.45pm daily.* **Admission** €14; €8-€11 concessions; free under-6s.

If the Seine palls, take a trip up the city's second waterway, the Canal St-Martin (*see p133*). The tree-lined canal is a pretty and characterful sight, and the 150-minute trip even goes underground for a stretch, where the tunnel walls are enlivened by a coloured light show. Call for cruises between the Musée d'Orsay and La Villette.

Vedettes de Paris

Port de Suffren, 7th (01.47.05.71.29/ www.vedettesdeparis.com). M° Bir-Hakeim. **Departs** *Easter-Oct every 30mins 10am-10pm daily. Nov-Easter every hr 11am-6pm daily.* **Admission** €9; €4 concessions; free under-4s.

Open boats give the most unobstructed views, and the recorded commentary can be avoided by choosing the children's cruise: the French-only tour guide on board soon tires of the bridge-naming game.

Vedettes du Pont-Neuf

square du Vert Galant, 1st (01.46.33.98.38/ www.vedettesdupontneuf.com). M° Pont Neuf. **Departs** *Mar-Oct 10am-10.30pm daily. Nov-Feb 10.30am-10pm Mon-Fri; 10.30am-10.30pm Sat, Sun.* **Admission** €10; €5 concessions; free under-4s.

Big boats that give you the option of sitting inside just a foot or two above water level or outside on the top deck – where you may get drenched by pranksters throwing water from bridges as you pass underneath.

Rooms with a view: fashionable residences on the **quai d'Anjou**. *See p77.*

on Sunday), quaint tearooms, stone-walled bars, restaurants and hotels – runs the length of the island. The grandiose Hôtel Lambert (No.2) was built by Le Vau in 1641 for Louis XIII's secretary and has sumptuous interiors by Le Sueur, Perrier and Le Brun. At No.51, Hôtel Chenizot, look out for the bearded faun adorning the rocaille doorway, which is flanked by stern dragons supporting the balcony; there's more sculpture on the courtyard façade, while a second courtyard hides craft workshops and an art gallery. Across the street, the Hôtel du Jeu de Paume at No.54 was once a real tennis court, while famous deluxe ice-cream maker Berthillon, at No.31, still draws a crowd. There are great views of the flying buttresses of Notre-Dame at the western end from the terraces of the Brasserie de l'Isle St-Louis and the Flore en l'Ile café. A footbridge crosses from here to the Ile de la Cité.

Baudelaire wrote part of *Les Fleurs du Mal* while living at the Hôtel de Lauzun; he and fellow poet Théophile Gautier also organised meetings of their dope-smokers' club here. A couple of centuries earlier, Racine, Molière and La Fontaine resided as guests of La Grande Mademoiselle, cousin of Louis XIV – and mistress of the Comte de Lauzan. The *hôtel*, built 1657, stands out for its scaly sea-serpent drainpipes and trompe-l'oeil interiors. There are further literary associations at 6 quai d'Orléans: the Adam Mickiewicz library-museum (01.43.54.35.61, open 2-6pm Thur) is dedicated to the Romantic poet, journalist and zealous campaigner for Polish freedom, who had set off for Poland to catch the failed 1831 uprising only to find himself unable to cross the border. He came to Paris to write poems and political pamphlets, all found here.

Eglise St-Louis-en-l'Ile

19bis rue St-Louis-en-l'Ile, 4th (01.46.34.11.60).
M° Pont Marie. **Open** 9am-noon, 3-7pm Tue-Sun.
Map p411 L7.
Tucked discreetly amid the street façades, the island's church was constructed between 1664 and 1765, following plans by Louis Le Vau and later completed by Gabriel Le Duc. The interior follows the classic baroque model, with Corinthian columns and a sunburst over the altar, and is also used as a venue for classical music concerts.

The Louvre

A palatial setting for the world's finest art collection.

Main entrance under the **Pyramide**.

The most famous museum in the world is, in fact, several museums in one. It's a vast palace (and one whose medieval origins were slowly unearthed during the course of President Mitterrand's Grand Louvre project), a veritable patchwork of architectural styles dating from the Middle Ages to modern times. Treasures from the Egyptians, Etruscans, Greeks and Romans each have their own extensive galleries, as do Middle Eastern and Islamic art. There are European decorative arts from the Middle Ages up to the 19th century, and in the Sully wing you can roam through rooms distinguished by lavish interior design. The main draw is the paintings and sculpture, most of which are contained in the vast Denon wing, with two glass-roofed sculpture courts, Italian and French painting, and Dutch masters. The minimalist galleries of Primitive Arts in the Pavillon des Sessions foreshadow and promote the Musée du Quai Branly (*see p152* **Chirac's grand projet**), which is due to open in 2006.

So where did all the art come from? It's not all a testament to imperial greed, although that played a part. Much of the royal collection was, after all, presented as offerings to the ruling monarchs and acted as diplomatic sweeteners.

The talent of Leonardo Da Vinci was fought over as a commodity and prestige point during the reign of Louis XII, who petitioned for a portrait in Lombardy while at the same time Milan was being sacked by his very own troops. It was François I who brought an entire Italian court to France, resulting in a rich collection of then contemporary art and antiquities. Some treasures were bequeathed to the state in lieu of death duties, and others are acquired in an ongoing process by the Réunion des Musées Nationaux. The Louvre became a museum in 1793, its Revolutionary opening to the people a true expression of the art-for-all ethic still in force every first Sunday of the month when the museum is free to enter.

Mitterrand's Grand Louvre project expanded the museum two-fold by throwing out the Ministry of Finance and other government offices that once inhabited the Cour Napoléon. But the organisation and restoration of the Louvre is still a work-in-progress: check the website or lists in the Carrousel du Louvre to see which galleries are closed on certain days to avoid missing out on what you really want to see. It is unrealistic to expect to cover more than two sections in a day before museum fatigue sets in, so choose what you want to see before you go and follow the signs. What's wonderful about the Louvre, however, is the element of surprise – from the grandeur of the *Winged Victory of Samothrace* crowning the grand stairway to the two tiny dice that have survived a thousand years. Then there is the almost operatic setting provided by the building itself: what is more incongruous than finding Louis XIV's bedchamber in the Egyptian department? Nothing is quite like it, and you will wish you had even more time to lose yourself in its 12 miles of corridors and 300,000 works of art. Fifty thousand others do every day.

ADVANCE TICKETS AND ENTRANCE
IM Pei's glass pyramid is a wonderful piece of architecture but it has the effect of making you think this is the only entrance. Avoid it or you'll be standing in a queue waiting for your bag to go through the scanner. There are three other ways in. Buying a ticket in advance means you can go in directly via the passage Richelieu off rue de Rivoli, or via the Carrousel du Louvre shopping mall (steps down either side of the Arc de Triomphe du Carrousel, at 99 rue de Rivoli or from the Métro). Advance tickets are valid for any day, and are available from the Louvre website, or from branches of **Fnac**, **Virgin Megastore** (for both, *see p244*) or any of the major department stores (*see p233*) or supermarkets. The Cour des Lions entrance in the south-west corner of the complex (closed Fridays) has its own ticket desk and gives directly on to the *Arts premiers* and entrance to the Italian collections – and the *Mona Lisa*.

The Louvre is also one of the museums accessible with the all-in **Carte Musées et Monuments** (www.parismuseumpass.fr; *see p67*), which is available in three formats.

The best Odd facts

● The name 'Louvre' is thought to come from 'lupara' (it was built on the site of a wolfhound kennel) or the word for 'fortress' in Anglo-Saxon.
● In 1939, 200 truckloads of art were evacuated to the Château de Chambord. On his fleeting visit to Paris in June 1940, Hitler didn't bother to look at the Louvre, much to Albert Speer's disappointment.
● The IM Pei pyramid has its own robot to clean the glass.
● In 1680 a bourgeois petitioned Louis XIV to put public water closets in the Louvre. The request was ignored.

OTHER TIPS
● Pick up a map at the information desk. The museum is divided into three wings: Denon (down the Seine side); Richelieu (down Rivoli), and Sully, which joins them up and runs around the Cour Carrée at the end. The eight collections are colour-coded on the map and signs show you to the way to the most popular exhibits. *Destination Louvre* (€7.50), from the Réunion des Musées Nationaux shop in the Carrousel du Louvre, is a good English-language guide.
● Printed cards, available in a variety of languages in each room, give good background information. Audioguides (€5) are available at the main entrances in the Carrousel du Louvre.
● Take breathers – your ticket is valid all day and you can leave and re-enter as you wish.
● Evening visits are on Wednesdays and Fridays till 9.45pm. Late on Friday the museum is free for the under-26s, but if you are planning to make several visits, the Carte Louvre Jeunes, at €15 for the year, is worth getting.
● Some rooms are closed on a weekly basis – check on 01.40.20.51.51 or www.louvre.fr.
● Save your shopping for the end. The RMN bookshop and separate souvenir shops are open an hour after closing, except when the museum stays open late.
● Don't try to see everything on one visit. You're bound to get lost, so think of it as an excuse to discover the unexpected.

The Louvre
rue de Rivoli, 1st (01.40.20.50.50/recorded information 01.40.20.51.51/disabled access 01.40.20.59.90/www.louvre.fr). M° Palais Royal Musée du Louvre or Louvre Rivoli. **Open** 9am-6pm Mon, Thur, Sat, Sun; 9am-9.45pm Wed, Fri. **Admission** *Permanent collections* €8.50 (incl entry to the Musée Delacroix but not shows at the Salle Napoléon); €6 6-9.45pm Wed, Fri; free under-18s at all times, under-26s 6-9.45pm Fri, all ages on 1st Sun of mth, CM. *Exhibitions* €8.50. *Combined ticket* €13; €11 6-9.45pm Wed, Fri. **Credit** MC, V. **Map** p403 G5.

REFRESHMENTS
Grab a bite at one of the cafés: **Richelieu**, **Denon** or **Mollien**, on the Mollien staircase, which has a terrace. Under the pyramid there's a sandwich bar, café and the **Grand Louvre** restaurant serving French cuisine. The **Restorama**, in the Carrousel du Louvre, has multiple self-service outlets. The terrace of fashionable **Café Marly** (93 rue de Rivoli, 1st, 01.49.26.06.60), with a view of the pyramid, serves pricey brasserie fare. Fast-food outlet **Aux Pains Perdus** (4 rue de l'Echelle, 1st, 01.49.26.96.96) has soups, salads, wraps and artisanal lemonades to take away or eat on their terrace; **Ragueneau** (202 rue St-Honoré, 1st, 01.42.60.29.20) has pastries, salads, soups and a full lunchtime menu.

The Collections

History of the Louvre

Sully: lower ground floor. Shown as dark brown on Louvre maps.

Here you can visit the medieval foundations of the Louvre, which were uncovered in 1985. A scale model shows the fortress at the time of Charles V. You can walk around the moat of Philippe-Auguste's outer wall to see the pillars of two drawbridges; La Taillerie tower, with heart symbols cut into the stone by masons; and the outside of the dungeon, where treasure and prisoners were kept. A well and a portion of ground are left undisturbed, showing artefacts just as they were found. An exhibition in the Saint-Louis room – a guard room from the era of Philippe-Auguste, which was discovered in 1882 – recounts the history of the Louvre through rare archeological finds, as well as an unfinished staircase and carved pillars.

Ancient Egypt

Denon: lower ground floor; Sully: lower ground, ground & 1st floors. Green on Louvre maps.

Announced by the Giant Sphinx in pink granite (1898-1866 BC), the Egyptian department divides into two routes. The Thematic Circuit on the ground floor presents Nile culture (fishing, agriculture, hunting, daily and cultural life, religion and death); one of the big draws is the Mastaba of Akhethetep, a decorated burial chamber from Sakkara dating to 2400 BC. Six small sphinxes, apes from Luxor and the lion-headed goddess Sekhmet recreate elements of temple complexes, while stone sarcophagi, mummies, amulets, jewellery and entrails form a vivid display on funeral rites. One of the best displays is on Egyptian furniture (room 8, ground floor): dating from 1550-1069 BC, the pieces look almost contemporary in design. On the first floor, the Pharoah Circuit is laid out chronologically, from the Seated Scribe and other stone figures of the Ancient Empire, via the painted figures of the Middle Empire, to the New Empire, with its animal-headed statues of gods and goddesses, papyrus scrolls and hieroglyphic tablets. Look for the double statue of the god Aman protecting Tutankhamun, and the black diorite 'cube statues' of priests and attendants. The collection, one of the largest hoards of Egyptian antiquities in the world, has its origins in Napoléon's Egyptian campaign of 1798-99, as well as Egyptologist Champollion, who deciphered hieroglyphics in 1824. The Coptic gallery, on the lower ground floor, shows textiles and manuscripts. **Photo** *right.*

Oriental antiquities

Richelieu: lower ground & ground floors; Sully: ground floor. Yellow on Louvre maps.

This section deals with Mesopotamia, Persia and the Levant from the fifth millennium BC to the first century AD. The huge Mesopotamian rooms contain glistening diorite sculptures of the Akkad dynasty and Gudea from the third millennium BC; for some of which, only their remarkable feet have survived intact. Make sure you don't miss the serene alabaster sculpture of Ebih-II, the superintendant of Mari (room 1b), and the earliest evidence of writing, in the form of fourth-century BC Sumerian tablets (room 1a). The Hammurabi Code, an essential document of Babylonian civilisation, is a black basalt stele recording 282 laws beneath reliefs of the king and the sun god; it's one of the most ancient collections of laws in the history of mankind (room 3).

Then come two breathtaking palace reconstructions: the great court, c713 BC, from the palace of Sargon II at Khorsabad (in present-day Iraq), with its giant bearded and winged bulls and friezes of warriors and servants (room 4); and the palace of Darius I at Susa (now Iran), c510 BC, with its fine glazed-brick reliefs of rows of archers, lions and griffins (room 12). The double-bull-headed column was one of a chequerboard of such gigantic columns. As you enter the Iranian section, you'll find 5,000-year-old statues from Suza housed in circular room 8, which provides a magnificent view of the Cour Napoléon. The Levantine section includes Cypriot animalistic vases and carved reliefs from Byblos.

Egyptian department.

Islamic arts

Richelieu: lower ground floor. Turquoise on Louvre maps.

The Islamic decorative arts here include early glass, tenth- to 12th-century dishes decorated with birds and calligraphy, traditional Iranian blue-and-white wares, Iznik ceramics, intricate inlaid metalwork from Syria, tiles, screens, weapons and funerary steles. The highlight is three magnificent 16th-century kelims. In 2005 a Saudi prince, Prince Walid bin Talal, gave over €17 million – one of the largest donations in French cultural history – for a new Islamic wing to be built as an extension to the Louvre's southern wing. It's expected to open by 2009.

Greek, Roman & Etruscan antiquities

Denon: lower ground & ground floors; Sully: ground & 1st floors. Blue on Louvre maps.

The *Winged Victory of Samothrace*, a headless Greek statue dating from the second century BC, stands sentinel at the top of the grand staircase, giving an idea of its original dramatic impact on a promontory overlooking the sea. This huge department is made up of pieces amassed by François I and Richelieu, plus the Borghese collection (acquired in 1808), and the Campana collection of thousands of painted Greek vases and small terracottas.

Endless dark rooms on the first floor harbour small bronze, silver and terracotta objects, but the really exciting stuff is on the ground floor.

Grandiose vaulted marble rooms are a fitting location for knockout masterpieces such as the 2.3m-high *Athena Peacemaker* and the *Venus de Milo* (room 12), and overflow with gods and goddesses, swords and monsters.

Also on the ground floor are examples of the culture of Etruscan civilisation of south-central Italy, spanning the seventh century BC until submission to the Romans in the first century AD. The highlight is the Sarcophagus of the Cenestien Couple (c530-510 BC) in painted terracotta, which illustrates a smiling couple reclining at a banquet. Key Roman antiquities include a vivid relief of sacrificial animals, intricately carved sarcophagi, mosaic floors and the Boscoreale Treasure: magnificent silverwork excavated at a villa near Pompeii. Pre-classical Greek art on the lower ground floor includes a large Cycladic head and Mycenean triad.

French painting

Denon: 1st floor; Richelieu: 2nd floor; Sully: 2nd floor. Red on Louvre maps.

There are around 6,000 of the most famous paintings in the world on show here, the most impressive being the huge 18th- to 19th-century canvases hanging in the Grande Galerie in the Denon wing. Here, art meets politics with Gros' suitably dashing *Napoléon Visitant le Champ de Bataille d'Eylau*, David's enormous *Sacre de Napoléon* and Delacroix's flag-flying *La Liberté Guidant le Peuple*. Géricault's beautiful but

Sightseeing

Inscrutable, unmissable: **Mona Lisa**.

disturbing *Le Radeau de la Méduse* illustrates his artistic vision of the true story of the abandoned men who resorted to cannibalism and murder after a famous shipwreck in 1816. Just as horrifying is Girodet's *Le Déluge*, where a wild-eyed man tries to cling on to a woman being pulled down by her own children. Biblical and historical scenes rub shoulders with aristocracy and grand depictions of great moments in mythology.

In the Richelieu wing you can find the earliest known non-religious French portrait, an anonymous portrait of French king Jean Le Bon (c1350); the *Pietà de Villeneuve-les-Avignon*, later attributed to Enguerrand Quarton; Jean Clouet's *Portrait of François I* (marking the influence of the Italian Renaissance on portraiture); and works from the Ecole de Fontainebleau, including the anonymous *Diana the Huntress*, an elegant nude who strangely resembles Diane de Poitiers, the mistress of Henri II. Poussin's religious and mythological subjects epitomise 17th-century French classicism, and are full of erudite references for an audience of cognoscenti. His works spill over into the Sully wing, where you'll also be able to find Charles Le Brun's wonderfully pompous *Chancellier Séguier* and his four grandiose battle scenes, in which Alexander the Great is a suitable stand-in for Louis XIV.

The 18th century begins with Watteau's *Gilles* and the *Embarkation for Cythera*. Works by Chardin include sober still lifes, but also fine figure paintings. If you're used to the sugary images of Fragonard, don't miss the *Fantaisies*, which forgo sentimentality for fluent, broadly-painted fantasy portraits, intended to capture moods rather than likenesses. Also in the Sully wing are sublime neo-classical portraits by David, Ingres' *La Baigneuse* and *Le Bain Turc*, portraits and Orientalist scenes by Chassériau, and landscapes by Corot.

French sculpture

Richelieu: lower ground & ground floors. Light brown on Louvre maps.

French sculpture is displayed in and around the two glazed sculpture courts created by the Grand Louvre scheme. A tour of the medieval regional schools takes in the *Virgins* from Alsace, 14th-century figures of Charles V and Jeanne de Bourbon that adorned the exterior of the Louvre, and the late 15th-century Tomb of Philippe Pot, an effigy of a Burgundian knight carried by eight black-clad mourners. Fine Renaissance memorials, fountains and portals include Jean Goujon's friezes from the Fontaine des Innocents. In the Cour Marly, pride of place goes to Coustou's *Chevaux de Marly*, rearing horses being restrained by their grooms, plus two earlier equestrian pieces by Coysevox. Hewn from single blocks of marble, they were sculpted for the royal château at Marly-le-Roi before being moved to the Tuileries gardens, where copies now stand. In Cour Puget are the four bronze captives by Martin Desjardins, Clodion's rococo frieze and Pierre Puget's twisting *Baroque Milo of Croton*. Amid the 18th-century heroes and allegorical subjects, look out for Pigalle's *Mercury* and *Voltaire*.

Italian and Spanish painting

Denon: 1st floor. Red on Louvre maps.

Starting from the Sully end of the Denon wing, two rooms of fragile Renaissance frescoes by Botticelli, Fra Angelico and Luini open the Italian department. Cimabue's *Madonna of the Angels* (c1270) combines the composition of Byzantine icons and prefigures the modelling of form of the Renaissance visible in Fra Angelico's *Coronation of the Virgin* and Mantegna's *Calvary*, for example. Highlights of the Sienese school are Simone Martini's *Christ Carrying the Cross* and Piero della Francesa's *Portrait of Sigismondo Malatesta*. High Renaissance treasures from Florence include Raphael's *La Belle Jardinière*, and two paintings of dragon slayers St George and St Michael. A small Spanish section takes in El Greco's *Christ on the Cross Adored by Two Donors* and Jusepe de Ribera's *Club Foot*.

Big changes have been taking place in this department. In spring 2005, the Salle des Etats (room 6) reopened after a four-year renovation programme, the museum's two most celebrated works, the *Mona Lisa* (aka *La Joconde*) and Veronese's monumental, lavish *Wedding at Cana*, were given pride of place in the glass-roofed room, funded – at vast expense – by Japanese television channel NTV. Mona is now more visible than previously, although the protective glass is still there, and there's a wooden barrier to keep the public at a safe distance. They will be surrounded by other Italian Renaissance masterpieces such as Leonardo's *Virgin of the Rocks, Virgin, Child and Saint-Anne* and *Saint-Jean Baptiste*, Caravaggio's *Fortune Teller*, the celebrated *Fête Champêtre* (attributed to Titian), and the fruit-and-leaf heads of Arcimboldo's *Four Seasons*, plus works by Tintoretto, Lotto and Bronzino. Queues for *La Joconde* are even more inevitable after the success of Dan Brown's bestselling phenomenon *The Da Vinci Code* – as if the bullet-proof glass wasn't off-putting already.

Graphic arts

Denon: 1st floor; Sully: 2nd floor. Pink on Louvre maps.
The Louvre's huge collection of drawings includes works by Raphael, Michelangelo, Dürer, Holbein and Rembrandt, but owing to their fragility, drawings are not shown as

Canova's **Psyche Revived by Cupid's Kiss**.

permanent exhibits. Four galleries (French and Northern schools on the 2nd floor; Italian and the latest acquisitions on the 1st) have changing exhibitions (*see below*). Other works can be viewed in the Salle de Consultation only upon written application to the management (01.40.20.52.51, fax 01.40.20.53.51).

Italian, Spanish and Northern sculpture

Denon: lower ground & ground floors. Light brown on Louvre maps.
Michelangelo's *Dying Slave* and *Captive Slave* (sculptures planned for the tomb of Pope Julius II in Rome) are the real showstoppers in this section, but other Renaissance treasures include a painted marble relief by Donatello, Adrien de Vriesse's bronze *Mercury and Psyche*, Giambologna's *Mercury* and the ethereal *Psyche Revived by Cupid's Kiss* by Antonio Canova. Benvenuto Cellini's *Nymph of Fontainebleau* relief is on the Mollien staircase. Aptly positioned between ancient and modern worlds on the ground floor, Napoléon III's former stables were reopened in 2004 to house princely collections of statuary acquired by Richelieu, and the Borghese and Albani families during the 17th and 18th centuries. The statues, either copies of classical works or heavily restored originals, demonstrate the relationship between antique and modern sculpture. The height of the room has also allowed oversized works such as *Jupiter* and *Albani Alexander* to be displayed here for the first time. Northern sculpture, on the lower ground floor, ranges from Erhart's Gothic *Mary Magdalene* to the neo-classical work of Thorvaldsen, while the pre-Renaissance Italian pieces include Donatello's clay relief *Virgin and Child*.

Northern schools

Richelieu: 2nd floor; Sully: 1st floor. Red on Louvre maps.
Works of the northern Renaissance include Flemish altarpieces by Memling and Van der Weyden, Bosch's fantastical, proto-Surrealist *Ship of Fools*, Metsys' *The Moneylender and his Wife*, and the northern Mannerism of Cornelius van Haarlem. The Galerie Médicis houses Rubens' Médicis cycle; the 24 canvases were commissioned in the 1620s for the Palais de Luxembourg by Marie de Médicis, the widow of Henri IV. Together they combine historic events and classical mythology for the glorification of the queen who was never afraid to put her best features on public display. Look out, too, for Rubens' more personal, glowing portrait of his second wife, *Hélène Fourment and her Children*, along with Van Dyck's *Charles I and his Groom*, and peasant-filled townscapes by David Teniers the Younger.

Who built the Louvre?

From Philippe-Auguste to Jacques Chirac, France's rulers have all added their *sou*'s worth to the Louvre. Here's who made it the behemoth of today – and how:

Philippe-Auguste 1180-1223

Built a medieval castle on the site of a seventh-century Roman wolfhound kennel in 1190 to protect Paris from invasion. In the centre was a dungeon, which also served as a treasure trove. The remains of Philippe-Auguste's Louvre were discovered under the Cour Carrée in 1985.

Louis IX (Saint-Louis) 1226-70

The Salle Saint-Louis, in one of the outer towers, is thought to date from the saintly king because of the carvings on the pillars.

Charles V (The Wise) 1364-80

Records show that Charles turned the Louvre into a sumptuous palace, with gardens, a zoo and a tennis court. There was little to show for it after the Hundred Years War.

François I (1515-47)

Having razed the medieval tower, a year before his death François I had Pierre Lescot build a new wing fit for a Renaissance prince.

Henri II (1547-59)

Henri II added the Pavillon du Roi, the earliest example of a Mansart-style roof (hidden by façades built by Napoléon). The architecture is decorated with figures and monograms (F for François I; H for Henri II, with C and D for his wife and favourite, Catherine de Médicis and Diane de Poitiers; K for Charles IX; and HdB for Henri IV). The Salle des Caryatides and Escalier Henri II are from this era.

Charles IX (1560-74)

Charles carried on the work of Lescot. A façade with his motto, 'Piety and Justice', dismantled by Napoléon, can be seen in the Rotonde Napoléon. At this time Catherine de Médicis had the Tuileries palace built. Thus began 'Le Grand Dessein', the plan to unite the two palaces finally achieved by Napoléon III 30 years before the Tuileries burnt down.

Henri III (1574-89); Henri IV (1589-1610)

To Charles IX's Petite Galerie, the two Henris added the perpendicular Grande Galerie, a show of power and order alongside the Seine. Henri IV's second wife, Marie de Médicis, felt the palace was far too gloomy and medieval.

Louis XIII (1610-43)

Louis had Jacques Lemercier continue the Lescot wing on the western side of the Cour Carrée. Lemercier created a mirror image of Lescot's work, with the magnificent Sully Pavilion receiving pride of place in the middle.

Louis XIV (1643-1715)

Superintendant Colbert had plans for the Louvre, but Louis XIV only spent a sixth of the sum he spent on Versailles on it. He added three sides to the Cour Carrée to complete the square. View it from the Pont des Arts on the south side, or on the east side from St-Germain l'Auxerrois, and you can appreciate the work of Louis Le Vau and François d'Orblay. Place du Carrousel, now a traffic roundabout, is named after an equestrian event held on this site in 1662.

Napoléon (1799-1815)

Though Napoléon credited himself with 'the construction of the Louvre' in his memoirs, he only built one wing along rue de Rivoli (its galleries now occupied by the **Musée des Arts Décoratifs**; *see p93*) and filled the museum with plunder from his campaigns. The Percier and Fontaine rooms in the Denon wing are all that is left of the grand staircase and entrance the Emperor ordered – this was

Dutch paintings in this wing include early and late self-portraits by Rembrandt, his *Flayed Ox* and the warmly glowing nude *Bathsheba at her Bath*. There are Vermeer's *Astronomer* and *Lacemaker* amid interiors by De Hooch and Metsu, and the meticulously finished portraits and framing devices of Dou, plus works from the Haarlem school. German paintings in side galleries include portraits by Cranach, Dürer's *Self-Portrait* and Holbein's *Anne of Cleves*.

The rooms of Northern European and Scandinavian paintings include Caspar David Friedrich's *Trees with Crows*, the sober, classical portraits of Christian Købke, and pared-back views by Peder Balke. A fairly modest but high-quality British collection located on the first floor of the Sully includes landscapes by Wright of Derby, Constable and Turner and portraits by such notables as Gainsborough, Reynolds and Lawrence.

where Napoléon married Marie-Louise in 1810. He also erected the handsome Arc de Triomphe du Carrousel, copied from the Arch of Septimus Severus in Rome.

Napoléon III (1852-70)

With the exception of the Grande Galerie, Napoléon I's galleries on rue de Rivoli and the Pavillon de Rohan (built by Louis XVIII), the whole of the Cour Napoléon was built in the Second Empire by Louis Visconti and Hector Lefuel. With Baron Haussmann at the helm, the whole project was completed in four years (1852-56). Though designed as a continuation, the stone decoration is more ornate than that of the 17th-century parts – note Denon's central *pavillon* with a statue of the Emperor in the centre.

François Mitterrand (1981-1995)

This president will be remembered for his daring Grand Louvre project. Mitterrand threw out the Ministry of Finance and opened the Richelieu wing, doubling the exhibition space, but his most inspired move was to make IM Pei's glass pyramid the main entrance to the museum. A spiral staircase descends into the Carrousel du Louvre, with shops, restaurants and an exhibition hall used for fashion shows.

Jacques Chirac (1995-present)

There was little Chirac could do to top the achievements of his Socialist predecessor, so he commissioned the **Musée du Quai Branly** (*see p152* **Chirac's *grand projet***) to house Primitive Arts from the Louvre and other collections. Jean-Michel Wilmotte's conversion of the Pavillon des Sessions in the Louvre in 2000 provide an hors d'oeuvre. The Salle des Etats and the Cour d'Apollon have also been renovated under Chirac's watch.

Decorative arts

Richelieu: 1st floor; Sully: 1st floor. Magenta on Louvre maps.

The decorative-arts collection runs from the Middle Ages to the mid 19th century, often with royal connections, and includes entire rooms decorated in the fashion of the day. Many of the finest medieval items came from the treasury of St Denis amassed by the powerful Abbot Suger, counsellor to Louis VI and VII, among them Suger's 'Eagle' (a porphyry vase), a serpentine

plate surrounded by precious stones, and the sacred sword of the kings of France, dubbed 'Charlemagne's sword' by the Capetian monarchs as they sought to legitimise their line.

The Renaissance galleries take in ornate carved chests, German silver tankards, and the *Hunts of Maximilien*, twelve 16th-century Brussels tapestries depicting months, the zodiac and hunting scenes. 17th- and 18th-century French decorative arts are displayed in superb panelled rooms, and include characteristic brass and tortoiseshell pieces by Boulle. Displays move on to French porcelain, silverware, watches and scientific instruments. Napoléon III's opulent apartments, used until the 1980s by the Ministry of Finance, have been preserved, with chandeliers and upholstery intact. Butting on to the Denon wing, the magnificent Galerie d'Apollon reopened in 2004 after four years of restoration work. A precursor to the Hall of Mirrors at Versailles, the gallery was built for Louis XIV and is a showcase of talents from this golden age: architecture by Louis Le Vau, painted ceilings by Charles Le Brun and sculpture by François Girardon, the Marsy brothers and Thomas Regnaudin. It was completed by Napoléon III, who had Delacroix paint the central medallion, *Apollo Vanquishing the Python*. It houses the crown jewels and Louis XIV vases. Merry-Joseph Blondel's *Chute d'Icare* graces the ceiling of an anteroom of the adjacent Rotonde d'Apollon.

African, Asian, Oceanic and American arts

Denon: ground floor. White on Louvre maps.

A new approach to '*arts premiers*' is seen in these eight rooms in the Pavillon des Sessions, prefiguring the Musée du Quai Branly (*see p152* **Chirac's *grand projet***). The spare, modern design of Jean-Michel Wilmotte allows each of the 100 key works to stand alone in something midway between an art gallery and a museum. The pure aesthetics of such objects as a svelte Zulu spoon with the breasts and buttocks of a woman, a sixth-century BC Sokoto terracotta head, a recycled iron sculpture of the god Gou that prefigures Picasso, and a pot-bellied, terracotta Chupicaro from Mexico can be appreciated in their own right, while printed boards provide fascinating explanations of their uses. Computer terminals with mahogany benches provide multimedia resources.

Temporary exhibitions

Major new exhibitions are to be found in the Salle Napoléon. The programme for 2006 includes a major Ingres retrospective (24 Feb-15 May) and a comprehensive round up of 18th- and 19th-century American painters with French connections (15 June-18 Sept).

MUSÉE
DE MONTMARTRE

Open Tuesday - Sunday
10.00am - 6.00pm
12 rue Cortot
75018   PARIS
Tel: 01. 49.25.89.37
www.museedemontmartre.com

- **More than 300 original works of art**

- **Fine art gallery**

- **Bookshop**

2 fascinating museums next to the Sacré Coeur in Montmartre

In its oldest property
including a beautiful garden
share the life and history o
Montmartre, its cabaret
and its artists
Toulouse-Lautrec
Utrillo
Suzanne Valador

Open daily
10.00am - 6.00pm
11 rue Poulbot
75018   PARIS
(1 min walk from Place du Tertre)
Metro Abbesses-Anvers-Funiculaire
Tel: 01.42.64.40.10
www.daliparis.com

DALÍ
ESPACE MONTMARTRE

The Right Bank

Bright lights, tourist cameras – action!

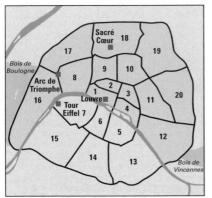

The Louvre to Concorde

In the 1st arrondissement.

It may no longer be the centre of French power but the Louvre (*see pp80-88* **The Louvre**) still exerts influence: first of all as a grandiose architectural ensemble, a palace within the city; and, secondly, as a symbol of cultural Paris. When the monarchs moved from the Ile de la Cité in the 14th century, the Louvre became the new base of royal power, and later that of the empire. What had been simply a fortress along Philippe-Auguste's city wall in 1190 was transformed into a residence with all the latest Gothic comforts by Charles V; François I turned it into a sumptuous Renaissance palace. For centuries it was a work in progress: everyone wanted to add his bit, even the most monarchical of presidents, François Mitterrand, who added IM Pei's glass pyramid, doubled the exhibition space and added the subterranean Carrousel du Louvre shopping mall, auditorium and food halls.

The palace has always attracted swarms of people – first courtiers and ministers, then artists and, since 1793, when the palace was first turned into a museum, art lovers (though the last department of the Finance Ministry only moved out as late as 1991). Around the palace, other subsidiary palaces grew up: Catherine de Médicis commissioned Philibert Delorme to begin work on one in the Tuileries; Richelieu built the Palais Cardinal, which later became the Palais-Royal.

On place du Louvre, opposite Claude Perrault's grandiose western façade of the Louvre, is **Eglise St-Germain-l'Auxerrois**, once the French kings' parish church and home to the only original Flamboyant Gothic porch in Paris, built in 1435. Mirroring it to the left of the belfry is the 19th-century neo-Gothic 1st arrondissement town hall, with its own fanciful rose window and classical porch. Next door is chic bar **Le Fumoir** (*see p215*), which has a Mona Lisa of its own – one made with Amaretto, orange juice and champagne. You can walk through the Louvre from here, through the ornate Cour Carrée, although the main museum entrance is now the pyramid or from métro Palais Royal Musée du Louvre.

Across rue de Rivoli from the Louvre, past the **Louvre des Antiquaires** antiques emporium (*see p266*) and nightspot **Le Cab** (*see p325*), stands the understatedly elegant **Palais-Royal**, once Cardinal Richelieu's private mansion and now the Conseil d'Etat and Ministry of Culture. With its quiet gardens, it's hard to believe that this was once the most debauched corner of the capital and the starting point of the French Revolution.

In the 1780s the Palais was a boisterous centre of Paris life, where aristocrats and the financially challenged inhabitants of the *faubourgs* rubbed shoulders, and the coffee-houses in its arcades generated radical debate. Here Camille Desmoulins called the city to arms on the eve of Bastille Day (*see p275*); and after the Napoleonic Wars, Wellington and Field Marshal von Blücher lost so much money in the gambling dens that Parisians claimed they had won back their entire dues for war reparations. Only haute cuisine restaurant **Le Grand Véfour** (*see p185*), founded as Café de Chartres in the 1780s, survives from this era, albeit with decoration from a little later. The **Comédie Française** theatre ('La Maison de Molière'; *see p339*) stands on the south-west corner. The company, created by Louis XIV in 1680, moved here in 1799. Molière himself is honoured with a fountain on the corner of rue Molière and rue de Richelieu. Brass-fronted Café Nemours on place Colette – Colette herself used to buy cigars from old-fashioned A la Civette nearby (157 rue St-Honoré, 1st, 01.42.96.04.99) is another thespian favourite; standing in front of it, the métro entrance by artist Jean-Michel Othoniel, all glass baubles and wonky aluminium struts, is a kitsch take on Guimard's famous art nouveau métro entrances.

Today the arcades of the Palais-Royal provide an eclectic succession of antique dealers, philatelists and specialists in tin soldiers and musical boxes. Here you'll find chic vintage clothes specialist **Didier Ludot** (*see p253*) and the elegant perfumery **Salons du Palais-Royal Shiseido** (*see p238*). Passing through the arcades to rue de Montpensier, the neo-rococo Théâtre du Palais-Royal and the centuries-old theatre café L'Entr'acte (47 rue de Montpensier, 1st, 01.42.97.57.76), you'll find narrow, stepped passages that run between here and rue de Richelieu. This small area, along with parallel rue Ste-Anne, is the focus of the city's Japanese community, and is packed with sushi restaurants and noodle bars.

On the other side of the palace towards Les Halles, off rue Jean-Jacques-Rousseau, galerie Véro-Dodat, built by rich *charcutiers* during the Restoration, has beautifully preserved neo-classical wooden shopfronts. Browse the bijou selection of antique dolls, the made-to-measure make-up boutiques and luxury leather goods. Where rue St-Honoré meets rue Croix-des-Petits-Champs, look out for the controversial new steel façade by architect Francis Solers on a Haussmannian Ministry of Culture annexe.

At the western end of the Louvre by rue de Rivoli are the **Musée des Arts Décoratifs**, the **Musée de la Mode et du Costume** and the **Musée de la Publicité**. All of these are administered independently of the Musée du Louvre, but were refreshed as part of the Grand Louvre scheme. Across the place du Carrousel from the Louvre pyramid, the Arc du Carrousel, a mini-Arc de Triomphe, was built in polychrome marble for Napoléon in 1806-09. The chariot on the top was originally drawn by the antique horses from San Marco in Venice, snapped up by Napoléon but returned in 1815. From the arch the extraordinary axis along the **Jardin des Tuileries**, the **Champs-Elysées** (*see p118*) up to the **Arc de Triomphe** (*see p119*) and on to the **Grande Arche de la Défense** (*see p177*) is plain to see.

Once stretching as far as the Tuileries palace, destroyed in the 1871 Paris Commune, the Tuileries gardens were laid out in the 17th century by André Le Nôtre and remain a key pleasure area, with a summer **funfair** (*see p285*); they also serve as an open-air gallery for modern art sculptures. Overlooking focal **place de la Concorde** is the **Musée de l'Orangerie** (which might – possibly – reopen in 2006) and the **Jeu de Paume**, the latter built as a court for real tennis, now a new centre for photographic exhibitions.

The stretch of rue de Rivoli running beside the Louvre towards Concorde, laid out by Napoléon's architects Percier and Fontaine in 1802-11, is most remarkable for its arcaded façades. It runs in a straight line between place de la Concorde and rue St-Antoine, in the **Marais** (*see p105*); at the western end it's heavy on tacky souvenir shops – though some old-fashioned hotels remain, and there are also gentlemen's outfitters, bookshop **WH Smith** (*see p244*) and tearoom Angelina (226 rue de Rivoli, 1st, 01.42.60.82.00). The area became a little England in the 1830s and 1840s as aristocrats, writers and artists flooded across the Channel after the Napoleonic Wars, sleeping at the **Hôtel Meurice** (*see p43*), buying the daily English newspaper published by bookseller **Galignani** (*see p242*), and dining in the fancy restaurants of the Palais-Royal.

Place des Pyramides, at the junction of rue de Rivoli and rue des Pyramides, contains a shiny gilt equestrian statue of Joan of Arc. One of four statues of her in the city, it's fêted as a proud symbol of French nationalism every May Day by supporters of the Front National. Ancient rue St-Honoré, running parallel to rue de Rivoli, is one of those streets that changes style in different districts: smart shops line it near place Vendôme, small cafés and inexpensive bistros towards Les Halles. No.296, the baroque **Eglise St-Roch**, is still pitted with bullet holes made by Napoléon's troops when they crushed a royalist revolt in 1795. With its old houses, adjoining rue St-Roch still feels wonderfully authentic; a couple of shops are even built into the side of the church. Further up, at No.263bis, the Chapelle Notre-Dame de l'Assomption (1670-76), now used by the city's Polish community, has a dome so disproportionately large locals dubbed it *sot dôme* ('stupid dome'), a pun on 'Sodom'. Much talked-about boutique **Colette** (*see p256* **High concept**) brought some oomph to what was once a staid shopping area, drawing a swarm of high-concept fashion stores in its wake. All are ideally placed for the fashionistas and film stars who touch down at **Hôtel Costes** (*see p43*) and its chic bar (*see p213* **Overnight sensations**).

Opposite Colette is rue du Marché St-Honoré, which once led to the covered Marché St-Honoré, since replaced by the shiny offices of the BNP-Paribas bank, in a square lined with trendy restaurants; to the north, rue Danielle-Casanova boasts fine 18th-century houses.

Further west along rue St-Honoré lies the wonderful, eight-sided **place Vendôme** and a perspective stretching from rue de Rivoli up to **Opéra** (*see p96*). At the end of the Tuileries, place de la Concorde, originally laid out for the glorification of Louis XV, is a masterclass in the

Jardin des Tuileries. *See p92.*

use of open space, and looks fabulous when lit up at night. The winged Marly horses, only copies as the originals are in the Louvre, frame the entrance to the Champs-Elysées. Smart rue Royale, leading to the **Madeleine** (*see p96*), boasts elite tearoom **Ladurée** (*see p218*) and the celebrated Maxim's restaurant (3 rue Royale, 1st, 01.42.65.27.94), which has a fabulous art nouveau interior and featured in Lehár's opera *The Merry Widow*. The rue Boissy d'Anglas proffers stylish shops and perennially popular Le Buddha Bar (No.8, 1st, 01.53.05.90.00); while the ultimate sporting luxuries can be found at **Hermès** (*see p248*) on rue du Fbg-St-Honoré (a westward extension of rue St-Honoré), as well as designer divas **Yves Saint Laurent** (*see p249*), Gucci (No.2, 1st, 01.42.96.83.27), Chloé (No.54, 1st, 01.44.94.33.00) and others. More tearooms and fine porcelain can be found in the galerie and passage Royale.

Eglise St-Germain-l'Auxerrois

2 pl du Louvre, 1st (01.42.60.13.96). M° Pont Neuf or Louvre Rivoli. **Open** 9am-7pm Mon-Sat; 9am-8.30pm Sun. **Map** p408 H6.
The architecture of this former royal church spans several eras: most striking, though, is the elaborate Flamboyant Gothic porch. Inside, there's the 13th-century Lady Chapel and splendid canopied, carved bench by Le Brun made for the royal family in 1682.

The church achieved notoriety on 24 August 1572, when its bell rang to signal the St Bartholomew's Day massacre (*see p14*).

Eglise St-Roch

296 rue St-Honoré, 1st (01.42.44.13.20). M° Pyramides or Tuileries. **Open** 8am-7pm daily. **Map** p403 G5.
Begun in the 1650s in what was then the heart of Paris, this long church was designed chiefly by Jacques Lemercier; work took so long, it was only consecrated in 1740. Famed parishioners and patrons are remembered in funerary monuments: Le Nôtre, Mignard, Corneille and Diderot are all here, as are busts by Coysevox and Coustou, Falconet's statue *Christ on the Mount of Olives* and Anguier's superb *Nativity*. There's also a baroque pulpit and a cherub-adorned retable behind the rear altar. Bullet holes from a 1795 shoot-out between royalists and conventionists still pit the façade, recently scrubbed to honeyed cleanliness thanks to an ongoing programme of restoration.

Jardin des Tuileries

rue de Rivoli, 1st. M° Tuileries or Concorde. **Open** 7.30am-7pm daily. **Map** p403 G5.
Stretching between the Louvre and place de la Concorde, the gravelled alleyways of the gardens, named after the tile factories that stood here in the Middle Ages, have been a chic promenade ever since they opened to the public in the 16th century, and the popular entertainment mood persists with the

House man

In Georges Perec's *La Vie Mode d'Emploi* (*Life: A User's Manual*), a multi-generational, multi-storey story takes place over a Haussmannian apartment building from the cellars with its boiler and gurgling pipes, via the two apartments on each floor up to the *chambres de bonne* (maid's rooms) in the mansard roof. In this jigsaw puzzle of different lives, the apartment building becomes a microcosm of French society.

The Haussmannian apartment model is perhaps the archetype of the *préfet*'s 19th-century transformation of Paris. Though derived – of course – from earlier rental building precursors, the new regulations of 1859 controlled details such as the pitch of the roof and ratio of building height to street width. It conveyed a sort of uniformity on the city, but also proved brilliantly habitable, and adaptable to different budgets (a similar format could be used for prosperous five-bedroom flats and humble two- bedroom ones, for large reception rooms or small), to varying degrees of decoration and to the

different architectural styles that followed. This continued well into the 20th century, as a similar floor plan was adopted by belle époque and art deco apartment blocks. A typical pattern developed. There were two flats on each floor on either side of a central staircase (18th-century rented buildings generally had one flat on each floor), full-length wrought-iron balconies along the second floor and the fifth floor, which was stepped back to allow additional daylight into the building, small balconies on other floors, and mansard windows in the sixth-floor roof. A second set of flats was often reached through a courtyard. The hierarchy of front and back staircases, the prime flats with grand balconies and the humble *chambres de bonne*, ensures a degree of social mix even in the grandest districts. This is perhaps even more true today, as *chambres de bonne* have become the domain of students and the single, and – as with the capital's earlier ancient tenements – continue to ensure a density of population in the city centre.

funfair that sets up along the rue de Rivoli side in summer. Renowned André Le Nôtre, who began his career as royal gardener here in 1664 before going on to such exalted commissions as Vaux-le-Vicomte and Versailles, created the prototypical French garden with terraces and central vista running through circular and hexagonal ponds, and down the Grand Axe, along what would become the Champs-Elysées. When the Tuileries palace was burned down by the Paris Commune in 1871, the park was expanded. As part of Mitterrand's Grand Louvre project (*see p86* **Who built the Louvre?**), fragile sculptures such as Coysevox's winged horses were transferred to the Louvre and replaced by copies, and the Maillol sculptures were returned to the Jardins du Carrousel. Replanting has restored parts of Le Nôtre's design and renewed damaged trees. A handful of modern sculptures have been added, including bronzes by Laurens, Moore, Ernst, Giacometti and Dubuffet's *Le Bel Costumé*. There's even a specialist gardeners' bookshop by place de la Concorde. **Photo** *p91*.

Jeu de Paume

1 pl de la Concorde, 8th (01.47.03.12.50/ www.jeudepaume.org). M° Concorde. **Open** noon-9.00pm Tue; noon-7pm Wed-Fri; 10am-7pm Sat, Sun (last admission 30mins before closing). **Admission** €6; €3 concessions. **Credit** MC, V. **Map** p403 F5.
New home of the Centre National de la Photographie, the Jeu de Paume is a light, airy building that was once a court for real tennis. It offers two large galleries, a hip café, and a video art and cinema suite in the basement. Programming includes ground-breaking films, and the video cycles, conceived as an integral part of the thematic exhibitions, often include modern, experimental works. The Jeu de Paume's second site is the old Patrimoine Photographique at the Hôtel de Sully (*see p110*).

Musée des Arts Décoratifs

107 rue de Rivoli, 1st (01.44.55.57.50/www.ucad.fr). M° Palais Royal Musée du Louvre or Pyramides. **Open** 11am-6pm Tue-Fri; 10am-6pm Sat, Sun. Closed some hols. **Admission** (with Musée de la Mode & Musée de la Publicité) €6; €4.50 18s-25s; free under-18s; CM. **Credit** MC, V. **Map** p404 H5.
This rich collection of decorative arts is undergoing a major facelift as part of the Grand Louvre project; with the exception of the much-fêted Galerie des Bijoux, two dramatic rooms linked by a glass bridge that were inaugurated in 2004, the museum is closed until June 2006. In the meantime, the 1,200 pieces on display give an impression of quality rather than quantity: clever spotlighting and black settings show the exquisite treasures – from *châtelaines* made for medieval royalty to Maison Falize enamel – to best advantage. The second gallery shows modern works made from unlikely materials like car inner tubes and celluloid. There are cases devoted to Chinese head jewellery and the Japanese art of seduction with combs. Reopening in 2006 are the Renaissance and Middle Ages galleries, with Flemish tapestries and 16th-century Venetian glass,

the 17th- and 18th-century, art deco and art nouveau, modern and contemporary collections, plus galleries of glass, wallpaper, drawings and toys.

Musée de la Mode et du Textile

107 rue de Rivoli, 1st (01.44.55.57.50/www.ucad.fr). M° Palais Royal. **Open** for exhibitions 11am-6pm Tue-Fri; 10am-6pm Sat, Sun. Closed Mon, some public hols. **Admission** €6; €4.50 18s-25s; free under-18s; CM. **Credit** MC, V. **Map** p404 H5.
This municipal fashion museum holds Elsa Schiaparelli's entire archive and hosts exciting themed exhibitions. Dramatic black-walled rooms make a fine background to the clothes, while video screens and a small cinema space show you how they move, and display interviews with the creators.

Musée de l'Orangerie

Jardin des Tuileries, 1st (01.40.20.67.71/www. rmn.fr). M° Concorde. **Open** 2006. **Map** p403 F5.
Discovery of chunks of the Louvre's original curtain wall in the basement means that renovation work on the Orangerie has been delayed. The museum, which houses Monet's eight huge, late *Nymphéas* (water lilies) paintings, left by the artist to the nation as a 'spiritual testimony', as well as the Jean Walter and Paul Guillaume collection of Impressionism and the Ecole de Paris, will not reopen until at least 2006.

Musée de la Publicité

107 rue de Rivoli, 1st (01.44.55.57.50/www.ucad.fr). M° Palais Royal Musée du Louvre. **Open** 11am-6pm Tue-Fri; 10am-6pm Sat, Sun. Closed some public hols. **Admission** (with Musée des Arts Décoratifs & Musée de la Mode) €6; €4.50 18s-25s; free under-18s; CM. **Credit** MC, V. **Map** p404 H5.
Upstairs element of the triumvirate of museums, the advertising museum occupies an artfully distressed interior by Jean Nouvel. Only a fraction of the vast collection of posters, promotional objects and packaging can be seen at one time; vintage posters can be accessed through the multimedia space.

Palais-Royal

pl du Palais-Royal, 1st, M° Palais Royal Musée du Louvre. **Open** *Gardens* 7.30am-8.30pm daily. **Map** p404 H5.
Built for Cardinal Richelieu by Jacques Lemercier, the building was known as the Palais Cardinal. Richelieu left it to Louis XIII, whose widow Anne d'Autriche preferred it to the chilly Louvre and rechristened it when she moved in with her son, the young Louis XIV. In the 1780s the Duc d'Orléans, Louis XVI's fun-loving brother, enclosed the gardens in a three-storey peristyle and filled it with cafés, theatres, sideshows, shops and accommodation to raise money for rebuilding the burnt-down opera. In complete contrast to Versailles, the Palais-Royal was a place for people of all classes to mingle, and its arcades were a trysting venue. Daniel Buren's controversial modern installation of black-and-white-striped columns of different heights graces the main courtyard; the stately buildings house the Conseil d'Etat and the Ministry of Culture.

Sightseeing

Place de la Concorde.

Place de la Concorde

1st/8th. Mº Concorde. **Map** p403 F5.

This is the city's largest square, its grand east-west perspectives stretching from the Louvre to the Arc de Triomphe, and north-south from the Madeleine to the Assemblée Nationale across the Seine. Royal architect Gabriel designed it in the 1750s, along with the two colonnaded mansions astride rue Royale; the west one houses the chic Hôtel de Crillon (*see p43*) and the Automobile Club de France, the other is the Naval Ministry. In 1792 the centre statue of Louis XV was replaced with the guillotine for Louis XVI, Marie-Antoinette and many more. The square was embellished in the 19th century with sturdy lamp-posts, the Luxor obelisk (from the Viceroy of Egypt), and ornate tiered fountains that represent navigation by water. The best view is by night, from the terrace by the Jeu de Paume. **Photo** *above.*

Place Vendôme

1st. Mº Tuileries or Opéra. **Map** p403 G4.

Elegant place Vendôme got its name from a *hôtel particulier* built by the Duc de Vendôme that stood on the site. Opened in 1699, the eight-sided square was conceived by Hardouin-Mansart to show off an equestrian statue of the Sun King, torn down in 1792 and replaced in 1806 by the Colonne de la Grande Armée. Modelled on Trajan's Column in Rome and featuring a spiral comic strip illustrating Napoléon's military exploits, it was made from 1,250 Russian and Austrian cannons captured at the Battle of Austerlitz. During the 1871 Commune this symbol of 'brute force and false glory' was pulled down; the present column is a replica. Hardouin-Mansart only designed the façades, with their ground-floor arcade and giant Corinthian pilasters; the buildings behind were put up by nobles and speculators. Today the square houses sparkling jewellers like Boucheron, Cartier (for both, *see p257*), Van Cleef & Arpels (*see p257*) and top fashion houses, as well as merchant banks, the Justice Ministry and the Hôtel Ritz (*see p45*) from where Lady Di and Dodi Al-Fayed set off on their last journey. At No.12, you can visit the Grand Salon where Chopin died in 1849; its fabulous allegorical decoration dates from 1777 and has been restored as part of the new museum above the venerable jewellers Chaumet (01.44.77.26.26).

The Bourse

In the 1st and 2nd arrondissements.

Paris' traditional business district is squeezed between the elegant calm of the Palais-Royal and shopping hub the **Grands Boulevards** (*see p98*). Along rue du Quatre-Septembre and around, **La Bourse** (the Stock Exchange) is where financiers and stockbrokers beaver away in vast, grandiose buildings. The Banque de France, France's national central bank, has occupied the 17th-century Hôtel de Toulouse since 1811, its long gallery still hung with old masters. Nearby, fashion and finance meet at stylish **place des Victoires**, designed by Hardouin-Mansart, forming an intimate circle of buildings today dedicated to *la mode*. West of the square, try and poke your nose into shop-lined galerie Vivienne, the smartest of all the covered passages in Paris, adjoining galerie Colbert. Also look out for temporary exhibitions at the **Bibliothèque Nationale Richelieu**. You can linger at the luxury food and wine merchant **Legrand** (*see p264*), or take a detour along the passage des Petits-Pères to see the 17th- to 18th-century Eglise Notre-Dame-des-Victoires, the remains of an Augustine convent, featuring a cycle of paintings around the choir by Carle van Loo.

Rue de la Banque now leads to the Bourse, behind a commanding neo-classical colonnade. Generally, the area has a relaxed feel (and is positively sleepy at weekends), but animated pockets exist at places like Le Vaudeville (29 rue Vivienne, 2nd, 01.40.20.04.62) and Gallopin (40 rue Notre-Dame-des-Victoires, 2nd, 01.42.36.45.38), brasseries where stockbrokers and journalists converge for lunch and post-work drinks. Rue des Colonnes is a quiet street lined with graceful porticos and acanthus motifs dating from the 1790s, while its design nemesis, the 1970s concrete-and-glass HQ of Agence France-Presse, the nation's biggest news agency, stands across busy rue du Quatre-Septembre. Although most newspapers have left, *Le Figaro* remains in rue du Louvre. From the corner of rue Montmartre and rue du Croissant, take a look at the Café du Croissant, where Jean Jaurès, Socialist politician and founder of newspaper *L'Humanité*, was assassinated in 1914.

Bibliothèque Nationale de France – Richelieu

58 rue de Richelieu, 2nd (01.53.79.53.79/www. bnf.fr). Mº Bourse. **Open** *Galeries Mansart/ Mazarine, exhibitions only* 10am-7pm Tue-Sat; 1-7pm Sun. *Cabinet des Médailles* 1-5.45pm Mon-Fri; 1-4.45pm Sat; noon-6pm Sun. **Admission** *Galeries* €5; €4 under-26s. *Cabinet des Médailles* free. **Credit** MC, V. **Map** p404 H4.

The history of the French National Library begins in the 1660s, when Louis XIV moved manuscripts that couldn't be housed in the Louvre to this lavish Louis XIII townhouse, formerly the private residence of Cardinal Mazarin. The library was first opened to the public in 1692, and by 1724 it had received so many new acquisitions that the adjoining Hôtel de Nevers had to be added. Some of the original painted decoration by Romanelli and Grimaldi can still be seen in Galeries Mansart and Mazarine, now used for exhibitions of manuscripts and prints. Antique coins (originally known as *médailles*) and curious royal memorabilia collected by kings from Philippe-Auguste onwards can be found in the Musée du Cabinet des Médailles (*see below*). Transformed in the 1860s by the innovative circular vaulted reading room designed by Henri Labrouste, the library is now curiously empty as most books have since been relocated to the Bibliothèque Nationale – François Mitterrand (*see p171*). Still, a number of medieval manuscripts, maps, engravings, musical scores and performing arts materials remain here.

La Bourse

Palais Brongniart, pl de la Bourse, 2nd (01.49.27.55.55/www.bourse-de-paris.fr). Mº Bourse. **Open** *Guided tours* call 1 wk in advance. **Admission** €8.50; €5.50 concessions. **No credit cards. Map** p404 H4.

After a century at the Louvre, the Palais-Royal and rue Vivienne, the Stock Exchange was transferred in 1826 to this building, a dignified testament to First Empire classicism designed at Napoléon's behest by Alexandre Brongniart. It was later enlarged in 1906 to create a cruciform interior, where brokers buzzed around a central enclosure, known as the *corbeille* ('basket' or 'trading floor'). Computers have made the design obsolete, but the daily dash remains frenetic.

Musée du Cabinet des Médailles

58 rue de Richelieu, 2nd (01.53.79.81.26/www. bnf.fr). Mº Bourse. **Open** 9am-6pm Mon-Fri; 9am-5pm Sat. Closed 2wks Sept, public hols. **Admission** *2-day pass for library* €4.50. **Credit** MC, V. **Map** p404 H4.

On the first floor of the old Bibliothèque Nationale is this collection of coins and medals – the Greek, Roman and medieval examples being the most interesting. Notable oddities include Merovingian king Dagobert's throne and Charlemagne's chess set.

Place des Victoires

1st, 2nd. Mº Bourse. **Map** p404 H5.

This circular square, the first of its kind, was designed by Hardouin-Mansart in 1685 to show off a statue of Louis XIV that marked victories against Holland. The original went after 1789 (although the massive slaves from its base are found in the Louvre) and was replaced in 1822 with an equestrian statue by Bosio. Its sweeping façades now house fashion boutiques Kenzo and Victoire. **Photo** *p96*.

Sightseeing

Sweeping **Place des Victoires**. *See p95.*

Opéra & Grands Boulevards

Mainly in the 2nd, 8th, 9th and 10th arrondissements.

Opéra and Madeleine

Charles Garnier's wedding-cake **Palais Garnier** (of *Phantom of the Opera* legend) is all gilt and grandeur, as an opera house should be. Garnier was also responsible for the ritzy Café de la Paix (12 bd des Capucines, 9th, 01.40.07.36.36) and **Le Grand Hôtel Inter-Continental** (*see p46*) overlooking place de l'Opéra. In the Jockey Club (now the Hôtel Scribe, the centre for Allied war correspondents after the Liberation) behind, the Lumière brothers held the world's first public cinema screening in 1895. Old England, just opposite on the boulevard des Capucines (No.12, 9th, 01.47.42.81.99) with its wooden counters, Jacobean-style ceilings and old-style goods and service, could have served as their costume consultants. The **Olympia** concert hall (*see p316*), the legendary venue of Piaf, the Beatles and anyone in *chanson*, was knocked down, but rose again nearby. Over the road at No.35, pioneering portrait photographer Nadar opened a studio in the 1860s, frequented by names such as Dumas père, Offenbach and Doré. In 1874 it

hosted the first Impressionists' exhibition. Pedestrianised rue Edouard-VII, laid out in 1911, leads to the octagonal square of the same name with an equestrian statue of the monarch by Landowski, and through an arch, another square contains the belle-époque **Théâtre de l'Athénée-Louis Jouvet** (*see p339*).

The Madeleine, a monument to Napoléon, guards the end of the boulevard. At the head of rue Royale, its classical portico mirrors the Assemblée Nationale on the other side of place de la Concorde over the river, while the interior is a riot of marble and altars. Worth a browse are extravagant delicatessens **Fauchon**, **Maison de la Truffe** (for both, *see p263*) and other luxury foodstores, plus haute cuisine restaurant **Senderens** (*see p191*), formerly the art nouveau landmark eaterie Lucas Carton.

Landmark department stores **Printemps** and the **Galeries Lafayette** (for both, *see p234*), which opened just behind the Palais Garnier in the late 19th century, also deserve investigation. Behind the latter stands the Lycée Caumartin, designed as a convent in the 1780s by La Bourse architect Brongniart to become one of the most prestigious *lycées* under Napoléon. West along Haussmann's boulevard is the small square containing the sober **Chapelle Expiatoire** dedicated to Louis XVI and Marie-Antoinette.

Chapelle Expiatoire

29 rue Pasquier, 8th (01.42.65.35.80). Mº St-Augustin. **Open** 1-5pm Thur-Sat. **Admission** €2.50; free under-18s. **Map** p403 F3.
The chapel was commissioned by Louis XVIII in memory of his executed predecessors, his brother Louis XVI and Marie-Antoinette. Their remains, along with those of almost 3,000 victims of the Revolution, including Camille Desmoulins, Danton, Malesherbes and Lavoisier, were found in 1814 on the exact spot where the altar stands. The year after, the bodies of Louis XVI and Marie-Antoinette were transferred to the Basilique St-Denis (*see p173*); they are now represented by marble statues of Louis XVI supported on an angle and Marie-Antoinette on her knees at the feet of Religion. In January the chapel draws ardent (if currently unfulfilled) royalists for an annual memorial service.

Eglise St-Augustin

46 bd Malesherbes, 8th (01.45.22.23.12). Mº St-Augustin. **Open** *Sept-June* 10am-6pm Mon-Fri; 10am-7.30pm Sat, Sun. *July, Aug* 10am-12.45pm, 3.30-6pm Tue-Fri; 10am-noon, 4-7.30pm Sat; 10am-noon, 4.30-6pm Sun. **Map** p403 F3.
St-Augustin, designed in 1860-71 by Victor Baltard, architect of the Les Halles pavilions, is not what it seems. The domed, neo-Renaissance stone exterior is merely a shell, inside is an iron vault structure; even the decorative angels are cast in metal. Bouguereau paintings hang in the transept.

Eglise de la Madeleine

pl de la Madeleine, 8th (01.44.51.69.00).
M° Madeleine or Concorde. **Open** 9am-7pm daily.
Map p403 G4.

The building of a church on this site began in 1764, and in 1806 Napoléon sent instructions from Poland for Barthélémy Vignon to design a 'Temple of Glory' dedicated to his Grand Army. After the emperor's fall, construction slowed and the building, by now a church again, was finally consecrated in 1845. The exterior is ringed by huge fluted Corinthian columns, with a double row of columns at the front and a frieze of the Last Judgement just above the portico. Inside are three-and-a-half giant domes, a striking organ and pseudo-Grecian side altars in a sea of multicoloured marble. The painting by Ziegler in the chancel depicts the history of Christianity, the ever-modest Napoléon prominent in the foreground. It's now a favourite venue for society weddings.

Musée de la Franc-Maçonnerie

16 rue Cadet, 9th (01.45.23.20.92). M° Cadet. **Open** 2-6pm Tue-Sat. Closed public hols, 2wks July, Aug. **Admission** €2; free under-12s. **No credit cards**. **Map** p404 H3.

At the back of the Grand Orient de France (French Masonic Great Lodge), the history of freemasonry is traced from medieval stonemasons' guilds to the prints of famous masons (General Lafayette and 1848 revolutionary leaders Blanc and Barbès).

Musée de l'Opéra

Palais Garnier, 1 pl de l'Opéra, 9th (01.40.01.24.93). M° Opéra. **Open** 10am-6pm daily. **Admission** €6; €4 10-25s, students, over-60s; free under-10s. **No credit cards**. **Map** p403 G4.

The Palais Garnier houses temporary exhibitions relating to current opera or ballet productions, and a permanent collection of paintings, scores and bijou opera sets housed in period cases. Entrance includes a visit to the auditorium, if rehearsals permit.

Musées des Parfumeries-Fragonard

9 rue Scribe, 9th (01.47.42.04.56) & 39 bd des Capucines, 2nd (01.42.60.37.14). M° Opéra. **Open** 9am-5.30pm Mon-Sat (Mar-Oct rue Scribe open 9.30am-3.30pm Sun). **Admission** free. **Map** p403 G4.
Get on the scent at the two museums showcasing the collection of perfume house Fragonard. The five rooms at rue Scribe range from Ancient Egyptian ointment flasks to Meissen porcelain scent bottles, while the second museum has bottles by Lalique and Schiaparelli. Both have displays on scent manufacture and an early 20th-century 'perfume organ'.

Palais Garnier

pl de l'Opéra, 9th (box office 08.92.89.90.90/www.operadeparis.fr). M° Opéra. **Open** 10am-5pm daily. **Admission** €6; €3 concs. *Guided tours in English* (01.40.01.22.63) 1pm & 2pm Tue-Sun €11; €6-€9 concs. **Credit** AmEx, DC, MC, V. **Map** p403 G4.
Brimming with gilt and red velvet, the Opera House designed by Charles Garnier is a monument to Second Empire high society. The opera company

had been founded by Louis XIV in 1669, moving home after fires and assassination attempts. In 1860 a competition for a grander – and safer – new opera house was launched. It was won by then unknown 35-year-old Charles Garnier, who described opera as 'a temple with art for divinity' and designed his new building with auditorium as sanctuary and foyer as nave. Held up by money, fire, the Franco-Prussian War and the Paris Commune, the building was only inaugurated in 1875. The comfortably upholstered auditorium seats more than 2,000 people and the exterior is just as opulent, with sculptures of music and dance on the façade, Apollo topping the copper dome and nymphs bearing torches. Carpeaux's sculpture *La Danse* shocked Parisians with its frank sensuality; in 1869 someone threw a bottle of ink over its thunderous marble thighs. The original is safe in the Musée d'Orsay (*see p159*), where there is now also a massive maquette of the building. The Garnier hosts productions of both opera and ballet (*see p312 and p288*). The Grand Foyer, its mirrors and parquet, coloured marble, moulded stucco, sculptures and allegorical paintings by Baudry have all recently been magnificently restored. This was a place of social exchange where during the interval the public of all origins could mix and observe. You can also visit the Grand Staircase, the auditorium with its false ceiling painted by Chagall in 1964, and red satin and velvet boxes (some of which have almost no view), as well as the library and museum – once the emperor's private salons where he could arrive directly by carriage by the ramp at the rear of the building.

Quartier de l'Europe

With its streets named after European cities, the district stretching from Gare St-Lazare towards place de Clichy was the Impressionists' quarter. In those days it epitomised modernity, when the station – the city's first – opened here in 1837 serving the line from Paris to St-Germain-en-Laye, later displaced and rebuilt in the 1880s. The long shabby commuter hub has had a revamp; a glass dome disgorges travellers from the métro interchange. Adjoining **Hôtel Concorde St-Lazare** (*see p46*) was the city's first great station hotel, with a grandiose hallway built by Eiffel in 1889 for visitors to the Exposition Universelle as he was putting up the Eiffel Tower. Monet, who lived nearby in rue d'Edimbourg, depicted the steam age in *La Gare St-Lazare* and *Pont de l'Europe*; Pissarro and Caillebotte painted views of the new boulevards, while Manet had a studio on rue de St-Petersbourg. Rue de Budapest remains a red-light district; rue de Rome, or '*rue des luthiers*', has long been home to stringed-instrument makers. East of St-Lazare are the **Eglise de la Trinité** and art nouveau brasserie Mollard (115 rue St-Lazare, 8th, 01.43.87.50.22).

Sightseeing

Eglise de la Trinité

pl Estienne-d'Orves, 9th (01.48.74.12.77).
M° Trinité. **Open** 11am-8pm Mon-Sat; 10.30am-8pm
Sun. **Map** p403 G3.

Dominated by the tiered belltower, this neo-
Renaissance church was built 1861-67 by Théodore
Ballu. Composer Olivier Messiaen (1908-92) was
organist here for over 30 years.

The Grands Boulevards

Contrary to popular belief, the string of Grands
Boulevards between Madeleine and République
(des Italiens, Montmartre, Poissonnière, Bonne-
Nouvelle, St-Denis, St-Martin) were not built by
Haussmann but by Louis XIV in 1670, replacing
the fortifications of King Philippe-Auguste's
city wall. Their ramparts have left their traces
in the strange changes of levels with stairways
climbing up to side streets at the eastern end.
They became a place of entertainment, crowded
with street sellers, hawkers and entertainers.
The boulevards burgeoned after the Revolution,
as new residences, theatres and covered
passages were built on land repossessed from
aristocrats and monasteries. They still offer a
glimpse of the city's divergent personalities –
a stroll from Opéra to République leads from
luxury shops to St-Denis prostitutes – and the
phrase *théâtre des boulevards* is still used for
lowbrow theatre. Between boulevard des
Italiens and rue de Richelieu is place Boïeldieu
and the **Opéra Comique** (*see p311*), where
Carmen was premièred in 1875. Alexandre
Dumas fils was born at No.1 in 1824.

The 18th-century Hôtel d'Angny, now the
Town Hall of the 9th arrondissement, was
once home to the infamous '*bals des victimes*',
where every guest had to have a relative who
had lost their head to the guillotine. The **Hôtel
Drouot** auction house (*see p272*) is ringed by
antiques shops, coin and stamp dealers and
wine bar Les Caves Drouot, where auction-
goers and valuers congregate. There are
several grand *hôtels particuliers* on rue de la
Grange-Batelière, which leads on one side
down curious passage Verdeau, occupied by
antiques dealers, and on the other back to the
boulevards via passage Jouffroy. With its
grand barrel-vaulted glass-and-iron roof,
this is home to the lovely Hôtel Chopin (10 bd
Montmartre, 9th, 01.47.70.58.10), shop
windows of doll's houses, walking sticks,
art books and film posters, and the colourful
entrance of the **Grévin** waxworks (*see p283*).

Over the boulevard, passage des Panoramas
is the oldest remaining covered passageway in
Paris. When it opened in 1800, panoramas –
vast illuminated circular paintings – of Rome,
Jerusalem, Athens, London and other cities

drew large crowds. Today it contains tearoom
L'Arbre à Cannelle (No.57, 2nd, 01.45.08.55.87),
coin and stamp sellers, furniture-makers and
old-fashioned printer Stern (No.47), established
here since 1840; it leads into a tangle of other
little passages and the stage door of the
Théâtre des Variétés (7 bd Montmartre, 2nd,
01.42.33.11.41), a pretty neo-classical theatre,
where Offenbach premièred *La Belle Hélène*.

Rue du Faubourg-Montmartre is home to
celebrated belle-époque *bouillon* Chartier (No.7,
9th, 01.47.70.86.29), which serves up hundreds
of meals a day to the budget minded, and at
No.8, late lamented nightspot Le Palace. The
street is also part of a Jewish quarter, less well
known than the Marais, which grew up in the
19th century. There are several kosher bakers,
restaurants and France's largest synagogue at
44 rue de la Victoire (01.45.26.95.36), an opulent
Second Empire affair completed in 1876.
Wander down cobbled Cité Bergère, constructed
in 1825 as desirable residences; though most are
now budget hotels, the pretty iron-and-glass
portes-cochères remain. On rue Bergère stands
the art deco Folies-Bergère (32 rue Richer, 9th,
08.92.68.16.50), now only sporadically used for
cabaret revues. South of boulevard Bonne-
Nouvelle lies **Sentier** (*see p101*), while to the
north rue du Faubourg-Poissonnière offers its
interesting mixture of rag-trade outlets and
grand *hôtels particuliers*.

Back on the boulevard is evidence of a move
north of the Marais by trendsetting hubs: gay
club **Le Vogue** (*see p302*), lesbian club **Pulp**
(*see p307*), DJ Laurent Garnier's fief **Le Rex**
(*see p325*) and chic **De la Ville Café** (*see
p216*). Palatial art deco cinema **Le Grand Rex**
(*see also p292*) completes the quintet. East of
here are Louis XIV's twin triumphal arches,
the **Porte St-Martin** and **Porte St-Denis**,
symbolic gateways erected at the same time
as the fortifications were taken down.

Le Grand Rex

*1 bd Poissonnière, 2nd (01.45.08.93.58/reservations
08.92.68.05.96/www.le grandrex.com). M° Bonne
Nouvelle.* **Tour** Les Etoiles du Rex every 5mins
10am-7pm Wed-Sun, daily during school hols.
Admission €7.50; €6.50 under-16s; €12.50/€11.50
tour & film. **Credit** AmEx, MC, V. **Map** p404 J4.

Opened in 1932, the huge art deco cinema was
designed by Auguste Bluysen with fantasy Hispanic
interiors by US designer John Eberson. Go behind
the scenes in the crazy 50-minute guided tour, which
includes a presentation about the construction of the
auditorium and a visit to the production room complete with nerve-jolting Sensurround effects.

Hôtel Drouot

*9 rue Drouot, 9th (01.48.00.20.20/www.drouot.fr).
M° Richelieu Drouot.* **Open** 11am-6pm Mon-Sat.
Auctions 2pm Mon-Sat. **Map** p404 H3.

A spiky 1970s aluminium-and-marble concoction is the unlikely location for the centre of France's secondary art market, though now rivalled by Sotheby's and Christie's. Inside, escalators whizz you up to several small salerooms, where at any one time, medieval manuscripts, antique furniture, oriental arts, modern paintings, posters, jewellery and fine wines might be up for sale. Details of upcoming auctions are published in the weekly *Gazette de L'Hôtel Drouot*, sold at newsstands. Prestige sales are at Drouot-Montaigne, the junkier sell-offs at Drouot Nord.

Other locations: Drouot-Montaigne, 15 av Montaigne, 8th (01.48.00.20.80); Drouot Nord, 64 rue Doudeauville, 18th (01.48.00.20.90).

Porte St-Denis & Porte St-Martin

rue St-Denis/bd St-Denis, 2nd/10th; 33 bd St-Martin, 3rd/10th. **Map** p404 K4.
These twin triumphal gates were erected in 1672 and 1674 at important entry points to the city as part of Colbert's strategy to glorify Paris and celebrate Louis XIV's victories on the Rhine. Modelled on the triumphal arches of Ancient Rome, the Porte St-Denis is particularly harmonious, based on a perfect square with a single arch, bearing Latin inscriptions and decorated with military trophies and battle scenes. Porte St-Martin bears allegorical reliefs of some of Louis XIV's many campaigns.

Fbg-St-Denis to Gare du Nord

North of Porte St-Denis and Porte St-Martin, around two of Paris' oldest thoroughfares leading out of the city, the Fbg-St-Denis and Fbg-St-Martin, is an area transformed in the 19th century by the railways – and the two stations of Gare du Nord and Gare de l'Est. The grubby rue du Fbg-St-Denis is almost souk-like with its food shops, narrow passages and sinister courtyards, and pimps surveying the prostitutes hanging in doorways. Amid this, brasserie Julien (16 rue du Fbg-St-Denis, 10th, 01.47.70.12.06) boasts one of the finest art nouveau interiors in Paris. Garishly lit passage Brady is a surprising piece of India in Paris, full of restaurants, hairdressers and costume shops, while the art deco passage du Prado is more a continuation of the Sentier rag trade. The Fbg-St-Martin follows the trace of the Roman road out of the city, full of children's clothes wholesalers, atmospheric courtyards and the ornate Mairie for the 10th. Rue des Petites-Ecuries ('Little Stables Street') was once known for saddlers but now has shops, cafés and top jazz venue **New Morning** (*see p319*), and is home to large Afro-Caribbean and Turkish

Sightseeing

Scandale! Dead on the job

The sternly guarded Palais de l'Elysée, official residence of French presidents since 1873, is off-limits to visitors and would seem to hold little historic interest for anyone. Wrong! For here that occured one of the great presidential scandals in history – even more mind-blowing than the recent one of popular lore, that involving Bill Clinton and Monica Lewinsky in the White House.

François Félix Faure – Félix to his friends – had been rising up the political ladder for 14 years when he got the top job – President of France – in 1895. A shrewd if vain man, the son of a Le Havre furniture-maker, he was the least offensive choice when the post became vacant in January 1895. Imposing but tactful, Faure was steering a careful path in foreign affairs when he became embroiled in the Dreyfus Affair (*see p142* **Scandale!**).

Faure foolishly entrusted secret documents relating to the affair to his mistress, Marguerite Steinheil. Well known in Paris social circles, 'Meg' Steinheil was a real piece of work. On the night of 16 February 1899, she was allegedly giving the serving French president oral pleasure in his Oval

Office when he dropped dead. Word quickly spread from attendant policemen and cheeky politicians. Jokes soon did the rounds. Clemenceau is alleged to have said that the orderly Faure 'wanted to be Caesar, but only ended up Pompey', *pompé* meaning 'sucked'. Steinheil became known as the 'Pompe Funèbre', either Funeral Director or Deadly Sucker.

Notoriety became her. Nine years later, Steinheil's stepmother and her husband were found dead at home near rue de Vaugirard – she strangled, he having choked on his false teeth. As Steinheil set about framing her servants, the tabloids happily dragged up the Dreyfus papers again. After the trial, she fled to London, published her scandalous memoirs in 1912 and was made a baroness through her marriage to the sixth Baron Abinger, in Tulse Hill in 1917. She died in a nursing home in Hove. An effigy of an exhausted-looking Faure can be seen on his grave at the top end of avenue Principale, directly ahead of you as you enter Père-Lachaise cemetery (*see p136*). He died, as they say, with a smile on his face.

The first taste many visitors get of Paris: the **Gare du Nord**. *See p101.*

communities. On nearby alleyway Cour des Petites-Ecuries, the Brasserie Flo (No.7, 10th, 01.47.70.13.59) has the allure of an Alsatian tavern; rue de Paradis is known for its porcelain and glass outlets, and the Musée du Cristal has become art space **La Pinacothèque de Paris**. Rue d'Hauteville contains hints of the area's grander days; at No.58, unseen from the street, hides the **Petit Hôtel Bourrienne**, a small privately owned time capsule. Opposite, the Cité Paradis is an alleyway of early industrial buildings. At the top of the street, **Eglise St-Vincent-de-Paul** has twin towers and cascading terraced gardens, and is about as close as Paris gets to Rome's Spanish Steps. Behind, on rue de Belzunce, are modern bistro **Chez Michel** (*see p202*) and offshoot Chez Casimir (No.6, 10th, 01.48.78.28.80). Down on boulevard Magenta, the covered Marché St-Quentin, built in the 1860s, is one of the city's few remaining cast-iron, covered market halls.

Popular theatres such as the mosaic-filled neo-Renaissance Théâtre Antoine-Simone Berriau (No.14, 10th, 01.42.08.77.71) and the art deco Eldorado (No.4, 10th, 01.42.38.22.22) line up on boulevard de Strasbourg, cut through in the 19th century to create a vista up to the Gare de l'Est. At No.2, another neo-Renaissance creation houses the last fan-maker in Paris and the **Musée de l'Eventail**; towards the station, Eglise St-Laurent (69 bd de Magenta/119 rue du Fbg-St-Martin, 10th) is one of the city's oldest churches, an eclectic composition

with 12th-century tower, Gothic nave, baroque lady chapel, 1930s stained glass and a 19th-century façade. Between the Gare de l'Est and **Canal St-Martin** are the restored **Couvent des Récollets** and Square Villemin park.

Couvent des Récollets

148 rue du Fbg-St-Martin, 10th. Mº Gare de l'Est. **Map** p404 L3.
Founded as a Franciscan monastery in the 17th century when still outside city walls, this barracks, spinning factory and hospice then became a military hospital between 1860 and 1968. Abandoned to dereliction, the convent was squatted by artists, les Anges des Récollets, at the start of the 1990s. The buildings were renovated and reopened in 2004. One half, the Maison des Architectes, hosts a café and architectural debates. The other half is the Centre International d'Accueil et d'Echanges des Récollets: 85 studios and duplexes for foreign 'creators' – artists and researchers (from painters to neurobiologists) – invited to stay here for extended periods. In rehabilitating the building, architect Frédéric Vincendon left traces of its chequered history, the ghostly 17th-century stonework, 20th-century reinforced concrete columns and squatters' graffiti.

Eglise St-Vincent-de-Paul

pl Franz-Liszt, 10th (01.48.78.47.47). Mº Gare du Nord. **Open** *Sept-June* 8am-noon, 2-7pm daily. *July, Aug* 8am-noon, 5-7pm Tue-Sun. **Map** p404 K2.
Set at the top of terraced gardens, this church was begun in 1824 by Lepère and completed 1831-44 by Hittorff. The twin towers, pedimented Greek temple

portico and sculptures along the parapet of the four evangelists are in classical mode. The interior has a double-storey arcade of columns, murals by Flandrin and church furniture by Rude.

Gare du Nord

rue de Dunkerque, 10th (08.91.36.20.20). M° Gare du Nord. **Map** p404 K2.

The grandest of the great 19th-century train stations (and Eurostar terminal since 1994) was designed by Hittorff in 1861-64. A conventional stone façade, with Ionic capitals and statues representing towns served by the station, hides a vast, iron-and-glass vault. The airy refurbishment of the suburban section by rue du Fbg-St-Denis makes the Eurostar's glass-topped digs look a little drab. **Photo** *left.*

Musée de l'Eventail

2 bd de Strasbourg, 10th (01.42.08.90.20/www.anne hoguet.com). M° Strasbourg St-Denis. **Open** 2-6pm Mon-Wed (Mon-Fri in school hols). *Children's activities* Wed afternoons. Closed Aug, public hols. **Admission** €6; €4 under-26s; €3 8-12s; free under-8s. **No credit cards. Map** p404 K4.

Anne Hoguet keeps the tradition of her ancestors alive in this arcane museum in a 19th-century apartment, a fan-maker's *atelier* since 1805. One room houses the tools of the trade; beside, Hoguet's studio where she works on fans for fashion and the stage. The former *salle d'exposition*, lined in blue silk, is where the collection of almost 1,000 historic fans – from 18th-century fans painted alternately with sacred or profane themes to modern versions – are shown in glass cases and stored in cabinets.

Petit Hôtel Bourrienne

58 rue d'Hauteville, 10th (01.47.70.51.14). M° Poissonnière. **Open** *Guided visits* 1-15 July, 1-30 Sept noon-6pm daily. Rest of year by appointment, Sat. **Admission** €6. **No credit cards.** Map p404 K3.

A rare example of the Consulaire style, this quite exceptional, small *hôtel particulier* was built by Célestin-Joseph Happé in 1789-98. From 1795 it was occupied by Fortunée Hamelin, born (like her friend the Empress Joséphine) in Martinique, and notorious for parading topless down the Champs-Elysées. A bedroom boudoir painted with detailed tropical birds was her only decoration before the site was taken over by Louis Fauvelet de Bourrienne, the private secretary of Napoléon. He decorated it according to the latest mode, making sure to keep his political options open (the dining room ceiling is painted with motifs favourable to both monarchy and empire). The two small wings overlooking the garden contain an Egyptian-style bathroom – where guests could be entertained – and a winter garden.

La Pinacothèque de Paris

30bis rue de Paradis, 10th (01.43.25.71.41/ www.pinacotheque.com). M° Bonne Nouvelle or Poissonnière. **Open** 10am-10.30pm Mon, Fri; 10am-7pm Tue-Thur, Sat, Sun. **Admission** €12; €8 13-25s, students; €6 8-12s; free under-12s. **Credit** MC, V. **Map** p404 H5.

Nearly 200,000 visitors came to inaugural show Picasso Intime at this privately funded venue in the former Musée Baccarat. This allowed for a renovation that will create 4,000sq m of space for permanent and temporary exhibitions (due to open early in 2006). Created by art historian Marc Restellini, responsible for major shows at the Musée du Luxembourg, its ambition is to bring over crowd-pulling shows, often as partnerships with exhibition centres in Japan and the USA. On the ground floor, a room will present changing displays of works on long-term loan from private collections. There's a café overseen by Alain Ducasse, too.

Les Halles & Sentier

In the 1st and 2nd arrondissements.

In Zola's novel *Le Ventre de Paris*, Les Halles is an area groaning with food, swarming and seething with the Parisian populace. While Les Halles remains the belly of Paris, a geographic and symbolic centre, a nexus of commerce and entertainment, with its daily discharge of some 800,000 people from its massive RER-métro interchange, it has become a place to avoid.

For centuries, Les Halles was the city's wholesale food market. Covered markets were set up here in 1181 by King Philippe-Auguste; in the 1850s Baltard's spectacular cast-iron and glass pavilions were erected, 'the lace of Vulcan' as Verlaine described them. In 1969 the market was relocated to the southern suburb of Rungis. Baltard's ten pavilions were knocked down (one was saved and reconstructed at Nogent-sur-Marne) leaving a giant hole – rudely nicknamed 'le trou des Halles'. After a long political dispute it was filled in the early 1980s by the miserably designed **Forum des Halles** underground shopping and transport hub and the unloved (except by tramps) Jardin des Halles.

The problem with what to do with a smelly, crime-ridden transport interchange and poorly conceived mall is a political one. Mayor Bertrand Delanoë asked four architects and planners to come up with proposals to improve Les Halles, to bring people back to the gardens, and a classier clientele to the shops and to combat the sense of insecurity. The plans of French architect David Mangin won the contest, with their vision of a vast plaza under an equally vast glass roof, larger gardens and a new shopping centre in the form of a massive, light-filled well. Still, it's going to be some time before the scheme is ready to be put into action.

East of the Forum in the middle of place Joachim-du-Bellay stands the Renaissance Fontaine des Innocents. The canopied fountain has swirling stone reliefs of water nymphs and titans by Jean Goujon (the ones you see today are copies; the originals are in the Louvre).

Sightseeing

It was inaugurated for Henri II's arrival in Paris on 16 June 1549 on the traditional royal route along the rue St-Denis. It was moved and reconstructed here when the nearby Cimetière des Innocents, the city's main burial ground, was demolished in 1786 after flesh-eating rats started gnawing into people's living rooms, and the bones were transferred to the catacombs.

Pedestrianised rue des Lombards is a beacon for live jazz, with **Sunset/Sunside**, **Baiser Salé** and **Au Duc des Lombards** (*see pp318-319*). King Henri IV was assassinated in 1610 by Catholic fanatic François Ravaillac on nearby rue de la Ferronnerie, when the royal carriage got held up in the traffic. The street has now become an extension of the Marais gay circuit, so the only thing Henri would be held up for today is, perhaps, ridicule.

The ancient easternmost stretch of rue St-Honoré runs into the southern edge of Les Halles. The Fontaine du Trahoir stands at the corner with rue de l'Arbre-Sec. Opposite, the superb Hôtel de Truden (52 rue de l'Arbre-Sec) was built in 1717 for a wealthy wine merchant; in the courtyard, a shop sells vintage magazines and newspapers, while on rue des Prouvaires, the old market-traders' haunt **La Tour de Montlhéry** (*see p185*) still serves up meaty fare all night long. Fashion chains line the commercial stretch of the rue de Rivoli south of Les Halles. Running towards the Seine, ancient little streets such as rue des Lavandiers-Ste-Opportune and narrow rue Jean-Lantier show a human side of Les Halles that has yet to be swept away. Stretching between the rue de Rivoli and the Pont Neuf is **La Samaritaine** department store (*see p233*), metamorphosed from ugly duckling into splendid swan after a takeover by luxury conglomerate LVMH – but currently closed for safety reasons for the next five years at least. Next door, a former part of the store contains the fashionable Kenzo flagship, spa and Philippe Starck-designed **Kong** restaurant and bar (*see p215*), offering more great views. From here quai de la Mégisserie, thickly lined with horticultural suppliers and pet shops, leads in the direction of **Châtelet** (*see p105*).

Looming over the northern edge of the Jardin des Halles is the massive **Eglise St-Eustache**, with Renaissance motifs inside and chunky flying buttresses without. At the western end of the gardens is the circular, domed **Bourse de Commerce**. In front of it, an astrological column is all that remains from a grand palace belonging to Marie de Médicis that once stood on this spot. Nearby, the delightfully dusty **E Dehillerin** (*see p269*) continues to supply colossal saucepans, knives and specialist implements to restaurants and regular clients.

The empire of **Agnès b** (*see p250*) stretches along most of rue du Jour, with streetwise outlets such as **Kiliwatch** (*see p252*) and **Diesel** (*see p251*) on rue Tiquetonne and rue Etienne-Marcel, getting progressively more upmarket towards the place des Victoires. The restored **Tour Jean Sans Peur** is a strange relic of the fortified medieval townhouse of Jean Sans Peur, Duc de Bourgogne.

If you're in the mood for food, head to buzzy, pedestrianised rue Montorgueil, lined with grocers, delicatessens and pavement cafés. Historic façades remain from when this was an area where the belle monde and the working class mingled: Pâtisserie Stohrer (No.51, 2nd, 01.42.33.38.20), founded in 1730 and credited with the invention of the sugary Puits d'Amour; Le Rocher de Cancale (No.78, 01.42.33.50.29) and, back towards Les Halles, the golden snail sign hanging out in front of L'Escargot Montorgueil (No.38, 1st, 01.42.36.83.51). Glass-roofed passage du Grand-Cerf has been restored and is home to several design consultancies.

Stretching north of here, bordered by boulevard du Bonne-Nouvelle to the north and boulevard Sébastopol to the east, lies Sentier, the historic garment district, while cocky rue St-Denis has long relied on strumpets and strip joints. The tackiness is unremitting into its northern continuation of rue du Fbg-St-Denis, which snakes north from the Forum des Halles.

Rue Réaumur houses striking art nouveau buildings with metal structures constructed as industrial premises in the early 1900s. Between rue des Petits-Carreaux and rue St-Denis is the site of the medieval Cour des Miracles – a refuge where, after a day's begging, paupers would 'miraculously' regain use of their eyes or limbs. An abandoned aristocratic estate, it was a sanctuary for the underworld for decades until it was cleared out in 1667.

Sentier's surrounding maze of streets and passages throng with porters shouldering linen bundles, while sweatshops churn out copies of catwalk creations. It comes as no surprise that the area has attracted hundreds of illegal and semi-legal foreign workers. Streets such as rue du Caire, rue d'Aboukir and rue du Nil reflect the Egyptian craze following Napoléon's Egyptian campaign in 1798-99 – make sure you look out for the sphinx heads and mock hieroglyphics at 2 place du Caire.

Bourse de Commerce

2 rue de Viarmes, 1st (01.55.65.78.41/tour booking 01.55.65.70.18). Mº Louvre Rivoli. **Open** *for tour groups* 9am-6pm Mon-Fri. **Admission** €42/tour group. **No credit cards. Map** p404 J5.
Housing offices of the Paris Chamber of Commerce, this trade centre for coffee and sugar was built as a grain market in 1767. The circular building was then

Eglise St-Eustache. *See p104*.

Take a good look – its days are numbered: **Forum des Halles.** *See p104.*

covered by a wooden dome, damaged by fire and replaced by an avant-garde iron structure in 1809. Once covered in copper, now in glass, it is sadly underused; recent proposals have put forward the idea of a hotel, restaurant or museum.

Eglise St-Eustache

rue du Jour, 1st (01.40.26.47.99/www.st-eustache. org). M° Les Halles. **Open** 9am-7.30pm daily. **Map** p404 J5.

This massive barn-like church, built 1532-1640, has a Gothic structure but Renaissance decoration in its pedimented façade and Corinthian capitals. Among the paintings in the side chapels are a *Descent from the Cross* by Luca Giordano; contemporary pieces by John Armleder were added in 2000. Works by Thomas Couture adorn the 19th-century Lady Chapel. There is a fine 8,000-pipe organ and also free recitals at 5.30pm on Sundays. **Photo** *p102.*

Forum des Halles

1st. M° Les Halles/RER Châtelet Les Halles. **Map** p404 J5.

The labyrinthine mall and transport interchange extends three levels underground and includes the Ciné Cité multiplex (*see p292*), the Forum des Images (*see p293*) and a swimming pool (*see p336*), as well as mass-market clothing chains, branches of Darty, Fnac (*see p244*) and Muji, and the Forum des Créateurs, a section given over to young designers. Despite a tiered open central courtyard, a sense of cavernous gloom prevails. On Saturdays it's invaded by kids pouring in on the RER. **Photo** *above.*

Pavillon des Arts

Les Halles, 101 rue Rambuteau, 1st (01.42.33.82.50/ www.paris.fr/musees). M° Châtelet Les Halles. **Open** 11.30am-6.30pm Tue-Sun. Closed public hols. **Admission** €5.50; €4 students; €2.50 14s-26s; free under-14s. **No credit cards. Map** p404 K5.

This gallery in Les Halles hosts exhibitions on anything from photography to local history.

Tour Jean Sans Peur

20 rue Etienne-Marcel, 2nd (01.40.26.20.28/http:// tour.jeansanspeur.free.fr). M° Etienne Marcel. **Open** *Term-time* 1.30-6pm Wed, Sat, Sun. *School hols* 1.30-6pm Tue-Sun. **Admission** €5; €3 7s-18s, students; free under-7s. **Tour** 3pm; €8. **No credit cards. Map** p404 J5.

This Gothic turret (1409-11) is the remnant of the townhouse of Jean Sans Peur, Duc de Bourgogne. His nickname ('The Fearless') is from his exploits in Bulgaria – but he was responsible for the assassination in 1407 of his rival Louis d'Orléans, which sparked the Hundred Years' War and saw Burgundy allied to the English crown. Jean had this show-off tower added to his mansion to protect him from vengeance by the aggrieved widow. In 1419 he was assassinated by a partisan of the dauphin, the future Charles VII. Today you can climb the multistorey tower, with rooms leading off the stairway. Carved vaulting halfway up depicts naturalistic branches of oak, hawthorn and hops, symbols of Jean Sans Peur and Burgundian power. The huge mansion originally spanned Philippe-Auguste's city wall. The base of a turret is still concealed within.

Beaubourg & the Marais

In the 3rd and 4th arrondissements.
Between boulevard Sébastopol and the Bastille
are Beaubourg – site of the **Centre Pompidou**
since 1977 – and the Marais, largely built
between the 16th and 18th centuries and now
jam-packed with boutiques, museums and bars.

Beaubourg & Hôtel de Ville

Contemporary Parisian architecture began with
the Centre Pompidou, designed by Richard
Rogers and Renzo Piano, and this international
benchmark of inside-out high-tech is as much of
an attraction as its contents, which include the
Musée National de l'Art Moderne. The
piazza outside attracts a motley crew of street
performers and pavement artists, while on one
side the reconstructed **Atelier Brancusi**, the
sculptor's studio, which he left to the state, was
moved here from the 15th arrondissement. On
the other side of the piazza is rue Quincampoix
with its galleries, bars and cobbled passage
Molière with its old shopfronts and the Théâtre
Molière (01.44.54.53.00). Beside the Centre
Pompidou is place Igor-Stravinsky and the
funky Fontaine Stravinsky, full of splashing,
spraying kinetic fountains, including a
colourful snake by the late artists Nikki de St-
Phalle and Jean Tinguély, and the red-brick
IRCAM music institute (*see p311*), also
designed by Renzo Piano.

The church of St-Merri (78 rue St-Martin, 4th,
01.42.71.93.93), which has a Flamboyant Gothic
façade complete with an androgynous demon
leering over the doorway, sits on the south side
of the square. Inside are a carved wooden organ
loft, the joint contender (along with **Eglise
St-Séverin**; *see p138*) for the oldest bell in
Paris (1331), and 16th-century stained glass.

South of here stands the spiky Gothic **Tour
St-Jacques**. Towards the river, on the site of
the Grand Châtelet, a fortress put up in the 12th
century to defend Pont au Change, place du
Châtelet features an Egyptian-themed fountain
in the middle framed on each side by twin
theatres designed by Davioud as part of
Haussmann's urban improvements in the 1860s.
They are now two of the city's leading arts
venues: the **Théâtre de la Ville** (*see p313
and p340*); and **Théâtre du Châtelet** (*see
p290 and p310*), an opera and concert hall.

Beyond Châtelet, the **Hôtel de Ville**, the
City Hall and home to the mayor, has been the
symbol of municipal power since 1260. The
equestrian statue on the embankment in front
of the building is of 14th-century merchant
leader and rebel Etienne Marcel. Subsequent
revolutionaries made it their base in the 1871
Commune, but the building was set on fire by
the Communards themselves and wrecked
during savage fighting. It was rebuilt according
to the original model, on a bigger scale in
fanciful neo-Renaissance style with knights in
armour along the roofline and statues of French
luminaries from Didot to Corot dotted all over
the walls. The square outside was formerly
called place de Grève, after the nearby riverside
wharf on which goods were unloaded for
market. *Grève* has come to be the French word
for 'strike', thanks to the large number of
demonstrations and protests that gathered here.
Protestant heretics were burnt in the square
during the 16th-century Wars of Religion, and
the dreadful guillotine stood here during the

Scandale! History lessons

In January 2005, at almost the same time
as President Jacques Chirac was solemnly
unveiling a new Holocaust Memorial, the
Mémorial de la Shoah (*see p113*) in the
heart of the old Jewish quarter of the Marais,
and as ceremonies were taking place all over
Europe to mark the 50th anniversary of the
liberation of Auschwitz – controversial right-
wing leader Jean-Marie Le Pen was giving
a newspaper interview in which he described
the Nazi occupation of France as not
'particularly inhumane'.

Family and friends of the deportees listed
on the vast 'Wall of Names' at the entrance
to the adjacent documentation centre – the
names belonging to the 76,000 men, women

and children who were transported from
France to the Nazi camps between 1942
and 1945 – may well disagree.

Speaking during the same week that the
memorial wall, permanent exhibition space
and vast reading room comprising a million
artefacts and 55,000 photographs were
made available to the public, Le Pen summed
up the Gestapo's role in wartime France as
'protecting the nation'. Himself the son of a
fisherman killed by a German mine, Le Pen
went on to explain to French right-wing paper
Rivarol that the Nazis may have committed
'a few blunders' during the Occupation.

Did he know that of the 76,000 victims
listed on the wall, only 2,500 survived?

Pipe dream: the inside-out **Centre Pompidou**. *See p107*.

Sightseeing

Terror, when Danton, Marat and Robespierre made the Hôtel de Ville their own seat of government. Today the square is used for outdoor events such as an ice rink in December for Paris sur glace (*see p277*) and screenings of major sports events. Just across the road stands the popular Bazar de l'Hôtel de Ville department store, or **BHV** (*see p233*).

Atelier Brancusi

Piazza Beaubourg, 4th (01.44.78.12.33/www. centrepompidou.fr). M° Hôtel de Ville or Rambuteau. **Open** 2-6pm Mon, Wed-Sun. **Admission** (incl with Centre Pompidou – Musée National d'Art Moderne) €7; €5 18s-26s; free under-18s, 1st Sun of mth. **Credit** AmEx, V. **Map** p408 K6.

When Constantin Brancusi died in 1957 he left his studio and its contents to the state. The studio has been faithfully reconstructed by the Centre Pompidou. His fragile works in wood and plaster, including his endless columns and streamlined bird forms, show how Brancusi revolutionised sculpture.

Centre Pompidou
(Musée National d'Art Moderne)

rue St-Martin, 4th (01.44.78.12.33/www.centre pompidou.fr). M° Hôtel de Ville or Rambuteau. **Open** 11am-9pm (last entry 8pm) Mon, Wed-Sun; until 11pm some exhibitions. **Admission** *Museum* €7; €5 18s-25s; free under-18s, 1st Sun of mth; CM. *Exhibitions* €7-€9; €5-€7 13s-25s. *Day pass* (exhibitions, collection & Atelier Brancusi) €10; €8 18s-25s. **Credit** AmEx, DC, MC, V. **Map** p408 K6.

The primary colours, exposed pipes and air ducts make this one of the most well-known sights in Paris. The then unknown Italo-British architectural duo of Renzo Piano and Richard Rogers won the competition with their 'inside-out' boilerhouse approach, which put air-conditioning, pipes, lifts and the escalators on the outside, leaving an adaptable space within. The multi-disciplinary concept of modern art museum (the most important in Europe), library, exhibition and performance spaces and repertory cinema was also revolutionary. When it opened in 1977, its success exceeded all expectations. After a two-year revamp the centre reopened in January 2000 with an enlarged museum, renewed performance spaces, vista-rich Georges restaurant and a mission to get back to the stimulating inter-disciplinary mix of old. Entrance to the forum is free (as is the library, which has a separate entrance), but you now have to pay to go up the escalators.

The Centre Pompidou (or 'Beaubourg') holds the largest collection of modern art in Europe, rivalled only in its breadth and quality by MOMA in New York. Sample the contents of its vaults (50,000 works of art by 5,000 artists) on the website, as only a fraction – about 600 works – can be seen for real at any one time. There is a partial rehang each year. For the main collection, buy tickets on the ground floor and take the escalators to level four for post-1960s art. Level five spans 1905 to 1960. There are four temporary exhibition spaces on each of these

two levels (included in the ticket). Main temporary exhibitions are on the ground floor, in gallery two on level six, in the south gallery, level one and in the new Espace 315 devoted to the under-40s.

On level five, the historic section takes a chronological sweep through modern art history, via Primitivism, Fauvism, Cubism, Dada and Surrealism up to American Color-Field painting and Abstract Expressionism. Masterful ensembles let you see the span of Matisse's career on canvas and in bronze, the variety of Picasso's invention and the development of cubic orphism by Sonia and Robert Delaunay. Others on the hit list include Derain, Braque, Duchamp, Picabia, Mondrian, Malevich, Kandinsky, Dix, Ernst, Miró, Klee, Magritte, Rothko and Bacon. Don't miss the reconstruction of a wall of André Breton's studio, combining the tribal art, folk art, flea-market finds and drawings by fellow artists that the Surrealist artist and theorist had amassed. The photography collection also has an impressive roll call, including Brassaï, Kertész, Man Ray, Cartier-Bresson and Doisneau. Slotted in tinier vitrines between the main rooms are works on paper, photography and archive material; other galleries are devoted to design and architecture.

Level four, post-'60s art, has been entirely rehung. Thematic rooms concentrate on the career of one artist; others focus on movements such as Anti-form or arte povera. Recent acquisitions line the central corridor, while at the far end you can find architecture and design. Video art and installations by the likes of Mathieu Mercier and Dominique Gonzalez-Foerster are in a frequently changing room devoted to *nouvelle création*.

Big shows for 2006 include a survey of sculpture by the German-born Surrealist Hans Bellmer (1 Mar-22 May), a multi-disciplinary overview of the Los Angeles art scene from 1960 to 1985 (8 Mar-26 June) and an exhibition devoted to French painter Yves Klein (20 Sept-8 Jan 2007). The winner of the Prix Marcel Duchamp creates a new work for Espace 315 every winter. Atelier Brancusi, a public library, cinemas, children's activities, trendy restaurant Georges and the contemporary music and dance factory IRCAM form part of the Centre Pompidou. *See also chapters* **Architecture**, **Right Bank**, **Children** *and* **Film**. *Photos left.*

Hôtel de Ville

29 rue de Rivoli, 4th (01.42.76.43.43/www.paris.fr). M° Hôtel de Ville. **Open** 10am-7pm Mon-Sat. **Map** p408 K6.

Rebuilt by Ballu after the Commune, the palatial, multi-purpose Hôtel de Ville is both the heart of the city administration and a place to entertain visiting dignitaries. Small exhibitions are held in the Salon d'accueil (*see p108*); the rest of the building accessible only by guided tour (weekly – book in advance) is awash with parquet floors, marble statues, crystal chandeliers and allegorical painted ceilings. Mayor Delanoë prefers to live in a dinky, bijou pad in the Marais rather than in the lofty apartment here.

Salon d'acceuil

29 rue de Rivoli, 4th (01.42.76.43.43). M° Hôtel de Ville. **Open** 10am-7pm Mon-Sat; 2-7pm Sun. **Admission** free. **Map** p408 K6.
Exhibitions at the Hôtel de Ville vary from nostalgia trips about Piaf to contemporary cartoons.

Tour St-Jacques

square de La-Tour-St-Jacques, 4th. M° Châtelet. **Map** p408 J6.
Loved by the Surrealists, this solitary Flamboyant Gothic belltower with its leering gargoyles is all that remains of the St-Jacques-La-Boucherie church, built for the powerful Butchers' Guild in 1508-22. The statue of Blaise Pascal at the base commemorates his experiments on atmospheric pressure carried out here in the 17th century. A weather station now crowns the 52m tower, not open to the public.

The Marais

The Marais, a bewitching area whose narrow streets are dotted with aristocratic *hôtels particuliers*, art galleries, fashion boutiques and stylish cafés, lies east of Roman rue St-Martin and rue du Renard. While browsing, look up at the beautiful carved doorways and the early street signs carved into the stone. The Marais, or 'marsh', started life as a piece of swampy ground inhabited by a few monasteries, sheep and market gardens. This was one of the last parts of central Paris to be built up. In the 16th century the elegant Hôtel Carnavalet and Hôtel Lamoignon saw the area's phenomenal rise as an aristocratic residential district; Henri IV began building the **place des Vosges** in 1605. Nobles and royal officials followed, building smart townhouses where famous literary ladies such as Mme de Sévigné and Mlle de Scudéry and influential courtesan Ninon de l'Enclos held court. The area fell from fashion a century later; happily, many of the narrow streets were essentially unchanged as mansions were transformed into industrial workshops, crafts studios, schools and tenements, and even the fire station on rue de Sévigné. Several can be visited as museums, others can be seen only on walking tours or on the **Journées du Patrimoine** (*see p276*). The Marais is a favourite spot for a Sunday stroll, as many of the shops are open, though if you come during the week you have more chance of wandering into some of the elegant courtyards.

Rue des Francs-Bourgeois, crammed with impressive mansions and original boutiques, runs like a backbone right through the Marais, becoming more aristocratic as it leaves the foodshops of rue Rambuteau behind. Two of the the most refined early 18th-century residences are Hôtel d'Albret (No.31), a venue for jazz concerts at the **Paris quartier d'été** festival (*see p275*), and the palatial Hôtel de Soubise (No.60), the national archives. Begun in 1704 for the Prince and Princesse de Soubise, interiors by Boucher and Lemoine can be seen as part of the **Musée de l'Histoire de France**, along with the neighbouring Hôtel de Rohan, and a surprising series of rose gardens. On one side of its grandiose, colonnaded Cour d'Honneur, architect Delamair incorporated the turreted, fortified medieval gateway of the Hôtel de Clisson visible on rue des Archives. Facing the Archives Nationaux, the Crédit municipal (No.55), successor of the historic Mont de Piété founded by Louis XVI in 1777, still acts as a sort of municipal pawnshop: people bring in valuables in exchange for cash; items never reclaimed are sold off at auction. Just beyond, by the Centre Culturel Suisse (No.38), an alleyway with overhanging houses, is typical of the little lanes that once ran between the mansions, and still has its central gutter and stone bollards down the side. On the corner of rue Pavée is the austere Renaissance Hôtel Lamoignon, with a magisterial courtyard adorned with giant Corinthian pilasters. Built in 1585 for Diane de France, Henri II's illegitimate daughter, it houses the Bibliothèque Historique de la Ville de Paris (No.24, 4th, 01.44.59.29.40). Further along, the **Musée Carnavalet**, dedicated to the history of Paris, runs across the Hôtel Carnavalet and the later Hôtel le Peletier de St-Fargeau. One of the finest houses in the Marais, the Hôtel Carnavalet set the pattern for many of the *hôtels* to follow with its U-shaped plan behind an entrance courtyard; the reliefs of the four seasons on the façade are possibly by Jean Goujon. It was once home to famous letter-writer Mme de Sévigné.

At its eastern end, rue des Francs-Bourgeois leads into the beautiful brick-and-stone place des Vosges. At one corner is the **Maison de Victor Hugo**, where the writer lived from 1833 to 1848, and across the square is the luxurious Ambroisie restaurant (No.9, 4th, 01.42.78.51.45). An archway in the south-west corner leads to the **Hôtel de Sully**, accommodating the Patrimoine Photographique. Designed in 1624, it belonged to Henri IV's minister, the Duc de Sully. Its two beautifully proportioned courtyards contain reliefs of the four seasons and a rare, surviving orangery.

Several other important museums are also in sumptuous *hôtels*. The Hôtel Salé on rue de Thorigny, built in 1656, was nicknamed ('salty') after its owner, Fontenay, who collected the salt tax. It was beautifully restored and extended in the 1980s to house the **Musée National Picasso**; it has an elegant semi-circular courtyard adorned by sphinxes and a grand baroque stairwell carved with garlands,

Musée National Picasso – an incomparable treasure trove. *See p111.*

imperial busts and gambolling cupids. Nearby, the pretty Hôtel Donon, built in 1598 for the royal building inspector, contains the **Musée Cognacq-Jay** and has remarkable 18th-century panelled interiors (both its own and those brought here from other mansions), while the Hôtel Guénégaud, attributed to François Mansart for its harmonious proportions and sobriety, contains the eclectic collection of the **Musée de la Chasse et de la Nature** hunting museum.

The Marais has also long been a focus for the Jewish community. Jews were expelled from France in the Middle Ages, but when they were granted citizenship after the Revolution, the Marais became the point of arrival. Today's community is centred on rue des Rosiers, rue des Ecouffes and rue Pavée (where there's a synagogue designed by Guimard). Originally made up mainly of Ashkenazi Jews who arrived after the pogroms in Eastern Europe at the end of the 19th century (many were later deported during World War II), the community expanded in the 1950s and '60s with a wave of Sephardic Jewish immigration after French withdrawal from North Africa. As a result, there are now many falafel shops alongside Central European Jewish bakers and delis, such as **Finkelstajn** (*see p262*) and late-opening Jo Goldenberg (7 rue des Rosiers, 4th, 01.48.87.20.16).

The lower ends of rue des Archives and rue Vieille-du-Temple are the centre of café life – including **Petit Fer à Cheval** (*see p221*) and

La Chaise au Plafond in the neighbouring rue du Trésor (No.10, 4th, 01.42.76.03.22) – and the hub of the gay scene. Gay bars such as the **Open Café** (*see p303*) draw merry crowds for the early-evening happy hour. In their midst at 22-26 rue des Archives, the 15th-century Cloître des Billettes is the only surviving Gothic cloister in Paris.

Workaday rue du Temple, once the road leading to the Templars' church, is full of surprises. Near rue de Rivoli, the **Latina** (*see p295*) specialises in Latin American films and holds tango balls in the room above. At No.41, an archway leads into the former Aigle d'Or coaching inn, now the **Café de la Gare** café-théâtre (*see p279*). Further north, at No.71, the grandiose Hôtel de St-Aignan, built in 1650 for the Conte d'Avaux, contains the **Musée d'Art et d'Histoire du Judaïsme**. A truly majestic courtyard, with giant Corinthian pilasters and carved armorial, the oval galleried staircase and traces of fresco in the café hint at just how splendid this must have been before it was converted into a town hall, workshops and a warren of apartments before being rescued in the 1990s. The top end of rue du Temple and adjoining streets such as rue des Gravilliers are packed with costume jewellery, handbag and rag-trade wholesalers in what is the city's oldest Chinatown. The Quartier du Temple was once a fortified, semi-independent entity under the Knights Templar, until the order grew so powerful it rivalled the monarchy and it was suppressed in 1313 by Philippe le Bel. Their Tour du Temple, a monastery under the Knights Hospitalier de St-Jean, became a prison in the Revolution, where the royal family was held in 1792. The round church and keep have been replaced by square du Temple and the Carreau du Temple clothes market.

The north-west corner of the Marais hinges on the **Musée des Arts et Métiers**, a science museum with early flying machines displayed in the 12th-century chapel of the former priory of St-Martin-des-Champs, and the adjoining Conservatoire des Arts et Métiers. Across rue St-Martin on square Emile-Chautemps, after a brief, disastrous interlude as a theme park, the Théâtre de la Gaîté Lyrique, which once premièred operettas by Offenbach, is to be renovated as a cultural centre. Of the many ancient streets here, 3 rue Volta, long considered the oldest house in Paris, is now thought to be a bit of retro design. It dates from the early 17th century in disobedience to the laws against half-timbered structures; a much older house is the Auberge de Nicolas Flamel at 51 rue de Montmorency built in 1407 by notorious alchemist Nicolas Flamel. He never lived here himself, but rented out the ground floor workshop (now a restaurant) and lodged the poor for free upstairs.

Despite the Marais' rise to fashion, the less-gentrified streets around the northern stretch of rue Vieille-du-Temple towards place de la République is awash with tiny local bars, designers on the rise and old craft workshops. Contemporary art galleries such as **Yvon Lambert** (*see p299*) hide in elegant *hôtels particuliers*. Amid the foodshops of rue de Bretagne is chic couscous stalwart **Chez Omar** (*see p197*) and the Marché des Enfants-Rouges, one of the city's oldest markets founded in 1615, once a red-uniformed orphanage.

Hôtel de Sully

62 rue St-Antoine, 4th (01.42.74.47.75). M° St-Paul or Bastille. **Open** noon-7pm Tue-Fri; 10am-7pm Sat, Sun (last admission 30mins before closing). **Admission** €5; €2.50 concessions. **Credit** MC, V. **Map** p411 L7.
The former Patrimoine Photographique forms part of the two-site home for the Jeu de Paume: the Centre National de la Photographie (*see p93*). Visiting exhibitions here tend to have a political slant.

Maison de Victor Hugo

Hôtel de Rohan-Guéménée, 6 pl des Vosges, 4th (01.42.72.10.16/www.paris.fr/musees). M° Bastille. **Open** 10am-6pm Tue-Sun. **Admission** free. *Exhibitions* prices vary. **Credit** MC, V. **Map** p411 L6.
Victor Hugo lived here 1832-48, the house today a museum for France's favourite son. On display are his first editions, nearly 500 drawings and, more bizarrely, the great man's home-made furniture.

Musée d'Art et d'Histoire du Judaïsme

Hôtel de St-Aignan, 71 rue du Temple, 3rd (01.53.01.86.60/www.mahj.org). M° Rambuteau. **Open** 11am-6pm Mon-Fri; 10am-6pm Sun. Closed Jewish hols. **Admission** €6.80; €4.50 18s-26s; free under-18s. **Credit** *Shop* MC, V. **Map** p411 K6.
Set in a Marais mansion, this museum sprung from the collection of a private association formed in 1948 to safeguard Jewish heritage after the Holocaust. Displays illustrate ceremonies, rites and learning, and show how styles were adapted across the globe through some fine examples of Jewish decorative arts: a silver Hannukah lamp made in Frankfurt, finely carved Italian synagogue furniture, embroidered Bar Mitzvah robes. There are also documents and paintings relating to the emancipation of French Jewry after the Revolution, and the Dreyfus case, from Zola's J'Accuse! to anti-Semitic cartoons. Paintings by the early 20th-century avant-garde and the Ecole de Paris include El Lissitsky and Chagall. The Holocaust is marked by Christian Boltanski's work commemorating the Jews who were living in the building in 1939, 13 of whom died in the camps. The Shoah Memorial (*see p113*) opened in 2005.

Musée des Arts et Métiers

60 rue Réaumur, 3rd (01.53.01.82.00/www.arts-et-metiers.net). M° Arts et Métiers. **Open** 10am-6pm Tue, Wed, Fri-Sun; 10am-9.30pm Thur. Closed public hols. **Admission** €6.50; €4.50 students, under-26s; free under-18s. *With exhibition* €7.50; €5.50 students, under-26s; free under-18s. *Exhibition only* €3; €2 students, under-26s. **Credit** V. **Map** p404 K5.
After the monks of this 11th-century priory lost their heads in the Revolution, Abbé Henri Grégoire kept his by thinking up a brilliant new use for the building – as a repository of technological marvels that could act as a 3D encyclopedia for investors and industrialists in the new republic. Three floors of the neighbouring building contain glass cases of beautifully crafted scientific instruments from astrolabes to steam engines including reconstructions of famous inventors' workshops. Though it is a bit short on moving-parts models, filmed diagrams explain the workings and there are themed talks by staff throughout the day. The best bit is the restored church – the earliest example of Parisian Gothic – containing Foucault's pendulum, Blériot's biplane and the history of the car on seven glass floors. The pleasant terrace restaurant offers an all-in brunch and museum deal on Sundays (€19.50; €17.50 concessions, students, under-18s; €10 children).

Musée Carnavalet

23 rue de Sévigné, 3rd (01.44.59.58.58/www.paris.fr/musees). M° St-Paul. **Open** 10am-6pm Tue-Sun. Closed some public hols. **Admission** free. *Exhibitions* €5.50; €4 over-60s; €2.50 14s-26s; free under-14s. **Credit** *Shop* AmEx, MC, V. **Map** p411 L6.
This fine Marais building houses 140 rooms depicting the history of Paris, from pre-Roman Gaul to the 20th century. Built in 1548, transformed by Mansart

in 1660, it became a museum when Haussmann persuaded the city in 1866 to buy the *hôtel* to preserve its beautiful interiors. Displays are chronological. The original 16th-century rooms house Renaissance collections with portraits by Clouet, and furniture and pictures relating to the Wars of Religion. The first floor shows the period up to 1789 with furniture, applied arts and paintings displayed in restored, period interiors. 1789 onwards is covered in neighbouring Hôtel Le Peletier de St-Fargeau. The Revolutionary items detail the convoluted politics and bloodshed of the period. There are portraits of all the major players, prints, objects and memorabilia including a chunk of the Bastille prison. There are items belonging to Napoléon, views of post-Haussmann Paris, a cradle given by the city to Napoléon III – and Proust's cork-lined bedroom.

Musée de la Chasse et de la Nature

Hôtel Guénégaud, 60 rue des Archives, 3rd (01.53.01.92.40/www.chassenature.org). M° Rambuteau. **Open** reopening May 2006; ring for hours and prices. **Map** p411 K5.
Housed on three floors of a fine, Mansart-designed 17th-century mansion is a store of objects with a hunting theme (including a stuffed polar bear and a pair of gorillas). Highlights are the ornate weapons: crossbows inlaid with ivory and mother-of-pearl, rifles decorated with hunting scenes, reminders that hunting's accoutrements were status symbols. There are bird and animal studies by the first great *animalier* in France, Alexandre-François Desportes, as well as his own portrait of Louis XIV's hunting dogs. The museum is linked to a nature reserve in the Ardennes woodland.

Musée Cognacq-Jay

Hôtel Donon, 8 rue Elzévir, 3rd (01.40.27.07.21/ www.paris.fr/musees/cognacq_jay). M° St-Paul. **Open** 10am-6pm Tue-Sun. Closed some public hols. **Admission** free. **Map** p411 L6.
This cosy museum in a carefully restored *hôtel particulier* houses the collection put together in the early 1900s by La Samaritaine founder Ernest Cognacq and his wife Marie-Louise Jay. They stuck mainly to 18th-century French, focusing on rococo artists like Watteau, Fragonard, Boucher, Greuze and pastellist Quentin de la Tour, though some English (Reynolds, Romney, Lawrence), Dutch and Flemish (an early Rembrandt, Ruysdael, Rubens) names, plus Canalettos and Guardis, have managed to slip in. Pictures are displayed in panelled rooms with furniture, porcelain, tapestries and sculpture of the same period.

Musée d'Histoire de France

Hôtel de Rohan, 87 rue Vieille-du-Temple, 3rd (01.40.27.60.96/www.archivesnationales.culture. gouv.fr/chan). M° Hôtel de Ville or Rambuteau. **Open** 10am-12.30pm, 2-5.30pm Mon, Wed-Fri; 2-5.30pm Sat, Sun. Closed public hols. **Admission** €3; €2.30 18s-25s; free under-18s. **Credit** V. **Map** p411 K6.

Housed in one of the grandest Marais mansions, this museum is to be renovated in order to present a more pluralistic historical interpretation. In the meantime, a changing selection of documents and artefacts covers major political people and events – the Wars of Religion, the French Revolution, Napoléon – plus social issues and quirky aspects of daily life, from the founding of the Sorbonne to an ordinance about umbrellas. The neighbouring Hôtel de Soubise boasts the finest rococo interiors decorated for the Prince and Princesse de Soubise in the 1730s and paintings by Boucher and Van Loo (visits can be arrranged on Sunday afternoons by reservation only on 01.40.27.62.18). The venue is also used for concerts and contains a decent resource library.

Musée National Picasso

Hôtel Salé, 5 rue de Thorigny, 3rd (01.42.71.25.21/ www.musee-picasso.fr). M° Chemin Vert or St-Paul. **Open** Oct-Mar 9.30am-5.30pm Mon, Wed-Sun. Apr-Sept 9.30am-6pm Mon, Wed-Sun. **Admission** €5.50; €4 18-25s; free under-18s, 1st Sun of mth; CM. *With exhibitions* €6.70; €5.20 18-25s, all on Sun; free under-18s. **Credit** *Shop* AmEx, MC, V. **Map** p411 L6.
This astonishing testament to one man's genius was acquired by the state in lieu of inheritance tax and is housed in a grand Marais mansion. The collection shows all phases of Picasso's long and varied career, revealing his continual inventiveness and sense of humour. Masterpieces include a gaunt, blue-period self-portrait, studies for the *Demoiselles d'Avignon*, *Paolo as Harlequin*, his Cubist and classical phases, the surreal *Nude in an Armchair*, beach pictures of the 1920s, sand-covered *tableaux-reliefs*, portraits of models Marie-Thérèse and Dora Maar, and even the ribald artist-and-model paintings of his later years. The unusual wallpaper collage, *Women at their Toilette*, has been given its own small room, and there are prints and ceramics, Minotaur etchings and his own collection of tribal art – all juxtaposed with 'primitive' wood figures he carved himself. Finds include his bizarrely wonderful sculptures, from the vast plaster head on the staircase and the spiky *Project for Monument to Apollinaire* to *Girl on a Swing*. Look out, too, for the sculpture of an ape – its face is actually made out of a toy car. Exhibitions for 2006 include works by and inspired by Maar (until mid April) and – in the pipeline, this one – a show on Picasso and Africa. You'll find an outdoor café here in the warmer months and a half-decent bookshop. **Photo** *p109*.

Passage de Retz

9 rue Charlot, 3rd (01.48.04.37.99). M° Filles du Calvaire. **Open** 10am-7pm Tue-Sun. **Admission** €6; €4 students under 26, over-60s; free under-12s. **Credit** (over €10) MC, V. **Map** p411 L5.
This gorgeous Marais mansion, once a toy factory, was resurrected as a gallery in the 1990s to host shows and installations by contemporary artists, architects, designers and photographers. Wooden floors, glass roof and walled garden give it a relaxing vibe, and there's a cool designer café.

Charm both raffish and historic – **Place des Vosges**.

Place des Vosges

4th. Mº St-Paul. **Map** p411 L6.

The first planned square in Paris (along with its contemporary place Dauphine) was commissioned in 1605 by Henri IV and inaugurated by his son Louis XIII in 1612. Intimate, with harmonious red-brick-and-stone arcaded façades and steeply pitched slate roofs, it is quite distinct from the pomp of later Bourbon Paris. Laid out on a symmetrical plan with carriageways through the taller Pavillon de la Reine on the north side and Pavillon du Roi on the south, the other lots were sold off as concessions to royal officials and nobles (note that some façades are imitation brick). Originally called place Royale, its name dates from the Napoleonic Wars, when the Vosges was the first region of France to pay its war taxes. Mme de Sévigné, salon hostess and letter-writer, was born at No.1bis in 1626. At that time the garden was the scene of duels and trysts; now it attracts children from the nearby nursery school. **Photo** *above.*

The St-Paul district

In 1559 Henri II was mortally wounded jousting on today's rue St-Antoine, commemorated by the marble *La Vierge de Douleur* by Pilon in the **Eglise St-Paul-St-Louis**. South of rue St-Antoine is the sedate residential area of St-Paul, still lined with dignified 17th- and 18th-century façades. The Village St-Paul is a colony of antiques sellers, set over linked courtyards between rue St-Paul, rue Charlemagne and quai des Célestins, and a promising source of 1930s and 1950s furniture, kitchenware and wine gadgets (open Mon, Thur-Sun). Over on rue des Jardins-St-Paul is the largest surviving section of the fortified wall of Philippe-Auguste. The infamous poisoner Marquise de Brinvilliers lived at Hôtel de Brinvilliers (12 rue Charles-V) in the 1630s. She killed her father and brothers to inherit the family fortune and was only caught after her lover died – of natural causes.

By St-Paul métro station on the corner of rue François-Miron and rue de Fourcy is another fine mansion, the Hôtel Hénault de Cantorbe, renovated and given a minimalist modern extension as the **Maison Européenne de la Photographie**. Down rue de Fourcy towards the river across a medieval formal garden you can see the rear façade of the Hôtel de Sens, a rare medieval mansion built as the Paris residence of the Archbishops of Sens at the end of the 15th century, with a lovely array of turrets. It houses the **Bibliothèque Forney**, specialising in posters, postcards and exhibitions about graphic design.

Across from Ile St-Louis near Pont Sully, the square Henri-Galli, with a rebuilt piece of Bastille prison, and the **Pavillon de l'Arsenal**, built by a rich timber merchant to put on art shows, and home to displays about Parisian architecture.

Winding rue François-Miron leads you back towards the Hôtel de Ville. At 17 rue Geoffroy l'Asnier, the Mémorial du Martyr Juif Inconnu is currently being extended as part of the **Mémorial de la Shoah**, a major museum, memorial and study centre devoted to the Holocaust, which was opened by Jacques Chirac in January 2005; note also the Cité des Arts complex of artists' studios and the ornate lion's head and giant shell motif on the doorway of 17th-century Hôtel de Châlon-Luxembourg at No.26. At 11 and 13 rue François-Miron, two wonky half-timbered houses are probably rare 14th-century structures, although they were both heavily rebuilt in the 1960s. Rue du Pont-Louis-Philippe contains funky jewellers, paper shops, and the designer furniture and gifts of the eye-catching **Sentou Galerie** (*see p268*), while stepped rue des Barres is tearoom territory, overlooking the spiky chevet of the **Eglise St-Gervais-St-Protais**.

Bibliothèque Forney

Hôtel de Sens, 1 rue du Figuier, 4th (01.42.78.14.60). M° Pont Marie. **Open** 1.30-8.30pm Tue-Fri; 10am-8.30pm Sat. Closed public hols. **Admission** €4; €2 students under 28, over-60s; free under-12s. **No credit cards. Map** p411 L7.
In the turrets of the oldest Marais mansion, the Forney library specialises in exhibitions and gifts of applied and graphic arts.

Eglise St-Gervais-St-Protais

place St-Gervais, 4th (01.48.87.32.02). M° Hôtel de Ville. **Open** varies. **Map** p411 K6.
Gothic at the rear, classical at the front (the west front is now attributed to Salomon de Brosse, the architect of the Palais de Luxembourg), most of the impressive Flamboyant Gothic interior dates from the 16th century. The nave gives an impression of enormous height with tall columns without capitals that soar up to the vault. There are plenty of fine funerary monuments dotted about, especially the baroque statue of Chancellor Le Tellier reclining on a marble sarcophagus. The Couperin family were organists here for generations.

Eglise St-Paul-St-Louis

99 rue St-Antoine, 4th (01.42.72.30.32). M° Bastille or St-Paul. **Open** 9am-8pm Mon-Sat; 9-8.30pm Sun. **Map** p411 L6.
This domed baroque Counter-Reformation church is modelled, like all Jesuit churches, on the Gesù in Rome. Completed in 1641, it features a single nave, side chapels and a three-storey hierarchical façade with statues of Saints Louis, Anne and Catherine – all replacements. The provider of confessors to the kings of France, the Eglise St-Paul-St-Louis was richly endowed until Revolutionary iconoclasts broke into it and pinched its treasures, including the hearts of Louis XIII and XIV. In 1802 it was converted back to a church and now houses Delacroix's *Christ in the Garden of Olives*.

Fortified wall of Philippe-Auguste

rue des Jardins-St-Paul, 4th (www.philippe-auguste. com). M° Pont Marie or St-Paul. **Map** p411 L7.
King Philippe-Auguste (1165-1223), the first great Parisian builder since the Romans, enclosed his city within a great wall. The largest surviving section, complete with towers, extends along rue des Jardins-St-Paul. Another chunk is at 3 rue Clovis (5th) and odd remnants of towers are dotted around the Marais, rue du Louvre and St-Germain-des-Prés.

Maison Européene de la Photographie

5-7 rue de Fourcy, 4th (01.44.78.75.00/www.mep-fr.org). M° St-Paul. **Open** 11am-8pm Wed-Sun (last admission 7.30pm). Closed public hols. **Admission** €6; €3 students, 8s-26s; free under-8s, all 5-8pm Wed. **Credit** MC, V. **Map** p411 L6.
Housed in a Marais mansion with a modern annexe, the MEP is devoted to contemporary photography and stores a huge permanent collection. Up to six exhibitions run concurrently, from photojournalism to experimental art photography, and the venue organises the biennial Mois de la Photo (the next one scheduled for November 2006) and the Art Outsiders festival of new media web art in September.

Le Mémorial de la Shoah

17 rue Geoffroy-l'Asnier, 4th (01.42.77.44.72/ www.memorialdelashoah.org). M° St-Paul or Pont Marie. **Open** 10am-6pm Mon-Wed; 10am-10pm Thur; 10am-6pm Fri-Sun. **Research** centre 10am-5.30pm Mon-Wed; 10am-7.30pm Thur; 10am-5.30pm Fri-Sun. **Admission** free **Map** p411 K6.
The Mémorial du Martyr Juif Inconnu reopened with a permanent collection and temporary exhibitions devoted to the Holocaust and the 76,000 Jews deported from France from 1942 to 1944. The new research centre and library is free to all. *See p105* **Scandale!**

Musée de la Magie

11 rue St-Paul, 4th (01.42.72.13.26/www.museedela magie.com). M° St-Paul. **Open** 2-6.30pm Wed, Sat, Sun (longer in hols). **Admission** €7; €5 3-12s; free under-3s. **No credit cards. Map** p411 L7.
This interactive museum of magic is run in the spirit of Robert-Houdin, the 19th-century French conjurer whose name was taken by Harry Houdini. The sleight of hand starts outside in the queue and gets craftier as you work your way through the exhibition. There's a broad array of conjuring tools, many of which are put into practice before your very eyes.

Pavillon de l'Arsenal

21 bd Morland, 4th (01.42.76.33.97/www.pavillon-arsenal.com). M° Sully Morland. **Open** 10.30am-6.30pm Tue-Sat; 11am-7pm Sun. **Admission** free. **Credit** *Shop* MC, V. **Map** p411 L7.
The Pavillon displays local building projects and acts as an archive. The fantastic 1880s gallery, with its iron frame and glass roof, has been refurbished; the ground floor houses a permanent exhibition on the history of Paris. Upstairs you'll find temporary displays, a library and *vidéothèque*. **Photo** *p115*.

Bastille & eastern Paris

Mainly in the 11th and 12th arrondissements.
Place de la Bastille, traditionally the frontier between central Paris and the more proletarian east, has remained a potent symbol of popular revolt ever since the prison-storming that inaugurated the Revolution. While the square is still a gathering point for demonstrations, and setting for the big Bastille Day ball every July (*see p275*), the area has been transformed since the 1980s with the arrival of the **Opéra Bastille** (*see p312*), and trendy cafés, restaurants and bars. The site of the prison itself is now a Société Générale bank while the gap left by the castle ramparts forms the present-day square, dominated by the massive, curved façade of the Opéra. Opened in 1989 on the bicentennial of Bastille Day, it remains controversial, criticised for its poor acoustics and construction – but productions usually sell out. South of the square is the Port de l'Arsenal marina, while north of the square, the canal continues underground, beneath the broad boulevard Richard-Lenoir, site of a long outdoor market on Sunday mornings.

Rue du Fbg-St-Antoine has been the heart of the furniture-makers' district for centuries. Some gaudy furniture showrooms still line the street, but it is increasingly being colonised by clothes shops and bars, including the popular salsa-themed Barrio Latino (Nos.46-48, 12th, 01.55.78.84.75), and you can't help but feel a twinge of regret for when the last Louis XVI chair or Nubian slave candelabra finally disappears. The cobbled rue de Lappe typifies the Bastille's seismic shift, as the last remaining furniture workshops, the 1930s Balajo dancehall (No.9, 11th, 01.47.00.07.87), old Auvergnat bistro La Galoche d'Aurillac (No.41, 11th, 01.47.00.77.15) and grocer Chez Teil (No.6, 11th, 01.47.00.41.28) hold out against gift shops and theme bars that teem with teens at weekends. Pockets of arty resistance remain on rue de Charonne with the hip Pause Café (No.41, 11th, 01.48.06.80.33) and its busy terrace, old-style bistro **Chez Paul** (No.13, 11th, 01.47.00.34.57), art nouveau Bistro du Peintre (116 av Ledru-Rollin, 11th, 01.47.00.34.39) and dealers in colourful 1960s furniture. On rue des Taillandiers and rue Keller, the patch is a focus for record shops, streetwear boutiques and, increasingly, young fashion designers.

The main thoroughfares reveal only half the story. Narrow street frontages hide cobbled alleys, lined with craftsmen's workshops or quirky bars and bistros dating from the 18th century. Peruse the cours de l'Ours, du Cheval Blanc, du Bel Air (with its hidden garden) and de la Maison Brûlée, the passage du Chantier

on Fbg-St-Antoine, the rustic-looking passage de l'Etoile d'Or and the passage de l'Homme with old wooden shopfronts on rue de Charonne. This area was originally located outside the city walls on the lands of the Convent of St-Antoine (parts of which survive as the Hôpital St-Antoine). In the Middle Ages skilled furniture- makers not belonging to the city's restrictive guilds began a tradition of free thinking, a development that made this an incendiary area during the 1789 Revolution.

Further down rue du Fbg-St-Antoine is place d'Aligre, home to a rowdy North African vegetable market (the cheapest in Paris), a more sedate covered market (*see p259* **Forward marché!**) and the only flea market within the city walls, where a handful of *brocanteurs* sell junk and old books and prints for reasonably high prices. Marketeers and locals meet on Sunday mornings at the **Baron Rouge** wine bar (*see p223*), where you can take your container to fill up from a cheap barrel of wine. The road ends in the major intersection place de la Nation, another grand square. Originally called place du Trône, after a throne that was placed here when Louis XIV and his bride Marie-Thérèse entered the city here in 1660. During the bloody aftermath of the Revolution, the guillotine was moved here and thousands were guillotined between 13 June and 28 July 1799, the bodies carted to the nearby **Picpus Cemetery**. The square still has two of Ledoux's toll houses and tall Doric columns from the 1787 Mur des Fermiers-Généraux. Right in the centre stands Jules Dalou's rather grandiose allegorical bronze sculpture *Le Triomphe de la République*, erected for the centenary of the Revolution in 1889. East of Nation, broad Cours de Vincennes has a busy street market on Wednesday and Saturday mornings and kerb crawlers by night.

North of place de la Bastille, boulevard Beaumarchais separates rowdy Bastille from the elegant Marais, and the polygonal **Cirque d'Hiver** winter circus (*see p280*), designed by Hittorff in 1852. East of place Voltaire, on rue de la Roquette, which heads eastwards towards **Ménilmontant** (*see p135*) and the cemetery of **Père-Lachaise** (*see p136*), a small park and playground surrounded by modern housing marks the site of the prison de la Roquette, where a plaque remembers the 4,000 Resistance members imprisoned here in World War II.

La Maison Rouge – Fondation Antoine de Galbert

10 bd de la Bastille, 12th (01.40.01.08.81/ www. lamaisonrouge.org). M° Quai de la Rapée.
Open 11am-7pm Wed, Fri-Sun; 11am-9pm Thur.
Admission €6.50; €4.50 students, 13s-25s; free under-13s. **Credit** MC, V. **Map** p408 M7.

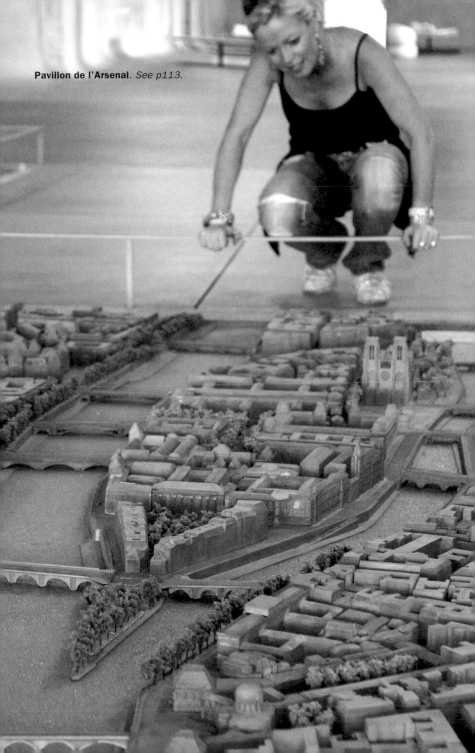

Pavillon de l'Arsenal. *See p113.*

This 2,000sq m art space opened in 2004 occupies an old printworks, comprising three large exhibition rooms and basement. It presents two private collections and two thematic shows a year.

Place de la Bastille

4th/11th/12th. M° Bastille. Map p409 M7.
Nothing remains of the prison that, on 14 July 1789, was stormed by the forces of the plebeian revolt. Though only seven prisoners remained, the event provided the rebels with arms and gave the insurrection momentum. It remains the eternal symbol of the Revolution, celebrated with a lively street ball here every 13 July. The prison itself was quickly torn down, its stones used to build Pont de la Concorde. Vestiges of the foundations can be seen in the métro; there's part of a reconstructed tower at square Henri-Galli, near Pont de Sully (4th). The Colonne de Juillet, topped by a gilded *génie* of Liberty, is a monument to Parisians who fell in the revolutions of July 1830 and 1848.

Bercy & Daumesnil

The **Viaduc des Arts** is the former Paris-Vincennes railway viaduct along avenue Daumesnil, whose glass-fronted arches now showcase a gentrified row of craft and design boutiques and workshops. Atop the viaduct, old ladies admire the blooms among the bamboo of the **Promenade Plantée**, which continues through the Jardin de Reuilly and east to the **Bois de Vincennes**. Further along, amid its comfortable residential blocks, avenue Daumesnil is fast becoming a Silicon Valley of computer outlets.

Eglise du St-Esprit is a curious 1920s concrete copy of Istanbul's Hagia Sofia, while nearby **Cimetière de Picpus** contains the graves of many of the Terror's victims, as well as American War of Independence hero General La Fayette. Just before the Périphérique, the fabulous **Palais de la Porte Dorée** (*see p284*) was built in 1931 for the Exposition Coloniale with striking, if politically incorrect, reliefs on the façade and two fabulous art deco offices designed by Ruhlmann. Originally the Musée des Colonies, then the Musée des Arts d'Afrique et d'Océanie (now in storage as the basis of the future Musée du Quai Branly; *see p152* **Chirac's grand projet**), it is currently being used for design exhibitions, but still has a popular aquarium complete with crocodiles in the basement.

As recently as the 1980s, wine was still unloaded off barges at Bercy but now this stretch of the Seine is firmly part of redeveloped Paris with the massive Ministère de l'Economie et du Budget and to the west the peculiar grass-covered pyramid of the **Palais Omnisports de Paris-Bercy**, a rock (*see p314*) as well as a

sports venue (*see p329*). To the east is the Bercy Expo exhibition and trade centre. Between the two lie the modern **Parc de Bercy** and the former American Center, built at the start of the 1990s by Frank Gehry, thus predating his Bilbao Guggenheim. For the last few years, it has been in the process of refitting for its new tenant, the **Cinémathèque Française** (*see p294* 'thèque five'). At the eastern edge of the park, in contrast to the contemporary **Ciné Cité** multiplex (*see p292*), is **Bercy Village**. Forty-two stone wine warehouses have been restored and opened as shops, wine bars and cafés on either side of a cobbled street, the Cour St-Emilon; the result is lively, if somewhat antiseptic. Typical is **Club Med World** (*see p328*), whose themed bars and juggling barmen evoke a holiday resort. Another group has been converted as the Pavillons de Bercy, with the **Musée des Arts Forains**, a charming collection of fairground rides and Venetian carnival salons.

Bois de Vincennes

12th. M° Porte Dorée or Château de Vincennes.
This is Paris' biggest park created, like the Bois de Boulogne in the west, when former royal hunting forest was landscaped by Alphand for Baron Haussmann. As well as lawns and woodland, there are cycle paths, four lakes, picnic areas, a Buddhist temple, a racetrack, restaurants, a baseball field (*see p331*) and a small farm. It also contains the city's main zoo (*see p284*), now largely closed because of lack of maintenance, though the rugged fake mountains look impressive against the skyline, and the Cartoucherie theatre complex. Boats can be hired out on Lake Daumesnil. The Parc Floral (*see p285*), something between a botanical garden and an amusement park, was laid out in a modern style in 1969, with mock hills, brick turrets, a spiral lake, an iris mound, pine trees and a bonsai garden. A first-rate programme of jazz (*see p319*) and classical concerts takes place on lazy summer weekends by the lake. Dotted around are unusual amusements such as Paris-themed crazy golf, with the water drained from the Seine. Next to the park stands the imposing Château de Vincennes, where England's Henry V died in 1422.

Cimetière de Picpus

35 rue de Picpus, 12th (01.43.44.18.54). M° Nation or Daumesnil or Picpus. **Open** *15 Apr-14 Oct* 2-6pm Tue-Sun. *15 Oct-14 Apr* 2-4pm Tue-Sun.
Admission €2.50. **No credit cards. Map** p409 Q8.
Redolent with revolutionary associations, both French and US, this cemetery in a working convent is the resting place for the thousands of victims of the Revolutionary aftermath, guillotined at place du Trône (now place de l'Ile de Réunion) between 14 June and 27 July 1794. At the end of a walled garden is a graveyard of aristocratic French families. In one corner is the tomb of General La Fayette, who fought

in the American War of Independence and was married to one of the aristocratic Noailles. Clearly marked are the sites of two communal graves and you can discern the doorway where the carts arrived. It was only thanks to a maid who had seen the carts that the site was rediscovered – plus the cemetery and adjoining convent founded by the descendants of the Noailles family. In the chapel, two tablets on either end of the transept list the names and occupation of the executed: 'domestic', 'farmer' and 'employee' figure alongside 'lawyer', 'abbess' and 'prince and priest'.

Cité de l'Architecture et du Patrimoine – Palais de la Porte Dorée

293 av Daumesnil, 12th (01.58.51.52.00/www. archi.fr/IFA-CHAILLOT). M° Porte Dorée. **Open** 10am-5pm Mon, Wed-Sun. **Admission** *Exhibitions* free. *Art deco rooms & aquarium* €5.50; €4 under-25s. **No credit cards.**

Until the inauguration of the Cité de l'Architecture in the Palais de Chaillot at the end of 2006, the combined Musée des Monuments Nationaux and Institut Français de l'Architecture has been given a temporary home in the old Musée des Arts d'Afrique et d'Océanie. Shows range from architects' projects to retrospectives on Auguste Perret. The fine building, designed for the 1931 Exposition Coloniale, has an art deco bas-relief glorying in France's colonial past – it will be the Cité Nationale de l'Histoire de l'Immigration in 2007. Meanwhile, the crocodiles brought in from Dakar in 1948 lurk in the basement. *See also chapter* **Children.**

Eglise du St-Esprit

186 av Daumesnil, 12th (01.44.75.77.50). M° Daumesnil. **Open** 9.30am-noon, 3-7pm Mon-Fri; 9.30am-noon, 3-6pm Sat; from 9am Sun. **Map** p409 P9.

Behind the red-brick exterior cladding, this unusual 1920s concrete church follows a square plan around a central dome, lit by a scalloped ring of windows. Architect Paul Tournon was directly inspired by the Hagia Sofia cathedral in Istanbul, though rather than mosaics, the inside is decorated with frescos by Maurice Denis and others.

Musée des Arts Forains

53 av des Terroirs-de-France, 12th (01.43.40.16.22). M° Cour Saint-Emilion. **Open** groups only, by appointment. **Admission** €11.80; €3.85 concessions. **No credit cards. Map** p409 P10.

Housed in a collection of Eiffel-era iron-framed wine warehouses is a fantastical collection of 19th- and early 20th-century fairground attractions, all working and imaginatively enhanced. The venue is hired out for functions most evenings, and staff may well be setting the tables when you visit. Of the three halls the most wonderful is the Salon de la Musique, where a musical sculpture by Jacques Rémus chimes and flashes lights in time with the 1934 Mortier organ and a modern-day digital grand piano playing *Murder on the Orient Express*. In the Salon de Venise you will be twirled round on a gondola carrousel to 18th-century music, while in Salon des Arts Forains you can play a ball-throwing game that sets off a race of mustachioed waiters, and live out *Belleville Rendezvous* fantasies on the Vélocipède, a nightmarish carousel of penny-farthings. Open only to groups of 15 or more, the venue can be visited as an individual as part of a guided visit. Call ahead.

Parc de Bercy

rue de Bercy, 12th. M° Bercy or Cour St-Emilion. **Open** *Winter* 8am-5.30pm Mon-Fri; 9am-5.30pm Sat, Sun. *Summer* 8am-9pm Mon-Fri; 9am-9pm Sat, Sun. **Map** p409 N9/10.

Created in the 1990s, the Bercy park combines the French love of geometry with that of food. There's a large lawn and a grid with square rose, herb and vegetable plots, an orchard and gardens laid out to represent the four seasons.

La Promenade Plantée

av Daumesnil, 12th. M° Ledru-Rollin or Gare de Lyon. **Map** p409 M8/N8.

The railway tracks atop the Viaduc des Arts have been replaced by a promenade planted with roses, shrubs and rosemary, offering a high-level view into Parisian lives. It continues at ground level through the Jardin de Reuilly and the Jardin Charles Péguy on to the Bois de Vincennes in the east. Rollerbladers are banned, but no one seems to have noticed.

Le Viaduc des Arts

15-121 av Daumesnil, 12th (www.viaduc-des-arts.com). M° Ledru-Rollin or Gare de Lyon. **Map** p409 M8/N8.

Glass-fronted workshops poke out from the arches beneath the Promenade Plantée, providing a showroom for craftspeople, including furniture and fashion designers, picture-frame gilders, tapestry restorers, porcelain decorators, and chandelier, violin and flute makers. There's the late-opening Viaduc Café too. Design industry body VIA puts on exhibitions of contemporary work at Nos.29-35.

The Champs-Elysées & western Paris

In the 8th, 16th and 17th arrondissements.

While the 'Elysian Fields' can be a letdown on first, tourist-filled sight, the avenue remains the symbolic gathering place of a nation for sports victories, New Year's Eve and displays of military might on 14 July. At night, the head and tail lights of ten lanes of honking traffic form a continuous red-and-white ribbon.

Over the past decade, the Champs-Elysées has undergone a renaissance, thanks initially to the facelift – underground car parks and granite paving – instigated by Jacques Chirac. Chi-chi shops and chic hotels have set up in the 'golden

Sightseeing

Focus of national pride and celebration – the **Champs-Elysées**. *See p117*.

triangle' (avenues George-V, Montaigne and the Champs), including **Louis Vuitton** (*see p249*), **Chanel** (*see p247*), **Jean-Paul Gaultier** (*see p248*), **Ladurée** tearoom (*see p218*), **Marriott** (70 av des Champs-Elysées, 8th, 01.53.93.55.00) and **Pershing Hall** (*see p51*) hotels. The **Four Seasons George V** (*see p49*) has undergone a revamp, while fashionable restaurants such as Spoon, Food & Wine (14 rue de Marignan, 8th, 01.40.76.34.44) and Senso (16 rue de la Trémoille, 8th, 01.56.52.14.14), and nightspots like loungey **La Suite** (*see p328*) draw an affluent and screamingly fashionable pack. Crowds line up for the glitzy Lido cabaret (116bis avenue des Champs-Elysées, 8th, 01.40.76.56.10), the now commercialised **Queen** nightclub (*see p328*) and numerous cinemas, or stroll down the avenue to floodlit **place de la Concorde** (*see p94*). Just down from the **Arc de Triomphe**, locals stock up on late-night wines, magazines and groceries at **Drugstore Publicis** (*see p234*), founded by an advertising agency in the 1960s, and recently given a tacky cladding of swirly metal bars by American architect Michele Saee.

This great spine of western Paris started life as an extension to the Tuileries gardens, laid out by Le Nôtre in the 17th century. By the time of the Revolution, the avenue had reached its full stretch, but it was more Sunday stroll territory than thoroughfare. During the Second Empire the Champs-Elysées became a focus of fashionable society, military parades and royal

processions. Bismarck was so impressed when he arrived with the conquering Prussian army in 1871 that he had a replica, the Ku'damm, built in Berlin. Here smart residences and hotels sprung up along its upper half, together with streetlights, sideshows, concert halls, theatres and exhibition centres. Hitler's troops made a point of marching down it in 1940; as did their Allied counterparts four years later.

The lower, landscaped reach of the avenue hides behind it two theatres and haute cuisine restaurants Laurent (41 av Gabriel, 8th, 01.42.25.00.39) and Ledoyen (1 av Dutruit, 8th, 01.53.05.10.01), in fancy Napoléon III pavilions. At the Rond-Point des Champs-Elysées, Nos.7 (now the Artcurial gallery, bookshop and auction house) and 9 hint at the magnificent mansions that once lined the avenue. From here, it's platinum cards and stick-thin women only as avenue Montaigne rolls out a full deck of fashion houses: **Christian Dior**, **Chanel** (for both, *see p247*) and **Prada** (*see p249*); as well as Jil Sander (No.52, 8th, 01.44.95.06.70), Loewe (No.46, 8th, 01.53.57.92.50), Céline (No.36, 8th, 01.56.89.07.92), Calvin Klein (No.53, 8th, 01.56.88.12.12), Ungaro (No.2, 8th, 01.53.57.00.00) and more. Models and magnates nibble on the terrace at fashionable eaterie L'Avenue (No.41, 8th, 01.40.70.14.91). You can admire the lavish **Hôtel Plaza Athénée** (*see p50),* and Auguste Perret's quite innovative 1911-13 **Théâtre des Champs-Elysées** concert hall (*see p313*), a monument to the early 20th-century avant-garde with reliefs by Bourdelle, an auditorium painted by Maurice Denis and lights by Lalique. Since 1990 it has been topped by the sleek glass-fronted Maison Blanche restaurant (No.15, 8th, 01.47.23.55.99) with magnificent views across the Seine to the Eiffel Tower.

South of the avenue, the glass-domed **Grand Palais** and Petit Palais, both built for the 1900 Exposition Universelle and still used for major art exhibitions, create a magnificent vista across elaborate Pont Alexandre III to Les Invalides. Both emerged from hoardings after major renovations in 2005. At the bridge end of the Petit Palais, a bronze statue of Winston Churchill stomps along in an overcoat, while old rival Charles de Gaulle strides at the Champs-Elysées end of the Grand Palais. The rear wing of the Grand Palais opening on to av Franklin-D.-Roosevelt contains the **Palais de la Découverte** science museum.

To the north of the avenue lie smart shops, antiques dealers and officialdom. On circular place Beauvau wrought-iron gates herald the Ministry of the Interior. The 18th-century Palais de l'Elysée, the official presidential residence, is at 55-57 rue du Fbg-St-Honoré. Nearby, with gardens extending down to avenue Gabriel are the equally palatial British Embassy and adjoining ambassadorial residence, once the Hôtel Borghèse, where Napoléon's favourite sister Pauline lived from 1803 to 1815.

At the western end of the Champs-Elysées, the Arc de Triomphe towers above place Charles-de-Gaulle, also known as l'Etoile. Initially a project to glorify the victories of Napoléon, the giant triumphal arch was later modified to celebrate the Revolutionary armies. The square with its 12 avenues radiating out was commissioned later by Haussmann. From the top, gaze upon prize Paris real estate: the swanky mansions along the grassy verges of avenue Foch or the prestige office buildings of avenues Hoche and Wagram.

South of the Arc de Triomphe, avenue Kléber leads to the monumental buildings and terraced gardens of the Trocadéro, with views over the river to the Eiffel Tower. The vast symmetrical 1930s **Palais de Chaillot** dominates the hill and houses four museums plus the **Théâtre National de Chaillot** (*see p288*). Descending in terraces, Trocadéro's bronze and stone statues showered by powerful fountains form a dramatic ensemble with the backdrop of the Eiffel Tower and Champ de Mars. Across place du Trocadéro is the **Cimetière de Passy**.

To the west of Chaillot on av du Président-Wilson is the **Palais de Tokyo**, which houses on one side the **Musée d'Art Moderne de la Ville de Paris**, and on the other, the wacky

Palais de Tokyo Site de Création Contemporaine, which has injected new life into this area. By night the art world mixes with young professionals. Facing the Palais de Tokyo (although you enter from av Pierre-1er-de-Serbie) is the **Musée Galliera**, used for fashion exhibitions, while just up the hill at place d'Iéna are the fabulous Asian and oriental art collections of the **Musée National des Arts Asiatiques – Guimet**. Back towards the Champs-Elysées amid the grand 19th-century mansions around place des Etats-Unis, the lavish former townhouse of avant-garde patron Marie-Laure de Noailles has been given a cheeky renovation by Philippe Starck and contains the showroom, museum and **Le Cristal Room** restaurant (*see p189*) of the **Galerie-Musée Baccarat**.

Arc de Triomphe

pl Charles-de-Gaulle (access via underground passage), 8th (01.55.37.73.77). Mº Charles de Gaulle Etoile. **Open** 10am-10.30pm daily. *Apr-Sept* 10am-11pm daily. Closed public hols. **Admission** €8; €5 18-25s; free under-18s. **Credit** MC, V. **Map** p402 C3.

Napoléon ordered the arch's construction in 1809 as a monument to the triumph of the Republican armies, but almost immediately the empire he'd built began to collapse. The arch, 50m high and 45m wide, was only completed in 1836. Nonetheless it is carved with the names of Napoléon's victories, and decorated with a frieze of battle scenes and sculptures on its flanks, including Rude's celebrated *Le Départ des Volontaires* (or *La Marseillaise*). In 1840 Napoléon's ashes were carried under it on their way to Les Invalides; French troops finally got to march through it victoriously to celebrate the end of World War I; in 1921 France's Unknown Soldier was buried here. The annual Bastille Day military procession begins here (*see p275*). Manic drivers race around the square – use the underpass for a wonderful radial view atop the arch. **Photo** *p121*.

Cimetière de Passy

2 rue du Commandant-Schloesing, 16th (01.53.70.40.80). Mº Trocadéro. **Open** 8am-5.45pm Mon-Fri; 8.30am-5.45pm Sat; 9am-5.45pm Sun. **Map** p402 B5.

Since 1874 this has been considered one of the most elegant Paris places in which to be laid to rest. Here you'll find composers Debussy and Fauré, painters Manet and his sister-in-law Berthe Morisot, writer Giraudoux, and various generals and politicians.

Espace Paul Ricard

9 rue Royale, 8th (01.53.30.88.00/www.espacepaul ricard.com). Mº Concorde. **Open** 10am-7pm Mon-Fri. Closed public hols. **Admission** free. **Map** p403 F4.

The Pastis firm promotes modern art, notably with the Prix Paul Ricard – young French artists shortlisted by an independent curator for an annual prize – to coincide with FIAC (*see p276*) each autumn.

Fondation Mona Bismarck

34 av de New-York, 16th (01.47.23.38.88). M° Alma Marceau. **Open** 10.30am-6.30pm Tue-Sat. Closed Aug, public hols. **Admission** free. **Map** p402 C5.
The Fondation provides a chic setting for eclectic exhibitions from Etruscan antiquities to folk art.

Fondation Pierre Bergé
Yves Saint Laurent

3 rue Léonce-Reynaud, 16th (01.44.31.64.00/www. fondation-pb-ysl.net). M° Alma Marceau. **Open** for exhibitions Tue-Sun 11am-6pm. **Closed** Aug. **Admission** €5; €2.50 students, 11s-16s; free under-11s. **Credit** AmEx, MC, V. **Map** p402 D5.
When Yves Saint Laurent bowed out of designing in 2002, he reopened his fashion house as this foundation, exhibiting Picasso and Warhol paintings with the dresses they closely inspired. Every sketch and every *toile* have been carefully catalogued, and many of Saint Laurent's friends and clients have presented the designer with the dresses he created for them, all stored in the upper floors of the building at precisely 18 degrees centrigrade and a hygrometeric level of 50%.

Galerie-Musée Baccarat

11 pl des Etats-Unis, 16th (01.40.22.11.00/www. baccarat.fr). M° Iéna. **Open** 10am-7pm Mon, Wed-Sat. Closed public hols. **Admission** €7; €3.50 students. **No credit cards**. **Map** p402 C4.
It didn't take long for this fantastical showcase to make the itinerary of every fashion victim in town. Philippe Starck has created a neo-rococo wonderland in the old Musée Baccarat, the former mansion of socialite, the Vicomtesse de Noailles. From the red carpet entrance with a chandelier in a fish tank to the Alchemy room decorated by Gérard Garouste, there's a play of light and movement that makes Baccarat's work, past and present, sing. See items by great designers like Georges Chevalier and Ettore Sottsass, services made for princes and maharajahs, and monumental show-off items made for the great exhibitions of the 1800s. Le Cristal Room (*see p189*) restaurant has a two-month waiting list.

Galeries Nationales
du Grand Palais

3 av du Général-Eisenhower, 8th (01.44.13.17.17/ reservations 08.92.68.46.94/www.rmn.fr/galeries nationalesdugrandpalais). M° Champs-Elysées Clemenceau. **Open** 10am-8pm Mon, Thur-Sun; 10am-10pm Wed; pre-booking compulsory before 1pm. **Admission** *Before 1pm with reservation* €11.10. *After 1pm without reservation* €10; €8 18s-26s; free under-13s. **Credit** MC, V. **Map** p403 E5.
Built for the 1900 Exposition Universelle, the Grand Palais was the work of three different architects, each of whom designed a façade. During World War II it accommodated Nazi tanks. In 1994 the magnificent glass-roofed central hall was suddenly closed when bits of metal started falling off the roof, although exhibitions continued to be held in the other wings. The Palais reopened after a major

restoration project in 2005, henceforth under the management of the Réunion des Musées Nationaux, the national museums authority. Exhibition themes for 2006 include 'Rousseau and the urban jungle' and the Italian avant-garde between 1910 and 1950.

Palais de la Découverte

av Franklin-D.-Roosevelt, 8th (01.56.43.20.21/www. palais-decouverte.fr). M° Champs-Elysées Clemenceau or Franklin D. Roosevelt. **Open** 9.30am-6pm Tue-Sat; 10am-7pm Sun (last entry 30mins before). **Admission** €6.50; €4 5s-18s, over-60s, students under 26; free under-5s. *Planetarium* €3.50.
Credit AmEx, MC, V. **Map** p403 E5.
The city's original science museum houses designs dating from Leonardo da Vinci's time to the present day. Models, real apparatus and audio-visual material manage to bring displays to life, while the permanent exhibits cover astrophysics, astronomy, biology, chemistry, physics and earth sciences. The pertinent Planète Terre section highlights the latest developments in meteorology, while one room is dedicated to the sun. There are shows at the Planetarium, too, and 'live' experiments (at weekends and during school holidays), ranging from the effect of pesticides to electrostatics. Exhibition themes for 2006 include light and – complete with high-end animatronics – dinosaurs.

Musée d'Art Moderne
de la Ville de Paris

11 av du Président-Wilson, 16th (01.53.67.40.00/ www.paris.fr/musees/MAMVP). M° Iéna or Alma Marceau. **Open** Set to reopen Jan 2006. **Open** noon-8pm Tue-Sun. **Admission** €4.50; €2.50 13s-25s; free under-13s. **No credit cards**. **Map** p408 H7.
The monumental 1930s building that houses the city's own modern art collection was, at the time of going to press, due to reopen in January 2006 with a Pierre Bonnard exhibition. The museum is particularly strong on the Cubists, Fauves, the Delaunays, Rouault, Schwitters and Ecole de Paris artists Soutine, Modigliani and Van Dongen.

Musée de la Contrefaçon

16 rue de la Faisanderie, 16th (01.56.26.14.00/ www.museedelacontrefacon.com). M° Porte Dauphine. **Open** 2-5.30pm Tue-Sun. Closed most public hols. **Admission** €4; free under-12s.
No credit cards. **Map** p402 A4.
This small museum was set up by the French anti-counterfeiting association with the aim of deterring forgers – but playing spot-the-fake with brands like Reebok, Lacoste and Vuitton is fun for visitors, too.

Musée Dapper

35bis rue Paul-Valéry, 16th (01.45.00.01.50/ www.dapper.com.fr). M° Victor Hugo. **Open** 11am-7pm Wed-Sun. Closed some public hols. **Admission** €5; €2.50 students, 16s-25s; free under-16s. **Credit** MC, V. **Map** p402 B4.
A specialist museum named after the 17th-century Dutch humanist Olfert Dapper, the Fondation Dapper began in 1983 as an organisation dedicated

Probably the city's second most recognisable monument: the **Arc de Triomphe**. *See p119.*

to preserving sub-Saharan art. Reopened in 2000, the new Alain Moatti-designed museum includes a performance space, bookshop and café. The exhibition space houses two themed exhibitions each year on Africa and the African diaspora; the performance space welcomes African musicians and storytellers.

Musée Galliera

10 av Pierre-1er-de-Serbie, 16th (01.56.52.86.00). M° Iéna. **Open** for exhibitions 10am-6pm Tue-Sun. Closed Mon, public hols. **Admission** (incl audioguide) €7.50; €5 over-60s; €3.50 14-26s; free under-13s. **Credit** MC, V. **Map** p402 D5.
This comprehensive look at clothes through history takes an academic approach to its subject. Housed in a *hôtel particulier* built by Eiffel, the Galliera has a huge costume collection: 1,300 garments from the 18th century alone. It has links with the industry, and its initiative with young designers shows examples of innovative work the moment it hits the shops.

Musée National des Arts Asiatiques – Guimet

6 pl d'Iéna, 16th (01.56.52.53.00/www.musee guimet.fr). M° Iéna. **Open** 10am-6pm (last entry 5.30pm) Mon, Wed-Sun. **Admission** €6; €4 students, 18-25s, Sun; free under-18s, 1st Sun of mth; CM. **Credit** *Shop* AmEx, MC, V. **Map** p402 C5.

Founded by Lyonnais industrialist Emile Guimet in 1889 to house his collection of Chinese and Japanese religious art, and later incorporating the oriental collections from the Louvre, the expanded Musée Guimet has 45,000 objects from Neolithic times on, in a voyage to Asia that conveys the flow of religions and civilisations. Lower galleries focus on India and South-east Asia, centred on the stunning collection of Hindu and Buddhist Khmer sculpture from Cambodia. You can't miss the vast Giant's Way, part of the entrance to a temple complex at Angkor Wat. Upstairs, Chinese antiquities include mysterious jade discs and an elephant-shaped Shang dynasty bronze pot. Afghan glassware, Tibetan mandalas and Moghul jewellery also feature. **Photo** *p122.*

Palais de Chaillot

pl du Trocadéro, 16th. M° Trocadéro. **Map** p402 C5.
Looming across the river from the Eiffel Tower, the immense pseudo-classical Palais de Chaillot was constructed by Azéma, Boileau and Carlu for the 1937 international exhibition, with giant sculptures of *Apollo* by Henri Bouchard and *Hercules* by Albert Pommier and inscriptions by Paul Valéry. Ironically, it stands on the foundations of an earlier complex put up for the 1878 World Fair. With two sweeping symmetrical wings astride the central esplanade, it

was home until 2005 to the Cinémathèque cinema (*see p294* **'thèque five**) and still houses the Musée de la Marine (*see below*) and what's left of the Musée de l'Homme in the western wing (*see below*). It is still staging temporary exhibitions while the ethnology and anthropology sections are in storage awaiting the new museum at quai Branly (*see p152* **Chirac's grand projet**). In the east wing are the Théâtre National de Chaillot, and the ex-Musée des Monuments Historiques, to open late in 2006 as the Cité de l'Architecture.

Musée de la Marine

Palais de Chaillot, pl du Trocadéro, 16th (01.53.65.69.69/www.musee-marine.fr). M° *Trocadéro.* **Open** 10am-6pm Mon, Wed-Sun. Closed public hols. **Admission** €9; €7 under-25s, over-60s; €3.85 6s-18s; free under-6s, CM, under-18s to main collection. **Credit** *Shop* MC, V. **Map** p402 B5.
French naval history is outlined in detailed models of battleships and Vernet's series of paintings of French ports (1754-65). There's also an imperial barge, built when Napoléon's delusions of grandeur were reaching their zenith in 1810. **Photo** *p134.*

Musée de l'Homme

Palais de Chaillot, 17 pl du Trocadéro, 16th (01.44.05.72.72/www.mnhn.fr). M° Trocadéro. **Open** 9.45am-5.15pm Mon, Wed-Fri; 10am-6.30pm Sat, Sun, most public hols. **Admission** €7; €5 concessions; €3 under-16s. **Credit** *Shop* MC, V. **Map** p402 B5.

Eastern promise: **Musée Guimet**. *See p121.*

The human department of the Muséum National d'Histoire Naturelle (*see p146*) considers human evolution, genetic diversity and the reasons and consequences of the population explosion. The prehistoric department covers from 3.7 million years ago to the Bronze Age with artefacts including the skeleton of Lucy and the skull of the Man of Tautavel. The subjects for temporary exhibitions here in 2006 include Birth and Treasure.

Palais de Tokyo: Site de Création Contemporaine

13 av du Président-Wilson, 16th (01.47.23.54.01/ 01.47.23.38.86/www.palaisdetokyo. com). M° Iéna or Alma Marceau. **Open** noon-midnight Tue-Sun. **Admission** €6; free under-18s, art students. **Map** p402 B5.
Curators Nicolas Bourriaud and Jérôme Sans' fresh approach has managed to secure the future of this contemporary art 'laboratory' for another three years. When it opened in 2002, many thought the stripped-back interior with visible air-conditioning and lighting gubbins was a statement. In fact, it was a practical answer to tight finances, but the 1937 building has come into its own as an open-plan space with a skylit central hall, permitting the co-existence of exhibitions and installations, fashion shows and performances. The extensive opening hours and funky café have succeeded in drawing a younger audience, and the roll call of artists is impressive (Pierre Joseph, Frank Scurti, Wang Du and others). Although the name dates back to the 1937 Exposition Internationale, it links in with a new generation of artists from the Far East.

Monceau & Batignolles

Parc Monceau, with its neo-Antique follies and large lily pond, lies at the far end of avenue Hoche (the main entrance is on boulevard de Courcelles, the circular pavilion by Ledoux). Three museums capture the extravagance of the area when it was newly fashionable in the 19th century: the **Musée Jacquemart-André**, with its magnificent collection of old masters; **Musée Nissim de Camondo** (superb 18th-century decorative arts); and **Musée Cernuschi** (all kinds of Chinese art). There are some nice exotic touches, too, such as the unlikely red lacquer Galerie Ching Tsai Too (48 rue de Courcelles, 8th), built in 1926 for a dealer in oriental art near the fancy wrought-iron gates of Parc Monceau, or the onion domes of the Russian Orthodox **Alexander Nevsky Cathedral** on rue Daru. Built in the mid 19th century when a stay in Paris was essential to the education of every Russian aristocrat, it is still at the heart of an émigré little Russia.

Famed for its stand during the 1871 Paris Commune, the Quartier des Batignolles to the north-east towards place de Clichy is more working class, with the lively rue de Lévis street market, tenements lining the deep railway canyon and the attractive square des Batignolles park with the pretty Eglise Ste-Marie-de-Batignolles overlooking a small semi-circular square. It is fast becoming fashionable, with an equally developing restaurant scene. On rue des Dames are the Eldorado hotel (No.18, 17th, 01.45.22.35.21), the cool **Lush** bar (*see p219*) and trendy bathroom shop SBR (No.29, 17th, 01.43.87.88.00).

Alexander Nevsky Cathedral

12 rue Daru, 17th (01.42.27.37.34). M° Courcelles. **Open** varies. **Map** p402 D3.
The edifice has enough onion domes, icons and incense to make you think you were in Moscow. This Russian Orthodox church was built 1859-61 in the neo-Byzantine Novgorod-style of the 1600s, by the tsar's architect Kouzmin, who was also responsible for the Fine Arts Academy in St Petersburg. Services, on Sunday mornings and Orthodox saints' days, are in Russian.

Cimetière des Batignolles

rue St-Just, 17th (01.53.06.38.68). M° Porte de Clichy. **Open** 8am-5.35pm Mon-Fri; 8.30am-5.35pm Sat; 9am-5.30pm Sun.
Squeezed inside the Périphérique are the graves of poet Paul Verlaine, Surrealist André Breton, and Léon Bakst, costume designer of the Ballets Russes.

Musée Cernuschi

7 av Velasquez, 8th (01.45.63.50.75/www.paris.fr/ musees). M° Villiers or Monceau. **Open** 10am-6pm Tue-Sun. Closed public hols. **Admission** free. **Map** p403 E2.
Since banker and Republican Henri Cernuschi built a *hôtel particulier* by the Parc Monceau for the treasures he found in the Far East in 1871, the collection has grown steadily: it now ranks as the fifth most important collection of Chinese art in Europe. The museum has been expanded to twice its size, and was reopened in 2005 with a total exhibition area of 3,200sq m and 1,000 exhibits – an increase of 300 over the previous line-up. The fabulous displays range from legions of Han and Wei dynasty funeral statues to refined Tang celadon wares and Sung porcelain. An exhibition of Chinese erotic painting runs until 7 May 2006.

Musée Jacquemart-André

158 bd Haussmann, 8th (01.45.62.11.59/www. musee-jacquemart-andre.com). M° Miromesnil or St-Philippe du-Roule. **Open** 10am-6pm daily. **Admission** €9.50; €7 7s-17s, students; free under-7s. **Credit** AmEx, MC, V. **Map** p403 E3.
The collection built by Edouard André and his wife Nélie Jacquemart – and the mansion they built to house it – are magnificent, and worth visiting for their illustration of life among the 19th-century haute bourgeoisie alone. On the ground floor are the circular Grand Salon, rooms of tapestries and French

furniture, Boucher mythological fantasies, library (with Dutch paintings including Rembrandts), the smoking room hung with English portraits, and the polychrome marble winter garden with double spiral staircase. On the stairway three Tiepolo frescos from the Villa Contarini depict the arrival of Henri III in Venice. Upstairs, what was to have been Nélie's studio became their 'Italian museum', a splendid early Renaissance collection that includes Uccello's *St George and the Dragon*, Mantegna's *Ecce Homo*, a superb Schiavone portrait, a Carpaccio panel and Della Robbia terracottas; even the tearoom has a Tiepolo ceiling. The free audio guide is useful.

Musée Nissim de Camondo

63 rue de Monceau, 8th (01.53.89.06.40/www. ucad.fr). M° Villiers or Monceau. **Open** 10am-5pm Wed-Sun. **Admission** €6; €4.50 18s-25s; free under-18s; CM. Closed some public hols. **Credit** AmEx, MC, V. **Map** p403 E3.
Put together by Count Moïse de Camondo, this collection is named after his son Nissim, killed in World War I. Moïse replaced the family's two houses near Parc Monceau with this palatial residence and lived here in a style in keeping with his love of the 18th century. Grand first-floor reception rooms are filled with furniture by leading craftsmen of the Louis XV and XVI eras, huge silver services and vast services of Sèvres and Meissen porcelain, Savonnerie carpets and Aubusson tapestries.

Parc Monceau

bd de Courcelles, av Hoche, rue Monceau, 8th. M° Monceau. **Open** *Nov-Mar* 7am-8pm daily. *Apr-Oct* 7am-10pm daily. **Map** p403 E2.
Surrounded by grand *hôtels particuliers* and elegant Haussmannian apartments, Monceau is a favourite with well-dressed children and their nannies. It was laid out in the late 18th century for the Duc de Chartres in the then fashionable English style, with an oval lake, spacious lawns and a variety of follies: an Egyptian pyramid, a Corinthian colonnade, Venetian bridge and sarcophagi. **Photo** *p126*.

Passy & Auteuil

To the west of l'Etoile, the extensive 16th arrondissement is the one that probably suffers the most from prejudices and preconceptions. This is an area of grandiose apartments and exclusive residences hidden down private roads, yet beyond its bourgeois respectability, it hides some seminal pieces of modernist architecture – and some of the city's most important museums.

When **Balzac** lived at 47 rue Raynouard in the 1840s, Passy was a country village where a fashionable clientele came to take cures for anaemia at its mineral springs – a name reflected in the rue des Eaux. The village – along with nearby Auteuil – was absorbed into the city with the annexation of 1860. Beyond the Maison de Balzac, at Nos.51-55, is the apartment building and former design offices by avant-garde architect August Perret in his material of predilection, reinforced concrete. The **Musée du Vin** is of interest if only for its atmospheric setting in the vaulted cellars of the wine-producing Abbaye de Minimes destroyed in the Revolution. Rue de Passy, formerly the village high street, and parallel rue de l'Assomption, are the focus of local life with fashion shops and *traiteurs*, the revamped department store Franck et Fils (80 rue de Passy, 16th, 01.42.15.00.37) and an upmarket covered market. The former Passy station is now La Gare restaurant (19 chaussée de la Muette, 16th, 01.42.15.15.31), ladies who shop watch from the lovely art deco La Rotonde café (12 chaussée de la Muette, 16th, 01.45.24.45.45)

or stack up on cakes at Japanese *pâtisserie* Yamakasi (6 chaussée de la Muette), while a nearby curiosity are three wooden dachas on Villa Beauséjour, constructed by Russian craftsmen for the 1867 Exposition Universelle and rebuilt here.

West of the Jardin du Ranelagh (originally high-society pleasure gardens, modelled on the endearingly bawdy 18th-century London version) is the Impressionist draw the **Musée Marmottan**, featuring a fabulous collection of Monet's late water-lily canvases, other Impressionists and Empire furniture.

Next to the Pont de Grenelle stands the circular **Maison de Radio-France**, the giant Orwellian home to the state broadcasting bureaucracy. Opened in 1963, it's a constant reminder of the pivotal role that the state still

Paris against the clock

You've got a mere 48 hours – or maybe 36, or perhaps only 24 – to spend in the city of light. As well as the must-do-must-see list – the Eiffel Tower, Notre-Dame, Arc de Triomphe, the Louvre, the Musée d'Orsay, the Sacré-Coeur – there are some other delights worth squeezing into a swift *séjour*. Here are a few ideas.

Day one

A delicious croissant is an vital Paris rite of passage. Start the day with mouthfuls of crispy, buttery flakes and soft, squishy dough – in other words, ideally, a croissant from **Au Levain du Marais** (32 rue de Turenne, 3rd), an easy stroll from the magnificent 17th-century place des Vosges. Sip an espresso at one of several cafés that face the square.

Now for a look at a bit more of the Marais. Traditionally the Jewish quarter, it's abuzz with culture, retail and bars. Many of its beautiful *hôtels particuliers* – old aristocratic mansions – now house important cultural institutions like the **Musée Carnavalet** (*see p110*), **Musée National Picasso** (*see p111*) and **Maison Européene de la Photographie** (*see p113*). Boutique safarists, meanwhile, will find joy in the streets leading off the main shopping thoroughfare of rue des Francs-Bourgeois. The area is also an enclave of contemporary art galleries and, particularly around rue Vieille-du-Temple, a thriving bar scene, both straight and gay.

There are several unsung panoramas in Paris. The **Institut du Monde Arabe** (*see p145*), a behemoth glass building designed by French superstar architect Jean Nouvel, has a fine collection of Middle Eastern art and a rooftop café with fabulous views looking down the Seine. Clambering up to the small temple that marks the summit of the **Parc des Buttes-Chaumont** (*see p136*) shows beautifully landscaped swaths of green below, and miles of city beyond. Save **Sacré-Coeur** (*see p129*) for dusk, when the tourists have largely departed and the night lights have begun to smoulder.

Meander along the stone quays that border the Seine and leaf through old *revues* and tatty paperbacks at the riverside *bouquiniste* stalls (*see p242*), which are folded away into their iconic green boxes at night. From the quays you can either hop on a sightseeing boat, or pause to explore the islands. The **Mémorial des Martyrs de la Déportation** (*see p77*) on the Ile de la Cité is an undervisited tribute to the people deported to concentration camps during World War II. On the Ile St-Louis, the deliciousness of the ice-cream from **Berthillon** (31 rue St-Louis-en-l'Ile, 4th, 01.43.54.31.61) is no secret; if the weather's warm you'll have to queue. We recommend the *cassis* (blackcurrant) flavour.

Evenings start with aperitifs. Join the sociable crowd on the terrace seats at **Le Bar du Marché** (*see p230*) and watch the Left Bank people-traffic pass by over a kir, served by one of the eccentric, dungaree-wearing waiters. And now you're almost certainly in the mood for a little nocturnal plays in people's lives. You can attend concerts (*see p311*) or take guided tours around its endless corridors; employees nickname the place 'Alphaville', after the Jean-Luc Godard film. From here, in more upmarket Auteuil, you can head up rue Fontaine, the best place to find art nouveau architecture by Hector Guimard, of métro entrance fame. Despite extravagant iron balconies, **Castel Béranger** at No.14 was originally low-rent lodgings; Guimard designed outside and in, right down to the wallpaper and stoves. He also designed the less ambitious Nos.19, 21 and tiny Café Antoine at No.17. The long neglected Hôtel Mezzara at No.60 has recently been renovated and is sometimes open for exhibitions. Pay literary homage at No.96 where Marcel Proust was born. Guimard lived in the house he built at 122 avenue Mozart.

Nearby around the métro station Jasmin is Le Corbusier territory. The **Fondation Le Corbusier** occupies a couple of his avant-garde houses in square du Dr-Blanche. A little further up rue du Dr-Blanche, rue Mallet-Stevens is almost entirely made up of refined houses by Robert Mallet-Stevens, while sculptor Henri Bouchard himself commissioned the studio and house that is now the endearingly dusty **Atelier-Musée Bouchard**. Much of the rest of Auteuil is firmly private territory with exclusive streets of residences off rue Chardon-Lagache, although you can still find somewhat more villagey bits around the Eglise d'Auteuil; the studio of 19th-century sculptor Jean-Baptiste Carpeaux also remains, looking rather lost, at 39 boulevard Exelmans. The top storey was later added by Guimard.

Sightseeing

revelry. Cross the river for the **Rex** nightclub (*see p325*) for an electronica blowout. Post-dancefloor hunger pangs can be satiated at welcoming Les Halles bistro **La Poule au Pot** (10 rue de Vauvilliers, 1st, 01.42.36.32.96), which thoughtfully stays open until 6am. Near the Champs, **La Maison de l'Aubrac** (37 rue Marbeuf, 8th, 01.43.59.05.14) is a bonhomie-filled outpost of the Auvergne, grilling *côte du boeuf* to perfection until 7am, every day of the week. Finish your *nuit blanche* in style with a coffee at gorgeous art deco brasserie **Le Vaudeville** (29 rue Vivienne, 2nd, 01.40.20.04.62), which opens its doors from 7am.

Day two

Cross the Pont des Arts and head south through the narrow Left Bank streets to St-Sulpice church, then stroll to the **Jardin du Luxembourg** (*see p153*), pull up two green chairs (this is the accepted protocol – you need the extra one as a footrest) and size up the park life: children sailing toy boats past the ducks on the central pond, tai chi groups doing bizarre stretches and old timers playing unhurried chess. The adjacent museum, the **Musée National du Luxembourg** (*see p153*), hosts world-class art exhibitions – Botticelli, Modigliani and so on.

Amble along the tree-lined **Canal St-Martin**, crossing from side to side over its romantic green bridges, to explore the little shops and gently buzzing bars that have made this an up-and-coming area. On Sundays, traffic

is outlawed from the quai de Valmy and the bar-lined quai de Jemmapes, replaced by streams of in-line skaters, cyclists and baby buggies. Boutiques such as princessy outfitter **Stella Cadente** (93 quai Valmy, 10th, 01.42.09.27.00) and kitsch merchants **Antoine et Lili** (*see p250*) are both open on Sundays. For coffee and a slice of chocolate cake, try wood-floored, chandeliered café **Le Sporting** (3 rue des Récollets, 10th, 01.46.07.02.00); for a swift *demi* that you can drink by the water, go for friendly bar **Le Jemmapes** (*see p227*).

Modern art lovers should make a point of visiting the superb collection at the **Musée de l'Art Moderne de la Ville de Paris** (*see p120*), which is neighbour to contemporary art space the **Palais de Tokyo** (*see p122*). From here you can walk to the Champs-Elysées and make a nighttime hike up the Arc de Triomphe to see the lit avenue stretching into the city.

As a parting gesture, sink into a comfy Chesterfield and relax with an expertly shaken cocktail at the classy neo-colonial **China Club** (*see p224*). Cigar and cigarette smokers can wallow in the fug of the *fumoir* upstairs.

WEEKEND TRAVEL TIPS

Buy a *carnet* of ten tickets (€10) if you're staying for less than two days; for long weekends it's worth investing in a *coupon hebdomadaire*, or weekly pass, for €14.50. You can use these tickets on the métro, RER and buses.

Classic elegance: **Parc Monceau**. *See p123.*

West of the 16th, across the Périphérique, sprawls the **Bois de Boulogne**, a royal hunting reserve turned park that includes a boating lake and cycle paths. At Porte d'Auteuil are the romantic **Serres d'Auteuil** and sports venues the **Parc des Princes** (*see p329*), home of flagship football club **Paris St-Germain** (*see p329*), and **Roland Garros** (*see p329*), host of the French tennis open.

Atelier-Musée Henri Bouchard

25 rue de l'Yvette, 16th (01.46.47.63.46/ www.musee-bouchard.com). M° Jasmin. **Open** 2-7pm Wed, Sat. Closed last 2wks Mar, June, Sept & Dec. **Admission** €4; €2.50 students under-26; free under-6s. **No credit cards**.
Sculptor Henri Bouchard had this house and studio built in 1924. Tended by his son, his dusty workroom, crammed with sculptures, sketchbooks and tools, gives an idea of the official art of his day. He began with Realist-style peasants and maidens, but around 1907 adopted a pared-down, linear style, as seen in his reliefs for the Eglise St-Jean-de-Chaillot and the monumental Apollo at the Palais de Chaillot.

Bois de Boulogne

16th. M° Porte Dauphine or Les Sablons.
Covering 865 hectares, the Bois was the old Forêt de Rouvray hunting grounds. It was landscaped in the 1860s, when romantic artificial grottos and waterfalls were created around the Lac Inférieur. The Jardin de Bagatelle (route de Sèvres à Neuilly, 16th, 01.40.67.97.00) is famous for its roses, daffodils and water lilies and contains an orangery that rings to the sound of tinkling Chopin in summer. The Jardin d'Acclimatation is a children's amusement park (*see p285*). The Bois also boasts two racecourses (Longchamp and Auteuil; *see p330*), sports clubs and stables, the Musée National des Arts et Traditions Populaires and restaurants, including the haute cuisine of Le Pré Catelan (route de Suresnes, 16th, 01.44.14.41.14).

Today there are plans to reduce the traffic and replant some of the scrubby woodland. Boats can be rented on the Lac Inférieur and there's cycle hire nearby. Crowded at weekends with romancing picnickers and dog walkers, at night the Bois is transformed into a parade ground for transsexuals and swingers of every stripe.

Castel Béranger

14 rue La Fontaine, 16th. M° Jasmin. Closed to the general public.
Guimard's masterpiece of 1895-98 epitomises art nouveau in Paris. Here you can see his love of brick and wrought iron, asymmetry and renunciation of harsh angles not found in nature. Along with the whiplash motifs characteristic of art nouveau, there are still many signs of Guimard's earlier taste for fantasy and the medieval: green seahorses climb the façade, and the faces on the balconies are thought to be a self-portrait, inspired by Japanese figures, to ward off evil spirits.

Fondation Le Corbusier

Villa La Roche, 8-10 square du Dr-Blanche, 16th (01.42.88.41.53/www.fondationlecorbusier.fr). M° Jasmin. **Open** 1.30-6pm Mon; 10am-12.30pm, 1.30-6pm Tue-Thur; 10am-12.30pm, 1.30-5pm Fri. Closed Aug. **Admission** €2.50; €1.50 13-18s; free under-12s. **No credit cards**.
This house, designed by Le Corbusier in 1923 for a Swiss art collector, shows the visionary architect's ideas in practice with its stilts, strip windows, roof terraces and balconies, built-in furniture and an unsuspected use of colour inside: sludge green, blue and pinky beige. Sculptural cylindrical staircase and split volumes create a variety of geometrical vistas, while inside is decked out with Corb and Perriand's furniture and Corb's own neo-Cubist paintings. The adjoining Villa Jeanneret, designed by Le Corbusier for his brother, houses the foundation's library.

Le Jardin des Serres d'Auteuil

3 av de la Porte d'Auteuil, 16th (01.40.71.75.23). M° Porte d'Auteuil. **Open** *Winter* 10am-5pm daily. *Summer* 10am-6pm daily. **Admission** €1; €3 during exhibitions. **No credit cards**.

These romantic glasshouses were opened in 1895 to cultivate plants for Parisian parks and public spaces. Today there are seasonal displays of orchids and begonias. Look out for the steamy tropical pavilion with palms, birds and Japanese ornamental carp.

Maison de Balzac

47 rue Raynouard, 16th (01.55.74.41.80/www. paris.fr/musees). M° Passy. **Open** 10am-6pm Tue-Sun. Closed public hols. **Admission** free. **Credit** MC, V. **Map** p406 B6.

Honoré de Balzac rented an apartment at this very address in 1840 to escape his creditors and quickly established a password to sift friends from bailiffs. Since converted into a museum, this collection of objects relating to his life and work is spread over several floors, and although the displays are rather dry, the garden gives an idea of the villas that lined this street when Passy was a chic spa in the 19th century. Memorabilia includes first editions, letters, proofs, portraits of friends and the novelist's mistress Mme Hanska, with whom he corresponded for years before marrying her – plus a 'family tree' of Balzac's characters that extends across several walls. You can see his desk and the monogrammed coffee pot that fuelled all-night work on his sprawling *Comédie Humaine*.

Musée Marmottan – Claude Monet

2 rue Louis-Boilly, 16th (01.44.96.50.33/www. marmottan.com). M° La Muette. **Open** 10am-6pm Tue-Sun (last entry 5.30pm). **Admission** €7; €4.50 8-25s; free under-8s. **Credit** MC, V.

Originally a museum of the Empire period left to the state by collector Paul Marmottan, this old hunting pavilion has become a famed holder of Impressionist art thanks to two bequests: the first by the daughter of the doctor of Manet, Monet, Pissaro, Sisley and Renoir; the second by Monet's son Michel. Its Monet collection, the largest in the world, numbers 165 – including the seminal *Impression Soleil Levant* – plus sketchbooks, palette and photos. A special circular room was created for the breathtaking series of late water lily canvases; upstairs are works by Renoir, Manet, Gauguin, Caillebotte and Berthe Morisot, 15th-century primitives, the Wildenstein collection of medieval manuscripts, a Sèvres clock and a collection of First Empire furniture.

Musée de Radio-France

Maison de Radio France, 116 av du Président-Kennedy, 16th (01.56.40.15.16/01.56.40.21.80/ www.tourisme.fr/radio-france). M° Ranelagh or Passy/RER Kennedy Radio France. **Open** *Guided tours* 10.30-11am, 2.30pm, 4pm Mon-Fri. **Admission** €5; €3 concessions. **No credit cards**. **Map** p406 A7.

Audio-visual history is presented with an emphasis on French pioneers such as Edouard Branly and Charles Cros, including documentary evidence of the first radio message transmitted between the Eiffel Tower and the Pantheon. Look out also for the London broadcast of the Free French carried out in delightfully obscure coded messages.

Musée du Vin

rue des Eaux, 16th (01.45.25.63.26/www.musee duvinparis.com). M° Passy. **Open** 10am-6pm Tue-Sun. **Admission** (with guidebook and glass of wine) €8; €7 over-60s; €5.70 students; free under-14s, diners in the restaurant. **Credit** *Shop, restaurant* AmEx, DC, MC, V. **Map** p406 B6.

Here the Confrères Bacchiques defend French wines from imports and advertising laws. In the cellars of an old wine-producing monastery are displays on the history of viticulture with waxwork peasants, old tools, bottles and corkscrews. Visits finish with a wine tasting and, a paid extra, a meal.

Montmartre & Pigalle

In the 9th and 18th arrondissements.

Montmartre, the highest point in the whole city, resembles some perched southern hill village, with its tight-packed houses spiralling up round the mound underneath the sugary-white oversized dome of **Sacré-Coeur**. Despite the onslaught of tourists, it is surprisingly easy to leave them all behind and to fall under the spell of the most unabashedly romantic district of Paris. Climb and descend quiet stairways, peer into little alleys, ivy-covered houses and deserted squares, and explore streets like rue des Abbesses, rue des Trois-Frères and rue des Martyrs with their cafés, quirky boutiques and young, arty community.

For centuries, Montmartre was a tranquil, windmill-packed village. When Haussmann sliced through the city centre, working-class families started to move out and peasant migrants poured into an industrialising Paris from across France. Montmartre swelled. The hill was absorbed into the city of Paris in 1860, but remained fiercely independent, and its role in the Paris Commune in 1871, when the Montmartrois fended off the government troops of Adolphe Thiers, is marked by a plaque on rue du Chevalier-de-la-Barre.

Artists moved into the area from the 1880s. Renoir found subject matter in the cafés and *guinguettes*. Toulouse-Lautrec patronised its bars and immortalised its cabarets in posters; later it was frequented by Picasso and artists of the Ecole de Paris, Utrillo and Modigliani.

The best starting point is the Abbesses métro station, one of only two in Paris (along with Porte Dauphine) to retain its original art nouveau metal-and-glass awning designed by Hector Guimard. Across place des Abbesses as you emerge from the dark depths of the station is the art nouveau church of St-Jean-de-Montmartre, a pioneering reinforced concrete structure behind the brick, studded with turquoise mosaics around the door. Along rue des Abbesses and adjoining rue Lepic, which winds its way up the hill, are many excellent

Gaudy, glorious, unignorable **Sacré Coeur**.

food shops, wine merchants, cafés, including popular **Le Sancerre** (*see p219*), and offbeat boutiques. The famous **Studio 28** cinema (*see p295*), opened in 1928, is where Buñuel's controversial Surrealist classic *L'Age d'Or* had its riotous première in 1930. It has a dinky bar.

In the other direction from Abbesses, at 11 rue Yvonne-Le-Tac, is the Chapelle du Martyr where, according to legend, St Denis picked up his head after his execution by the Romans in the third century (hence the name Montmartre – martyr's mount; *see also p11*). Rue Orsel, with a typically Montmartrois cluster of retro design, ethnic and second-hand clothes shops, leads to place Charles-Dullin where cafés overlook the respected Théâtre de l'Atelier (1 pl Charles-Dullin, 18th, 01.46.06.49.24).

Up the hill, the cafés of rue des Trois-Frères are popular for an evening drink. The street leads into sloping place Emile-Goudeau, whose staircases, wrought-iron streetlights and old houses are particularly evocative. The Bateau Lavoir, a piano factory that stood at No.13, witnessed the birth of Cubism. Divided into a warren of studios in the 1890s for impoverished artists of the day, it was here that Picasso painted *Les Demoiselles d'Avignon* in 1906-07, when he, Braque and Juan Gris all happened to be residents. The building burned down in 1970 but has since been reconstructed. On rue Lepic, which winds up the hill from rue des Abbesses, are the village's two remaining windmills: the Moulin du Radet, moved here in the 17th century from its hillock in rue des Moulins near the Palais-Royal; and the Moulin de la Galette, site of the celebrated dancehall famously depicted by Renoir (now in the Musée d'Orsay; *see p158*) and today a restaurant. Vincent Van Gogh and his beloved brother Theo resided at No.54 from 1886 to 1888.

On tourist-swamped place du Tertre at the top of the hill, portrait painters compete to sketch you or flog lurid sunset views of Paris; nearby Espace Dali (11 rue Poulbot, 18th, 01.42.64.40.10) offers a slightly more illustrious alternative. Round here, according to legend, the word 'bistro' was born in the early 1800s at the restaurant La Mère Catherine when Russian soldiers shouted '*Bistro!*' ('Quickly!') to be served. Just off the square is the oldest church in the district, St-Pierre-de-Montmartre, whose columns have grown bent with age. Founded by Louis VI in 1133, it is a fine example of early Gothic, and a contrast to its extravagant neighbour, the basilica of Sacré-Coeur.

For all its kitsch and swarms of tourists, though, Sacré-Coeur is well worth the visit for its sheer 19th-century excess. Rather than the main steps, take the staircase down rue Maurice-Utrillo to pause on a café terrace on the small square at the top of rue Muller, or wander down through the adjoining park to the Halle St-Pierre. The former covered market is now used for exhibitions of naïve art, but the surrounding square and streets, known as the Marché St-Pierre, are packed with fabric shops, laden with rolls of material, and a great source of discounted bin ends.

On the north side of place du Tertre in rue Cortot is the quiet 17th-century manor, which today houses the **Musée de Montmartre**, dedicated to the neighbourhood and its former famous inhabitants. Dufy, Renoir and Utrillo all used to have studios in the entrance pavilion. Nearby in rue des Saules is the Montmartre vineyard, planted by local artist Poulbot in 1933 in commemoration of the vines that once covered the area. The grape picking here every autumn is a much-loved local ritual celebrated with great pomp.

Further down the hill, amid rustic, shuttered houses, is **Au Lapin Agile** cabaret (*see p279*). This old meeting point for local artists got its name from André Gill, who painted the inn sign of a rabbit (lapin A. Gill). Singers still churn out nostalgia here today.

A series of pretty squares leads to rue Caulaincourt, crossing the ravine of the oddly romantic **Cimetière de Montmartre** (enter on avenue Rachel, reached by staircase from rue Caulaincourt or place de Clichy). Winding down the back of the hill, avenue Junot is lined with exclusive residences, such as the avant-garde house built by Adolf Loos for Dadaist poet Tristan Tzara at No.15, exemplifying his Modernist maxim: 'Ornament is crime'.

Cimetière de Montmartre

20 av Rachel, access by stairs from rue Caulaincourt, 18th (01.53.42.36.30). M° Blanche. **Open** *6 Nov-15 Mar* 8am-5.30pm Mon-Fri, 8.30am-5.30pm Sat; 9am-5.30pm Sun & public hols. *16 Mar-5 Nov* 8am-6pm Mon-Fri; 8.30am-6pm Sat; 9am-6pm Sun & public hols. **Map** p405 G1.
You stumble over the famous and infamous here: Truffaut, Nijinsky, Berlioz, Degas, Offenbach, German poet Heine and Surrealist painter Victor Brauner are all buried here. Also La Goulue, the first great cancan star and model for Toulouse-Lautrec, celebrated local beauty Mme Récamier, and the consumptive heroine Alphonsine Plessis, inspiration for Dumas' *La Dame aux Camélias* and Verdi's *La Traviata*. Flowers and messages are still left daily for Egyptian pop diva and gay icon Dalida, who lived on nearby rue d'Orchampt.

Musée d'Art Halle St-Pierre

2 rue Ronsard, 18th (01.42.58.72.89/www.hallesaint pierre.org). M° Anvers. **Open** 10am-6pm daily. Closed Aug. **Admission** €7; €5.50 students, 4s-26s; free under-4s. **Credit** Shop AmEx, MC, V. **Map** p404 J2.
The former covered market in the shadow of Sacré-Coeur specialises in *art brut*, *art outsider* and *art sin-gulier* from its own and other collections. The exhibitions programme for 2006 includes a show of Australian 'outsider art' (until July).

Musée de Montmartre

12 rue Cortot, 18th (01.46.06.61.11/www.museede montmartre.com). M° Lamarck Caulaincourt. **Open** 10am-6pm Tue-Sun. **Admission** €5.50; €3.50 students, over-60s; free under-10s. **Credit** *Shop* MC, V. **Map** p404 H1.
At the back of a garden, this 17th-century manor shows the history of the historic hilltop, with rooms devoted to revolutionary Louise Michel, composer Gustave Charpentier, the porcelain factory at Clignancourt, and a tribute to the Lapin Agile cabaret, with original Toulouse-Lautrec posters. There are paintings by Suzanne Valadon, who had a studio above the entrance pavilion, as did Renoir, Raoul Dufy and Valadon's son Maurice Utrillo.

Sacré-Coeur

35 rue du Chevalier-de-la-Barre, 18th (01.53.41.89.00). M° Abbesses or Anvers. **Open** *Basilica* 6am-10.30pm daily. *Crypt & dome Winter* 10am-5.45pm daily. *Summer* 9am-6.45pm daily. **Admission** free; *crypt & dome* €5. **Credit** MC, V. **Map** p404 J1.
Commissioned as an act of penance after the nation's defeat by the Prussians in 1870, voted by the Assemblée Nationale and financed from public subscription, work began on this enormous mock Romano-Byzantine edifice in 1877. It was finished in 1914 and consecrated in 1919, by which time a jumble of architects had succeeded Paul Abadie, winner of the original competition. The interior is lavishly adorned with gaudy neo-Byzantine mosaics. There's a fantastic view from the dome – although at the time of going to press, both crypt and dome were closed to the public in the wake of the July 2005 bomb attacks in London. **Photo** *left.*

Pigalle

Pigalle has long been the sleaze centre of Paris, but that may be changing. A recent police blitz, instigated in response to increased tourist rip-offs and rough-ups, has shooed away the streetwalkers and many an erotic cabaret, peep show and go-go bar with them. While locals bemoan the sanitising of their atmospherically seedy neighbourhood, the recent relandscaping of boulevards de Clichy and de Rochechouart looks set to continue the clean up.

In the 1890s Toulouse-Lautrec's posters of Jane Avril at the Divan Japonais, Le Chat Noir, the Moulin Rouge, and of *chansonnier* Aristide Bruant, immortalised the area's cabarets and the art of advertising. At the end of the 19th century, of the 58 houses on rue des Martyrs, 25 were cabarets (a few, such as the drag shows Michou and Madame Arthur, remain today); others were *maisons closes*. But it's still a pretty cool street: Le Divan Japonais is now **Le Divan du Monde** (*see p316*), club and music venue; a hip crowd packs into **La Fourmi** (*see p219*) across the street, and up the hill there's a cluster of *atelier*-boutiques where designers have set up their sewing machines at the back of the shop. Along the boulevard, behind its bright red windmill, the **Moulin Rouge**, once the image of naughty 1890s Paris, is now a cheesy tourist draw. Its befeathered dancers still cancan across the stage but are no substitute for La Goulue and Joseph Pujol – *le pétomane* who could pass wind melodically. In stark contrast is the Cité Véron next door, a cobbled alley with curlicue iron entrance sign, a small theatre and cottagey buildings, among them 6bis where writer and jazz musician Boris Vian lived between 1953 and 1958. The famous **Elysée**

Paris promenade Cemetery greats

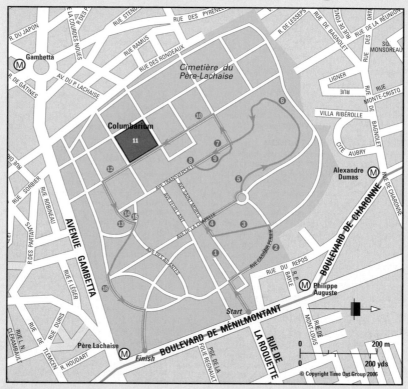
Père-Lachaise cemetery (*see p136*) has as starry a line-up of illustrious corpses as anywhere in the world. Here lie Delacroix, Proust, Bizet – in fact almost anyone French, talented and dead that you care to mention. Not even French, for that matter. Creed and nationality have never prevented entry – you just had to have lived or died in Paris or have an allotted space in a family tomb.

It was opened after the Terror of the 1790s, when the city's graveyards were full. The state passed a law to buy land for cemeteries and created a large out-of-town alternative, the Cimetière de l'Est. Later named after the Jesuit Père de La Chaise, Louis XIV's confessor who lived on this estate, it was designed by Alexandre Brongniart as a public park and cemetery, a green and pleasant place in which Parisians could wander and ponder.

But people wanted to be buried where they had lived, in their native *quartiers*, and snubbed the new project. In a bid to gain popularity, the presumed remains of medieval lovers Abélard and Héloïse were moved here in 1817, along with those of Molière and La Fontaine. In next to no time, great ceremonial burials became the norm, and thousands of trees were cut down to make space for new graves: Sarah Bernhardt, Ingres, Balzac, Chopin, Colette, Edith Piaf and more.

Space and demand mean it's not easy to buy eternal rest. Since 2003, leases for ten, 30 and 50 years have been introduced, in addition to existing leases that are *temporaires* (about a century) and *perpetuelles* (until abandoned). Of the one million originally buried here, only 200,000 have enjoyed uninterrupted slumber. Some

500 graves a year are classified 'abandoned', either no longer visited and/or fallen into dangerous disrepair. Walk the labyrinthine cobbled alleys and avenues, and you'll see ashen layers of pollution, decrepit masonry, slowly disappearing epitaphs and tree roots clamped over gravestones. While this adds to the mystery, such an incredible reliquary cannot be left to decay. With the bicentennial of the cemetery in 2004, its preservation policy came under review. On the agenda is the revival of Brongniart's '*jardin-cimetière*' concept, with new plantings and fewer fellings.

So when should you visit Père Lachaise? The quiet early mornings can be magical, especially in spring, when the white chesnut blossoms come out; a late sunny September afternoon can have its special moments, too. Luckily, for all its two million annual visitors, Père-Lachaise is too sprawling to ever be bustling. This is a place for *flâneurs*: allow at least a morning or an afternoon.

Finding a particular grave can be tricky without a map. Requests for information from the entry guards will be met with a shrug, so buy a €2 map from the hawkers at the Père Lachaise métro entrance or from shops nearby – or follow our pocket-sized tour of some of the headline headstones.

Start at the main entrance, opposite rue de la Roquette, and proceed up the hill to the first major crossroads. If you're not in a hurry, walk a short way further to see the tomb of former president **Félix Faure** (❶ *See p99* **Scandale!**); otherwise, turn right onto the avenue du Puits. After 150 metres, step off to the right to peruse the mausoleum of **Abélard and Héloïse** (❷ *See p13* **Love hurts**), a neo-Gothic pavillion that shelters their tomb, topped with recumbent stone effigies.

Return to the main path and walk on, looking out on your left for a mausoleum marked 'Sépulture de Bence'; take the left-hand path immediately after it and walk on another 100m. Ahead of you on the right, invariably festooned with flowers, is the pristine tomb of **Chopin** (❸), with its medallion portrait of the composer and the muse of Music, head bowed in mourning, on top. Chopin's heart is buried in Warsaw.

Where the path joins another running across it, turn right, ascend a short flight of steps and turn right again. Almost immediately, on the right, is the last resting place of painter **Géricault** (❹), whose best-known canvas,

The Raft of the Medusa – now in the Louvre – is replicated here in bronze bas relief; Géricault himself, palette and brush at the ready, reclines in a languourous pose (surely he didn't paint like this?) above it.

Continue along the path to the roundabout and take the first exit (avenue des Acacias). A few steps along, on the right, is the grave – in apt obelisk form, fenced in with low iron railings – of the great Egyptologist **Jean-François Champollion** (❺), who first deciphered hieroglypics. Keep going. You'll pass the grave of **Nadar** (❻), real name Félix Tournachon, pioneer of photography and 19th-century man-about-town, and, some 250m further on, the **Sépulture Greffulhe** (❼) on the right, a neo-Gothic mausoleum the size of a small house – one of the first to be built (in 1810) in the cemetery. A further 75m or so brings you to two ground-level stones (❽), both covered in flowers, candles and handwritten notes. The first belongs to French crooner **Gilbert Bécaud**, who died in 2001; the second is that of actress **Marie Trintignant**, killed by her lover Bertrand Cantat (singer with rock band Noir Désir). Her burial in 2003 was the biggest media event here since Edith Piaf moved in 40 years before.

Now turn around, cross over and take the left-hand path, chemin Laplace, on the other side. After a short way you come to another pair of famous neighbours (❾), **La Fontaine** and **Molière**, who knew each other in real life and now share the same fenced-off plot. Next, take a left after the green sign, cross the main path again, and mount to the right of the water tap. Walk 100m to the crossroads and turn left.

Next up is **Victor Noir** (❿), a journalist shot in 1870, aged 22, by Napoléon's cousin Prince Pierre. He rests underneath a bronze likeness by Dalou; its groin is rubbed so often by women hoping to conceive that it gleams. A good walk further on, after the **Colombarium** (⓫), is the plain black grave of Proust (⓫); carrying on to the crossroads and turning left will bring you to more literary luminaries, namely **Balzac** (⓬) and, directly opposite, **Gérard de Nerval** (⓭), who hanged himself from a lamp-post in 1855. At the next junction, a short detour left will bring you to **Delacroix** (⓮). From here, it's a gentle curving walk downhill to the exit, via the eccentric-looking bust on the grave of cinema pioneer **Georges Méliès** (⓯).

Montmartre belle-époque music hall today programmes an eclectic array of music concerts (*see p316*) and cool club nights, but the **Folies Pigalle** nightspot (*see p323*) still retains undeniable Pigalle flavour with its after-parties and drag queens.

Musée de l'Erotisme

72 bd de Clichy, 18th (01.42.58.28.73/www.erotic museum.com). M° Blanche. **Open** 10am-2am daily. **Admission** €7; €5 students. **Credit** MC, V. **Map** p403 H2.

Seven floors of erotic art and artefacts amassed by collectors Alain Plumey and Joseph Khalif. The first three run from first-century Peruvian phallic pottery through Etruscan fertility symbols to Yoni sculptures from Nepal; the fourth gives a history of Paris brothels; and the recently refurbished top floors host exhibitions of modern erotic art. In the basement you'll find titillations like a vagina dinner plate.

La Nouvelle Athènes

Just south of Pigalle and east of the rue Blanche lies this mysterious, often overlooked quarter dubbed the New Athens when colonised by quantities of artists, writers and composers in the early 19th century. Long-forgotten actresses and demi-mondaines had mansions built here and some of the prettiest can be found in tiny rue de la Tour-des-Dames, which refers to one of the many windmills owned by the once-prosperous Couvent des Abbesses. Wander through the adjoining streets and passageways to glimpse further angles of these miniature palaces, especially on rue St-Lazare (painter Paul Delaroche lived in the Italianate house at No.58) and rue de La Rochefoucauld.

Just off rue Taitbout stands square d'Orléans, a remarkable housing estate built in 1829 by English architect Edward Cresy. This ensemble of flats and artists' studios attracted the glitterati of the day, including George Sand and her lover Chopin. In the house originally built for Dutch painter Ary Scheffer in nearby rue Chaptal, the **Musée de la Vie Romantique** displays the writer's mementoes.

The **Musée Gustave Moreau** on rue de La Rochefoucauld, meanwhile, is reason enough for a visit, featuring the artist's cramped apartment and magnificent studio. Fragments of bohemia can still be gleaned in the area, although the Café La Roche, where Moreau would meet Degas for drinks and more, has been downsized to La Joconde (57 rue Notre-Dame-de-Lorette, 9th, 01.48.74.10.38). Degas painted most of his memorable ballet scenes round the corner in rue Frochot and Renoir hired his first decent studio at 35 rue St-Georges. A few streets away in Cité Pigalle, a collection of studios, is Van Gogh's last Paris house (No.5), from where he moved to

Auvers-sur-Oise. There is a plaque here, but nothing on the building in rue Pigalle where Toulouse-Lautrec sat and drank himself to death in 1903.

The area round the neo-classical Eglise Notre-Dame-de-Lorette, built in the form of a Greek temple, was built up in Louis-Philippe's reign and was famous for its courtesans or *lorettes*, elegant young ladies named after their haunt of rue Notre-Dame-de-Lorette. From 1844 to 1857, Delacroix had his studio at No.58 (by No.56, where Gauguin was born in 1848). The painter later moved to place de Furstenberg in the 6th (now **Musée Delacroix**). Rue St-Lazare still contains some delightfully old-fashioned shops and bistros, including perfumier **Détaille 1905** (*see p237*), and bistro **Chez Jean** (*see p193*). The lower stretch of rue des Martyrs is packed with food shops, while a little further up the hill look out for the prosperous residences of the Cité Malesherbes and avenue Trudaine. Place Gustave-Toudouze contains tearoom Tea Folies (No.6, 9th, 01.42.80.08.44) and the No Stress café (No.2, 9th, 01.48.78.00.27), and glorious circular place St-Georges was home to the true Empress of Napoléon III's Paris: the notorious Madame Païva. She lived in the neo-Renaissance No.28, thought to be outrageous at the time of its construction. 'La Païva' shot herself in the head following the termination of her passionate love affair with the millionaire cousin of Chancellor Otto von Bismarck.

Musée Gustave Moreau

14 rue de La Rochefoucauld, 9th (01.48.74.38.50/ www.musee-moreau.fr). M° Trinité. **Open** 10am-12.45pm, 2-5.15pm Mon, Wed-Sun. Closed Tue. **Admission** €4; €2.60 18s-25s, Sun; free under-18s; CM. **Credit** MC, V. **Map** p403 G3.

A wonderful private museum, this combines the small private apartment of Symbolist painter Gustave Moreau (1825-98) with the vast two-floor gallery he built to display his work – set out as a museum by the painter himself. Downstairs shows his obsessive collector's nature with family portraits, Grand Tour souvenirs and a boudoir devoted to the object of his unrequited love, Alexandrine Durem. Upstairs is his fantasy realm, which plunders Greek mythology and biblical scenes for canvases filled with writhing maidens, trance-like visages, mystical beasts and strange plants. Printed on boards that you can carry around are Moreau's lengthy, rhetorical and mad commentaries. Don't miss the trippy masterpiece *Jupiter et Sémélé* on the second floor.

Musée de la Vie Romantique

16 rue Chaptal, 9th (01.55.31.95.67/www.paris.fr/ musees). M° Blanche or St-Georges. **Open** 10am-6pm Tue-Sun. Closed public hols. **Admission** free. *Exhibitions* €7; €5.50 18s-26s; €3.80 14s-18s; free under-14s. **Credit** AmEx, DC, MC, V. **Map** p403 G2.

When Dutch artist Ary Scheffer lived in this villa, this area south of Pigalle was home to so many composers, writers and artists, it was known as 'New Athens'. Aurore Dupin, Baronne Dudevant (George Sand) was a guest at Scheffer's soirées, and many other great names crossed the threshold, including Chopin, Delacroix and Liszt. The museum has a lovely rose garden and tearoom, but Sand fans will be disappointed: the watercolours, lockets and jewels she left behind reveal little of her ideas or affairs.

La Goutte d'Or

For a less orthodox Paris experience, head for Barbès Rochechouart métro station and the area north of it. Zola used it as a backdrop for *L'Assommoir*, his novel set among the district's laundries and absinthe cafés. Today heroin has replaced absinthe as the means of escape.

Primarily an African and Arab neighbourhood, La Goutte d'Or can seem like a colourful slice of Africa or a state under perpetual siege due to the frequent police raids. Down rue Doudeauville, you'll find African music shops, while rue Polonceau contains African grocers and Senegalese restaurants. Mayor Delanöe has tried to attract young designers to the area by designating rue des Gardes 'rue de la mode', while square Léon is the focus for **La Goutte d'Or en Fête** in June (*see p275*), which brings together local musicians. Some of them, such as Africando and the Orchestre National de Barbès, have become well known across Paris. There is a lively street market under the métro tracks (Mon, Wed, Sat morning) along boulevard de la Chapelle, with stalls of exotic vegetables and rolls of African fabrics.

On the northern edge of the city at Porte de Clignancourt is the city's largest flea market, the **Marché aux Puces de St-Ouen.**

North-east Paris

In the 10th, 11th, 19th and 20th arrondissements.
Gigantic place de la République stands like a frontier between the old aristocratic Marais and the more proletarian north-east, an area in transition with charming areas abreast grotty, dodgy ones, and modern housing developments beside relics from the old villages of La Villette, Belleville, Ménilmontant and Charonne.

Canal St-Martin to La Villette

Canal St-Martin, built 1805-25, begins at the Seine at Pont Morland – where there's a small marina at Port de l'Arsenal – disappears underground at Bastille, hides under boulevard Richard-Lenoir, then re-emerges after crossing rue du Faubourg-du-Temple, east of place de la République. Faubourg-du-Temple itself, once the country lane that led to Belleville, is scruffy and cosmopolitan, lined with cheap grocers and everything-for-one-euro stores, a number of surprising hidden courtyards and colourful stalwarts of Paris nightlife: **Le Gibus** (*see p325*), lively Brazilian bar-restaurant **Favela Chic** (18 rue du Fbg-du-Temple, 11th, 01.40.21.38.14), the vintage dancehall **La Java** (*see p326*), as well as the Palais des Glaces (No.37, 10th, 01.42.02.27.17), which programmes seasons of French comics.

The first stretch of the canal lined with shady trees and crossed by iron footbridges and locks has the most appeal. The canal is a favourite spot with local families on Sunday when the quays are traffic-free. Many of the remaining canalside warehouses have been snapped up by artists and designers or turned into loft apartments and the *quais* and nearby streets have been colonised by trendy bars. You can take a boat up the canal as far as La Villette.

East of here, the Hôpital St-Louis (main entrance rue Bichat) was commissioned in 1607 by Henri IV to house plague victims, and was built as a series of isolated pavilions in the brick-and-stone style as **place des Vosges** (*see p112*), far enough from the town to prevent risk of infection. Behind the hospital, the rue de la Grange-aux-Belles housed the infamous Montfaucon gibbet, put up in 1233, where victims were hanged and left to the elements. Today the street contains music cafés **Chez Adel** (*see p317*) and L'Apostrophe (No.23, 10th, 01.42.08.26.07). East of the hospital, delightful

Canal St-Martin.

To dive for: **Musée de la Marine**. *See p122.*

cobbled rue Ste-Marthe and place Ste-Marthe have a provincial air, busy at night with multiethnic restaurants and cafés Le Panier (32 pl Ste-Marthe, 10th, 01.42.01.38.18) and the Sainte-Marthe (32 pl Ste-Marthe, 10th, 01.44.84.36.96).

To the north is the Parti Communiste Français, on the place du Colonel-Fabien, a surrealist, curved glass curtain wall raised off the ground on a concrete wing, built in 1968-71 by Brazilian architect Oscar Niemeyer with Paul Chemetov and Jean Deroche. The canal disappears briefly again under place de Stalingrad, one of Paris' dodgiest districts by night. The square was landscaped in 1989 to showcase the Rotonde de La Villette, one of Ledoux's grandiose 1780s toll houses that once marked the boundary of Paris and now houses exhibitions and archaeological finds. Here the canal widens into Bassin de La Villette, and the new developments along the quai de Loire and further quai de la Marne, as well as some of the worst of 1960s and '70s housing in the colossal blocks that stretch along rue de Flandres. At 104 rue d'Aubervilliers the old Pompes Funèbres – former municipal undertaker – is being turned into a multimedia art space, and is scheduled to open towards the end of 2006.

At the eastern end of the basin is an unusual 1885 hydraulic lifting bridge, Pont de Crimée. Thursday and Sunday mornings add vitality with a canalside market at place de Joinville.

East of here, the Canal de l'Ourcq (created in 1813 to provide drinking water, as well as for freight haulage) divides: Canal St-Denis runs north through St-Denis towards the Seine, Canal de l'Ourcq continues through La Villette and suburbs east. Long the city's main abattoir district, still reflected in the Grande Halle de La Villette and by some of the old meaty brasseries along boulevard de La Villette, the neighbourhood has been revitalised since the late 1980s by the postmodern **Parc de La Villette** leisure and education complex with the **Cité des Sciences et de l'Industrie** science museum (also incorporating the **Cité des Enfants**; *see p283*), the **Cité de la Musique** concert hall (*see p310 and p318*), and its eclectic programme of ethnic music, jazz and classical events.

La Cité des Sciences et de l'Industrie

La Villette, 30 av Corentin-Cariou, 19th (01.40.05.80.00/08.92.69.70.72/www.cite-sciences.fr). M° Porte de la Villette. **Open** 10am-6pm Tue-Sat; 10am-7pm Sun. Closed public holidays. **Admission** €7.50; €5.50 7s-16s, students under 25, over-60s; free under-7s; CM. **Credit** MC, V. **Map** p405 (inset).

The ultra-modern science museum at La Villette pulls in five million visitors every year. Explora, the permanent show, occupies the upper two floors, whisking visitors through 30,000sq m of space, life, matter and communication, where scale models of satellites including the Ariane space shuttle, planes and robots make for an exciting journey. Experience weightlessness in the section devoted to the conquest of space. In the Espace Images, try out the delayed camera and other optical illusions, draw 3D images on a computer or lend your voice to the *Mona Lisa*. The hothouse garden investigates futuristic developments in agriculture and bio-technology. The lower floors host temporary exhibitions; the Cité des Enfants runs workshops for children. *See also chapter* **Children**).

Musée de la Musique

Cité de la Musique, 221 av Jean-Jaurès, 19th (01.44.84.44.84/www.cite-musique.fr). M° Porte de Pantin. **Open** noon-6pm Tue-Sat; 10am-6pm Sun. Closed public hols. **Admission** €6.10; €4.57 18-25s; €2.29 6-18s; free under-6s, over-60s; CM. **Credit** MC, V. **Map** p405 (inset).

Alongside the concert hall, the innovative music museum houses a gleamingly restored collection of instruments from the old Conservatoire, interactive computers and scale models of opera houses and concert halls. On arrival you are supplied with an audio guide in a choice of languages. The musical commentary is a joy, playing the appropriate instrument as you approach each exhibit. Alongside the trumpeting brass, curly woodwind instruments and precious strings are more unusual items, such as the

Indonesian gamelan orchestra, whose sounds influenced the work of Debussy and Ravel. Some of the concerts in the museum's amphitheatre use historic instruments from the collection. A major exhibition on John Lennon runs until 26 June 2006.

Parc de La Villette

av Corentin-Cariou, 19th (01.40.03.75.03). M° Porte de La Villette/av Jean-Jaurès, 19th. M° Porte de Pantin. **Map** p405 inset.

La Villette's programmes range from avant-garde music to avant-garde circus. Once the city's main cattle market and abattoir, it was to be replaced by a high-tech slaughterhouse but instead was transformed into the Cité des Sciences et de l'Industrie, a futuristic, interactive science museum. Outside you'll find the shining, spherical La Géode IMAX cinema (*see p292*) and the Argonaute submarine. Dotted with red pavilions or *folies*, the park itself designed by Swiss architect Bernard Tschumi is a postmodern feast (guided tours 08.03.30.63.06, 3pm Sun in summer). The *folies* serve as glorious giant climbing frames, as well as a first-aid post, burger bar and children's art centre. Kids shoot down a Chinese dragon slide and an undulating suspended path follows the Canal de l'Ourcq. As well as the big lawns, which are used for an open-air film festival in summer, there are ten themed gardens bearing evocative names such as the Garden of Mirrors, of Mists, of Acrobatics and of Childhood Horrors (all this can be terribly spooky if you lose your way en route to the Cabaret Sauvage circus or nightclub venue; *see p280 and p328*). South of the canal are the Zénith (*see p314*), used for rock concerts and the Grande Halle de La Villette – remnant of the former cattle market – now used for trade fairs, exhibitions and September's Villette Jazz Festival (*see p276*). It is winged by the Conservatoire de la Musique music school and the Cité de la Musique, wonderfully designed by Christian de Portzamparc, with its concert halls, rehearsal rooms and the Musée de la Musique (*see above*).

Belleville, Ménilmontant & Charonne

When the city boundaries were expanded in 1860, Ménilmontant, Belleville and Charonne, once villages that kept the capital supplied with wine and fruit and where Parisians would escape at weekends, were all absorbed. They were built up with housing for migrants, first from rural France and later from former French colonies in North Africa and South-east Asia. The main tourist attraction is **Père-Lachaise** cemetery, but the area also encompasses one of the city's most beautiful parks, the romantic **Buttes-Chaumont**. Despite clever attempts to dissipate workers' agitation by splitting the village between the 11th, 19th and 20th administrative arrondissements, Belleville became the

centre of opposition to the Second Empire. Cabarets, artisans and workers typified 1890s Belleville; colonised by artists in the 1990s and a centre of counter-culture, now Belleville is becoming a trendy hangout.

On boulevard de Belleville, Chinese and Vietnamese shops rub up against Muslim and kosher groceries, couscous and falafel eateries, and there's a busy street market on Tuesday and Friday mornings. Legend has it that Edith Piaf was born on the pavement outside 72 rue de Belleville, as commemorated on the plaque: 'On the steps of this house was born on the 19 December 1915, in the greatest poverty, Edith Piaf, whose voice would later move the world'. Aficionados run the nearby appointment-only **Musée Edith Piaf**, a modest two-room museum full of her memorabilia.

North of here, along avenue Simon-Bolivar, is the romantically landscaped Parc des Buttes-Chaumont. This is the most des-res part of north-east Paris with Haussmannian apartments overlooking the park and to the east, near place de Rhin-et-Danube, a small area of tiny, hilly streets lined with small houses and gardens, known by locals as the Quartier Mouzaïa. The gallery space **Le Plateau** (*see p297*) a short walk south of the park attracts contemporary art aficionados.

Up on the slopes of the Hauts de Belleville, there are picturesque old stairways and views from rue Piat and rue des Envierges, which lead to the modern but charming Parc de Belleville with its Maison des Vents devoted to birds and kites. Below the park, rue Ramponneau mixes new housing and relics of old Belleville. At No.23 an old smithy has been transformed into La Forge, an artists' squat, many of them members of La Bellevilloise association, which is trying to save the area from redevelopment and preserve its original charm.

Mesnil-Montant used to be a few houses on a hill with vines and fruit trees, then came the bistros, bordellos and workers' housing. It became part of Paris in 1860 along with Belleville and shares a similar history. These days it's a thriving centre of alternative Paris, as artists and young professionals have moved in. Boulevard de Ménilmontant divides this trendy nightlife quarter from the cemetery of Père-Lachaise. While side streets still display male-only North African cafés, rue Oberkampf is home to some of the city's most humming bars, many following the runaway success of the pivotal Café Charbon (*see p226 and p220* **Paris promenade**).

The area mixes 1960s and 1970s monster housing projects with older dwellings, some gentrified, some derelict. Just below rue des Pyrénées, which cuts through the 20th

Sightseeing

arrondissement, you can rummage around the rustic Cité Leroy or Villa l'Ermitage, cobbled cul-de-sacs of little houses and gardens, and old craft workshops. Rue de l'Ermitage has a curious neo-Gothic house at No.19 – and a bird's eye view from the junction with rue de Ménilmontant, right down the hill to the Centre Pompidou and Tour St-Jacques. Across on rue Boyer, the **Maroquinerie** (*see p316*) puts on an eclectic cultural programme of literary events, political debate and live music, and at 88 rue de Ménilmontant, graffiti-covered art squat La Miroiterie opens house for art shows and the *magasin gratuit*, a free swap shop.

East of Père-Lachaise on rue de Bagnolet, La Flèche d'Or, a converted station on the Petite Ceinture railway line, is a landmark bar and music establishment recently reopened after an overhaul. Nearby Le Gambetta (8 place Gambetta, 20th, 01.46.36.83.02) provides more of the same formula with its party crowd and live music. Just beyond, medieval **Eglise St-Germain-de-Charonne** is at the heart of what is left of the village of Charonne. Sitting at the top of a flight of stairs next to its presbytery, below a hill that was once covered with vines, it is the city's only church, apart from St-Pierre-de-Montmartre, still to have its own graveyard.

Below here, centred on the old village high street of rue St-Blaise, is a prettified backwater of quiet tearooms and bistros, such as Le Damier (No.29, 20th, 01.43.72.16.95) and Café Noir (No.15, 20th, 01.40.09.75.80), where old shops have since been taken over by art classes. Place des Grès, once the location of the public pillory where rough justice was meted out to thieves, and nearby renovated houses and modest garden squares, form a pristine village fragment before the grim housing estates lower down the street and a humungous tower block on rue Vitruve.

Towards Porte de Bagnolet, where rue de Bagnolet and rue des Balkans meet on the edge of a small park, the Pavillon de l'Hermitage is a small aristocratic relic built in the 1720s for Françoise-Marie de Bourbon, the daughter of Louis XIV, when it was in the grounds of the Château de Bagnolet. A little further south at Porte de Montreuil, cross the Périphérique for the Puces de Montreuil flea market.

Cimetière du Père-Lachaise

bd de Ménilmontant, 20th (01.55.25.82.10). M° Père-Lachaise. **Open** *6 Nov-15 Mar* 8am-5.30pm Mon-Fri; 8.30am-5.30pm Sat; 9am-5.30pm Sun & public hols. *16 Mar-5 Nov* 8am-6pm Mon-Fri; 8.30am-6pm Sat; 9am-6pm Sun & public hols. **Map** p409 P5.
Oscar Wilde, Colette and Edith Piaf reside among the thousands of tombs in the city's enormous main cemetery. *See p130* **Paris promenade**.

Eglise St-Germain-de-Charonne

pl St-Blaise, 20th (01.43.71.42.04). M° Porte de Bagnolet. **Open** varies.
The old village church of Charonne dates mainly from the 15th century, though one massive column and the belltower remain from an earlier structure. The interior is almost square with a triple nave and a simple organ loft. Two side altars have striking modern paintings (a crucifixion and a pietà) by Paul Rambié; a niche contains a wood statue of St Blaise.

Musée Edith Piaf

5 rue Crespin-du-Gast, 11th (01.43.55.52.72). M° Ménilmontant. **Open** by appointment 1-6pm Mon-Wed; 9am-noon Thur (call 2 days ahead). Closed June, Sept. **Admission** donation. **No credit cards**. **Map** p405 N5.
The association Les Amis d'Edith Piaf runs this tiny two-room museum in the heart of the singer's old stomping ground. The Little Sparrow's little black dress and tiny shoes are touching, and letters and photos provide a personal touch. There's a sculpture of her by Suzanne Blistène, wife of Marcel, who produced most of Piaf's films.

Musée du Fumeur

7 rue Pache, 11th (01.46.59.05.51/www.museedu fumeur.net). M° Voltaire. **Open** 1-7pm Tue-Sat; 12.30-7.30pm Sun. **Admission** free. **Map** p409 N6.
If an organic café in a museum about smoking is strange, the Musée du Fumeur relates to nature. 'Fumer moins et fumer mieux,' is the philosophy of enthusiastic director Monsieur Tigrane: smoking has lost touch with its purpose as an aid to religious or philosophical contemplation. Here you'll find obscure smoking contraptions and their history and different tobacco strains in the 'plantarium'. Relax at the end of your tour with a plant-based cocktail in the air-conditioned café.

Parc des Buttes-Chaumont

rue Botzaris, rue Manin, rue de Crimée, 19th. M° Buttes Chaumont. **Open** *Oct-Apr* 7am-8.15pm daily. *May, mid Aug-end Sept* 7am-9.15pm daily. *June-mid Aug* 7am-10.15pm daily. **Map** p409 N2.
With its meandering paths and vertical cliffs, this lovely park was designed by Adolphe Alphand for Haussmann in the 1860s. A former gypsum quarry, tip and public gibbet, waterfalls now cascade out of a man-made cave, which even has its own fake stalactites. A bridge (cheerfully named the Pont des Suicides) crosses the lake to an island crowned by a mini-temple. Always popular with kids (*see p284*).

Le Plateau

rue des Alouettes, 19th (01.53.19.84.10/www. fracidf-leplateau.com). M° Buttes Chaumont. **Open** 2-7pm Wed-Fri; 11am-7pm Sat-Sun. **Admission** free.
This modern art space has become the low-budget challenger to the Palais de Tokyo. Born out of a campaign for an arts centre in north-east Paris, the small exhibition space addresses the diversity of current art practice with installations, painting, photography, experimental cinema, music and dance.

The Left Bank

Chi-chi pockets amid the academic, literary and political institutions.

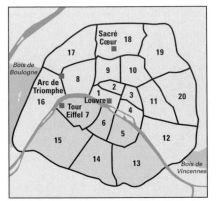

The Latin Quarter

In the 5th arrondissement.

The university quarter since medieval times, the Latin Quarter abounds in fine churches, wonky ancient buildings, studenty bars and learning or learned institutions. Despite the rocketing prices of flats, it still has a distinctly intellectual edge. It got its name from the use of Latin as the common language among students who came here from all over Europe in the Middle Ages, but it could just as well refer to the vestiges of Roman Lutetia, of which it was the heart. The first two Roman streets ran where rue St-Jacques (later the pilgrims' route to Compostela) and rue Cujas run today; the forum was probably underneath rue Soufflot. The area has the city's most important Roman remains: the Cluny baths, now part of the **Musée National du Moyen Age**, and the **Arènes de Lutèce** amphitheatre (*see p145*).

Quartier de la Huchette

The boulevard St-Michel, at one time synonymous with student rebellion, is now a ribbon of fast-food giants and shoe and clothing shops, though **Gibert Joseph** and **Gibert Jeune** (for both, *see p243*) continue to furnish books and stationery to students. East of here, the semi-pedestrianised Quartier de la Huchette has retained much of its medieval street plan. Rue de la Huchette and rue de la Harpe are now best known for their kebabs and pizzas, though

if you look past the Turks and tavernas there are 18th-century wrought-iron balconies and carved masks in the latter street. At the tiny **Théâtre de la Huchette** (*see p340*), Ionesco's absurdist drama *La Cantatrice Chauve* ('The Bald Soprano') has been playing continuously since 1957, with some of its original cast. Also of interest are rue du Chat-qui-Pêche, supposedly the city's narrowest street, and rue de la Parcheminerie, named after the parchment sellers and copyists who once lived here. Amid the tourist paraphernalia (and usually fringed by a row of tramps) stands the city's most charming medieval church, the **Eglise St-Séverin**, with leering gargoyles, spiky gabled side chapels and an exuberantly vaulted Flamboyant Gothic interior.

Across ancient rue St-Jacques is the **Eglise St-Julien-le-Pauvre**, built as a resting place for 12th-century pilgrims. Nearby rue Galande has old houses and the Trois Maillez cabaret at No.56 (5th, 01.43.54.00.79). The medieval cellars of the **Caveau des Oubliettes** jazz club (*see p319*) were used as a prison after the French Revolution (*oubliette* is the French word for a pit into which prisoners were thrown, then forgotten). At No.42, the **Studio Galande** (*see p295*) arts cinema still draws goths bearing rice and umbrellas for late screenings of the *Rocky Horror Picture Show* every Friday and Saturday. Just outside the church in square Viviani stands what is possibly the city's oldest tree, a false acacia planted in 1602, now half-swamped by an vast thatch of ivy and propped up by some impressive concrete buttresses. Nearby, on rue de la Bucherie, expats in worn tweed jackets sporting leather elbow patches gather at second-hand English bookshop **Shakespeare & Co** (*see p243*), opposite the **bouquinistes** (*see p242*), the book and print sellers whose green boxes line the quays.

The little streets between here and the eastern stretch of boulevard St-Germain are among the city's oldest: streets like rue de Bièvre, which follows the course of the River Bièvre that flowed into the Seine in the Middle Ages, rue du Maître-Albert, and rue des Grands-Degrés, with traces of old shop signs painted on its buildings' façades. Remnants of the Collège des Bernardins, built for the Cistercian order, can be seen in rue de Poissy, where the 13th- to 14th-century Gothic monks' refectory is being restored after long service as firemen's barracks. Nearby stand Eglise St-Nicolas-de-Chardonnet (23 rue Bernardins, 5th, 01.44.27.07.90), which is associated with the most reactionary wing of the Catholic Church and still performs Mass in Latin, and the art deco Maison de la Mutualité (24 rue St-Victor, 5th, 01.40.46.12.00), whose uses range from trades unions' meetings to rock concerts.

At 47 quai de la Tournelle, the 17th-century Hôtel de Miramion now contains the **Musée de l'Assistance Publique**, devoted to the history of Paris hospitals. You'll find food for all budgets along quai de la Tournelle, starting at the top with landmark haute-cuisine restaurant Tour d'Argent (No.15, 5th, 01.43.54.23.31), which claims to have been founded as an inn in 1582, and running to the populist Tintin shrine, *café-tabac* Le Rallye (No.11, 5th, 01.43.54.29.65). Place Maubert, today a breezy morning marketplace (Tue, Thur, Sat), witnessed the grim hanging of Protestants during the 16th-century Wars of Religion. Just behind the square, the hideous modern police station is home to a curious array of grisly criminal evidence in the **Musée de la Préfecture de Police**.

On the corner of boulevard St-Germain and boulevard St-Michel stand the striking ruins of the late second-century Thermes de Cluny, the Romans' main baths complex; the adjoining Gothic Hôtel de Cluny provides a suitable setting for the **Musée National du Moyen Age**, the national collection of medieval art. Adjoining boulevard St-Germain, its garden has been replanted with species portrayed in medieval tapestries, paintings and treatises.

Eglise St-Julien-le-Pauvre

rue St-Julien-le-Pauvre, 5th (01.43.54.52.16).
M° Cluny La Sorbonne. **Open** 9.30am-1pm, 3-6.30pm daily. **Map** p410 J7.
A former sanctuary for pilgrims en route to Compostela, this much-mauled church dates from the late 12th century, on the cusp of Romanesque and Gothic, and has capitals richly decorated with vines, acanthus leaves and winged harpies. Once part of a priory, it became the university church when colleges migrated to the Left Bank, and was the site of riotous university assemblies. Since 1889 it has been used by the Greek Orthodox Church.

Eglise St-Séverin

3 rue des Prêtres-St-Séverin, 5th (01.42.34.93.50).
M° Cluny La Sorbonne or St-Michel. **Open** 11am-7.30pm daily. **Map** p410 J7.
Built on the site of the chapel of the hermit Séverin, itself on top of a much earlier Merovingian burial ground, this lovely Flamboyant Gothic edifice was long the parish church of the Left Bank. It was rebuilt on various occasions to repair damage after ransacking by Normans and to meet the needs of the

growing population. The church dates from the 15th century, though the doorway, carved with foliage, was added in 1837 from the demolished Eglise St-Pierre-aux-Boeufs on Ile de la Cité.

The double ambulatory is famed for its forest of 'palm tree' vaulting, which meets at the end in a unique spiral column that inspired a series of paintings by Robert Delaunay. The belltower, a survivor from one of the earlier churches on the site, has the oldest bell in Paris (1412). Around the nave are stained-glass windows dating from the 14th and 15th centuries (most of those in the side chapels are by 19th-century Chartres master Emile Hersh); the choir apse has striking stained glass designed by artist Jean René Bazaine in the 1960s. Next door, around the former cemetery, is the only remaining charnel house in Paris, where the bones taken from common burial grounds were placed.

Musée de l'Assistance Publique

Hôtel de Miramion, 47 quai de la Tournelle, 5th (01.40.27.50.05/www.aphp.fr). M° Maubert Mutualité. **Open** 10am-6pm Tue-Sun. Closed Aug & public hols. **Admission** €4; €2 concessions; free under-13s, CM. **No credit cards**. **Map** p408 K7.
The history of Paris hospitals, from the days when they were receptacles for abandoned babies to the dawn of modern medicine with anaesthesia, is shown through paintings, prints, grisly medical devices and a mock ward and pharmacy.

Musée National du Moyen Age – Thermes de Cluny

6 pl Paul-Painlevé, 5th (01.53.73.78.00/www.musee-moyenage.fr). M° Cluny La Sorbonne. **Open** 9.15am-5.45pm Mon, Wed-Sun. **Admission** €5.50; €4 18-25s, all on Sun; free under-18s, all on 1st Sun of mth, CM. **Credit** *Shop* MC, V. **Map** p410 J7.
The national museum of medieval art is best known for the beautiful, allegorical *Lady and the Unicorn* tapestry cycle, but also has important collections of medieval sculpture and enamels. The building itself, commonly known as Cluny, is also a rare example of 15th-century secular Gothic architecture, with its foliate Gothic doorways, hexagonal staircase jutting out of the façade and vaulted chapel. It was built from 1485 to 1498 – atop a Gallo-Roman baths complex dating from the second and third centuries – to lodge priests, at the request of Jacques d'Amboise, abbot of the powerful Abbaye de Cluny in Burgundy. The baths, built in characteristic Roman bands of stone and brick masonry, are the finest Roman remains in Paris. The vaulted frigidarium (cold bath), tepidarium (warm bath), caldarium (hot bath) and part of the hypocaust heating system are all still visible. A themed garden fronts the complex.

With its U-shaped residential building set behind an entrance courtyard, Cluny was a precursor of the Marais *hôtels particuliers* of the 16th and 17th centuries. After serving as a printworks and laundry, the *hôtel* was rented in the 1830s by the fervent medievalist Alexandre du Sommerand to house his collection, which laid the foundations for this

Rue Mouffetard – 'that wonderful narrow crowded market street'. *See p143*.

Le Panthéon. *See p144.*

museum created in 1844. Recent acquisitions include the illuminated manuscript *L'Ascension du Christ* from the Abbey of Cluny, dating back to the 12th century, and the 16th-century triptych *Assomption de la Vierge* by Adrien Isenbrant of Bruges. The mesmerising *Lady and the Unicorn* cycle depicts convoluted allegories of the five senses via six, late 15th-century Flemish millefleurs tapestries, beautifully displayed in a special circular room. Other textiles include fragile Coptic embroidery, Edward III's emblazoned saddle cloth and a cycle of the life of St Stephen. One room covers chivalric and everyday life at the end of the Middle Ages. Heads of the Kings of Judah from Notre-Dame cathedral, mutilated in the Revolution and rediscovered (minus noses) in 1979, are the highlight of the sculpture collection.

Musée de la Préfecture de Police

4 rue de la Montagne-Ste-Geneviève, 5th (01.44.41.52.50/www.prefecturepolice-paris.interieur. gouv.fr). M° Maubert Mutualité. **Open** 9am-5pm Mon-Fri; 10am-5pm Sat. Closed public hols. **Admission** free. **No credit cards. Map** p408 J7.
Housed in a hideous police station, this museum looks at criminal Paris history since the establishment of the Paris police force in the 16th century. The eclectic collection includes prisoners' expenses from the Bastille (including those of dastardly jewel thief the Comtesse de la Motte), the crafty exploding flowerpot planted by Louis-Armand Matha in 1894, and the gory Epée de Justice, a 17th-century sword blunted by a succession of noble necks.

The Sorbonne, Montagne Ste-Geneviève & Mouffetard

The days of horn-rims, pipes and turtlenecks are long gone, thanks to an influx of well-heeled residents in the 1980s: accommodation here is well beyond most students' reach. But at least the intellectual tradition persists. The Montagne Ste-Geneviève is a concentration of academic institutions, from the Sorbonne to *grandes écoles* such as the Ecole Normale Supérieure; students throng the many specialist bookstores and the art cinemas on rue Champollion and rue des Ecoles.

The district's long association with learning began in about 1100, when a number of renowned scholars, including Pierre Abélard (*see p13* **Love hurts**), began to reside and teach on the Montagne, independent of the established cathedral school of Notre-Dame. This loose association of scholars came to be referred to as a 'university'. The Paris schools attracted disciples from all over Europe, and the 'colleges' – in reality student residences dotted round the area (some still survive) – multiplied, until the University of Paris was eventually given official recognition with a charter from Pope Innocent III in 1215.

By the 16th century the university – named the **Sorbonne**, after the most famous of its colleges – had been co-opted by the Catholic Church. A century later, Cardinal Richelieu rebuilt it. Following the Revolution, when the university was forced to close, Napoléon revived the Sorbonne as the cornerstone of his new, centralised education system. The university participated enthusiastically in the uprisings of the 19th century, and was also a seedbed of the 1968 revolt (*see p24*). These days it is decidedly less turbulent. The present buildings are mostly of 19th-century origin; of Bonaparte's rebuild, only the baroque Chapelle de la Sorbonne survives. In contrast, independent **Collège de France**, also on rue des Ecoles, was founded in 1530 by a group of humanists led by Guillaume Budé under the patronage of François I. Neighbouring Brasserie Balzar (No.49, 5th, 01.43.54.13.67) is a long-standing supplier of fuel for philosophising.

From here, climb rue St-Jacques to rue Soufflot for the most impressive introduction to place du Panthéon. Otherwise, follow rue des Carmes – with its baroque chapel, now used by the Syrian Church – and continue on rue Valette past the brick-and-stone entrance of the Collège Ste-Barbe, where Ignatius Loyola, Montgolfier and Eiffel studied. Alternatively, wend along serpentine rue de la Montagne-Ste-Geneviève; at the junction of rue Descartes, cafés and eccentric wine bistros overlook the sculpted 19th-century entrance to what was formerly the elite Ecole Polytechnique (since moved to the suburbs) and is now the research ministry. There's a small park here, too, and bistro **L'Ecurie** (2 rue Laplace, 5th, 01.46.33.68.49) – an old stable burrowed into medieval cellars.

The huge domed **Panthéon**, inspired by the Pantheon in Rome, was commissioned by Louis XV to honour Geneviève, the city's patron saint, but was converted during the Revolution into a secular temple for France's *grands hommes*. The surrounding place du Panthéon, also conceived by Panthéon architect Jacques-Germain Soufflot, is one of the city's grand set pieces: looking on to it are the elegant 5th arrondissement town hall and, opposite, the law faculty. On the north side, the Ste-Geneviève university library (No.10, 5th, 01.44.41.97.97), built by Labrouste with an iron-framed reading room, contains medieval manuscripts. On the other side you'll find the historic Hôtel des Grands Hommes (No.17, 5th, 01.46.34.19.60, www.hoteldesgrandshommes.com), where Surrealist mandarin André Breton invented 'automatic writing' in the 1920s.

Pascal, Racine and the remains of Ste Geneviève are all interred in **Eglise St-Etienne-du-Mont**, on the north-east corner of the square. Just behind it, within the illustrious and elitist Lycée Henri IV, is the Gothic-Romanesque Tour de Clovis, part of the former Abbaye Ste-Geneviève. Take a look through the entrance (open during term-time) and you'll also catch glimpses of the cloister and other sundry monastic structures. Further from place de Panthéon, along rue Clovis, is a chunk of Philippe-Auguste's 12th-century city wall (other chunks can be spotted at 62 rue du Cardinal-Lemoine and at the rear of buildings on rue Descartes). Exiled monarch James II resided at 65 rue du Cardinal-Lemoine, in the severe buildings of the former Collège des Ecossais (now a school), founded in 1372 to house Scottish students; King James' brain was preserved here until carried off and lost during the French Revolution. Other well-known ex-

residents include Hemingway, who lived at both 79 rue du Cardinal-Lemoine (note the plaque) and 39 rue Descartes in the 1920s; James Joyce completed *Ulysses* while staying at 71 rue du Cardinal-Lemoine; and Rimbaud also lived in rue Descartes. Descartes himself lived on nearby rue Rollin.

This area is still a mix of tourist picturesque and gentle village, where some of the buildings hide surprising courtyards and gardens. Pretty place de la Contrescarpe has been a famous rendezvous since the 1530s, when writers Rabelais, Ronsard and Du Bellay frequented the Cabaret de la Pomme de Pin at No.1; it still has some lively cafés. When George Orwell stayed at 6 rue du Pot-de-Fer in 1928 and 1929 (he described his time here and his work as a dishwasher in *Down and Out in Paris and*

Scandale! The wrong man

One of the biggest and most acrimonious scandals in modern French history – concluded a hundred years ago, in 1906 – was bookended by elaborate ceremonies in the courtyard of the Ecole Militaire.

The first took place on the frosty morning of 5 January 1895, when French army captain Alfred Dreyfus was stripped of his stripes, insignia, buttons, sword and dignity during a degrading ritual accompanied by the barking of a 20,000-strong mob outside the main gate. 'Death to the traitor!' they cried. 'Death to the Jew!'

Dreyfus was the only Jew at that level of his chosen profession. Born to a wealthy Alsace family in 1859, he decided on a career in the army and moved up through the ranks. In the early 1880s, in the climate of suspicion following the Franco-Prussian war, the French authorities thought someone had been passing military secrets to the German embassy – possibly the work of a certain 'scoundrel D'. Letters had been found, in script vaguely resembling Dreyfus's, and with his unpopular Jewish and German-border background, the captain was the perfect fit. A gullible French public was happy to swallow the story. Outrage ensued.

After a swift court case, there followed the dramatic ceremony at the Ecole Militaire. Dreyfus's sword was snapped across a French sergeant's knee; he was whisked away in a prison van before being shipped to Devil's Island on the north coast of South America. The most notorious penal colony of its day, Devil's Island meant desperate exile

in a disease-ridden jungle surrounded by piranha-infested waters. Only a quarter of its inmates returned to France.

Back in France, a more enlightened chief of counter-intelligence had been appointed – Lieutenant-Colonel Marie-Georges Picquart. Looking into the flimsy case, Picquart soon found the real culprit: a high-living Franco-Hungarian by the name of Esterhazy. While Dreyfus rotted in his tropical hell, it took a number of plots, sub-plots, the suicide of culpable Major Henry and, most famously, a front-page declaration in liberal daily *L'Aurore* by Emile Zola for the case to be reopened. As the French public bitterly debated Zola's polemical 'J'Accuse!', and the military fussed over losing face, *l'affaire Dreyfus* dragged on. Esterhazy was exonerated and escaped, like Zola, to England. Picquart was sent to Tunisia. By the time the case was solved and Dreyfus cleared in 1906, Zola had died and the now reinstated army captain had published his own memoirs. On 20 July 1906 Dreyfus took part in another official ceremony in the courtyard of the Ecole Militaire – that of receiving the Légion d'honneur, France's highest military honour.

In February 1998, at another ceremony in this same courtyard, then French Defence Minister Alain Richard gave a speech to mark the centenary of Zola's sensational front-page plea. He began it with a quote from a leading writer of the day, a staunch Catholic and Dreyfus supporter Charles Péguy: 'The more this affair is over, the more it's clear that it will never go away'.

London), it was a place of astounding poverty; today the street is lined with bargain bars and restaurants, while the restored houses along rue Tournefort bear little relation to the garrets of Balzac's *Le Père Goriot*. Rue Mouffetard, originally the road to Rome and one of the oldest streets in the city, winds southward as a suite of cheap bistros, Greek and Lebanese tavernas and knick-knack shops thronged with tourists; the vibe described by Hemingway – 'that wonderful narrow crowded market street, beloved of bohemians' – has somewhat faded. The busy street market (Tue-Sat, Sun morning) on the lower half seethes on weekends when it spills on to the square and around the cafés in front of the **Eglise St-Médard**. There's another busy market, more frequented by locals, at **place Monge** (Wed, Fri, Sun morning; *see p259* **Forward *marché!***).

Back to the west of the Panthéon, head south beyond rue Soufflot, and you'll notice rue St-Jacques becomes prettier. Here you'll find several ancient buildings, including the elegant *hôtel* at No.151, good food shops, vintage bistro Perraudin (No.157, 5th, 01.46.33.15.75), and the Institut Océanographique (No.195, 5th, 01.44.32.10.70, www.oceano.org/io), which has plentiful aquariums much loved by schoolkids. Rue d'Ulm contains the blue-chip Ecole Normale Supérieure (No.45, 5th, 01.44.32.30.00, www.ens.fr), occupied in protest by the unemployed in January 1998; in an echo of 1968, students also joined in.

Turn off up hilly rue des Fossés-St-Jacques to discover place de l'Estrapade; in the 17th century the *estrapade* was a tall wooden tower from which deserters were dropped repeatedly until they died. Nearby, in rue des Irlandais, the **Centre Culturel Irlandais** (*see p69*) hosts concerts, exhibitions, films, plays and spoken-word events promoting Irish culture. Back to the west of rue St-Jacques, rue Soufflot and broad rue Gay-Lussac (a hotspot of the May 1968 revolt), with their Haussmannian apartment buildings, lead to boulevard St-Michel and the **Jardin du Luxembourg** (*see p153*). Further south along rue St-Jacques, in the potters' quarter of Roman Lutetia, is another landmark, the **Eglise du Val-de-Grâce**, the least altered and most ornate of the city's baroque churches. Round the corner, at 6 rue du Val-de-Grâce, is the former home of Alfons Maria Mucha, the Czech art nouveau painter, best known for his posters of actress Sarah Bernhardt.

Collège de France

11 pl Marcelin-Berthelot, 5th (01.44.27.12.11/ 01.44.27.11.47/www.college-de-france.fr). M° Cluny La Sorbonne or Maubert Mutualité/RER Luxembourg. **Map** p410 J7.

Founded in 1530 with the patronage of François I, the college is both a place of learning and a research institute. The present building dates from the 16th and 17th centuries; there's a later annexe. All lectures are free and open to the public; some have been given by such eminent figures as anthropologist Claude Lévi-Strauss, philosopher Maurice Merleau-Ponty and mathematician Jacques Tits.

Eglise St-Etienne-du-Mont

pl Ste-Geneviève, 5th (01.43.54.11.79). M° Cardinal Lemoine/RER Luxembourg. **Open** 10am-7pm Tue-Sun. **Map** p410 J8.

Geneviève, patron saint of Paris, is credited with having miraculously saved the city from the ravages of Attila the Hun in 451, and her shrine has been a popular site of pilgrimage ever since. The present church was built in an amalgam of Gothic and Renaissance styles between 1492 and 1626, and once adjoined the abbey church of Ste-Geneviève. The façade mixes Gothic rose windows with rusticated classical columns and reliefs of classically draped figures. The interior is wonderfully tall and light, with soaring columns and a classical balustrade. The stunning Renaissance rood screen, with its double spiral staircase and ornate stone strapwork, is the only surviving one in Paris, and was possibly designed by Philibert Delorme. Also worth a look is the ornate canopied wooden pulpit by Germaine Pillon dating from 1651, adorned with figures of the Graces and supported by a muscular Samson sitting on the defeated lion. St Geneviève's elaborate neo-Gothic brass-and-glass shrine (shielding the ancient tombstone) is located to the right of the choir, surrounded by assorted reliquaries and dozens of marble plaques bearing messages of thanks. At the back of the church (reached via the sacristy), the catechism chapel built by Baltard in the 1860s has a cycle of paintings relating the saint's life story.

Eglise St-Médard

141 rue Mouffetard, 5th (01.44.08.87.00). M° Censier Daubenton. **Open** 8am-noon, 2.30-7.30pm daily. **Map** p408 J9.

The original chapel was a dependency of the Abbaye Ste-Geneviève; rebuilding at the end of the 15th century created a much larger, late Gothic structure with an elaborate vaulted ambulatory.

Eglise du Val-de-Grâce

pl Alphonse-Laveran, 5th (01.40.51.47.28). RER Luxembourg or Port-Royal. **Open** noon-6pm Tue, Wed, Sat, Sun. **Admission** €5; €2.50 students, 6-12s; free under-6s. **No credit cards**. **Map** p408 H9.

Anne of Austria, wife of Louis XIII, vowed to erect 'a magnificent temple' if God blessed her with a son. She got two. The resulting church and surrounding Benedictine monastery – now a military hospital and the Musée du Service de Santé des Armées – were built by François Mansart and Jacques Lemercier. This is the most luxuriously baroque of the city's 17th-century domed churches, its ornate altar decorated with twisted barley-sugar columns.

Sightseeing

The swirling colours of the dome frescoes painted by Pierre Mignard in 1669 (which Molière once eulogised) are designed to give a foretaste of heaven. In contrast, the surrounding monastery is the perfect example of Mansart's classical restraint. Be sure to phone ahead to arrange a guided visit.

Musée du Service de Santé des Armées

Val de Grâce, pl Alphonse-Laveran, 5th (01.40.51.51.94). RER Luxembourg or Port Royal. **Open** noon-6pm Tue, Wed, Sat, Sun. **Admission** €5; €2.50 6-12s; free under-6s. **No credit cards.** **Map** p408 J9.

Housed in the royal convent designed by Mansart, next door to a military hospital, this museum traces the history of military medicine, via replicas of field hospitals and ambulance trains, and antique medical instruments. The chilling section on World War I demonstrates how speedily the conflict propelled progress in medical science.

Le Panthéon

pl du Panthéon, 5th (01.44.32.18.00). Mº Cardinal Lemoine/RER Luxembourg. **Open** 10am-5.15pm (until 5.45pm summer) daily. **Admission** €7; €4.50 18s-25s; free under-18s (if accompanied by an adult). **Credit** MC, V. **Map** p410 J8.

Soufflot's neo-classical megastructure, with its huge dome, was the architectural *grand projet* of its day, commissioned by a grateful Louis XV as an appropriately grandiose way to thank Ste Geneviève for his recovery from illness. But by the time it was ready in 1790, a lot had changed; during the Revolution, the Panthéon was rededicated as a 'temple of reason' and the resting place of the nation's great men. The austere barrel-vaulted crypt now houses Voltaire, Rousseau, Hugo and Zola; new heroes are installed but rarely: Pierre and Marie Curie's remains were transferred here in 1995. André Malraux, writer, Resistance hero and de Gaulle's culture minister, arrived in 1996; Alexandre Dumas in 2002. Inside are Greek columns and domes, and 19th-century murals of Geneviève's life by Symbolist painter Puvis de Chavannes, a formative influence on Picasso during his blue period.

Mount the steep spiral stairs to the colonnade encircling the dome for superb views across the city. A replica of Foucault's pendulum hangs here; the original proved that the earth does indeed spin on its axis, via a universal joint that lets the direction of the pendulum's swing rotate as the earth revolves. **Photo** *p140.*

La Sorbonne

12 rue de la Sorbonne, 5th (01.40.46.22.11/www. sorbonne.fr). Mº Cluny La Sorbonne. **Open** *Tours* by appointment. Closed July & Aug. **Map** p410 J7.

Founded in 1253 by Robert de Sorbon, the University of the Sorbonne was at the centre of the Latin Quarter's intellectual activity from the Middle Ages until 1968, when it was occupied by students and stormed by the riot police. The authorities then split the University of Paris into safer outposts, but the Sorbonne still houses the Faculté des Lettres. Rebuilt by Richelieu and reorganised by Napoléon, the present buildings date from the late 1800s, and have a labyrinth of classrooms and lecture theatres, as well as an observatory tower. The elegant dome of the 17th-century chapel dominates place de la Sorbonne; Cardinal Richelieu is buried inside. It's only open to the public for exhibitions or concerts.

The Jardin des Plantes district

The quiet, easternmost part of the 5th arrondissement is home to more academic institutions, the Paris mosque and another Roman relic. Old-fashioned bistros on rue des Fossés-St-Bernard contrast with the slab-sided 1960s architecture of the massive university campus of Paris VI and VII, the science faculty (known as Jussieu) built on what had been the site of the important Abbaye St-Victor. Between the Seine and Jussieu is the strikingly modern, glass-faced **Institut du Monde Arabe**, which has a busy programme of concerts and exhibitions and a restaurant with a great view. The **Jardin Tino Rossi**, along the river, contains the slightly dilapidated **Musée de la Sculpture en Plein Air**, and in summer is a favourite stop for dancing and picnicking.

Hidden among the many hotels of rue Monge is the entrance to the **Arènes de Lutèce**, a Roman amphitheatre. The circular arena and its tiers of stone seating were rediscovered in 1869 when the street was being built. Their excavation started in 1883, thanks to lobbying by Victor Hugo. Nearby you can see the white minaret and green pan-tiled roof of the **Mosquée de Paris**, built in 1922. This is the official focus for the city's Muslim community, as opposed to more makeshift or clandestine mosques that have since sprung up elsewhere around the city. Its beautiful Moorish tearoom is a favourite student haunt.

The mosque looks over the **Jardin des Plantes** botanical garden. Opened in 1626 as a garden for medicinal plants, it features an 18th-century maze and a winter garden bristling with rare species. It also houses the **Museum National d'Histoire Naturelle**, with its brilliantly renovated Grande Galerie de l'Evolution, and to a zoo, La Ménagerie, an unlikely by-product of the Revolution, when royal and noble collections of wild animals were impounded. Street names and the lovely animal-themed fountain on the corner of rue Cuvier pay homage to the many naturalists and other scientists who worked here. A short distance away, at 11-13bis rue Geoffroy-St-Hilaire, the words 'Chevaux', 'Poneys' and 'Anes' are still visible on the façade of the old horse market.

Yabba Dabba Doo! It's the **Muséum National d'Histoire Naturelle.** *See p147.*

Arènes de Lutèce

rue Monge, rue de Navarre or rue des Arènes,
5th. M° Cardinal Lemoine or Place Monge. **Open**
Summer 8am-10pm daily. *Winter* 8am-5.30pm
daily. **Map** p408 K8.
This Roman arena, where wild beasts and gladia-
tors fought, could seat 10,000 people. It was still visible during the reign of Philippe-Auguste in the 12th
century, then disappeared under rubble. The site
was rediscovered in 1869 and now incorporates a
romantically planted garden. These days, it attracts
skateboarders, footballers and boules players.

Institut du Monde Arabe

1 rue des Fossés-St-Bernard, 5th (01.40.51.38.38/
www.imarabe.org). M° Jussieu. **Open** *Museum* 10am-
6pm Tue-Sun. *Library* 1-8pm Tue-Sat. *Café* noon-
6pm Tue-Sun. **Admission** *Roof terrace, library*
free. *Museum* €5; €4 concessions; free under-12s.
Exhibitions varies. **Credit** MC, V. **Map** p408 K7.
A clever blend of high-tech, steel-and-glass architecture and Arab influences, this wedge-shaped
Grand Projet was built between 1980 and 1987 to a
design by French architect Jean Nouvel. Shuttered
windows, inspired by the screens of Moorish
palaces, act as camera apertures according to the
amount of available light. Inside is a collection of
Middle Eastern art, archaeological finds, a library
and a popular café. Displays include items on long-
term loan from museums in Syria and Tunisia, and
the Institut's own permanent collection covers a
huge geographical and historical span from prehis-
tory to the present. Of special interest are the collections of urns and masks from Carthage, early
scientific tools, and 19th-century Tunisian costume
and jewellery. The Institut also runs a varied agenda
of dance and classical Arab music, and there's a
great view from the roof.

Jardin des Plantes

36 rue Geoffroy-St-Hilaire, 2 rue Bouffon,
pl Valhubert or 57 rue Cuvier, 5th. M° Gare
d'Austerlitz, Place Monge or Jussieu. **Open** *Main*
garden winter 8am-dusk daily; summer 7.30am-dusk
daily. *Alpine garden* Apr-Sept 8-11am, 1.30-5pm
daily; closed Oct-Mar. *Greenhouses* (closed 2006)
Apr-Sept 1-5pm Mon, Wed-Fri; 10am-5pm Sat, Sun.
Ménagerie Apr-Sept 9am-5pm daily. **Admission**
Jardin des Plantes free. *Greenhouses* €3. *Ménagerie*
€7; €5 4s-18s; free under-4s. **No credit cards.**
Map p408 L8.
Although small and a tad dishevelled, the Paris
botanical garden – which contains more than 10,000
species and includes tropical greenhouses and rose,
winter and Alpine gardens – is worth a visit. Begun
by Louis XIII's doctor as the royal medicinal plant
garden in 1626, it opened to the public in 1640. It also
comprises the Ménagerie (a small zoo) and the

Notre-Dame de l'Arche de l'Alliance. *See p160.*

Muséum National d'Histoire Naturelle (*see below*). Ancient trees on view include a false acacia planted in 1636 and a cedar in 1734; an 18th-century spiral yew maze climbs up a little hill. A plaque on the old laboratory declares that this is where Henri Becquerel discovered radioactivity in 1896.

Jardin Tino Rossi (Musée de la Sculpture en Plein Air)

quai St-Bernard, 5th. M° Gare d'Austerlitz. **Open** 8am-dusk Mon-Fri; 9am-dusk Sat, Sun. **Admission** free. **Map** p408 K8.

Despite recent replanting, the open-air sculpture museum by the Seine fights a constant battle against graffiti. Still, it's a pleasant enough, if traffic-loud, place for a stroll. Most of the works are second-rate aside from Etienne Martin's bronze *Demeure I* and the Carrara marble *Fenêtre* by Cuban artist Careras.

La Mosquée de Paris

2 pl du Puits-de-l'Ermite, 5th (01.45.35.97.33/ tearoom 01.43.31.38.20/baths 01.43.31.18.14/ www.mosquee-de-paris.net). M° Monge. **Open** *Tours* 9am-noon, 2-6pm Mon-Thur, Sat, Sun (closed Muslim hols). *Tearoom* 10am-11.30pm daily. *Restaurant* noon-2.30pm, 7.30-10.30pm daily. *Baths* (women) 10am-9pm Mon, Wed, Sat; 2-9pm Fri; (men) 2-9pm Tue; 10am-9pm Sun. **Admission** €2.30; €1.50 7s-25s, over-60s; free under-7s. *Tearoom* free. *Baths* €15-€35. **Credit** MC, V. **Map** p408 K9.

The mosque's stunning green-and-white square minaret is the spiritual heart of France's Algerian-dominated Muslim population. Built from 1922 to 1926 in Hispano-Moorish style, with elements inspired by the Alhambra and Fez's Mosque Bou-Inania, the mosque is a series of buildings and courtyards in three sections: religious (grand patio, prayer room and minaret, all for serious worshippers and not inquisitive tourists); scholarly (Islamic school and library); and, via rue Geoffroy-St-Hilaire, commercial (domed hammam, Turkish baths, and relaxing Moorish tearoom). *See also p240.*

Muséum National d'Histoire Naturelle

36 rue Geoffroy-St-Hilaire, 2 rue Bouffon or pl Valhubert, 5th (01.40.79.54.79/56.01/www.mnhn.fr). M° Gare d'Austerlitz or Jussieu. **Open** *Grande Galerie* 10am-6pm Mon, Wed-Fri, Sun; 10am-8pm Sat. *Other galleries* 10am-5pm Mon, Wed-Fri; 10am-6pm Sat, Sun. **Admission** *Grande Galerie* €8; €7 4s-18s; free under-4s. *Other galeries* (each) €6; €4 4s-18s; free under-4s. **No credit cards. Map** p408 K9.

The brilliant renovations to the Grande Galerie de l'Evolution, located within the Jardin des Plantes (*see above*), has taken the city's natural history museum out of the dinosaur age. Architect Paul Chemetov set modern lifts and the latest audio-visual techniques into the 19th-century iron-framed structure. Upon entry, you're confronted with the 14m-long skeleton of a whale; the rest of the ground floor is dedicated to other sea creatures. On the first floor are the mammals, including Louis XVI's rhinoceros. Videos and interactive displays give information on life in the wild. Glass-sided lifts take you up through suspended birds to the second floor, which deals with man's impact on nature and considers demographic problems and pollution. The third floor traces endangered and extinct species. The separate Galerie d'Anatomie Comparée et de Paléontologie contains over a million skeletons – of every creature you can imagine – and a fossil collection of world importance. *See chapter* **Children**. **Photo** *p145.*

St-Germain-des-Prés & Odéon

In the 6th arrondissement.

The Left Bank once symbolised scholarship; now it has some of the most expensive property in Paris. It's also serious fashion territory, but still home to publishers.

The lore of Paris café society and intellectual life has been amply fed by the tales that leaked out of St-Germain-des-Prés. Verlaine and Rimbaud drank here; later, Sartre, Camus and de Beauvoir scribbled and squabbled, and musicians congregated around Boris Vian in the post-war jazz boom. Today earnest types still pose with weighty tomes, and the literati and glitterati assemble on café terraces – to give interviews: with all the local price hikes, the only writers living here these days will be the well-established ones.

In 1997 a band of intellectuals founded 'SOS St-Germain' to halt the tide of commercialism. Fashion designer **Sonia Rykiel** (*see p249*), long in the camp of the *germanopratins* (as residents are called), joined the campaign. The campaigners' efforts have been largely in vain: St-Germain almost rivals avenue Montaigne (*see p118*) for designer boutiques. Armani, Louis Vuitton, Dior, Cartier and Céline have all set up shop here, and **Karl Lagerfeld** (*see p248*) opened his photography gallery on rue de Seine, but the jazz clubs and musicians have largely moved away.

From the boulevard to the Seine

Hit by shortages of coal during World War II, Sartre shunned his cold flat on rue Bonaparte. 'The principal interest of the Café de Flore,' he noted at the time, 'was that it had a stove, a nearby métro and no Germans.' Although you can spend more on a few coffees here than a week's heating these days, the **Café de Flore** (*see p230*) remains an arty favourite and hosts *café-philo* evenings in English. Its rival, **Les Deux Magots** (*see p230*), facing historic **Eglise St-Germain-des-Prés**, is frequented largely by tourists. Nearby is the celebrity favourite Brasserie Lipp (151 bd St-Germain, 6th, 01.45.48.53.91); art nouveau fans prefer Brasserie Vagenende (142 bd St-Germain, 6th,

Sightseeing

Eglise St-Sulpice shows classical design unmatched – and unmatching. *See p153.*

01.43.26.68.18). The swish late-night bookshop **La Hune** (*see p243*) provides sustenance of a more intellectual kind.

St-Germain-des-Prés grew up around the medieval abbey, the oldest church in Paris and site of an annual fair that drew merchants from across Europe. There are traces of its cloister and part of the abbot's palace behind the church on rue de l'Abbaye. Constructed in 1586 in red brick with stone facing, the palace prefigured the architecture of **place des Vosges** (*see p112*). Charming place Furstenberg (once the palace stables) is home to upmarket furnishing fabric stores and the house and studio where the elderly Delacroix lived when painting the murals in St-Sulpice; today it accommodates the **Musée National Delacroix**. Wagner, Ingres and Colette lived on nearby rue Jacob; its elegant 17th-century *hôtels particuliers* now contain specialist book, design and antiques shops, a handful of pleasant hotels and the odd bohemian establishment.

Further east, rue de Buci hosts a street market and upmarket food shops, and is home to cafés Les Etages (No.5, 6th, 01.46.34.26.26) and Bar du Marché (No.16, 6th, 01.43.26.55.15). Hôtel La Louisiane (60 rue de Seine, 6th, 01.44.32.17.17, www.hotellalouisiane.com) has housed jazz stars Chet Baker and Miles Davis, and Existentialist powerhouses Sartre and de Beauvoir. Rue de Seine, rue des Beaux-Arts and

rue Bonaparte (Manet was born in the latter, at No.5, in 1832) are still packed with small art galleries, mostly specialising in 20th-century abstraction, tribal art and art deco furniture. It was in rue des Beaux-Arts, at the Hôtel d'Alsace, that Oscar Wilde complained about the wallpaper and then checked out for good. Now renovated and fashionably over-the-top, it has rechristened itself **L'Hôtel** (*see p58*). La Palette (43 rue de Seine, 6th, 01.43.26.68.15) and Bistro Mazarin (42 rue Mazarine, 6th, 01.43.29.99.01) are good stopping-off points with enviable terraces; rue Mazarine, with boutiques selling lighting, vintage toys and jewellery, also has Terence Conran's brasserie **L'Alcazar** at No.62 (*see p207 and p229*) and hipster club **Wagg** (*see p326*) located in a former cabaret.

On quai de Conti stands the neo-classical Hôtel des Monnaies, built at the demand of Louis XV by architect Jacques-Denis Antoine; formerly the mint (1777-1973), it's now the **Musée de la Monnaie**, a coin museum. Behind the colonnaded façade is a curious combination of elegant salons and industrial premises; commemorative medals are still engraved and struck here today. Next door stands the domed **Institut de France**, cleaned to within an inch of its crisp, classical life. Opposite, the iron Pont des Arts footbridge leads directly to the **Louvre** (*see pp80-88*).

Further along, the city's main fine-arts school, the **Ecole Nationale Supérieure des Beaux-Arts**, occupies an old monastery.

Coffee was first drunk in Paris in 1686 at Café Procope (13 rue de l'Ancienne-Comédie, 6th, 01.40.46.79.00), whose customers have included Voltaire, Rousseau, Benjamin Franklin, Danton, Verlaine – and, today, tourists. Look out for Voltaire's desk and a postcard from Marie-Antoinette. The back opens on to the twee, cobbled passage du Commerce St-André, home to toy shops, jewellers, chintzy tearooms and tapas trove Bistrot La Catalogne (No.4, 6th, 01.55.42.16.19). In the 18th century Dr Joseph-Ignace Guillotin first tested out his notorious device – designed, believe it or not, to make executions more humane – in the cellars of what is today the **Pub St-Germain** (17 rue de l'Ancienne-Comédie, 6th, 01.56.81.13.13); the first victim was, reputedly, a sheep. Jacobin regicide Billaud-Varenne was among those who felt the steel of Guillotin's gadget; his former home (45 rue St-André-des-Arts, 6th) was the site of the first girls' *lycée* in Paris, the Lycée Fénelon, founded in 1883. Today rue St-André-des-Arts, which winds toward boulevard St-Michel, features gift shops, crêperies and an arts cinema. Veer off the main drag into quiet side streets such as rue des Grands-Augustins, rue de Savoie and rue Séguier, and you find printers, bookshops and dignified 17th-century *hôtels particuliers*. On the corner of rue and quai des Grands-Augustins, **Lapérouse** restaurant (*see p207*) has a series of private dining rooms, where gentlemen would entertain their demi-monde mistresses; contemporary **Les Bouquinistes** (53 quai des Grands-Augustins, 6th, 01.43.25.45.94) is easier to peek into. The turreted Hôtel de Fécamp, at 5 rue de Hautefeuille, was the medieval townhouse of the abbots of Fécamp, begun in 1292; a few doors down, at No.13, is the birthplace of poet Baudelaire. Legend has it that rue Gît-le-Coeur ('here lies the heart') is so called because one of Henri IV's mistresses lived here; at No.9 is the rather luxurious Hôtel du Vieux Paris (6th, 01.44.32.15.90), the 'Beat Hotel' where William Burroughs revised *Naked Lunch*.

Ecole Nationale Supérieure des Beaux-Arts (Ensb-a)

14 rue Bonaparte, 6th (01.47.03.52.15/www. ensba.fr). M° St-Germain-des-Prés. **Open** *Courtyard* 9am-5pm Mon-Fri. *Exhibitions* 1-7pm Tue-Sun. **Admission** *Exhibitions* prices vary. **Credit** V. **Map** p410 H6.
The city's most prestigious fine-arts school resides in what's left of the 17th-century Couvent des Petits-Augustins, the 18th-century Hôtel de Chimay, some 19th-century additions and some chunks of assorted French châteaux moved here after the Revolution

(when the buildings briefly served as a museum of French monuments, before becoming the art school in 1816). Exhibitions are often held here; the entrance is on quai Malaquais.

Eglise St-Germain-des-Prés

3 pl St-Germain-des-Prés, 6th (01.55.42.81.33/ www.eglise-sgp.org). M° St-Germain-des-Prés. **Open** 8am-7.45pm Mon-Sat; 9am-8pm Sun. **Map** p410 H7.
The oldest church in Paris. On the advice of Germain (later Bishop of Paris), Childebert, son of Clovis, had a basilica and monastery built here around 543. It was first dedicated to St Vincent, and then came to be known as St-Germain-le-Doré ('the gilded') for its copper roof, and later as St-Germain-des-Prés ('of the fields'). During the Revolution the abbey was burnt and a saltpetre refinery installed; the spire was only added in a clumsy 19th-century restoration. Still, most of the present structure is 12th century, and some ornate carved capitals and the tower remain from the 11th. Illustrious tombs include those of Jean-Casimir, the deposed King of Poland who became Abbot of St-Germain in 1669, and of Scottish nobleman William Douglas. Under the window in the second chapel is the funeral stone of philosopher-mathematician René Descartes; his ashes have been here since 1819.

Institut de France

23 quai de Conti, 6th (01.44.41.44.41/www.institut-de-france.fr). M° Louvre Rivoli or Pont Neuf. **Open** *Guided tours* Sat, Sun (01.44.54.19.30/www. monum.fr; call for times).* **Admission** €8; €6 under-25s. **No credit cards. Map** p410 H6.
This elegant domed building with two sweeping curved wings was designed as a school (founded by Cardinal Mazarin for provincial children) by Louis Le Vau and opened in 1684. The five academies of the Institut (Académie Française, Académie des Inscriptions et Belles-Lettres, Académie des Beaux-Arts, Académie des Sciences, Académie des Sciences Morales et Politiques) moved here in 1805. Inside is Mazarin's ornate tomb by Hardouin-Mansart, and the Bibliothèque Mazarine (open to over-18s with ID and two photos; €15/year). The Académie Française, zealous guardian of the French language, was founded by Cardinal Richelieu in 1635 with the aim of preserving the purity of French from corrupting outside influences (such as English). Les Immortels, as Academy members are still modestly known, have never stopped trying to impose rules on a language and population that embrace multicultural input.

Musée de la Monnaie de Paris

11 quai de Conti, 6th (01.40.46.55.35/www.monnaie deparis.fr). M° Odéon or Pont Neuf. **Open** 11am-5.30pm Tue-Fri; noon-5.30pm Sat, Sun. Closed Aug and public holidays. **Admission** (includes audio guide) €8; free under-16s. **Credit** *Shop* MC, V. **Map** p410 H6.
Housed in the handsome neo-classical mint built in the 1770s, this high-tech museum tells the tale of global and local coinage from its pre-Roman origins,

using sophisticated displays and audio-visual presentations. The history of the franc, from its wartime debut in 1360, is outlined in great detail.

Musée National Delacroix

6 pl Furstenberg, 6th (01.44.41.86.50/www.musee-delacroix.fr). M° St-Germain-des-Prés. **Open** 9.30am-4.30pm Mon, Wed-Sun. **Admission** €5; free under-18s, all on 1st Sun of mth, CM. **Credit** MC, V. **Map** p410 H6.

Romantic painter Eugène Delacroix moved to this apartment and studio in 1857 in order to be near the Eglise St-Sulpice, where he was painting murals. The Louvre and the Musée d'Orsay house his major canvas works, but this collection includes small oil paintings – among them an early self-portrait in the stance of a Walter Scott hero and *Madeleine au Désert* – free pastel studies of skies, sketches and lithographs, as well as his palette and some Moroccan memorabilia. Exhibits include correspondence between Baudelaire and George Sand.

St-Sulpice & the Luxembourg

The quarter south of boulevard St-Germain between Odéon and Luxembourg, crammed with historic buildings and interesting shops, epitomises civilised Paris. Just off the boulevard lies the covered market of St-Germain, once the site of the medieval St-Germain fair. It's now the site of a shopping arcade, auditorium, food hall and underground swimming pool. There are bars and bistros along rue Guisarde, nicknamed rue de la Soif ('thirst street') thanks to its carousers; it has the late-night Birdland bar (No.8, 6th, 01.43.26.97.59) and a couple of notable bistros: Mâchon d'Henri (No.8, 6th, 01.43.29.08.70) and Brasserie Fernand (No.13, 6th, 01.43.54.61.47). Rue Princesse and rue des Canettes are a beguiling mix of budget eateries, pizzerias and nocturnal haunts known to a determined few: the Bedford Arms pub (17 rue Princesse, 6th, 01.46.33.43.54) and nightspot Castel (15 rue Princesse, 6th, 01.40.51.52.80).

Pass the fashion boutiques, high-class pâtisseries and antiquarian book and print shops and you come to **Eglise St-Sulpice**, a surprising 18th-century exercise in classical form with two unmatching turrets and a colonnaded façade. The square in front was designed in the 19th century by Visconti; it contains his imposing, lion-flanked Fontaine des Quatre Points Cardinaux (a pun on cardinal points and the statues of Bishops Bossuet, Fénelon, Massilon and Flechier, none of whom was actually a cardinal) and is the centrepiece for today's **Foire St-Germain** (*see p275*), a summer fair for antiques, books and poetry. The Café de la Mairie (8 pl St-Sulpice, 6th, 01.43.26.67.82) is a favourite with Left-Bank intellectuals and students.

Amid shops of religious artefacts, the chic boutiques on place and rue St-Sulpice include **Yves Saint Laurent** (*see p249*), Christian Lacroix (2-4 pl St-Sulpice, 6th, 01.46.33.48.95, www.christian-lacroix.com), **Agnès b** (*see p250*), **Vanessa Bruno** (*see p252*), Catherine Memmi (11 rue St-Sulpice, 6th, 01.44.07.02.02), popular perfumier Annick Goutal (12 pl St-Sulpice, 6th, 01.46.33.03.15) and milliner **Marie Mercié** (*see p255*). Prime shopping continues further west: clothes on rue Bonaparte and rue du Four, and accessory and fashion shops on rue du Dragon, rue de Grenelle and rue du Cherche-Midi. If you spot a queue in the latter street, it's most likely for the famous bread at **Poilâne** (*see p260*). Across the street, at the junction of rue de Sèvres and rue du Cherche-Midi, César's spiky bronze *Centaur* is a tribute by the French sculptor to Picasso.

The early 17th-century chapel of St-Joseph-des-Carmes – once a Carmelite convent, now hidden within the Institut Catholique (21 rue d'Assas, 6th, 01.44.39.52.00, www.icp.fr) – was the scene of the murder of 115 priests during the Terror in 1792. To the east lies wide rue de Tournon, lined by such grand 18th-century residences as the elegant Hôtel de Brancas (No.6), with figures of Justice and Prudence over the door. This street opens up to the **Palais du Luxembourg**, which now serves as the Senate, and the adjoining **Jardin du Luxembourg**, the quintessential Paris park.

Towards boulevard St-Germain is the neoclassical **Odéon, Théâtre de l'Europe** (*see p340*), built in 1779 and recently renovated. Beaumarchais' *Le Mariage de Figaro* was first performed here in 1784. A house in the square in front was home to Revolutionary hero Camille Desmoulins, who incited the mob to attack the Bastille in 1789. Now it's occupied by La Méditerranée (2 pl de l'Odéon, 6th, 01.43.26.02.30); an arty rendezvous in the 1940s, the restaurant's menus and plates were designed by Jean Cocteau. Joyce's *Ulysses* was first published in 1922 by Sylvia Beach at the iconic Shakespeare & Co at 12 rue de l'Odéon (no relation to the current Latin Quarter bookshop, whose first owner was given permission to use the name).

Further along the street, at 12 rue de l'Ecole-de-Médecine, is the colonnaded neo-classical Université René Descartes (Paris V) medical school, and the **Musée d'Histoire de la Médecine**. The Club des Cordeliers, set up by Danton in 1790, devised revolutionary plots across the street at the Couvent des Cordeliers (No.15); the 14th-century refectory, all that remains of the monastery founded by St Louis, houses contemporary art exhibitions. Marat, one of the club's leading lights, was stabbed to

Boules, boats and sun-dappled bonhomie – the **Jardin du Luxembourg**. *See p153*.

Chirac's *grand projet*

Every French president, it seems, needs a pet project. Pompidou had his Centre, Mitterrand his Bibliothèque, and Jacques Chirac, clearly not the man to be left out, will shortly have the Musée du Quai Branly. A museum dedicated to the ethnic art of Africa, Oceania, Asia and the Americas, it joins together the collections of the Musée des Arts d'Afrique et d'Océanie and the Laboratoire d'Ethnologie du Musée de l'Homme, as well as contemporary indigenous art. The aim of the museum is to 'officially recognise the rightful place of these civilisations, together with the heritage of peoples who are sometimes forgotten, in the present culture of the world'.

Factor in an extraordinary building by Jean Nouvel (whose last foray in the Paris museums circuit was the stunning Fondation Cartier; *see p166*) on a prime riverside site within spitting distance of the Eiffel Tower and covering 40,000 square metres, and Paris has a new big hitter in its powerful museum line-up. It looks to be a pleasing addition to the *quartier*: the landscaped gardens that will take up half the site incorporate an open-air amphitheatre and extend to the building itself, with a 'vertical garden' of 15,000 plants scaling the façade.

The museum's remit goes beyond merely presenting relics from the 300,000 strong collection, which includes ceremonial objects from the Pacific islands, costumes and textiles from the Far East, statuary and musical instruments from a variety of African cultures, and pre-Columbian treasures and sacred objects from more recent times from throughout the Americas. There will be audio-visual displays to provide cultural and historic context, a multimedia library and a 500-seat auditorium. Plans for the latter include a full programme of theatre, music and dance performances, plus the opportunity to relay the oral tradition that is inherent to so many global cultures.

Despite a frustrating number of delays – including an alarming spot of flooding in June 2005 – the Musée du Quai Branly looks set to open at last in the summer of 2006. All in all, it promises to be an extraordinary, and much-needed, addition to the capital's traditionally stuffy museum scene.

Musée du Quai Branly

29-55 quai Branly, 7th (01.56.61.70.00/ www.quaibranly.fr). RER Pont de l'Alma. **Open** ring for details. **Map** p406 C6.

death in the bathtub at his home in the same street; David depicted the moment after the crime in his iconic painting, the *Death of Marat*. This was the surgeons' district: observe the sculpted doorway of the neighbouring *hôtel* and the domed building at No.5, once the barbers' and surgeons' guild (the two nearly the same thing in early medicine), now university premises. Climb rue André-Dubois to rue Monsieur-le-Prince to reach budget restaurant Polidor (No.41, 6th, 01.43.26.95.34), in business since 1845; further along is arts cinema Les 3 Luxembourg (No.67, 6th, 01.46.33.97.77).

Eglise St-Sulpice
pl St-Sulpice, 6th (01.46.33.21.78). M° St-Sulpice. **Open** 7.30am-7.30pm daily. **Map** p410 H7.
It took 120 years (starting in 1646) and six architects to finish the church of St-Sulpice. The grandiose Italianate façade, with its two-tier colonnade, was designed by Jean-Baptiste Servandoni. He died in 1766 before the second tower was finished, leaving one tower a good five metres shorter than the other. Three murals by Delacroix in the first chapel – *Jacob's Fight with the Angel, Heliodorus Chased from the Temple* and *St Michael Killing the Dragon* – create a suitably sombre atmosphere. **Photo** *p148*.

Jardin & Palais du Luxembourg
pl Auguste-Comte, pl Edmond-Rostand or rue de Vaugirard, 6th (01.42.34.23.89/www.senat.fr/visite). M° Odéon/RER Luxembourg. **Open** *Jardin* summer 8am-dusk daily; winter 9am-dusk daily. **Map** p410 H8.
The palace was built in the 1620s for Marie de Médicis, widow of Henri IV, by Salomon de Brosse on the site of the former mansion of the Duke of Luxembourg. Its Italianate style, with Mannerist rusticated columns, was intended to remind her of the Pitti Palace in her native Florence. In 1621 she commissioned Rubens to produce for the palace the 24 huge paintings, now in the Louvre, celebrating her life. Reworked by Chalgrin in the 18th century, the palace now houses the French parliament's upper house, the Sénat (open only by guided visits or on the *Journées du Patrimoine; see p276*).

The mansion next door (Le Petit Luxembourg) is the residence of the Sénat's president. The gardens, though, are the real draw: part formal (terraces and gravel paths), part 'English garden' (lawns and mature trees), they are the quintessential Paris park. The garden is almost crowded with sculptures: a looming Cyclops (on the 1624 Fontaine de Médicis), queens of France, a mini Statue of Liberty, wild animals, busts of literary giants Flaubert and Baudelaire, and a monument to Delacroix. There are orchards (300 varieties of apples and pears) and an apiary where you can take beekeeping courses. The Musée du Luxembourg (*see below*) hosts prestigious art exhibitions, with lesser art shows in the former Orangerie. Most interesting, though, are the people: an international mixture of *flâneurs* and *dragueurs*,

chess players and martial arts practitioners; as well as children on ponies, in sandpits, up climbing frames, on roundabouts and playing with the old-fashioned sailing boats on the pond (*see p285*). Then there are the tennis courts (*see p336*), boules pitches (*see p331*), a bandstand showcasing concerts on summer afternoons – and hundreds and hundreds of park chairs. **Photo** *p151*.

Musée d'Histoire de la Médecine
Université René Descartes, 12 rue de l'Ecole-de-Médecine, 6th (01.40.46.16.93). M° Odéon. **Open** *Mid July-Sept* 2-5.30pm Mon-Fri. *Oct-mid July* 2-5.30pm Mon-Wed, Fri, Sat. Closed public hols. **Admission** €3.50; €2.50 students; free under-8s. **No credit cards. Map** p410 H7.
The history of medicine is the subject of the medical faculty collection. There are ancient Egyptian embalming tools, a 1960s electrocardiograph and a gruesome array of saws used for amputations. As well, you'll find the instruments of Dr Antommarchi, who performed the autopsy on Napoléon, and the scalpel of Dr Félix, who operated on Louis XIV.

Musée des Lettres et Manuscrits
8 rue de Nesle, 6th (01.40.51.02.25/www.museedes lettres.fr). M° Odéon. **Open** 1-9pm Wed; 10am-6pm Thur-Sun. Closed public hols. **Admission** €8; €5.50 students, over-60s, 12-15s; free under-12s. **Credit** (€16 minimum) MC, V. **Map** p410 H7.
This intimate space in the heart of the Latin Quarter presents modern history as recorded on paper. More than 2,000 documents and letters give an insight into the lives of the great and the good, from Magritte to Mozart and Freud to François Mitterrand. Einstein arrives at the theory of relativity on notes scattered in authentic disorder, Napoléon boards HMS *Northumberland* in its log-book on the day it took him to St Helena, and Baudelaire complains about his money problems in a letter to his mother.

Musée National du Luxembourg
19 rue de Vaugirard, 6th (01.42.34.25.95/www. museeduluxembourg.fr). M° Cluny La Sorbonne/RER Luxembourg. **Open** 11am-10.30pm Mon, Fri; 11am-7pm Tue-Thur, Sat; 9am-7pm Sun. **Admission** €10; €7 students, 8-25s; free under-8s. **Credit** MC, V. **Map** p410 H7.
When it opened in 1750, this small but imposing museum was the first public gallery in France. Its current stewardship by the national museums and the French Senate has brought imaginative touches and some impressive coups. Kicking off 2006 is an exhibition (until 26 Mar) of European masterworks loaned by Washington's Phillips Collection, including Renoir's *Luncheon of the Boating Party*. Book ahead to avoid queues.

The 7th & western Paris
Mainly 7th arrondissement, parts of 15th.
Townhouses spread out westwards from St-Germain into the profoundly establishment 7th arrondissement, as the streetlife and café

Sightseeing

culture give way to tranquil residential blocks and government offices. The 7th divides into the intimate Faubourg St-Germain, with historic mansions and fine shops, and Les Invalides, its wide windswept avenues and the Eiffel Tower.

The Faubourg St-Germain

In the early 18th century, when the Marais went out of fashion, aristocrats built palatial new residences on the Faubourg St-Germain, the district developing around the site of the former city wall. It is still a well-bred part of the city, government ministries and foreign embassies colouring the area with flags and diplomatic number plates. Many fine *hôtels particuliers* survive; glimpse their stone gateways and elegant entrance courtyards on rues de Grenelle, St-Dominique, de l'Université and de Varenne.

Just west of St-Germain, the 'Carré Rive Gauche' or 'Carré des Antiquaires' – the quadrangle of streets enclosed by quai Voltaire,

Scandale! Marble marvel

Walk through the main entrance of the Musée d'Orsay (*see p159*), stroll 50 yards up the central aisle, and there – slap bang in the middle – is the writhing figure of a naked siren captured, for all the world, in the throes of orgasm. Auguste Clésinger's *Woman Bitten by a Snake* (if so, where's the snake, eh?) was the scandal of 1847, its success ensured by the rumour, orchestrated by literary critic Théophile Gautier, that Clésinger had cast his work from real life.

Whatever she was doing at the time, Clésinger's model, Apollonie Sabatier, had achieved enough notoriety without further recourse to snakes or sexual gymnastics. Born of unknown parentage as Aglaé-Joséphine Savatier in 1822, this bedtime companion of much of the literary set of 19th-century Paris was better known as 'La Présidente', after manifold *galanteries* in the pornographic letters written to her by Gautier himself. (Apollonie, née Aglaé-Joséphine,

swiftly changed Savatier to Sabatier after it was pointed out to her that *savate* meant worn-out slipper.)

La Présidente was one of the 'grandes horizontales', ladies who frequented literary salons, entertaining writers and bestowing occasional favours. The Sunday salon Sabatier ran herself, 'La Nouvelle Athènes', gave its name to a small corner of the 9th arrondissement, and many influential visitors – Gautier, Baudelaire, the philanthropist Richard Wallace – were invited to her bed. (Wallace spent some of his family fortune on the hundred or so ornate public drinking fountains still dotted around Paris today.)

In the same year as the scandal, Clésinger married George Sand's daughter, but the resultant daughter Nini died soon after the couple separated in 1855. Some of his more sober sculptures – such as the one of Gustave Flaubert – can be seen in the Jardin du Luxembourg (*see p153*).

rue des Sts-Pères, rue du Bac and rue de l'Université – is filled with antiques shops. On rue des Sts-Pères, *chocolatier* **Debauve & Gallais** (*see p261*), with its classic period interior, has been making chocolates since 1800, originally for medicinal purposes. Rue du Pré-aux-Clercs, named after a field where students used to sort out their differences by duelling, is today a favourite with fashion insiders. There are still students to be found on adjoining rue St-Guillaume, home to the prestigious Fondation Nationale des Sciences-Politiques (No.27, 7th, 01.45.49.50.50, www.sciences-po.fr), more commonly known as 'Sciences-Po'.

Rue de Montalembert is home to two of the Left Bank's smartest hotels: the **Hôtel Montalembert** (*see p62*) and the Hôtel du Pont-Royal, a gastronomic magnet since the addition of the trendy **Atelier de Joël Robuchon** (*see p210*). By the river, a Beaux Arts train station – the towns once served still listed on the façade – houses the unmissable art collections of the **Musée d'Orsay**; outside on the esplanade are 19th-century bronze *animalier* sculptures. Next door is the lovely 1780s Hôtel de Salm, a mansion built for a German prince and now the Musée National de la Légion d'Honneur (2 rue de la Légion d'Honneur, 7th, 01.40.62.84.25), devoted to France's honours system. Across the street, a modern footbridge, the Passerelle Solférino, crosses the Seine to the Tuileries. Fancy Hôtel Bouchardon today houses the **Musée Maillol**. Beside its curved entrance, the Fontaine des Quatre-Saisons by Bouchardon has statues of the seasons surrounding allegorical figures of Paris above the rivers Seine and Marne.

You'll have to wait for the open-house Journées du Patrimoine (*see p276*) to see the decorative interiors and private gardens of other *hôtels*, such as the Hôtel de Villeroy (Ministry of Agriculture; 78 rue de Varenne, 7th), Hôtel Boisgelin (Italian Embassy; 47 rue de Varenne, 7th), Hôtel d'Avaray (Dutch ambassador's residence; 85 rue de Grenelle, 7th), Hôtel d'Estrées (Russian ambassador's residence; 79 rue de Grenelle, 7th), or Hôtel de Monaco (Polish Embassy; 57 rue St-Dominique, 7th). Among the most beautiful is the Hôtel Matignon (57 rue de Varenne, 7th), residence of the prime minister. Once used by French statesman Talleyrand for lavish receptions, it contains the biggest private garden in Paris. The Cité Varenne at No.51 is a lane of exclusive houses with private gardens.

Rue du Bac is home to the city's oldest and most elegant department store, **Le Bon Marché** ('the good bargain'; *see p233*), and to an unlikely pilgrimage spot, the **Chapelle de la Médaille Miraculeuse**. On nearby rue de

Babylone, handy budget bistro Au Babylone (No.13, 7th, 01.45.48.72.13) has been serving up lunches for decades, but the Théâtre de Babylone, where Beckett's *Waiting for Godot* was premièred in 1953, is long since gone.

At the foot of boulevard St-Germain, facing place de la Concorde across the Seine, is the **Assemblée Nationale**, the lower house of the French parliament. Behind, elegant place du Palais-Bourbon leads into rue de Bourgogne, a rare commercial thoroughfare amid the official buildings, with some delectable pâtisseries and designer furniture showrooms. Nearby, the mid 19th-century Eglise Ste-Clothilde (12 rue Martignac, 7th, 01.44.18.62.60), with its skeletal twin spires, is an early example of Gothic Revival. Beside the Assemblée is the Foreign Ministry, often referred to by its address, 'quai d'Orsay'. Beyond it, a long, grassy esplanade leads up to the golden-domed **Invalides**. The vast military hospital complex, with its Eglise du Dôme and St-Louis-des-Invalides churches, all built by Louis XIV, epitomises the official grandeur of the Sun King as expression of royal and military power. It now houses the **Musée de l'Armée**, as well as Napoléon's tomb inside the Eglise du Dôme. Stand with your back to the dome to survey cherubim-laden Pont Alexandre III and the **Grand** and **Petit Palais** (*see p120*) over the river, all three put up for the 1900 Exposition Universelle. Just beside Les Invalides is the **Musée Rodin**, occupying the charming 18th-century Hôtel Biron and its romantic gardens. Rodin was invited here in 1908, on the understanding that he would give his work to the state. Many of his great sculptures, including the *Thinker*, the *Burghers of Calais* and the swarming *Gates of Hell*, are displayed in his house and around the gardens.

Assemblée Nationale

33 quai d'Orsay, 7th (01.40.63.60.00/www. assemblee-nat.fr). M° Assemblée Nationale. **Map** p407 F5.

Like the Sénat, the Assemblée Nationale (also known as the Palais Bourbon) is another royal building adapted for republicanism. It was built in 1722-28 for the Duchesse de Bourbon, daughter of Louis XIV and Madame de Montespan, who also put up the neighbouring Hôtel de Lassay (official residence of the Assembly's president) for her lover, the Marquis de Lassay. The *palais* was modelled on the Grand Trianon at Versailles, with a colonnaded *cour d'honneur* opening on to rue de l'Université and gardens running down to the Seine. The Prince de Condé extended the palace, linked the two *hôtels* and laid out the place du Palais-Bourbon. The Greek temple-style façade facing Pont de la Concorde (actually the rear of the building) was added only in 1806 to mirror the Madeleine. Flanking this riverside façade are statues of four great statesmen: L'Hôpital, Sully,

Sightseeing

Built by Bourbons, debated in daily by *députés* – the **Assemblée Nationale**. *See p155.*

Colbert and Aguesseau. The Napoleonic frieze on the pediment was replaced by a monarchist one after the restoration: between 1838 and 1841 Cortot sculpted the figures of France, Power and Justice. After the Revolution, the palace became the meeting place for the Conseil des Cinq-Cents, the new legislative body. It was the forerunner of the parliament's lower house, which set up here for good in 1827, radically altering the interior with the building of the Hémicycle debating chamber. Visits are only possible by arrangement through a *député* (if you're French) – or, after long queuing, during the Journées du Patrimoine (*see p276*). **Photo** *above.*

Chapelle de la Médaille Miraculeuse
Couvent des Soeurs de St-Vincent-de-Paul, 140 rue du Bac, 7th (01.49.54.78.88). M° Sèvres Babylone. **Open** 7.45am-1pm, 2.30-7pm daily. **Map** p407 F7.
In 1830 saintly Catherine Labouré was said to have been visited by the Virgin, who gave her a medal that performed miracles. This kitsch chapel – murals, mosaics, statues and the embalmed bodies of Catherine and her mother superior – is one of France's most visited sites, attracting two million pilgrims every year. Reliefs in the courtyard tell the nun's story – and slot machines sell medals.

Espace EDF Electra
6 rue Récamier, 7th (01.53.63.23.45/www.edf.fr). M° Sèvres Babylone. **Open** noon-7pm Tue-Sun. Closed public hols. **Admission** free. **Map** p407 G7.
This former electricity substation, converted by Electricité de France for PR purposes, is now used for varied, well-presented exhibitions examining the

likes of garden designer Gilles Clément and pioneer filmmaker Georges Méliès. First up in 2006 is an exhibition of contemporary Franco-British art.

Les Invalides & Musée de l'Armée
esplanade des Invalides, 7th (01.44.42.40.69/www. invalides.org). M° La Tour Maubourg or Varenne. **Open** *Apr-Sept* 10am-5.45pm daily. *Oct-Mar* 10am-5pm daily. Closed 1st Mon of mth & public hols. **Admission** *Courtyard* free. *Musée de l'Armée & Eglise du Dôme* €7.50; €5.50 students under 26; free under-18s, CM. **Credit** MC, V. **Map** p407 E6.
Its imposing gilded dome is misleading: the Hôtel des Invalides was (and in part still is) a hospital. Commissioned by Louis XIV for wounded soldiers, it once housed as many as 6,000 invalids. Designed by Libéral Bruand (the foundations were laid in 1671) and then later completed by Jules Hardouin-Mansart, it's a magnificent monument to Louis XIV and Napoléon. Behind lines of topiaried yews and cannons, the main (northern) façade has a relief of Louis XIV (Ludovicus Magnus) and the Sun King's sunburst. Wander through the main courtyard and you'll see grandiose two-storey arcades, sundials on three sides and a statue of Napoléon glaring out from the end; the dormer windows around the courtyards are sculpted in the form of suits of armour.
The complex contains two churches – or, rather, a sort of double church: the Eglise St-Louis was for the soldiers, the Eglise du Dôme for the king, and each had its own separate entrance. You'll find an opening behind the altar between the two. The long, barrel-vaulted nave of the church of St-Louis is hung with flags captured from enemy troops. Since 1840

Where the Sun King meets Napoléon – **Les Invalides & Musée de l'Armée**. *See p156.*

the baroque Eglise du Dôme has been solely dedicated to the worship of Napoléon, whose body was supposedly brought here from St Helena (although this is now in doubt).

On the ground floor, under a dome painted by De la Fosse, Jouvenet and Coypel, are chapels featuring monuments to such generals as Vauban, Foch and Joseph Napoléon (Napoléon's older brother and King of Italy and Spain). Napoléon II (King of Rome) is buried in the crypt with his father the emperor. Two dramatic black figures holding up the entrance to the crypt, the red porphyry tomb, the ring of giant figures, and the friezes and texts eulogising the emperor's heroic deeds give the measure of the cult of Napoléon, cherished in France for ruling large swaths of Europe and for creating an administrative and educational system that endures to this day.

The Invalides also houses the Musée de l'Ordre de la Libération and the Musée des Plans-Reliefs, the collection of scale models of cities begun by Vauban, and once used as an aid to military strategy. Also included in the entry price is the impressive Musée de l'Armée. For the military historian, the museum is a must, but even if sumptuous uniforms and hefty cannons are not your thing, the building is itself a splendour. Besides military memorabilia, the rooms are filled with fine portraiture, such as Ingres' *Emperor Napoléon on his Throne*. The World War I rooms are moving, with the conflict brought into vivid focus by documents and photos. The Général de Gaulle wing deals with World War II, taking in not only the Resistance but also the Battle of Britain and the war in the Pacific, alternating artefacts with contemporary film footage. **Photos** *above.*

Musée Maillol

59-61 rue de Grenelle, 7th (01.42.22.59.58/www. museemaillol.com). M° Rue du Bac. **Open** 11am-6pm (last admission 5.15pm) Mon, Wed-Sun. **Admission** €8; €6 students; free under-16s. **Credit** *Shop* AmEx, MC, V. **Map** p407 G7.

Dina Vierny was 15 when she met Aristide Maillol (1861-1944) and became his principal model for the next decade, idealised in such sculptures as *Spring*, *Air* and *Harmony*. In 1995 she opened this delightful museum above the renovated 18th-century Hôtel Bouchardon, exhibiting Maillol's drawings, engravings, pastels, tapestry panels, ceramics and early Nabis-related paintings, as well as the sculptures and terracottas that epitomise his calm, modern classicism. Vierny also set up a Maillol Museum in his Pyrenean village of Banyuls-sur-Mer. This Paris venue also has works by Picasso, Rodin, Gauguin, Degas and Cézanne, a whole room of Matisse drawings, rare Surrealist documents and works by naïve artists. Vierny has also championed Kandinsky and Ilya Kabakov, whose *Communal Kitchen* installation recreates the atmosphere of Soviet domesticity. Monographic exhibitions are devoted to modern and contemporary artists; the highlight for 2006 is a Magritte retrospective (8 Mar-19 June).

Musée National Rodin

Hôtel Biron, 77 rue de Varenne, 7th (01.44.18.61.10/www.musee-rodin.fr). M° Varenne. **Open** *Apr-Sept* 9.30am-5.15pm Tue-Sun (gardens until 6.45pm). *Oct-Mar* 9.30am-4.15pm (gardens until 5pm) Tue-Sun. **Admission** €5; €3 18-25s, all on Sun; free under-18s, all on 1st Sun of mth, CM. *Gardens* €1. **Credit** MC, V. **Map** p407 F6.

Trains and busts and panes – the **Musee d'Orsay**. *See p159.*

Sightseeing

The Rodin museum occupies the *hôtel particulier* where the sculptor lived at the end of his life. The *Kiss*, the *Cathedral*, the *Walking Man*, portrait busts and early terracottas are exhibited indoors, as are many of the individual figures or small groups that also appear on the *Gates of Hell*. Rodin's works are accompanied by several pieces by his mistress and pupil, Camille Claudel. The walls are hung with paintings by Van Gogh, Monet, Renoir, Carrière and Rodin himself. Most visitors have greatest affection for the gardens, spotted with trees and treasures: look out for the *Burghers of Calais*, the elaborate *Gates of Hell* (inspired by Dante's *Inferno*), the *Thinker*, *Orpheus* under shade, and unfinished nymphs emerging from their marble matrix. Fans can also visit the Villa des Brillants at Meudon (19 av Rodin, Meudon, 01.41.14.35.00, closed Mon-Thur and Oct-Apr), where Rodin worked from 1895.

Musée d'Orsay

1 rue de la Légion-d'Honneur, 7th (01.40.49.48.14/ recorded information 01.45.49.11.11/www.musee-orsay.fr). M° *Solférino/RER Musée d'Orsay.* **Open** 10am-6pm (from 9am June-Sept) Tue, Wed, Fri, Sat; 10am-9.30pm (from 9am June-Sept) Thur; 9am-6pm Sun. **Admission** €7.50; €5.50 concessions, all on Sun; free under-18s, all on 1st Sun of mth. **Credit Shop** MC, V. **Map** p407 G6.
The building was originally a train station, designed by Victor Laloux to coincide with the 1900 Exposition Universelle. The platforms proved too short for modern trains and, by the 1950s, the station was threatened with demolition; it then became home to a theatre (the Renaud-Barrault), and scenes in Orson Welles' *The Trial* were filmed here. It was saved in the late 1970s when President Giscard d'Estaing decided to turn it into a museum spanning the fertile art period between 1848 and 1914. (The painter Edouard Détaille had said it looked like a palace of fine art when it was built.) Italian architect Gae Aulenti remodelled the interior, keeping the iron-framed, coffered roof and creating galleries either side of a light-filled canyon. The arrangement has its drawbacks – upstairs, the Impressionists and post-Impressionists are knee-deep in tourists, while too much space is given downstairs to Couture's languid nudes and Meissonier's history paintings – but it somehow manages to keep its open-plan feel.

The museum follows a chronological route, from the ground floor to the upper level and then to the mezzanine, showing links between Impressionist painters and their forerunners. Running down the centre of the tracks, a central sculpture aisle takes in monuments and maidens by artists including Rude, Barrye and Carrier-Belleuse, but the outstanding pieces are by Carpeaux, including his controversial *La Danse* for the façade of the Palais Garnier. The Lille side, on the right of the central aisle, is dedicated to the Romantics and history painters: Ingres and Amaury-Duval contrast with the Romantic passion of Delacroix's North African period, Couture's vast *Les Romains de la Décadence* and the cupids of Cabanel's *Birth of Venus*. Further

on are a number of early Degas canvases and works by Symbolists Moreau and Puvis de Chavannes; another gallery provides space for selections from the Orsay's vast holdings of early photography.

The first rooms to the Seine side of the main aisle are given over to the Barbizon landscape painters: Corot, Daubigny and Millet. One room is dedicated to Courbet, with the *Artist and his Studio*, the monumental *Burial at Ornans* and show-stopping *L'Origine du Monde*. This floor also covers pre-1870 works by Impressionists, including Manet's provocative *Olympia*, and their precursor Boudin.

Upstairs are the Impressionists, with masterworks by Pissarro, Renoir and Caillebotte, Manet's *Déjeuner sur l'Herbe*, Monet's paintings of Rouen cathedral and works by Degas. Among the Van Goghs are later works *Church at Auvers* and *Wheat Field with Crows*. You'll also find the primitivist jungle of Le Douanier Rousseau, the gaudy lowlife of Toulouse-Lautrec, the colourful exoticism of Gauguin's Breton and Tahitian periods and Cézanne's still lifes, landscapes and the *Card Players*, as well as works by Seurat and Signac, and the mystical pastel drawings of Odilon Redon.

On the mezzanine are works by the Nabis painters – Vallotton, Denis, Roussel, Bonnard and Vuillard. Several rooms are given over to art nouveau decorative arts, including furniture by Majorelle, and Gallé and Lalique ceramics. Paintings by Klimt and Burne-Jones reside here, and there are sections on architectural drawings and early photography. The sculpture terraces include busts by Rodin, heads by Rosso and bronzes by Bourdelle and Maillol.

The exhibitions scheduled for 2006 include the blockbuster-in-waiting *Cézanne and Pissarro* (28 Feb-18 May); *From Symbolism to Expressionism*, a retrospective of the Danish artist Jens Ferdinand Willumsen (27 June-17 Sept); and a confrontation of sculpture by Rodin and paintings by his friend Eugène Carrière (11 July-1 Oct). **Photos** *left and p154.*

West of Les Invalides

South-west of the Invalides is the massive Ecole Militaire (av de la Motte-Picquet, 7th), the military academy built by Louis XV to educate the children of penniless officers; it would later train Napoléon. The severe neo-classical building was designed by Jacques Ange Gabriel. It's still used by the army and closed to the public. From the north-western side of the Ecole Militaire begins the vast Champ de Mars, a market garden converted into a military drilling ground in the 18th century. It has long been home to the most celebrated Paris monument of all, the **Eiffel Tower**. At the south-eastern end of the Champ de Mars stands the Mur pour la Paix ('wall for peace'), erected in 2000 to articulate hopes for peace. South-east of the Ecole are the Y-shaped **UNESCO** building, built in 1958, and the modernist

Sightseeing

Ministry of Labour. Smart apartments line broad avenues Bosquet and Suffren, though there's much architectural eclecticism in the area: look at the pseudo-Gothic and pseudo-Renaissance houses on avenue de Villars, Lavirotte's fabulous art nouveau doorway at 27 avenue Rapp and the striking, box-shaped Notre-Dame de l'Arche de l'Alliance church (81 rue d'Alleray, 15th, 01.56.56.62.56), which was completed in 1998. For signs of life, visit the **Saxe-Breteuil** street market (*see p259* **Forward *marché!***), and old-fashioned bistros Thoumieux (79 rue St-Dominique, 7th, 01.47.05.49.75) and, on an arcaded square next to a pretty fountain, Fontaine de Mars (129 rue St-Dominique, 7th, 01.47.05.46.44). The upper reaches of rue Cler contain classy food shops.

Les Egouts de Paris

Entrance opposite 93 quai d'Orsay, by Pont de l'Alma, 7th (01.53.68.27.81). M° Alma Marceau/RER Pont de l'Alma. **Open** 11am-4pm (until 5pm May-Sept) Wed-Sat. Closed 3wks Jan. **Admission** €3.80; €3.05 5-12s; free under-5s, CM. **No credit cards. Map** p402 D5.
For centuries the main source of drinking water in Paris was the Seine, which was also the main sewer. Construction of an underground sewerage system began in 1825 under Napoléon. Today the Egouts de Paris is a smelly museum; each sewer in the 2,100km system is marked with a replica of the street sign above. The Egouts can be closed after periods of heavy rain.

Eiffel Tower

Champ de Mars, 7th (01.44.11.23.45/recorded information 01.44.11.23.23/www.tour-eiffel.fr). M° Bir-Hakeim/RER Champ de Mars Tour Eiffel. **Open** *14 June-31 Aug* 9am-midnight daily. *1 Sept-13 June* 9.30am-11pm daily. **Admission** *By stairs* (1st & 2nd levels, 9.30am-6.30pm) €3.80; €3 under-25s. *By lift* (1st level) €4.10; €2.30 3-12s; (2nd level) €7.50; €4.10 3-12s; (3rd level) €10.70; €5.90 3-12s; free under-3s. **Credit** AmEx, MC, V. **Map** p406 C6.
No building better symbolises Paris than the Tour Eiffel. Maupassant claimed he left Paris because of it, William Morris visited daily to avoid having to see it from afar, and it was meant to be a temporary structure. The radical cast-iron tower was built – for the 1889 World Fair and the centenary of the 1789 Revolution – by engineer Gustave Eiffel (whose construction company still exists today). Eiffel made use of new technology that was already popular in iron-framed buildings. Construction took more than two years and used some 18,000 pieces of metal and 2,500,000 rivets. The 300-metre tower stands on four massive concrete piles, and was the tallest structure in the world until overtaken by New York's Empire State Building in the 1930s. Vintage double-decker lifts ply their way up and down, or you can walk as far as the second level. There are souvenir shops, an exhibition space, café and even a post office on the first and second levels. The smart Jules Verne

restaurant, on the second level, has its own lift in the north tower. At the top (third level), there's Eiffel's cosy salon and a viewing platform with panels pointing out what to see in every direction. Views can reach over 65km on a good day, although the most fascinating perspectives are of the ironwork itself, whether gazing up from underneath or enjoying the changing vision as the lift rises. At night, for ten minutes on the hour, 20,000 flashbulbs attached to the tower provide a beautiful shimmering effect. The tower has some six million visitors a year; to avoid the queues, come late at night. **Photo** *right.*

UNESCO

7 pl de Fontenoy, 7th (01.45.68.10.00/tours 01.45.68.16.42/www.unesco.org). M° Ecole Militaire. **Open** 10am-3pm Mon-Fri. *Tours* 3pm Mon-Fri (in English on Tue). **Admission** free. **Map** p407 D7.
The Y-shaped UNESCO headquarters, built in 1958, is home to a swarm of international diplomats. It's worth visiting for the sculptures and paintings – by Picasso, Arp, Giacometti, Moore, Calder and Miró – and the Japanese garden, with its contemplation cylinder by minimalist architect Tadao Ando.

Village Suisse

38-78 av de Suffren or 54 av La Motte-Picquet, 15th (www.levillagesuise.com). M° La Motte Picquet Grenelle. **Open** 10.30am-12.30pm, 1.30-7pm Mon, Thur-Sun. **Map** p406 D7.
The mountains and waterfalls created for the Swiss Village at the 1900 Exposition Universelle are long gone, but the village lives on. Rebuilt as blocks of flats, the street level has been colonised by some 150 boutiques offering high-quality, though pricey, antiques and collectibles.

Along the Seine

Downstream from the Eiffel Tower, the high-tech **Maison de la Culture du Japon** stands near Pont Bir-Hakeim on quai Branly. Beyond, the 15th-arrondissement Fronts de Seine riverfront, with its tower block developments, was the site of some of the worst architecture of the 1970s. This would-be brave new world of walkways, suspended gardens and tower blocks had no easily discoverable means of access. The adjacent Beaugrenelle shopping centre is more straightforward to get into, but remains woefully dingy – though there are plans for an extensive redevelopment in the next few years. Further west, things look up: the sophisticated former headquarters of the Canal+ TV channel (2 rue des Cévennes, 15th), designed by American architect Richard Meier, is surrounded by fine modern housing; and the pleasant **Parc André Citroën**, created in the 1990s on the site of the former Citroën car works, runs down to the Seine quayside – where you'll find the occasional cruise ship and August party-goers.

Sightseeing

The **Eiffel Tower**. *See p160.*

Maison de la Culture du Japon

101bis quai Branly, 15th (01.44.37.95.00/www.
mcjp.asso.fr). Mº Bir-Hakeim/RER Champ de Mars
Tour Eiffel. **Open** noon-7pm Tue, Wed, Fri, Sat;
noon-8pm Thur. Closed Aug. **Admission** free.
Map p406 C6.

Built in 1996 by the Anglo-Japanese architectural
partnership of Masayuki Yamanaka and Kenneth
Armstrong, this opalescent glass cultural centre
screens films and puts on exhibitions and plays. It
also has a library, an authentic Japanese tea pavilion on the roof, where you can watch the tea ceremony, and a well-stocked book and gift shop.

Parc André Citroën

rue Balard, rue St-Charles or quai Citroën, 15th.
Mº Javel or Balard. **Open** 8am-dusk Mon-Fri; 9am-
dusk Sat, Sun, public hols. **Map** p406 A9.

This park is a fun, postmodern version of a French
formal garden by Gilles Clément and Alain Prévost.
It comprises glasshouses, computerised fountains,
waterfalls, a wilderness and themed gardens with
different coloured plants and even sounds. Stepping
stones and water jets make it a garden for pleasure
as well as philosophy. The tethered Eutelsat helium
balloon takes visitors up for marvellous panoramic
views over the city. If the weather looks unreliable,
call 01.44.26.20.00 to check the day's programme.

Montparnasse & beyond

Mainly 14th & 15th arrondissements, parts of 6th.
Artists such as Picasso, Léger and Soutine
fled to 'Mount Parnassus' in the early 1900s to
escape the rising rents of Montmartre. They
were soon joined by Chagall, Zadkine and other
escapees from the Russian Revolution, and by
Americans such as Man Ray, Henry Miller,
Ezra Pound and Gertrude Stein. Between the
wars the neighbourhood symbolised modernity:
studio buildings with large north-facing

Paris promenade Writer way

No spot on the planet has as many literary
associations in so small an area as St-
Germain-des-Prés. The myth of the struggling
writer in a garret might have died now Louis
Vuitton is next door to the Deux Magots, but
the ghosts – and the bookshops, wholesalers
and publishers – are still there.

Once you've emerged from the métro onto
place St-Michel, take the rue de l'Hirondelle
(more passageway than street, to the right
of the fountain). This brings you to rue Gît-le-
Coeur. At No.9, on your right, is the **Hôtel
du Vieux Paris** (❶ 6th, 01.43.54.41.66) –
otherwise known as the Beat Hotel. It's been
smartened up since William Burroughs wrote
Naked Lunch in a drug-crazed frenzy, and Ted
Joans' mural *The Chick Who feels off a Rhino*
is no more, but photos of the Beats adorn the
wall and Mme Odillard will show fans photos
of those wild times in a signed copy of Brian
Chapman's book, *The Beat Hotel.*

Continue to the quai des Grands-Augustins,
which supplies literary nourishment with its
bouquinistes (*see p242*). No.21 was an
early home of George Sand. The restaurant
Lapérouse (❷ *see p207*), at No.51, was a
literary hot-spot from 1870: its small salons
– designed for dangerous liaisons – hosted
Sand, Maupassant, Zola, Dumas, Musset
and Hugo. Photos of some of this crowd
are on the wall of the ground-floor bar.

Walk on to rue Dauphine, and drop down
little rue Mazet. At No.3, the former
restaurant Magny (now **Azabu**; ❸ 6th,

01.46.33.72.05) is where George Sand
smoked cigars with Flaubert, Gautier and
Turgenev at Sainte-Beuve's literary dinners.

Cross rue St-André-des-Arts and go through
the archway at No.59 to find a charming
covered passage (cour du Commerce St-
André) and the rear entrance of **Le Procope**
(❹ 13 rue de l'Ancienne Comédie, 6th,
01.40.46.79.00), the oldest café in Paris. In
business since 1686, it claims Balzac, Sade,
Voltaire, Rousseau, Beaumarchais, Verlaine,
Hugo, La Fontaine and Anatole France as
former customers. The food, sadly, is as dull
as such patrons were great, but upstairs you
can see a strange memorial of sorts, with
Voltaire's marble desk and a cringeworthy
letter from the imprisoned Marie-Antoinette.

Leave by the café's front entrance, turn left
to get to boulevard St-Germain, bear right and
then turn right again two roads up, into rue de
Seine, which is peppered with literary haunts.
At No.60 is the modest **Hôtel La Louisianne**
(❺ 6th, 01.44.32.17.17). Cyril Connolly's
Unquiet Grave describes the ferrets with bells
on that were here during World War II;
Simone de Beauvoir and Sartre, as well as
many other regulars of the Café de Flore,
lodged here towards the end of the war, and
Sartre rehearsed his play *Huis Clos* here with
Camus. The only memorabilia is a newspaper
interview with Juliette Gréco, but the hotel
does have a living poet *in situ*: the 93-year-
old Albert Cossery, known as 'the last dandy',
who has been here for over 50 years. At

windows were built by avant-garde architects all over this part of Paris; artists, writers and intellectuals drank and debated in the quarter's showy bars; and naughty pastimes – such as the tango – flourished.

Today Montparnasse has lost much of its soul. The high-rise **Tour Montparnasse**, the first skyscraper in central Paris, is the most visible of several redevelopment projects of the 1970s; horror at its construction prompted a change in building regulations for central Paris. At least there are fabulous views from the panoramic café on the 56th floor, and the tower is an inescapable landmark. At its foot are a shopping centre, the **Red Light** and **Club Mix** nightclubs (*see p325 and p326*) and, in winter, an open-air **ice rink** (*see p277*). The old Montparnasse railway station witnessed two events of historic significance: in 1898 a runaway train burst through its façade (you've

almost certainly seen the photo), and on 25 August 1944 the Germans surrendered Paris here. The train station was rebuilt in the 1970s, a grey affair that contains the surprising **Jardin Atlantique**, and the **Mémorial du Maréchal Leclerc** and **Musée Jean Moulin**, above its tracks.

Rue du Montparnasse, appropriately enough for a street near the station that sends trains to Brittany, is clustered with crêperies. Nearby, strip joints have replaced most of the theatres on ever-saucy rue de la Gaîté, but boulevard Edgar-Quinet has pleasant cafés and a street market (Wed, Sat), and the entrance to the **Cimetière du Montparnasse**. Nearby boulevard du Montparnasse still buzzes at night, thanks to its many cinemas and eating and drinking spots: giant art deco brasserie La Coupole (*see p208*); opposite, classic café **Le Select** (*see p231*); Le Dôme (No.108, 14th,

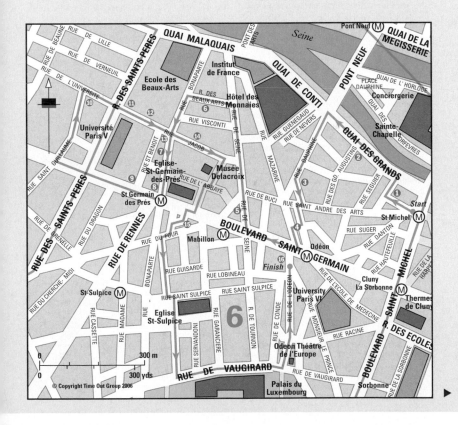

01.43.35.25.81), now a top-notch fish restaurant and bar; and restaurant La Rotonde (No.105, 6th, 01.43.26.48.26). All were popularised by the heavyweight literary and arty set between the wars, and all now use this heritage to their advantage. Of the bunch, Le Select seems the least forced – but only just. Nearby, on boulevard Raspail, stands Rodin's statue of Balzac, whose rugged rather than flattering appearance caused such a scandal that it was only put in place in 1937.

For a whiff of Montparnasse's artistic past, wander down rue de la Grande-Chaumière. Bourdelle and Friesz taught at the venerable Académie de la Grande-Chaumière (No.14),

frequented by Calder, Giacometti and Pompon among others (it still offers drawing lessons today); Modigliani died at No.8 in 1920, ruined by tuberculosis, drugs and alcohol; nearby **Musée Zadkine** occupies the sculptor's old house and studio. Rue Vavin and rue Bréa, leading to the **Jardin du Luxembourg** (*see p153*), have become an enclave of children's shops. Make sure you look out for Henri Sauvage's sleek, white-tiled apartment building at 6 rue Vavin, built in 1912.

Further east on boulevard du Montparnasse, literary café La Closerie des Lilas (No.171, 6th, 01.40.51.34.50) was a pre-war favourite with everyone from Lenin and Trotsky to Picasso

► ## Writer way (continued)

No.63, a plaque marks the house where Polish poet Adam Mickiewicz lived when his *Pan Tadeusz* was published in 1834. At No.57, behind the door crowned with the words 'Henri Diéval Maître Imprimeur', lived Baudelaire in the years when, stricken by debt, he dared emerge only at night.

Take a left into rue des Beaux-Arts, where, at No.13, **L'Hôtel** (❻ *see p58*) was where Oscar Wilde died after a long battle with the wallpaper. The place has been opulently done up by Jacques Garcia, and Wilde's room now has a peacock print inspired by his London home. A plaque on the outside remembers Argentine writer Jorge Luis Borges, who was a frequent visitor in the 1970s and 1980s. Opposite, at No.10, is the unmarked former offices of the *Revue des Deux Mondes*, the main journal of the Romantic movement, and focus for its salons from 1834 to 1845.

Turn left into rue Bonaparte, and a quick detour into rue Visconti, where, at No.24, Racine lived for the last seven years of his life, dying here in 1699. No.17, now a second-hand bookshop, was where Balzac set up a printer's (1826-28), only to fall badly in debt. He installed his mistress, Mme de Berny, on the first floor, and her blue room is described in *Le Lys dans la Vallée*. In 1928, Henry Miller taught his wife June to ride a bike on this road.

Miller's home when he arrived in Paris in 1930 was on the top floor of 36 rue Bonaparte, the present-day **Hôtel St-Germain-des-Prés** (❼ *see p59*). The hotel also housed American lesbian columnist Janet Flanner, whose 'Letter from Paris' appeared for almost 50 years in the *New Yorker*; Jean Cocteau smoked opium in room 6. Perhaps the most

famous address in this road is the plaque-free No.42, where the 40-year-old Sartre moved in to a fourth-floor flat in 1945 with his mother and a piano and stayed until 1962, when the apartment was bombed in protest at his stance against the war in Algeria. Were he still here today, the communist Sartre would be able to look out on a Dior boutique.

It's only a few steps from here to **Les Deux Magots** (❽ *see p230*), a favourite hangout of Sartre and de Beauvoir in the closing years of the war. Resistance messages were passed in the café's loos, which today are presided over by a charming *dame pipi* (toilet attendant). The Magots' literary memories are many, and on the walls inside are photos of Hemingway and the Surrealists. Although the terrace is filled with St-Tropez types in Chanel shades, the interior still has dignity and is calm enough to write in. To the right along boulevard St-Germain is **Café de Flore** (❾ *see p230*), also frequented by Sartre and de Beauvoir. Black American writers James Baldwin and Richard Wright also enjoyed the liberated spirit of both cafés, and Baldwin completed *Go Tell it on the Mountain* in the Flore.

Carry on along the boulevard and take the second street on the right, pretty rue St-Guillaume, which becomes rue du Pré-aux-Clercs. At the top of this road, turn right into rue de l'Université, whose No.9, the **Hôtel Lenox** (❿ *see p62*), was Joyce's first home in Paris. The hotel, more comfortable than in Joyce's day, has an art deco foyer and jazz-themed bar. Joyce used to eat with his family at Michaud's (now the **Comptoir des Saints-Pères**; ⓫ 29 rue des Sts-Pères, 6th, 01.40.20.09.39), at the intersection where

and Hemingway; brass plaques on the tables illustrate which historic figure used to sit where. Next to it is the lovely Fontaine de l'Observatoire, featuring bronze turtles and thrashing sea horses by Frémiet and figures of the four continents by Carpeaux. From here, the Jardins de l'Observatoire form part of the green axis running between the **Palais du Luxembourg** (*see p153*) and the **Observatoire de Paris**, the original royal observatory. A curiosity next door is the Maison des Fontainiers, built over an expansive (now dry-ish) underground reservoir originally commissioned by Marie de Médicis to supply water to fountains around the city.

A recent addition to boulevard Raspail is the glass-and-steel **Fondation Cartier**; designed by Jean Nouvel, it contains the jewellery company's headquarters and an exhibition centre for contemporary art.

West of the train station, the redevelopment of Montparnasse is also evident in the circular place de Catalogne, a piece of 1980s postmodern classicism by Mitterrand's favourite architect, Ricardo Bofill, and the housing estates of rue Vercingétorix. Traces of old, arty Montparnasse remain, too: in impasse Lebouis, an avant-garde studio building has recently been converted into the **Fondation Henri Cartier-Bresson**; at 21 avenue du Maine, an ivy-clad alleyway of

Sightseeing

rue de l'Université becomes rue Jacob. Hemingway recounts in *A Moveable Feast* how F Scott Fitzgerald showed him his wedding tackle in the loos after Zelda had complained about its size. In 1921 Hemingway and Hadley lived at 44 rue Jacob, the **Hôtel d'Angleterre** (⑫ 6th, 01.42.60.34.72). On the corner with rue Bonaparte, **Le Pré-aux-Clercs** (⑬ 30 rue Bonaparte, 6th, 01.43.54.41.73), Hemingway's favourite restaurant when he lived in rue Jacob, is an unpretentious art deco café where locals prop up the bar and read the racing press. The place hasn't cashed in on its literary fame and remains a typical St-Germain café. A little further, at No.20 (⑭), is the former home of Natalie Barney, known as the Amazon, whose literary salon was one of the few that Hemingway didn't disdain. In her garden, Pound and Hemingway hatched a fund-raising plan to rescue TS Elliot from his job in a bank, but Hemingway bet the money he'd set aside on a horse and lost.

Cut down rue Cardinale and passage de la Petite Bûcherie, then cross boulevard St-Germain in front of Café Mabillon. If you walk right, you'll come to place Copeau, where Boris Pasternak stayed at the **Hôtel Madison** (⑮ 143 bd St-Germain, 6th, 01.41.51.60.00) in 1935, sent by Stalin to attend the Congrès International des Ecrivains. Psychologically damaged, he refused to dine with Malraux and Cocteau and later had a nervous breakdown.

Go south down rue des Ciseaux and (jogging to the right) rue des Canettes to reach place St-Sulpice. As well as its notorious part in Dan Brown's *Da Vinci Code*, the church features in the Abbé Prévost's 18th-century libertine tale *Manon Lescaut*.

Continue south on rue Jouvenel, which becomes rue Férou, where the attractive house at No.6 (with its two sphinxes) is where Hemingway lived in 1926-28 with Pauline Pfeiffer, who was to become his second wife, and worked on *A Farewell to Arms*. Ahead, busy rue de Vaugirard runs along the Jardin du Luxembourg; on the right, at No.58, Zelda and F Scott F rented an apartment in 1928. Turn left and walk past the Palais du Luxembourg to reach rue Rotrou, which leads up to place de l'Odéon, the home of classical French theatre. Take rue de l'Odéon opposite.

On your left, at No.12, a plaque marks the site where Sylvia Beach published *Ulysses* in 1922. This was the second home of the original Shakespeare & Co bookshop (after a brief spell on nearby rue Dupuytren), where Hemingway borrowed books and remarked of the snapshots on the wall that 'even the dead writers looked as though they had really been alive.' The Marquis de Sade was born behind here in parallel rue de Condé in 1740. Opposite, at 7 rue de l'Odéon (now a hairdressers), was La Maison des Amis du Livre, whose salons drew French writers Gide, Valéry and Claudel.

On the carrefour de l'Odéon, drop into the *papeterie* on the right, where you can pick up a Moleskine notebook and talk philosophy with the owner, then rest your weary feet at modern-day literary café **Les Editeurs** (⑯ No.4, 6th, 01.43.26.67.76, www.lesediteurs.fr). Perhaps the first place on this walk where you might meet a living writer, it's packed with editors marking proofs, runs its own literary prize and has an extensive library.

old studios contains the artist-run exhibition space Immanence, as well as the **Musée du Montparnasse**, housed in the former academy and canteen of Russian painter Marie Vassilieff; on rue Antoine-Bourdelle, the **Musée Bourdelle** includes another old cluster of studios, where sculptor Bourdelle, Symbolist painter Eugène Carrière and, briefly, Marc Chagall worked. Towards Les Invalides, on rue Mayet, craft and restoration workshops still hide in old courtyards.

Cimetière du Montparnasse

3 bd Edgar-Quinet, 14th (01.44.10.86.50). M° Edgar Quinet or Raspail. **Open** *16 Mar-5 Nov* 8am-5.45pm Mon-Fri; 8.30am-5.45pm Sat; 9am-5.45pm Sun. *6 Nov-15 Mar* 8am-5.15pm Mon-Fri; 8.30am-5.15pm Sat; 9.30am-5.15pm Sun. **Admission** free. **Map** p407 G9.

This 1,800-acre cemetery was formed by commandeering three farms (you can still see the ruins of a rural windmill by rue Froidevaux) in 1824. As with much of the Left Bank, the Montparnasse cemetery scores rates highly for literary credibility: Beckett, Baudelaire, Sartre, de Beauvoir, Maupassant, Ionesco and Tristan Tzara all reside here; the artists include Brancusi, Henri Laurens, Frédéric Bartholdi (sculptor of the Statue of Liberty) and Man Ray. The celebrity roll-call continues with Serge Gainsbourg, André Citroën (of automobile fame), comic Coluche and actress Jean Seberg.

Fondation Cartier pour l'Art Contemporain

261 bd Raspail, 14th (01.42.18.56.72/recorded info 01.42.18.56.51/www.fondation.cartier.fr). M° Raspail. **Open** noon-8pm Tue-Sun. **Admission** €6.50; €4.50 concessions; free under-10s. **Credit** AmEx, MC, V. **Map** p407 G9.

Jean Nouvel's glass-and-steel building, an exhibition centre with Cartier's offices above, is as much a work of art as the installations inside. Shows by contemporary artists and photographers often have wide-ranging themes, such as 'Birds' or 'Desert'. Live events around the shows are called Nuits Nomades.

Fondation Dubuffet

137 rue de Sèvres, 6th (01.47.34.12.63/www. dubuffetfondation.com). M° Duroc. **Open** 2-6pm Mon-Fri. Closed Aug & public hols. **Admission** €4; free under-10s. **No credit cards. Map** p407 E8.

You have to walk up a winding garden path to get to this museum housed in an old three-storey mansion. Set up a decade before his death in 1985 by Jean Dubuffet, wine merchant and master of *art brut*, the foundation ensures that a fair body of his works is accessible to the public. There's a changing display of his lively drawings, paintings and sculptures, plus models of the architectural sculptures from the *Hourloupe* cycle. The foundation looks after the *Closerie Falbala*, 3D masterpiece of the *Hourloupe* cycle, located at Périgny-sur-Yerres, east of Paris (viewings by appointment only, €8).

Fondation Henri Cartier-Bresson

2 impasse Lebouis, 14th (01.56.80.27.00/www.henri cartierbresson.org). M° Gaîté. **Open** 1-8.30pm Wed; 1-6.30pm Thur, Fri, Sun; 11am-6.45pm Sat. Closed 20 Dec-11 Jan & Aug. **Admission** €4; €3 students, 12-26s; free under-12s, all 6.30-8.30pm Wed. **No credit cards. Map** p407 F10.

Opened in 2003, this two-floor gallery is dedicated to the great photographer Henri Cartier-Bresson. Built in 1913, it consists of a tall, narrow *atelier* with a minutely catalogued archive open to researchers, and a lounge on the fourth floor screening films. In the spirit of Cartier-Bresson, who assisted on films Jean Renoir films and drew and painted all his life (some drawings are also found on the fourth floor), the Fondation opens its doors to other disciplines with three annual shows. The convivial feel of the Fondation, and its Le Corbusier armchairs, foster relaxed discussion with staff and other visitors.

Jardin Atlantique

Gare Montparnasse or pl des Cinq-Martyrs-du-Lycée-Buffon, 15th. M° Montparnasse Bienvenüe or Gaîté. **Open** 8am-dusk Mon-Fri; 9am-dusk Sat, Sun. **Map** p407 F9.

Perhaps the hardest of all the gardens in Paris to find, the Jardin de l'Atlantique was opened in 1995. It's an engineering feat in itself: a modest oasis of granite paths, trees and bamboo is spread over the roof 18m above the tracks of Montparnasse train station. Small openings allow you to peer down on the trains below; children seem to love the randomly triggered fountain jets.

Mémorial du Maréchal Leclerc de Hauteclocque et de la Libération de Paris & Musée Jean Moulin

Jardin Atlantique, 23 allée de la 2e DB (above Gare Montparnasse), 15th (01.40.64.39.44/www.paris.fr). M° Montparnasse Bienvenüe. **Open** 10am-6pm Tue-Sun. Closed public hols. **Admission** free. *Exhibitions* €4; €3 students, over-60s; €2 under-26s; free under-13s. **Credit** *Shop* MC, V. **Map** p407 F9.

This double museum retraces World War II and the Resistance, through the Free French commander General Leclerc and left-wing hero Jean Moulin. Documentary material and film archives complement an impressive 270° slide show, complete with sound effects retelling the Liberation of Paris.

Musée-Atelier Adzak

3 rue Jonquoy, 14th (01.45.43.06.98). M° Plaisance. **Open** usually 3-7pm Sat, Sun but call in advance. **Admission** free.

The eccentric house, studio and garden built by the late Roy Adzak harbours traces of the conceptual artist's plaster body columns and dehydrations. Now a registered, British-run charity, it gives artists (generally foreign) a chance to exhibit in Paris.

Musée Bourdelle

16-18 rue Antoine-Bourdelle, 15th (01.49.54.73.73/ www.paris.fr/musees/bourdelle). M° Montparnasse Bienvenüe or Falguière. **Open** 10am-6pm Tue-Sun.

Closed public hols. **Admission** free. *Exhibitions* prices vary (approx €4.50/€3 concessions). **No credit cards. Map** p407 F8.

The sculptor Antoine Bourdelle (1861-1929), pupil of Rodin, produced monumental works like the Modernist relief friezes at the Théâtre des Champs-Elysées, inspired by Isadora Duncan and Nijinsky. Set around a small garden, the museum includes the artist's apartment, and studios used by him, as well as by Eugène Carrière, Dalou and Chagall. A 1950s extension tracks the evolution of Bourdelle's equestrian monument to General Alvear in Buenos Aires, and his masterful *Hercules the Archer*. A new wing by Christian de Portzamparc houses bronzes such as studies of Beethoven in various guises.

Musée du Montparnasse

21 av du Maine, 15th (01.42.22.91.96/www.musee dumontparnasse.net). M° Montparnasse Bienvenüe. **Open** 12.30-7pm Tue-Sun. **Admission** €5; €4 students, 12-18s; free under-12s. **No credit cards. Map** p405 F8.

Set in one of the last surviving alleys of studios, this was home to Marie Vassilieff, who opened her own academy and canteen, where penniless artists – Picasso, Cocteau and Matisse – came for cheap food; Trotsky and Lenin were also guests. Shows focus on the area's creative past and present-day artists.

Musée Pasteur

Institut Pasteur, 25 rue du Dr-Roux, 15th (01.45.68.82.83/www.pasteur.fr). M° Pasteur. **Open** 2-5.30pm Mon-Fri. Closed Aug. **Admission** €3; €1.50 students. **Credit** MC, V. **Map** p407 E9.

The flat where the famous chemist and his wife lived at the end of his life (1888-95) has not been touched; you can see their furniture and possessions, photos and instruments. An extravagant mausoleum on the ground floor houses Pasteur's tomb, decorated with mosaics depicting his scientific achievements.

Musée de la Poste

34 bd de Vaugirard, 15th (01.42.79.23.45/www. museedelaposte.fr). M° Montparnasse Bienvenüe. **Open** 10am-6pm Mon-Sat. Closed public hols. **Admission** €5; €3.50 students under 26; free under-13s. *Permanent & temporary exhibitions* €5.50-€7; free under-18s. **Credit** MC, V. **Map** p407 E9.

Among uniforms, pistols, carriages, official decrees and fumigation tongs are snippets of history: during the 1871 Siege of Paris, hot-air balloons and carrier pigeons were used to get post out of the city, and *boules de Moulins*, balls crammed with hundreds of letters, were floated down the Seine in return, mostly never to arrive. The second section covers French and international philately.

Musée Zadkine

100bis rue d'Assas, 6th (01.55.42.77.20/www.paris. fr/musees/zadkine). M° Notre-Dame-des-Champs/ RER Port-Royal. **Open** 10am-6pm Tue-Sun. Closed public hols. **Admission** free. *Exhibitions* €4; €3 students, over-60s; €2 under-26s; free under-13s, CM. **Credit** (€15 minimum) MC, V. **Map** p410 G8.

Works by the Russian-born Cubist sculptor Ossip Zadkine are displayed around this tiny house and garden near the Jardin du Luxembourg, where he lived from 1928 until his death in 1967. Zadkine's works cover musical, mythological and religious subjects, and his style varies with his materials: bronzes tend to be geometrical, wood more sensuous. Sculptures are displayed at eye level, with drawings and poems by Zadkine and paintings by his wife, Valentine Prax. Changing exhibitions of contemporary artists are held in the former studio.

Observatoire de Paris

61 av de l'Observatoire, 14th (www.obspm.fr). M° St-Jacques/RER Port-Royal. **Open** *Tours* 1st Sat of mth (except Aug) by written reservation only to: Service de la communication (service des visites), Observatoire de Paris, 61 av de l'Observatoire, 75014 Paris. **Map** p407 H10.

The Paris observatory was founded by Louis XIV's finance minister, Colbert, in 1667; it was designed by Claude Perrault (who worked on the Louvre), with labs and an observation tower. The French meridian line drawn by François Arago in 1806 (in use before the Greenwich meridian was adopted as an international standard) runs north–south through the centre of the building. The dome on the observation tower was added in the 1840s, but what with urban light pollution, most stargazing is now done in Meudon and Provence. A visit entails a prior written appointment, but check the website for openings linked to astronomical happenings – or visit on the Journées du Patrimoine (*see p276*).

Tour Montparnasse

33 av du Maine, 15th (01.45.38.52.56/www.tour montparnasse56.com). M° Montparnasse Bienvenüe. **Open** *Winter* 9.30am-10.30pm daily. *Summer* 9.30am-11.30pm daily. **Admission** €8.50; €7.50 students; €5.50 5-14s; free under-5s. **Credit** MC, V. **Map** p407 F9.

Built in 1974 on the site of the old station, this 209m steel-and-glass monster is shorter than the Eiffel Tower, but more central. A lift whisks you up to the 56th floor, where you'll find a display of aerial views of Paris. Classical concerts are held on the terrace.

Denfert-Rochereau & Montsouris

In the run-up to the 1789 Revolution, the bones of six million Parisians were taken from the handful of overcrowded city cemeteries and wheelbarrowed to the **Catacombs**, a network of tunnels that spreads under much of the 13th and 14th arrondissements. The gloomy Denfert-Rochereau public entrance to one section is next to one of the toll gates of the Mur des Fermiers-Généraux built by Ledoux in the 1780s.

The bronze *Lion de Belfort* dominates the traffic-laden place Denfert-Rochereau, a favourite starting point for the city's countless political demonstrations. The regal beast was sculpted by Bartholdi, and is a scaled-down

Sightseeing

replica of one in Belfort that commemorates Colonel Denfert-Rochereau's brave defence of the town in 1870. Nearby, the southern half of rue Daguerre is a sociable, pedestrianised market street (Tue-Sat, Sun morning) brimming with cafés and food shops.

One of the big draws here is the **Parc Montsouris**, containing lovely lakes, dramatic cascades and an unusual history. Surrounding the western edge of the park are a number of modest, quiet streets – including rue du Parc Montsouris and rue Georges-Braque – that used to be lined in the 1920s and 1930s with charming villas and artists' studios by avant-garde architects including Le Corbusier and André Lurçat. On the southern edge of the park sprawls the **Cité Universitaire** complex, containing three dozen internationally themed halls of residence and 6,000 students.

Les Catacombes

1 av Colonel Henri-Rol-Tanguy, 14th (01.43.22.47.63/www.catacombes.info). M° Denfert Rochereau. **Open** *9.30am-4pm Tue-Sun.* **Admission** *€5; €3.30 over-60s; €2.50 students, 14-26s; free under-14s.* **Credit** *(€15 minimum) MC, V.* **Map** *407 H10.*

Official entrance for the extensive network of subterranean passages that runs under much of the city, particularly the 13th and 14th arrondissements. The 3,000-km tunnel network originated as quarries, providing limestone for huge building projects such as Notre-Dame. By the late 18th century, when the city had extended this far south, many streets began to collapse. The authorities set about building tunnels and supports to prop up the earth. At the same time, with public burial pits rising in the era of the Revolutionary Terror, the bones of six million people were transferred to the *catacombes*. The bones of Marat, Robespierre and their cronies are tightly

The kindness of strangers

'We are glad to see folks from abroad. We are travellers. We aren't guides. We can't tell you when such-and-such a church was built – people are just free to speak about what they want.' The irresistibly enthusiastic Aurélie Taupin (*pictured, right*) is co-founder and chief organiser of a revolutionary scheme that allows visitors to Paris to meet with interested locals, experience the daily life of the city through the eyes of a native and discuss ideas. The choice of venues naturally depends on the weather, what's on around town and the mood of the group. Music goes down well, especially at jazz clubs and on the *péniches* that ply the Seine.

Devised in 2004 by **Aventures du Bout du Monde**, Paris-based travel enthusiasts, it got Town Hall backing in January 2005. Aurélie's above-board escorts are the most personable element of the Mairie's current drive to make notoriously snooty Paris more welcoming to its 26 million annual visitors. Most ABM hosts have a good level of English, but if visitors have no French at all, they should make it clear. The service is free: you only pay the usual entrance fee for any events that require it, and for any drinks you might have.

Our own visit began in a suitably smoky Latin Quarter jazz cellar. Our host, Catherine, a thirtysomething teacher, explained that packed in with wall upon wall of their fellow citizens. It's an extraordinary sight, and one not for the claustrophobic: you descend an 85-step spiral staircase that takes you 20m below ground, to a mass of bones and carvings. Do carry a torch – and don't try to take away one of the bones as a souvenir: your bags are checked at the end.

Cité Universitaire
bd Jourdan, 14th (01.44.16.64.00/www.ciup.fr). RER Cité Universitaire.
The Cité Internationale Universitaire de Paris is an odd mix. Created between the wars in a mood of internationalism and inspired by the model of Oxbridge colleges, the 37 halls of residence spread across landscaped gardens were designed in a variety of supposedly appropriate national styles, some by appropriate national architects (Dutchman Willem Dudok drew the De Stijl-style Collège Néerlandais); others, like the Asie du Sud-Est build-ing, with its Khmer sculptures and bird-beak roof, are exotic pastiches. The Brits get what looks like a minor public school; the Maison Internationale is based on Fontainebleau; the Swiss and Brazilians get Le Corbusier. You can visit the sculptural white Pavillon Suisse (01.44.16.10.10, www.fondation suisse.fr), which has a Le Corbusier mural on the ground floor. The Cité's spacious landscaped gardens are open to the public, and the newly renovated theatre stages a mix of drama and modern dance.

Parc Montsouris
bd Jourdan, 14th. RER Cité Universitaire. **Open** 8am-dusk Mon-Fri; 9am-dusk Sat, Sun.
The most colourful of the capital's parks was laid out for Baron Haussmann by Jean-Charles Adolphe Alphand. It boasts sweeping, gently sloping lawns, an artificial lake and artificial cascades. On its opening day in 1878 the lake inexplicably emptied and the engineer responsible committed suicide.

Sightseeing

when members join ABM, they can tick a box to offer their hosting services; and, like inter-cultural superheroes, they never know when the call may come. ABM also functions as a social network, and several members responded to the call and joined our party at intervals during the evening. No one knew anyone else, so the conversation was on an enjoyably equal footing. Inevitably – desirably, even – discussions tiptoed towards conversational minefields such as racism and the Iraq war; views were civilly and tactfully expressed. It was good, grown-up chat, and though plenty of travel experiences were traded, there was none of that tedious backpacker-circuit talk.

Hoping to make use of local knowledge, we asked for suggestions for the rest of our weekend. Lots of ideas were forthcoming: a walk along the 'Coulée Verte' (a former railway line), rummages around markets and strolls around squares, ice skating at La Défense, virtuoso rollerblading at Montparnasse. 'What would a local do on a Sunday?' we asked. 'Nothing at all,' replied the charming Emmanuel.

The question remains: why would anyone give up a Saturday evening to come and hang out with a couple of Brits? Guillaume, a computer programmer, explained his own reasons: 'Paris is nice but Parisians can be cold. I'd love to have this chance when I go to other places. If we start here, the scheme may spread elsewhere.'

This is echoed by Aurélie, whom we met the next day. With her was another Guillaume, high up in Chip and PIN by day and an improv impresario by night, and Olivier, who works for the local Ministry of Defence but isn't at all scary. We ambled round the Jardin des Plantes (*see p145*) and explored the zoo, then moved on to the lovely tiled café at the nearby Paris mosque, an atmospheric venue we wouldn't have thought to visit but apparently a people-magnet in summer (and where the hammam steam with massage is an absolute bargain, according to Guillaume).

Over pastries and mint tea, Aurélie explained how she had the idea after meeting people through a similar scheme in New York. There, she said with some wonder, people talk to each other on the subway. Here, she had to help out a young American who had caught her finger in a closing métro train door while other passengers ignored her. Ever since, she has been working out a way to bring visitor and local together.

'I love introducing Paris to people. I've made friends out of the strangers I've met on the scheme. If this kind of dynamic catches on it would be great.'

● There are two ways to enjoy the benefits of the Aventures du Bout du Monde scheme: you can either check the agenda for the year-long programme of organised events (www.abm.fr); or email the group (pja@abm.fr) to see if a rendezvous can be tailored to time with your visit or meet your particular interest.

The 15th arrondissement

Centred on the shopping streets of rue du Commerce and rue Lecourbe, the expansive 15th has little to offer tourists, though as a largely residential district it has plenty of good restaurants and street markets. It's worth making a detour to visit **La Ruche** ('beehive'), designed by Eiffel as a wine pavilion for the 1900 Exposition Universelle and moved here to serve as artists' studios. Nearby is **Parc Georges Brassens**, opened in 1983, while at the Porte de Versailles, the sprawling **Paris-Expo** exhibition centre was created in 1923.

Parc Georges Brassens

rue des Morillons, 15th. M° Porte de Vanves or Porte de Versailles. **Open** 8am-dusk Mon-Fri; 9am-dusk Sat, Sun. **Map** p406 D10.

Built on the site of the old Abattoirs de Vaugirard, Parc Georges Brassens prefigured the industrial regeneration of Parc André Citroën and La Villette. The gateways, crowned by bronze bulls, have been kept, as have a series of iron meat-market pavilions, which house a second-hand book market at weekends. The Jardin des Senteurs is planted with aromatic species, and a small vineyard yields 200 bottles of Clos des Morillons every year.

La Ruche

passage de Dantzig, 15th. M° Convention or Porte de Versailles. **Map** p406 D10.

Take a peek through the grille or sneak in behind an unsuspecting resident to see the iron-framed former wine pavilion built by Eiffel for the 1900 Exposition Universelle, and rebuilt by philanthropic sculptor Alfred Boucher to be let as studios for struggling artists. Chagall, Soutine, Brancusi, Modigliani, Lipchitz and Archipenko spent periods here, and the 140 studios are still sought after by artists today.

Paris-Expo

Porte de Versailles, 15th (01.72.72.17.00/www. paris-expo.fr). M° Porte de Versailles. **Map** p406 B10.

The vast exhibition centre, spread over different halls, hosts all kinds of trade and arts fairs. Many, such as the Foire de Paris (*see p273*) and art fair FIAC (*see p276*), are open to the public.

The 13th arrondissement

The contrasts are immediate in the 13th, where villagey clusters of little houses alternate with 1960s tower blocks and the new ZAC Rive Gauche (ZAC, 'zone d'aménagement concerté', means multi-partner development zone).

Les Gobelins & La Salpêtrière

Its defining features may be tower blocks, but the 13th arrondissement is also historic, especially in the area bordering the 5th. The **Manufacture Nationale des Gobelins**, home to the state weaving companies, continues a tradition founded in the 15th century, when tanneries, dyers and weaving workshops lined the River Bièvre. The waterway became notorious for its pollution, and the slums that grew up around it were depicted in Hugo's *Les Misérables*. The area was tidied up in the 1930s when square René-Le-Gall, a small park, was laid out on the allotments used by tapestry workers. The river was built over, but local enthusiasts have opened up a small stretch in the park. Nearby, through a gateway at 17 rue des Gobelins, you can spot the turret and first floor of a medieval house, recently renovated as apartments. The so-called Château de la Reine Blanche on rue Gustave-Geffroy is named after Queen Blanche of Provence, who had a château here; it was probably rebuilt in the 1520s for the Gobelin family. Blanche was also associated with a nearby Franciscan monastery, of which a fragmentary couple of arches survive on the corner of rue Pascal and rue de Julienne.

In the northern corner of the 13th, next to Gare d'Austerlitz (the station that serves most of central France), sprawls the huge Hôpital de la Pitié-Salpêtrière founded in 1656, with its striking **Chapelle St-Louis**.

The busy intersection of place d'Italie has seen further recent developments. Opposite the 19th-century town hall stands the Centre Commercial Italie 2, a bizarre high-tech confection designed by Kenzo Tange. It houses a shopping centre and the **Gaumont Grand Ecran Italie** cinema (*see p292*). You'll also find a thrice-weekly food market on boulevard Auguste-Blanqui (Tue, Fri, Sun).

Chapelle St-Louis-de-la-Salpêtrière

47 bd de l'Hôpital, 13th (01.42.16.04.24). M° Gare d'Austerlitz. **Open** 8.30am-6pm Mon-Fri, Sun; 11am-6pm Sat. **Admission** free. **Map** p408 L9.

The austerely beautiful chapel, designed by Libéral Bruand and completed in 1677, features an octagonal dome in the centre and eight naves in which they used to separate the sick from the insane, the destitute from the debauched. Around the chapel sprawls the vast Hôpital de la Pitié-Salpêtrière, founded on the site of a gunpowder factory (hence the name, derived from saltpetre) by Louis XIV to house rounded-up vagrant women. It became a centre for research into insanity in the 1790s, when renowned doctor Philippe Pinel began to treat some of the inmates as sick rather than criminal; Charcot later pioneered neuro-psychology here, receiving a famous visit from Freud. Salpêtrière is today one of the city's main teaching hospitals, but the chapel is also used for contemporary art installations, notably for the Festival d'Automne (*see p276*), when its striking architecture provides a backdrop for artists such as Bill Viola, Anish Kapoor and Nan Goldin.

Manufacture Nationale des Gobelins

42 av des Gobelins, 13th (tours 01.44.54.19.33). M° Les Gobelins. **Open** *Tours* 2pm, 2.45pm Tue-Thur. **Admission** €8; €6 7s-24s; free under-7s. **No credit cards. Map** p408 K10.

The royal tapestry factory was founded by Colbert, when he set up the Manufacture Royale des Meubles de la Couronne in 1662; it's named after Jean Gobelin, a dyer who owned the site. It reached the summit of its renown during the *ancien régime*, when Gobelins tapestries were produced for royal residences under artists such as Le Brun and Oudry. Tapestries are still made here (mainly for French embassies), and visitors can watch weavers at work. The tour (in French) through the 1912 factory takes in the 18th-century chapel and the Beauvais workshops. Arrive 30 minutes before the tour starts.

Chinatown & La Butte-aux-Cailles

South of rue de Tolbiac, the shop signs suddenly turn Chinese or Vietnamese, and even McDonald's is decked out *à la chinoise*. The city's main Chinatown runs along avenue d'Ivry, avenue de Choisy and into the 1960s tower blocks between. While many of the tower blocks in the Paris suburbs are bleak, here they have a distinctly Eastern vibe, with restaurants, Vietnamese *pho* noodle bars and Chinese pâtisseries, hairdressers and purveyors of exotic groceries, as well as the large **Tang Frères** supermarket (*see p262*). There's even a Buddhist temple hidden in a car park beneath the tallest tower (avenue d'Ivry, opposite rue Frères d'Astier-de-la-Vigerie, 13th). Lion and dragon dances take place on the streets at Chinese New Year (*see p277*).

In contrast to Chinatown, the villagey Butte-aux-Cailles, occupying the wedge between boulevard Auguste-Blanqui and rue Bobillot, is a neighbourhood of old houses, winding cobblestone streets, funky bars and restaurants. This workers' neighbourhood, home in the 19th century to many small factories, was one of the first to fight during the 1848 Revolution and the Paris Commune. The Butte has preserved its rebellious character: residents wear Fidel Castro T-shirts and resist the aggressive forces of city planning and construction companies. The cobbled rue de la Butte-aux-Cailles and rue des Cinq-Diamants are the hub of the arty, *soixante-huitard* forces, where you'll find relaxed, inexpensive bistros like the eccentric Le Temps des Cérises (18 rue Butte-aux-Cailles, 13th, 01.45.89.69.48), run as a co-operative, Chez Gladines (30 rue des Cinq-Diamants, 13th, 01.45.80.70.10) and the more upmarket **Chez Paul** (*see p203*). The cottages built in 1912 in a mock-Alsatian style around a central green at

10 rue Daviel were one of the earliest public-housing schemes in Paris. Just across rue Bobillot, the **Piscine de la Butte-aux-Cailles** (*see p336*) is a charming Arts and Crafts-style swimming pool, fed by artesian wells. Further south, you can explore passage Vandrezanne, the little houses and gardens of square des Peupliers, rue des Peupliers and rue Dieulafoy, and the flower-named streets of the Cité Florale. By the Périphérique, the Stade Charléty (17 av Pierre-de-Coubertin, 13th, 01.44.16.60.60), designed by father and son Henri and Bruno Gaudin, is a superb piece of stadium architecture headed by swooping, bird-like floodlights.

The developing east

The erection of the **Bibliothèque Nationale de France** breathed life into the desolate area between Gare d'Austerlitz and the Périphérique, formerly just lonesome railway yards and now known as the ZAC Rive Gauche. The ZAC project calls for office and residential development and a new university quarter, an eastwards extension of the Latin Quarter.

Further east, towards Porte d'Ivry, curious rue Watt is the lowest street in Paris (it runs below river level). At 12 rue Cantagrel you can see Le Corbusier's Cité de Réfuge de l'Armée de Salut hostel, a long, reinforced-concrete structure built from 1929 to 1933 to accommodate 1,500 homeless men, and a precursor of the architect's Unités d'Habitation.

Bibliothèque Nationale de France François Mitterrand

quai François-Mauriac, 13th (01.53.79.59.59/ www.bnf.fr). M° Bibliothèque François Mitterrand or Quai de la Gare. **Open** 2-7pm Mon; 9am-7pm Tue-Sat; noon-7pm Sun. **Admission** *1 day* €3. *2 days* €4.50. *2 weeks* €15-€30. *1 year* €23-€46. **Credit** MC, V. **Map** p409 M10.

Opened in 1996, the new national library was the last and costliest of Mitterrand's *Grands Projets*. Its architect, Dominique Perrault, was criticised for his curiously dated design, which hides readers underground and stores the books in four L-shaped glass towers. He also forgot to specify blinds to protect books from sunlight; they had to be added afterwards. In the central void is a garden (filled with 140 trees, transported from Fontainebleau at vast expense). The library houses over ten million volumes, and can accommodate 3,000 readers. The research section, just below the public reading rooms, opened in 1998. Much of the library is open to the public: books, newspapers and periodicals are accessible to anyone over 18, and you can browse through photo, film and sound archives in the audio-visual section. There are classical music concerts and exhibitions, too.

Sightseeing

Beyond the Périphérique

Done Paris? Next stop: the suburbs.

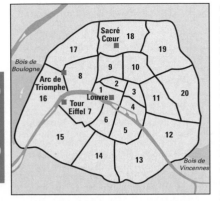

Across the Périphérique ring road lies another world. It starts with the dense housing and industrial estates of the inner suburbs, built up since the 19th century as old villages and rural churches were absorbed into the urban sprawl, and stretches to the outer edge of new towns that colonised old farmland after the war.

For many Parisians, an expedition to the *banlieue* (especially the undesirable northern and eastern suburbs) takes on the aura of a journey to a foreign land, a land ventured into only for cheap supermarket petrol and DIY stores. For them, the *banlieue* (a term rarely used to include the sought-after districts such as Neuilly, St-Cloud or Boulogne, but with much the same implied shudder as 'inner-city' when applied to UK towns) is as much a mindset as a physical reality, with its image of housing estates, large immigrant populations, car rodeos, unemployment, drugs and urban gangs, even its own accent, argot and style of dress. Part of the negative rep is accurate: there are dangerous, no-go housing estates, the *quartiers sensibles* (for 'sensitive' read 'problem'), where even the fire brigade is attacked as it puts out blazes, and where attempts to reopen local shops are answered by vandalism. But there are also swaths of very respectable residential districts, with their own self-contained provincial atmosphere quite different from the city itself.

There are signs of change, too. The rising property prices within Paris mean that many families are being forced out into the inner ring of suburbs. High business rents have seen companies, notably in the advertising and media sectors and, more recently, financial services, moving outwards. And if many Parisians wouldn't contemplate living anywhere other than Paris itself, the mistrust works both ways – there are also *banlieusards* proud of belonging to the *neuf-trois* (slang for the 93 *département* of Seine St-Denis) rather than to the 'elitist' *soixante-quinze* (75) of Paris.

St-Denis & the north

North of Paris, the *département* of Seine St-Denis (and part of adjoining Val d'Oise) is the one that best fulfils the negative image of the *banlieue*. It's a victim of its own 19th-century industrial boom and the 20th-century housing shortage, when colossal estates went up in places like La Corneuve (where a tower block was recently dynamited), Aulnay-sous-Bois and Sarcelles; it includes some of the poorest *communes* in all of France. Yet the *département* also boasts a buzzing theatre scene, such as the MC93 in Bobigny, the Théâtre Gérard Philipe in St-Denis and the Théâtre de la Commune in Aubervilliers, as well as prestigious jazz and classical music festivals. And amid all the sprawl stands one of the treasures of Gothic architecture: the **Basilique St-Denis**, the spot where most of France's monarchs were buried. St-Denis also contains the atmospheric **Musée d'Art et d'Histoire de St-Denis**, located in a scrupulously preserved Carmelite convent, and also a busy covered market. Its fine modern buildings include Niemeyer's head offices for Communist newspaper *L'Humanité* and Gaudin's extension to the town hall. Across the canal is the landmark **Stade de France** (*see p329*). Built for the 1998 World Cup, it has provided a spur to the renewal of this long run-down area of small terraced houses, council flats, factories and wasteland. Indeed, it could be said that the area of La Plaine St-Denis is on the up.

The canal has been nicely landscaped with a footpath along the quay, the noisy motorway has been covered over by a series of garden squares and playgrounds, and smart canalside apartments, a multiplex cinema, shopping centre and a DIY superstore have all gone up near the stadium, which is now attracting businesses to the area. Over in nearby Aubervilliers, acres of 19th-century brick warehouses buzz with import-export businesses and recently arrived audio-visual companies.

Le Bourget, home to the city's first airport and still used for private business jets and an air fair, contains the **Musée de l'Air et de l'Espace** in its original passenger terminals and hangars. North-east of Paris, Pantin arrived on the cultural scene with the opening in June 2004 of the **Centre National de la Danse** (*see p288*) in a cleverly rehabilitated office block. North-west of St-Denis, Ecouen, noted for its beautiful Renaissance château, now the **Musée National de la Renaissance**, allows for a glimpse of a more rural past.

Basilique St-Denis

1 rue de la Légion-d'Honneur, 93200 St-Denis (01.48.09.83.54). M° Basilique de St-Denis/tram 1. **Open** *Apr-Sept* 10am-5.45pm Mon-Sat; noon-5.45pm Sun. *Oct-Mar* 10am-4.45pm Mon-Sat; noon-4.45pm Sun. *Tours* 11.15am, 3pm Mon-Sat; 12.15pm, 3pm Sun. **Admission** €6.10; €4.10 18s-25s; free under-18s. **Credit** MC, V.

Legend has it that when St Denis was beheaded, he picked up his noggin and walked with it to Vicus Catulliacus (now St-Denis) to be buried. The first church, parts of which can be seen in the crypt, was built over his tomb in around 475. The present edifice was begun in the 1130s by Abbot Suger, the powerful minister of Louis VI and Louis VII. It is considered the first example of Gothic architecture, by uniting the elements of pointed arches, ogival vaulting and flying buttresses. In the 13th century master mason Pierre de Montreuil erected the spire and rebuilt the choir, nave and transept. This was the burial place for all but three French monarchs between 996 and the end of the *ancien régime*, so the ambulatory is a museum of French funerary sculpture, among them a fanciful Gothic tomb for Dagobert, the austere effigy of Charles V and richly sculpted Renaissance tomb of Louis XII and Anne de Bretagne. In 1792 all these tombs were desecrated and the royal remains thrown into a pit.

Musée de l'Air et de l'Espace

Aéroport de Paris-Le Bourget, 93352 Le Bourget Cedex (01.49.92.71.99/recorded information 01.49.92.71.71/www.mae.org). M° Gare du Nord, then bus 350/RER Le Bourget, then bus 152. **Open** *Apr-Sept* 10am-6pm Tue-Sun. *Oct-Mar* 10am-5pm Tue-Sun. **Admission** €7; €5 students; free under-18s. **Credit** MC, V.

The air and space museum is a reminder that France is a technical and military, as well as cultural, power. Set in the former passenger terminal at Le Bourget airport, the collection begins with the pioneers, including fragile-looking biplanes, the contraption in which Romanian Vivia succeeded in flying 12m (40ft) in 1906, and the command cabin of a Zeppelin airship. On the runway are Mirage fighters, a US

Pavillon Baltard. *See p175.*

Thunderchief with painted shark-tooth grimace and Ariane launchers 1 and 5. A hangar houses the prototype Concorde 001 and wartime survivors. Other sections are devoted to ballooning and space travel.

Musée d'Art et d'Histoire de St-Denis

22bis rue Gabriel-Péri, 93200 St-Denis (01.42.43.05.10). M° St-Denis – Porte de Paris. **Open** 10am-5.30pm Mon, Wed, Fri; 10am-8pm Thur; 2-6.30pm Sat, Sun. Closed public hols. **Admission** €4; €2 over-60s, students; free under-16s. **No credit cards**.

This museum in St-Denis is set around the cloister of a former Carmelite convent, home to Louis XV's daughter, Louise de France, in the 1700s. Along with displays of archaeology, prints about the Paris Commune, post-Impressionist drawings and documents relating to local poet Paul Eluard, the most vivid part is the first floor, where items are displayed within the nuns' austere cells.

Musée National de la Renaissance

Château d'Ecouen, 95440 Ecouen (01.34.38.38.50/ www.musee-renaissance.fr). Train from Gare du Nord to Ecouen-Ezanville, then bus 269 or walk. **Open** 9.30am-12.30pm, 2-5.45pm Mon, Wed-Sun. **Admission** €4; €2.60 18s-25s, all on Sun; free under-18s, all on 1st Sun of mth. **Credit** MC, V.

The Renaissance château completed in 1555 for Royal Constable Anne de Montmorency and wife Margaret de Savoie is the setting for a wonderful collection of

La Défense: one feat of civil engineering after another. *See p177.*

16th-century decorative arts, arranged over three floors (some parts only open at certain times – phone ahead). Best are the original painted chimney pieces, decorated with biblical and mythological scenes.

Vincennes & the east

The more upmarket residential districts in the east surround the Bois de Vincennes, such as Vincennes, with its royal château, St-Mandé and Charenton-le-Pont. Joinville-le-Pont and Champigny-sur-Marne draw weekenders for the riverside *guinguette* dancehalls.

Château de Vincennes
av de Paris, 94300 Vincennes (01.48.08.31.20). M° Château de Vincennes. **Open** *Apr-Sept* 10am-noon, 1.15-6pm daily. *Oct-Mar* 10am-noon, 1.15-5pm daily. **Admission** *Short visit* €4.60; €3.10 18s-25s,

students; free under-18s. *Long visit* €6.10; €4.10 18s-25s, students; free under-18s. **Credit** MC, V.
An imposing curtain wall punctuated by towers encloses this medieval fortress, still home to an army garrison. The square keep was begun by Philippe VI and completed by Charles V, who added the curtain wall. Henry V died here in 1422; Louis XIII used the château for hunting expeditions and had the Pavillon du Roi and Pavillon de la Reine built by Louis Le Vau, though their decoration disappeared when they were turned into military barracks.

Musée de la Résistance Nationale
Parc Vercors, 88 av Marx-Dormoy, 94500 Champigny-sur-Marne (01.48.81.00.80/www.musee-resistance.com). RER Champigny, then bus 208. **Open** 9am-12.30pm, 2-5.30pm Tue-Fri; 2-6pm Sat, Sun. Closed public hols, weekends in Aug, all Sept. **Admission** €4; €2 over-60s; free under-18s, students. **No credit cards.**

Occupying five floors of a 19th-century villa, the Resistance museum starts at the top with the pre-war political background and works down, via defeat in 1940, through the Occupation and the rise of the Maquis, to victory. Hundreds of photographs aside, the material consists of newspaper files, three short archive films, a wall of machine guns and a railway saboteur's kit. Commendably, displays steer clear of Resistance hero tub-thumping.

Pavillon Baltard

12 av Victor-Hugo, 94130 Nogent-sur-Marne (01.43.24.76.76/www.pavillon-baltard.fr). RER Nogent-sur-Marne. **Open** *during exhibitions only.*
When Les Halles was demolished some bright spark had the foresight to save one of its Baltard-designed iron-and-glass market pavilions (No.8, the egg and poultry shed) and resurrect it for the benefit of the suburbs. **Photo** *p173.*

Boulogne & the west

The capital's most desirable suburbs lie to the west, where expensive properties were built between the wars. La Défense, Neuilly-sur-Seine, Boulogne-Billancourt, Levallois-Perret and, across the river, Issy-les-Moulineaux have become work locations for Parisians, notably in the advertising, media and service industries. Neuilly-sur-Seine is home to many of France's finance brains and captains of industry, as well as the fief of politician Nicolas Sarkozy (*see p26* **The heir apparent?**).

Boulogne-Billancourt is the main town in the region outside Paris, and a lively centre in its own right. In 1320 the Gothic Eglise Notre-Dame was begun in tribute to a miraculous statue of the Virgin washed up at Boulogne-sur-Mer. By the 18th century Boulogne was known for its wines and laundries and, early in the 20th century, for its artist residents (Landowski, Lipchitz, Chagall, Gris), while Billancourt was known for car manufacture, aviation and its film studios. In the 1920s and '30s Boulogne-Billancourt was proud of its modernity: Tony Garnier built the elegant new town hall on avenue André-Morizet; a new post office, apartments and schools all went up in the modern style; and private houses were built by the leading avant-garde architects of the day – Le Corbusier, Perret, Lurçat, Mallet-Stevens, Pingusson and Fischer – notably on rue Denfert-Rochereau near the Bois de Boulogne and rue du Belvedère. The **Musée des Années 30** focuses on artists and architects who lived or worked in the town at the time. The innovative glass-fronted apartment block by Le Corbusier – including the flat where he lived from 1933 to 1965 – can be visited each Wednesday morning at

24 rue Nungesser et Coli (reserve ahead with the Fondation Le Corbusier on 01.42.88.41.53, www.fondationlecorbusier.asso.fr).

The former Renault factory has sat in the Seine like a beached whale since it closed in 1992. In 2000 billionaire François Pinault decided to convert it, and the Ile Seguin stands on, as a contemporary art museum. The musuem was to be designed by Japanese architect Tadao Ando, with a projected opening date of 2005. However, the deadline was moved back a year, then another, until finally, in May 2005, Pinault, frustrated by the inertia of the Boulogne-Billancourt local council and the lack of investment on the site, abandoned the idea. The *Fondation Pinault* will still go ahead – but it will be located in Venice.

Across the Seine, villas in large gardens surround the Parc de St-Cloud, one of the loveliest bits of open space around Paris. South of St-Cloud is Sèvres, where the former royal porcelain manufacturer is now the **Musée National de la Céramique**.

In the 19th century riverside towns like Chatou, Asnières and Argenteuil, accessible by train, became places of entertainment – for promenades, *guinguettes* and rowing on the Seine – depicted by the Impressionists. Ile de la Grande Jatte, between Neuilly and Courbevoie, was immortalised in Seurat's *La Grande Jatte*, and Renoir frequented the Ile de Chatou, where the old restaurant and dancehall, the Maison Fournaise, is now a small museum.

At Rueil-Malmaison, the romantic **Château de Malmaison** was loved by Napoléon and Joséphine. Joséphine had a second château, La Petite Malmaison (229bis av Napoléon-Bonaparte, 01.47.32.02.02, by appointment only), built nearby. The empress is buried in the Eglise St-Pierre St-Paul in the old centre, as is her daughter Hortense de Beauharnais, Queen of Holland and mother of Napoléon III. At Port Marly, the fanciful Château de Monte-Cristo (01.39.16.49.49), built for Alexandre Dumas *fils*, has a tiled Moorish room; in its leafy grounds is the Château d'If, a folly inscribed with the names of Dumas' numerous works.

Suresnes, across the Seine from the Bois de Boulogne, has been a wine-producing village since Roman times, and still celebrates the Fête des Vendanges grape harvest every autumn. The 162-metre-high (532-foot) Mont Valérien was a place of pilgrimage – one of the nearby streets is still named rue du Calvaire. In 1841 a huge fortress was built here to defend Paris. It was occupied by the German army during World War II; French Resistants were brought here at night and shot. The fortress itself still belongs to the French army and is the centre of its eavesdropping network. On the surrounding hill is the American Cemetery (190 bd de Washington), which contains the graves of American soldiers from World Wars I and II.

St-Germain-en-Laye is a smart suburb with a historic centre and a château, rebuilt by François I on the foundations of the fortress of Charles V. Here Henri II lived in style with his wife Catherine de Médicis and his mistress Diane de Poitiers; it was here also that Mary Queen of Scots grew up, Louis XIV was born and the deposed James II lived for 12 years. Napoléon III turned the château into the **Musée des Antiquités Nationales**.

Château de Malmaison

av du Château, 92500 Rueil-Malmaison (01.41.29.05.55/www.chateau-malmaison.fr). RER La Défense, then bus 258. **Open** *Apr-Sept* 10am-5pm Mon-Fri; 10am-5.30pm Sat, Sun. *Oct-Mar* 10am-noon, 1.30-4.45pm Mon-Fri; 10am-noon, 1.30-5pm Sat, Sun. **Admission** €4.50; €3 18-25s, all on Sun; free under-18s. **Credit** AmEx, MC, V.

Napoléon and Joséphine's love nest was purchased by Joséphine in 1799, and was the emperor's favourite retreat during the Consulate (1800-03). After their divorce, Napoléon gave the château to his ex, who died here in 1814. All that romance has not gone to waste: today the château is used for weddings as well as for sightseeing. The couple redesigned the entrance as a military tent; you can also see the emperor's office, the billiard room and Joséphine's tented bedroom.

Maison de Chateaubriand

La Vallée aux Loups, 87 rue de Chateaubriand, 92290 Chatenay-Malabry (01.55.52.13.00/recorded information 01.47.02.08.62). RER Robinson, then walk. **Open** (guided tours only except Sun) *Apr-Sept* 10am-noon, 2-5.15pm Tue-Sun. *Oct-Mar* 2-4.15pm Tue-Sun. Closed Jan. **Admission** €4.50; €3 over-60s; free students, under-12s. **No credit cards**.

In 1807, attracted by the quiet Vallée aux Loups, René, Vicomte de Chateaubriand (1768-1848), set about turning a simple 18th-century country house into his own Romantic idyll, and planted the park with rare trees as a reminder of his travels. Most interesting is the double wooden staircase, based on a maritime design: a reminder of the writer's noble St-Malo birth. Anyone familiar with David's *Portrait of Mme Récamier* in the Louvre will find the original chaise longue awaiting the sitter, one of Chateaubriand's many lovers. After publishing an inflammatory work, he was ruined, and in 1818 was forced to sell up. The house offers free concerts in June, and literary evenings in spring and autumn.

Mémorial de la France Combattante

rue du Professeur-Léon-Bernard, 92150 Suresnes (01.41.44.56.34/reservations 01.49.74.34.00). Train to Suresnes-Mont-Valérien/RER La Défense, then bus 360, 160 or tram 2. **Open** *Guided tours* (in French) *Apr-Sept* 3pm, 4.30pm Sun, public hols. *Oct-Mar* 3pm Sun, public hols. Other times by appointment. **Admission** free.

Inaugurated in 1960 by Charles de Gaulle, and set against a massive Cross of Lorraine in pink granite from the Vosges, 16 bronze relief sculptures by 16 artists represent France's struggle for liberation – from a Gaullist perspective. Behind an eternal flame, the crypt contains 16 tombs of 16 heroes from 16 French battles in World War II (with a 17th left empty for the last liberation hero). The memorial was built on the site where members of the Resistance were brought from prisons in Paris. A staircase from within the crypt leads visitors inside the curtain wall, then up around the hill to the chapel where prisoners were locked before execution, and down to the Clairière des Fusillés, the clearing where the shootings took place. The chapel walls were covered in their last, desperate graffiti (of which only a small patch remains); it also contains five of the wooden firing posts against which the condemned were tied. Over 1,000 men were shot here (women were deported); no one is known to have escaped. A monument by artist Pascal Convert lists the names of the victims, including figures such as Communist politician Gabriel Péri.

Musée des Années 30

Espace Landowski, 28 av André-Morizet, 92100 Boulogne-Billancourt (01.55.18.46.45/www.annees 30.com). M° Marcel Sembat. **Open** 11am-6pm Tue-Sun. Closed 2wks Aug. **Admission** (incl Musée-Jardin Paul Landowski) €4.20; €3.20 concessions; free under-16s. **Credit** MC, V.

The Musée des Années 30 shows how much second-rate art was produced in the 1930s, though there are decent modernist sculptures by the Martel brothers, graphic designs and Juan Gris still lifes and drawings. The highlights are the designs by avant-garde architects like Perret, Le Corbusier and Fischer. 2006 will see a retrospective devoted to Polish art deco painter Tamara de Lempicka.

Musée des Antiquités Nationales

Château St-Germain, pl Charles-de-Gaulle, 78105 St-Germain-en-Laye (01.39.10.13.00/www.musee-antiquitesnationales.fr). RER St-Germain-en-Laye. **Open** *May-Sept* 10am-6.15pm Mon, Wed-Sun. *Oct-Apr* 9am-5.15pm Mon, Wed-Sun. **Admission** €4; €2.60 students, 18-25s, all on Sun; free under-18s, all on 1st Sun of mth. **Credit** *Shop* MC, V.

Thousands of years spin by from one cabinet to the next in this awe-inspiring museum tracing France's rich archaeological heritage: some of the Paleolithic animal sculptures existed long before the Ancient Egyptians. The redesigned Neolithic galleries feature statue-menhirs, female statues and an ornate tombstone from Cys-la-Commune. Exhibits are well presented and full of curiosities, like the huge antlers from a prehistoric Irish deer or the 18th-century cork models of ancient sites.

Musée Départemental Maurice Denis, 'Le Prieuré'

2bis rue Maurice-Denis, 78175 St-Germain-en-Laye (01.39.73.77.87/www.musee-mauricedenis.fr). RER St-Germain-en-Laye. **Open** 10am-5.30pm Tue-Fri;

10am-6.30pm Sat, Sun. **Admission** €3.80; €2.20 concessions; free under-12s. *Exhibitions* (with museum) €5.30; €3.80 concessions; free under-12s. **Credit** MC, V.

This former royal convent and hospital was bought to use as a home and studio by Nabi painter Maurice Denis; in 1915 he decorated the chapel in the garden. The remarkable collection comprises decorative objects, prints and paintings by the Nabis – the name means 'Prophets' – whose ranks included Sérusier, Bonnard, Vuillard, Roussel and Valloton. Seeking a renewed spirituality in painting, they took inspiration from Gauguin and Toulouse-Lautrec, who also have some paintings on show here.

Musée-Jardin Paul Landowski

14 rue Max-Blondat, 92100 Boulogne-Billancourt (01.46.05.82.69). Mº Boulogne Jean Jaurès. **Open** 10am-noon, 2-5pm Wed, Sat, Sun. **Admission** €3.20; €2.20 students; free under-16s. *With Musée des Années 30* €4.20; €3.20 concessions; free under-16s. **No credit cards.**

Sculptor Paul Landowski (1875-1961) won the Prix de Rome in 1900, and never lacked for state commissions, his work treating classical and modern themes on a monumental scale. One of his most intriguing creations is *Temple* – four sculpted walls depicting the history of humanity. Some 100 sculptures are on show in this garden and studio.

Musée National de la Céramique

pl de la Manufacture, 92310 Sèvres (01.41.14.04.20). Mº Pont de Sèvres. **Open** 10am-5pm Mon, Wed-Sun. Closed most public hols. **Admission** €4; €2.60 18-25s, all on Sun; free under-18s, all on 1st Sun of mth. *Temporary exhibition*s €5.20; €3.80 CM. **Credit** MC, V.

Founded in 1738 as a private concern, the famous porcelain factory moved to Sèvres from Vincennes in 1756 and was taken on by the state. Finely painted, delicately modelled pieces that epitomise French rococo style, together with later Sèvres, adorned with copies of Raphaels and Titians, demonstrate a technical virtuosity. The collection also includes Delftware, Meissen and wonderful Ottoman plates.

La Défense

The skyscrapers and walkways of La Défense – named after a stand against the Prussians in 1870 – create a whole new world. La Défense has been a showcase for French business since the mid 1950s, when the CNIT hall was built to host trade shows, but it was the arrival of the **Grande Arche** that gave the district its most dramatic monument. Today, more than 100,000 people work here, and another 35,000 live in the blocks of flats on the southern edge, served by the inevitable mall, an IMAX cinema – and, from 2006, a new 16-screen multiplex cinema and a vast leisure and restaurant complex. On the central esplanade are fountains and sculptures by Miró and Serra. No particular skyscraper

The grand view from **La Grande Arche**.

displays architectural distinction, although together they make an impressive sight. A kiosk in front of the CNIT building has local maps.

La Grande Arche de La Défense

92044 Paris La Défense (01.49.07.27.57/www. grandearche.com). Mº La Défense. **Open** *Apr-Sept* 10am-8pm daily. *Oct-Mar* 10am-7pm daily. **Admission** €8; €6 students, 6-18s; free under-6s. **Credit** MC, V.

Completed for the bicentenary of the Revolution, in 1989, the Grande Arche was designed by Danish architect Johan Otto von Spreckelsen. Though it lines up neatly on the Grand Axe – from the Louvre, up the Champs-Elysées to the Arc de Triomphe – the building itself is skewed. A vertigo-inducing glass lift soars up through the 'clouds' to the roof, and a fantastic view over Paris. **Photo** *p174*.

Musée Mémorial Ivan Tourguéniev

16 rue Ivan-Tourguéniev, 78380 Bougival (01.45.77.87.12). Mº La Défense. then bus 258. **Open** *Apr-Oct* 10am-6pm Sun. Also by appointment for groups (weekdays). **Admission** €5.50; €2.60 students, 12-25s; free under-12s. **No credit cards.**

The dacha where novelist Ivan Turgenev lived until his death in 1883 was a gathering spot for composers Saint-Saëns and Fauré, divas Pauline Viardot and Maria Malibran, and writers Henry James, Flaubert, Zola and Maupassant. Letters and editions (mainly Russian) are on the ground floor; above, there's the music room where Viardot held court, and the writer's deathbed. The guided tour (5pm Sun) is worthwhile if you speak French.

Eat, Drink, Shop

Features

Restaurants

Paris chefs are shaking off their shackles.

Mon Vieil Ami. *See p183.*

Eat, Drink, Shop

Somehow, in the past few years, Paris has become the underachiever of European dining. Spain pushes the culinary boundaries, London sets the standard for cool, and Italians understand the sandwich in a way that the French, with their ubiquitous *jambon-beurre*, never will. Yet Paris restaurants – perhaps in response to competition from elsewhere – are not standing still. Increasingly, young chefs (and older ones, such as Joël Robuchon with his **Atelier de Joël Robuchon** or Alain Senderens of **Senderens**; *see p195* **Return to Senderens**) are rejecting the rigid, hierarchical

system that was once the only road to success. They are opening their own bistros, inventing their own styles, choosing their own tableware, and even encouraging kitchen staff to create their own restaurants in turn. Perhaps for the first time, Paris chefs feel free to do their own thing – and their contentment shows in the food. The most notable example is Yves Camdeborde, who sold his landmark bistro La Régalade to a promising young chef and now runs a chic St-Germain-des-Prés hotel with a low-key restaurant, **Le Comptoir**. Even haute cuisine chefs are daring to have fun: at lofty hotel restaurant **Les Ambassadeurs**, Jean-François Piège invents desserts inspired by childhood sweets; Alain Ducasse has also been indulging his soft spot for marshmallows.

Yes, it's possible to eat badly in Paris, as in any world capital – but this is still a city that worships food, as proved by its 90 or so markets and hundreds of specialist shops (*see p259* **Forward *Marché*!** and *pp258-265*). The new generation of bistro chefs has been making the most of this plethora of ingredients, offering regularly changing, market-inspired menus that let them keep prices reasonable – though the days of the €10 three-course lunch are well and truly over. Many of the best are listed in this chapter, and while it can be hard

Prices

With our reviews, we give the average price for a standard main course chosen from the à la carte menu. If 'Main courses' is not listed, only *prix fixe* options are available. 'Prix fixe' indicates the price of the venue's set menu at lunch and/or dinner. All bills include a service charge, but an additional tip of a few euros (for the whole table) is polite unless you're unhappy with the service.

Memorable **Le Meurice**. *See p185.*

to secure a last-minute reservation for dinner, they're usually quieter at lunchtimes. Note that the scribbled blackboard menus typical of these bistros rarely come with English translations, unless you're lucky enough to be served by a bilingual waiter.

Still, for all the ups and downs, something about the world's original gastronomic capital keeps people coming back in search of the bistro that hasn't changed its menu in decades, the brasserie where oyster-slurping is really just an excuse to indulge in some of the world's finest people-watching, and the haute cuisine temple where food becomes art. Thankfully,

only the most unprepared visitors leave without having experienced a meal that justifies the city's high culinary reputation.

MEALTIME MAXIMS

Before spending a week's salary at a high-end gastronomic restaurant, consider what's important to you. Some of the best bistros and contemporary restaurants serve cooking of comparable skill and quality, albeit using fewer costly ingredients like truffles, foie gras, caviar and lobster. Unless you're looking for an all-out *luxe* experience – where you're made to feel like royalty for a few hours – a visit to an haute cuisine restaurant might not be so vital. Remember, too, that most of these restaurants offer more affordable lunch menus, though keep an eye on the often hair-raising cost of extras like aperitifs, wine and coffee.

As a general rule, avoid eating in cafés if food is a priority. The exceptions are easy to spot (they're filled with happy locals tucking into duck confit with sautéed potatoes or delicious-looking steak tartare), but if frankfurters are on the menu, flee the place before it fleeces you. The hundreds of Asian traiteurs that have popped up in recent years are almost uniformly mediocre, too, reheating pre-made dishes in the microwave before your eyes. It would be wiser to eat a sandwich in a park at lunch and save your money for a memorable dinner (expect to spend €80 or more per couple for a meal with drinks). Asian fast-food joints aside, non-French options are multiplying by the minute as Parisians grow more open to flavours from around the world: Moroccan, South Indian, Chinese, Laotian, Italian and Jewish cuisines are well represented, if you know where to look.

Except for the very simplest restaurants, it's wise to book ahead. This can usually be done on the same day as your intended visit. More time should be allowed for really top-notch establishments, which require bookings weeks in advance and confirmation the day before.

All listings have been checked at time of press, but are often liable to change. Many venues close for their annual break in August, some at Christmas. It pays to phone ahead. Restaurants in this chapter are presented by area, then by type: French, haute cuisine and international. For more reviews, refer to *Time Out Paris Eating & Drinking*, available at www.timeout.com/shop.

Purple '❶' numbers given in this chapter correspond to the location of each restaurant as marked on the street maps. *See pp402-411.*

The Islands

French

Brasserie de l'Ile St-Louis

55 quai de Bourbon, 4th (01.43.54.02.59). M° Pont Marie. **Open** noon-midnight Mon, Tue, Fri-Sun; 6pm-midnight Thur. Closed Aug. **Main courses** €20. **Credit** MC, V. **Map** p408 K7 **①**

Happily, this old-fashioned brasserie soldiers on while exotic juice bars and fancy tea shops on the Ile St-Louis come and go. The terrace has one of the best summer views in Paris, and is invariably packed; the dining room exudes shabby chic. Nicotined walls make for an agreeably authentic Paris mood, as does the slightly gruff waiter, though nothing here is gastronomically gripping: a well dressed *frisée aux lardons*, a slab of fairly ordinary terrine, a greasy slice of *foie de veau* prepared *à l'anglaise* with a rasher of bacon, and a more successful pan of warming tripes. A dash more sophistication in the kitchen would transform this delightful place into something more exceptional.

Mon Vieil Ami

69 rue St-Louis-en-l'Ile, 4th (01.40.46.01.35). M° Pont Marie. **Open** 12.30am-2.30pm, 7.30-10.30pm daily. Closed 3wks Jan & 3wks Aug. **Main courses** €20. **Prix fixe** €39. **Credit** AmEx, DC, MC, V. **Map** p411 K7 **②**

You don't have to work too hard on the Ile St-Louis to pull a crowd, as its many candlelit places serving indifferent food prove. So it's a thrill that Antony Clemot, a protégé of Strasbourg's Antoine Westermann, should be here. The menu offers a short but tempting assortment. Outstanding starters include *pâté en croûte* (buttery pastry enclosing delicious terrine with a cap of beef aspic and a lobe of foie gras) and mixed root vegetables in bouillon with foie gras. Among the mains, a slow-braised shoulder of roebuck comes with celery, quince, chestnuts and prunes, served with a pretty Alsatian earthenware dish generously filled with white beans stewed with garlic cloves, bay leaf and tomato, and topped with tender squid. *Photo p181.*

Le Vieux Bistro

14 rue du Cloître-Notre-Dame, 4th (01.43.54.18.95). M° Cité or St-Michel. **Open** noon-10.15pm daily. **Main courses** €50. **Credit** MC, V. **Map** p408 J7 **③**

Given the place's touristy name and location opposite Notre-Dame, it's a surprise to discover that the food here is generally excellent and the dining room comfortable and well run. Choose a spot in the spacious front room, cosy back room or on the romantic terrace, and start with sliced, pistachio-studded sausage and potatoes dressed in vinegar and oil, or the sublime *pâté de tête* (chunks of head cheese in a dark amber-coloured beef aspic). Then sample the renowned *bourguignon*, a first-rate rib of beef for two, or scallops sautéed in whisky. The house Bordeaux, a Château Layauga Médoc 2000, is superb and goes down a treat with cheese or one of the homely desserts.

The Louvre, Palais-Royal & Les Halles

French

L'Ardoise

28 rue du Mont-Thabor, 1st (01.42.96.28.18). M° Concorde or Tuileries. **Open** noon-2.30pm, 6.30-11pm Tue-Sun. Closed Aug. **Main courses** €18. **Prix fixe** €31. **Credit** MC, V. **Map** p403 G5 **④**

One of the city's outstanding modern bistros, L'Ardoise is one of the few to open on Sundays. The rather anonymous room gets packed with gourmets eager to explore the €31 blackboard menu of Pierre Jay's reliably delicious cooking. A wise choice might be six oysters with warm chipolatas and a pungent shallot dressing, an unusual combination from Bordeaux; dishes like a 'gamey' hare pie with an escalope of foie gras nestling in its centre, or firm,

The best Restaurants

Bistros

L'Ardoise (*see p183*); **Le Bistrot d'à Côté Flaubert** (*see p189*); **Le Petit Caboulot** (*see p194*); **Restaurant L'Entredgeu** (*see p191*).

Brasseries

A la Bière (*see p202*); **La Coupole** (*see p208*); **Au Pied de Cochon** (*see p185*).

Haute cuisine

L'Arpège (*see p210*); **Le Grand Véfour** (*see p185*); **Le Meurice** (*see p185*); **Taillevent** (*see p191*).

International

Chez Vong (Chinese; *see p186*); **Dong Huong** (Vietnamese; *see p201*); **The Kitchen** (British; *see p186*); **Takara** (Japanese; *see p186*).

Regional

L'Ambassade d'Auvergne (*see p194*); **Chez Savy** (Auvergne; *see p189*); **Mon Vieil Ami** (Alsace; *see p183*); **L'Ourcine** (Basque; *see p205*).

Trendy

Alcazar (*see p207*); **Anahi** (*see p197*); **Le Petit Marché** (*see p197*); **Le Square Trousseau** (*see p199*).

Vegetarian

Chez Omar (*see p197*); **Le Petit Marché** (*see p197*).

shelled langoustines placed around a delicate *mousseline* of celery and coated in a luscious chervil sauce, are just as attractive. A lightly chilled, raspberry-scented Chinon, from a wine list sensibly arranged by price, provides a perfect complement.

Chez La Vieille

37 rue de l'Arbre-Sec, 1st (01.42.60.15.78). Mº Louvre Rivoli. **Open** noon-2pm Mon-Wed, Fri; noon-2pm, 7.30-9.30pm Thur. **Main courses** €26. **Prix fixe** *Lunch* €27. **Credit** AmEx, MC, V. **Map** p408 J6 **❺**
The rustic ground floor of this bistro bursts with well-rounded regulars, while upstairs is plain and bright. A wondrous ad-lib selection of starters might include hot *chou farci* and home-made terrine de foie gras, both delivered by a smiling waitress. Equally impressive is *foie de veau*, coated in a pungent reduction of shallots and vinegar and served with potato purée. Puddings follow the same cornucopian principle as the starters, and the wine list includes a fine selection of wines from Corsica (birthplace of the eponymous *vieille* who now runs the dining room). Opening hours are limited and booking is essential, but the *prix fixe* is a bargain for the quantity and quality of the fare.

Le Grand Véfour

17 rue de Beaujolais, 1st (01.42.96.56.27/www. relaischateaux.com). Mº Palais Royal Musée du Louvre. **Open** 12.30-2pm, 8-10pm Mon-Thur; 12.30-2pm Fri. Closed Aug. **Main courses** €74. **Prix fixe** *Lunch* €75. *Dinner* €250. **Credit** AmEx, DC, MC, V. **Map** p404 H5 **❻**
Opened in 1784 (as the Café de Chartres), this is one of the oldest and most historical restaurants in Paris. Many of the greats of this world feasted on this very spot, from Napoléon and his Joséphine to the literary elite – André Malraux, Colette, Sartre, Simone de Beauvoir and Victor Hugo, who was a regular. Each member of staff is perfectly charming, particularly the knowledgeable sommeliers and the dashing maître d'hôtel, Christian David. An à la carte meal begins with a fantasia suite of delicacies: tiny frogs' legs, say, artistically arranged within a circle of sage sauce; a first course of creamed Breton sea urchins served in their spiny shells with a quail's egg and topped with caviar; flash-fried langoustines with tangy mango sauce nestling inside a curled shell, with tiny girolles and a swirl of coriander juice. Fish dishes may be a tad overcooked, and the adventurous desserts are not always successful – but you'll forgive all after a glass of vintage armagnac.

Le Meurice

Hôtel Meurice, 228 rue de Rivoli, 1st (01.44.58.10.10/www.meuricehotel.com). Mº Tuileries. **Open** noon-2pm, 7.30-10pm Tue-Fri; 7.30-10pm Sat. Closed Aug. **Main courses** €50. **Prix fixe** *Lunch* €75. *Dinner* €170. **Credit** AmEx, DC, MC, V. **Map** p403 G5. **❼**
Yannick Alléno, chef here since 2003, has hit his stride and is doing some glorious if understated contemporary French luxury cooking. Few chefs working in Paris today exercise such restraint when it comes to

letting superb produce star at the table, but Alléno has a light touch, teasing the flavour out of every leaf, frond, fin or fillet that passes through his hands. Turbot is sealed in clay before cooking and then sauced with celery cream and a coulis of flat parsley, while Bresse chicken stuffed with foie gras and served with truffled *sarladais* potatoes (cooked in the fat of the bird) is breathtakingly good. A fine cheese tray, with a stunning extra-aged comté, comes from Quatrehomme (*see p260*), and the pastry chef amazes with his signature millefeuilles. The bemused complicity of the courtly but friendly waiters and sommeliers makes for a memorable meal. **Photos** *p182*.

Au Pied de Cochon

6 rue Coquillière, 1st (01.40.13.77.00/www. pieddecochon.com). Mº Les Halles. **Open** 24hrs daily. **Main courses** €20. **Credit** AmEx, DC, MC, V. **Map** p404 J5 **❽**
Open 24 hours a day, this brasserie is a reminder of the time when Les Halles was a wholesale market and barrow boys would sit down to a bowl of onion soup in the early hours of the morning. Nowadays it's an ornate, pig-oriented tourist favourite, but its smart professional approach to catering does not disgrace its heritage. Go the whole hog with the signature pig's trotters, ears or tails, or order the celebrated cheese-capped onion soup – but avoid any dishes that sound too ambitious, as the kitchen's forte lies in simple fare. Finish with crêpes flambées or some discreet people-watching over coffee.

La Tour de Montlhéry (Chez Denise)

5 rue des Prouvaires, 1st (01.42.36.21.82). Mº Les Halles/RER Châtelet Les Halles. **Open** noon-3pm, 7.30pm-6.30am Mon-Fri; noon-3pm Sat, Sun. Closed 14 July-15 Aug. **Main courses** €20. **Credit** MC, V. **Map** p404 J5 **❾**
At the stroke of midnight, the place is packed, jovial and hungry. The red-checked dining room is intimate – you end up tasting a portion of your neighbour's roasted lamb or chatting by the barrels of wine stacked atop the bar. Savoury traditional dishes, washed down by litres of the house Brouilly, are the order of the day. Les Halles was the city's wholesale meat market, and game, beef and offal still rule here. Diners devour towering rib steaks served with marrow and a heaping platter of fries, home-made and among the best in Paris. Adventurous souls can try *tripes au calvados*, grilled *andouillette* or lamb's brain, or go for an interesting stewed venison, served with succulent celery root and home-made jam.

Willi's Wine Bar

13 rue des Petits-Champs, 1st (01.42.61.05.09/ www.williswinebar.com). Mº Pyramides. **Open** noon-2.30pm, 7-11pm Mon-Sat. Closed 2wks Aug. **Main courses** €15. **Prix fixe** *Lunch* €25. *Dinner* €32. **Credit** MC, V. **Map** p404 H5 **❿**
If you haven't discovered Willi's, you're missing something. A narrow passage beside the long bar gives way to a small and elegant beamed room

Eat, Drink, Shop

accented with crisp white linen. From some tables you can look through the hatch at the derring-do in François Yon's tiny, perfect kitchen and whet your appetite on stray aromas. Courses are ambitious, but never gratuitously so. Starters – succulent quail breasts sizzled in a sophisticated version of barbecue sauce, say, or a creamy *cassoulet* of cockles, puy lentils and shredded leek – set the tone, but the mains, classic and innovative, are more than you'd hope for. Yon is a fine meat chef who matches precise cooking and fine sauces with superb presentation. A thick fillet steak, crowned with a tiny shallot *Tatin*, is tender and just-right rare; a flaky chunk of roast cod, set in a dark, earthy sauce of chanterelles and artichokes, is robust. Willi's wine list is appropriately long (Côtes du Rhône looms large) and the bilingual staff offer informed, enthusiastic advice.

International

Chez Vong

10 rue de la Grande-Truanderie, 1st (01.40.26.09.36). *M° Etienne Marcel.* **Open** noon-2.30pm, 7pm-midnight Mon-Sat. **Main courses** €50. **Prix fixe** *Lunch* €23. **Credit** AmEx, DC, MC, V. **Map** p404 J5 ⓫
The staff at this intimate Chinese restaurant take pride in its excellent cooking, which covers the great dishes of Canton, Shanghai, Beijing and Sichuan. From the greeting at the door to the knowledgeable and trilingual service (Cantonese, Mandarin and French), each part of the experience is thoughtfully orchestrated to showcase China's diverse and delicious cuisines. Tables, draped in pink cloth, are widely spaced; low lighting and green ceramic bamboo partitions heighten the sense of intimacy. Any doubts about authenticity are extinguished with the first arrival of the beautifully presented dishes, which are placed on heated stands at the table. Expertly cooked spicy shrimp glistens in a smooth, characterful sauce of onions and ginger, while Ma Po tofu melts in the mouth, its spicy and peppery flavours melding with those of the fine pork mince.

Takara

14 rue Molière, 1st (01.42.96.08.38). M° Palais *Royal Musée du Louvre or Pyramides.* **Open** 12.30-2.15pm, 7-10.15pm Tue-Fri; 7-10.15pm Sat, Sun. Closed 2wks Aug & 2wks Dec. **Main courses** €20. **Prix fixe** *Lunch* €23, €26. *Dinner* €47, €62. **Credit** MC, V. **Map** p404 H5 ⓬
Takara does some of the best Japanese food in Paris. Start with four plump raw oysters, served out of the shell in a light vinegar sauce topped with shredded green onions and a pinch of peppery, grated radish. Follow with the monkfish liver sushi, an unusual and delightful *mélange* of cubed, creamy monkfish liver and rice wrapped in crispy nori. Move on to the fresh turbot sashimi: roll up each translucent sliver with a sprig of chives, a sprinkle of chopped green onion and a dab of grated radish, dip it into the vinaigrette and chew slowly. The *maguro* (tuna) with

blanched leeks in miso paste provides just the right kick. Then try the astonishing *agedashi dofu*, deep-fried cubes of the silkiest tofu coated in a light, subtly elastic batter, softened by a warm, mirin-based broth. Takara also specialises in *sukiyaki* and a self-serve Japanese hotpot called *shabu shabu*.

Opéra & Grands Boulevards

French

Angl'Opéra

39 av de l'Opéra, 2nd (01.42.61.86.25/www. *anglopera.com). M° Opéra.* **Open** noon-2.30pm, 7.30-11.30pm Mon-Fri. **Main courses** €38. **Prix fixe** *Lunch* €19. **Credit** AmEx, MC, V. **Map** p403 H4. ⓭
Gilles Choukroun, one of the more daring young chefs in Paris, is behind this hotel restaurant. Office types keep it busy at noon, but after hours this is a relaxed and charming place for a meal in a stylish dining room with excellent service. 'Hot bouillon, herbs, ginger, soft-boiled egg… and foie gras' turns out to be tiny cubes of raw foie gras garnished with fresh mint, tarragon and lemon verbena, which you douse with hot bouillon and eat with spoonfuls of scrambled egg with 'apéro-peanuts' (peanuts with a crunchy shell). Deep-fried camembert wedges with a salad of celery root and apple in a soy dressing are lovely, but the best conclusion to a meal here, from a menu that changes often, is a dessert inspired by childhood sweets. The wine list is nicely international, with reds from Spain, Argentina and Morocco.

Aux Lyonnais

32 rue St-Marc, 2nd (01.42.96.65.04). M° Bourse *or Richelieu Drouot.* **Open** noon-2pm, 7.30-11pm Tue-Fri; 7.30-11pm Sat. Closed 3wks Aug & 1wk Dec. **Main courses** €25. **Prix fixe** €28. **Credit** AmEx, MC, V. **Map** p404 H4 ⓮
Still with its Majorelle interior and gorgeous belle-époque tiles, this classic bistro run by Alain Ducasse and Thierry de la Brosse has an antique zinc bar in the back dining room and comfortable dark wood furniture. The menu of intelligently modernised Lyonnais, Bressane and Beaujolais classics is just as comforting. After pleasant glasses of Bugey sparkling wine, served with cheese and sausage nibbles, first courses of charcuterie from Sibilla (the best in Lyon) and luscious suckling-pig confit with foie gras, are superb. Steak served with sautéed shallots and a side of cheesy, garlicky mash is similarly fine. A sublime st-marcellin and a Cointreau soufflé will have you coming back as soon as you possibly can.

International

The Kitchen

153 rue Montmartre, 2nd (01.42.33.33.97/www. *thekitchen.fr). M° Grands Boulevards or Bourse.* **Open** 8am-3.30pm, 7-11pm Mon-Fri; 7-11pm Sat; 11am-3.30pm Sun. **Main courses** €15. **Credit** AmEx, MC, V. **Map** p404 J4 ⓯

Aveyron cuisine, art deco character – **Chez Savy**. See p189.

Airy, clean, crisp, playful – the vast kitchen in which you're invited to pull up a seat is familiar, probably because it embodies the ideal set for your fantasy cooking show. Opened by a pair of Irishmen, the Kitchen excels in putting creative twists on old standards, such as a spinach soup with coconut, or a salmon fillet rolled in gingerbread crumbs and served with a tangy mustard sauce. Brunch, with an accent on fresh produce and herbs, is also popular. But it's the attention to detail that wins you over – the board games and cookbooks; the smoke-free ground floor; earnest anglophone staff daintily pouring tea; and simple, bright foods that actually taste of each individual vegetable. After one dingy Parisian bistro too many, it's no small joy to relax in a wooden-and-white decor reminiscent of Habitat, and to absorb its anglo-inflected sensibility.

Champs-Elysées & western Paris

French

Alain Ducasse au Plaza Athénée
Hôtel Plaza Athénée, 25 av Montaigne, 8th (01.53.67.65.00/www.alain-ducasse.com). M° Alma Marceau. **Open** 7.45-10.15pm Mon-Fri. Closed mid July-mid Aug & 2wks Dec. **Prix fixe** €300. **Credit** AmEx, DC, MC, V. **Map** p402 D5 ⑯
The sheer glamour factor would be enough to recommend this restaurant, Alain Ducasse's most lofty Paris undertaking (though he himself is rarely seen in its kitchen). The once-subdued dining room has a cheerful new clementine-and-white colour scheme, while the ceiling drips with 10,000 crystals. The dining room's layout makes the waiters conspicuous, but they're personable, with none of the stiffness sometimes encountered in this style of restaurant. Christophe Moret, the former Spoon, Food & Wine

chef, recently took over the kitchen and seems to still be finding his identity. An *amuse-bouche* of a single langoustine in a lemon cream with a touch of Iranian caviar starts the meal off beautifully, but other dishes are inconsistent: a part-raw/part-cooked salad of autumn fruit and veg in a red, Chinese-style sweet-and-sour dressing; Breton lobster in an overwhelming sauce of apple, quince and spiced wine. Cheese is predictably delicious, as is the rum baba *comme à Monte-Carlo*, with the finest rums for dousing.

Les Ambassadeurs
Hôtel de Crillon, 10 pl de la Concorde, 8th (01.44.71.16.17/www.crillon.com). M° Concorde. **Open** 7.30-10pm Mon; 12.30-2pm, 7.30-10pm Tue-Sat; 12.30-2pm Sun. **Main courses** €90. **Prix fixe** *Lunch* (Mon-Fri) €70. *Dinner* €200. *Brunch* (Sun) €60. **Credit** AmEx, DC, MC, V. **Map** p403 F5 ⑰
To mark the arrival of former Ducasse chef Jean-Francois Piège, the hotel updated the decor of its prized restaurant, choosing softer tones and subtle colours to enhance the light-flooded space that already blazes with magnificent Baccarat chandeliers. Despite the new chef and the contemporary touches, the dining experience in this former 18th-century ballroom, opulently gilded and furnished with sky-high mirrors and seven types of marble, is rooted in classicism. The menu is predictably expensive and even a little predictable: caviar, foie gras, lobster, duck and venison, among other upper-crust classics. These luxury ingredients are expertly prepared, but the subtlety of flavours can verge on blandness. Service is courteous and professional, even friendly for such a formal ambience.

Astrance
4 rue Beethoven, 16th (01.40.50.84.40). M° Passy. **Open** 12.15-3pm, 8.15-9pm Tue-Fri. Closed 1wk Feb, 4wks Aug & 1wk Dec. **Main courses** €50. **Prix fixe** *Lunch* €70, €120. *Dinner* €150. **Credit** AmEx, DC, MC, V. **Map** p406 B6 ⑱

When Pascal Barbot opened Astrance, he was praised for creating a new style of Paris restaurant – refined, yet casual and affordable. Three years later, this small, slate-grey dining room feels exactly like an haute cuisine restaurant, with seemingly as many staff as there are customers and prices comparable to Taillevent's (*see p191*). Most customers, having secured their reservations at least a month ahead, give free rein to the chef with the 'menu Astrance' (€150). Barbot has an indisputably original touch, combining foie gras with thin slices of white mushrooms and a lemon condiment, or sweet lobster with candied grapefruit peel, a grapefruit and rosemary sorbet, and raw baby spinach. Beautiful as this is, it won't necessarily send you into ecstasies; rather, the experience is quietly pleasurable. Wines by the glass are reasonably priced but not always elegant enough to stand up to the food.

Ballon & Coquillages

71 bd Gouvion-St-Cyr, 17th (01.45.74.17.98). M° Porte Maillot. **Open** noon-3pm, 7pm-midnight daily. Closed Aug. **Main courses** €25. **Credit** AmEx, MC, V. **Map** p402 B2 ⑲

Almost no larger than an oyster itself, this charming little bar is a great asset in the neighbourhood around the Porte Maillot and Palais des Congrès, its round mosaic-topped counter a sun of conviviality in corporate precincts. Take one of the red leather stools and design your feast. The oysters (Utah Beach, Gillardeau, *spéciales de Normandie* and *plates de Bretagne*) are sold by threes, and your first order should comprise a minimum of nine. Otherwise, garnish your tray with *bigorneaux* (sea snails), red prawns, grey shrimp, langoustines, clams, cockles and mussels, or opt for one of the chef's suggested platters, including a tempting four-oyster sampler. From a curious and rather dear wine list with twice as many reds as whites, a good pick is the Château Theullet Bergerac, a dry white suited to shellfish.

Le Bistrot d'à Côté Flaubert

10 rue Gustave-Flaubert, 17th (01.42.67.05.81/ www.michelrostang.com). M° Courcelles. **Open** 12.30-2.30pm, 7.30-10.45pm daily. **Main courses** €25. **Prix fixe** *Lunch* €25. **Credit** AmEx, MC, V. **Map** p402 D2 ⑳

Star chef Michel Rostang took over this old *épicerie*, kept the pretty, period interior and began serving up what he thought genuine bistro food should be. Starters, though, have a degree of sophistication that reflects haute cuisine roots. They include a wonderfully complex *pressé* of asparagus, sundried tomatoes and coppa ham accompanied by a raw artichoke and parmesan salad, and marinated *lisette* (small mackerel) with mushrooms, carrots and mesclun. Main courses are simpler but well prepared, with the emphasis on fine-quality meat (there's always a beef offering of the day), and a choice of accompaniments. Lamb from the Pyrenees comes in a crumble crust with garlic shortbread biscuit and a bowl of smooth purée; and *dos de lieu* (pollack) comes with spicebread crust and jus, served with vegetables.

Chez Savy

23 rue Bayard, 8th (01.47.23.46.98). M° Franklin D. Roosevelt. **Open** noon-2.30pm, 7.30-11pm Mon-Fri. Closed Aug. **Main courses** €22. **Prix fixe** *Lunch* €19.50, €23.50. *Dinner* €26.50. **Credit** MC, V. **Map** p403 E4 ㉑

It's comforting that this 1923 art deco bistro, with its intimate rows of mirrored booths, continues to produce simple regional food based on the fine products of the Aveyron. Starters include a generous plate of Cantal charcuterie, a creamy *oeuf en cocotte* with roquefort, and the unusual *farçou aveyronnais* (fried herb and chard patties). Main courses feature light and delicate *tripoux* (highly seasoned tripe and trotter parcels), a generous slice of *foie de veau*, and a meaty Auvergne sausage served with a wholesome purée of split peas. A fine hunk of st-nectaire cheese and a timeless chocolate mousse finish a satisfactory meal, accompanied by well-priced red Morgon. The service is old-fashioned, although challenged by any large parties. **Photo** *p187*.

Le Cristal Room

11 pl des Etats-Unis, 16th (01.40.22.11.10). M° Iéna. **Open** 8.30-10.30am, noon-2pm, 8-10pm Mon-Sat. **Main courses** €50. **Credit** AmEx, DC, MC, V. **Map** p402 C4 ㉒

This sumptuous townhouse is the glittering HQ, boutique and showroom of Baccarat, the venerable French crystal company. The restaurant, Le Cristal Room, has decor by Philippe Starck and a light, luxury menu by chef Thierry Burlot. The salon shows Starck's pastiche of grandeur, exposing the bricks to create a brilliant contrast to the ox-blood red marble mouldings and huge Baccarat chandeliers. The expensive menu was conceived to please puckish rich types, but you can still eat well here. Start with chestnut soup with white truffles, or scallops with Petrossian caviar – then go for risotto with white truffles, spaghetti with cherry tomatoes, hare with quince, or lobster spit-roasted with vanilla beans.

Flora

36 av George-V, 8th (01.40.70.10.49). M° George V. **Open** noon-2.30pm Mon-Fri; 7-11pm Mon-Sat. Closed 3wks Aug. **Main courses** €30. **Prix fixe** *Lunch* €26. *Dinner* €34. **Credit** AmEx, MC, V. **Map** p402 D4 ㉓

Engaging chef Flora Mikula, founder of Les Olivades and former second to Alain Passard at L'Arpège (*see p210*), runs this stylish restaurant. She has broadened her horizons to include an international version of Provence that extends to Morocco, Turkey, India and Vietnam. The hospitality is southern, too, as a meal begins with delicious *amuse-bouches* and generously concludes with *mignardises*, including chocolate caramels, Turkish delight and miniature *cannelés*. Starters – such as a *croustillant de crabe* in tomato soup, and lacquered prawns and aubergine – are excellent, as is a main of lobster with broad beans and tiny girolles in a jus of its own coral. Desserts include a macaroon in rose syrup with lime sorbet, and the wine list is reasonable.

Worth fuming about?

Like a carafe of tap water or a basket of baguette, second-hand smoke comes free with nearly any restaurant meal in Paris. Are we a touch paranoid or is there something nonchalant yet calculated in the way the French hold cigarettes, aiming that curly stream of toxic waste at the nearest non-smoker's face? Protests most often draw a look of innocent surprise, then hostility and occasionally a diatribe on *la liberté* – but what about *égalité* and *fraternité*?

But even the French have had enough. In 2004 a survey by market researchers Sofres found that 72 per cent would support a total ban on cigarette smoking in restaurants, even though 30 per cent of adults smoke. (The ban on smoking in TGV trains has proved popular among smokers.) Encouraged by these figures, the government has vowed to enforce the *Loi Evin*, which, according to a non-smoker's rights association, was applied all of ten times between its creation in 1992 and 2004. Restaurateurs who fail to identify smoking and non-smoking areas and who lack proper ventilation can be fined €1,500, and customers caught puffing away in a non-smoking area can be asked to cough up as much as €450.

It's understandable that the owner of a historic little bistro might find it impractical to create a properly ventilated non-smoking area; more puzzling that a spacious modern restaurant, such as **Ze Kitchen Galerie** (4 rue des Grands-Augustins, 6th, 01.44.32.00.32), can ignore the law altogether. A few brave restaurateurs, encouraged by the Mairie de Paris, have opted for the '100% sans tabac' label, making their restaurants entirely non-smoking. To put this initiative in perspective, only about 60 such establishments are listed on the city's official website, www.parisinfo.com, and eight of these are branches of Starbucks (Paris has around 12,000 hotels, restaurants and bars).

Still, it's a significant step forward for the city, and one that's already proving profitable for the restaurants involved. Starbucks aside, there are plenty of styles to choose from on the tobacco-free list. **L'Atelier de Joël Robuchon** (*see p210*), a tapas-style restaurant run by the star chef, is certainly the most *gastronomique* of the bunch – the haute cuisine set clearly doesn't want to alienate its cigar-puffing clientele, though a few encourage their customers to retire to the *fumoir*.

Among the bistros that have gone against tradition to declare themselves entirely non-smoking are **La Cerisaie** (70 bd Edgar-Quinet, 14th, 01.43.20.98.98), known for its delicious traditional grub; the down-to-earth **Chez Germaine** (30 rue Pierre Leroux, 7th, 01.42.73.28.34), and the newly opened wine bar **Le Vin dans les Voiles** (8 rue Chapu, 16th, 01.46.47.83.98). **L'Artisan des Saveurs** (72 rue du Cherche-Midi, 6th, 01.42.22.46.64), a sedate tearoom, has chosen not to pollute its perfect pastries with Gauloise effluvia, while the Italian restaurant **Sale e Pepe** (30 rue Ramey, 18th, 01.46.06.08.01) is packed every night thanks to its great-value *prix fixe* menu and clean air.

Elsewhere, too, there seems to be a growing awareness of the issue – so don't be afraid to assert your right to a non-smoking table when you make your reservation.

Pierre Gagnaire

6 rue Balzac, 8th (01.58.36.12.50/www.pierre-gagnaire.com). M° George V or Charles de Gaulle Etoile. **Open** noon-1.30pm, 7.30-9.30pm Mon-Fri; 7.30-9.30pm Sun. Closed 1wk Feb, 2wks July & 1wk Oct/Nov. **Main courses** €100. **Prix fixe** *Lunch* €90. *Dinner* €225. **Credit** AmEx, MC, V. **Map** p402 D3 ㉔

Most starters alone cost over €90 at Pierre Gagnaire, which seems to be the price of culinary experimentation (Gagnaire is something of a scientist, often working with 'molecular gastronomy' specialist Hervé This). The more accessibly priced €90 lunch menu is far from being the same experience as the *carte*: the first is conventionally presented in three courses, while the second involves four or five plates for each course. Even the *amuse-bouches* fill the table: an egg 'raviole' (interesting technically but jarring to the palate), crisp-like waffled potatoes with chilli, ricotta with apple, fish in a cauliflower 'jelly', and glazed monkfish. The langoustine, at €122, has four variations: raw, skewered, grilled and in a creamy sauce. The best thing about the lunch menu is that it brings you four very indulgent desserts (half of 'le grand dessert'): clementine, raspberry and vanilla, chocolate and passion fruit. Coffee is priced at €8.50, but at least if you don't finish your wine, the staff will let you take it home.

Restaurant L'Entredgeu

83 rue Laugier, 17th (01.40.54.97.24). M° Porte de Champerret. **Open** noon-2pm, 7-11pm Tue-Sat. Closed 3wks Aug & 1wk Dec. **Prix fixe** *Lunch* €22. *Dinner* €28. **Credit** MC, V. **Map** p402 C2 ㉕
This snug bistro has been packed since it opened, thanks to fine food at fair prices. Chef Philippe Tredgeu mastered this sure-fire formula while heading the kitchen at Chez Casimir. You almost can't complain about the squeeze-'em-in seating, slow service or clouds of cigarette smoke (and we'd like a jazzier wine list, for that matter). The blackboard menu changes daily; scallops cooked in their shells with salted butter and crumbled cauliflower and a *croustillant* of pig's trotter with celeriac *rémoulade* are fine starters, followed by main courses of chewy, flavourful roast pork with braised chicory, and lamb stuffed with foie gras. Book and be on time – latecomers are sent to the cramped back dining room.

Senderens

9 pl de la Madeleine, 8th (01.42.65.22.90/www. lucascarton.com). M° Madeleine. **Open** 7-10.30pm Mon, Sat; noon-2.30pm, 7-10.30pm Tue-Fri. Closed 3wks Aug & 1wk Dec. **Main courses** €70. **Prix fixe** *Lunch* €76. *Dinner* €264; (with wine) €434. **Credit** AmEx, DC, MC, V. **Map** p403 F4 ㉖
Long live Alain Senderens. The ageing chef has reinvented his art nouveau institution with a *Star Trek* interior and a mind-boggling fusion menu. Now instead of his famed *canard à l'Apicius*, Senderens serves roast duck foie gras with a warm salad of black figs and licorice powder, or monkfish steak with Spanish mussels and green curry sauce. Each dish comes with a suggested wine, whisky, sherry or punch (to accompany a rum-doused *savarin* with slivers of ten-flavour pear), and while these are perfectly matched, the mix of flavours and alcohols can be a tad overwhelming by the end of a meal. The chef seems to be getting to grips with his new style – a sole tempura was not as crisp as it might have been – but even a faintly flawed meal here is an event, as much for the eclectic clientele as the adventurous food. *See p195* **Return to Senderens**.

La Soupière

154 av de Wagram, 17th (01.42.27.00.73). M° Wagram. **Open** 12.30-2pm, 7.30-10.30pm Mon-Fri; 7.30-10.30pm Sat. **Main courses** €19. **Prix fixe** €30, €55. **Credit** AmEx, MC, V. **Map** p402 D2 ㉗

This quiet and well-mannered little spot specialises in mushrooms all year round. Autumn is, of course, the best season here, as ceps, girolles, morels and other fleshy fodder of the forest floor appear in local markets and on menus. They come in a variety of guises, including a sublime salad of finely sliced raw ceps sprinkled with olive oil and sea salt as a starter, along with a lusciously earthy mushroom soup, followed by brill with a sauté of mixed mushrooms, or a superb sauté of girolles in wine sauce with cinammon. The wine list is a bit dull and service leisurely, especially at noon, but the cooking is impeccable.

La Table du Lancaster

Hôtel Lancaster, 7 rue de Berri, 8th (01.40.76.40.18/ www.hotel-lancaster.fr). M° George V. **Open** 12.30-1.45pm, 7.30-10pm Mon-Fri; 7.30-10pm Sat, Sun. **Main courses** €40. **Credit** AmEx, DC, MC, V. **Map** p402 D4 ㉘
The intimate dining room of the Hôtel Lancaster is open to anyone willing to dig up the €70-plus for a meal here. Chef Michel Troisgros has created a fascinating (if not always perfect) menu divided into six themes: tomatoes; citrus; condiments and spices; wine and vinegar; vegetables, herbs and fruit; and dairy produce. Each offers several starters and main courses. With good advice from the waiters, you'll eat very well indeed, as Troisgros cleverly draws on global inspirations and also knows what the fashionable folk here will want. Dishes such as a scallop tartare with sea urchin roe make for successful starters; mains are similarly racy and satisfying, including a brilliant dish of perfect cooked cod, smeared with Japanese mustard and set on a bed of Japan's best rice before being doused with cod bouillon. Desserts are great fun, too. The wine list tilts heavily towards Bordeaux, though there are also some lovely New World bottles to be had.

Taillevent

15 rue Lamennais, 8th (01.44.95.15.01/www. taillevent.com). M° George V. **Open** 12.30-2pm, 7.30-10pm Mon-Fri. Closed Aug. **Main courses** €60. **Prix fixe** *Lunch* €70. *Dinner* €130, €180. **Credit** AmEx, DC, MC, V. **Map** p402 D3 ㉙
Taillevent owes much of its ongoing success to the personality of its owner, Jean-Claude Vrinat. Change (including a recent refurbishment) always seems to occur seamlessly, yet Vrinat is not afraid to hire young chefs with character. A recent decision was to put Alain Solivérès in charge of the kitchen, which is turning out flawless food. Past the spacious and rather subdued front room is a livelier, almost brasserie-like second room. Prices here are not as shocking as in some restaurants at this level; there's a €70 lunch menu, though you might have to make a point of asking for it. *Rémoulade de coquilles St-Jacques* is a technical feat, with slices of raw, marinated scallop wrapped in a tube shape around a finely diced apple filling, encircled by a mayonnaise-like *rémoulade* sauce. An earthier and lip-smacking dish is the trademark *épeautre* – known in English as spelt – cooked 'like a risotto' with bone marrow,

DINING OUT IN PARIS AND LONDON?

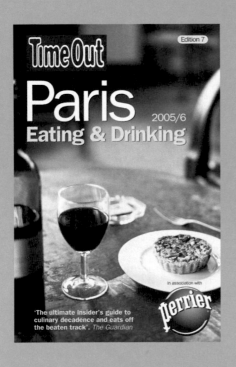

black truffle, whipped cream and parmesan, and topped with sautéd frogs' legs. *Ravioli au chocolat araguani* is a surprising and wonderful dessert: pillowy pockets of soft chocolate pasta explode in the mouth, releasing liquid bitter chocolate.

International

Le Bistrot Napolitain

18 av Franklin-D.-Roosevelt, 8th (01.45.62.08.37). M° Philipe du Roule. **Open** noon-2.30pm, 7-10.30pm Mon-Fri; noon-3pm Sat. Closed Aug. **Main courses** €25. **Credit** MC, V. **Map** p403 E4 ③⓪

This chic Italian bistro off the Champs-Elysées is as far from a tourist joint as it is possible to be. On weekday lunchtimes (it doesn't open on Saturday night or Sunday) it is full of suave Italianate businessmen in modish pinstripes. The decor is plain, the tablecloths starched white, and the kitchen open with the *pizzaiolo* shoving fluffy pizzas in and out of the oven while orders are shouted over the heads of diners. Generosity defines the food – not just big plates but lashings of the ingredients that others skimp on, such as the slices of tangy parmesan piled high over rocket on the fresh and tender beef carpaccio. The pizzas are as good as they say they are: the Enzo comes with milky, almost raw mozzarella di bufala and tasty tomatoes, which prove how good the crust is as it doesn't become a soggy mush. For pasta you can choose between dried and fresh, with variations such as fresh saffron tagliatelle.

Man Ray

34 rue Marbeuf, 8th (01.56.88.36.36/www.manray. fr). M° Franklin D. Roosevelt. **Open** 7pm-midnight daily. Closed Aug. **Main courses** €25. **Prix fixe** €27, €35. **Credit** AmEx, MC, V. **Map** p402 D4 ③①

At Man Ray the conversation involves whispering, 'Don't look now, but that's Mick Jagger', punctuated by lengthy gawping at the extravagant pan-Asian decor. The food is an afterthought, and comically bland, though you might have more luck with the sashimi. Normally safe-bet fried spring rolls, labelled '*comme je les aime*', are greasy, and the insipid foie gras with chutney is like a butter and fig-jam breakfast. Dry tuna steak is beached on spinach leaves drowned in tangy ginger sauce, turning blacker by the minute as you wait for your partner's course to arrive. Tiramisu comes in a sundae glass, with coffee jelly lurking beneath. Be warned. Better to taste the buzz from the mezzanine bar for the 'After Work' drink and free massage in the week.

Montmartre & Pigalle

French

Casa Olympe

48 rue St-Georges, 9th (01.42.85.26.01). M° St-Georges. **Open** noon-2pm, 8-11pm Mon-Fri. Closed 1wk May, 3wks Aug & 1wk Dec. **Prix fixe** €37. **Credit** AmEx, MC, V. **Map** p404 H3 ③②

Dominique Versini (aka Olympe) is one of the rare female chefs in Paris to have achieved a sort of celebrity status, thanks to the jet-set restaurant she once ran in the 15th arrondissement. In her current location, the mood is far more businesslike, with Roman ochre-painted walls, a pretty Murano chandelier, oil paintings and an almost entirely male, suit-wearing crowd. In truffle season, you might order a potato salad laced with this earthy treasure for a €15 supplement to the €37 *prix fixe*. The luxury continues with squash soup dressed up with chestnut and foie gras, and home-made sorbets for dessert. A fine choice for dinner with someone you want to impress.

Chez Jean

8 rue St-Lazare, 9th (01.48.78.62.73). M° Notre-Dame-de-Lorette. **Open** noon-2.30pm, 7.30-10.30pm Mon-Fri. Closed Aug. **Main courses** €30. **Prix fixe** €35. **Credit** AmEx, DC, MC, V. **Map** p404 H3 ③③

Despite a staff-to-diner ratio near that of a haute cuisine purveyor, and a sumptuous high-ceilinged dining room with pine panelling and comfy banquettes, the *prix fixe* at Chez Jean remains good value. Food is well prepared and creative, while service combines politeness and efficiency. Served with a light verbena sauce, fine yellow Chinese-style ravioli stuffed with crab burst with flavour, while a ramekin of plump snails with quartered fresh artichokes is set off well by tasty poultry gravy. Mains range from foie gras *mi-cuit*, scattered with toasted almonds and served with a bracing rhubarb sauce, to a delicious slow-cooked farmhouse pork with a chutney of apricots, preserved lemons and sage. Pleasingly alcoholic cherries soaked in eau de vie and scattered with pistachios make for a fine dessert.

Chez Toinette

20 rue Germain-Pilon, 18th (01.42.54.44.36). M° Abbesses or Pigalle. **Open** 7.30-11pm Tue-Sat. Closed Aug. **Main courses** €16. **Credit** MC, V. **Map** p403 H2 ③④

This stalwart purveyor of bistro fare behind the Théâtre de Montmartre has steadily upped its prices in line with its burgeoning success. However, the blackboard menu is still good value in an area known for rip-offs. As you squeeze into the seats, the amiable waiter describes each dish with pride, then presents an appetiser of olives, ripe cherry tomatoes and crisp radishes. Of the starters, try the red-blooded wild boar terrine, the pleasing *chèvre chaud* with a glorious creamy st-marcellin on a bed of rocket and lettuce, or the soufflé-like asparagus quiche. Carnivorous mains include *mignon de porc*, spring lamb and assorted steaks – the lamb seared in rosemary is a deliciously lean morsel. The desserts cover standard ground, but you can round off on a high note with armagnac-steeped prunes.

Georgette

29 rue St-Georges, 9th (01.42.80.39.13). M° St-Georges. **Open** noon-2.45pm, 7.30-11pm Tue-Fri. Closed 3wks Aug. **Main courses** €13. **Credit** AmEx, MC, V. **Map** p404 H3 ③⑤

Eat, Drink, Shop

A mix of 1950s formica tables and ancient wooden beams provides external charm, but what has won Georgette a loyal following since this bistro opened three years ago is the chef's loving use of seasonal ingredients. Forget pallid supermarket tomatoes; here they're orange, yellow and green, layered in a salad or blended up in a flavour-packed gazpacho. Hearty meat dishes satisfy the local business crowd, while lighter options might include slightly bony sea bream with Provençal vegetables, or a charlotte of juicy lamb chunks and aubergine. For calorie counters there's an unsweetened prune and pear compote – though the creamy, cloudlike fontainebleau cheese with raspberry coulis is worth abandoning a diet for.

Le Petit Caboulot

6 pl Jacques-Froment, 18th (01.46.27.19.00).
M° Guy Môquet. **Open** noon-2.30pm, 8-11pm Mon-Sat. **Main courses** €13.50. **Prix fixe** *Lunch* €10. **Credit** DC, MC, V. **Map** p403 G1 **36**
This has all the trappings of a friendly neighbourhood bistro. *Brik de chèvre aux pommes*, a crisp pastry of apple and melting goat's cheese on a bed of salad, starts things off nicely. Foie gras *maison* is also well worth a try. The duck confit (ask for it *bien grillé*) is dark and succulent, with a skin that crunches wonderfully; the haddock *brandade* features flakes of smoked fish blended with moist potato purée, oven-browned. Then the *tarte Tatin* arrives. Ubiquitous in bistros but so rarely right, this one, caramelised to the core, will have you booking a return visit. Mosaic pillars, a huge curved bar and a vast collection of old enamel adverts (look for the Arabic Kodak) evoke a bygone era.

Pétrelle

34 rue Pétrelle, 9th (01.42.82 11.02). M° Anvers. **Open** 8-10pm Tue-Sat. Closed 4wks July/Aug & 1wk Dec. **Main courses** €23. **Prix fixe** €27. **Credit** MC, V. **Map** p404 J2 **37**
Jean-Luc André is as inspired a decorator as he is a cook, and the quirky charm of his dining room has made it popular with fashion designers and film stars. A faded series of early 20th-century tableaux is one recent flea market find, but behind this style is some serious substance. André seeks out the very best ingredients from local producers. The €27 no-choice menu is huge value (on our last visit, marinated sardines with tomato relish, rosemary roasted rabbit with roasted vegetables, deep purple poached figs), or you can splash out with luxurious à la carte dishes such as tournedos Rossini. If you're looking for a quick and delicious lunch near Montmartre, visit his annexe, Les Vivres, next door.

International

Kastoori

4 pl Gustave-Toudouze, 9th (01.44.53.06.10). M° St-Georges. **Open** 6.30-11.30pm Mon; 11.30am-2.30pm, 6.30-11.30pm Tue-Sun. **Main courses** €16. **Prix fixe** *Lunch* (Mon-Fri) €8, €10. *Dinner* €15. **Credit** MC, V. **Map** p403 H2 **38**

It's no surprise that Kastoori's terrace, on a delightful 19th-century square, is often full: this friendly, family-run Indian restaurant is one of the few good-value eateries in the area. Each dish on the lunch and dinner set menus is prepared with care and home-mixed spices; you can taste the difference. Amid dangling lanterns, Indian fabrics and (perhaps too much) incense inside, or under hot lamps outside, order some popadoms to taste the home-made chutneys served in an ornate metal boat, and choose from tangy raita and *kaleji* (coriander-sprinkled, curried lamb liver) as starters, followed by a choice of tandoori chicken, chicken curry, *saag paneer* or the dish of the day, selected from the à la carte menu. You can bring your own wine for no corkage fee, and don't miss the delicious lassis or kulfis for afters. **Photos** *p198 and p199.*

Beaubourg & the Marais

French

L'Ambassade d'Auvergne

22 rue du Grenier-St-Lazare, 3rd (01.42.72.31.22/ www.ambassade-auvergne.com). M° Rambuteau. **Open** noon-2pm, 7.30-10.30pm daily. Closed mid July-mid Aug. **Main courses** €15. **Prix fixe** €32. **Credit** AmEx, MC, V. **Map** p404 K5 **39**
This rustic auberge is a fitting embassy for the hearty, filling fare of central France. Go easy on the complimentary pâté and thick-sliced country bread while you look at the menu – you're going to need your appetite later. An order of cured ham comes as two hefty, plate-filling slices, as does the salad bowl chock-full of green lentils cooked in goose fat, studded with bacon bits and shallots. The *rôti d'agneau* arrives as a pot of melting chunks of lamb in a rich meaty sauce with a helping of tender white beans. Dishes arrive with the flagship *aligot*, served with great pomp as the waiter lifts great strands of the creamy, elastic mash-and-cheese concoction into the air and lets it plop on to the plates with a dramatic flourish. Of the regional wines (Chanturgue, Boudes, Madargues), the rather fruity AOC Marcillac makes a worthy partner for a successful meal.

Le Dôme du Marais

53bis rue des Francs-Bourgeois, 4th (01.42.74.54.17). M° Rambuteau. **Open** noon-2.30pm, 7.15-11pm Tue-Sat. Closed 2wks Jan & 3wks Aug. **Main courses** €18. **Prix fixe** *Lunch* €17, €23. *Dinner* €32, €45. **Credit** AmEx, MC, V. **Map** p411 L6 **40**
Lying somewhere between casual and formal, bistro and haute cuisine, Le Dôme du Marais seems to have got it just about right. The staff won't turn a hair if you show up in jeans, but should you feel the urge to mark the occasion with finery, the octagonal, domed dining room would provide a stunning backdrop. The building predates the French Revolution and once served as the auction room for state-owned pawnbrokers; today it has been done up (but thankfully not overdone) in burgundy and gilt, with tables dressed in sparkling white linen. Owner-chef Pierre

Lecoutre loves to work with seasonal produce, serving, say, *filet de courbine*, a white fish available for three weeks a year, in a chorizo cream sauce next to fresh little broad beans that also have a brief season. *Monceau de chocolat* and strawberry *dacquoise* live up to their stunning good looks.

Le Hangar

12 impasse Berthaud, 3rd (01.42.74.55.44). Mº Rambuteau. **Open** noon-2.30pm, 7-11.30pm Tue-Sat. Closed Aug. **Main courses** €16. **No credit cards. Map** p404 K5 ⑪
It's worth making the effort to check out this bistro by the Centre Pompidou, with its terrace and excellent cooking. The exposed stone walls and smartly set tables are immediately welcoming, and the airy, long room fills with locals and slightly baffled tourists. A bowl of tapenade and toast is supplied to keep you fed while choosing from the fairly comprehensive *carte*. It yields, for starters, tasty and grease-free *rillettes de lapereau* (rabbit) alongside

perfectly balanced pumpkin and chestnut soup. Main courses include a well-seasoned steak tartare, served with a crisp salad and some *pommes dauphines*, and a superb *ris de veau* on a bed of melting chicory. You may also be tempted by the puddings: the chocolate soufflé and warm white wine tart with cinnamon – but if you're going to splurge, remember that payment is by cash only.

Le Pamphlet

38 rue Debelleyme, 3rd (01.42.72.39.24). Mº Filles du Calvaire. **Open** 7.30-11pm Mon, Sat; noon-2.30pm, 7.30-11pm Tue-Fri. Closed 2wks Jan & 2wks Aug. **Prix fixe** €30, €45. **Credit** MC, V. **Map** p411 L5 ⑫
A beamed room with elegantly dressed and widely spaced tables, and cooking that's modern and sophisticated without being insubstantial or over elaborate, make Le Pamphlet's €30 menu one of the best deals in town. Here you can chew on fragrant *saucisson sec* with your aperitif, before a ladle of creamy lentil soup arrives as a pre-starter. The first course

Return to Senderens

At age 65, with a 28-year run as a Michelin three-star chef behind him, Alain Senderens might have gracefully bid adieu to the Paris restaurant scene. Instead, he ripped out the interior of his landmark art nouveau diner – an act akin to painting the Eiffel Tower purple – and reopened the former Lucas Carton as a 'luxury brasserie' as **Senderens** (*see p191*).

Senderens is not the only Michelin-starred chef in the past few years to have experienced a late-life crisis: the manic-depressive Bernard Loiseau committed suicide rather than risk a downward slide, and Joël Robuchon took a less dramatic early retirement at age 51 before resurfacing to open a chain of eponymous restaurants from Las Vegas to Tokyo. Alain Ducasse keeps fingers in many different pots, heading three luxury restaurants (in Paris, Monaco and New York), a chain of contemporary restaurants in locations such as Hong Kong and Mauritius, country auberges in France and Italy, and two classic Paris bistros, **Aux Lyonnais** (*see p186*) and Benoît. Even the fanatically experimental Pierre Gagnaire oversees the fashionable restaurant Sketch in London and recently took over fish bistro Gaya Rive Gauche in Paris.

If Senderens is not the first established chef to thumb his nose at the all-powerful Michelin inspectors, he is perhaps the cheekiest. Bronze banquettes, crater-like ceiling lights and easy-wipe tables – set against the carved wood and etched glass

background as if to remind you of how glorious this restaurant used to be – recall Alain Ducasse's freshly refurbished, space age dining room at the **Plaza Athénée** (*see p187*). An *amuse-bouche* of avocado mousse topped with shredded crab and Granny Smith apple matchsticks echoes a dish served by Robuchon, who himself acknowledges borrowing the idea from young chef Pascal Barbot at **Astrance** (*see p187*). The Asian and Mediterranean-inspired dishes resemble those of William LeDeuil at the contemporary bistro **Ze Kitchen Galerie** (4 rue des Grands-Augustins, 6th, 01.44.32.00.32) and are just as moderately successful; it's not easy to go from three-star chef to fusion cook overnight. The difference at Senderens lies in the suggested drink for each dish, a subject that fascinates this chef (who believes that food should accompany wine and not vice versa). Warm semi-smoked salmon with Thai spices and iced cucumber comes with ten-year-old Talisker whisky from the Isle of Skye, while manzanilla sherry accompanies roast foie gras with fig salad and licorice powder.

Senderens, who made a show of giving his three stars back to Michelin, declares himself relieved to be cooking with sardines instead of turbot after all these years, at more democratic prices (less then €100 per person with wine). Who can blame him if he has realised, like so many other French chefs young and old, that he can make more money by charging less?

keeps up the high standard of presentation: an outstanding combination of escargots and rabbit *rillettes*, while a mini *brandade* is enlivened by the addition of tasty haddock. Mains include a well prepared *parmentier de canard* (a duck version of shepherd's pie) glazed suckling pig, served French-style astride some roasted root vegetables. Charming service and a carefully chosen Pouilly Fumé make you feel as if you have eaten at a prestigious address for half the price. **Photo** *p201*.

Le Petit Marché

9 rue de Béarn, 3rd (01.42.72.06.67). M° Chemin Vert. **Open** noon-3pm, 8pm-midnight daily. **Main courses** €16. **Prix fixe** *Lunch* (Mon-Fri) €13.50. **Credit** MC, V. **Map** 408 L6 **43**
Just a step away from place des Vosges, the Petit Marché has become a hip Marais bistro, attracting a fashion-conscious crowd. The woody interior is warm and welcoming, while the heated terrace offers a view of the gendarmerie. The menu is short and modern with Asian touches. The raw tuna is flash-fried in sesame seeds, and served with a Thai sauce, making for an original and refreshing starter; the crispy-coated deep-fried king prawns have a similar oriental lightness. The main vegetarian risotto is rich in basil, coriander, cream and al dente green beans, contrasting winningly with the unctuous rice. Pan-fried scallops with lime are precision-cooked to avoid any hint of rubberiness, and accompanied by a good purée and more beans. There's a short wine list; the carafe of house red is unusually good.

International

Anahi

49 rue Volta, 3rd (01.48.87.88.24). M° Arts et Métiers, Temple or République. **Open** 8pm-midnight daily. **Main courses** €20. **Credit** MC, V. **Map** p411 K5 **44**
A rickety old building in a narrow and ill-lit street deep in the Marais houses this trendy Argentinian restaurant. Slabs of grilled beef fresh (well, vacuum-packed) from the pampas pull in the crowds, cheerily welcomed by Carmina and Pilat, the sisters who started up in this old *charcuterie* some 20 years ago. The original white tiled walls feature black-and-white photos of the pair, and the art deco ceiling was painted by Albert Camus' brother. Tuck into *torta pascualina*, a sweetish spinach tart with onions, or try the standout *ceviche* made with sea bass. Mains of skewered chicken breast marinated in lemon and served with apple and pineapple salsa and sweet potato purée, and *cururù de camarào* (grilled gambas with peanuts and okra) are satisfying, but the *bif angosto* – a juicy fillet served with a green salad – is the star. Match it with a choice Chilean red.

Chez Omar

47 rue de Bretagne, 3rd (01.42.72.36.26). M° Temple or Arts et Métiers. **Open** noon-2.30pm, 7-11.30pm Mon-Sat; 7-11.30pm Sun. **Main courses** €14. **No credit cards. Map** p404 L5 **45**

The once-fashionable Omar doesn't take reservations, and the queue can stretch the length of the zinc bar and out the door. Everyone is waiting for the same thing: couscous. Prices range from €11 (vegetarian) to €24 (*royale*); there are no tagines or other traditional Maghreb mains, only a handful of French classics (duck, fish, steak). Overstretched waiters slip through the crowds with mounds of semolina, steaming vats of vegetable-laden broth and steel platters heaving with meat and more meat, including the stellar merguez. Even on packed nights there's an offer of seconds – gratis, of course – to encourage you to stay; big appetites might find room for the giant platter of Algerian pastries the waiter leaves at your table. Non-smokers beware: the proximity of your neighbours means you'll share more than just their conversation.
Other locations: Café Moderne, 19 rue Keller, 11th (01.47.00.53.62).

Al Filo delle Stagioni

8 rue de Beauce, 3rd (01.48.04.52.24). M° Temple or Filles du Calvaire. **Open** 11.30am-3pm, 7.30pm-midnight Mon-Sat. **Main courses** €17. **Prix fixe** *Lunch* €24, €28. *Dinner* €28, €34. **Credit** MC, V. **Map** p404 L5 **46**
A young team with Auvergnat-Italian origins is behind this fashionable new northern Marais restaurant. The dressed-up, stone-walled dining room buzzes even at lunch, and the cellar room, though less desirable than the airy main floor, is a good choice for a large group. The owner has been known to dash from table to table with a truffle (black, not the priceless white Alba variety), which he shaves over everything – not a touch you would normally expect from such an affordable menu, which for €28 includes three courses plus a glass of wine and coffee. Breaded and fried mozzarella is a generous plate of high-quality, crunchy-crusted fried cheese made colourful with rocket and cherry tomatoes. Pigeon roasted with pine nuts is a juicy choice, served perhaps inauthentically with a plate of pasta on the side – but who's complaining when it's topped with fresh truffle? A hybrid millefeuille de tiramisu layers still-crisp ladyfingers and coffee-infused cream, served with a matching ice-cream.

Bastille & eastern Paris

French

Astier

44 rue Jean-Pierre-Timbaud, 11th (01.43.57.16.35). M° Parmentier. **Open** noon-2pm, 8-10pm Mon-Fri. Closed 1wk Apr, Aug & 1wk Dec. **Prix fixe** *Lunch* €23.50. *Dinner* €28. **Credit** MC, V. **Map** p405 M4 **47**
On entering Astier your senses tell you this is a serious bastion of traditional French cooking: the unmistakeable smell of fine French cooking, the look of unbridled contentment on the crimson faces of businessmen, and the sound of frantic ordering across a crowded, unassumingly decorated room. The charming

patronne finds you a table and gives you the handwritten menu. This is a place where home-made terrines lead the way, so go for the chicken liver and seafood versions, both highly flavoured. Firm yet tender lamb sweetbreads, served generously with tiny *mousseron* mushrooms, replace the controversial calf variety with aplomb, and the accompanying *gratin dauphinois* is sinfully good. Book ahead for the bargain lunch menu.

Le Bistrot Paul Bert

18 rue Paul Bert, 11th (01.43.72.24.01).
M° Charonne. **Open** noon-2pm, 7.30-11pm Tue-Thur;
noon-2pm, 7.30-11.30pm Fri, Sat. Closed Aug. **Main
courses** €19. **Prix fixe** *Lunch* €16. *Dinner* €30.
Credit MC, V. **Map** p409 N7
This haunt of businessmen and artisans has a well-worn interior filled with smells of garlic and red wine. The boss here chooses superb bottles, his list interesting but not without affordable treats. The food is not of the sophisticated modern bistro type but good old-fashioned, no-nonsense cuisine. Egg mayo is raised from mundanity by a particularly good potato salad; mains include a substantial and perfectly cooked piece of salmon with hollandaise sauce, served with pasta; and a tender chuck steak with two spoonfuls of flavoursome beef reduction, accompanied by melting potato wedges. The cinnamon-rich apple crumble with crème fraîche sustains the high standards. The *prix fixe* menu features nobler products prepared with the same honest care.

Bofinger

5-7 rue de la Bastille, 4th (01.42.72.87.82/www.
bofingerparis.com). M° Bastille. **Open** noon-3pm,
6.30pm-1am Mon-Fri; noon-1am Sat, Sun. **Main
courses** €28. **Prix fixe** *Lunch* (Mon-Fri) €23.50.
Dinner €34.50. **Credit** AmEx, DC, MC, V.
Map p411 M7
Opposite the Bastille opera house, Bofinger is a post-show haunt, and draws big crowds at other times for its authentic art nouveau setting and brasserie

atmosphere. Downstairs is the prettiest place to eat; upstairs is air-conditioned. As at many Flo group restaurants, the food is always adequate but rarely aspires to great culinary heights. An à la carte choice might start with plump, garlicky escargots or a well-made langoustine terrine, followed by an intensely seasoned salmon tartare, a generous (if uneventful) cod steak, or calf's liver accompanied by cooked melon. Alternatively, you could go for the foolproof brasserie meal of oysters and fillet steak, followed by a rabidly pungent plate of munster cheese and accompanying bowl of cumin, washed down by the fine Gigondas at €35.50 a bottle.

C'Amelot

*50 rue Amelot, 11th (01.43.55.54.04). M° Chemin
Vert.* **Open** 7-10.30pm Mon, Sat; noon-2pm, 7-
10.30pm Tue-Fri. **Prix fixe** *Lunch* €17, €24. *Dinner*
€32. **Credit** AmEx, DC, MC, V. **Map** p411 M6
Didier Varnier is a young bistro chef who relishes the contrast of serving inventive and often refined food in low-key settings. With its panelling and bare wood tables, C'Amelot's long, narrow dining room in gloomy rue Amelot has a countrified, even dated, feel. There are two options for each course. You could start with a typically South-western lentil soup with foie gras – earthy, with morsels of oozy goodness – or unusual cured salmon with braised chicory, whose bitterness contrasts nicely with the sweet vinegar sauce. Lamb chops in *poivrade* sauce with porridgy polenta are remarkable for the quality of the rosy meat, and prunes in spiced wine provide a wintry end to a market-inspired meal.

Crêperie Bretonne Fleurie

67 rue de Charonne, 11th (01.43.55.62.29).
M° Ledru-Rollin or Charonne. **Open** noon-2.30pm,
7pm-11pm Mon-Fri; 7-11pm Sat. Closed Aug.
Main courses €5. **Credit** MC, V. **Map** p409 M7
Everything about this restaurant is authentic, including the crêpe chef's own pointy chin thatch, wiggly pipe and striped sailor shirt. The menu is

Kastoori. See p194.

straightforward: to fill your savoury, freshly cooked buckwheat *galette*, choose a ham/cheese/egg combination (all three is a *complète*, presented in a square topped with a gleaming egg yolk), *andouille* (tripe sausage) or the more unusual camembert with walnuts. Old-fashioned manners prevail: the sashaying waitresses serve ladies first as gents politely contemplate the Celtic flags, Breton Tintin book and puzzling tribal mask. Dessert crêpes feature pear 'n' chocolate and banana 'n' chocolate fillings. Dry cider would be the logical accompaniment, but a Breton Breizh cola in its nifty glass bottle is hard to resist.

L'Encrier

55 rue Traversière, 12th (01.44.68.08.16). Mº Ledru-Rollin or Gare de Lyon. **Open** noon-2.15pm, 7.30-11pm Mon-Fri; 7.30-11pm Sat. Closed Aug. **Main courses** €14. **Prix fixe** *Lunch* €13. *Dinner* €17, €21. **Credit** MC, V. **Map** p409 M8 52

Through the door and past the velvet curtain, you find yourself face-to-face with the kitchen – and a crowd of locals, many of whom seem to know the charming boss personally. Value is tremendous here, with a €13 lunch menu and a choice of €17 or €21 menus in the evening, as well as a few à la carte choices. Start with fried rabbit kidneys on a bed of salad dressed with raspberry vinegar, an original and wholly successful combination, and follow with goose magret with honey – a welcome change from the usual duck version and served with crunchy, thinly sliced sautéed potatoes. To end, share a chocolate cake, or try the popular profiteroles. The fruity Chinon is a classy red at a rather steep €24, but worth every centime.

Juan et Juanita

82 rue Jean-Pierre-Timbaud, 11th (01.43.57.60.15). Mº Couronnes. **Open** 8pm-2am Tue-Sat. **Main courses** €15. **Credit** AmEx, MC, V. **Map** p405 N4 53

J 'n' J attracts a fresh-faced clientele with its refined cuisine. With dripping candelabras on every table and one in the ladies, the look is polished and flirty

– as are the staff. Starters include mesclun salads with toasted hazelnuts, one of them including a crispy st-marcellin *brik*. They are followed by the special of the night, perhaps a buttery rabbit with thyme, or a leg of lamb with mint, a house speciality so tender it needs no urging off the bone. Desserts are too good to pass up; try a lime sorbet with vodka or the vanilla ice-cream with a red fruit coulis. The ambitious wine list is strong on Graves and Gaillacs.

Le Square Trousseau

1 rue Antoine-Vollon, 12th (01.43.43.06.00). Mº Ledru-Rollin. **Open** noon-2.30pm, 8-11.30pm Tue-Sat. **Main courses** €20. **Prix fixe** *Lunch* €20, €25. **Credit** MC, V. **Map** p409 N7 54

This restaurant, with its superb 1900s interior, is a favourite with a fashion and media crowd; the friendly waiters, handsome in their long white aprons, appear as if in a film. The food, though, is for real. Start with a silky timbale of smoked salmon and candied lemon, or a tomato, cucumber and avocado millefeuille with mozzarella, its refreshing red, green and white layers showered with chives – or poached eggs in a fine, nutmeg-scented cheese sauce with Japanese herbs. A main dish of plump farm chicken is served with a creamy risotto or set in Moroccan-style pastry; tender strips of duck arrive with a delicious cherry sauce. The wine prices are a surprise, given the good-value food, but the selection does unearth the best from Touraine, Burgundy, Auvergne and Vaucluse.

Le Temps au Temps

13 rue Paul-Bert, 11th (01.43.79.63.40). Mº Faidherbe Chaligny. **Open** noon-2pm, 8-10.30pm Tue-Sat. **Main courses** €16. **Prix fixe** *Lunch* €11, €13, €16. *Dinner* €27. **Credit** MC, V. **Map** p409 N7 55

This bistro's friendly new owners have retained the name, but replaced the bric-a-brac of inaccurate timepieces with just two or three clocks, opening up the room with a clear glass frontage and cheering up the interior with a paint job. Chef Sylvain Sendra is a bright talent. The €27 menu might begin with a home-made *fromage de tête*, well worth the three days it took in the making, or a cleverly balanced dish of warm *ratte* potatoes and sundried tomatoes topped with anchovies. The quality of the main courses doesn't flag, with, for instance, a delicate fillet of verbena-steamed John Dory on a bed of cauliflower 'couscous'. Ice-creams are home-made, and include an exquisite violet sorbet.

Le Train Bleu

Gare de Lyon, cour Louis-Armand, 12th (01.43.43.09.06/www.le-train-bleu.com). Mº Gare de Lyon. **Open** 11.30am-3pm, 7-11pm daily. **Main courses** €26. **Prix fixe** €43. **Credit** AmEx, DC, MC, V. **Map** p409 M8 56

This listed dining room – with vintage frescoes of the alluring destinations served by the Paris-Lyon-Marseille railway and big oak benches with shiny brass coat racks – exudes a pleasant air of expectation. Don't expect cutting-edge cooking, but rather

Eat, Drink, Shop

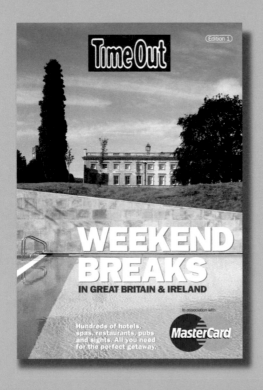

fine renderings of French classics using first-rate produce. Lobster served on walnut-oil-dressed salad leaves is a generous, beautifully prepared starter, as is the pistachio-studded *saucisson de Lyon* with a warm salad of small *ratte* potatoes. Mains of veal chop topped with a cap of cheese, and *sandre* (pike-perch) with a 'risotto' of *crozettes* are also pleasant, although given the size of the starters and the superb cheese tray, you could have a satisfying meal here even if you forgo a main course. A few reasonably priced wines would be a welcome addition.

International

Dong Huong
14 rue Louis-Bonnet, 11th (01.43.57.18.88).
Mº Belleville. **Open** noon-11pm Mon, Wed-Sun.
Closed 3wks Aug. **Main courses** €7. **Credit**
(€15 minimum) MC, V. **Map** p405 M4 **⑤**
The excellent food attracts a buzzy crowd, but this is also, significantly, one of the few Paris restaurants to banish smokers to a separate room (on the lower floor). Dishes arrive promptly and in generous portions. The delicious *bành cuôn*, steamed Vietnamese ravioli, stuffed with minced meat, bean sprouts, spring onions and deep-fried onion, are served piping hot. *Com ga lui*, chicken kebabs with tasty lemongrass, though not as delicate, come with tasty rice. *Bò bùn chà giò* (noodles with beef and small *nem* topped with onion strips, spring onion and crushed peanuts) makes a meal in itself. For dessert, the mandarin, lychee and mango sorbets are tasty and authentic – and don't miss out on the dark, sickly sweet iced lotus-flower tea, with lotus seeds, lychees and seaweed jelly.

Ile de Gorée
70 rue Jean-Pierre-Timbaud, 11th (01.43.38.97.69).
Mº Parmentier. **Open** 7pm-1am daily. **Main**
courses €14. **Credit** MC, V. **Map** p405 M4 **⑤**
Gorée Island is a 15-minute ferry ride off the Senegal coast. At for its namesake in the most happening bar quarter of Paris, mango and peach punch and live kora music set the mood. Simple but well prepared *boudin créole* (black pudding with cinnamon) and *aloco* (sautéd plantains) with sweet tomato relish can be followed with a hearty *dem farci* (stuffed mullet) in brown sauce or *thiou poisson* (whole fish) with tomatoes, bell peppers, carrots, potatoes and basmati rice, richly marinated with a sauce tingling with flavour. Muomuo, the friendly house cat, will happily lap up the rest of your rum-raisin ice-cream from the bowl, but disdains the exotic selection of coconut, mango and pistachio sorbets. The cooks wave goodbye – an enchanted isle indeed.

Kazaphani
122 av Parmentier, 11th (01.48.07.20.19).
Mº Parmentier or Goncourt. **Open** noon-3pm,
7.30pm-midnight Tue-Fri, Sun; 7.30pm-midnight Sat.
Closed last 2wks Aug. **Main courses** €30. **Prix**
fixe *Lunch* €18. *Dinner* €27, €32. **Credit** AmEx,
MC, V. **Map** p405 M5 **⑤**

The welcome at this family-run Cypriot restaurant is so relaxed that you might feel you've walked into someone's home. The room is pleasantly decorated with rhododendron boughs and paintings of Cyprus. Highlights of the €32 meze menu are octopus in olive oil, lemon and garlic; wonderfully lemony mushrooms; a tasty paste of broad beans; and a tara-masalata so pale and creamy it's a world away from the usual lurid concoction that dares to bear the same name. Next arrive plates of calamari, deep-fried whitebait and huge, aniseed-flavoured gambas. Meat dishes are of excellent quality, particularly the crisp meatballs and stuffed pork. You can match the food with any of the good red wines on offer – Hatzimichalis, say, or Nemea.

Le Souk
1 rue Keller, 11th (01.49.29.05.08). Mº Ledru-Rollin
or Bastille. **Open** 7.30-11.30pm Tue-Fri; noon-
2.30pm, 7.30-10.30pm Sat, Sun. **Main courses** €15.
Prix fixe (for 8 or more) €31, €35. **Credit** MC, V.
Map p409 N7 **⑥**
Potted olive trees mark the entrance to this lively den of Moroccan cuisine. Start with savoury *b'stilla*, a pasty stuffed with duck, raisins and nuts, flavoured with orange-blossom water and sprinkled with cinnamon and powdered sugar; or creamy aubergine dip scooped up with fluffy Moroccan bread, made on the premises. Don't fill up, though, as the first-rate tagines and couscous are enormous. The *tagine canette*, duckling stewed with honey, onions, apricots, figs and cinnamon then showered with toasted almonds, is terrific; *couscous bidaoui* arrives in handsome earthenware, a hefty shank of lamb on the side. Cold beer goes down well, but you might prefer a bottle of Algerian or Moroccan red wine. For dessert try the excellent millefeuille with fresh figs, while sweet mint tea is poured in a long stream by a djellaba-clad waiter.

Le Pamphlet. *See p195.*

French

A la Bière

104 av Simon-Bolivar, 19th (01.42.39.83.25).
M° Colonel Fabien. **Open** noon 3pm, 7pm-1.30am
daily. **Main courses** €8.60. **Prix fixe** €12.30.
Credit AmEx, MC, V. **Map** p405 M3 **⑥**
A la Bière looks like one of those nondescript corner
brasseries with noisy pop music and lots of smoke,
but what makes it stand out is an amazingly good-
value €12.30 *prix fixe* full of fine bistro favourites,
all served with a smile. White tablecloths and finely
balanced kirs set the tone; starters of thinly sliced
pig's cheek with a nice French dressing on the salad,
and a home-made rabbit terrine exceed expectations.
The mains live up to what's served before: charcoal-
grilled entrecôte with hand-cut chips, and juicy
Lyonnais sausages with potatoes drenched in olive
oil, garlic and parsley. The staff know their wine and
never hurry the diners; there's usually jolly banter
going on at the bar. This is one of the few bargains
left in Paris – let's hope it stays that way.

Chez Michel

*10 rue de Belzunce, 10th (01.44.53.06.20). M° Gare
du Nord.* **Open** 7pm-midnight Mon; noon-2pm, 7pm-
midnight Tue-Fri. Closed 3wks Aug. **Prix fixe** €30.
Credit MC, V. **Map** p404 K2 **⑥**
Thierry Breton is from Brittany, and so proud of his
origins he sports the Breton flag on his chef's
whites. His menu is stacked with hearty offerings
from said hearty region. Marinated salmon with purple potatoes served in a preserving jar, pickled herring style, is succulently tender; so, too, is the fresh
abalone. As for the rabbit, braised with rosemary
and Swiss chard, it might just be the best bunny in
town. Blackboard specials, which carry a €5-€25
supplement, follow the seasons: game lovers are
spoilt in the cooler months with wood pigeon, wild
boar and venison, and there are usually some juicy,
fat, fresh scallops on offer, too.

International

Bharath Café

*67 rue Louis-Blanc, 10th (01.58.20.06.20). M° La
Chapelle.* **Open** 9am-midnight daily. **Main courses**
€7. **Prix fixe** €7.50, €13.50. **Credit** AmEx, DC, MC,
V. **Map** p404 L2 **⑥**
For the most authentic South Indian/Sri Lankan
food in town, venture to La Chapelle. Don't be
deterred by the basic decor, brusque service or the
throngs of men loitering round about. These Tamil
immigrants are fussy about their food. Start with
tempting meat rolls, compact deep-fried pancakes
stuffed with mutton, potatoes and spices – though
don't take more than two or you'll have no room for
the more tantalising main dishes, such as lamb *kotta
roti* (shredded thick chapattis mixed with tender
meat, eggs, green chillies and onions), big enough

for two. Another house speciality is the *masala dosai*
(crêpes filled with yellow curry, potatoes and mustard seed), originally a filling breakfast dish but
equally suitable at dinner. Braver souls should try
the stronger dishes, including the spicy chicken
curry with rice and a small helping of lentil curry.

La Madonnina

*10 rue Marie-et-Louise, 10th (01.42.01.25.26).
M° Goncourt.* **Open** noon-2.30pm, 8-11pm Mon-Sat.
Closed 2wks Aug. **Main courses** €13. **Prix fixe**
Lunch €11. **Credit** MC, V. **Map** p404 L4 **⑥**
Host Gianni will pull up a chair to explain the entire
(if small) menu and recommend a wine (like a dry,
ruby-red Rupicolo). Otherwise, there are no red-
checked clichés here, no blinking lights, no Virgin
Mary shrines. Food worship, though – lots of that,
as seen in the luscious salads and roasted veg displayed on an antipasti altar. Every dish is made with
fresh ingredients: starters of tender marinated calamari amid potatoes and rocket, and a scrumptious
aubergine *parmiggiano*, also served with a generous
heap of rocket; mains such as the exquisite pesto-
truffle-mushroom ravioli. There's a special €9 children's menu on Saturdays. **Photo** *p210.*

French

Atelier Maître Albert

*1 rue Maître-Albert, 5th (01.56.81.30.01/www.
ateliermaitrealbert.com). M° St-Michel or Maubert
Mutualité.* **Open** noon-2.30pm, 6.30-11.30pm Mon-
Wed; noon-2.30pm, 6.30pm-1am Thur, Fri; 6.30pm-
1am Sat; 6.30-11.30pm Sun. **Main courses** €24.
Prix fixe *Lunch* €23, €28. **Credit** AmEx, DC, MC,
V. **Map** p408 J7 **⑥**
This Guy Savoy outpost has slick decor by Jean-
Michel Wilmotte, who designed Savoy's eponymous
restaurant. The grey-marble-floored dining room
with open kitchen and *rôtisseries* on view is attractive but noisy – book a table in the quieter bar area.
The short menu lets you have a Savoy classic or two
to start with, including oysters in sea-water gelée or
more inventive dishes like the ballotine of chicken,
foie gras and celery root in a chicken liver sauce.
Next up, perhaps, a roast faux-filet, or a chunk of
tuna served with tiny iron casseroles of dauphinois
potatoes, and cauliflower in béchamel sauce.

L'Avant-Goût

*26 rue Bobillot, 13th (01.53.80.24.00). M° Place
d'Italie.* **Open** noon-2pm, 7.30-11pm Tue-Fri. Closed
1wk Jan, 1wk May & 3wks Aug/Sept. **Prix fixe**
Lunch €14. *Dinner* €31. **Credit** MC, V.
Owner-chef Christophe Beaufront has resisted the
temptation to raise prices, lower quality and turn
tables faster. The blackboard menu doesn't change
much, but who cares when you eat so well at this
price? Starters – like the tuna tartare with roasted
vegetables, and a medley of spring vegetables in a
light bouillon with a poached egg – are all first rate.

Water with your meal?

The Seine is one of the French capital's key sights, so it's surprising so few eating venues capitalise on views of it. The richest pickings are to be had on and around the Ile St-Louis. The **Brasserie de l'Ile St-Louis** (*see p183*) has a fine terrace, as does **Bertillon** (31 rue St-Louis-en-l'Ile, 4th, 01.43.54.31.61) – a Paris institution and tourist magnet that's justifiably famous for its stellar if steeply priced ice-cream. A short walk across the river brings you to the **Kiosque Flottant** (port Montebello, 5th, 01.43.54.19.51), one of the city's four floating cafés with a river terrace. It serves snacks by day and a €20 Sunday brunch, and offers live jazz after dark. A short stroll away, you'll find **Metamorphosis** (port Montebello, 5th, 01.43.54.08.08). This kitsch barge is a

venue for magic shows and ably doubles up as a daytime café, serving one of the most copious brunches (€20) in central Paris.

Further out from the centre, and thus less overrun with tourists, there's **La Guinguette de Neuilly** (12 bd Georges-Seurat, 92200 Neuilly-sur-Seine, 01.46.24.25.04), which is set on an island in the Seine at the end of the No.3 métro line. It's a *guinguette* bistro with a fishing-themed decor and gingham tablecloths, as well as a wonderful terrace that slinks down to the river's edge. The food is, reassuringly, traditional French. **Quai Ouest** (quai Marcel-Dassault, 92210 St-Cloud, 01.46.02.35.54) is a Californian loft-style restaurant with a terrace for 250 people and great views over the Seine. The food is French and there's a good €18 lunch deal.

Eat, Drink, Shop

Beaufront's signature dish is a *pot-au-feu de cochon*, a big casserole brimming with pork cuts, fennel and sweet potato, served with gherkins, horseradish sauce and ginger chips. Across the street, the Avant-Goût *épicerie* sells hot dishes in cast-iron pots to take away, solving weeknight dinner-party dilemmas.

Le Bistrot Côté Mer
16 bd St-Germain, 5th (01.43.54.59.10/www. bistrocotemer.com). M° Maubert Mutualité. **Open** 12.15-2.15pm, 7.15-10.15pm Mon-Sat. Closed 2wks Aug. **Prix fixe** *Lunch* €19, €24. *Dinner* €29. **Credit** AmEx, MC, V. **Map** p408 K7 ⑥
Bistrot Côté Mer may be way inland, but its blue-and-yellow entrance is reminiscent of a beach cabin, its stone walls could be seaside St-Malo and even the plates are wave-shaped. A creamy mushroom *amuse-bouche* arrives with the menus, which is written on a ceramic platter. Skip standards like oysters

and tuna; instead opt for the succulent ravioli stuffed with scallops, taramasalata and a hint of ginger. The main courses include sea bass, chard and artichokes in a tangy broth steamed in an iron pot; and yellow pollock, whose crispy skin is accompanied by a green pea sauce, sautéed mustard greens and a winter vegetable mash. Desserts are pricey but tasty.

Chez Paul
22 rue Butte-aux-Cailles, 13th (01.45.89.22.11). M° Place d'Italie. **Open** noon-2.30pm, 7.30pm-12.30am daily. **Main courses** €14. **Credit** MC, V.
Chez Paul is heaven to local professional types, its wood and white drapery setting a chic alternative to other offbeat spots along the strip. Tradition takes pride of place – *pot-au-feu*, beef knuckle, bone marrow – and you can eat your way from one end of a beast to the other. Seafood makes an appearance on the blackboard menu in the shape of oysters, whelks,

Le Pamphlet. *See p195*.

La Gourmandise.

an excellent starter of pan-fried mullet fillets with olive tapenade, and a main of monkfish nuggets in a creamy garlic sauce served with gleaming green spinach. Liquorice ice-cream and carafes of chilled Brouilly also go down well. This joint is jumping, so if you want a bone to pick, book ahead.

Chez René

14 bd St-Germain, 5th (01.43.54.30.23). M° Maubert Mutualité. **Open** 12.15-2.15pm, 7.45-10.30pm Tue-Sat. Closed Aug & 1wk Dec. **Main courses** €20. **Prix fixe** *Lunch* €30. *Dinner* €41. **Credit** MC, V. **Map** p408 K7 ⑰

Every decade since René Cinquin opened this place in 1957, the staff have gathered for a photo, which is framed and added to the others hanging by the door. And as far as change is concerned, that's pretty much it. These days it's René's son Jean-Paul who chats with the diners, but the silver cutlery, starched linen and hard work in the kitchen are all still here. The *coq au vin* is the reason for coming, the secret of whose dark, succulent sauce is no stock, just a good 20 minutes stirring flour and butter over the feeblest of flames before adding the wine – just as René's granny taught him. Similar skills go into the *boeuf bourguignon*. Cheese, impressively, comes in two courses: cow's milk and goat's milk.

L'Ourcine

92 rue Broca, 13th (01.47.07.13.65). M° Les Gobelins. **Open** noon-2pm, 7-10.30pm Tue-Sat. Closed 2wks July/Aug. **Prix fixe** *Lunch* (Tue-Fri) €21. *Dinner* €29. **Credit** MC, V. **Map** p408 J10 ⑱

This cream-and-red restaurant near Gobelins is a wonderful destination for anyone who really loves Basque and Béarnais cooking, since the kitchen sends out homely, delicious and impeccably prepared regional classics. Start with pipérade, succulent chorizo or maybe an original spread of sliced beef tongue with piquillo peppers. Then try the sautéed baby squid with parsley, garlic and Espelette peppers or the piquillos stuffed with puréed cod and potato. Service is friendly, and an appealing atmosphere is generated by a growing band of regulars. The wine list is quite short but offers several pleasant South-western bottles (the Madiran is a better buy than the Irouleguey). Homely desserts include *gâteau basque* and ewe's milk cheese with black cherry preserves.

Le Pré Verre

8 rue Thénard, 5th (01.43.54.59.47). M° Maubert Mutualité. **Open** noon-2pm, 7.30-10.30pm Tue-Sat. Closed 1st 2wks Aug. **Prix fixe** *Lunch* €12.50. *Dinner* €25.50. **Credit** MC, V. **Map** p408 J7 ⑲

Philippe Delacourcelle knows how to handle spices like few other French chefs, having lived in Asia for long enough to master ingredients like cassia bark and tamarind. He also trained with the late Bernard Loiseau, and learned the art of French pastry at Fauchon. A classic on his menu is the salt cod with cassia bark and smoked potato purée: what the fish lacks in size it makes up for in crunchy texture and

rich, cinnamon-like flavour, and the super-smooth potato cooked in a smoker makes a startling accompaniment. Spices have a way of making desserts seem esoteric rather than decadent, but the roast figs with olives make a convincing case. The purple-grey walls are lined with jazz album covers, which echo the music. The main floor is non-smoking.

Le Reminet

3 rue des Grands-Degrés, 5th (01.44.07.04.24). M° Maubert Mutualité or St-Michel. **Open** noon-2.30pm, 7.30-11pm Mon, Thur-Sun. Closed 3wks Aug. **Main courses** €15. **Prix fixe** *Lunch* (Mon, Thur, Fri) €15. **Credit** MC, V. **Map** p408 J7 ⑳

Le Reminet has always been a favourite Left Bank bistro, serving a €50 tasting menu for those looking to splash out, and a €15 lunch menu on three days in the week. Hugues Gournay's cooking remains accurate and delicious. Start off with some crisp fried filo parcels of black pudding, or even ravioli – whole gambas in a light, pliable dough, bathing in coconut milk. Main courses include a perfectly timed fillet of beef with a shallot purée, and some tender scallops on firm, well-sauced tagliatelle. A bottle of red Gigondas bears up well at €29.50, but the wine of the month can be alarmingly pricey.

International

Rouammit & Huong Lan

103 av d'Ivry, 13th (01.53.60.00.34). M° Corvisart. **Open** noon-3pm, 7-11pm Tue-Fri; noon-11pm Sat, Sun. **Main courses** €20. **Credit** MC, V.

Local fans of South-east Asian food learn to seek out Laotian holes in the wall rather than splurge on flashier Thai restaurants. A perfect example is this plainly decorated (bare tables, strips of carved wood here and there) Chinatown joint, easy to spot thanks to the queue outside the door. Show up early or be prepared to wait: the food here is cheap and delicious and the service super-efficient and friendly. To try the full span of flavours – hot, sour, aromatic, sweet – it's best to go in a group and order compendiously. Among the highlights are *lap neua*, a tongue tickling, chilli-spiked salad made with slivers of beef and tripe; lacquered duck in curry sauce; *khao nom kroc*, Laotian ravioli filled with shrimp; and sweet, juicy prawns stir-fried with Thai basil. Even the sticky rice is exceptional. If you're in the mood for an adventurous dessert, try the assortment of gelatins, all worm-like shapes and fluorescent colours.

St-Germain-des-Prés & Odéon

French

Allard

41 rue St-André-des-Arts, 6th (01.43.26.48.23). M° Odéon. **Open** noon-2.30pm, 7-11.30pm Mon-Sat. Closed 3wks Aug. **Main courses** €20. **Prix fixe** *Lunch* €24, €32. *Dinner* €32. **Credit** AmEx, DC, MC, V. **Map** p410 H7 ㉑

Eat, Drink, Shop

Menu lexicon

For a selection of handy phrases to use when ordering or paying the bill, see p387.

Meals

petit déjeuner breakfast. **déjeuner** lunch. **dîner** dinner. **souper** late dinner, supper.

Preparation

en croûte in a pastry case. **désossé** deboned. **farci** stuffed. **au four** baked. **flambé** flamed in alcohol. **forestière** with mushrooms. **fricassé** fried and simmered in stock, usually with creamy sauce. **fumé** smoked. **garni** garnished. **glacé** frozen or iced. **gratiné** topped with breadcrumbs or cheese and grilled. **à la grècque** vegetables served cold in the cooking liquid with oil and lemon juice. **grillé** grilled. **haché** minced. **julienne** (vegetables) cut into matchsticks. **lamelle** very thin slice. **mariné** marinated. **pané** breaded. **en papillote** cooked in a packet. **parmentier** with potato. **pressé** squeezed. **râpé** grated. **salé** salted.

Cooking type (la cuisson)

cru raw. **bleu** practically raw. **saignant** rare. **rosé** (of lamb, duck, liver, kidneys) pink. **à point** medium rare. **bien cuit** well done.

Basics (essentiels)

ballotine stuffed, rolled-up piece of meat or fish. **crème fraîche** thick, slightly soured cream. **épices** spices. **feuilleté** 'leaves' of (puff) pastry. **fromage** cheese. **fruits de mer** shellfish. **galette** round flat cake of flaky pastry, potato pancake or buckwheat savoury crêpe. **gelée** aspic. **gibier** game. **gras** fat. **légume** vegetable. **maison** of the house. **marmite** small cooking pot. **miel** honey. **noisette** hazelnut; small round portion of meat. **noix** walnut. **noix de coco** coconut. **nouilles** noodles. **oeuf** egg; – **en cocotte** baked egg; – **en meurette** egg poached in red wine; – **à la neige** see île flottante. **parfait** sweet or savoury mousse-like mixture. **paupiette** slice of meat or fish, stuffed and rolled. **timbale** dome-shaped mould, or food cooked in one. **tisane** herbal tea. **tourte** covered pie or tart, usually savoury.

Meat (viande)

agneau lamb. **aloyau** beef loin. **andouillette** sausage made from pig's offal. **bavette** beef flank steak. **biche** venison. **bifteck** steak. **boudin noir/blanc** black (blood)/white pudding. **boeuf** beef; – **bourguignon** beef

It's reassuring to come across this fine (if pricey) traditional bistro. With its vanilla-coloured walls and a coat rack in the narrow hall connecting the two small dining rooms, Allard has a pre-war feel – a first impression confirmed by the kitchen itself, which sends out just the sort of glorious Gallic grub you come to Paris for. It's perfect in winter. Start with sliced Lyonnais sausage studded with pistachios and served with potato salad in delicious vinaigrette, or maybe a sauté of wild mushrooms; then choose between roast shoulder of lamb, roast Bresse chicken with sautéed ceps, or roast duck with olives. Finish up with the *tarte fine de pommes* and go for one of the good Bordeaux.

Le Comptoir

Hôtel Relais Saint-Germain, 9 carrefour de l'Odéon, 6th (01.44.27.07.97). M° Odéon. **Open** noon-midnight daily. Closed 3wks Aug. **Main courses** €12. **Prix fixe** *Dinner* (Mon-Fri) €40. **Credit** AmEx, DC, MC, V. **Map** p408 H7 **72**

Yves Camdeborde was one of the first chefs to introduce the accessibly priced, market-inspired menu (at La Régalade in the early 1990s). With proceeds from the sale of La Régalade, he bought the bijou 17th-century hotel Le Relais Saint-Germain, whose art deco dining room, modestly dubbed Le Comptoir, serves brasserie fare from noon to 6pm and on weekend

nights – salads and a hot *plat du jour*, such as duck confit with smooth mashed potatoes – and a five-course, no-choice meal for €40 on weekday evenings. The single dinner sitting lets the chef take real pleasure in his work. On the daily menu, you might find dishes like an iced cream of chicken soup spiked with *vin jaune du Jura* and dotted with chanterelle mushrooms, or rolled saddle of lamb with vegetable-stuffed 'Basque ravioli' (Camdeborde is from Southwest France). In warm weather, the handful of pavement tables makes for fine people-watching.

Josephine 'Chez Dumonet'

117 rue du Cherche-Midi, 6th (01.45.48.52.40). M° Duroc. **Open** 12.30-2.30pm, 7.30-10.30pm Mon-Fri. **Main courses** €22. **Credit** AmEx, MC, V. **Map** p407 F8 **73**

At this bastion of bistro cooking luxury ingredients bring a tad of glamour and a well-heeled loyal clientele. The dining room is comfortingly old-fashioned and formal staff give the impression of serious eating. Dishes are available as half portions, letting you try some classy numbers without breaking the bank. In truffle season, the salad of lamb's lettuce, warm potatoes and truffle shavings is €31 in its half-portion version. Delicious sautéed potatoes, rich in goose fat and garlic, accompany both the tournedos and a quality *andouillette*. Puddings are sumptuous, too.

cooked Burgundy style, with red wine, onions and mushrooms; – **gros sel** boiled beef with vegetables. **carbonnade** beef stew with onions and stout or beer. **carré d'agneau** rack of lamb. **cassoulet** stew of white haricot beans, sausage and preserved duck. **cervelle** brains. **châteaubriand** thick fillet steak. **chevreuil** young roe deer. **civet** game stew. **cochon de lait** suckling pig. **contre-filet** sirloin steak. **côte** chop; – **de boeuf** beef rib. **croque-madame** sandwich of toasted cheese and ham topped with an egg. **croque-monsieur** sandwich of toasted cheese and ham. **cuisses de grenouille** frogs' legs. **daube** meat braised in red wine. **entrecôte** beef rib steak. **escargot** snail. **estouffade** meat that's been marinated, fried and braised. **faux-filet** sirloin steak. **filet mignon** tenderloin. **foie** liver; – **de veau** calf's liver. **gigot d'agneau** leg of lamb. **hachis parmentier** shepherd's pie. **jambon** ham; – **cru** cured raw ham. **jarret** ham shin or knuckle. **langue** tongue. **lapin** rabbit. **lard** bacon. **lardon** small cube of bacon. **lièvre** hare. **marcassin** wild boar. **merguez** spicy lamb/beef sausage. **mignon** small meat fillet. **moelle** bone marrow; **os à la** – marrow bone. **navarin** lamb and vegetable stew. **onglet** cut

of beef, similar to bavette. **pavé** thick steak. **petit salé** salt pork. **pied** foot (trotter). **pot-au-feu** boiled beef with vegetables. **queue de boeuf** oxtail. **ragoût** meat stew. **rillettes** potted pork or tuna. **ris de veau** veal sweetbreads. **rognons** kidneys. **rôti** roast. **sanglier** wild boar. **saucisse** sausage. **saucisson sec** small dried sausage. **selle** (*d'agneau*) saddle (of lamb). **tagine** slow-cooked North African stew. **tartare** raw minced steak (also tuna or salmon). **tournedos** small slices of beef fillet, sautéed or grilled. **travers de porc** pork spare ribs. **tripes** tripe. **tripoux** dish of sheep's offal and sheep's feet. **veau** veal.

Poultry (volaille)

aiguillettes (*de canard*) thin slices (of duck breast). **blanc** breast. **caille** quail. **canard** duck; **confit de** – preserved duck. **coquelet** baby rooster. **dinde** turkey. **faisan** pheasant. **foie gras** fattened goose or duck liver. **gésiers** gizzards. **magret** duck breast. **oie** goose. **perdrix** partridge. **pintade/pintadeau** guinea fowl. **poulet** chicken. **suprême** (*de poulet*) fillets (of chicken) in a cream sauce.

▶

Lapérouse

51 quai des Grands-Augustins, 6th (01.43.26.68.04). M° St-Michel. **Open** noon-2.30pm, 7.30-10.30pm Mon-Fri; 7.30-10.30pm Sat. Closed Aug. **Main courses** €28. **Prix fixe** *Lunch* €30. *Dinner* €90. **Credit** AmEx, DC, MC, V. **Map** p410 J6 **74**

One of the most romantic spots in Paris, Lapérouse was formerly a clandestine rendezvous for French politicians and their mistresses; the tiny private dining rooms upstairs used to lock from the inside. Chef Alain Hacquard does a modern take on classic French cooking: his beef fillet is smoked for a more complex flavour; a tender saddle of rabbit is cooked in a clay crust, flavoured with lavender and rosemary and served with ravioli of onions. The only snag is the cost, especially wine – a half-bottle of Pouilly Fuissé is nearly €35. The lunch menu is limited, but frankly, the seductive Seine-side dining room has always been best savoured at night.

Le Timbre

3 rue Ste-Beuve, 6th (01.45.49.10.40). M° Vavin. **Open** noon-2pm, 7.30-11pm Mon-Sat. Closed 3wks Aug. **Main courses** €17. **Prix fixe** *Lunch* €22. **Credit** MC, V. **Map** p407 G8 **75**

Chris Wright's restaurant, open kitchen included, might be the size of the average student garret, but this native of Manchester aims high. His menu of

three to four starters, main courses and desserts changes every week, and he uses the same suppliers as the city's top chefs. Typical of his cooking is a plate of fresh green asparagus elegantly cut in half lengthwise and served with dabs of anise-spiked sauce and balsamic vinegar, and a little crumbled parmesan. Main courses are also pure in presentation and flavour – a thick slab of pork, pan-fried but not the least bit dry, comes with petals of red onion that retain a light crunch, while juicy guinea fowl is served on a bed of tomato and pineapple 'chutney'. Should you opt for cheese, you'll have a choice between 'le vrai' (British cheddar) and 'le faux' (a goat's cheese from the Ardèche).

International

Alcazar

62 rue Mazarine, 6th (01.53.10.19.99/www.alcazar. fr). M° Odéon. **Open** noon-3pm, 7pm-12.30am daily. **Main courses** €22. **Prix fixe** *Lunch* €24. *Dinner* €39. **Credit** AmEx, DC, MC, V. **Map** p408 H7 **76**

The success of Conran's Paris gastrodome might have more to do with its see-and-be-seen cachet than with the food. The space is certainly impressive, but the open kitchen is more likely to have you knock on the window and complain about your chips than

Fish & seafood
(poisson & fruits de mer)
anguille eel. **bar** sea bass. **belon** smooth, flat oyster. **bisque** shellfish soup. **bouillabaisse** Mediterranean fish soup. **bourride** bouillabaisse-like soup, without shellfish. **brochet** pike. **bulot** whelk. **cabillaud** fresh cod. **carrelet** plaice. **colin** hake. **coquille** shell. **coquilles St-Jacques** scallops. **crevettes** prawns (UK), shrimp (US). **crudités** assorted raw vegetables. **crustacé** shellfish. **daurade** sea bream. **eglefin** haddock. **escabèche** sautéd and marinated fish, served cold. **espadon** swordfish. **fines de claire** crinkle-shelled oysters. **flétan** halibut. **goujon** breaded, fried strip of fish; also a small catfish. **hareng** herring. **homard** lobster. **huître** oyster. **langoustine** Dublin Bay prawns, scampi. **limande** lemon sole. **lotte** monkfish. **maquereau** mackerel. **merlan** whiting. **merlu** hake. **meunière** fish floured and sautéd in butter. **moules** mussels; – **à la marinière** cooked with white wine and shallots. **morue** dried, salted cod; **brandade de** – cod puréed with potato. **oursin** sea urchin. **palourde** type of clam. **poulpe** octopus. **quenelle** light, poached fish (or poultry) dumpling. **raie** skate. **rascasse** scorpion fish. **rouget** red mullet. **St- Pierre** John Dory. **sandre** pikeperch. **saumon** salmon. **seiche** squid. **supion** small squid. **truite** trout.

Vegetables (légumes)
aligot mashed potatoes with melted cheese and garlic. **asperge** asparagus. **céleri** celery. **céleri rave** celeriac. **cèpe** cep mushroom. **champignon** mushroom; – **de Paris** button mushroom. **chanterelle** small, trumpet-like mushroom. **choucroute** sauerkraut; – **garnie** served with cured ham and sausages. **ciboulette** chive. **citronelle** lemongrass. **coco** large white bean. **cresson** watercress. **duxelles** chopped, sautéd mushrooms. **échalote** shallot. **endive** chicory (UK), Belgian endive (US). **épinards** spinach. **frisée** curly endive. **frites** chips (UK); fries (US). **gingembre** ginger. **girolle** small, trumpet-like mushroom. **gratin dauphinois** sliced potatoes baked with milk, cheese and garlic. **haricot** bean; – **vert** green bean. **mâche** lamb's lettuce. **morille** morel mushroom. **navet** turnip. **oignon** onion. **oseille** sorrel. **persil** parsley. **pignon** pine kernel. **pipérade basque**

express admiration for the deft preparation. Seafood is a safe bet, and the lunchtime *menu minceur* is a nice alternative to the salad and Marlboros diet favoured by calorie-counting Parisians. As disappointing as dinner can be, staff can rustle up a good brunch: perfect scrambled eggs, fluffy muffins and a diet-starts-on-Monday chocolate cake.

Il Gattopardo
29 rue Dauphine, 6th (01.46.33.75.92). M° Odéon. **Open** noon-2.30pm, 7.30-11.30pm Mon-Sat; 8-11.30pm Sun. **Main courses** €14. **Prix fixe** *Lunch* €14. **Credit** AmEx, MC, V. **Map** p410 H7 ⓱
This cosy restaurant is up a steep flight of stairs of an old Left Bank house. The cheerful, slightly corny service sets a laid-back mood for some good eating – and Angelo Procopio knows what locals want from Italian food. One of the best pasta cooks in town, he does a short but tempting menu, tantalising with tagliolini under white truffle shavings (costly but worth it), fettuccine with a superb, home-made tomato sauce, ravioli and tortellini. Another of his signature dishes, *tagliata*, is a delicious, thinly sliced steak in a herby, garlicky green sauce. A changing line-up of fish is also available. Desserts aren't very interesting, but the wine list has some good buys, especially in the Sardinian and Sicilian categories. A great little hole in the wall for dinner with friends.

Montparnasse & beyond

Bistros & brasseries

Apollo
3 pl Denfert-Rochereau, 14th (01.45.38.76.77/ 01.43.22.02.15). M° Denfert Rochereau/RER Denfert Rochereau. **Open** noon-3pm, 8pm-midnight daily. **Main courses** €20. **Prix fixe** *Lunch* €18. **Credit** AmEx, DC, MC, V. **Map** p407 H10 ⓲
From the same team that conceived Quai Ouest, this high-design restaurant in the former RER offices of Denfert Rochereau brings a breath of novelty into a staid part of Paris. The decor fits nicely with the original design, but the menu is firmly in the 21st century. Modern takes on comfort food here include herring caviar and potatoes, *blanquette de coquilles St-Jacques*, and braised beef with carrots. The food is generally good and generously served, as are desserts such as pineapple and bananas sautéd in vanilla-flavoured rum.

La Coupole
102 bd du Montparnasse, 14th (01.43.20.14.20). M° Vavin. **Open** 8.30am-1am Mon-Thur, Sun. 8.30am-1.30am Fri, Sat. **Main courses** €40. **Prix fixe** €34.50. **Credit** AmEx, DC, MC, V. **Map** p407 G9 ⓲

dish of green peppers, onions, bayonne ham and tomatoes, often served with scrambled egg. **poivre** pepper. **poivron** red or green (bell) pepper. **pomme de terre** potato. **pommes lyonnaises** potatoes fried with onions. **potiron** pumpkin. **riz** rice. **tapenade provençal** olive and caper paste. **truffes** truffles.

Fruit (fruits)

ananas pineapple. **cassis** blackcurrants; blackcurrant liqueur. **citron** lemon; **– vert** lime. **groseille** redcurrant; **– à maquereau** gooseberry. **mirabelle** tiny yellow plum. **myrtille** bilberry, blueberry. **pamplemousse** grapefruit. **pomme** apple. **prune** plum. **pruneau** prune. **quetsche** damson.

Desserts & cheese (desserts & fromage)

bavarois moulded cream dessert. **beignet** fritter or doughnut. **chèvre** goat; goat's cheese. **clafoutis** batter filled with fruit, usually cherries. **crème brûlée** creamy custard dessert with caramel glaze. **crème chantilly** sweetened whipped cream. **fraise** strawberry. **framboise** raspberry. **fromage blanc** smooth cream cheese. **glace** ice-cream. **île flottante** whipped egg white floating in vanilla custard. **marquise** mousse-like cake. **réglisse** liquorice. **tarte aux pommes** apple tart. **tarte Tatin** warm, caramelised apple tart cooked upside-down. **vacherin** cake of layered meringue, cream, fruit and ice-cream; a soft, cow's milk cheese.

Herbs, spices, soups & sauces (herbes, épices, soupes & sauces)

aïoli garlic mayonnaise. **anchoïade** spicy anchovy and olive paste. **béarnaise** sauce of butter and egg yolk. **blanquette** 'white' stew made with eggs and cream. **cannelle** cinnamon. **chaud-froid** sauce used to glaze cold dishes. **mousseline hollandaise** sauce with whipped cream. **potage** soup. **velouté** stock-based white sauce; creamy soup. **vichyssoise** cold leek and potato soup.

Drinks

bière beer. **eau** water; **– de robinet** tap water; **– gazeuse/pétillante** sparkling mineral water; **– plate** still mineral water. **eau de vie** fruit spirit or liqueur. **vin** wine; **– blanc** white wine; **– rouge** red wine.

Though Montparnasse today is a far cry from its avant-garde heyday when this restaurant opened in 1927 – as a 'bar américain' with cocktails and basement dancing where you could savour the indecency of the tango – La Coupole still glows with some of the old glamour. The people-watching is superb, inside and out, while the long ranks of linen-covered tables, highly professional waiters, 32 art deco columns painted by different artists, mosaic floor and the sheer *scale* still make coming here an event. What's more, it continues to be a favourite with Parisians of all ages, as well as out-of-towners and tourists. The set menu offers unremarkable steaks, foie gras, fish and autumn game stews, but the real treat is the shellfish, displayed along a massive counter. You can take your pick from among the *claires*, *spéciales* and *belons*, or go for a platter brimming with crabs, oysters, prawns and periwinkles.

Wadja

10 rue de la Grande-Chaumière, 6th (01.46.33.02.02). M° Vavin. **Open** 12.30-2.30pm, 7.30-11pm Mon-Sat. **Main courses** €23. **Prix fixe** *Lunch* €11, €14. *Dinner* (2 courses) €14. **Credit** MC, V. **Map** p407 G9 ⑳

Striking the right balance between simplicity and sophistication, this creamy yellow bistro has become a favourite destination for families, foreign visitors and artists from the adjacent studios. A la carte, you might find foie gras sautéd with prunes, monkfish with bacon, seasonal game or a classic *agneau de sept heures*, but you can opt for the daily changing *menu du jour*. With a choice of two main courses (one meat, one fish) and either a starter or dessert for only €14, this is one of the best bargains in town. Wadja is also a place for some interesting wine discoveries – say, a little-known white Burgundy, or an unfiltered organic red Bergerac.

The 7th & the 15th

French

L'Ami Jean

27 rue Malar, 7th (01.47.05.86.89). M° Invalides. **Open** noon-2pm, 7pm-midnight Tue-Sat. Closed Aug. **Main courses** €18. **Prix fixe** €28. **Credit** MC, V. **Map** p407 D6 ㉛

This long-running Basque address has become a hit since the arrival of chef Stéphane Jégo. Excellent bread from Poujauran is a perfect nibble when slathered with a tangy, herby *fromage blanc* – as are starters of sautéd baby squid on a bed of ratatouille, and little rolls of aubergine stuffed with perfectly seasoned braised lamb. Tender veal shank comes

Eat, Drink, Shop

Cafés & Bars

Traditional cafés soldier on and lounge bars shake up the scene – at a price.

Luxurious libations at the Louvre – **Cafe Marly**. *See p215.*

The traditional Paris café is a dying breed. A few years ago there was one on almost every street corner, 10,000 in all; today only 1,500 are still in business, providing regulars with strong coffee, cheap plonk and lively conversation from early morning to long past dusk.

Many bars in prominent locations have had a modern makeover. Names once delicately curled over the door in neon are now displayed in lower-case lettering, above the sign that the venue is now a 'lounge bar'. The furniture is softer, the decor funkier and the vibe friendlier to women. The food is far more varied than a casual *croque-monsieur* and covers all the bases from breakfast to late-night munchies. You'll find a couple of decent Belgian beers (by the bottle at least), the wines listed by origin and an electronic or Latin music CD on random play. For this, Parisians now pay a pretty penny.

Pink '**❶**' numbers given in this chapter mark the location of each café as shown on the street maps. *See pp402-411.*

In some cases, modernisation has been a boon. Commendable examples include **Bar Ourcq, L'Alimentation Général** and **L'Ile Enchantée**. More established venues of cosmopolitan character are clustered in the city's nightlife hub in the 11th arrondissement between Parmentier and Ménilmontant métro stops, an area named after its main bar-lined street: Oberkampf. Parallel to rue Oberkampf runs rue Jean-Pierre-Timbaud, which delivers a more off-beat and varied selection of bars (*see p220* **Eleventh heaven**). Other destinations include the Canal St-Martin in the 10th, the Marais (and its north-western overspill between Etienne Marcel and Arts et Métiers métro stations), and the area around Abbesses in Montmartre. The Left Bank and Montparnasse boast a proud if overplayed literary heritage, while the west still has its swank and glitz.

Despite the recent changes, the process of getting a drink is similar throughout. A draught beer, or *pression*, is served in 25cl measures as a *demi*, and costs €2-€3. It's cheaper to drink at the counter than be served at table, cheaper inside than on the terrace, and cheaper before

10pm, when a *tarif de nuit* might be imposed. Wine in three colours is ubiquitous, and coffee comes as a strong espresso unless otherwise requested. Modern venues also offer a standard selection of cocktails. The sturdy brasserie and noble bistro provide food with formality akin to a restaurant, so if you're just there for a drink, you'll pay more for the social nicety of aproned-and-waistcoated service. You can usually run a tab, and tipping is optional, generally a few small coins left in the silver dish.

The Louvre, Palais-Royal & Les Halles

Le Café des Initiés

3 pl des Deux-Ecus, 1st (01.42.33.78.29). M° Louvre Rivoli or Les Halles. **Open** 7.30am-1am Mon-Sat. **Credit** AmEx, MC, V. **Map** p404 H5 **❶**

Once a crumbling corner café, now a designer hangout, the Café des Initiés is a top spot for a trendy tipple. The main room is lined with ergonomic red

Overnight sensations

Perhaps it's the possibility of slipping upstairs to a suite after a few too many that makes hotel bars such sexy places, or maybe it's the likelihood of spying an A-lister in the loos. Whatever the reason, Paris hotel bars make for some of the best drinking dens in the city – and for that matter, in the world.

The daddy of them all, the **Hemingway Bar at the Ritz** (15 pl Vendôme, 1st, 01.43.16.33.65), is a wonderfully civilised place in which to get smashed. Bartenders Colin and Ludo dispense fabulous cocktails (and compliments and flowers for the ladies) in a gloriously suave manner. A little more lively, the refurbed **Bar Cambon** opposite (entrance at 38 rue Cambon, 1st, 01.43.16.30.90) is a good spot for posh partying, but the **Bar Vendôme** (01.43.16.33.63) at the front of the hotel is still a little grim – though its terrace is sublime in summer.

Stunning sundowners can also be found on the roof terrace of the **Hôtel Raphaël** (17 av Kléber, 16th, 01.53.64.32.00). The interior bar, while not the prettiest in Paris, is the place at which to live out any Jane Birkin fantasies: Serge Gainsbourg apparently wrote many of his songs while propping up the bar here.

Equally sexy, champagne bar **Le Dokhan's** (Hôtel Trocadéro Dokhan's, 117 rue Lauriston, 16th, 01.53.65.66.99) is the perfect choice for amorous encounters. Think high ceilings, ornate gilt, decorative panelling and service so discreet it's practically invisible. Superb cocktails served, too.

Those looking for something just a little less subtle should head to the **V** (Four Seasons George V, 31 av George-V, 8th, 01.49.52.70.06) for a glitzy beverage or three. It's sure swank at the Cinq. Higher on the see-and-be-seen scale is **Le Bar du Plaza** (Hôtel Plaza Athénée, 25 av Montaigne, 8th, 01.53.67.66.00), a cocktail bunny's most outré fantasy, with flattering lighting, high chairs offering maximum leg-crossing opportunities and ridiculous drinks. Avoid the savoury concoctions and speciality vodka jellies and instead go for an old-fashioned but expertly mixed standard or join the PR crowd in a Fashion Ice: alcoholic ice lollies that offer maximum flirting and slurping potential.

Traditionalist trendies still make a beeline for the **Costes** (239 rue St-Honoré, 1st, 01.42.44.49.80), with its plentiful supply of champers and air kisses, but a hotter hotel bar can be found at the **Murano Urban Resort** (13 bd du Temple, 3rd, 01.42.71.20.00). With an inventive interior, glamorous rather than glacial staff and great drinks (go for the Red Fruits and Love combo: vodka and summer fruits served in test tubes), this is the place at which to get rip-roaringly drunk, take a room and live out your rock-star fantasies.

Of the latest boutique hotels, **Le Sezz** (*see p55* **Reet boutique**) features the only dedicated Veuve Clicquot champers bar in Paris: **la Grande Dame**.

banquettes, a long zinc bar provides character and sleek black articulated lamps peer down from the ceiling. Dotted across the windowsills are tall, slender vases filled with fresh, scented lilies. The friendly staff and central location have helped put this place firmly on the aperitif map.

Café Marly

93 rue de Rivoli, cour Napoléon du Louvre, 1st (01.49.26.06.60). M° Palais Royal Musée du Louvre. **Open** 8am-2am daily. **Credit** AmEx, DC, MC, V. **Map** p403 H5 ❷

A class act this, as you might expect of a Costes café whose lofty arcaded terrace overlooks the Louvre's glass pyramid. Accessed through the passage Richelieu (the entrance for advance Louvre ticket holders), Marly offers an elegant, sophisticated and pricey break from the world's most famous collection of art. It's €6 a Heineken, so you're as well splashing out €12 on a Chocolate Martini or Shark of vodka, lemonade and grenadine. Most of the well-chosen wines are under €10 a glass and everything is impeccably served by razor-sharp smart staff. Brasserie fare and sandwiches on offer, too. **Photo** *p212.*

Etienne Marcel

34 rue Etienne-Marcel, 2nd (01.45.08.01.03). M° Les Halles. **Open** 9am-2am Mon-Thur, Sun; 9am-3am Fri, Sat. **Credit** AmEx, MC, V. **Map** p404 J5 ❸

Typical of the new urban drinking establishments springing up on the main drags of Paris, the Etienne Marcel offers pricey fare from breakfast to bedtime. Simple formula, really. Run the name in lower-case lettering outside, throw in some wacky retro sci-fi furniture and arty transparent light fittings, hire a team of glam waitresses and print up a bunch of stylish menus with silly prices in them. Smoothies €8! Breakfasts (coffee, fruit juice, pastries) €11! Brunches €15 and €22! To be fair, Parisians are paying these kinds of prices in similar establishments elsewhere – and the vodka smoothies and Polish Martinis with Krupnik or Zubrowka are top notch.

Le Fumoir

6 rue de l'Amiral-de-Coligny, 1st (01.42.92.00.24/ www.lefumoir.fr). M° Louvre Rivoli. **Open** 11am-2am daily. Closed 2wks Aug. **Credit** AmEx, MC, V. **Map** p404 H6 ❹

Run by the same people as the China Club (*see p224*), this elegant bar facing the Louvre has become a local institution: neo-colonial fans whirr lazily, oil paintings adorn the walls and even the bar staff seem to have sprung from the interior decorator's sketches. A sleek crowd sips Martinis or reads papers at the long mahogany bar (originally from a Chicago speakeasy), giving way to young professionals in the restaurant and pretty things in the library. It can feel try-hard and well behaved, but expertly mixed cocktails should take the edge off any evening.

Kong

1 rue du Pont-Neuf, 1st (01.40.39.09.00). M° Pont Neuf. **Open** noon-2am Sun-Thur; noon-3am Fri, Sat. **Credit** AmEx, MC, V. **Map** p408 J6 ❺

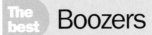

The best Boozers

L'Alimentation Générale
Kitsch, funky DJ bar within the Oberkampf orbit. *See p226.*

L'Antenne Bastille
Quayside retro chic within earshot of the Bastille opera. *See p223.*

L'Atmosphère
Easily the best and least pretentious of the Canal St-Martin venues. *See p226.*

Bar Ourcq
Canalside gem and boho haunt. *See p226.*

Le Cinquante
Get your fill of retro chic and reasonably priced 50cl pitchers of wine till last orders at 1.20am. *See p227.*

L'Ile Enchantée
Stylish, popular DJ haunt flooded by acres of natural light. *See p227.*

Le Mange Disque
The name to drop. *See p228.*

Au P'tit Garage
Grunge with style. *See p228.*

Philippe Starck's latest addition to the Paris scene, set on the top two floors of the Kenzo building overlooking the Pont Neuf, is one of the city's hottest places for cocktails. The bright mishmash interior is manga-inspired with lots of neon, Hello Kitty knick-knacks, grey leather sofas and (best avoided after a few *coupes*) rocking chairs in the main dining area. The best bet is to perch at the long bar, flirt with the too-beautiful-to-bartend staff and order an excellent Vodkatini or three. After dark you can make a music suggestion with each order; at weekends they carve out a tiny dancing space for the trendy crowd to strut their stuff. Wear lots of labels and remember to look cool even when half-cut.

Opéra & Grands Boulevards

Café de la Paix

12 bd des Capucines, 9th (01.40.07.36.36). M° Opéra. **Open** 7am-midnight daily. **Credit** AmEx, DC, MC, V. **Map** p403 G4 ❻

The sumptuous street-level terrace café-restaurant of the Grand InterContinental (*see p46*) exudes history. Your table, beneath the ornate, stucco ceiling or overlooking Garnier's opera house, may be the one patronised by Oscar Wilde, Josephine Baker, Emile Zola – or Bartholdi and the Franco-American

Union as they sketched out the *Statue of Liberty*. You'll be treated as one of their equals by the immaculate staff, and presented with little bowls of crisps, nuts and olives to accompany your €9 kir or €7 glass of draught Grimbergen. They mix a classy cocktail, too, from a range of ten standards, although your €15 could be just as enjoyably spent on a flute of Moët & Chandon. This is once-in-a-holiday stuff, so lap it up. **Photo** *below*.

Le Café Noir

*65 rue Montmartre, 2nd (01.40.39.07.36). M°
Sentier.* **Open** 8am-2am Mon-Fri; 4pm-2am Sat.
Credit DC, MC, V. **Map** p404 J5 **7**
This justifiably buzzing and enticingly kitsch corner bar is Noir in name, scarlet in tone and brash in attitude. A framed Gainsbourg portrait and quotation exhort 'Music Above All', although they're fighting for your attention with leopard-spotted bicycles, reindeer-antlered fishheads and dinky hanging baskets and papier-mâché lightshades, offset by a tiled bar counter – and all of it the size of a communal changing cubicle at your local swimming baths. The regulars make the place nice and naughty, bright, bitchy and boho, forever picking up on the giggling conversation on the next banquette or prized pavement table. There's a modest lunchtime menu, too.

De la Ville Café

*34 bd Bonne-Nouvelle, 10th (01.48.24.48.09).
M° Bonne Nouvelle.* **Open** 11am-2am daily.
Credit MC, V. **Map** p404 J4 **8**
Opened by the Café Charbon (*see p226*) crew and other Ménilmontant movers, De la Ville has brought good news to Bonne Nouvelle. A major expansion and refurb have upped the ante, so much so that the in-crowd is migrating from the Marais to this otherwise ignored quarter. Inside, the distressed walls and hippie feel remain, but the curvy club section at the back has become terribly cool. A grand staircase leads to a first-floor lounge and exhibition space, and the interior is ambitious and arty with a fashion edge (Agnès b designed the staff aprons). After elevating the 11th to bar legend, can the crew transform the 10th, and bring a café boom back to the boulevards?

Dok's Café

*46 rue Lamartine, 9th (01.53.16.32.49). M° Cadet
or Notre-Dame-de-Lorette.* **Open** 8am-9pm daily.
No credit cards. Map p404 J3 **9**
This 'salon de thé contemporain' is really a laid-back lounge bar with a long list of teas and coffees (nothing by way of alcohol), and a free internet service for customers. The three terminals are almost always in use, so you'll have time to muse over your black *mocca banane* or fresh mint caffè latte and take in

Where Wilde mused and Bartholdi drew the Statue of Liberty – **Café de la Paix**. *See p215.*

the cosmopolitan ambience before you check your email. The drinks menu has dozens of perfumed teas (try the *pomme d'amour* of caramelised apple and maraschino cherry, or the red-fruit variety of cherry, strawberry, raspberry and redcurrant) and ten green teas; slices of rhubarb tart beckon from the bar counter. Home-made lemonade is another speciality, in orgeat, cinnamon or green banana flavour.

Fogão

8 bd Montmartre, 9th (01.47.70.27.20). M° Grands Boulevards. **Open** 10am-4am daily. **Credit** AmEx, MC, V. **Map** p404 J4 ⑩

Opened to coincide with 2005's Year of Brazil in Paris, Fogão styles itself as a *churrascaria*. But if you're expecting a sizzling grill with gauchos, sawdust and spittoons, forget it. This bar-restaurant-club is an upmarket contemporary café in the modern European style: brown, high-backed banquettes, dinky chairs and twisted light-bulb arrangements. Caipirinhas and Batidas come at €8, cocktails likewise; bottled Brahma at €5.50 is steep, though if you sneak in between 5.30pm and 8pm it's €3. The mainly South American wines (Chilean Santa Digna, Los Medanos from Uruguay) are €20 a bottle, and the grills – hulking sculptures of pork, beef and chicken – are just what the gaucho ordered.

Harry's New York Bar

5 rue Daunou, 2nd (01.42.61.71.14/www.harrys-bar.fr). M° Opéra. **Open** 10.30am-4am daily. **Credit** AmEx, DC, MC, V. **Map** p403 G4 ⑪

The city's quintessential American bar is still the smoky, pennant-bedecked institution beloved of expats, visitors and hard-drinking Parisians. The white-coated bartenders mix some of the finest and most lethal cocktails in town, from the trademark Bloody Mary (invented here, so they say) to the well-named Pétrifiant, a paralysing elixir of half a dozen spirits splashed into a beer mug. They can also whip up a personalised creation: we remember (patchily) a string of delicious vodka concoctions that had us swooning in the downstairs piano bar and outrageously overtipping the artiste.

La Jungle

56 rue d'Argout, 2nd (01.40.41.03.45/www.la-jungle.com). M° Sentier. **Open** 10am-2am Mon-Fri; 4pm-2am Sat, Sun. **Credit** AmEx, MC, V. **Map** p404 J5 ⑫

A zebra-striped patch of Africa between the financial district and the newly hip north-west of the Marais, this Jungle rocks with easy sociability and unaffected fun – despite its morose collection of scruffy animal skins. There's a programme of live Afro-jazz on Wednesdays and Fridays (€2 extra on drinks), some of it half decent – but really you're here for exotic cocktails (€6) such as 'Ti Georges, Zoulou and vodka-soaked Gazelle Allumée, plus ethnic dishes with a Cameroon bent. Hearty N'Dôle soup, chicken *yassa* and *boudin créole* can be washed down with Flag beer from Senegal. A branch at nearby 15 rue d'Aboukir is run in the same vein. **Photo** *right*.

Somo

168 rue Montmartre, 2nd (01.40.13.08.80/www.hip-bars.com). M° Sentier or Grands Boulevards. **Open** noon-2am Mon-Fri; 6pm-4am Sat. **Credit** AmEx, MC, V. **Map** p404 J4 ⑬

The thoroughbred among the expat-owned Hip Bars stable, Somo is a sleeker, more grown-up offering than the Lizard Lounge (*see p221*), Stolly's (*see p223*) and the Bottle Shop (5 rue Trousseau, 11th, 01.43.14.28.04). Popular with suits from the nearby Bourse after work, it chills out later on in the evening and at weekends, when bright young things arrive to party amid the fairy lights, aided and abetted by well-mixed €9 Absolut-based cocktails. There's a full menu, too: the €13.90 dinner's a snip, the €9 bar snacks not so. Weekend DJ spots here have become a fixture on the Saturday night circuit.

Le Tambour

41 rue Montmartre, 2nd (01.42.33.06.90). M° Sentier. **Open** 6pm-6am daily. **Credit** MC, V. **Map** p404 J5 ⑭

A classic nighthawks' bar, decked out with vintage transport chic, its slatted wooden banquettes and bus-stop-sign bar stools occupied by chatty regulars who give the 24-hour clock its best shot. Neither tatty nor threatening, Le Tambour comprises a small counter area where staff and souses banter,

Punch drunk at **La Jungle**.

a busy conservatory, and a long dining room memorable for its retro métro map from Stalingrad station and iconic image of Neil Armstrong.

Le Truskel

10 rue Feydeau, 2nd (01.40.26.59.97/www.truskel. com). M° Bourse. **Open** 8pm-2am Tue, Wed; 8pm-5am Thur-Sat. Closed Aug. **Credit** MC, V. **Map** p404 H4 ⓳

Oirish meets indie at this pub-cum-disco a stone's throw from the stock exchange. The formula is quite simple: an excellent selection of beers, fruity Belgian and quality Czech included, attends to your throat while an extensive repertoire of Britpop assaults your ears. The back area is for dancing, just like a school disco. Malcontent expats love it, but not as much as French boys who can't hold their Murphy's. To add to the mystique, a bar bell rings for no reason whatsoever, causing first-time UK visitors to down their drinks in one and dive for the bar.

Champs-Elysées & western Paris

Le Dada

12 av des Ternes, 17th (01.43.80.60.12). M° Ternes. **Open** 6am-2am Mon-Sat; 6am-10pm Sun. **Credit** AmEx, MC, V. **Map** p402 C3 ⓰

Perhaps the hippest café on this classy avenue in a stuffy part of town, Le Dada is best known for its well-placed, sunny terrace, though the kookily Dada-influenced two-floor interior is ideal for a cheeky afternoon tipple. The wood-block carved tables and red walls provide a warm atmosphere for a crowd that tends towards the well-heeled, well-spoken and, well, loaded. That said, the atmosphere is friendly and relaxed and, if terracing is your thing, you could happily spend a summer's day here.

Impala Lounge

2 rue de Berri, 8th (01.43.59.12.66). M° George V. **Open** 9.30am-2am Mon, Tue, Sun; 9.30am-3am Wed, Thur; 9.30am-5am Fri, Sat. **Credit** AmEx, MC, V. **Map** p402 D4 ⓱

Dubbed the 'African Bar' by regulars, this wannabe hip spot hams up the colonial with zebra skins, tribal masks and a throne hewn from a tree trunk. Beer, wine, tea and standard favourites can all be had, but best are the cocktails, one of which claims to boost a waning libido with its mystery mix of herbs and spices. DJs rock Sunday afternoon away, and the snack-and-mains menu includes ostrich.

Ladurée

75 av des Champs-Elysées, 8th (01.40.75.08.75/ www.laduree.fr). M° George V or Franklin D. Roosevelt. **Open** 7.30am-midnight Mon-Thur; 7.30am-midnight Fri-Sun. **Credit** AmEx, DC, MC, V. **Map** p402 D4 ⓲

Everything in this elegant tearoom suggests decadence, from the 19th-century-style interior and service to the labyrinthine corridors that lead to the

toilets. But you came here not merely to wallow in bygone wealth: you came for the teas, pastries and, most of all, the hot chocolate. It's thick, bitter, creamier than heaven; on a first tasting, you'll say to yourself, 'This is tar.' And so it is, a rich, velvety tar that will leave you in the kind of stupor requisite for any lazy afternoon. The original branch at 16 rue Royale (8th, 01.42.60.21.79) is more well known for its macaroons.

Petit Défi de Passy

18 av du Président-Kennedy, 16th (01.42.15.06.76/ www.defidepassy.com). M° Passy/RER Avenue du Pdt Kennedy. **Open** 10am-midnight daily. **Credit** AmEx, DC, MC, V. **Map** p406 B6 ⓳

In permanent rebellion against its posh postcode, this refreshingly no-fuss bar-restaurant challenges the local chi-chi rule, jollying along friendly students and English teachers through happy hour in a distinct whiff of late adolescence. It's positively bursting with toff totty (albeit rather on the young side) and the best bit is, it's cheap. Chaps can impress the fillies by buying a bottle of Absolut for €60 and keeping it behind the bar with their name on.

Le Rival

20 av George V, 8th (01.47.23.40.99). M° George V. **Open** 7am-2am daily. **Credit** MC, V. **Map** p402 D4 ⓴

Stylish but low-key, this four-star contemporary bar makes a mean Martini: either fresh fruit, Polish or Detroit, with a wellyful of Zubrowka or Krupnik chucked in and served with pzzazz. Other highlights of the €12 cocktail range are a Saigon Extra Mule with Poire Williams, lemon and ginger beer, and a Spiced Swizzle of rum and amaretto. A decent glass of Brouilly or Chablis sets you back €7, par for the course – but God knows how they can charge €18 for a cheeseburger and hash browns or €10 for a *croque-monsieur*. Still, the shopaholic and business clientele seem happy to pay up.

Sir Winston

5 rue de Presbourg, 16th (01.40.67.17.37). M° Charles de Gaulle Etoile. **Open** 9am-3am Mon-Wed, Sun; 9am-4am Thur-Sat. **Credit** AmEx,V. **Map** p402 C4 ㉑

A bit of an anomaly, this. Grand and imperial in a location on the corner of avenue d'Iéna within sight of very high-end glitz, Sir Winston does a nice line in jazz and gospel brunches on a Sunday; chicken tandoori and Scottish salmon feature among the main dishes (€15-€20). Colonial knick-knacks, chesterfields and chandeliers make up the decor, while Winnie himself is framed behind a sturdy bar counter equipped with a well-worn arm-rest groove. A battalion of whiskies stands guard beside him, and the wine list is equally recherché; nothing wrong with the €10 cocktails, either. Where the place falters is in veering from the established standards, especially in its girly cocktails. A Sir Winston Breezer of Bacardi, melon liqueur, pineapple and banana juice? Harrumph!

Andy Wahloo.

Montmartre & Pigalle

La Divette de Montmartre

136 rue Marcadet, 18th (01.46.06.19.64). Mº Lamarck Caulaincourt. **Open** 5pm-1am Mon, Fri, Sat; 3pm-1am Tue-Thur. **Credit** MC, V.

This cavern of colourful nostalgia is run by Serge, its barrel-bellied barman. Tucked away among Montmartre's hilly backstreets but worth the trek, this is Serge's *Recherche du temps perdu* in album cover, poster and table-football form. Beatles albums line up over the bar, Rolling Stones ones under it and an Elvis clock ticks in between; this decorative trinity is interrupted by *yé-yé* pop tack, the occasional green of St-Etienne football iconography and an old red telephone box. On tap are Wieckse Witte, Afflighem, Pelforth, and gossip about the days when Manu Chao were regulars.

La Fourmi

74 rue des Martyrs, 18th (01.42.64.70.35). Mº Pigalle. **Open** 8.30am-2am Mon-Thur; 8.30am-4am Fri, Sat; 10am-2am Sun. **Credit** MC, V. **Map** p404 H2 ㉒

Set on the cusp of the 9th and 18th, La Fourmi is retro-industrial at its best. It's an old bistro that has been converted for today's tastes, with picture windows giving natural light and visual bustle to the spacious, roughshod, sand-coloured main interior, whose prime seats are on the podiums at the back. The classic zinc bar counter is crowned by industrial lights, the ornately carved back bar featuring the odd titular ant. An excellent music policy and cool clientele – although they'd have to go some to beat the bar staff – ensure a pile of flyers. As good a place as any to find out what's happening in town.

Lush

16 rue des Dames, 17th (01.43.87.49.46/ www.lushbars.com). Mº Place de Clichy. **Open** 6pm-2am daily. **Credit** MC, V. **Map** p403 G1 ㉓

Lush is a sleek lair for chilled-out drinking with a loyal clientele of laid-back trendies. Soft grape purples and comfy banquettes provide a suitable setting for inexpensive pints, well-chosen New World wines and delicious cocktails. Premiership football and rugby on big-screen TV, and half-decent live music, drag punters from across the city.

Le Sancerre

35 rue des Abbesses, 18th (01.42.58.08.20). Mº Abbesses. **Open** 7am-2am Mon-Thur; 7am-4am Fri, Sat; 9am-2am Sun. **Credit** MC, V. **Map** p404 H1 ㉔

Of the many choices on rue des Abbesses, this is the most popular, its terrace full, its large, dark wood interior an attractive mix of cool and cosy. Taps of Paulaner, Grimbergen and Record accompany bottled Belgian beauties Kriek and Mort Subite; standard cocktails, €5.50 on Mondays, are presented with the same care as the couple of *plats du jour* and a good range of mains and salads. Sadly, the service can be teeth-grindingly slow, truly galling when a duo is murdering your favourite Roy O number.

Beaubourg & the Marais

Andy Wahloo

69 rue des Gravilliers, 3rd (01.42.71.20.38). Mº Arts et Métiers. **Open** 4pm-2am Mon-Sat. **Credit** AmEx, MC, V. **Map** p411 K5 ㉕

Andy Wahloo – created by the people behind its neighbour 404 and London's Momo and Sketch – is Arabic for 'I have nothing'. Bijou? The place brings

Paris promenade Eleventh heaven

Everyone says that the best bar crawl in Paris is up rue Oberkampf, a two-sided strip of joints in the 11th arrondissement between Parmentier and Ménilmontant métro stops. And they're probably right, even now. New bars such as **L'Abreuvoir** (**❶** *see p225*) and **La Maizon** (**❷** *see p228*) complement landmarks like **La Mercerie** (**❸** *see p228*) and the **Café Charbon** (**❹** *see p226*) that started the phenomenon in the first place.

So what's wrong with Oberkampf? Nothing, really, except that everyone and their moped occupies its narrow pavements and there's something annoying about being in the same bar or kebab shop as a city of ten million people, suburbanites included. Happily, a more laid-back, less stressful scene is burgeoning five minutes away, in a parallel street to the north: rue Jean-Pierre-Timbaud. Free of the pressure to provide the next hip thing, away from the beat of the No.96 bus, it offers a refreshing range of bars and change of tempo. Sassy restaurants, such as **Ile de Gorée** (**❺** *see p201*) and **Juan et Juanita** (**❻** *see p199*), also provide ethnic sustenance.

Start your crawl near boulevard Richard Lenoir (M° Oberkampf or Parmentier), where a small clutch of bars lines either side of a pedestrianised central strip. On the left, **Le Record** (**❼** No.25, no phone) provides a constant buzz throughout the day and simple

offerings at mealtimes, when tables dot the pavement. The terrace atmosphere is enhanced by the more foodie option of nearby **Aux Tables de la Fontaine** (**❽** No.33, 01.43.57.26.00), which covers half of the traffic-free middle section with chatting diners. On the other side, at No.46, **Les Trois Têtards** (**❾** 01.43.14.27.37) is one of the livelier of the boho bars of the locality. Stripped-down, with picture windows and a mural of the cover from *Electric Ladyland*, it offers old-school music, simple salads and flavoured vodkas at €3.50.

At the junction with avenue Parmentier, **L'Idéal Bar** (**❿** no phone), with its Belgian pinball machine, and neat **L'Industrie** (**⓫** no phone), with its €12 lunches, provide unpretentious fun. Further down on the right-hand side, the rather more gastronomically pretentious **L'Autre Café** (**⓬** No.62, 01.40.21.03.07) serves up well conceived mains amid the dark wood and foliage. The **Bakara Lounge** opposite (**⓭** No.61, 01.48.07.17.04) is of a similar stripe. Next door, **Le Rapide** (**⓮** No.61bis, no phone) is an authentic African football bar whose counter is fringed by the colourful worship of the JS Kabylie club of Algeria.

It's here that rue J-P-T starts to get funky – around the junction with rue St-Maur and its line of oddball ethno and boho bars – beginning with the two landmark venues:

new meaning to the word. A formidably fashionable set crowds in here and fights for a coveted place on an upturned paint can (who needs a divan when you've got Dulux?). From head to toe, it's a beautifully designed venue crammed with Moroccan artefacts, and enough colours to fill a Picasso. It's quiet early on, but there's a surge around nine and the atmosphere heats up as the night gets longer. **Photo** *p219*.

L'Etoile Manquante
34 rue Vieille-du-Temple, 4th (01.42.72.48.34/www. cafeine.com). M° Hôtel de Ville or St-Paul. **Open** 9am-2am daily. **Credit** MC, V. **Map** p411 K6 **㉖**
This is one of a small coterie of Vieille-du-Temple venues owned and designed by Xavier Denamur – and is the hippest of the bunch. The cocktails are punchy, the traditional tipples just as good, the salads and cold snacks reasonably priced and tasty – but it's the design and buzz that are the draws here. The decor is trendy and comfortable, embellished with wonderful lighting and interesting art spread over the walls. As ever with Denamur's places, no visit is complete without a trip to the toilets: here, an

electric train shuttles between cubicles, starlight beams down from the ceiling and a hidden camera films you washing your hands. Just watch the small screen set up on the wall behind you.

Guillaume
32 rue de Picardie, 3rd (01.44.54.20.60). M° Temple. **Open** 11am-2am Mon-Fri; 7pm-2am Sat. **Credit** MC, V. **Map** p411 L5 **㉗**
Opened in 2005, this trendy bar-restaurant has an expansive back room equipped with a gallery and a huge peacock-feather chandelier, though the smart set prefers a spot on the modest terrace facing the Carreau du Temple market. During 'bubble hours', 5.30-7.30pm, custom is encouraged with cheapish Jaeger-Ligneut champers and *crostini* with red tuna or guacamole. The rest of the time, cocktails (standards and specials itemised as 'Mais Aussi') are €8 a pop; flavoured lemonades, pistachio or rose, for instance, are key ingredients. Among the unusual eats is Piña Colada soup (€5), but most pick at a salad, sip a cocktail and fight the temptation to scowl at whoever arrives in more fashionable shoes.

Eat, Drink, Shop

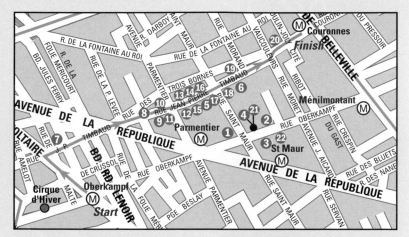

the arty **L'Alimentation Générale** (⑮ *see p226*) and rocking **Au P'tit Garage** (⑯ *see p228*). Both merit investigation, as does the wine bar **Les Crâneuses** (⑰ No.72bis, 01.47.00.37.59), recommended in reliable local circles. Facing each other at the St-Maur crossroads, the foxy **Au Chat Noir** (⑱ No.76, 01.48.06.98.22) and the funky **Marquise** (⑲ No.75, no phone) do battle for business.

As the street rises up to meet Couronnes métro, the landscape becomes more down-at-heel, with nondescript North African bars surrounded by cheap international phone centres and a mosque. The one exception

is the **Cannibale Café** (⑳ No.93, 01.49.29.95.59), considered to be the prime mover behind the street's new buzz, but these days a self-satisfied mainstream bar-restaurant where couples come to dine.

For all the talk of bar heaven in the 11th, the district only opens late at weekends. During the week, it's a strict 2am curfew, the streets becoming so dark they would satisfy the most finickety ARP warden. So for a late drink on a Thursday night, you'll still have to head back down to rue Oberkampf and the **Nouveau Casino** (㉑ *see p325*) or **Cithéa** (㉒ No.112, 01.40.21.70.95).

Lizard Lounge
18 rue du Bourg-Tibourg, 4th (01.42.72.81.34/ www.hip-bars.com). Mº Hôtel de Ville. **Open** noon-2am daily. **Credit** MC, V. **Map** p411 K6 ㉘
Anglophone/phile favourite deep in the Marais, this loud and lively (hetero) pick-up joint provides lager in pint glasses (€6), strong, well-mixed cocktails (€7) by the bucketload and a viewing platform from which the beer-goggled can ogle their prey. Bare brick and polished woodwork are offset by the occasional lizard, but the main backdrop is provided by a trip hop and house soundtrack of consistent quality, as happy hours upstairs and in the sweaty cellar meet at 8pm. Mercifully, given the five straight hours of bargain boozing from 5pm, the downstairs dancefloor is minuscule, a straitjacket for those unco-ordinated or incapacitated through drink. Show off your catch at the popular weekend brunch.

La Perle
78 rue Vieille-du-Temple, 3rd (01.42.72.69.93). Mº Chemin Vert or St-Paul. **Open** 6am-2am Mon-Fri; 8am-2am Sat, Sun. **Credit** MC, V. **Map** p411 L6 ㉙

This recent Marais hit is commendably simple. Cool little touches – arty dabblings on the walls, the old locomotive over the bar – meet sleek rows of grey chairs spread on the quiet corner of rue de la Perle and rue Vieille-du-Temple, and patterned banquettes within. The Pearl's real triumph is its all-day and late-night hetero/homo mix: it feels like a neighbourhood bar, with labourers and cravatted screen-writers rubbing elbows at the bar counter. There's unpretentious and inexpensive attention to detail and the menu runs from hearty omelettes to a delicate *salade marine*. Expect a DJ later on.

Le Petit Fer à Cheval
30 rue Vieille-du-Temple, 4th (01.42.72.47.47). Mº St-Paul. **Open** 9am-2am daily. **Credit** MC, V. **Map** p411 K6 ㉚
If Glasgow's Horseshoe boasts the UK's longest bar counter, its Paris near-namesake contains one of the smallest to be found across the Channel. Certainly by Paris standards it's small, and far too charming by half, a marble ring surrounded by old film and promotional posters and headed by a vintage clock

and an ornate mirror backdrop. Everything is done with mirrors, in fact, because behind the glassy façade hides a friendly dining room lined with old métro benches, offering space, but not scenery – for that, try the handful of small tables out front looking at Vieille-du-Temple's bustle. In business since 1903, the Little Horseshoe enjoyed a retro makeover by Xavier Denamur and his team in the 1990s.

Stolly's

16 rue Cloche-Perce, 4th (01.42.76.06.76/www.hip-bars.com). M° Hôtel de Ville or St-Paul. **Open** 4.30pm-2am daily. **Credit** MC, V. **Map** p411 K6 **③**
This seen-it-all drinking den has been serving a mainly anglophone crowd with expert vodka tonics and old Velvets tunes for nights immemorial. The staff make the place what it is, helping you feel like part of what passes for furniture, and smoothing a passage from arriving sober to sinking them relentlessly until you're rotten. A summer terrace eases libation, as do long happy hours, but don't expect anyone to faff about with food. There's football on TV and a plastic shark to compensate.

Le Troisième Lieu

62 rue Quincampoix, 4th (01.48.04.85.64). M° Rambuteau. **Open** 6pm-2am. **Credit** AmEx, MC, V. **Map** p408 K5 **③**
This self-styled 'Cantine des Ginettes Armées' turns into the Cantine Electro after dark. Day or night, the industrial, low-ceilinged interior embellished with retro advertising provides a cheapish antidote to the tourist traps in the area around the Centre Pompidou, serving €9 couscous and dishes of the day, strong punch (€4.50) and standard beers. A youngish crowd occupies the banquettes, looking for a little action with members of the opposite sex. La Cantine makes no bones about what it's here for: 'On bouffe. On boit. On danse.' Scoff, glug and bop. And it takes its music pretty seriously, with DJs playing Wednesday to Saturday, including the occasional lower-drawer international name *(see p323)*.

Bastille & eastern Paris

L'Antenne Bastille

32ter bd de la Bastille, 12th (01.43.43.34.92). M° Bastille. **Open** 8am-2am Mon-Fri; noon-2am Sat; 2-9pm Sun. Closed Aug. **Credit** MC, V. **Map** p408 M7 **③**
A great little retro bar a quayside stroll from the Bastille opera, L'Antenne has a terrace overlooking the Port de l'Arsenal marina and a simple interior that's light and airy. It's appeal lies not just in the Maurice Chevalier posters, but also in the fact you can get a humble *jambon-beurre* sandwich for under €3 or a chocolate bar from the rows arranged in sweet-shop fashion. There's more substantial food and equally cheap, too: a *plat du jour* at €8.50 and an €11.50 daily *formule*. A thirtysomething clientele banters quietly, leaving hedonism to the younger mob who dive into the nearby snakepits of rue de la Roquette and rue de Lappe.

Bar à Nenette

26bis rue de Lappe, 11th (01.48.07.08.18). M° Bastille or Ledru-Rollin. **Open** 5pm-2am daily. **Credit** AmEx, DC, MC, V. **Map** p409 M7 **③**
This lovely little wooden bar has character in spades – something lacking in the somewhat rocking-by-rote of modern competitors nearby. Circa 1988, rue de Lappe was *the* place to bar-hop, soon surpassed by Oberkampf further north. Recently, Sister May (No.25), Bar Sans Nom (No.49) and L'Or en Bar (No.30) have revived the scene – while the Nenette has been doing steady trade at its traditional rows of tables. Happy hours until 10pm (*demis* of St-Omer at €2) help, as do plates of cheeses or sausages (€10) and the friendly mix of foreigners and regulars.

Le Baron Rouge

1 rue Théophile-Roussel, 12th (01.43.43.14.32). M° Ledru-Rollin. **Open** 10am-3pm, 5-10pm Tue-Thur; 10am-10pm Fri, Sat; 10am-3pm Sun. **Credit** AmEx, MC, V. **Map** p409 N7 **③**

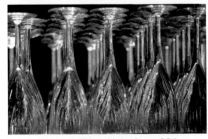
Cool, convivial **China Club**. *See p224.*

Eat, Drink, Shop

Au P'tit Garage. *See p228.*

Calling this simply a wine bar might give the wrong impression. It sells wine, certainly – bloody great barrels of the stuff piled on the tiled floor by the entrance; take a look at the board over the corner bar counter and you'll see Merlots and Muscadets chalked up at very reasonable prices by the glass. But there are draught beers, too, the ever more present St-Omer and far rarer Jenlain and Corsican Pietra. Most aptly of all, though, the Red Baron could be described as a chat room. Regulars congregate around the simple space to yak, their glasses sat on upturned barrels, perhaps with a plate of sausages to pick at or a few oysters. Given the 10pm closing time, it's used as an early-evening pick-me-up, half the customers occupying the pavement outside. Popular, so don't expect much elbow room.

China Club

50 rue de Charenton, 12th (01.43.43.82.02/ www.chinaclub.cc). M° Bastille or Ledru-Rollin. **Open** 7pm-2am daily. Closed Aug. **Credit** AmEx, MC, V. **Map** p409 M7 36

With huge chesterfields, low lighting and a sexy long bar, it's impossible not to feel glamorous here. In fact, if you've had a few, it's hard not to drop into a gentle snooze. Yes, this is the domain of the extremely relaxed gentlemen's club, all with a distinctly colonial Cohibas-and-cocktails feel. They take their Martinis seriously, but if you're more Pussy Galore than James Bond you can't go wrong with a well-made champagne cocktail. This is also ideal seduction territory – although China Club is equally suited to a hands-off first date. Those unconcerned by brewers' droop should plan to schedule any rendezvous during the inhibition-demolishing happy hour (7-9pm). **Photo** *p223.*

Le Fanfaron

6 rue de la Main-d'Or, 11th (01.49.23.41.14). M° Ledru-Rollin. **Open** 6pm-2am Tue-Sat. Closed 2wks Aug. **No credit cards**. **Map** p409 N7 37

On a small backstreet, Le Fanfaron (named after Dino Risi's cult 1962 movie) is the favoured haunt for musically inclined retro dudes. Envious buffs come from far and wide for owner Xavier's collection of rare film soundtracks, while others pop in for the cheap (€2.30) beer and sound of needle against crackly vinyl. The decor is an ode to kitsch-cool with Stones and Iggy memorabilia, second-hand furniture, 1960s film posters, wooden panelling and Lucy the legless mannequin who props up one side of the bar. There are reasonably priced goat's cheese and *saucisson* bar snacks, too.

La Liberté

196 rue du Fbg-St-Antoine, 12th (01.43.72.11.18). M° Faidherbe Chaligny. **Open** 9am-2am Mon-Fri; 11am-2am Sat, Sun. **Credit** MC, V. **Map** p409 N7 38

By day this is a relaxed spot; the decor is a little primitive and rubbing elbows is inevitable, but convivial is the word you're looking for. Good food, too, a notch above the average bar grub and a notch cheaper. By night, though, it's ripped to the tits and still thirsty with it. La Lib comprises a small terrace

and a narrow bar area dangling with knick-knacks and invariably packed; a back room is for groups who actually want to talk to each other. The rest are perfectly happy to guzzle (house punch or decent Belgian brews by the bottle), guffaw and cop off; at some point someone dances like a maniac on the bar counter. The music is always right: African beats, Burning Spear or Little Richard howling *Lucille*.

Pop In

105 rue Amelot, 11th (01.48.05.56.11). M° St-Sébastien Froissart. **Open** 6.30pm-1.30am Tue-Sun. Closed Aug. **Credit** AmEx, MC, V. **Map** p408 L5 **㊳**
The Pop In seems to be a contradiction in terms – or at the very least, an exercise in postmodern irony. A bar so uncool that it is, in fact, cutting edge, the place is all things to all men. Since it hosted a Christian Dior after-show party and was subsequently colonised by fashion-hangers-on, the Pop In has won a reputation as a place that doesn't care, doesn't try, but manages to be cool anyway. It's scruffy, cheap and the staff are genuinely nice. Add a cellar bar that alternates between open-mic venue and club for DJs and you have a recipe for a top night out.

Trucmush

5 passage Thiéré, 11th (01.48.07.11.91). M° Ledru-Rollin. **Open** 6pm-2am daily. Closed Aug. **Credit** MC, V. **Map** p409 M7 **㊵**
A handy little DJ bar near the bottom end of rue de Lappe – look out for the Carlsberg pub sign. Inside, such is the dense, conspiratorial atmosphere and

rather splendid wall of electronic noise, you'll barely notice the deft decorative touches such as the false windows overlooking the Eiffel Tower or upturned sinks and bidets used as tables. You will notice it's red, though, no escaping that, nor the €5.50 cocktails (Ti Punch, Pina Colada). Wooden tables at the back offer a little privacy, at a premium by the tiny bar counter and DJ set-up built from a car bumper.

Le Zéro Zéro

89 rue Amelot, 11th (01.49.23.51.00). M° St-Sébastien Froissart. **Open** 6pm-2am daily. **Credit** AmEx, MC, V. **Map** p404 L5 **㊶**
Revolutionary when it opened in 1999, the ZZ still has a chip on its shoulder. It's as wee as a wardrobe, it drinks like a fish and its music kicks like a mule. Men gather round the tiny L-shaped bar and mutter musings, profound at the time, pitiful when chalked up above the counter. The extensive cocktail blackboard lists (among others) a potent Zéro Zéro of dark rum, ginger and lime; discounted during happy hour (6.30-8.30pm) despite a reasonable pricing structure. Oh, and the decorators don't seem to have touched it since the day it opened.

North-eastern Paris

L'Abreuvoir

103 rue Oberkampf, 11th (01.43.38.87.01). M° Parmentier. **Open** 5pm-2am Mon-Sat. Closed 2wks Aug. **Credit** (€16 minimum) MC, V. **Map** p405 N5 **㊷**

Another relative newcomer to the Oberkampf beat, this *sympa* little bar is set on the other side of rue St-Maur from the more popular venues, keeping it relatively underused. Nabbing a low stool at a candlelit table is a cinch, and you might even get a spot at the bar counter done out in signed Chuck Berry posters and other rock 'n' roll memorabilia. The speciality here is beer cocktails (€6), such as the Casse-Tête of beer, rum and peach liqueur, or the Tchek of vodka, beer and lemon. You'll feel it in the morning – but that's a million miles away. Tidy choice of music, too.

L'Alimentation Générale

64 rue Jean-Pierre-Timbaud, 11th (01.43.55.42.50). M° Parmentier. **Open** 5pm-2am Mon-Sat. **Credit** AmEx, MC, V. **Map** p405 N5 **43**
The 'Grocery Store' is rue J-P-Timbaud's answer to Oberkampf's 'Haberdashery' (La Mercerie; *see p228*): it, too, is a big old space filled with junk. Cupboards of kitsch china or plastic peppers face the long bar counter, while elsewhere, Miró-esque touches inform much of the decor – the lampshades made from kitchen sponges are an inspired choice. The beer is equally well chosen – Flag, Sagres, Picon and Orval by the bottle – and the €8 house speciality involves obscure combinations of fruit, spices and alcohol, throwing basil, figs and apricot into the mix. Salads are equally imaginative. Professional sounds emerge from a DJ booth the size of a small airport terminal – expect a €5 cover price for big names or live bands. Oh, yes – and the most brazen toilet walls on this side of town. *See also p220* **Seventh heaven**.

L'Atmosphère

49 rue Lucien-Sampaix, 10th (01.40.38.09.21). M° Gare de l'Est or Jacques Bonsergent. **Open** 9.30am-1.45am Mon-Sat; 9.30am-midnight Sun. **No credit cards. Map** p404 L3 **44**
L'Atmosphère remains at the centre of the Canal St-Martin renaissance and sums up the spirit of the area. Parisians of all kinds chat, read and gaze from the waterside terrace while, within, the simple, tasteful interior, animated conversation and cheapish drinks provide entertainment enough. It's always packed, but brave the crowds on Sundays for the early-evening world and experimental music slots.

Bar Ourcq

68 quai de la Loire, 19th (01.42.40.12.26/www.barourcq.com). M° Laumière. **Open** 3pm-midnight Wed-Sun. **No credit cards. Map** p405 N1 **45**
Best new bar in Paris? It's certainly got an awful lot going for it. A little turquoise-framed corner bar, it's set back from a canal embankment broad enough to accommodate *pétanque* games (ask at the bar), a cluster of deckchairs and a kids' playground nearby. It's a completely different scene from the crowded, narrow bustle along Canal St-Martin a pleasant walk the other side of Jaurès métro station. Inside, Ourcq is a vivacious, boho cabin of parrot wallpaper and busted sofas, with an intimate raised area at the back. Drinks are listed in a hit parade of prices, starting with €1 for coffee, €2 for a *demi* or glass of red

wine, €3 for a Pelforth or kir, and €4 for a lively Mojito. €7 pastas, exhibitions and a regular DJ agenda keep the cool clientele sated and entertained.

Café Charbon

109 rue Oberkampf, 11th (01.43.57.55.13/www. nouveaucasino.net). M° Parmentier or Ménilmontant. **Open** 9am-2am Mon-Thur, Sun; 9am-4am Fri, Sat. **Credit** MC, V. **Map** p405 N5 **46**
This beautifully restored belle-époque building sparked the Oberkampf nightlife boom, its booths, mirrors, chandeliers and adventurous music policy putting trendy locals at their ease, capturing the essence of café culture spanning each end of the 20th century. It was cool, it was grand: fine dining, sound DJing, retro chic and high ceilings. After 15 years or more, the formula still works, inspiring scores of bars nearby. The management opened the equally popular Nouveau Casino nightclub next door (*see p325*) and has continued the empire-building with the groovified De la Ville Café (*see p216*) in the 10th.

Café Chéri(e)

44 bd de la Villette, 19th (01.42.02.02.05). M° Belleville. **Open** 8am-2am daily. **Credit** MC, V. **Map** p405 M3 **47**
This splendid DJ bar (*see p320*) has expanded its brief and its opening hours to become an all-day café – without watering down any of the funky chic that keeps it well ahead of the pack after dark. Set in a gloomy corner of Belleville, the Chéri(e) sparkles with wit and invention. Large sealed jars on the bar counter pack all kinds of punches, such as the €5 Chéri(e) of dark rum; fruit vodkas are another speciality. DJ nights are conceived with equal craft, and

the atmosphere around the red interior dotted with low-key artwork is one of suss and seduction. There's a front terrace if you need a little conversational respite from the BPM.

Le Cinquante

50 rue de Lancry, 10th (01.42.02.36.83). Mᵒ Jacques Bonsergent. **Open** 5.30pm-2am daily. Closed Mon in Aug. **No credit cards. Map** p404 L4 ④⑧
Spunky little place this, just down from the Canal St-Martin. Bare brick, formica and framed ads from the immediate post-war period form the decor, although ambience comes with the inner circle of regulars: boho types in on the scene. Reasonable prices – 50cl pitchers of Sauvignon, Brouilly and Chablis in the €10 range, all available by the glass – attract a mixed bag of tastes and generations in the cabin-sized space. The two rooms behind the main bar are for dining (affordable classics) and performances (minimal and generally acoustic). Last orders are at 1.20am – no arguments there, then.

Les Couleurs

117 rue St-Maur, 11th (01.43.57.95.61). Mᵒ Parmentier. **Open** 11am-2am daily. **No credit cards. Map** p405 M4 ④⑨
Rue St-Maur at its squat-chic best. Plastic furniture, a tacky desert island mural, bare brick and naked lightbulbs compose the decor. Abrupt service, arty underground films and pool balls in primary colours on the beer taps are other features. Locals flock here in droves (clock the mounted Kodak shots). The soundtrack is as good as you'll find anywhere in these parts, the cocktails sharp, and the vibe is vibrant and vital. Food is a recent innovation.

L'Ile Enchantée

65 bd de la Villette, 10th (01.42.01.67.99). Mᵒ Colonel Fabien. **Open** 8am-2am Mon-Fri; 5pm-2am Sat, Sun. **Credit** MC, V. **Map** p405 M3 ⑤⓪
The latest DJ bar on the burgeoning scene northwest of nearby Belleville, the Enchanted Island has just the right understated touches of chic and retro – wacky Renault Mégane advertising on the terrace tabletops – and equally minimal house/electro sounds to keep the focus firmly fixed on conversation. It's light, too, in the sense that the tall, tall ceilings and French windows let in acres of Belleville skyline, and there's space aplenty amid the studded banquettes and tables. The wine list is formidable, there's Kriek by the bottle and sturdy cocktails come in at €6.50 a hit. An up-for-it and slightly older crowd keeps a steady buzz without any pressing need to be the next best thing in town. On busier DJ nights (*see p320*), a cool lounge operates upstairs.

Le Jemmapes

82 quai de Jemmapes, 10th (01.40.40.02.35). Mᵒ Jacques Bonsergent or République. **Open** 11am-2am daily. **No credit cards. Map** p404 L4 ⑤①
A destination canalside café and a fine reason to join the lazy throng along the St-Martin embankment. In fine weather, this leads to a bottleneck of content couples mini-picnicking on the waterfront, while others brunch on the narrow bar terrace, where weekend tables are at a premium. Inside is small and arty, but not so much so it puts you off – not with Chimay Bleue and Duval available, anyway. Rare flavoured vodkas are another speciality – there's a slight Polish touch to the extensive lunchtime menu – but

5th Bar. *See p228.*

location is the deciding factor here. Visit during the week for a more boho crowd than the somewhat self-satisfied contingent of bric-a-brac browsers.

La Maizon

123 rue Oberkampf, 11th (01.58.30.62.12). M°
Ménilmontant. **Open** 4pm-2am Mon-Thur, Sun; 4pm-6am Fri, Sat. **Credit** AmEx, MC, V. **Map** p405 N5 🄲
The best DJ bar on the Oberkampf strip – although inexplicably less frequented than the cod salsa and pseudo Brazilian bars you have to pass to get here. This means you're guaranteed a cosy spot, if not by the bar, then certainly at a table in the back of the narrow room, fringed with Arabic touches. Its location opposite madly popular late-night music venue Cithéa helps, but stick around here for Maes on draught, Gin Fizz and other long drinks at €7 and thumping but imaginative sounds. Actually, that might be a drawback, as conversation gets tricky once the DJ hits his groove approaching dawn of a Saturday – but hey, who needs talk at that time?

Le Mange Disque

58 rue de la Fontaine, 11th (01.58.30.87.07/
www.mangedisque.fr). M° Goncourt. **Open** 5pm-2am Tue-Sat. Closed Aug. **No credit cards.**
Map p405 M4 🄳
This remarkably cool bar shows just what you can do with a little art, a fine taste in music, the most mundane of furniture and the right connections. If you want to launch a CD, introduce a DJ or throw any kind of bash where word of mouth counts, do it here. There are other factors, of course. Savvy owner Hubert has brought in choice wines from little-known producers in South-west France but only charges €2-€3 a glass for them. Likewise, the small-ish snacks at under €10. Stacks of vinyl are left out for browsing – is there anything more satisfying than browsing through vinyl? – and with the constant traffic of events and launches, no two evenings are the same. A good name to drop.

La Mercerie

98 rue Oberkampf, 11th (01.43.38.81.30). M°
Parmentier. **Open** 7pm-2am daily. **Credit** MC, V.
Map p405 N5 🄴
Opposite the landmark Charbon (*see p226*) and infinitely more grungy, the spacious Mercerie does indeed look like a haberdasher's – one that's been stripped out and then scuffed by the collective feet of boho Paris. Bare walls – bare everything, in fact – allow room for the usual Oberkampf shenanigans of death-wish drinking against a loud, eclectic musical backdrop. A DJ programme is lipsticked on to the back-bar mirror. Happy hour stretches to 9pm, so you can cane the house vodkas (apricot, mango, honey) and still have enough euros to finish the job after dusk. The back area, with its tea lights, provides intimacy if that's where the evening takes you.

Au P'tit Garage

63 rue Jean-Pierre-Timbaud, 11th (01.48.07.08.12).
M° Parmentier. **Open** 6pm-2am daily. **Credit** AmEx, MC, V. **Map** p405 M4 🄵

As sweetly tuned as Chuck Berry's cherry-red '53, this quite marvellous rock 'n' roll bar is the pick of the bunch on rue J-P-T. Not that the owners have fitted it with Americana or waitresses on rollerskates; the Garage is as rough and ready as the real car-fit business a few doors down the road. The stuffing bursts out of the bar stools and skip-salvage chairs accompany wobbly tables of ill-matched colours; an old fridge and radiogram are tucked away in the back. But while motorcyclists talk over the Andrews Sisters and black-palmed mechanics clutch the first cold one of the day, music-savvy Frenchettes giggle and gossip, lending the place an understated sass. El Toro spins Fonz-era faves at his Keep On Rockin' residency and you'll find flyers for similar events in town. *See also p220* **Seventh heaven**. **Photo** *p224.*

Rosso

4bis rue Neuve Popincourt, 11th (01.49.29.06.36).
M° Parmentier. **Open** 6pm-2am daily. **Credit** MC, V.
Map p405 M5 🄶
Fans of the nearby Zéro Zéro (*see p225*) take note: boss Ben's new venture, Rosso, is just as funky, equally snug and somewhat less religious. More arty, too: as well as having kitsch cherub designs on the wallpaper and a perspective-wobbling, iconic red square motif, Rosso is a regular host of exhibition openings and attracts a more bohemian – rather than no-nonsense hedonistic – clientele. Not that you can't get trashed. Among the dozen or so cocktails (€6.50) are the Rosso (vodka, Triple Sec and framboise) and Daiquiris in several fruit flavours, while draught Kilkenny and Hoegaarden complement the Carlsberg Special on tap. Happy hour (6-8pm) and a €5 cocktail *du jour* encourage dalliance at this quiet, off-Oberkampf location.

Le Sainte Marthe

32 rue Ste-Marthe, 10th (01.44.84.36.96). M°
Coloniel Fabien or Belleville. **Open** 11am-2am daily.
No credit cards. Map p405 M3 🄷
The most accommodating bar on a narrow street lined with boho dives and ethnic eateries, this little gem is also the most culinary of the drinking options. It may not have the sunlit terrace of Le Panier next door, but the SM does have a cool interior and wantonly shabby clientele, who create a mildly louche atmosphere of loose, arty talk and easy pick-ups. Poets and priapic fiftysomethings on the pull prop up the half-moon bar counter, but don't let that put you off – this is a class-A bar in a class-A bar zone.

The Latin Quarter & 13th

5th Bar

62 rue Mouffetard, 5th (01.43.37.09.09). M° Place
Monge. **Open** 5pm-2am Mon-Thur, Sun; 4pm-3am Fri, Sat. **Credit** MC, V. **Map** p408 J8 🄸
The 5th is perhaps the most intimate of the numerous expat pubs of Paris. Tucked away in quaint, hilly rue Mouffetard, the 5th is easily overlooked but has been here for five years or more. Small, dark and

squeezed into two floors, it boasts Sky Sports, a pool table at the back and pub-type bonhomie and banquettes downstairs. A mounted, illuminated bicycle nods towards the zany, but staff and punters here are mainstream residents from over the Channel or the Atlantic, happy to pay a little extra for the convenience of discussing familiar topics with their own kind. Prices for the standard cocktails rise as the evening progresses. There's nothing by way of all-day breakfasts or big roasts, but this lack of pretend pub professionalism is part of the attraction. **Photo** *p227*.

Le Crocodile

6 rue Royer-Collard, 5th (01.43.54.32.37). RER Luxembourg. **Open** 10pm-late Mon-Sat. Closed Aug. **Credit** MC, V. **Map** p410 J8 ⑤

Ignore the apparently boarded-up windows for a cocktail at Le Crocodile – if you're here late, it's open. Young, friendly regulars line the sides of this small, narrow bar and try to decide on a drink: not easy, given the length and complexity of the cocktail list. It trots out 311 choices (the number increases on a yearly basis), each one more potent than the last. Pen and paper are provided to note your decision; the pen comes in handy for point-and-choose decisions when it all gets hazy. Given the €6-per-cocktail happy hour (Mon-Thur before midnight; €9 other times), this can be patient. We think we can recommend an *accroche-coeur*, a supremely 1970s mix of champagne and Goldschläger, served with extra gold leaf; after that, we had to start pointing.

Le Pantalon

7 rue Royer-Collard, 5th (no phone). RER Luxembourg. **Open** 5.30pm-2am Mon-Sat. **No credit cards. Map** p410 J8 ⑥

Mad as a bag of frogs, Le Pantalon is a local café that seems familiar yet utterly surreal. It has the standard fixtures and fittings, including the old soaks at the bar – plus a strange vacuum-cleaner sculpture, disco-light toilets and the world's most prosaic proposal of marriage. Offbeat decor aside, the regulars and staff are enough to tip the balance firmly into eccentricity. Friendly and very funny French grown-ups and foreign students chat in a mishmash of languages; happy hours are generous, but drinks are always cheap enough to make you tipsy without the worry of a cash hangover.

Le Piano Vache

8 rue Laplace, 5th (01.46.33.75.03/www.lepiano vache.com). M° Maubert Mutualité. **Open** noon-2am Mon-Fri; 9pm-2am Sat, Sun. **Credit** AmEx, MC, V. **Map** p410 J8 ⑥

A Left Bank drinking haunt for many a decade, this has all the hallmarks of what any beer-stained, smoky hovel should be: dark, cramped, filled with a hardcore drinker/student clientele, walls covered four times over with posters and indeterminate pub grime, and the hits of alternative 1980s synth-pop on repeat on the stereo. This is what the French mean by grunge, bless them. Note that weekday opening hours switch to evenings out of term-time.

Rhubarb

18 rue Laplace, 5th (01.43.25.35.03). M° Maubert Mutualité. **Open** 5pm-2am daily. **Credit** MC, V. **Map** p410 J8 ⑥

A wonderful little spot near Mouffetard, Rhubarb is the latest offering from the crew that put the Fu Bar (in the 6th) on the map. The cocktails here are excellent, and while Sean's famous Apple Martini is still sublime, we think we might plump for his watermelon concoction or Chocolate Martini in future. A relaxed vibe abounds and a mixed crowd mingle happily at the bar. The cellar is all crumbling pale stone and high ceilings, and while a quiet corner is ideal seduction territory, the space works equally well for gaggles of mates on a big night out.

St-Germain-des-Prés & Odéon

Alcazar

62 rue Mazarine, 6th (01.53.10.19.99/www.alcazar.fr). M° Odéon. **Open** 7pm-2am daily. **Credit** AmEx, DC, MC, V. **Map** p410 H7 ⑥

It would be fair to assume that the Alcazar would be over by now, hip bars tending to fade once their first flush of youth is gone. But the 'AZ bar' still somehow pulls it off. The sleek velvet banquettes, polished aluminium bar and the vantage point over the oh-so-trendy restaurant (*see p207*) and into the private dining room all help, of course, but really this place is worth paying for because it's posh without being poncey – and the drinks are great. The Monday night easy-listening sessions are *un must* in local hip circles, and the weekend aperitif crowd still shows no sign of defecting.

Le Bar

27 rue de Condé, 6th (01.43.29.06.61). M° Odéon. **Open** 8pm-late Mon-Sat. **No credit cards. Map** p410 H7 ⑥

Le Bar is one of those strange little places that you only ever visit when it's very, very late and you're very, very drunk. It'll all come back to you: how it's almost completely pitch black, has a shrine-type affair at the back of the bar and gravel on the floor; and how everyone talks in whispers – and the drinks are very strong. A couple of words of warning about this place: once you've been here, you'll find yourself strangely drawn back at inappropriate times when you really should be going home to bed, and at least one member of the party will fall asleep on the comfy black leather banquettes. There's a weird echo effect in the corridor down to the toilet, so if Le Bar is your last chance to pull before the sun comes up, don't discuss your strategy too loudly.

Le Bar Dix

10 rue de l'Odéon, 6th (01.43.26.66.83). M° Odéon. **Open** 6pm-2am daily. **No credit cards. Map** p410 H7 ⑥

It's been here forever, this homely cavern of a bar, certainly longer than the brash Irish Horse's Tavern at one end of the street. Generations of students have glugged back jugs of home-made sangria while

Eat, Drink, Shop

Le Rostand.

squeezed into the cramped, twilit upper bar, tattily authentic with its Jacques Brel record sleeves, Yves Montand handbills and pre-war light fittings. The jukebox sadly no longer runs on vinyl, but the CDs weep suitably nostalgic pop nectar. Spelunkers and hopeless romantics negotiate the hazardous stone staircase for the cellar bar, with its candlelight and century-old advertising murals. Someone slap a preservation plaque on this place, please.

Le Bar du Marché

75 rue de Seine, 6th (01.43.26.55.15). M° Mabillon or Odéon. **Open** 8am-2am daily. **Credit** MC, V. **Map** p410 H7 ⑥⑥
The market in question is the Cours des Halles, the bar a convivial corner café opening out on to a pleasing blur of St-Germain-des-Prés bustle. It's all wonderfully simple, with easy dishes like a ham omelette or plate of herring in the €7 range, half-decent Brouilly or Muscadet at €4-€5 a glass, a few retro posters – Campari, Piaf, the Frères Jacques – and the regular passing of a beret-topped waiter. It couldn't be anywhere else in the world. Locals easily outnumber the tourists, though, the long afternoons underlining Rod Stewart's unusually astute observation that Paris gives you the impression that no one is ever working. Recommended.

Café de Flore

172 bd St-Germain, 6th (01.45.48.55.26/www.cafe-de-flore.com). M° St-Germain-des-Prés. **Open** 7.30am-1.30am daily. **Credit** AmEx, DC, MC, V. **Map** p410 H7 ⑥⑦
Bourgeois locals crowd the terrace tables at lunch, eating club sandwiches with knives and forks, as anxious waiters frown at couples with pushchairs or single diners occupying tables for four. This historic café, former HQ of the Lost Generation intelligentsia, attracts many tourists who eye passers-by hopefully. And, yes, celebs have been known to alight here from time to time. But a *café crème* is €4.60, a Perrier €5 and the omelettes and *croque-monsieurs* are best passed over for better dishes on the menu (€15-€25). Upstairs, play readings are held on Mondays and philosophy discussions on the first Wednesday of the month, both at 8pm, in English.

Les Deux Magots

6 pl St-Germain-des-Prés, 6th (01.45.48.55.25/ www.lesdeuxmagots.com). M° St-Germain-des-Prés. **Open** 7.30am-1am daily. Closed 1wk Jan. **Credit** AmEx, DC, MC, V. **Map** p410 H7 ⑥⑧
Stand outside here too long and be prepared to photograph visitors wanting proof of their encounter with French philosophy. The former haunt of Sartre, de Beauvoir et al now draws a less pensive crowd that can be all too '*m'as-tu vu*', particularly on weekends when anglophone and Anglophile hordes pack the terrace. The hot chocolate is still good (and the only item served in generous portions) – but, like everything else, it's pricey. Visit on a weekday afternoon when the editors return, manuscripts in hand, to the inside tables, leaving enough elbow room to engage in some serious discussion.

Au Petit Suisse

16 rue de Vaugirard, 6th (01.43.26.03.81). M° Odéon. **Open** 7am-midnight Mon-Sat; 7am-10.30pm Sun. **Credit** DC, MC, V. **Map** p410 H7 ⑥⑨
Named after Marie de Médicis' Swiss Guards, the compact Au Petit Suisse has an enviable location next to the Jardin du Luxembourg and so pulls in a

so brews you'll find the best of Belgium, but it's the choice of French beers that really sets it apart. Don't miss the house special – L'Epi, brewed in three different versions: Blond (100% barley), Blanc (oats) and Noir (buckwheat) – or Corsican Pietra on tap.

Montparnasse

Le Select
99 bd de Montparnasse, 6th (01.42.22.65.27).
M° Vavin. **Open** 7am-2am Mon-Thur, Sun; 7am-4am Fri, Sat. **Credit** MC, V. **Map** p407 G9 **72**
For a decade between the wars, the junction of boulevards Raspail and Montparnasse was the centre of the known universe. Man Ray, Cocteau and Lost Generation Americans hung out at its vast glass-fronted cafés (Le Dôme, La Coupole), socialising, snubbing and snogging. Eight decades on, Le Select is the best of these inevitable tourist traps. Sure, its pricey menu is big on historical detail but short on authenticity ('Cockney Brunch' of eggs, bacon and jam at €15), but generally Le Select holds on to its heyday with dignity. *Intello* locals hang out at the bar, spreading out the highbrow culture section as Mickey the house cat walks over the newsprint. Happy hour from 7pm makes history affordable, the cocktail and whisky list is extensive, and pleasingly it's Mickey (not Ern Hemingway) who's honoured with a prominent framed portrait.

The 7th & the 15th

Le Café du Marché
38 rue Cler, 7th (01.47.05.51.27). M° Ecole Militaire. **Open** 7am-midnight Mon-Sat; 7am-5pm Sun. **Credit** MC, V. **Map** p407 D6 **73**
This well-loved address is frequented by trendy locals, shoppers hunting down a particular type of cheese along this busy market street or tourists who've managed to make it this far from the Eiffel Tower. Le Café du Marché really is a hub of neighbourhood activity. Its *pichets* of decent house plonk go down a treat, and while it's fine just to drink here, mention must be made of the food – such as the huge house salad with lashes of foie gras and Parma ham.

Café Thoumieux
4 rue de la Comète, 7th (01.45.51.50.40/www. thoumieux.com). M° La Tour Maubourg. **Open** noon-2am Mon-Fri; 5pm-2am Sat. Closed 3wks Aug. **Credit** AmEx, MC, V. **Map** p407 E6 **74**
The little brother to vintage bistro Thoumieux is a laid-back destination for cocktails, tapas or big-screen sport. Banquettes snake around the room and spiky Aztec-pattern lamps send light flickering up the walls and the faces of pretty young locals who have made this place their own. The flavoured vodkas are delicious and include vanilla, caramel and banana. Don't blame them for any difficulties you might be suffering with the extra-high bar stools (the banquettes are safest) or for the sight of the monstrous, pebble-dashed sink in the toilets – it's real.

range of posh locals, au pairs escaping from their charges, and Gauloise-puffing Sorbonne students. The formal waiters excel in French snottiness, but do at least make this place all the more authentic and tourist-free. Brave the haughty stares for one of the handful of tables, order a kir with a side of sneer and lap up a genuine 6th arrondissement café experience.

Le Rostand
6 pl Edmond-Rostand, 6th (01.43.54.61.58). RER Luxembourg. **Open** 8am-2am daily. **Credit** MC, V. **Map** p410 H6 **70**
Le Rostand has a truly wonderful view of the Jardin du Luxembourg from its classy interior, decked out with oriental paintings, a long mahogany bar and wall-length mirrors. It's a terribly well-behaved place, and you should definitely consider arriving in fur or designer sunglasses if you want to fit in with the well-heeled regulars. The drinks list is lined with whiskies and cocktails, pricey but not as steep as the brasserie menu. Perfect for a civilised drink after a spin round the gardens. **Photo** *above.*

La Taverne de Nesle
32 rue Dauphine, 6th (01.43.26.38.36). M° Odéon. **Open** 6pm-4am Mon-Thur, Sun; 6pm-6am Fri, Sat. **Credit** V. **Map** p410 H6 **71**
La Taverne, a late-night staple for people who just can't go home before daylight, has four distinct drinking areas: a zinc bar at the front, a sort of Napoleonic campaign tent in the middle, a trendily lit ambient area at the back, and a dreadful 1980s disco downstairs, where girls in pearls do their best to look sexy. The separate spaces correspond to stages of drunkenness and encourage a gradual progression to the horizontal state. Among the 100 or

Eat, Drink, Shop

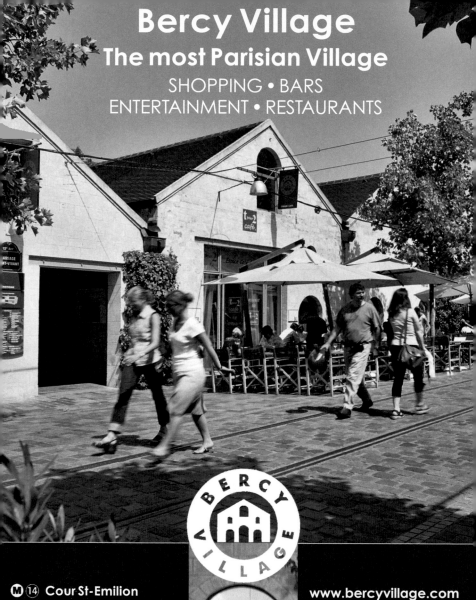

Shops & Services

From super-chic showcases to family-run *fromageries* – they're all here.

The world's fashion capital suffered a few tremors in 2005. The biggest news was the lengthy closure of esteemed department store La Samaritaine but there were other stories, too. Helmut Lang stormed out of his own *maison*, sold the remaining shares in his loss-making brand to owner Prada and then stood by as his shops were closed down worldwide – chic rue St-Honoré address included.

Elsewhere on the *mode* merry-go-round, Louis Vuitton reopened its flagship store on the Champs-Elysées after extensive renovation; and fashion darling Marc Jacobs, responsible for the triumphant revamping of the LV label, followed suit by announcing he would open the first Marc by Marc Jacobs store in central Paris at the start of 2006. The tantrums of the luxury groups and their cronies are not the only factor shaping the commercial landscape. Real Paris shopping is found in specialist boutiques, family-run food shops, outlets for artisan tradition and rustic markets barely changed in over a century (*see p259* **Forward *marché!***).

Recent years have seen the closure of many family-run *fromageries, boulangeries, charcuteries* and quirky little treasure troves. Although the chain concept is catching on quickly, the overall quality remains impressive, and almost everything, from a vintage bottle of armagnac to a single praline chocolate, is lovingly served, wrapped and presented, whatever the store. Informative discussion is still very much part of the purchasing process; and beautiful, old-style arcades – such as the galerie Vivienne or passage Jouffroy – make shopping a sightseeing pleasure as well.

Different areas have different specialities. There are clusters of antiques shops in the 7th and second-hand and rare book outlets in the 5th (a reminder of the days when there were publishing guilds there); crystal and porcelain manufacturers still dot rue de Paradis in the 10th; furniture craftsmen inhabit rue du Faubourg-St-Antoine; and the world's top jewellers can be found on place Vendôme. Street-chic and lifestyle boutiques live side by side in the Marais and around rue Etienne-Marcel, while quirky newcomers settle in Abbesses or near the Canal St-Martin. Designer labels are scattered all over the 1st, 6th and 8th; specialist enclaves include bikes and cameras on boulevard Beaumarchais.

No shopping trip would be complete without a visit to one of the city's flea markets, the only place where haggling is still *de rigueur*, and cash, not plastic, is the payment of choice.

OPENING HOURS

Shops open 10am-7pm Monday to Saturday, with specialist boutiques closing for an hour at lunch. Sunday shopping is no longer frowned upon, but is not as common as in the UK. Small corner grocery stores open late for essentials, and many family-run concerns close in August.

One-stop shops

Department stores

The revamped *grands magasins* have brought in trendy designers and luxury spaces to lure shoppers away from independent boutiques. 2005 was notable for the closure of venerable old dame La Samaritaine for at least five years. LVMH, owner since 2004, was forced to close the landmark belle-époque building after it failed to satisfy safety regulations.

For the trendier one-stop 'concept stores', *see p256* **High concept**.

BHV (Bazar de l'Hôtel de Ville)

52-64 rue de Rivoli, 4th (01.42.74.90.00/DIY hire 01.42.74.97.23/www.bhv.fr). M° Hôtel de Ville. **Open** 9.30am-7.30pm Mon, Tue, Thur-Sat; 9.30am-9pm Wed. **Credit** AmEx, MC, V. **Map** p408 J6.
DIY buffs spend hours in this hardware heaven, drooling over hinges, screws, nuts and bolts in the basement or dithering over paint colours upstairs; there's even a Bricolage Café, with internet access. Upper floors of the store have a good range of men's outdoor wear, women's underwear, upmarket bed-linen, toys, books, household appliances – and large space devoted to every type of storage utility.

Le Bon Marché

24 rue de Sèvres, 7th (01.44.39.80.00/www.bon marche.fr). M° Sèvres Babylone. **Open** 9.30am-7pm Mon-Wed, Fri; 10am-9pm Thur; 9.30am-8pm Sat. **Credit** AmEx, DC, MC, V. **Map** p407 G7.
The capital's oldest department store (it opened in 1848) is also its most swish and user-friendly, thanks in large part to an extensive redesign by LVMH. The prestigious Balthazar men's section offers a cluster of designer boutiques, while the Théâtre de la Beauté provides a comfort zone for women. Seven

luxury boutiques, occupied by Dior and Chanel among others, take pride of place on the ground floor; escalators designed by Andrée Putman take you up to the fashion floor, which has a fabulous selection of global designer labels, from Martin Margiela and Marni to APC and Isabel Marant. The neighbouring Grande Epicerie luxury food hall (01.44.39.81.00, www.lagrandeepicerie.fr, 8.30am-9pm Mon-Sat) contains its own antiques gallery, café and restaurant.

Galeries Lafayette

40 bd Haussmann, 9th (01.42.82.34.56/ fashion shows 01.42.82.30.25/fashion advice 01.42.82.35.50/www.galerieslafayette.com). M° Chaussée d'Antin La Fayette/RER Auber. **Open** 9.30am-7.30pm Mon-Wed, Fri, Sat; 9.30am-9pm Thur. **Credit** AmEx, DC, MC, V. **Map** p403 H3.

This department store has revamped its fashion, beauty and accessories sections, and, in hot competition with Printemps (*see below*), opened a lingerie department on the third floor. On the first, Le Labo and Trend have introduced progressive international creators, while more than 90 established designers are spread over the rest of the first and second floors. There are five fashion and beauty consultants to guide you through the sartorial maze, and the men's fashion space on the third floor of Lafayette Homme is a must, with its natty designer corners and 'Club' area with net access. On the first floor, Lafayette Gourmet has exotic and high-end foods galore, and the second-biggest wine cellar in Paris. The exquisite domed ceiling in the main shop is eminently photogenic, and there's a rooftop café. On the other side of boulevard Haussmann, the old M&S building has become Lafayette Maison (www.lafayettemaison.com), with five floors of design for the home.

Printemps

64 bd Haussmann, 9th (01.42.82.50.00/www. printemps.com). M° Havre Caumartin/RER Auber. **Open** 9.35am-7pm Mon-Wed, Fri, Sat; 9.30am-10pm Thur. **Credit** AmEx, DC, MC, V. **Map** p403 G3.

Printemps is the home of superlatives: the largest shoe department in Paris is on the men's fifth floor, and – wait for it – the biggest beauty department in the world opened here in 2003, with some 200 brands in stock. The lingerie department is the stuff of fantasy, too, selling luxury brands such as Erès and far-out frillies from Gaultier and Pucci. In all, there are six floors of fashion in both the men's and women's stores. On the second floor of Printemps de la Mode, French designers APC and Zadig et Voltaire sit side by side with Dolce e Gabbana and Moschino; Miss Code, on the fifth floor, targets the teen miss and offers a huge selection of jeans and sportswear. The Printemps de la Maison store, along with home decoration and furnishings, contains the more conceptual 'function floor', where saucepans and coffee machines are neatly organised on steel shelving. The stylish ninth-floor terrace restaurant sports an art nouveau cupola. **Photo** *right*.

Tati

4 bd de Rochechouart, 18th (01.55.29.52.50/ www.tati.fr). M° Barbès Rochechouart. **Open** 10am-7pm Mon-Sat. **Credit** MC, V. **Map** p404 J2.

Expect to find anything from T-shirts to wedding dresses, as well as bargain children's clothes and household goods at this discount heaven. It's unbeatably cheap, but don't expect high quality.

Other locations: Centre Commercial Italie 2, 30 av d'Italie, 13th (01.53.80.97.70); Galerie Gaîté Montparnasse, 68 av du Maine, 14th (01.56.80.06.80); 76 av de Clichy, 17th (01.58.22.28.90).

Shopping centres

Drugstore Publicis

133 av des Champs-Elysées, 8th (01.44.43.79.00/ www.publicisdrugstore.com). M° Charles de Gaulle Etoile. **Open** 8am-2am Mon-Fri; 10am-2am Sat, Sun. **Credit** MC, V. **Map** p402 D4.

A 1960s legend for the likes of Jacques Dutronc and Fernand Raynaud, the landmark Drugstore Publicis was a convenient rendezvous point for gilded youth in the days when everything closed on Sundays. After a long renovation completed in 2004, the 1970s building has been clad with desultory neon swirls by American architect Michele Saee, and a carbuncular glass-and-steel café oozes on to the pavement. On the ground floor are a newsagent, pharmacy, bookshop and upmarket deli full of quality olive oils and elegant biscuits; a video screen reminds you that Publicis is an advertising agency. The basement is a macho take on Colette (*see p256* **High concept**), keeping the selected design items (some exclusive) and lifestyle mags, but replacing high fashion with fine wines (all New World) and a smart cigar cellar. **Photo** *p237*.

La Galerie du Carrousel du Louvre

99 rue de Rivoli, 1st (01.43.16.47.10/www. lecarrouseldulouvre.com). M° Palais Royal Musée du Louvre. **Open** 10am-8pm daily. **Credit** AmEx, MC, V. **Map** p408 J6.

Paris doesn't have many shopping malls, but this massive underground centre – open every day of the year – surely qualifies. It's home to more than 35 shops: big-name chains such as Virgin, Esprit, Sephora, Nature et Découvertes, L'Occitane, Agatha, Bodum and Périgot, all vying for your attention and your cash. It's great for last-minute gifts.

Beauty

Cosmetics

L'Artisan Parfumeur

24 bd Raspail, 7th (01.42.22.23.32). M° Rue du Bac. **Open** 10.30am-7pm Mon-Sat. **Credit** AmEx, DC, MC, V. **Map** p407 G7.

Among scented candles, potpourri and charms, you'll find the best vanilla perfume Paris can offer – Mûres et Musc, a bestseller for over 20 years.

Printemps. *See p234*.

Roger Vivier. *See p258.*

New good ol' **Drugstore Publicis**. *See p234.*

By Terry

*36 galerie Véro-Dodat, 1st (01.44.76.00.76/www.
byterry.com). M° Palais Royal Musée du Louvre.*
Open 10.30am-7pm Mon-Sat. **Credit** AmEx, MC, V.
Map p404 H5.
Terry de Gunzburg, who earned her reputation at
Yves Saint Laurent, offers made-to-measure 'haute
couleur' make-up, by skilled chemists and colourists
combining high-tech treatments and handmade pre-
cision. There's prêt-à-porter, too.
Other locations: 1 rue Jacob, 6th (01.46.34.00.36);
10 av Victor-Hugo, 16th (01.55.73.00.73).

Détaille 1905

*10 rue St-Lazare, 9th (01.48.78.68.50/www.detaille.
com). M° Notre-Dame-de-Lorette.* **Open** 3-7pm Mon;
10am-1.30pm, 3-7pm Tue-Sat. **Credit** MC, V. **Map**
p403 H3.
Step back in time at this shop, opened, as the name
suggests, in 1905 by the war artist Edouard Détaille
shortly before his death. Six fragrances (three for
men and three for women) are still being made from
century-old recipes.

Editions de Parfums Frédéric Malle

*37 rue de Grenelle, 7th (01.42.22.77.22/www.
editionsdeparfums.com). M° Rue du Bac or St-
Sulpice.* **Open** 1-7pm Mon; 11am-7pm Tue-Sat.
Credit AmEx, DC, MC, V. **Map** p407 F6.
Olfactory minimalism: choose from a mere eight per-
fumes made by Frédéric Malle, former consultant to
Chaumet, Hermès and Lacroix.

Galerie Noémie

*92 av des Champs-Elysées, 8th (01.44.76.06.26/
www.galerienoemie.com). M° George V.* **Open** 11am-
7pm Mon-Thur; 11am-9pm Fri, Sat. **Credit** AmEx,
DC, MC, V. **Map** p404 J5.
You can tell boutique owner Noémie is a painter by
the way all the make-up is set out in palettes, all very
artful indeed. Little pots of gloss (starting from a reasonable €7.50) in myriad colours triple as lip gloss,
eyeshadow or blusher. Now with a couple of stores
in the commercial end of town and one out in the
suburbs, Noémie has enough of a reputation to offer
seasonal creations to a loyal following.
Other locations: Galeries Lafayette, 40 bd
Haussmann, 9th (01.42.82.34.56).

The best Late shops

City of the night? Perhaps surprisingly, not
when it comes to shopping. The following
make up a large proportion of the few
places in Paris whose opening hours
almost keep up with yours.

Black Block
This spot sells kooky Japanese gadgets
and original art works until midnight, every
day except Monday. *See p265.*

Drugstore Publicis
The Paris version of a mall sells stylish last-
minute gifts until 2am every day. *See p234.*

La Hune
Buying reading matter gets no sexier than
11pm purchases of sleek art books or
existential tomes at this bookish St-
Germain beacon. *See p243.*

Librairie Flammarion
An outstanding selection of art books and
children's titles until 10pm, every day
except Tuesday. *See p243.*

Printemps
Most department stores stay open late on
Thursday; here until 10pm you can delve
into fantasy lingerie and the world's biggest
beauty department. *See p234.*

Sephora
For emergency repairs, this prominent
make-up and perfume emporium is open
until midnight all week. *See p239.*

Virgin Megastore
Two mega branches of this CD and DVD
bazaar are open until midnight, seven days
a week. *See p244.*

Eat, Drink, Shop

Guerlain

68 av des Champs-Elysées, 8th (01.45.62.52.57/ www.guerlain.com). M° Franklin D. Roosevelt. **Open** 10.30am-8pm Mon-Sat; 3-7pm Sun. **Credit** AmEx, DC, MC, V. **Map** p403 E4.

This bijou boutique harks back the golden age of the Champs-Elysées. Although the family sold to LVMH years ago, the brand still produces fine creations and old faves like Samsara, Mitsouko and L'Heure Bleue.

Iunx

48-50 rue de l'Université, 7th (01.45.44.50.14/www. iunx.com). M° Rue du Bac. **Open** 10.30am-7pm Mon-Sat. **Credit** AmEx, MC, V. **Map** p407 G6.

Invisible from the street, this minimal, mysterious space reinvents the way we choose and buy perfume. Iunx is Greek for 'seduction by scent', and this futuristic temple to fragrance sells its own delicious lines of perfumes, gels and candles. Sniff out the Eau Interdite, a curious, absinthe-scented eau de cologne.

L'Occitane

55 rue St-Louis-en-l'Ile, 4th (01.40.46.81.71/ www.loccitane.com). M° Pont Marie. **Open** 11am-7pm Mon; 10am-7pm Tue-Fri; 10am-8pm Sat, Sun. **Credit** AmEx, DC, MC, V. **Map** p411 K7.

The many branches of this popular Provençal chain proffer natural beauty products in neat packaging. Soap rules, along with essential oils and perfumes. **Other locations**: throughout the city.

Salons du Palais-Royal Shiseido

Jardins du Palais-Royal, 142 galerie de Valois, 1st (01.49.27.09.09/www.salons-shiseido.com). M° Palais Royal Musée du Louvre. **Open** 10am-7pm Mon-Sat. **Credit** AmEx, DC, MC, V. **Map** p403 H5.

Under the arcades of the Palais-Royal is this luxury perfume laboratory where Shiseido's perfumer Serge Lutens practises his aromatic arts. Lutens, a former photographer at Paris Vogue and artistic director of make-up at Christian Dior, is a maestro of rare taste.

Shopping by area

Châtelet & Les Halles

The **Forum des Halles** shopping centre is the commercial and transport centre of Paris. In the streets fanning out from this underground hub are good vintage clothes and streetwear shops. And along **rue de Rivoli** between the métro stations Châtelet and Louvre Rivoli you'll find the pick of high-street fashion.
adidas (Fashion, *p252*); **Agnès b** (Fashion, *p250*); **Boutique M Dia** (Fashion, *p252*); **La Bulle Kenzo** (Beauty, *p240*); **By Terry** (Beauty, *p237*); **Castelbajac Concept Store** (*p256* **High concept**); **Clery Brice** (Fashion, *p252*); **E Dehillerin** (Home, *p269*); **Ekivok** (Fashion, *p252*); **L'Esthétique de Demain** (Beauty, *p240*); **Go Sport** (Sport & games, *p269*); **Laguiole Galerie** (Home, *p269*); **Legrand Filles et Fils** (Food & drink, *p264*); **Monster Melodies** (Books, CDs, DVDs, *p244*); **Papeterie Moderne** (Gifts, *p265*); **Puma Store** (Fashion, *p253*); **Rag** (Fashion, *p253*); **Son et Image** (Fashion, *p254*); **Surface to Air** (*p256* **High concept**); **Le Vestibule** (Fashion, *p253*).

Rue Etienne-Marcel & environs

When Rei Kawakubo set up the first **Comme des Garçons** Paris boutique in this grungy area just north of Les Halles in the 1980s, she set in motion its transformation into the rebellious but chic neighbour of fashionable place des Victoires.
Barbara Bui (Fashion, *p251*); **Diesel** (Fashion, *p251*); **Et Vous** (Fashion, *p251*); **Jean-Paul Gaultier** (Fashion, *p248*); **Kabuki Femme** (Fashion, *p246*); **Kanabeach** (Fashion, *p252*); **Kiliwatch** (Fashion, *p252*); **Kokon To Zai** (Fashion, *p246*); **Mandarina Duck** (Fashion, *p258*); **Marithé et François Girbaud** (Fashion, *p251*); **Patrick Cox** (Fashion, *p258*); **Royal Cheese** (Fashion, *p253*); **Yohji Yamamoto** (Fashion, *p249*).

Rue St-Honoré & environs

The poshest part of the 1st, hugging the Louvre, this area spreads out from rue St-Honoré, and encompasses glamorous, diamond-studded place Vendôme. The success of concept store **Colette** has seen a recent influx of new boutiques setting up on and off rue St-Honoré.
Alice Cadolle (Fashion, *p254*); **American Apparel** (Fashion, *p250*); **Astier de Villatte** (Home, *p267*); **Bali Barret** (Fashion, *p250*); **Boucheron** (Fashion, *p257*); **Cabane de Zucca** (Fashion, *p247*); **Chanel** (Fashion, *p247*); **Chanel Joaillerie** (Fashion, *p257*); **Christian Louboutin** (Fashion, *p257*); **Colette** (*p256* **High concept**); **Costume National** (Fashion, *p247*); **Didier Ludot** (Fashion, *p253*); **Dior Joaillerie** (Fashion, *p257*); **Erès** (Fashion, *p254*); **Fauchon** (Food & drink, *p263*); **Fifi Chachnil** (Fashion, *p254*); **La Galerie du Carrousel du Louvre** (One-stop shops, *p234*); **Galignani** (Books, CDs, DVDs, *p242*); **Hédiard** (Food & drink, *p263*); **Institut Payot** (Beauty, *p241*); **John Galliano** (Fashion, *p248*); **Kioko** (Food & drink, *p262*); **Lavinia** (Food & drink, *p264*); **Louvre des Antiquaires** (Home, *p266*); **Madelios**

Bottles of his concoctions – 'Tubéreuse Criminelle', 'Rahat Loukoum' and 'Ambre Sultan' – can be sampled by visitors to this attractive wood-and-marble space. Many are exclusive to the Salons; prices start at around €100.

Sephora

70 av des Champs-Elysées, 8th (01.53.93.22.50/ www.sephora.fr). M° Franklin D. Roosevelt. **Open** 10am-midnight daily. **Credit** AmEx, DC, MC, V. **Map** p403 E4.
The flagship of the cosmetic supermarket chain houses 12,000 French and foreign brands of scent and slap. Sephora Blanc (14 cour St-Emilion, 12th, 01.40.02.97.79) features beauty products in a blindingly minimalist interior.
Other locations: Carrousel du Louvre, 1st (01.42.44.27.47); Forum des Halles, 1st (01.40.13.72.25); 75 rue de Rivoli, 1st (01.40.13.16.50); 21-23 bd Haussmann (01.53.24.99.65).

Salons & spas

Anne Sémonin

Le Bristol, 108 rue du Fbg-St-Honoré, 8th (01.42.66.24.22/www.lebristolparis.com). M° Miromesnil or Champs Elysées Clemenceau. **Open** 10.30am-7pm Mon-Sat. **Credit** AmEx, DC, MC, V. **Map** p403 E3.
Facials are the thing here, delicious ones with basil, lavender, lemongrass, ginger and plant essences that smell and feel so good you'll have to fight the urge to lick them off. Anne Sémonin has an impressively international selection of massage styles, too: Thai, Shiatsu, Korean, Ayurvedic… And there's the reflexologist who can study your feet to see how everything is holding up. Body treatments here cost from €70 to €210. Her renowned seaweed skin-care products and essential oils are also available at the hotel and other high-end outlets.

(Fashion, *p251*); **La Maison de la Truffe** (Food & drink, *p263*); **La Maison du Whisky** (Food & drink, *p264*); **Maria Luisa** (Fashion, *p246*); **Martin Margiela** (Fashion, *p249*); **Au Nain Bleu** (Children, *p246*); **Philippe Model** (Fashion, *p255*); **Pierre Hardy** (Fashion, *p258*); **Rodolphe Menudier** (Fashion, *p258*); **Salons du Palais-Royal Shiseido** (Beauty, *p238*); **Toni & Guy** (Beauty, *p241*); **Torréfacteur Verlet** (Food & drink, *p263*); **Van Cleef & Arpels** (Fashion, *p257*); **WH Smith** (Books, CDs, DVDs, *p244*); **Yoba** (Fashion, *p255*).

Rue du Fbg-St-Honoré & the Champs-Elysées

When St-Honoré crosses into the 8th and becomes **rue du Faubourg-St-Honoré**, it takes on an air of exclusivity. This neighbourhood encompasses the gorgeous shops around **Madeleine**, the famous A-grade fashion strip of **avenue Montaigne**, as well as the brash and buzzing **Champs-Elysées**.
Alléosse (Food & drink, *p260*); **Anne Sémonin** (Beauty, *p239*); **Balenciaga** (Fashion, *p247*); **Black Block** (Fashion, *p265*); **Les Caves Taillevent** (Food & drink, *p264*); **CFOC** (Home, *p268*); **Christian Dior** (Fashion, *p247*); **Comme des Garçons** (Fashion, *p247*); **Décathlon** (Sport & games, *p269*); **Drugstore Publicis** (One-stop shops, *p234*); **Equistable** (Sport & games, *p269*); **Etam** (Fashion, *p254*); **La Flûte de Pan** (Books, CDs, DVDs, *p242*); **Fnac** (Books, CDs, DVDs, *p244*); **Galérie Noémie** (Beauty, *p237*); **Guerlain**

(Beauty, *p238*); **Hermès** (Fashion, *p248*); **Institut Lancôme** (Beauty, *p241*); **Jabugo Ibérico & Co** (Food & drink, *p262*); **Loft Design by** (Fashion, *p251*); **Louis Vuitton** (Fashion, *p249*); **La Maison du Chocolat** (Food & drink, *p261*); **Marni** (Fashion, *p249*); **Monceau Fleurs** (Gifts, *p265*); **Petrossian** (Food & drink, *p262*); **Prada** (Fashion, *p249*); **Roger Vivier** (Fashion, *p258*); **Sephora** (Beauty, *p239*); **Virgin Megastore** (Books, CDs, DVDs, *p244*).

Opéra & Grands Boulevards

The department stores provide the commercial heartbeat to this busy *quartier*.
Brentano's (Books, CDs, DVDs, *p242*); **Cartier** (Fashion, *p257*); **Les Caves Augé** (Food & drink, *p264*); **Citadium** (Sport & games, *p269*); **Du Pareil au Même** (Children, *p244*); **Galeries Lafayette** (One-stop shops, *p234*); **Jamin Puech** (Fashion, *p258*); **Lafont** (Fashion, *p255*); **Pa Design** (Gifts, *p265*); **Printemps** (One-stop shops, *p234*); **René Pierre** (Sports & games, *p269*); **Velan** (Food & drink, *p262*); **Village Joué Club** (Children, *p246*).

Montmartre

On the winding streets around Sacré-Coeur are clustered many funky, independent designers. From Barbès Rochechouart métro station, **bd de Rochechouart** is one elongated strip of discount shops.
Arnaud Delmontel (Food & drink, *p260*); **Arnaud Lahrer** (Food & drink, *p262*); **Base One** (Fashion, *p246*); **Detaille 1905** (Beauty,

▶

Les Bains du Marais

*31-33 rue des Blancs-Manteaux, 4th (01.44.61.02.02/
www.lesbainsdumarais.com). M° St-Paul.* **Open** *Men*
11am-11pm Thur; 10am-8pm Fri. *Women* 11am-8pm
Mon; 11am-11pm Tue; 10am-7pm Wed. *Mixed* 10am-
8pm Sat; 11am-7pm Sun. Closed Aug. **Credit** AmEx,
MC, V. **Map** p411 K6.
This chic hammam and spa mixes modern and traditional (lounging beds and mint tea). Facials, waxing and essential oil massages are also available.
The hammam only costs €30; a massage is €30.

La Bulle Kenzo

*1 rue du Pont-Neuf, 1st (01.73.04.20.04/www.labulle
kenzo.com). M° Pont Neuf.* **Open** 10am-8pm Mon-
Sat. **Credit** AmEx, DC, MC, V. **Map** p408 J6.
Kenzo's flagship store houses a chic beauty salon of
high concept. Their two massage rooms offer two
different vibes: Pétillante has a disco ball, while the
Japanese Zen cocoon provides calmer pleasures.

L'Esthétique de Demain

*15 rue de la Grande-Truanderie, 1st (01.40.26.53.10).
M° Châtelet or Etienne Marcel.* **Open** 2-7pm Mon;
10am-7pm Tue-Sat. **Credit** MC, V. **Map** p404 J5.
If you're just looking to get the job done without a
lot of hoopla, this low-key, low-cost salon specialising in hair removal is for you. Waxing for men and
women starts at €8, facials from €30.

Hammam de la Grande Mosquée

*1 pl du Puits-de-l'Ermite, 5th (01.43.31.18.14).
M° Censier Daubenton.* **Open** *Men* 2-9pm Tue; 10am-
9pm Sun. *Women* 10am-9pm Mon, Wed, Sat; 2-9pm
Fri. **Credit** MC, V. **Map** p408 K9.
To the sound of soft voices and Arabic music, clients
are steamed, scrubbed and massaged in this 1920s
mosque. Follow your session with a *gommage* (exfoliation with a rough mitt), then a massage. The hammam is €15, *gommage* €10 and massage €10.

▶ # Shopping by area
(continued)

p237); **Espace Lab 101** (*p256* **High concept**);
Gaspard de la Butte (Children, *p245*); **La
Grande Récré** (Children, *p246*); **Spree** (*p256*
High concept); **Tati** (One-stop shops, *p234*);
Wochdom (Fashion, *p254*).

Canal St-Martin

This mini *quartier* provides the perfect canal-
side esplanade for relaxed browsing.
Antoine et Lili (Fashion, *p250*); **Artazart**
(Books, CDs, DVDs, *p242*).

Bastille

Traditionally home to fine furniture craftsmen,
rue du Fbg-St-Antoine and nearby **rue de
Charonne** and **rue Keller** are peppered with
new designer fashion and furniture shops.
Allicante (Food & drink, *p262*); **L'Autre
Boulange** (Food & drink, *p260*); **Blue Moon
Music** (Books, CDs, DVDs, *p244*); **Caravane
Chambre 19** (Home, *p267*); **Come On Eileen**
(Fashion, *p253*); **Les Domaines qui Montent**
(Food & drink, *p264*); **Galerie Patrick Seguin**
(Home, *p268*); **Silvera** (Home, *p268*); **Isabel
Marant** (Fashion, *p251*); **Ladies & Gentlemen**
(Fashion, *p251*); **The Lazy Dog** (Fashion,
p253); **Moisan** (Food & drink, *p260*);
Résonances (Gifts, *p265*).

The Marais

Particularly around **rue des Rosiers** and **rue
des Francs-Bourgeois**, this trendy area is a
treasure trove of designer boutiques, with a
concentration of design and interiors shops.
Anne et Valentin (Fashion, *p255*); **A-poc**
(Fashion, *p247*); **Arche de Noé** (Children,

p245); **L'Art du Buro** (Gifts, *p265*); **Les Bains
du Marais** (Beauty, *p240*); **Bains Plus** (Home,
p269); **Les Belles Images** (Fashion, *p246*);
BHV (One-stop shops, *p233*); **Cappellini**
(Home, *p267*); **Chône** (Home, *p268*);
Christophe Delcourt (Home, *p268*); **CSAO**
(Home, *p268*); **L'Eclaireur** (Fashion, *p246*);
L'Eclaireur Homme (Fashion, *p246*);
L'Epicerie (Food & drink, *p263*); **Espace
Lumière** (Home, *p268*); **Finkelsztajn** (Food &
drink, *p262*); **FR 66** (Home, *p268*); **Free 'P'
Star** (Fashion, *p253*); **Gaspard Yurkievich**
(Fashion, *p247*); **Goumanyat** (Food & drink,
p263); **L'Habilleur** (Fashion, *p253*); **Izraël**
(Food & drink, *p261*); **Jack Henry** (Fashion,
p251); **Jean-Paul Gardil** (Food & drink, *p263*);
Julien, Caviste (Food & drink, *p264*); **Librairie
Flammarion** (Books, CDs, DVDs, *p243*); **Martin
Grant** (Fashion, *p252*); **Nodus** (Fashion,
p252); **Au Nom de la Rose** (Gifts, *p265*);
L'Occitane (Beauty, *p238*); **Ozone** (Home,
p268); **Paris-Musées** (Gifts, *p265*); **Pasta
Linea** (Food & drink, *p262*); **The Red
Wheelbarrow Bookstore** (Books, CDs, DVDs,
p243); **Sentou Galerie** (Home, *p268*); **Shine**
(Fashion, *p247*); **Tsumori Chisato** (Fashion,
p249); **Le Village St-Paul** (Home, *p267*);
Zadig & Voltaire (Fashion, *p252*).

St-Germain-des-Prés & Odéon

This is the fashionable shopping paradise of
the Left Bank, with stores lined up down the
boulevard St-Germain, around **St-Sulpice
church** and along **rue de Buci**.

Hammam Med Centre

43-45 rue Petit, 19th (01.42.02.31.05/www. hammammed.com). M° Ourcq. **Open** *Women* 11am-10pm Mon-Fri; 9am-7pm Sun. *Mixed* 9am-7pm Sat. **Credit** MC, V. **Map** p405 N5.

This hammam is hard to beat – spotless mosaic-tiled surroundings, flowered sarongs and a pool. The exotic 'Forfait florale' option (€139) has you cloaked in rose petals and massaged with *huile d'Argan* from Morocco. Hammam and *gommage* are €39.

Institut Lancôme

29 rue du Fbg-St-Honoré, 8th (01.42.65.30.74/ www.lancome.fr). M° Madeleine or Concorde. **Open** 10am-7pm Mon-Sat. **Credit** AmEx, DC, MC, V. **Map** p403 F4.

Lancôme has been in business since introducing five original perfumes in 1935. Its classy flagship salon offers its affluent clientele just about every treatment you can imagine, for both men and women:

exfoliation, massage, facials, waxing, tans, manicures… Facials cost €45 to €90, body treatments €90 to €830 for 12 hours of bliss.

Institut Payot

10 rue de Castiglione, 1st (01.42.60.32.87). M° Concorde or Tuileries. **Open** 10am-6.30pm Mon, Wed, Fri; 9.30am-8.30pm Tue, Thur; 11am-6.30pm Sat. **Credit** AmEx, DC, MC, V. **Map** p403 G5.

The former home of Countess Castiglione is as beautifully preserved as its clientele. Created by Dr Nadia Payot, one of the leading ladies in French skincare, the institute offers the entire gamut of luxurious face and body treatments. Prices range from €40 to €80.

Toni & Guy

248 rue St-Honoré, 1st (01.40.20.98.20/www.toni andguy.com). M° Palais Royal Musée du Louvre or Pyramides. **Open** 10am-8pm Mon-Sat. **Credit** AmEx, DC, MC, V. **Map** p403 G5.

Alain Mikli (Fashion, *p255*); **APC** (Fashion, *p250*); **L'Artisan Parfumeur** (Beauty, *p234*); **Le Bon Marché** (One-stop shops, *p233*); **Bonton** (Children, *p244*); **Bruno Frisoni** (Fashion, *p257*); **Cacao et Chocolat** (Food & drink, *p261*); **Camper** (Fashion, *p257*); **Christian Constant** (Food & drink, *p261*); **Christian Liaigre** (Home, *p268*); **Christian Tortu** (Gifts, *p265*); **Corinne Sarrut** (Fashion, *p251*); **Da Rosa** (Food & drink, *p263*); **Debauve & Gallais** (Food & drink, *p261*); **Deyrolle** (Gifts, *p265*); **Editions de Parfums Frédéric Malle** (Beauty, *p237*); **Fnac Junior** (Children, *p246*); **Gérard Mulot** (Food & drink, *p262*); **Hervé Chapelier** (Fashion, *p257*); **Huilerie Artisanale Leblanc** (Food & drink, *p263*); **La Hune** (Books, CDs, DVDs, *p243*); **Irié Wash** (Fashion, *p251*); **Iris** (Fashion, *p258*); **Iunx** (Beauty, *p238*); **Jacadi** (Children, *p245*); **Jean-Paul Hévin** (Food & drink, *p261*); **Lagerfeld Gallery** (Fashion, *p248*); **Librairie 7L** (Books, CDs, DVDs, *p243*); **Marie Mercié** (Fashion, *p255*); **Miu Miu** (Fashion, *p249*); **Le Mouton à Cinq Pattes** (Fashion, *p253*); **Onward** (Fashion, *p247*); **Patrick Roger** (Food & drink, *p261*); **Paul and Joe** (Fashion, *p252*); **Paul Smith** (Fashion, *p252*); **Peggy Huyn Kinh** (Fashion, *p258*); **Petit Bateau** (Children, *p245*); **Pierre Hermé** (Food & drink, *p262*); **Pierre Marcolini** (Food & drink, *p261*); **Poilâne** (Food & drink, *p260*); **Princesse Tam Tam** (Fashion, *p255*); **Richart** (Food & drink, *p261*); **Robert Clergerie** (Fashion, *p258*); **Ryst Dupeyron** (Food & drink, *p265*); **Sabbia Rosa** (Fashion, *p255*); **Sadaharu Aoki** (Food

Bouquinistes. *See p242.*

& drink, *p262*); **San Francisco Book Co** (Books, CDs, DVDs, *p243*); **Sennelier** (Gifts, *p266*); **Six Pieds Trois Pouces** (Children, *p245*); **Sonia Rykiel** (Fashion, *p249*); **Swarovski** (Fashion, *p257*); **Traction** (Fashion, *p255*); **Vanessa Bruno** (Fashion, *p252*); **Village Voice** (Books, CDs, DVDs, *p244*); **Yves Saint Laurent** (Fashion, *p249*).

St-Michel & the 5th

St-Germain's bookish, intellectual cousin is the hub of the Paris publishing world.
Le Boulanger de Monge (Food & drink, *p260*); **Bouquinistes** (Books, CDs, DVDs, *p242*); **Crocodisc** (Books, CDs, DVDs, *p244*); **Diptyque** (Gifts, *p265*); **Gibert Jeune** (Books, CDs, DVDs, *p243*); **Gibert Joseph** (Books, CDs, DVDs, *p243*); **Hammam de la Grande Mosquée** (Beauty, *p240*); **Kayser** (Food & drink, *p260*); **La Maison des Trois Thés** (Food & drink, *p263*); **Mexi & Co** (Food & drink, *p262*); **Shakespeare & Co** (Books, CDs, DVDs, *p243*); **Au Vieux Campeur** (Sport & games, *p269*).

Eat, Drink, Shop

La Hune. *See p243.*

At prime spots around Paris, these hairdressing salons charge from €49 to €92, depending on the 'artist' working on your hair. Drop in (or, rather, book) for a cut on a Friday and Saturday afternoon and you can tax your hairdresser by nodding along to the resident DJ. Or you can have students experiment on you for free at Toni & Guy's training academy (122 rue du Fbg-St-Honoré, 8th, 01.40.20.15.93). **Other locations**: 18 rue Tiquetonne, 2nd (01.40.41.11.00); 264 bd St-Germain, 7th (01.44.18.33.72); 6 rue de Charonne, 11th (01.43.14.01.43).

Books, CDs, DVDs

Books

Trawl around the 5th and 6th arrondissements and you'll find racks of €1 English-language paperbacks, heavyweight academic specialists and **bouquinistes** bursting with literary treasure. *See also p244* **Fnac** and **Virgin Megastore**; for cinema bookshops, *see p296*.

Artazart
83 quai de Valmy, 10th (01.40.40.24.00/www. artazart.com). M° Jacques Bonsergent. **Open** 10.30am-7.30pm Mon-Fri; 2-8pm Sat, Sun. **Credit** AmEx, MC, V. **Map** p404 L4.
A bright yellow beacon on trendy Canal St-Martin, this bookshop and gallery stocks cutting-edge publications on fashion, art, architecture and design.

Bouquinistes
Along the quais, especially quai de Montebello & quai St-Michel, 5th. M° St-Michel. **Open** times vary from stall to stall, generally Tue-Sun. **No credit cards.** **Map** p408 J7.

The green, open-air boxes along the *quais* are one of the city's oldest institutions. Most, as the name suggests, sell books (second-hand) – ignore those specialising in nasty postcards and rummage through those packed with ancient paperbacks for something existential. You're allowed to haggle. **Photo** *p241.*

Brentano's
37 av de l'Opéra, 2nd (01.42.61.52.50/www. brentanos.fr). M° Opéra or Pyramides. **Open** 10am-7.30pm Mon-Sat. **Credit** (€45 minimum) AmEx, DC; (€17 minimum) MC, V. **Map** p403 G4.
In business for a century or more but no longer in the same family as the namesake bookstore on Fifth Avenue, Brentano's is good for American classics, modern fiction and bestsellers, plus business titles. The children's section is in the basement, the French part towards the rear. Dinky gifts are available next to the greetings cards. Monthly reading groups, children's clubs and a knitting circle in the Café Tricot.

La Flûte de Pan
49, 53 & 59 rue de Rome, 8th (01.42.93.65.05). M° Europe. **Open** 10am-6.30pm Mon, Tue, Thur-Sat; 2.30-6.30pm Wed. **Credit** MC, V. **Map** p403 F3.
Three shops stock books on classical music and – more importantly – scores for all kinds of instrument: strings, wind and orchestra. There's also learning material at No.49; brass, sax and percussion at No.53; and piano, organ and vocal at No.59.

Galignani
224 rue de Rivoli, 1st (01.42.60.76.07). M° Tuileries. **Open** 10am-7pm Mon-Sat. **Credit** MC, V. **Map** p403 G5.
Opened in 1802, Galignani was reputedly the first English-language bookshop in Europe, and even published its own daily newspaper. Today it stocks fine and decorative arts books, French and English literature, and a range of magazines.

Gibert Jeune

10 pl St-Michel, 5th (01.56.81.22.22/www.gibert jeune.fr). Mº St-Michel. **Open** 9.30am-7.30pm Mon-Sat. **Credit** MC, V. **Map** p410 J7.

This 'Langues et lettres' branch of the Left Bank chain stocks books published in 320 languages.
Other locations: 23, 27 quai St-Michel, 5th; 36 rue de la Huchette, 5th; 5 pl St-Michel, 5th; 2, 4, 6 pl St-Michel, 6th; 15bis bd St-Denis, 2nd (01.55.34.75.75).

Gibert Joseph

26 bd St-Michel, 6th (01.44.41.88.88/www.gibert joseph.com). Mº St-Michel. **Open** 10am-7.30pm Mon-Sat. **Credit** MC, V. **Map** p410 J7.

Best known as a bookshop for the Left Bank seats of learning, Gibert Joseph (a separate company from Gibert Jeune, *see above* – both were formed by splitting parent company Gibert in 1929) also has stationery, CDs, DVDs and art supply branches further up the boulevard.
Other locations: 30, 32, 34 bd St-Michel, 6th.

La Hune

170 bd St-Germain, 6th (01.45.48.35.85). Mº St-Germain-des-Prés. **Open** 10am-11.45pm Mon-Sat; 11am-7.45pm Sun. **Credit** AmEx, MC, V.
Map p407 G7.

This Left Bank institution boasts a global selection of art and design books, and a magnificent collection of French literature and theory. **Photo** *left*.

Librairie Flammarion

Centre Pompidou, 19 rue Beaubourg, 4th (01.44.78.43.22/www.flammarioncentre.com). Mº Rambuteau. **Open** 11am-10pm Mon, Wed-Sun. Closed 2wks Sept. **Credit** AmEx, MC, V.
Map p404 K5.

This bookshop, on the ground floor of the Centre Pompidou, is one of the most pleasant places in Paris in which to peruse first-rate art, design, architecture, photography and cinema titles. It also stocks children's books, a huge selection of postcards (the post office next door is the quietest in town), arty magazines and other odds and ends.

Librairie 7L

7 rue de Lille, 7th (01.42.92.03.58). Mº Rue du Bac or Solférino. **Open** 10.30am-7pm Tue-Sat. **Credit** AmEx, DC, MC, V. **Map** p407 G6.

Karl Lagerfeld's love of books gets street frontage in this chic shop, with a mix of fashion, architecture, design, contemporary art and poetry titles – and every magazine worth reading.

The Red Wheelbarrow Bookstore

22 rue St-Paul, 4th (01.48.04.75.08/www.thered wheelbarrow.com). Mº St-Paul. **Open** 10am-7pm Mon-Sat; 2-6pm Sun. **Credit** MC, V. **Map** p411 L7.

There's more literature than pulp fiction in this small but passionate English-language bookshop, home also to a well-stocked children's corner.

San Francisco Book Co

17 rue Monsieur-le-Prince, 6th (01.43.29.15.70/ www.sanfranciscobooksparis.com). Mº Odéon. **Open** 11am-9pm Mon-Sat; 2-7.30pm Sun. **Credit** MC, V.
Map p410 H7.

A well-established second-hand bookshop with a wide range of English-language fiction and more cheap paperbacks than you can shake a stick at.

Shakespeare & Co

37 rue de la Bûcherie, 5th (01.43.26.96.50/http:// shakespeareco.org). Mº St-Michel. **Open** noon-midnight daily. **Credit** MC, V. **Map** p408 J7.

George Whitman founded this institution, consisting of three floors crammed with books, in 1951. It's staffed by struggling expat writers who calmly play chess while you browse through the books. Now 91, Whitman still pops in every now and then.

Fnac.
See p244.

Eat, Drink, Shop

Village Voice

6 rue Princesse, 6th (01.46.33.36.47/www.village voicebookshop.com). M° Mabillon. **Open** 2-7.30pm Mon; 10am-7.30pm Tue-Sat; noon-6pm Sun. **Credit** AmEx, DC, MC, V. **Map** p407 H7.

Village Voice stocks an excellent range of new fiction, non-fiction and literary magazines in English. It also holds literary events and poetry readings.

WH Smith

248 rue de Rivoli, 1st (01.44.77.88.99/www.whsmith. fr). M° Concorde. **Open** 9am-7.30pm Mon-Sat; 1-7.30pm Sun. **Credit** AmEx, MC, V. **Map** p403 G5.

Some 70,000 English-language titles and a near impenetrable crush around the magazine section; the first floor has more books, as well as British DVDs and audio books. Knowledgeable expat staff, too.

CDs & DVDs

Gibert Joseph (*see p243*) stocks CDs and DVDs; **WH Smith** (*see above*) stocks British DVDs. For vinyl, head to rue Keller in the 11th for electronica and rue de Navarre (5th) for jazz.

Blue Moon Music

84 rue Quincampoix, 3rd (01.40.29.45.60). M° Rambuteau. **Open** 11am-7pm Mon-Sat. **Credit** AmEx, MC, V. **Map** p408 J6.

This shop specialises in reggae and ragga. Come for authentic Jamaican sounds, as it receives new imports on a weekly basis.

Crocodisc

40-42 rue des Ecoles, 5th (01.43.54.47.95). M° Maubert Mutualité. **Open** 11am-7pm Tue-Sat. Closed 2wks Aug. **Credit** MC, V. **Map** p410 J7.

An excellent, if expensive, range includes rock, funk, African, country and classical. For jazz and blues try sister shop Crocojazz.

Other locations: Crocojazz, 64 rue de la Montagne-Ste-Geneviève, 5th (01.46.34.78.38).

Fnac

74 av des Champs-Elysées, 8th (01.53.53.64.64/ticket office 08.92.68.36.22/www.fnac.com). M° George V. **Open** 10am-midnight Mon-Sat; noon-midnight Sun. **Credit** AmEx, MC, V. **Map** p402 D4.

To call Fnac a supermarket of culture would misrepresent its modern, quietly classy mien – but would give a good idea of its expansive and competitively priced array of books, DVDs, CDs, audio kit, computers and photographic equipment. Several of its branches – notably the vast Forum des Halles address – stock all of the above; others specialise. There are even Fnacs dedicated to kids (*see p246*). All of the generalist branches operate as a main concert box office. Staff in the electronics departments, though often a little curt, are knowledgeable and impartial; and if you plan to make a large purchase – a television, say – you can usually make big savings by signing up to Fnac's *adhérents* (members) programme beforehand. **Photo** *p243*.

Other locations: throughout the city.

Monster Melodies

9 rue des Déchargeurs, 1st (01.40.28.09.39). M° Les Halles. **Open** 12am-7pm Mon-Sat. **Credit** MC, V. **Map** p404 J5.

The owners of this store are prepared to help customers on their treasure hunt – and with more than 10,000 second-hand, well-priced CDs of every variety, that's just as well.

Virgin Megastore

52-60 av des Champs-Elysées, 8th (01.49.53.50.00/ www.virginmega.fr). M° Franklin D. Roosevelt. **Open** 10am-midnight Mon-Sat; noon-midnight Sun. **Credit** AmEx, DC, MC, V. **Map** p403 E4.

The luxury of perusing the latest CDs and DVDs till midnight makes this a choice spot, and the listening posts let you sample any CD by scanning its barcode. Tickets for concerts and sports events are available here, too. This main branch has the most comprehensive selection of books.

Other locations: Carrousel du Louvre, 99 rue de Rivoli, 1st (01.44.50.03.10); 5 bd Montmartre, 2nd (01.40.13.72.13); 15 bd Barbès, 18th (01.56.55.53.70).

Children

Clothes & shoes

Stroll through St-Germain-des-Prés and you'll see toddlers decked out in designer gear that has never been near a sandpit. If you're looking for cheap 'n' cheerful, you'll find lots of funky fashions at the chain **Du Pareil au Même**. Look for small boutiques with their own style, too, like **Gaspard de la Butte**. Children's shops are clustered on rue Bréa (6th), rue Vavin (6th) and rue du Fbg-St-Antoine (12th).

Bonton

82 rue de Grenelle, 7th (01.44.39.09.20/www. bonton.fr). M° Rue du Bac. **Open** 10am-7pm Mon-Sat. Closed 2wks Aug. **Credit** AmEx, DC, MC, V. **Map** p407 F6.

At this concept store for kids and trendy parents, T-shirts, skirts and trousers come in rainbow colours, albeit at pretty steep prices. You'll also find furniture, gadgets and accessories available, plus a children's hairdresser.

Du Pareil au Même

15-17, 23 rue des Mathurins, 9th (01.42.66.93.80/ www.dpam.com). M° Havre Caumartin/RER Auber. **Open** 10am-7pm Mon-Sat. **Credit** AmEx, MC, V. **Map** p403 G3.

Bright, cleverly designed basics for children aged three months to 14 years, at attractively low prices. The Du Pareil au Même Bébé branch, with fashionable accessories and clothing for kiddies up to two years, makes gifts that look more expensive than they are; note the musical cuddly chicken, a godsend at changing time.

Other locations: throughout the city.

Gaspard de la Butte

10bis rue Yvonne-Le-Tac, 18th (01.42.55.99.40).
M° Abbesses. **Open** 10am-7pm Tue-Sun. Closed Aug.
Credit DC, MC, V. **Map** p404 H2.
Catherine Malaure creates the prototypes for the
bright, graphic kids' wear (nought to six years) that
she sells in this natty boutique. Malaure does a great
line in sparky undersized accessories such as gloves
and funky aviator hats.

Jacadi

76 rue d'Assas, 6th (01.45.44.60.44/www.jacadi.fr).
M° Vavin. **Open** 10am-7pm Mon-Sat. **Credit** MC, V.
Map p407 G8.
Jacadi's well-made clothes for babies and children –
pleated skirts, smocked dresses, dungarees and Fair
Isle knits – are a hit with well-to-do parents. There's
funkier party stuff, too.
Other locations: throughout the city.

Petit Bateau

26 rue Vavin, 6th (01.55.42.02.53/www.petit-bateau.
com). M° Vavin. **Open** 10am-7pm Mon-Sat. **Credit**
AmEx, MC, V. **Map** p407 G8.
Renowned for comfortable, well-made cotton T-
shirts, vests and other separates in an extensive
range of colours and cuts, Petit Bateau carries an
equally coveted teen range. A hundred stores across
France and 14 in Paris alone.
Other locations: throughout the city.

Six Pieds Trois Pouces

222 bd St-Germain, 7th (01.45.44.03.72).
M° Solférino. **Open** 10.30am-7pm Mon-Sat.
Credit AmEx, DC, MC, V. **Map** p407 F6.
The excellent array of children's and teens' shoes
runs from classics by Start-rite, Aster and Little
Mary to trendy Reeboks and Timberlands, as well
as shoes under the shop's less-expensive own label.
Other locations: 19 rue de la Monnaie, 1st
(01.40.41.07.79); 85 rue de Longchamp, 16th
(01.45.53.64.21); 78 av de Wagram, 17th
(01.46.22.81.64).

Toys & books

Traditional toyshops abound. **Department
stores** (*see p233*) go overboard at Christmas.
For children's books in English, go to **WH
Smith** (*see p244*) or **Brentano's** (*see p242*).

Arche de Noé

70 rue St-Louis-en-l'Ile, 4th (01.46.34.61.60).
M° Pont Marie. **Open** 10.30am-7pm daily. **Credit**
AmEx, MC, V. **Map** p411 K7.
Far from the chaos of the *grands magasins*, 'Noah's
Ark' on the Ile St-Louis is a great place for Christmas
shopping, with traditional wooden toys from
Eastern Europe, games and jigsaw puzzles, Babar
paraphernalia and finger puppets.

Sales technique

Twice a year, Paris boutiques sell off what's
left of their seasonal stock at hugely reduced
prices – up to 75 per cent – to make way for
incoming collections. Winter stock is sold off
during four weeks in January, and summer
stock gets the boot in July. The exact national
dates for the much-anticipated sales, or
soldes, are, not surprisingly for this most
bureaucratic of countries, imposed by the
government – or, more specifically, by La
Direction départementale de la Concurrence,
de la Consommation et de la Répression des
Fraudes. Dates for 2006 were not confirmed
at the time of writing; call 01.40.27.16.00.

Not all shops keep their sale on for the
entire period; and because some prices drop
progressively during the *solde*, the shopper
has to address some prickly dilemmas. Are
a pair of size-40 Gaultier-designed Hermès
boots going to last till the price drops to half?
Or will they be so in demand that a fellow
shopper will happily snap them up with a
mere 25 per cent off the full price?

In other cases, though, it's first in, best
dressed. Significant price cuts from day one
of the sales mean that being at the door of

the **Bon Marché** (*see p233*) when it opens –
often as early as 8am especially for the start
of the sales – means you're in with half a
chance of getting your hot hands on bargain-
priced must-haves. Some of the smaller
boutiques, Prada shoes (5 rue de Grenelle,
6th, 01.45.48.53.14) for example, put
bouncers on the door to limit entry to ten
hysterical bargain-hunters at a time.

Other effective tactics for successful sales
shopping include reconnaissance patrols the
week before the sales begin, in order to
identify your sartorial targets; once the sales
start you'll be able to swoop on them, aided
by a little elbowing. Wear a shopping uniform
that's easy to get in and out of – shoes with
laces are a no-no. And if queues for the
changing room are starting to resemble those
for the toilets at Munich's Oktoberfest, your
foresight in wearing a skirt will let you save
time trying on, in a discreet corner of the
shop, other skirts or trousers underneath it.
And finally, shopping at department stores
means you can cover lots of ground without
running the risk of staining your new
Rodolphe Menudier (*see p258*) stilettos.

Eat, Drink, Shop

Au Nain Bleu

406-410 rue St-Honoré, 8th (01.42.60.39.01/
www.au-nain-bleu.com). Mº Madeleine or Concorde.
Open 10.15am-6.30pm Mon-Sat. **Credit** AmEx, DC,
MC, V. **Map** p403 G4.
Founded in 1836, France's most prestigious toy shop
is stuffier and more old-fashioned than London's
Hamleys. Its stock features toys from all around the
world, from furry animals to electronic games.

Fnac Junior

19 rue Vavin, 6th (01.56.24.03.46/www.eveiletjeux.
com). Mº Vavin. **Open** 10am-7.30pm Mon-Sat.
Credit AmEx, MC, V. **Map** p407 G8.
Fnac carries books, toys, DVDs, CDs and CD-Roms
for the under-12s. Storytelling and activities (Wed,
Sat) take place for three-year-olds and up.
Other locations: throughout the city.

La Grande Récré

13 bd Barbès, 18th (01.42.64.90.19/www.lagrande
recre.com). Mº Barbès Rochechouart. **Open** 10am-
7.30pm Mon-Fri; 10am-8pm Sat. **Credit** AmEx, DC,
MC, V. **Map** p404 J1.
France's answer to Toys R Us, this gargantuan toy
chain stocks all manner of goodies.
Other locations: throughout the city.

Village Joué Club

3-5 bd des Italiens, 2nd (01.53.45.41.41/www.joue
club.fr). Mº Richelieu Drouot. **Open** 10am-8pm Mon-
Sat. **Credit** AmEx, MC, V. **Map** p404 H4.
The largest toy store in Paris is spread out on
ground level in and around the passage des Princes.

Fashion

Fashion shopping in Paris is not always about
designer labels and selective boutiques. In
addition to pan-European brands like Mango,
H&M and Zara, the high street has its fair share
of Gallic cheapies: think **Etam** (*see p254*),
Jennyfer and Pimkie. The highest density of
these chains is in the Forum des Halles (1st) and
on nearby rue de Rivoli, between métro stations
Châtelet and Louvre Rivoli.

Designerwear

Base One

47bis rue d'Orsel, 18th (01.53.28.04.52). Mº Anvers.
Open 12.30-7.30pm Tue-Sat; 3-7pm Sun. Closed
2wks Aug. **Credit** MC, V. **Map** p404 J2.
Princesse Léa and Jean-Louis Faverole, the couple
behind Espace Lab 101 (44 rue Rochefoucauld, 9th,
01.49.95.95.85) and Project 101 (*see p323*), squeeze a
mix of items from unknown local and international
designers (Cart the Airport, Elephant 47, Tanya
Dove), plus small, established brands (Fenchurch,
Motel, Consortium) into their sitting-room style boutique. Calling it an underground Colette (*see p256*
High concept) would be somewhere near the mark.

Les Belles Images

74 rue Charlot, 3rd (01.42.76.93.61). Mº Filles du
Calvaire. **Open** 11am-7.30pm Mon-Sat. **Credit** MC,
V. **Map** p404 L5.
Formerly a buyer for Onward, Sandy Bontout has a
sharp eye and taste. She assembles a chic, global
selection of womenswear with labels like Melodie
Wolf, Véronique Leroy and Vivienne Westwood.

L'Eclaireur

3ter rue des Rosiers, 4th (01.48.87.10.22/
www.leclaireur.com). Mº St-Paul. **Open** 11am-7pm
Mon-Sat. **Credit** AmEx, DC, MC, V. **Map** p411 L6.
Housed in a dandified warehouse, L'Eclaireur stocks
the most uncompromising of top labels' designs,
including Comme des Garçons, Martin Margiela,
Dries van Noten, Carpe Diem and Junya Watanabe.
Other locations: 131 galerie de Valois, 1st
(01.40.20.42.52); 10 rue Hérold, 1st (01.40.41.09.89).

L'Eclaireur Homme

12 rue Malher, 4th (01.44.54.22.11/
www.leclaireur.com). Mº St-Paul. **Open** 11am-7pm
Mon-Sat. **Credit** AmEx, DC, MC, V. **Map** p411 L6.
Amid the exposed ducts of this old printerworks
you'll find items by Prada, Comme des Garçons,
Dries van Noten and Martin Margiela. The star is
Italian Stone Island, whose radical clothing features
parkas with a steel shell to counteract pollution.
Other locations: 26 av des Champs-Elysées, 8th
(01.45.62.12.32).

Kabuki Femme

25 rue Etienne-Marcel, 2nd (01.42.33.55.65/www.
babarabui.com). Mº Etienne Marcel. **Open** 10.30am-
7.30pm Mon-Sat. **Credit** AmEx, DC, MC, V. **Map**
p404 J5.
On the ground floor there's intrepid footwear and
bags by Costume National, Miu Miu and Prada,
along with Fendi's cult creations; Burberry belts and
Miu Miu sunglasses are also stocked. Upstairs is
home to no-flies-on-me suits by Helmut Lang,
Véronique Leroy, Prada and Costume National.

Kokon To Zai

48 rue Tiquetonne, 2nd (01.42.36.92.41/
www.kokontozai.co.uk). Mº Etienne Marcel. **Open**
11.30am-7.30pm Mon-Sat. **Credit** AmEx, DC, MC, V.
Map p404 J5.
Always a spot-on spotter of the latest creations, this
tiny, cutting-edge style emporium is sister to the
Kokon To Zai in London. The neon and club feel of
the mirrored interior match the dark glamour of the
designs. Unique pieces straight off the catwalk share
space with creations by Alexandre et Matthieu,
Marjan Peijoski and new Norwegian designers.

Maria Luisa

40 rue de Mont-Thabor, 1st (01.47.03.48.08).
Mº Concorde. **Open** 10.30am-7pm Mon-Sat. **Credit**
AmEx, DC, MC, V. **Map** p403 G4.
Venezuelan Maria Luisa Poumaillou was one of the
city's first stockists of Galliano, McQueen and the
Belgians, and has an eye for rising stars such as

Bernhard Willhelm, Elie Kishimoto, Undercover and Emma Cook. Nearby branches cover up-and-coming young designers (No.38, 01.42.96.47.81), menswear (No.19bis, 01.42.60.89.83) and shoes and accessories (2 rue Cambon, 01.47.03.96.15).

Onward

147 bd St-Germain, 6th (01.55.42.77.56). M° St-Germain-des-Prés. **Open** 11am-7pm Mon, Sat; 10.30am-7pm Tue-Fri. **Credit** AmEx, DC, MC, V. **Map** p407 G6.

Onward has a rapid turnover of young talents, who seem to compete to see who can produce the most far-fetched, priciest design. It currently stocks over 20 established and up-and-coming designers, including Hussein Chalayan, The People of the Labyrinth and Martin Margiela. Accessories, too, are astutely chosen: try funky pieces by Tatty Devine, Pièce à Conviction or Yazbukey on for size.

Shine

15 rue de Poitou, 3rd (01.48.05.80.10). M° Filles du Calvaire. **Open** 11am-7.30pm Mon-Sat. **Credit** AmEx, DC, MC, V. **Map** p409 M7.

If you're looking for a funkier, more youthful batch of cutting-edge clothes than Maria Luisa (*see p246*) can supply, Vinci d'Helia has just what you need: sexy T-shirts with unusual detailing, Luella's chunky knits and Earl Jeans trousers and jackets. A plethora of original if pricey accessories are here for the taking, and you could end up sharing shop space with Laetitia Casta and Emma de Caunes.

A-list

A-poc

47 rue des Francs-Bourgeois, 4th (01.44.54.07.05). M° St-Paul or Rambuteau. **Open** 11am-7pm Mon-Sat. Closed 3wks Aug. **Credit** AmEx, DC, MC, V. **Map** p411 L6.

Its unusual name an acronym for 'A Piece of Cloth', Issey Miyake's lab-style boutique takes a conceptual approach to clothes manufacture. Alongside ready-to-wear cotton Lycra clothes are rolls of seamless tubular wool jersey that is cut *sur mesure*; Miyake's assistants will be more than happy to advise you on a unique ensemble. Miyake's original shop (3 pl des Vosges, 4th, 01.48.87.01.86) today houses the creations of Naoki Takizawa, design protégé to the old master since 1989.

Balenciaga

10 av George-V, 8th (01.47.20.21.11/www. balenciaga.com). M° Alma Marceau or George V. **Open** 10am-7pm Mon-Sat. **Credit** AmEx, DC, MC, V. **Map** p402 D5.

With Nicolas Ghesquière at the Balenciaga helm, the venerable Spanish fashion house has jumped ahead of Japanese and Belgian designers in the hipness stakes. Floating fabrics contrast with dramatic cuts, producing a sophisticated urban style that the fashion *haut monde* can't wait to slip into. Übercool bags and shoes also available.

Cabane de Zucca

8 rue St-Roch, 1st (01.44.58.98.88/www.a-net.com). M° Tuileries. **Open** 11am-7pm Mon-Sat. Closed 3wks Aug. **Credit** AmEx, DC, MC, V. **Map** p403 G5.

Belonging to the Issey Miyake group, this funky Japanese label produces expensive urban wear distinguished by beautiful fabrics and detailing. Strong on accessories, it has a range of out-there watches.

Chanel

31 rue Cambon, 1st (01.42.86.28.00/www.chanel. com). M° Concorde or Madeleine. **Open** 10am-7pm Mon-Sat. **Credit** AmEx, DC, MC, V. **Map** p403 G4.

Practically synonymous with Paris, fashion legend Chanel has managed to stay relevant – thanks to Karl Lagerfeld. Coco opened her first boutique in this street, at No.21, in 1910, and the tradition continues in this elegant space. Lagerfeld has been designing for Chanel since 1983, and keeps on rehashing Chanel classics, like the little black dress and the Chanel suit, with great success.

Other locations: 42 av Montaigne, 8th (01.47.23.74.12).

Christian Dior

30 av Montaigne, 8th (01.40.73.54.44/www.dior. com). M° Franklin D. Roosevelt. **Open** 10am-7pm Mon-Sat. **Credit** AmEx, DC, MC, V. **Map** p402 D5.

To judge from the gaggles of girls who arrive en masse from the suburbs, life savings in hand, to choose a Dior bag, Nick Knight's sexy ad campaigns have been successful. Outrageous, gifted and acclaimed designer John Galliano is behind this label's upbeat, youthful and sexy image.

Other locations: throughout the city.

Comme des Garçons

54 rue du Fbg-St-Honoré, 8th (01.53.30.27.27/www. doublestreetmarket.com). M° Madeleine or Concorde. **Open** 11am-7pm Mon-Sat. **Credit** AmEx, DC, MC, V. **Map** p403 F4.

Rei Kawakubo's design ideas and revolutionary mix of materials have greatly influenced fashions of the past two decades, and are superbly showcased in this fire-engine-red, fibreglass store. Exclusive perfume lines get a futuristic setting at Comme des Garçons Parfums (23 pl du Marché-St-Honoré, 1st, 01.47.03.15.03).

Costume National

5 rue Cambon, 1st (01.40.15.04.36/www.costume national.com). M° Concorde. **Open** 11.30am-7pm Mon; 10.30am-7pm Tue-Sat. **Credit** AmEx, MC, V. **Map** p403 G4.

This Milan-based label produces young, sexy clothes for men and women. Its designer, Ennio Capasa, used to work for Yohji Yamamoto and is as keen on black as he is on giving women hourglass figures. A nice line in shoes and perfumes, too.

Gaspard Yurkievich

43 rue Charlot, 3rd (01.42.77.42.48/www.gaspard yurkievich.com). M° Filles du Calvaire. **Open** 10am-7pm Mon-Sat. **Credit** MC, V. **Map** p404 L5.

Eat, Drink, Shop

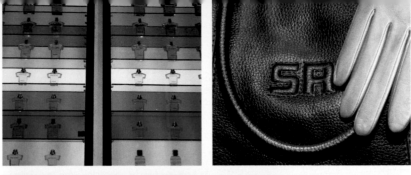

All hail the queen of stripes – **Sonia Rykiel**. *See p249.*

This native Parisian fashion missile thinks romance is on the rise. Hot men's and women's designs and a dangerous line of shoes are on display in this, his first boutique.

Hermès

24 rue du Fbg-St-Honoré, 8th (01.40.17.46.00/ www.hermes.com). M° Concorde or Madeleine. **Open** 10.30am-6.30pm Mon-Sat. **Credit** AmEx, DC, MC, V. **Map** p403 F4.

Originally a prestigious saddler, this fashion and accessories house has managed to remain an independent, family-run business as well as a fashion star. For a long time, its horse-themed scarves were associated with ladies who lunch, but after hiring avant-garde designer Martin Margiela as the womenswear head in 1997, Hermès brought its style right up to date. In 2004 Margiela handed the reins to Jean-Paul Gaultier. The fifth generation of the Hermès family continues to direct the company from this venerable building, built in the 1930s.

Jean-Paul Gaultier

6 rue Vivienne, 2nd (01.42.86.05.05/www. jeanpaulgaultier.fr). M° Bourse. **Open** 10am-7pm Mon-Fri; 11am-7pm Sat. **Credit** AmEx, DC, MC, V. **Map** p404 H4.

King of couture Gaultier has restyled his original boutique as a boudoir with trapunto-quilted, peach taffeta walls. Men's and women's ready-to-wear, accessories and the cheaper JPG Jeans lines are sold here, with haute couture upstairs (01.42.97.48.12, by appointment only).

Other locations: 44 av George-V, 8th (01.44.43.00.44).

John Galliano

384-386 rue St-Honoré, 1st (01.55.35.40.40/www. johngalliano.com). M° Concorde or Madeleine. **Open** 11am-7pm Mon-Sat. **Credit** AmEx, DC, MC, V. **Map** p403 G4.

Though at Christian Dior since 1996, Gibraltar-born Galliano still has his own range that confirms his reputation as one of the most original designers in Britain. Passers-by can view the small but diverse collection of flamboyant and feminine delights through the shop's showcase window, or survey the fashions and accessories from the Louis XVI-style leather chairs inside.

Lagerfeld Gallery

40 rue de Seine, 6th (01.55.42.75.51). M° Odéon. **Open** 11am-7pm Tue-Sat. Closed Aug. **Credit** AmEx, DC, MC, V. **Map** p410 H6.

Andrée Putman helped create this shrine to King Karl's brand of stylish minimalism: Lagerfeld's fashion creations and photography are both on display. You could just sneak in to browse the latest fashion, beauty and art collections, scattered over a handsome round table at the front of the gallery.

Louis Vuitton

101 av des Champs-Elysées, 8th (08.10.81.00.10/ www.vuitton.com). Mº George V. **Open** 10am-8pm Mon-Sat. **Credit** AmEx, DC, MC, V. **Map** p402 D4.
After major renovation work, the flagship Champs-Elysées store reopened with all attendant hoo-ha in October 2005 to reveal a stunning spiralled interior. Since 1998, Marc Jacobs has been the artistic director of the luxury label, and was responsible for its successful first ready-to-wear and shoe line in the same year. Bringing the august label screamingly up to date, Jacobs has made Vuitton's luggage and accessories, as well as its fashion line, as much in demand as water in the Sahara. The non-millionaires among us should just about be able to afford a monogrammed pencil case.
Other locations: 6 pl St-Germain-des-Prés, 6th; 22 av Montaigne, 8th.

Marni

57 av Montaigne, 8th (01.56.88.08.08/www.marni. com). Mº Franklin D. Roosevelt. **Open** 10am-7pm Mon-Sat. **Credit** AmEx, DC, MC, V. **Map** p402 D5.
This neo-romantic Italian label was born in 1994 to a family fur company. Consuelo Castiglioni has fun mixing leather, fur, silk, cashmere and prints, creating an eccentric but cool jostle of textures and colours. There are men's and children's lines, too.

Martin Margiela

23, 25bis rue de Montpensier, 1st (01.40.15.07.55/ www.maisonmartinmargiela.com). Mº Palais Royal Musée du Louvre. **Open** 11am-7pm Mon-Sat. **Credit** AmEx, DC, MC, V. **Map** p404 H5.
The first Paris boutique for the JD Salinger of the fashion world (MM refuses to be photographed and only gives interviews by fax) is a pristine white, unlabelled space. His collection for women (line 1), bearing a blank label but recognisable by external white stitching, is famous among those in the know. Here you can also find line 6 (women's basics) and line 10 (menswear), plus other lines covering magazines, accessories for men and women, and shoes.
Other locations: 7 rue de Grenelle, 7th (01.45.49.06.45).

Miu Miu

16 rue de Grenelle, 7th (01.53.63.20.30/www. miumiu.com). Mº Sèvres Babylone. **Open** 11am-7pm Mon; 10am-7pm Tue-Sat. **Credit** AmEx, DC, MC, V. **Map** p407 G7.
A diminutive of Miuccia, first name of Prada's savvy director, Miu Miu is the principal label's colourful younger (and cheaper) sister – notable for its frivolous, reckless style and fabulous shoes. In this simply decorated, massive two-storey boutique you'll find both men's and women's fashions.

Prada

10 av Montaigne, 8th (01.53.23.99.40/www.prada. com). Mº Alma Marceau. **Open** 11am-7pm Mon; 10am-7pm Tue-Sat. **Credit** AmEx, DC, MC, V. **Map** p402 D5.
Miuccia Prada dusted off her family's fine old leather company in the 1980s, turning Prada's handbags into the cognoscenti's accessory of choice. The ready-to-wear line was launched in 1989, and fashionistas haven't been able to get enough of Prada's elegant designs since. The Paris boutiques are recognisable for the trademark cool, lime-green walls.
Other locations: 5 rue de Grenelle, 6th (01.45.48.53.14); 6 rue du Fbg-St-Honoré, 8th (01.58.18.63.30).

Sonia Rykiel

175 bd St-Germain, 6th (01.49.54.60.60/www. soniarykiel.fr). Mº St-Germain-des-Prés or Sèvres Babylone. **Open** 10.30am-7pm Mon-Sat. **Credit** AmEx, DC, MC, V. **Map** p407 G6.
Even if her fabrics aren't as super-soft as they once were, the queen of stripes is still producing skinny rib knitwear evoking the Left Bank babes of Sartre's time. Menswear can be found across the street, while two newer boutiques stock the younger, more affordable 'Sonia by Sonia Rykiel' range (59 rue des Sts-Pères, 6th, 01.49.54.61.00) and kids' togs (4 rue de Grenelle, 6th, 01.49.54.61.10). Next door to the latter, on the site of Sonia's original 1966 shop, the Rykiel Woman store at No.6 (01.49.54.66.21) stocks a range of designer sex toys – give the vibrating black rubber duck (€45) a whirl. **Photos** *left*.
Other locations: throughout the city.

Tsumori Chisato

20 rue Barbette, 3rd (01.42.78.18.88). Mº St-Paul or Hôtel de Ville. **Open** 11am-7pm Mon-Sat. Closed 3wks Aug. **Credit** AmEx, MC, V. **Map** p411 L6.
Known for her inventive use of colour and wispy fabrics, this Japanese designer has a cult following among fashion-conscious *parisiennes*. Artistic director of Issey Sports in the 1980s, Chisato set up her own label in 1990 as part of Miyake's stable; her poetic, romantic designs are big on ingenious detail.

Yohji Yamamoto

25 rue du Louvre, 1st (01.42.21.42.93/www.yohji yamamoto.co.jp). Mº Sentier or Les Halles. **Open** 10.30am-7pm Mon-Sat. **Credit** AmEx, DC, MC, V. **Map** p407 G7.
One of the few true pioneers working in the fashion industry today, Yohji Yamamoto is a master of cut and finish, both strongly inspired by the kimono and traditional Tibetan costume. His dexterity with form makes for unique shapes and styles, largely in black, but when he does colour, it's a blast of brilliance. This is the women's store; the men's branch is nearby (47 rue Etienne-Marcel, 1st, 01.45.08.82.45).

Yves Saint Laurent

6 pl St-Sulpice, 6th (01.43.29.43.00/www.ysl.com). Mº St-Sulpice. **Open** 11am-7pm Mon; 10.30am-7pm Tue-Sat. **Credit** AmEx, DC, MC, V. **Map** p410 H7.

Yves Saint Laurent retired in 2002 after a 40-year career which began at Dior and continued with the androgynous revolution he fomented in the 1960s under his own name, getting women into dinner and jump suits. This is the women's store; menswear is at No.12 (01.43.26.84.40).

Other locations: 9 rue de Grenelle, 7th (01.45.44.39.01); 32, 38 rue du Fbg-St-Honoré, 8th (men 01.53.05.80.80/women 01.42.65.74.59).

Boutiques

Agnès b

2, 3, 6, 10 & 19 rue du Jour, 1st (men 01.42.33.04.13/ women 01.45.08.56.56/www.agnesb.com). M° Les Halles. **Open** 10am-7pm Mon-Sat. **Credit** AmEx, MC, V. **Map** p404 J5.

Agnès b rarely wavers from her design vision: pure lines in fine quality cotton, merino wool and silk. Best buys are shirts, pullovers and cardigans that keep their shape for years. Her mini-empire of men's, women's, children's, travel and sportswear shops is compact; see the website for details.

American Apparel

31 pl du Marché-St-Honoré, 1st (01.42.60.03.72/ www.americanapparel.net). M° Pyramides, Opéra or Tuileries. **Open** 10.30am-7.30pm Mon-Sat. **Credit** AmEx, DC, MC, V. **Map** p403 G4.

Paris clearly has acquired a taste for American Apparel's brand of ethically spotless, colourful cotton basics. After establishing its headquarters off überchic rue du Faubourg-St-Honoré in 2005, the LA brand followed later in the year with a second store off the Canal St-Martin, then one in the Marais, getting more in touch with the down-to-earth style that has made its slim-fit T-shirts such an impressive hit on the rock scene.

Other locations: 41 rue du Temple, 4th; 10 rue Beaurepaire, 10th.

Antoine et Lili

95 quai de Valmy, 10th (01.40.37.41.55/www. antoineetlili.com). M° Jacques Bonsergent or Gare de l'Est. **Open** 11am-7pm Mon, Sun; 11am-8pm Tue-Fri; 10am-8pm Sat. **Credit** AmEx, DC, MC, V. **Map** p404 L3.

Fuchsia-pink and apple-green shopfronts, reflected in the canal on a fine day, are a colour therapist's dream. Vibrant jumpers and neo-hippie skirts hang amid Mexican shrines, Hindu postcards and all sorts of miscellaneous kitsch. The three-shop Canal St-Martin 'Village' has an equally colourful home decoration shop, florist and self-service café.

Other locations: 51 rue des Francs-Bourgeois, 4th (01.42.72.26.60).

APC

3, 4 rue de Fleurus, 6th (01.42.22.12.77/www.apc.fr). M° St-Placide. **Open** 11am-7.30pm Mon-Sat. **Credit** AmEx, MC, V. **Map** p407 G8.

APC is very, very cool. Think of Muji crossed with a rough-cut Agnès b (*see above*) and you'll get an idea why Jean Touitou's gear is much sought after by the Japanese in-crowd. He recently collaborated with Jessica Ogden on an understated summer range, Madras. Men's clothes are at No.4, along with quirky accessories; cross the road to No.3 for the women's collection. All items can be bought online.

Other locations: 112 rue Vieille-du-Temple, 3rd (01.42.78.18.02).

Bali Barret

36 rue du Mont-Thabor, 1st (01.49.26.01.75/ www.balibarret.com). M° Concorde. **Open** 2.30-7.30pm Mon; 10.30am-7.30pm Tue-Sat. **Credit** AmEx, MC, V. **Map** p403 G5.

This French label opened its first boutique in 2002, stocking four different colours each season and offering an androgynous take on classic styles with a sexy twist. These days it's worth keeping a look out for the funky belts and bags and the matching

For businesswomen who like to cut to the chase – **Barbara Bui**. *See p251.*

stripy knickers, stockings and cotton polo necks; you'll also find a small menswear collection here with soft, logoed sweatshirts.

Barbara Bui
23 rue Etienne-Marcel, 1st (01.40.26.43.65/www. barbarabui.fr). M° Etienne Marcel. **Open** 10.30am-7.30pm Mon-Sat. **Credit** AmEx, DC, MC, V. **Map** p404 J5.

Businesswomen who like to cut to the chase have a sartorial ally in Bui: lean, finely cut trousers, figure-hugging shirts and jackets, and dagger heels. Bui has branched out into loungey CDs, and there's a café two doors up (No.27, 01.45.08.04.04). **Photo** *left.*
Other locations: 13 rue de Turbigo, 2nd (01.42.36.44.34); 35 av de Grenelle, 7th (01.45.44.85.14); 50 av Montaigne, 8th (01.42.25.05.25).

Corinne Sarrut
4 rue du Pré-aux-Clercs, 7th (01.42.61.71.60). M° Rue du Bac or St-Germain-des-Prés. **Open** 10.30am-7pm Mon-Sat. **Credit** AmEx, MC, V. **Map** p407 F7.

Fans of *Amélie* will be charmed by the work of Corinne Sarrut, who dressed Audrey Tautou for the part. Anyone with a weakness for the 1940s silhouette will love her trapeze creations in silky viscose.

Diesel
21 rue Montmartre, 1st (01.42.36.55.55/www.diesel. com). M° Etienne Marcel. **Open** 11am-7.30pm Mon-Sat. **Credit** AmEx, DC, MC, V. **Map** p404 K4.

After 20 years in the jeans business, Renzo Rossi is still tapping into teen dreams with brio. Plenty of branches to choose from in Paris.
Other locations: (accessories) 35 rue Etienne-Marcel, 1st (01.42.21.37.55); 26 rue de La Reynie, 1st (01.40.26.73.85); 38 av de l'Opéra, 2nd (01.44.94.09.40); 19 rue Pavée, 4th (01.42.72.34.86).

Et Vous
42 rue Etienne-Marcel, 2nd (01.55.80.76.10). M° Etienne Marcel. **Open** 11am-7pm Mon; 10.30am-7pm Tue-Sat. **Credit** AmEx, DC, MC, V. **Map** p404 J5.

Fashionable, mid upmarket womenswear in muted, neutral colours are the cornerstone of the Et Vous label. Its latest branch is ultra-minimal, with the collection displayed on pale plywood units.
Other locations: *Women* 6 rue des Francs-Bourgeois, 3rd (01.42.71.75.11); 46 rue du Four, 6th (01.45.44.70.21); 72 rue de Passy, 16th (01.45.20.47.15). *Men & women* 271 rue St-Honoré, 1st (01.47.03.00.31); 69 rue de Rennes, 6th (01.40.49.01.64).

Irié Wash
8 rue du Pré-aux-Clercs, 7th (01.42.61.18.28). M° Rue du Bac or St-Germain-des-Prés. **Open** 10.15am-7pm Mon-Sat. Closed 3wks Aug. **Credit** MC, V. **Map** p407 F7.

The more elegant Parisians have fallen for this Japanese designer, whose search for new methods and materials might include laser cutting or hologram prints. In 2005 the label took the adventurous step of releasing three perfumes for three different moods and times in any one day, for men and women: 9.25, 15.10 and 20.50.

Isabel Marant
16 rue de Charonne, 11th (01.49.29.71.55). M° Ledru-Rollin. **Open** 10.30am-7.30pm Mon-Sat. **Credit** AmEx, MC, V. **Map** p409 M7.

Marant's style is recognisable in her ethno-babe brocades, blanket-like coats and decorated sweaters.
Other locations: 1 rue Jacob, 6th (01.43.26.04.12).

Jack Henry
54 rue des Rosiers, 4th (01.44.59.89.44). M° St-Paul. **Open** 1.30-8pm Tue-Sat. **Credit** MC, V. **Map** p411 K6.

This New Yorker's spare, dark suits offer a fine, elongated silhouette, enhanced by chest-hugging knitwear. The look is inspired by US combat gear – meaning discipline in hidden details, rather than pockets in unlikely places.
Other locations: *Women* 1 rue Montmartre, 1st (01.42.21.46.01).

Ladies & Gentlemen
4 passage Charles-Dallery, 11th (01.47.00.86.12). M° Ledru-Rollin. **Open** noon-7pm Tue-Sat; 2-7pm Sun. Closed Aug. **Credit** MC, V. **Map** p409 N7.

Amid paintings and techno beats, red dummies are lovingly swathed in the classic yet slightly surreal creations of designers Isabelle Ballu (womenswear) and Moritz Rogorsky (menswear). Most clothes are hidden away in special alcoves – seek them out.

Loft Design by
12 rue du Fbg-St-Honoré, 8th (01.42.65.59.65/www. loftdesignby.com). M° Madeleine or Concorde. **Open** 10.30am-7pm Mon-Fri; 10am-7pm Sat. **Credit** AmEx, DC, MC, V. **Map** p403 F4.

Patrick Frêche makes clothes to match the urban skyline: heavy on grey and black. A shrewd move, seeing LDb's rating with the media and fashion crowd.
Other locations: 12 rue de Sévigné, 4th (01.48.87.13.07); 56 rue de Rennes, 6th (01.45.44.88.99); 175 bd Pereire, 17th (01.46.22.44.20); 22 av de la Grande-Armée, 17th (01.45.72.13.53).

Madelios
23 bd de la Madeleine, 1st (01.53.45.00.00/www. madelios.com). M° Madeleine. **Open** 10am-7pm Mon-Sat. **Credit** AmEx, DC, MC, V. **Map** p403 G4.

A one-stop-shop for men's fashion, with two floors and more than 100 labels. The decor's dull, but it's the stock that matters: suits by Kenzo, Paul Smith and Givenchy, as well as shoes and accessories.

Marithé et François Girbaud
38 rue Etienne-Marcel, 2nd (01.53.40.74.20/www. girbaud.com). M° Etienne Marcel. **Open** 11.30am-7.30pm Mon; 10.30am-7.30pm Tue-Sat. **Credit** AmEx, DC, MC, V. **Map** p407 J5.

The pioneering *soixante-huitard* Girbaud pair came up with streetwear in high-tech fabrics using laser cutting and welding. Their flagship store has four floors and a garden.
Other locations: 20 rue Malher, 4th (01.44.54.99.01); 7 rue du Cherche-Midi, 6th (01.53.63.53.63); 8 rue de Babylone, 7th (01.45.48.78.86); 49 av Franklin-D.-Roosevelt, 8th (01.45.62.49.15).

Martin Grant

10 rue Charlot, 3rd (01.42.71.39.49/www.martin grantparis.com). M° Temple. **Open** 10am-6pm Mon-Fri. Closed 3wks Aug. **Credit** MC, V. **Map** p408 K6.

Grant's shop is now tucked away on a second-floor Marais apartment: chipped tiled floor and worn velvet chairs recalling a retrofied Prada ad. This is couture, though, as interpreted by Australian designer Martin Grant. If you're a stickler for steady cuts, pure textiles and unfussy designs, pay him a visit.

Nodus

22 rue Vieille-du-Temple, 4th (01.42.77.07.96/ www.nodus.fr). M° St-Paul or Hôtel de Ville. **Open** 2-7.30pm Mon, Sun; 10.45am-7.30pm Tue-Sat. **Credit** AmEx, DC, MC, V. **Map** p411 K6.

Under the wooden beams of this cosy men's shirt specialist are neat rows of striped, checked and plain dress shirts, stylish silk ties with subtle, graphic designs and silver-plated crystal cufflinks.

Paul and Joe

64 rue des Sts-Pères, 7th (01.42.22.47.01/www.paul andjoe.com). M° Rue du Bac or St-Germain-des-Prés. **Open** 10am-7pm Mon-Sat. **Credit** AmEx, DC, MC, V. **Map** p407 G6.

Fashionistas have taken a great shine to Sophie Albou's weathered 1940s-style creations (named after her sons), so much so that she has opened a menswear branch in addition to this flagship, with its out-to-be-noticed, bubblegum-pink gramophone. **Other locations**: Men 40 rue du Four, 6th (01.45.44.97.70). Men & women 46 rue Etienne-Marcel, 2nd (01.40.28.03.34).

Paul Smith

22-24 bd Raspail, 7th (01.42.84.15.30/www.paul-smith.co.uk). M° Sèvres Babylone or Rue du Bac. **Open** 11am-7pm Mon-Sat; 10am-7pm Tue-Sat. **Credit** AmEx, DC, MC, V. **Map** p407 G7.

Le style anglais in a wood-panelled interior. Smith's great suits and classic shoes are on the upper floor; women and kids get a funkier space below.

Vanessa Bruno

25 rue St-Sulpice, 6th (01.43.54.41.04). M° Odéon or St-Sulpice. **Open** 10.30am-7.30pm Mon-Sat. **Credit** AmEx, DC, MC, V. **Map** p410 H7.

Bruno's feminine and highly characterful clothes have a cool Zen-like quality that no doubt derives from her stay in Japan. She also makes great bags, seen hanging from the coolest wrists. **Other locations**: 12 rue de Castiglione, 1st (01.42.61.44.60).

Zadig & Voltaire

42 rue des Francs-Bourgeois, 3rd (01.44.54.00.60/ www.zadig-et-voltaire.com). M° St-Paul or Hôtel de Ville. **Open** 1.30-7.30pm Mon, Sun; 10.30am-7.30pm Tue-Sat. **Credit** AmEx, DC, MC, V. **Map** p411 K6.

Z&V branches are popping up all over Paris – its relaxed, urban collection is clearly a winner. Popular separates include cotton tops, shirts and faded jeans; its winter range of cashmere jumpers is superb. **Other locations**: throughout the city.

Streetwear & clubwear

adidas

150 rue de Rivoli, 1st (01.58.62.51.60/www.adidas. com). M° Louvre Rivoli. **Open** 10am-7.30pm Mon-Sat. **Credit** AmEx, DC, MC, V. **Map** p404 H5.

Three techno floors of adidas products, whose shiny newness contrasts beautifully with this flagship store's raw surfaces. You'll be pressed to find all these hard-to-find models on display anywhere else in the world; look out for re-issues of 1970s models (of course) as they nestle up with the entire Yohji Yamamoto-designed range.

Boutique M Dia

5-7 rue des Innocents, 1st (01.40.26.03.31/www. mdiawear.com). M° Châtelet/RER Châtelet Les Halles. **Open** 1-8pm Mon; 11am-8pm Tue-Sat. **Credit** AmEx, DC, MC, V. **Map** p408 J6.

Mohammed Dia, a rebel from the Sarcelles *banlieue*, went to America and came back with an idea to get him out of the ghetto: fashion design. €20 million later, he has his own line of men's and women's urban sports clothes, plus shoe line Tariq, worn by the NBA's Dallas Mavericks. His first boutique is a shrine to his vision, offering all from the Dia range.

Clery Brice

11 rue Pierre-Lescot, 1st (01.45.08.58.70). M° Les Halles/RER Châtelet Les Halles. **Open** 11am-12.30pm, 1.30-8pm Mon-Sat. **Credit** MC, V. **Map** p404 J5.

Here you pay lofty prices to get limited editions of the coolest trainers six months before the rest of the world even finds out they should be wearing them.

Ekivok

39 bd de Sébastopol, 1st (01.42.21.98.71/www. ekivok.com). M° Les Halles/RER Châtelet Les Halles. **Open** 11am-7.30pm Mon-Sat. **Credit** MC, V. **Map** p404 J5.

The reality of Paris fashion is not just Dior and Chanel; *banlieue*-cultivated hip hop and streetwear cultures flourish in a parallel universe. Here you'll find the major brands like Royal Wear, Zoo York, Billal, Hardcore Session, Hixsept and Punky Fish. **Other locations**: 6 rue de Cygne, 1st (01.40.39.97.07).

Kanabeach

78 rue Jean-Jacques-Rousseau, 1st (01.40.26.41.66/ www.kanabeach.com). M° Etienne Marcel. **Open** 11am-7.30pm Mon-Sat. **Credit** MC, V. **Map** p404 J5.

With its mini waterfall, astroturf garden, mini caravan and changing rooms resembling beach cabins, this French youthwear store has a campsite vibe. The autumn/winter men's and women's collections include Jacquard check red and apricot coats, navy and cream trousers, and colourful separates.

Kiliwatch

64 rue Tiquetonne, 2nd (01.42.21.17.37/www. kiliwatch.com). M° Etienne Marcel. **Open** 2-7pm Mon; 11am-7.30pm Tue-Sat. **Credit** AmEx, DC, MC, V. **Map** p404 J5.

The trailblazer of the rue Etienne-Marcel revival is filled to bursting with hoodies, casual shirts and washed-out jeans. Featured brands such as G-Star and Kulte accompany a selection of pricey but good-condition second-hand garb (adidas tracksuit tops and mini-kilts especially) for that retro-chic look.

The Lazy Dog
2 passage Thiéré, 11th (01.58.30.94.76/www.the lazydog.fr). M° Ledru-Rollin. **Open** noon-7pm Mon; 11am-7pm Tue-Sat. **Credit** MC, V. **Map** p409 M7.
In the basement gallery you'll find exhibitions of the Dog's favourite artists; upstairs, this trendy boutique stocks graphic design-related objects and books, plus manga-style toys and clothes.

Puma Store
22 bd de Sébastopol, 4th (01.44.59.88.02/www.puma. com). M° Rambuteau/RER Châtelet Les Halles. **Open** 10.30am-7.30pm Mon-Fri; 10.30am-7pm Sat. **Credit** AmEx, MC, V. **Map** p404 J5.
Puma offers its particular brand of sport, lifestyle and fashion at this flashy, two-floor flagship store. Speciality fixtures show off Christy Turlington's yoga clothes, and there are obscure versions of Puma's popular Mostro trainer.

Royal Cheese
24 rue Tiquetonne, 2nd (01.40.28.06.56/www.royal cheese.com). M° Etienne Marcel. **Open** 11am-1pm, 2-8pm Mon-Sat. **Credit** AmEx, DC, MC, V. **Map** p404 J5.
Clubbers pop down to Royal Cheese to snaffle up hard-to-find imports – Stussy, Evisu, Duffer, Gravy and Original Shopper for the boys, and Shariff, Bonds, Kitten and Evisu Donna for the girls. Prices are hefty, though: its Japanese jeans cost €200.

Le Vestibule
3 pl Ste-Opportune, 1st (01.42.33.21.89). M° Châtelet. **Open** 10.30am-8pm Mon-Sat. **Credit** AmEx, MC, V. **Map** p404 J5.
An eye-popping showcase for the wildest creations of vintage streetwear and club gear, with exhibits by mainstream labels such as Dolce e Gabbana and Castelbajac. For effortless flash and panache, Cultura, Diesel StyleLab and Replay (and its Coca-Cola Ware label) are hard to beat.

Vintage & discount

The craze for vintage fashion has seen second-hand clothes flourish, though demand ensures that bargains are rare. *See also p266* **Antiques & flea markets**.

Come On Eileen
16-18 rue des Taillandiers, 11th (01.43.38.12.11). M° Ledru-Rollin. **Open** 11.30am-8.30pm Mon-Thur; 11.30am-7.30pm Fri; 4-8pm Sun. **Credit** DC, MC, V. **Map** p409 M7.
The owners of this three-floor vintage wonderland have an eye for what's funky, from cowboy gear to 1960s debutantes frocks. With customers like Kylie

Minogue, they can well afford to charge high prices (Hermès scarves cost around €100), but the stock is well sourced and in good condition.

Didier Ludot
20-24 galerie de Montpensier, 1st (01.42.96.06.56/ www.didierludot.com). M° Palais Royal Musée du Louvre. **Open** 11am-7pm Mon-Sat. **Credit** AmEx, DC, MC, V. **Map** p404 H5.
Didier Ludot's temples to vintage haute couture have been such a hit that he now has outlets in Printemps, London's Harrods and New York's Barneys, his own line of little black dresses – also sold at the aptly named La Petite Robe Noire (125 galerie de Valois, 1st, 01.40.15.01.04) – a perfume and a book (*The Little Black Dress*, natch). Prices are exorbitant, but then the pieces are stunning: Fath, Dior, Molyneux, Balenciaga, Pucci, Féraud, Stern and, of course, Chanel, from the 1920s onwards.

Doursoux
3 passage Alexandre, 15th (01.43.27.00.97/www. doursoux.com). M° Pasteur. **Open** 10am-7.30pm Tue-Sat. **Credit** MC, V. **Map** p407 E9.
This place is something of a essential in the army-surplus community. The stock is quite small, but includes good-quality coats, boots and gloves.

Free 'P' Star
8 rue Ste-Croix-de-la-Bretonnerie, 4th (01.42.76.03.72). M° St-Paul. **Open** noon-11pm Mon-Sat; 2-10pm Sun. **Credit** MC, V. **Map** p411 K6.
This veritable Aladdin's cave of retro glitz, ex-army jackets and 1960s, '70s and '80s glad rags is the best-priced of the bargain basements.

L'Habilleur
44 rue de Poitou, 3rd (01.48.87.77.12). M° St-Sébastien Froissart. **Open** noon-8pm Mon-Sat. **Credit** MC, V. **Map** p404 L5.
Urbanites prowl this slick store for its severely cut men's and women's togs by Dries van Noten, Helmut Lang, John Richmond, Plein Sud, Martine Sitbon and Bikkembergs, and dagger-toed shoes by Patrick Cox. All items, which are end of line or straight from the catwalk, are 50% to 70% off.

Le Mouton à Cinq Pattes
138 bd St-Germain, 6th (01.43.26.49.25). M° Odéon. **Open** 10.30am-7.30pm Mon-Fri; 10.30am-8pm Sat. **Credit** AmEx, MC, V. **Map** p410 H7.
Designer vintage and last season's collection in mint condition: Vittadini, Buscat, Donn Adriana, Chanel and Lagerfeld. Turnover is fast, so this is no place for indecision. Labels are cut out, too, so make sure you know what you're buying. **Photo** *p254*.
Other locations: *Men & women* 18 rue St-Placide, 6th (01.42.84.25.11). *Women* 8 rue St-Placide, 6th (01.45.48.86.26).

Rag
83-85 rue St-Martin, 4th (01.48.87.34.64). M° Rambuteau or Châtelet/RER Châtelet Les Halles. **Open** 10am-8pm Mon-Sat; noon-8pm Sun. **No credit cards. Map** p404 K5.

Mint **Mouton à Cinq Pattes**. *See p253*.

One half focuses on casual *fripes* – pilots' navy jumpers and 1970s shirts at €15, racks of colourful puffer jackets, '70s heels and more; the other might yield a vintage Hermès scarf, 1960s Paco Rabanne dresses or Gucci and Dior accessories.

Son et Image

87 rue St-Denis, 1st (01.40.41.90.61). M° Châtelet. **Open** 10.30am-7.30pm Mon-Sat. **Credit** AmEx, DC, MC, V. **Map** p404 J6.
This popular little second-hand clothes store is filled with vintage leather, fur coats and hip boots.

Wochdom

72 rue Condorcet, 9th (01.53.21.09.72). M° Pigalle or Anvers. **Open** noon-8pm Mon-Sat. **Credit** AmEx, DC, MC, V. **Map** p404 J2.
This temple to vintage stocks a mainly female collection, inclined towards the spotty and stripy 1980s. The shop sells copies of *Interview, Elle* and *Vogue*, old vinyl and opposite at No.69, vintage shoes. There's a concession at Printemps (*see p234*), too.

Lingerie & swimwear

Most of the third floor of **Galeries Lafayette** (*see p234*) is devoted to underwear; for swimwear, *see also p269* **Sport & games**.

Alice Cadolle

4 rue Cambon, 1st (01.42.60.94.22/www.cadolle. com). M° Concorde or Madeleine. **Open** 10am-1pm, 2-7pm Mon-Sat. Closed Aug. **Credit** AmEx, MC, V. **Map** p403 G4.

Five generations of lingerie-makers are behind this boutique, founded by Hermine Cadolle, the inventor of the brassière. Her great-great-granddaughter, Poupie Cadolle, continues the family tradition in a cosy space devoted to its luxury ready-to-wear line. The *couture* division has its own *très* contemporary setting, Loft Couture (255 rue St-Honoré, 1st, 01.42.60.94.94; by appointment only).

Erès

2 rue Tronchet, 8th (01.47.42.28.82/www.eres.fr). M° Madeleine. **Open** 10am-7pm Mon-Sat. **Credit** AmEx, DC, MC, V. **Map** p403 G4.
Don't be misled by the demure interior: the label's beautifully cut, minimalist bikinis and swimsuits are hot and designed to make a splash. One advantage for the natural woman is that the top and bottom can be purchased in different sizes, or you can buy just one piece of a bikini.
Other locations: 4bis rue du Cherche-Midi, 6th (01.45.44.95.54); 40 av Montaigne, 8th (01.47.23.07.26); 6 rue Guichard, 16th (01.46.47.45.21).

Etam

21 rue Tronchet, 8th (01.40.06.05.93/www. etam.com). M° Havre Caumartin/RER Auber. **Open** 10am-7pm Mon-Sat. **Credit** AmEx, MC, V. **Map** p403 G3.
This high-street brand has recently closed many of its daywear branches in favour of its underwear shops (its original speciality). The result is all-round underwear and swimsuits, catering to all tastes – from sex kitten to cotton candies on a budget.
Other locations: throughout the city.

Fifi Chachnil

26 rue Cambon, 1st (01.42.60.38.86/www. fifichachnil.com). M° Madeleine. **Open** 11am-7pm Mon-Sat. **Credit** AmEx, MC, V. **Map** p403 G4.
Chachnil has a new approach to frou-frou underwear in the pin-up tradition. Her chic mixes – such as deep red silk bras with boudoir pink bows, and pale turquoise girdles with orange trim – will have you and your admirer purring in delight. Check out the transparent black babydoll negligées with an empire-line bust. **Photo** *right*.
Other locations: 68 rue Jean-Jacques-Rousseau, 1st (01.42.21.19.98.); 231 rue St-Honoré, 1st (01.42.61.21.83).

Princesse Tam Tam

52 bd St-Michel, 6th (01.42.34.99.31). M° Cluny La Sorbonne. **Open** 1.30-7pm Mon; 10am-7pm Tue-Sat. **Credit** AmEx, MC, V. **Map** p410 J7.
The commendable but inexpensive underwear and swimwear brand favoured by Parisian trendies has launched out with provocative traffic-stopping promotions. Bright colours and sexily transparent and sporty gear are most certainly in – though sadly not for well-endowed girls.

Sabbia Rosa

73 rue des Sts-Pères, 6th (01.45.48.88.37). M° St-Germain-des-Prés. **Open** 10am-7pm Mon-Sat. **Credit** AmEx, MC, V. **Map** p407 G7.

Frou-frou **Fifi Chachnil**. See p254.

Settle yourself on the soft green leather sofa in this lingerie heaven and let Moana Moatti tempt you with feather-trimmed satin mules or spread out satin, silk and chiffon negligées in fine shades of tangerine, lemon, mocha or pistachio. All sizes here are medium, others are made *sur mesure*; prices are just the right side of extortionate for a slice of luxury.

Yoba
11 rue du Marché St-Honoré, 1st (01.40.41.04.06/ www.yobaparis.com). M° Tuileries. **Open** 11am-8pm Mon-Fri; noon-8pm Sat. **Credit** MC, V. **Map** p403 G5.
One for the liberated woman, this smart boutique runs the gamut from an exclusive range of wispy lingerie to cheeky sex toys.

Accessories

Eyewear

Get an eye test at an *ophtalmologiste*, then take along your prescription for some cool French specs to wow your friends back home.

Alain Mikli
74 rue des Sts-Pères, 7th (01.53.63.87.40/www. mikli.fr). M° Sèvres Babylone or Saint Sulpice. **Open** 10am-7pm Mon-Sat. **Credit** AmEx, DC, MC, V. **Map** p407 G7.
This cult French designer was among the first to inject some vroom into prescription peepers. Alain Mikli's signature material is cellulose acetate, a delicate blend of wood and cotton sliced from blocks. This flagship Starck-designed boutique features a

glass counter where the frames are laid out like designer sweeties, while upstairs, 'travel wear' is displayed in an 18th-century setting. Now boasting branches in Paris, New York, Shanghai and Tokyo. **Other locations**: 4 rue Bachaumont, 2nd (01.42.82.08.42); 1 rue des Rosiers, 4th (01.42.71.01.56).

Anne et Valentin
4 rue Ste-Croix-de-la-Bretonnerie, 4th (01.40.29.93.01/www.anneetvalentin.com). M° Hôtel de Ville or St-Paul. **Open** 11am-8pm Tue-Sat. **Credit** AmEx, DC, MC, V. **Map** p411 K6.
This modish French eyewear company occupies a cosy three-floor Marais boutique. Anne et Valentin design chic but unpretentious unisex frames: lightweight titanium models have names like Tarzan, Titus and Truman, and her coloured acetate frames have inventive details and colour combinations.

Lafont
11 rue Vignon, 8th (01.47.42.25.93/www.lafont-paris.com). M° Madeleine. **Open** 10am-7pm Mon-Sat. **Credit** AmEx, MC, V. **Map** p403 G4.
Philippe Lafont carries on the impeccable, finely hand-finished work of his grandfather. The speciality of Philippe's designer wife Laurence is small oval frames that tilt upwards like cat's eyes.
Other locations: 2 rue Duphot, 1st (01.42.60.01.02); 1 bd Raspail, 7th (01.45.48.24.23).

Traction
6 rue du Dragon, 6th (01.42.22.28.77/www.traction-lunettes.com). M° St-Germain-des-Prés or Sèvres Babylone. **Open** 2-7pm Mon; 10.30am-7pm Tue-Sat. **Credit** AmEx, DC, MC, V. **Map** p407 H7.
This brand marries four generations of Gros family know-how with a keen sense of modernity. Try the heavy metal specs or the conversation-making frames with quirky details on the arms.
Other locations: 56 galerie Vivienne, 2nd (01.44.50.58.88).

Hats

Marie Mercié
23 rue St-Sulpice, 6th (01.43.26.45.83). M° Odéon. **Open** 11am-7pm Mon-Sat. **Credit** AmEx, DC, MC, V. **Map** p410 H7.
Mercié's creations make you wish you lived in an era when hats were de rigueur. Step out in one shaped like curved fingers (complete with shocking-pink nail varnish and pink diamond ring) or a beret like a face with red lips and turquoise eyes. Ready-to-wear starts at €30; *sur mesure* takes ten days.

Philippe Model
33 pl du Marché-St-Honoré, 1st (01.42.96.89.02). M° Pyramides or Tuileries. **Open** 10am-7pm Tue-Sat. Closed Aug. **Credit** AmEx, DC, MC, V. **Map** p403 H5.
With his exuberant colours and two-tone designs, Model is your man if you're determined to stand out in the wedding, racing or boating crowd. Prices go from around €50 for a beret to more than €3,000 for a sumptuous, made-to-measure headdress.

Eat, Drink, Shop

High concept

Paris can't get enough of the designerish one-stop shop trend, as kicked off by **Colette** (which now has a branch in Tokyo). With their fusion of art, fashion and other creative pursuits, these so-called concept stores bring a cool and popular alternative to the traditional highbrow designer boutiques.

Castelbajac Concept Store

10 rue Vauvilliers, 1st (01.55.34.10.10/ www.jc-de-castelbajac.com). Mº Les Halles or Louvre Rivoli. **Open** 11am-7pm Mon-Sat. **Credit** AmEx, DC, MC, V. **Map** p404 J5.
Jean-Charles de Castelbajac's humorous, colourful world of fashion – developed by the aristo designer during 30 years on both sides of the Atlantic – is showcased in this gleaming white store.

Colette

213 rue St-Honoré, 1st (01.55.35.33.90/ www.colette.fr). Mº Tuileries or Pyramides. **Open** 11am-7pm Mon-Sat. **Credit** AmEx, DC, MC, V. **Map** p403 G4.
Nine years on, the original concept/lifestyle store (*pictured*) is still the most cutting edge. As well as exporting the one-stop concept to Tokyo in 2004, Colette releases CDs on its own label and produces regular, weighty style catalogues. This shrine to the limited edition displays must-have accessories inside clinical glass cases away from sticky fingers. Hipster books, media, Sony cameras, fancy Nokias,

and the hair and beauty brands själ, Kiehl's and uslu airlines, are scattered amid the ultra-cool reviews, magazines and photo albums on the ground floor and mezzanine. Upstairs has a selection of 'in' clothes (think Bless and Bernard Wilhelm), and accessories such as the Chrome Hearts line. Lunch, with a global selection of mineral water, can be nibbled at in the basement Water Bar.

Espace Lab 101

44 rue de La Rochefoucauld, 9th (01.49.95.95.85). Mº Pigalle or St-Georges. **Open** 12.30-8pm Tue-Thur, Sat; 12.30pm-2am Fri. **No credit cards. Map** p403 H2.
An offshoot of creative clubbers Project 101 (*see also p246* Base One), Espace Lab stocks a changing collection of streetwear labels (check out the customised military jackets by Super Sapin), plus electronic music on independent labels and DVDs.

Spree

16 rue de La Vieuville, 18th (01.42.23.41.40). Mº Abbesses. **Open** 2-7pm Mon; 11am-7.30pm Tue-Sat. Closed 1wk Aug. **Credit** AmEx, MC, V. **Map** p404 H1.
Managed by artistic director Bruno Hadjadj and fashion designer Roberta Oprandi, Spree offers fashion, design and contemporary art with a distinctly Montmartre vibe. Here you'll find 1960s chairs draped in the latest fashions by designers such as Preen or Isabel Marant.
Other locations: 1 rue St-Simon, 7th (01.42.22.05.04).

Surface to Air

46 rue de l'Arbre-Sec, 1st (01.49.27.04.54/ www.surface2air.com). Mº Pont Neuf. **Open** 12.30-7.30pm Mon-Sat. Closed 2wks Aug. **Credit** MC, V. **Map** p408 J6.
This indefinable, non-concept concept store also acts as a gallery and graphic design agency. The cult clothing selection takes in cute T-shirt dresses, Sila and Maria's trashy tank tops, Tatty Devine's hair accessories and men's themed sweatshirts. On its way to rivalling Colette for tastemaking supremacy, Surface to Air now runs biannual fashion salons, has launched its own menswear label, and has been called upon by multinationals such as Motorola to inject funkiness into their products. Surface to Air's other branch is in Grand Street, New York.

Jewellery

Dotted in and around **place Vendôme**, the key *joailliers* define the luxurious spirit of Paris.

Boucheron

26 pl Vendôme, 1st (01.42.61.58.16/www.boucheron. com). M° Opéra. **Open** 10.30am-7pm Mon-Sat. **Credit** AmEx, DC, MC, V. **Map** p403 G4.
The grandest shop on place Vendôme, Boucheron was the first to set up here, eager for celebrity custom from the nearby Ritz hotel. Now owned by Gucci, the venerable jeweller still manages to produce voluptuous pieces. Its uses traditional motifs with new accents: witness, for example, its fabulous chocolate-coloured gold watch.

Cartier

3 rue de la Paix, 2nd (01.42.18.53.70/www.cartier. com). M° Opéra. **Open** 10.30am-7pm Mon-Sat. **Credit** AmEx, DC, MC, V. **Map** p403 G4.
This mythic French jeweller and watchmaker has refocused on jewellery production after decades of concentrating on fine leather goods and watches. Its designs draw inspiration from its long, rich heritage: panthers, pearls and the 'trinity' ring (interjoined bands of white, yellow and rose gold).
Other locations: 3 rue de la Paix, 2nd (01.42.18.53.70); 10 cité du Retiro, 8th (01.58.18.18.18).

Chanel Joaillerie

18 pl Vendôme, 1st (01.55.35.50.05/www.chanel. com). M° Tuileries or Opéra. **Open** 10.30am-6.30pm Mon-Fri; 10.30am-1pm, 2-6.30pm Sat. **Credit** AmEx, DC, MC, V. **Map** p403 G4.
You almost expect Coco to walk through the door of this chic boutique, decorated in a style evocative of 1930s Paris. When Chanel launched its fine jewellery department in the early 1990s, it reissued the single jewellery collection – strong on platinum and diamonds – that Coco had designed 60 years before. The current collection reinterprets Coco's key motifs – camellias, stars and comets – in a modern way.

Dior Joaillerie

8 pl Vendôme, 1st (01.42.96.30.84/www.dior.com). M° Tuileries or Opéra. **Open** 11am-7pm Mon, Sat; 10.30am-7pm Tue-Fri. **Credit** AmEx, DC, MC, V. **Map** p403 G4.
Dior Jewellery leads the pack, thanks to the whimsical but unabashed bling of Victoire de Castellane's designs. The former Chanel accessories designer jumped ship to Dior in 1998, and is responsible for the fad of semi-precious, coloured stones.

Swarovski

52 rue Bonaparte, 6th (01.56.24.15.60/www. swarovski.com). M° St-Germain-des-Prés or Mabillon. **Open** 10am-7pm Mon-Sat. **Credit** AmEx, MC, V. **Map** p407 H6.
This lavish boutique sells the costume jewellery lines by century-old Austrian company Swarovski, which produces glamorous pieces from top quality crystals – a big hit with the celebrity set.

Van Cleef & Arpels

22, 24 pl Vendôme, 1st (01.53.45.45.45/www. vancleef.com). M° Tuileries or Opéra. **Open** 10.30am-7pm Mon-Fri; 11am-7pm Sat. **Credit** AmEx, DC, MC, V. **Map** p403 G4.
At this address since 1906, the legendary French dynasty grew from an alliance of two diamond merchant families. The girl's best friend continues to take centre-stage in its elegant designs.

Shoes & bags

The luxury floor at **Printemps** (*see p234*) is a good source of designer footwear labels. **Rue du Dragon** (métro Saint-Germain-des-Prés or Saint-Sulpice) in the 6th is crammed with accessory boutiques offering young designers' creations.

Bruno Frisoni

34 rue de Grenelle, 7th (01.42.84.12.30). M° Rue du Bac. **Open** 10.30am-7pm Tue-Sat. **Credit** AmEx, MC, V. **Map** p407 G7.
Innovative Frisoni used to work for Christian Lacroix and Jean-Louis Scherrer. Inspired by the 1960s, he makes shoes with a cinematic, pop edge; his modern theatrics are not for the conventional.

Camper

1 rue du Cherche-Midi, 6th (01.45.48.22.00/www. camper.com). M° St-Sulpice. **Open** 11am-7pm Mon-Sat. **Credit** AmEx, DC, MC, V. **Map** p407 G7.
This chic Spanish cobbler was the first to bring asymmetry to popular shoe design.
Other locations: 9 rue des Francs-Bourgeois, 3rd (01.48.87.09.09); 14-16 rue du Fbg-St-Honoré, 8th (01.42.68.13.65).

Christian Louboutin

19 rue Jean-Jacques-Rousseau, 1st (01.42.36.05.31). M° Palais Royal Musée du Louvre. **Open** 10.30am-7pm Mon-Sat. Closed 3wks Aug. **Credit** AmEx, MC, V. **Map** p404 J5.
Each of Louboutin's creations (with hallmark red soles) is displayed in individual frames. His Trash mules – incorporating old métro tickets, glitter, torn letters and postage stamps – are especially coveted.
Other locations: 38 rue de Grenelle, 7th (01.42.22.33.07).

Hervé Chapelier

1bis rue du Vieux-Colombier, 6th (01.44.07.06.50/ www.hervechapelier.fr). M° St-Sulpice. **Open** 10.15am-7pm Mon-Sat. **Credit** AmEx, DC, MC, V. **Map** 407 G7.
The top stop for the ultimate-chic, hard-wearing, bi-coloured totes. Often copied, never equalled, they're available in pretty much every colour. Sizes and prices range from a dinky little purse at €22 to a stonking weekend bag at €130.

Iris

28 rue de Grenelle, 7th (01.42.22.89.81). M° Rue du Bac or St-Sulpice. **Open** 10.30am-7pm Mon-Sat. **Credit** AmEx, MC, V. **Map** p407 F7.

Eat, Drink, Shop

This dazzling white boutique stocks shoes by the likes of Marc Jacobs, Chloé and John Galliano, as well as impeccably Belgian Véronique Branquinho.

Jamin Puech
61 rue de Hauteville, 10th (01.40.22.08.32). Mº Poissonnière. **Open** 11am-7pm Mon-Fri; noon-7pm Sat. **Credit** AmEx, MC, V. **Map** p404 K3.
The full collection of Isabelle Puech and Benoît Jamin's dazzling handbags – which use anything from tapestry and raffia to sequins – is on show in a boho setting complete with antler-horn chairs.

Mandarina Duck
36 rue Etienne-Marcel, 2nd (01.40.13.02.96/www. mandarinaduck.com). Mº Etienne Marcel. 11am-7pm Mon-Sat. **Credit** AmEx, DC, MC, V. **Map** p404 J5.
The yellow-and-white geometric Mandarina Duck features sleek, trendy, monotone handbags; the Italian brand's wallets, luggage, sunglasses and watches are also available.
Other locations: 7 bd de la Madeleine, 1st (01.42.86.08.00); 4 rue Pavée, 4th (01.42.77.75.15); 51 rue Bonaparte, 6th (01.43.26.68.38).

Patrick Cox
62 rue Tiquetonne, 2nd (01.40.26.66.55/www. patrickcox.co.uk). Mº Etienne Marcel. **Open** 10.30am-7.30pm Mon-Sat. **Credit** AmEx, MC, V. **Map** p404 J5.
If the slipper fits, chances are it's one of Cox's. Elegance off the catwalk is Patrick's forte, with ultra-feminine designs and fabrics. His stiletto boots and kitten heels are guaranteed to make your feet feel like a million euros.
Other locations: 21 rue de Grenelle, 7th (01.45.49.24.28).

Peggy Huyn Kinh
9-11 rue Coëtlogon, 6th (01.42.84.83.83/www.phk. fr). Mº St-Sulpice. **Open** 10am-7pm Mon-Sat. **Credit** AmEx, MC, V. **Map** p407 G7.
This street may not scream fashion, but it doesn't deter Peggy Huyn Kinh, former creative director for Cartier and others, whose bags use boarskin and python. She does minimalist silver jewellery, too.

Pierre Hardy
156 galerie de Valois, 1st (01.42.60.59.75/www. pierrehardy.com). Mº Palais Royal Musée du Louvre. **Open** 11am-7pm Mon-Sat. **Credit** AmEx, DC, MC, V. **Map** p404 H5.
This classy black-and-white shoebox is home to Hardy's range of superbly conceived footwear – with a price tag to match – for men and women. A shoe designer at Hermès, he has a feel for street-smart glamour that keeps him ahead of the pack.

Robert Clergerie
5 rue du Cherche-Midi, 6th (01.45.48.75.47). Mº St-Sulpice. **Open** 10am-7pm Mon-Sat. **Credit** AmEx, DC, MC, V. **Map** p407 G7.
Robert Clergerie has thankfully settled back into designing exquisitely practical daywear; he's even managed to revive the two-tone loafer he created at

the start of his career way back in 1981. Clergerie's highly stylised 'boxing trainer' knocks the socks off other models.
Other locations: 46 rue Croix-des-Petits-Champs, 1st (01.42.61.49.24); 18 av Victor-Hugo, 16th (01.45.01.81.30).

Rodolphe Menudier
14 rue de Castiglione, 1st (01.42.60.86.27/www. rodolphemenudier.com). Mº Concorde or Tuileries. **Open** 11am-7.30pm Mon; 10.30am-7.30pm Tue-Sat. **Credit** AmEx, MC, V. **Map** p403 G5.
This silver-and-black cylinder of a boutique is a perfect backdrop for Rodolphe Menudier's racy designs, which mingle moods and materials. Dozens of open, silver-handled drawers display his stilettos in profile; top of the range are outrageous thigh-high boots with Plexiglass soles, but more demure customers can opt for ballerina pumps or stock up on exclusive hosiery from Gerbé and Chantal Thomass.

Roger Vivier
29 rue du Fbg-St-Honoré, 8th (01.53.43.00.00/ www.rogervivier.com). Mº Madeleine or Concorde. **Open** 10.30am-7pm Mon-Sat. **Credit** AmEx, DC, MC, V. **Map** p403 F4.
Before Blahnik there was Vivier. This extravagent shoe designer approached his craft like a sculptor, fashioning extraordinarily intricate forms for feet. Vivier is widely credited with inventing the stiletto and made fans of celebrities as big as Queen Elizabeth II and the Beatles way back when. The master's legend lives on in this exclusive boutique, which sells signature vintage models and new designs by Bruno Frisoni (*see p257*). **Photo** *p260*.

Food & drink

Though *charcutiers* and quirky little places are becoming increasingly rare, Paris still has plenty to offer the food-obsessed. It would be easy to spend an entire holiday (if not a lifetime) exploring the enormous variety of breads, pastries, cheeses and chocolate, and open-air markets continue to beckon with their displays of fresh, seasonal goods (*see p259* **Forward marché!**). The chain concept is catching on: there seems to be a **Paul** bakery on every corner and even renowned *fromageries* such as **Quatrehomme** have been popping up in different neighbourhoods. The good news is that overall quality remains impressive – and you need only look around to realise that cream-filled pastries won't make you fat.

Arnaud Delmontel
39 rue des Martyrs, 9th (01.48.78.29.33). Mº St-Georges. **Open** 7am-8.30pm Mon, Wed-Sun. **No credit cards. Map** p404 H2.

Forward *marché*!

When pressed, Parisians will shop at the *supermarché*, but they're far happier queuing (or jostling, as often as not) at their local open-air market. Markets have eternal appeal and their products – like a farmer's pungent goat's cheese, a dozen fresh Cancale oysters, a bunch of ruby chard or a jar of sunflower-yellow honey – are seen as more 'natural' alternatives to supermarket fare. The city council has made markets more accessible to working people by extending their opening hours and planting late-afternoon markets in previously overlooked areas. There are now more than 70 markets – including a handful of the covered variety – in Paris, and even if quality can be unpredictable, there's no better place in which to soak up neighbourhood atmosphere. The city council's website (www.paris.fr) has comprehensive details of each one; below is a selection of the best:

Marché Monge (place Monge, 5th; 7am-2.30pm Wed, Fri; 7am-3pm Sun), though compact, is pretty, and set on a leafy square. It has an unusually high proportion of producers and is much less touristy than nearby rue Mouffetard, a long-established street market. Be prepared to queue for the best quality.

Saxe-Breteuil (av de Saxe, 7th; 7am-2.30pm Thur; 7am-3pm Sat; *pictured*) has an unrivalled setting facing the Eiffel Tower, as well as the city's most chic produce. Look for farmer's goat's cheese, rare apple varieties, Armenian specialities, abundant oysters and a handful of dedicated small producers.

Marché Anvers (pl d'Anvers, 9th; 3-8pm Fri) is a recently created afternoon market that adds to the village atmosphere of a peaceful *quartier* down the hill from Montmartre. Among its highlights are untreated vegetables, hams from the Auvergne, lovingly aged cheeses and award-winning honey.

Marché Bastille (bd Richard-Lenoir, 11th; 7am-2.30pm Thur; 7am-3pm Sun) is one of the biggest and most boisterous in Paris. A favourite of political campaigners, it's also a great source of local cheeses, farmer's chicken and excellent affordable fish.

Marché Beauvau (pl d'Aligre, 12th; 8.30am-1pm, 4-7.30pm Tue-Sat; 8.30am-1.30pm Sun), a covered market, is proudly working class. Stallholders do their utmost to out-shout each other while price-conscious

shoppers don't compromise on quality. The city's only central flea market runs nearby, open every day but Monday (*see p266*).

Marché Président-Wilson (av Président-Wilson, 16th; 7am-2.30pm Wed; 7am-3pm Sat) is a classy market attracting the city's top chefs, who snap up ancient vegetable varieties. Genuine Breton crêpes and buckwheat galettes lure you as you shop.

Marché Batignolles (bd de Batignolles, 17th; 9am-2pm Sat) is more down to earth than the better-known **Raspail** organic market, with a quirky selection of stallholders, many of whom produce what they sell. Prices are higher than at ordinary markets, but the goods are worth it.

Before Blahnik – **Roger Vivier**. *See p258.*

With its crisp crust and chewy crumb shot through with irregular holes, Delmontel's Renaissance bread is easily one of the finest in Paris. He puts the same skill and perfectionism into his pastries, biscuits and unsurpassable almond croissants.
Other locations: 57 rue Damrémont, 18th (01.42.64.59.63).

L'Autre Boulange
43 rue de Montreuil, 11th (01.43.72.86.04).
M° Nation or Faidherbe Chaligny. **Open** 7.30am-1.30pm, 3.30-8pm Tue-Sat. Closed Aug. **Credit** MC, V. **Map** p409 P7.
Michel Cousin bakes up 23 kinds of organic loaves in his wood-fired oven – types like the *flutiot* (rye bread with raisins, walnuts and hazelnuts), the *sarment de Bourgogne* (sourdough and a little rye) and a spiced cornmeal bread ideal for foie gras. Great croissants and *chaussons* for superior snacking.

Le Boulanger de Monge
123 rue Monge, 5th (01.43.37.54.20). M° Censier Daubenton. **Open** 7am-8.30pm Tue-Sun. **Credit** MC, V. **Map** p408 K9.
Dominique Saibron uses spices in his starter to give inimitable flavour to his organic sourdough *boule*. About 2,000 bread lovers a day visit his boutique, which also produces one of the city's best baguettes.

Kayser
8, 14 rue Monge, 5th (01.44.07.01.42/ 01.44.07.17.81). M° Maubert Mutualité. **Open** 6.45am-8.30pm Mon, Wed-Sun. **Credit** MC, V. **Map** p408 J7.
In a few years, Eric Kayser has established himself as one of the city's star bakers – even if his baguette is a little on the salty side. The bakery at 14 rue Monge is devoted to organic loaves.

Moisan
5 pl d'Aligre, 12th (01.43.45.46.60). M° Ledru-Rollin. **Open** 7am-8pm Tue-Sat; 7am-2pm Sun. **Credit** (€15 minimum) MC, V. **Map** p409 N7.
Moisan's organic bread, *viennoiseries* and rustic tarts are outstanding. At this branch, near the busy market on place d'Aligre, there's always a queue snaking out the door.
Other locations: 4 av du Général-Leclerc, 14th (01.43.22.34.13).

Le Moulin de la Vierge
166 av de Suffren, 15th (01.47.83.45.55). M° Sèvres Lecourbe. **Open** 7am-8pm Mon-Sat. **Credit** MC, V. **Map** p407 E8.
Basile Kamir learned breadmaking after falling in love with an abandoned bakery. Each of Kamir's branches has an irresistible fragrance, matched by the quality of his sourdough breads.
Other locations: 82 rue Daguerre, 14th (01.43.22.50.55); 105 rue Vercingétorix, 14th (01.45.43.09.84); 6 rue de Lévis, 17th (01.43.87.42.42).

Poilâne
8 rue du Cherche-Midi, 6th (01.45.48.42.59/www. poilane.com). M° Sèvres Babylone or St-Sulpice. **Open** 7.15am-8.15pm Mon-Sat. **Credit** (€20 minimum) MC, V. **Map** p407 G7.
Apollonia Poilâne took over the family business after her father died in 2002. Nothing has changed in the tiny original shop, where locals queue for freshly baked country *miches*, flaky-crusted apple tarts and buttery shortbread biscuits.
Other locations: 49 rue de Grenelle, 15th (01.45.79.11.49).

Cheese

The sign *maître fromager affineur* denotes merchants who buy young cheeses from farms and age them on their premises; *fromage fermier* and *fromage au lait cru* signify farm-produced and raw milk cheeses respectively.

Alléosse
13 rue Poncelet, 17th (01.46.22.50.45). M° Ternes. **Open** 9am-1pm, 4-7pm Tue-Thur; 9am-7pm Fri, Sat; 9am-1pm Sun. **Credit** MC, V. **Map** p402 C2.
People cross town for these cheeses – wonderful farmhouse camemberts, delicate st-marcellins, a choice of *chèvres* and several rarities.

Fromagerie Dubois et Fils
80 rue de Tocqueville, 17th (01.42.27.11.38). M° Malesherbes or Villiers. **Open** 9am-1pm, 4-8pm Tue-Fri; 8.30am-7.30pm Sat; 9am-1pm Sun. Closed 3wks Aug. **Credit** AmEx, MC, V. **Map** p403 E2.
Superchef darling Dubois stocks 80 types of goat's cheese plus prized, aged st-félicien.

Fromagerie Quatrehomme
62 rue de Sèvres, 7th (01.47.34.33.45). M° Vaneau. **Open** 8.45am-1pm, 4-7.45pm Tue-Thur; 8.45am-7.45pm Fri, Sat. **Credit** MC, V. **Map** p407 F8.

The award-winning Marie Quatrehomme runs this inviting *fromagerie*. Justly famous for classics such as comté fruité, beaufort and a squishy st-marcellin, she sells more unusual specialities such as goat's cheese with pesto and truffle-flavoured brie.
Other locations: 118 rue Mouffetard, 5th (01.45.35.13.19); 9 rue du Puteau, 18th (01.46.06.26.03).

Marie-Anne Cantin

12 rue du Champ-de-Mars, 7th (01.45.50.43.94/ www.cantin.fr). Mº Ecole Militaire. **Open** 8.30am-7.30pm Mon-Sat. **Credit** AmEx, MC, V. **Map** p406 D6.
Cantin, a vigorous defender of unpasteurised cheese and supplier to many posh Paris restaurants, is justifiably proud of her aged *chèvres*, roquefort réserve and amazing morbier, mont d'or and comté cheeses.

Chocolate

Cacao et Chocolat

29 rue de Buci, 6th (01.46.33.77.63). Mº Mabillon. **Open** 10.30am-7.30pm daily. **Credit** AmEx, DC, MC, V. **Map** p407 H7.
This shop, decorated in burnt orange and ochre, recalls chocolate's ancient Aztec origins with spicy fillings (honey and chilli, nutmeg, clove and citrus), chocolate masks and pyramids.
Other locations: 63 rue St-Louis-en-l'Ile, 4th (01.46.33.33.33); 36 rue Vieille-du-Temple, 4th (01.42.71.50.06).

Christian Constant

37 rue d'Assas, 6th (01.53.63.15.15). Mº St-Placide or Rennes. **Open** 8.30am-9pm Mon-Fri; 8.30am-8.30pm Sat, Sun. **Credit** MC, V. **Map** p407 G8.
A master chocolate-maker and *traiteur*, Constant is revered by all. Trained in the arts of *pâtisserie* and chocolate, he scours the globe for new and delectable ideas. His ganaches are subtly flavoured with verbena, jasmine or cardamom.

Debauve & Gallais

30 rue des Sts-Pères, 7th (01.45.48.54.67/www. debauve-et-gallais.com). Mº St-Germain-des-Prés or Rue du Bac. **Open** 9am-7pm Mon-Sat. **Credit** DC, MC, V. **Map** p407 G7.
This former pharmacy, a historic monument whose façade dates from 1800, sold chocolate for medicinal purposes. Its intense tea, honey and praline-flavours still heal the soul today.
Other locations: 33 rue Vivienne, 2nd (01.40.39.05.50).

Jean-Paul Hévin

3 rue Vavin, 6th (01.43.54.09.85/www.jphevin.com). Mº Vavin. **Open** 10am-7pm Mon-Sat. Closed Aug. **Credit** AmEx, MC, V. **Map** p407 G8.
Jean-Paul Hévin dares to fill his chocolates with potent cheeses; loyal customers like to serve them with wine as an apéritif. Even more risqué are his aphrodisiac chocolates, another favourite.
Other locations: 231 rue St-Honoré, 1st (01.55.35.35.96); 16 av de La Motte-Picquet, 7th (01.45.51.77.48).

La Maison du Chocolat

89 av Raymond-Poincaré, 16th (01.40.67.77.83/ www.lamaisonduchocolat.com). Mº Victor Hugo. **Open** 10am-7pm Mon-Sat. **Credit** AmEx, MC, V. **Map** p402 B4.
Robert Linxe opened his first Paris shop in 1977 and has been inventing new chocolates ever since, using Asian spices, fresh fruits and herbal infusions.
Other locations: 19 rue de Sèvres, 6th (01.45.44.20.40); 225 rue du Fbg-St-Honoré, 8th (01.42.27.39.44); 8 bd de la Madeleine, 9th (01.47.42.86.52).

Patrick Roger

108 bd St-Germain, 6th (01.43.29.38.42/ www.patrickroger.com). Mº Odéon. **Open** 10.30am-7.30pm Tue-Sat. **Credit** MC, V. **Map** p410 H7.
With a sculptor's sensibility and a concern for ethics that leads him to work only with small producers, Sceaux-based Patrick Roger is shaking up the Parisian art of chocolate-making. While other *chocolatiers* aim for the glossiest possible finish, Roger might create a brushed effect or sprinkle cocoa powder on hens so realistic you almost expect them to lay (chocolate) eggs.

Pierre Marcolini

89 rue de Seine, 6th (01.44.07.39.07/www.marcolini. com). Mº Mabillon. **Open** 2-7pm Mon; 10.30am-7pm Tue-Sat. **Credit** AmEx, MC, V. **Map** p407 H7.
This Belgian newcomer to Paris is known for his 44 ganache flavours, including ginger, jasmine and tea with lemon. In Brussels, Marcolini's chocolate cakes are considered edible works of art.

Richart

258 bd St-Germain, 7th (01.45.55.66.00/www. richart.com). Mº Solférino. **Open** 10am-7pm Mon-Sat. **Credit** AmEx, MC, V. **Map** p407 F6.
Each chocolate ganache has an intricate design, packages look like jewel boxes, and each purchase comes with a tract on how best to savour the stuff. Chic Richart boutiques now set up in Barcelona, Milan, Tokyo and New York.

Global

Les Délices d'Orient

52 av Emile-Zola, 15th (01.45.79.10.00). Mº Charles Michels. **Open** 8.30am-9pm Tue-Sun. **Credit** MC, V. **Map** p406 B8.
Shelves here groan under stuffed aubergines, halva, Lebanese bread, falafel, olives and all manner of Middle Eastern delicacies.
Other locations: 14 rue des Quatre-Frères-Peignot, 15th (01.45.77.82.93).

Izraël

30 rue François-Miron, 4th (01.42.72.66.23). Mº Hôtel de Ville. **Open** 9.30am-1pm, 2.30-7pm Tue-Fri; 10am-7pm Sat. Closed Aug. **Credit** MC, V. **Map** p411 K6.
A Marais fixture, this narrow shop stocks spices and other delights from Mexico, Turkey and India.

Jabugo Ibérico & Co

11 rue Clément-Marot, 8th (01.47.20.03.13).
M° Alma Marceau or Franklin D. Roosevelt. **Open**
10am-9pm Mon-Sat. **Credit** AmEx, MC, V. **Map**
p402 D4.
This shop specialises in Spanish hams with the
Bellota-Bellota label, meaning the pigs have feasted
on acorns. Manager Philippe Poulachon compares
the complexity of his cured hams (at €98 a kilo) to
the delicacy of truffles. They also sell hams at the
épicerie attached to restaurant Bellota-Bellota (18 rue
Jean-Nicot, 7th, 01.53.59.96.96).

Kioko

46 rue des Petits-Champs, 2nd (01.42.61.33.65).
M° Pyramides. **Open** 10am-8pm Tue-Sat; 11am-7pm
Sun. **Credit** MC, V. **Map** p403 H4.
From *koshi-hikari* rice to Kikkoman, this two-level
supermarket has everything that fans of Japanese
cooking might crave – including ready-made sushi.

Merry Monk

87 rue de la Convention, 15th (01.40.60.79.54).
M° Boucicaut. **Open** 10am-7pm Mon-Sat. **Credit**
MC, V. **Map** p406 B9.
Provides expatriates with essentials such as ginger
biscuits and loose tea, and even houses a section
specifically dedicated to South Africa.

Mexi & Co

*10 rue Dante, 5th (01.46.34.14.12). M° Cluny La
Sorbonne.* **Open** noon-midnight daily. **No credit
cards. Map** p410 J7.
All you need for organising your own fiesta: mari-
nades for fajitas, dried chillies, Latin American
beers, *cachaça* and tequilas.

Pasta Linea

9 rue de Turenne, 4th (01.42.77.62.54). M° St-Paul.
Open noon-9pm Tue-Sun. **Credit** AmEx, DC, MC, V.
Map p411 L6.
Artichoke ravioli with truffle cream sauce or fresh
linguine with tomato and rocket are among the heavenly hot pastas you might find here. Pasta Linea also
stocks quality dried pastas and prepared sauces to
eat at home.

Petrossian

*18 bd de La-Tour-Maubourg, 7th (01.44.11.32.22/
www.petrossian.fr). M° Invalides or La Tour
Maubourg.* **Open** 9.30am-8pm Mon-Sat. **Credit**
AmEx, DC, MC, V. **Map** p407 E6.
This Russian delicatessen downstairs from a trendy
restaurant of the same name and nationality sells
silky smoked salmon, Iranian caviar and gift boxes
with little drawers to impress even the most jaded
of the jet set.

Tang Frères

48 av d'Ivry, 13th (01.45.70.80.00). M° Porte d'Ivry.
Open 9am-7.30pm Tue-Sun. **Credit** MC, V.
The main supplier to Chinatown, this is the best one-
stop shop for a Chinese or South-east Asian stir-fry.
Other locations: 168 av de Choisy, 13th
(01.44.24.06.72).

Velan

*87 passage Brady, 10th (01.42.46.06.06/www.e-
velan.com). M° Château d'Eau.* **Open** 10am-8.30pm
Mon-Sat. **Credit** AmEx, DC, MC, V. **Map** p404 K4.
In a crumbling arcade lined with Indian restaurants,
this is a prime source of spices and Indian produce.

Pâtisseries

Arnaud Lahrer

53 rue Caulaincourt, 18th (01.42.57.68.08).
M° Lamarck Caulaincourt. **Open** 10am-7.30pm
Tue-Sat. **Credit** MC, V. **Map** p403 H1.
Look out for the strawberry-and-lychee flavoured
bonheur and the chocolate-and-thyme *récif*.

Finkelsztajn

27 rue des Rosiers, 4th (01.42.72.78.91). M° St-Paul.
Open 11am-7pm Mon; 10am-7pm Wed-Sun. Closed
15 July-15 Aug. **Credit** (€20 minimum) AmEx, MC,
V. **Map** p411 L6.
This motherly shop stocks dense Jewish cakes filled
with poppy seeds, apples or cream cheese.

Gérard Mulot

76 rue de Seine, 6th (01.43.26.85.77). M° Odéon.
Open 6.45am-8pm Mon, Tue, Thur-Sun. Closed
Easter & Aug. **No credit cards. Map** p410 H7.
Mulot rustles up stunning pastries. Typical is the
mabillon: caramel mousse with apricot marmalade.
Other locations: 92 rue de la Glacière, 13th
(01.45.81.39.09).

Pierre Hermé

*72 rue Bonaparte, 6th (01.43.54.47.77). M° St-
Sulpice.* **Open** 10am-7pm Tue-Sun. **Credit** AmEx,
DC, MC, V. **Map** p407 G7.
Pastry superstar Hermé attracts connoisseurs from
St-Germain and afar with his seasonal collections.
Other locations: 185 rue de Vaugirard, 15th
(01.47.83.89.96).

Sadaharu Aoki

*35 rue de Vaugirard, 6th (01.45.44.48.90). M° St-
Placide.* **Open** 11am-7pm daily. **Credit** MC, V.
Map p407 G8.
This Japanese pastry chef uses French techniques
and ingredients like green tea to produce original
(and pristine) pastries.
Other locations: 56 bd de Port-Royal, 5th
(01.45.35.36.80).

Treats & *traiteurs*

Allicante

*26 bd Beaumarchais, 11th (01.43.55.13.02/
www.allicante.com). M° Bastille or Chemin Vert.*
Open 10am-7.30pm Mon-Sat. **Credit** AmEx, DC,
MC, V. **Map** p411 M6.
A trove of oily delights, including rare olive oils from
Liguria, Sicily and Greece, fragrant pine nut, pistachio and almond varieties, oils extracted from apricot, peach and avocado pits – even pricey argania
oil, hand-pounded by the Berber women of Morocco.

Da Rosa

62 rue de Seine, 6th (01.40.51.00.09/www.darosa.fr).
M° Odéon. **Open** 10am-11pm daily. **Credit** AmEx,
MC, V. **Map** p410 H7.
José Da Rosa sourced ingredients for top Paris
restaurants before opening his own shop, stuffed
with Spanish hams, Olivier Roellinger spices, and
truffles from the Luberon.

L'Epicerie

51 rue St-Louis-en-l'Ile, 4th (01.43.25.20.14).
M° Pont Marie. **Open** *Oct-Apr* 10.30am-7pm daily.
May-Sept 11am-8pm daily. **Credit** MC, V.
Map p411 K7.
This glorious gift shop is crammed with nice bottles
of blackcurrant vinegar, five-spice mustard, tiny
pots of jam, orange sauce, honey with figs and indul-
gent boxes of chocolate snails.

Fauchon

26 & 30 pl de la Madeleine, 8th (01.47.42.60.11/
www.fauchon.com). M° Madeleine. **Open** *No.26* 8am-
9pm Mon-Sat. *No.30* 9am-8pm Mon-Sat. **Credit**
AmEx, DC, MC, V. **Map** p403 F4.
It may be the city's most famous food shop, but
glitzy Fauchon seems to lack soul after a series of
revamps. Still, it's worth a visit – particularly for its
beautifully packaged gift items.

Goumanyat

3 rue Dupuis, 3rd (01.44.78.96.74/www.goumanyat.
com). M° Temple or République. **Open** 2-7pm Tue-
Fri; 11am-7pm Sat. **Credit** AmEx, DC, MC, V.
Map p404 L5.
Jean-Marie Thiercelin's family has been in the spice
trade since 1809, and his spacious, rather secretive
shop (buzzer entry) is a treasure trove of super-fresh
flavourings. Star chefs come here for Indonesian
cubebe pepper, gleaming fresh nutmeg, long pepper
(an Indian variety), and Spanish and Iranian saffron.

Hédiard

21 pl de la Madeleine, 8th (01.43.12.88.88/
www.hediard.fr). M° Madeleine. **Open** 8.30am-9pm
Mon-Sat. **Credit** AmEx, DC, MC, V. **Map** p403 F4.
The first establishment to introduce exotic foods to
Paris, Hédiard specialises in rare teas and coffees,
spices, jams and candied fruits. The original shop,
dating from 1880, has a posh tearoom upstairs, La
Table d'Hédiard, offering buffet breakfasts during
the week for €22.
Other locations: 31 av George-V, 8th
(01.47.20.44.44); 70 av Paul Doumer, 16th
(01.45.04.51.92); 106 bd de Courcelles, 17th
(01.47.63.32.14).

Huilerie Artisanale Leblanc

6 rue Jacob, 6th (01.46.34.61.55). M° St-Germain-
des-Prés. **Open** 2-7pm Mon; 12.30-7pm Tue-Fri;
10am-7pm Sat. Closed 2wks Aug. **No credit cards.**
Map p407 H6.
The Leblanc family started out making walnut oil
from its family tree in Burgundy before branching
out to press pure oils from hazelnuts, almonds, pine
nuts, grilled peanuts, pistachios and olives.

Jean-Paul Gardil

44 rue St-Louis-en-l'Ile, 4th (01.43.54.97.15). M°
Pont Marie. **Open** 9am-12.45pm, 4-7.45pm Tue-Sat;
9am-12.30pm Sun. **Credit** MC, V. **Map** p411 K7.
Rarely has meat looked so beautiful as in this fairy-
tale shop, where a multitude of plaques confirm the
butcher's skill in choosing the finest meats – like
milk-fed veal and lamb, free-range Barbary duck-
lings and Bresse poulards and geese.

La Maison des Trois Thés

1 rue St-Médard, 5th (01.43.36.93.84). M° Place
Monge. **Open** 11am-7.30pm Tue-Sun. Closed Aug.
Credit MC, V. **Map** p408 K8.
Yu Hui Tseng, one of the world's leading tea experts,
has moved to these larger premises. Hush reigns as
connoisseurs dip their lips into more than 1,000 varieties of tea (most of them costing a small fortune –
the cheapest you'll find goes for €10). La Maison can
get very busy at the weekend.

La Maison de la Truffe

19 pl de la Madeleine, 8th (01.42.65.53.22/
www.maison-de-la-truffe.com). M° Madeleine.
Open 9.30am-9pm Mon-Sat. **Credit** AmEx, DC,
MC, V. **Map** p403 F4.
Come to Guy Monier's esteemed establishment in
winter for truffles worth more than gold, or for the
more affordable (artificial) truffle oils, sauces and
vinegars. Truffle-enhanced foies gras also available,
plus an extensive selection of wines.

Mariage Frères

30 rue du Bourg-Tibourg, 4th (01.42.72.28.11/
www.mariagefreres.com). M° Hôtel de Ville. **Open**
Shop 10.30am-7.30pm daily. *Salon* noon-7pm daily.
Credit AmEx, MC, V. **Map** p411 K6.
A wood-panelled, wonderfully aromatic, old-fashioned tea emporium – one of the few places in Paris
where queuing is the rule. Come here to buy (or, in
the salon, sample) teas of every provenance, colour
and strength, plus tea accessories. **Photo** *p264.*
Other locations: 13 rue des Grands-Augustins,
6th (01.40.51.82.50); 260 rue du Fbg-St-Honoré, 8th
(01.46.22.18.54).

Poissonnerie du Dôme

4 rue Delambre, 14th (01.43.35.23.95). M° Vavin.
Open 8am-1pm, 4-7pm Tue-Sat; 8am-1pm Sun.
Credit MC, V. **Map** p407 G9.
The fish here are individually selected, many com-
ing straight from small boats off the Breton coast.
Each one is bright of eye and sound of gill. Try the
drool-inducing (but bank-breaking) turbot, the giant
crabs or the scallops, when in season.

Torréfacteur Verlet

256 rue St-Honoré, 1st (01.42.60.67.39). M° Palais
Royal Musée du Louvre. **Open** 9.30am-6.30pm Mon-
Sat. **Credit** MC, V. **Map** p403 G5.
The freshly roasted coffee here smells as heavenly
as the priciest perfume. Eric Duchaussoy roasts rare
beans to perfection – sip a *p'tit noir* at a wooden
table, or take home some of the city's finest coffee.

Eat, Drink, Shop

Mariage
Frères.
See p263.

Julien, Caviste.

Don't expect to see an international selection
in Paris wine shops. Instead, nab reasonably
priced French wines that rarely get beyond
its borders. The food hall on the first floor of
Galeries Lafayette (*see p234*) also stocks
spirits of impressive vintage.

Les Caves Augé

*116 bd Haussmann, 8th (01.45.22.16.97). M° St-
Augustin.* **Open** 1-7.30pm Mon; 9am-7.30pm Tue-
Sat. Closed Mon in Aug. **Credit** AmEx, MC, V.
Map p403 E3.
The oldest wine shop in Paris – Marcel Proust was
a regular customer – is serious and professional.

Les Caves Taillevent

*199 rue du Fbg-St-Honoré, 8th (01.45.61.14.09/
www.taillevent.com). M° Charles de Gaulle Etoile or
Ternes.* **Open** 2-7.30pm Mon; 9am-7.30pm Tue-Sat.
Closed 3wks Aug. **Credit** AmEx, DC, MC, V.
Map p402 D3.
Half a million bottles make up the Taillevent cellar.
Order one with your meal at the Taillevent restau-
rant at nearby 15 rue Lamennais (01.44.95.15.01).

Les Domaines qui Montent

136 bd Voltaire, 11th (01.43.56.89.15). M° Voltaire.
Open 10am-8pm Tue-Fri; 10.30am-10pm Sat.
Credit MC, V. **Map** p405 N6.
A shop and café, where wines cost the same as they
would at the producers. Saturday tastings, too.

Julien, Caviste

*50 rue Charlot, 3rd (01.42.72.00.94). M° Filles du
Calvaire.* **Open** 9.30am-1.30pm, 3.30-8.30pm Tue-Fri;
9.30am-8.30pm Sat; 10am-1pm Sun. **Credit** MC, V.
Map p404 L5.
The tireless Julien overflows with enthusiasm for the
small producers he has discovered, and often holds
free wine tastings on Saturdays.

Lavinia

*3 bd de la Madeleine, 1st (01.42.97.20.20/www.
lavinia.fr). M° Madeleine.* **Open** 10am-8pm Mon-
Fri; 9am-8pm Sat. **Credit** AmEx, DC, MC, V.
Map p403 G4.
This three-floor emporium stocks some 5,000 wines,
half of them from outside France. There is a vast
selection of spirits, too.

Legrand Filles et Fils

*1 rue de la Banque, 2nd (01.42.60.07.12).
M° Bourse.* **Open** 11am-7pm Mon; 10am-7.30pm
Tue-Fri; 10am-7pm Sat. Closed Mon in Aug.
Credit AmEx, DC, MC, V. **Map** p404 H4.
This old-fashioned shop offering fine wines and
brandies, teas and *bonbons* also has a showroom for
its tasting glasses and gadgets, housed in galerie
Vivienne. There are wine tastings on Thursdays.

La Maison du Whisky

*20 rue d'Anjou, 8th (01.42.65.03.16/www.whisky.fr).
M° Madeleine.* **Open** 9.30am-7pm Mon; 9.30am-8pm
Tue-Fri; 9.30am-7.30pm Sat. **Credit** AmEx, MC, V.
Map p403 F4.

Jean-Marc Bellier explains which whisky matches which food, waxes lyrical about flavours such as honey and tobacco, and hosts a whisky club.

Ryst Dupeyron

79 rue du Bac, 7th (01.45.48.80.93/ www.dupeyron.com). M° Rue du Bac. **Open** 12.30-7.30pm Mon; 10.30am-7.30pm Tue-Sat. Closed 1wk Aug. **Credit** AmEx, MC, V. **Map** p407 F7.

The Dupeyron family has sold armagnac for four generations, and has bottles dating from 1868. Treasures include some 200 fine Bordeaux wines, vintage port and rare whiskies.

Gifts

Florists

Au Nom de la Rose

87 rue St-Antoine, 4th (01.42.71.34.24/www.aunom delarose.fr). M° St-Paul. **Open** 9am-9pm Mon-Sat; 9am-2pm, 3-6pm Sun. **Credit** AmEx, DC, MC, V. **Map** p411 L7.

Specialising in roses, Au Nom can supply a bouquet, as well as rose-based beauty products and candles. **Other locations**: 33 rue de Bretagne, 3rd (01.42.78.12.12); 1 bd du Montparnasse, 6th (01.40.56.05.15); 50 rue du Cherche-Midi, 6th (01.42.22.84.84).

Christian Tortu

6 carrefour de l'Odéon, 6th (01.43.26.02.56). M° Odéon. **Open** 10am-8pm Mon-Sat. Closed 3wks Aug. **Credit** AmEx, DC, MC, V. **Map** p410 H7.

The city's most celebrated florist is famed for turning flowers, twigs, bark and moss into lovely still lifes. Buy his vases at 17 rue des Quatre-Vents, 6th.

Monceau Fleurs

92 bd Malesherbes, 8th (01.53.77.61.77/www. monceaufleurs.com). M° Villiers. **Open** 8.30am-8.30pm daily. **Credit** AmEx, MC, V. **Map** p402 B6.

The city-wide branches sell an affordable range of fresh *fleurs*. Order and pay for bouquets online too. **Other locations**: throughout the city.

Souvenirs & eccentricities

L'Art du Buro

47 rue des Francs-Bourgeois, 4th (01.48.87.57.97). M° St-Paul. **Open** 10.30am-7pm Mon-Sat; 2-7pm Sun. **Credit** AmEx, DC, MC, V. **Map** p411 L6.

Sells sleek, modern desk accessories, and sexy ones that bring a new meaning to the term 'stress balls'.

Black Block

Palais de Tokyo, 13 av du Président-Wilson, 16th (01.47.23.37.04/www.blackblock.org). M° Iéna. **Open** noon-midnight Tue-Sun. **Credit** DC, MC, V. **Map** p402 C5.

Kooky Japanese items – toys, trainers, mayonnaise – in big fridges, with limited-edition artworks.

Deyrolle

46 rue du Bac, 7th (01.42.22.30.07). M° Rue du Bac. **Open** 10am-1pm, 2-7pm Mon; 10am-7pm Tue-Sat. **Credit** MC, V. **Map** p407 G6.

Established in 1831, this dusty taxidermists' overflows with stuffed animals. Have your pet stuffed (€500 for a cat) or hire a beast for a few days.

Diptyque

34 bd St-Germain, 5th (01.43.26.45.27/www. diptyqueparis.com). M° Maubert Mutualité. **Open** 10am-7pm Mon-Sat. **Credit** AmEx, MC, V. **Map** p407 G6.

Diptyque's divinely scented candles in 48 different varieties are probably the best you'll ever find.

Pa Design

2bis rue Fléchier, 9th (01.42.85.20.85/www.pa-design.com). M° Notre-Dame-de-Lorette. **Open** 11am-2pm, 3-7pm Wed-Fri; 10am-1pm, 2-7pm Sat. **Credit** MC, V. **Map** p404 H3.

This design company produces a range of ingenious, playful domestic products: tablecloths, vases, toys and photo frames with a twist. It also sells a hand-picked selection of other local designers' works.

Papeterie Moderne

12 rue de la Ferronnerie, 1st (01.42.36.21.72). M° Châtelet. **Open** 10am-6pm Mon-Sat. **Credit** MC, V. **Map** p408 J6.

The source of those enamel plaques that adorn Paris streets and forbidding gateways ('Attention! Chien bizarre' and the like) for less than €10 a pop.

Paris Accordéon

80 rue Daguerre, 14th (01.43.22.13.48). M° Gaîté or Denfert Rochereau. **Open** 9am-noon, 1-7pm Tue-Fri; 9am-noon, 1-6pm Sat. **Credit** AmEx, DC, MC, V. **Map** p407 G10.

This joint brims with accordions, from simple squeeze-boxes to the most beautiful tortoiseshell models, both second-hand and new.

Paris-Musées

29bis rue des Francs-Bourgeois, 4th (01.42.74.13.02). M° St-Paul. **Open** 2-7pm Mon; 11am-1pm, 2-7pm Tue-Fri; 11am-7pm Sat; noon-7.30pm Sun. **Credit** AmEx, DC, MC, V. **Map** p411 L6.

Run by the city's museums federation, this shop sells funky lamps and ceramics by young designers, along with reproductions from Paris museums. **Photo** *p266*. **Other locations**: 1 rue Pierre Lescot, 1st (01.40.26.56.75).

Résonances

9 cour St-Emilion, 12th (01.44.73.82.82/www. resonances.fr). M° Cour St-Emilion. **Open** 11am-9pm daily. **Credit** AmEx, MC, V. **Map** p409 P10.

A well-chosen array of supplies and gadgets for the home. DIY enthusiasts will appreciate the tape measures, paints and brushes, and interior design books; sybarites will dig the bath products. **Other locations**: 99 rue de Rivoli, 1st (01.42.97.06.00); 3-5 bd Malesherbes, 8th (01.44.51.63.70).

Eat, Drink, Shop

Funky gifts for your loved ones from **Paris-Musées**. *See p265*.

Sennelier

3 quai Voltaire, 7th (01.42.60.72.15/www.magasin sennelier.fr). M° St-Germain-des-Prés. **Open** 2-6.30pm Mon; 10am-12.30pm, 2-6.30pm Tue-Sat. **Credit** AmEx, DC, MC, V. **Map** p407 G6.
Old-fashioned colour merchant Sennelier has been supplying artists since 1887. The array of oil paints, watercolours and pastels includes rare pigments, and there are primered boards, varnishes and paper. **Other locations**: 4bis rue de la Grande-Chaumière, 6th (same phone).

Home

Antiques & flea markets

Knowing who specialises in what is essential for antique buying in Paris. Classy traditional antiques can be found in the **Louvre des Antiquaires**, **Carré Rive Gauche** (6th), **Village Suisse** and rue du Fbg-St-Honoré (1st). You'll find art deco in St-Germain-des-Prés (7th) and retro by rue de Charonne (11th). For books, look in the *bouquinistes* by the Seine and at parc Georges Brassens (15th).

As well as flea markets, don't forget auction house **Drouot** (01.48.00.20.17). There are also frequent *brocantes* and *braderies* – antiques' and collectors' markets.

Louvre des Antiquaires

2 pl du Palais-Royal, 1st (01.42.97.27.27/www. louvre-antiquaires.com). M° Palais Royal Musée du Louvre. **Open** 11am-7pm Tue-Sun. Closed Sun in July & Aug. **Credit** varies. **Map** p408 H5.
This upmarket antiques centre behind the façade of an old *grand magasin* houses 250 antiques dealers: perfect for Louis XV furniture, tapestries, porcelain, jewellery, model ships and tin soldiers. **Photo** *right*.

Marché aux Puces d'Aligre

pl d'Aligre, rue d'Aligre, 12th. M° Ledru Rollin. **Open** 7.30am-1.30pm Tue-Sun. **Map** p409 N7.
This is the only flea market in central Paris. Aligre's origins pre-date the Revolution, and it stays true to its junk tradition with a handful of *brocanteurs* peddling books, phone cards, kitchenware and oddities at what seem to be optimistic prices. It shares space with one of the city's cheapest fruit and veg markets (*see p259* Forward *marché*!).

Marché aux Puces de Montreuil

av de la Porte de Montreuil, 20th. M° Porte de Montreuil. **Open** 7am-7.30pm Mon, Sat, Sun.
The anarchic Montreuil disgorges veritable mountains of second-hand clothing, car parts and a jumble of rubbish. You'll find few pre-1900 items, but lots of fun collectibles like Pastis jugs and old hats. Stallholders shout out prices above the din and feisty women push prams over your toes, but the souk-like soul of the place will win you over in the end.

Marché aux Puces de Clignancourt

av de la Porte de Clignancourt, 18th. M° Porte de Clignancourt. **Open** 7am-7.30pm Mon, Sat, Sun.

This, the mother of all flea markets, is home to some 2,500 dealers at ten main markets, most of which are on or off spinal rue des Rosiers. For classic furniture, head to the Marché Dauphine (No.138-140) or the Marché Biron (No.85); for jewellery, try the Marché Serpette (No.110) and for vintage bric-a-brac, the Marché Paul Bert (No.104). Don't bother to arrive early for bargains – most stalls don't open till 9am.

Marché aux Puces de Vanves

av Georges-Lafenestre & av Marc-Sangnier, 14th. M° Porte de Vanves. **Open** 7am-7.30pm Sun.

Begun in the 1920s, Vanves is the smallest and friendliest of the flea markets. Conviviality and civility reign, and a stroll round the colourful stands makes for a peaceful, gently stimulating Sunday morning outing. If you get there early enough, there are decent second-hand clothes, dolls, 1950s costume jewellery and silverware.

Le Village St-Paul

rue St-Paul, rue Charlemagne & quai des Célestins, 4th. M° St-Paul. **Open** 10am-7pm Mon-Sat. **No credit cards. Map** p411 L7.

This colony of antiques sellers, spread across small courtyards linking rues St-Paul and Charlemagne, and quai des Célestins, is a source of 1930s and 1950s furniture, kitchenware and wine gadgets.

Design & interiors

The vast **Lafayette Maison** (*see p234*) offers a selection of current design and homewares.

Astier de Villatte

173 rue St-Honoré, 1st (01.42.60.74.13/www.astier devillatte.com). M° Palais Royal Musée du Louvre. **Open** 11am-7.30pm Mon-Sat. Closed 3wks Aug. **Credit** AmEx, MC, V. **Map** p403 G4.

Once home to Napoléon's silversmith, Biennet, this ancient warren of small rooms now houses white and platinum ceramics inspired by 17th- and 18th-century designs, handmade by the Astier de Villatte siblings in their Bastille workshop.

Other locations: 99 rue du Bac, 7th (01.42.22.81.59).

Cappellini

4 rue des Rosiers, 4th (01.42.78.39.39/www.cappellini.it). M° St-Paul. **Open** 10.30am-7pm Mon-Sat. **Credit** AmEx, DC, MC, V. **Map** p411 L6.

This major global design company knows talent when it sees it. In this former Marais hammam you'll find all the usual suspects – Jasper Morrison, Hella Jongerius, Tom Dixon, the Bourroullec brothers – and their first-rate contemporary pieces.

Caravane Chambre 19

19 rue St-Nicolas, 12th (01.53.02.96.96/www.caravane.fr). M° Ledru-Rollin. **Open** 11am-7pm Tue-Sat. Closed 2wks Aug. **Credit** AmEx, MC, V. **Map** p409 M7.

Eat, Drink, Shop

Upmarket antiques offered by the 250 dealers at **Louvre des Antiquaires**. *See p266.*

This offshoot of Françoise Dorget's original Marais shop has goodies such as exquisite hand-sewn quilts from West Bengal, crisp cotton and organdie tunics, Berber scarves, lounging sofas and daybeds. Also chic accessories such as silk-sheet sleeping bags and stripy neckrests with matching eyemasks.
Other locations: 6 rue Pavée, 4th (01.44.61.04.20).

CFOC
170 bd Haussmann, 8th (01.53.53.40.80). Mº St-Philippe-du-Roule. **Open** 10am-7pm Mon-Sat. **Credit** AmEx, DC, MC, V. **Map** p403 E3.
La Compagnie Française de l'Orient et de la Chine is full of Eastern promise, from Chinese teapots and celadon bowls, to Iranian blown glass.
Other locations: 163, 167, 260 bd St-Germain, 6th (01.45.48.00.18/01.45.48.10.31/01.47.05.92.82); 65 av Victor-Hugo, 16th (01.45.00.55.46).

Chône
60 rue Vieille-du-Temple, 3rd (01.44.78.90.00). Mº Rambuteau. **Open** 2-7pm Mon; 11am-7pm Tue-Sat. Closed Aug. **Credit** AmEx, DC, MC, V. **Map** p411 K6.
Camille Unglik designed shoes for Louis Vuitton before opening this boutique dedicated to exclusive and limited-edition tableware. Big on Scandinavian designers, it houses glassware, cutlery and crockery by Tapio Virkkala; other featured designers include Karim Rashid, Ross Lovegrove and Philippe Starck.

Christian Liaigre
42 rue du Bac, 7th (01.53.63.33.66/www.christian-liaigre.fr). Mº Rue du Bac. **Open** 10am-7pm Mon-Sat. Closed 3wks Aug. **Credit** AmEx, MC, V. **Map** p407 G6.
This famous French interior decorator fitted out Marc Jacobs' boutiques, New York's Mercer Hotel and the Market restaurant in Paris. His showroom displays his elegant lighting designs and furniture, in trademark tones of cream and brown.
Other locations: 61 rue de Varenne, 7th (01.47.53.78.76).

Christophe Delcourt
12 rue Volney, 2nd (01.42.78.44.97/www.christophe delcourt.com). Mº Opéra. **Open** 9am-noon, 1-6pm Mon-Fri. Closed Aug. **Credit** AmEx, DC, MC, V. **Map** p403 G4.
Delcourt's art deco-influenced, geometrical lights and furniture are given a contemporary spin by their combination of stained wood with black steel.

CSAO
1-3 rue Elzévir, 3rd (01.44.54.55.88/www.csao.fr). Mº St-Paul. **Open** 11am-7pm Mon-Sat; 2-7pm Sun. **Credit** AmEx, DC, MC, V. **Map** p411 L6.
Its name standing for 'Compagnie du Sénégal et de l'Afrique de l'Ouest', this spacious, lively boutique offers African craftwork constructed according to fair-trade principles. The artisans often fashion their objects out of recycled materials, so you'll find funky furniture made out of tins and colourful mats out of plastic. Some decorate CSAO's nearby bar Jokko, 5 rue Elzévir, and Petit Dakar restaurant (No.6).

Espace Lumière
17 rue des Lombards, 4th (01.42.77.47.71). Mº Châtelet. **Open** Mon-Sat (times vary). **Credit** AmEx, MC, V. **Map** p408 K6.
These sober showrooms stock the best European and American lighting designs around today, with pieces by Starck, Wilmotte and Artemide.
Other locations: 48 rue Mazarine, 6th (01.43.54.06.28); 167-169 bd Haussmann, 8th (01.42.89.01.15).

FR 66
25 rue de Renard, 4th (01.44.54.35.36/www.fr66. com). Mº Hôtel de Ville. **Open** 10am-7pm Mon-Sat. Closed 2-3wks Aug. **Credit** MC, V. **Map** p408 K6.
Somewhere between a gallery and a shop, this two-level experimental space accommodates contemporary artists and designers who produce exciting and original products for the home – not only furniture, but electrical fittings, and floor and wall coverings.

Galerie Patrick Seguin
5 rue des Taillandiers, 11th (01.47.00.32.35/www. patrickseguin.com). Mº Ledru-Rollin or Bastille. **Open** 10am-7pm Mon-Sat. **Credit** AmEx, DC, MC, V. **Map** p409 M7.
Seguin specialises in modern French design from the 1950s: items by Jean Prouvé and Charlotte Perriand on display in a showroom designed by Jean Nouvel.

Ozone
49 rue de Saintonge, 3rd (01.53.01.93.01/www.ozone light.com). Mº Filles du Calvaire. **Open** 11am-7pm Mon-Sat. **Credit** AmEx, MC, V. **Map** p404 L5.
Ozone produces elegant, modern lighting designs at this smart Marais showroom/workshop. Young duo Eric Jaehnke and Etienne Gounot make deceptively simple and original pieces like the X lamp – a glowing X-shaped light box that can be hung from the ceiling or stacked on the floor.

Sentou Galerie
18, 24 rue du Pont-Louis-Philippe, 4th (01.42.77.44.79/01.42.71.00.01/www.sentou.fr). Mº Pont Marie. **Open** 11am-7pm Tue-Sat. **Credit** AmEx, MC, V. **Map** p411 K7.
Favoured by *Marie Claire Maison*, this is a trend-setting shop for colourful tableware and furniture. Look out for painted Chinese flasks, vases and a lime-green accordion bench.
Other locations: 29 rue François-Miron, 4th (01.42.78.50.60); 26 bd Raspail, 7th (01.45.49.00.05).

Silvera
41 rue du Fbg-St-Antoine, 11th (01.43.43.06.75/ www.silvera.fr). Mº Bastille or Ledru-Rollin. **Open** 2-7pm Mon; 10am-7pm Tue-Sat. Closed 2wks Aug. **Credit** AmEx, DC, MC, V. **Map** p409 M7.
Amid shops selling clothes and mock Louis XV gear, the former Le Bihan is a three-floor showcase for the best of modern design, taken over by Silvera in spring 2005. Look out for furniture and lighting from Perriand, Santachiara, Gray, Mies van der Rohe, Pesce, Pillet, Morrison, Arad and others.
Other locations: 58 av Kléber, 16th (01.53.65.78.78).

Kitchen & bathroom

Bains Plus
51 rue des Francs-Bourgeois, 4th (01.48.87.83.07).
Mº Hôtel de Ville. **Open** 2-7pm Mon, Sun; 11am-
7.30pm Tue-Sat. **Credit** AmEx, MC, V. **Map** p411 K6.
This is the ultimate gentlemen's shaving shop: stock
includes duck-shaped loofahs, seductive dressing
gowns, chrome mirrors, bath oils and soaps.

E Dehillerin
18 rue Coquillière, 1st (01.42.36.53.13/www.
e-dehillerin.fr). Mº Les Halles. **Open** 9am-12.30pm,
2-6pm Mon; 9am-6pm Tue-Sat. **Credit** MC, V.
Map p404 J5.
Suppliers to great chefs since 1820, this no-nonsense
warehouse stocks just about every kitchen utensil
ever invented. A saucepan from Dehillerin is for life.

Kitchen Bazaar
11 av du Maine, 15th (01.42.22.91.17).
Mº Montparnasse Bienvenüe. **Open** 10am-7pm
Mon-Sat. **Credit** AmEx, MC, V. **Map** p407 F8.
All chrome gadgetry and modish fixtures, Kitchen
Bazaar is perfect for luxury items. Sister shop Bath
Bazaar, at No.6 on the other side of avenue du Maine
(01.45.48.89.00), sells bathroom goodies.
Other locations: 23 bd de la Madeleine, 1st
(01.42.60.50.30).

Laguiole Galerie
1 pl Ste-Opportune, 1st (01.40.28.09.42/www.forge-
de-laguiole.com). Mº Châtelet. **Open** 10.30am-1pm,
2-7pm Mon-Sat. **Credit** AmEx, MC, V. **Map** p408 J6.
Philippe Starck designed this chic and sharp boutique, a showcase for France's classic knife, the
Laguiole, and limited-edition versions thereof.

Sport & games

For general sports equipment and clothes, the
chains **Go Sport** and **Décathlon** are best; if
you just want to *look* sporty, *see p252*
Streetwear & clubwear. For **Agnès b**
sportswear, *see p250*; for **Paris St-Germain**
football gear (and match tickets), *see p329*.

Au Vieux Campeur
48 rue des Ecoles, 5th (01.53.10.48.48/www.au-
vieux-campeur.com). Mº Maubert Mutualité or Cluny
La Sorbonne. **Open** 11am-7.30pm Mon-Fri; 10am-
7.30pm Sat. **Credit** AmEx, MC, V. **Map** p410 J7.
This Paris institution runs several specialist shops
between rue des Ecoles and boulevard St-Germain.
Between them, they can provide all the advice and
equipment you need for just about any kind of sporting activity with the exception of golf.

Citadium
50-56 rue de Caumartin, 9th (01.55.31.74.00/www.
citadium.com). Mº Havre Caumartin. **Open** 10am-
8pm Mon-Wed, Fri, Sat; 10am-9pm Thur. **Credit**
AmEx, DC, MC, V. **Map** p403 G3.

Citadium is one of France's biggest sports stockists
– hip watches to cross-country skis – and a cult to
boot. The latest surf 'n' skater vids blast out into the
four, themed floors, all manned by expert staff.

Décathlon
26 av de Wagram, 8th (01.45.72.66.88/www.
decathlon.fr). Mº Charles de Gaulle Etoile. **Open**
10am-8pm Mon-Fri; 9.30am-8pm Sat. **Credit** MC, V.
Map p402 C3.
Sports megastore with a comprehensive catalogue
and helpful staff to ensure you're decked out with the
right equipment at a competitive price. The range is
awesome; it's also a camper's heaven.
Other locations: 17 bd de la Madeleine, 1st
(01.55.35.97.55); 4 rue Louis-Armand, 15th
(01.45.58.60.45).

Equistable
177 bd Haussmann, 8th (01.45.61.02.57). Mº St-
Philippe-du-Roule. **Open** 10am-7pm Mon-Fri; 10am-
6pm Sat. **Credit** AmEx, DC, MC, V. **Map** p403 E4.
Well-stocked emporium selling quality equine gear,
from Hermès saddles to horsey trinkets.

Go Sport
Forum des Halles, 1st (01.53.00.81.70/www.go-
sport.com). Mº Les Halles/RER Châtelet Les Halles.
Open 10am-7.30pm Mon-Sat. **Credit** AmEx, MC, V.
Map p408 J6.
Gear for an Olympian list of sports is covered by this
well-priced chain: home exercise machines, saddle
wax, wet suits and much more. Accessorise with
Nike, adidas and cheaper house clobber.
Other locations: throughout the city.

Nauti Store
40 av de la Grande-Armée, 17th (01.43.80.28.28/
www.nautistore.fr). Mº Argentine. **Open** 11am-7pm
Mon; 10.30am-7pm Tue-Sat. **Credit** MC, V. **Map**
p402 C3.
This shop stocks a vast range of sailing clothes and
shoes from labels such as Helly Hansen and Sebago.

René Pierre
35 rue de Maubeuge, 9th (01.44.91.91.21/www.rene-
pierre.fr). Mº Poissonnière. **Open** 10am-1pm,
2-6.30pm Mon-Sat. **Credit** MC, V. **Map** p404 H3.
Paris showroom for France's finest table-football
tables, crafted at the Chalon-sur-Saône factory of
René Pierre, *maître billardier* since 1952. Spun, swiv-
elled and slammed in cafés around the world, his
classic models Onze, Leader et al can be admired and
ordered here. For UK *baby-foot* aficionados, tables
can be delivered free of charge as far as Calais.
Jukeboxes and billiard tables are also on sale.

Subchandlers – Plongespace
80 rue Balard, 15th (01.45.57.01.01/www.
subchandlers.com). Mº Balard. **Open** 10.30am-
7.30pm Tue-Sat. **Credit** MC, V. **Map** p406 A9.
This diving specialist stocks all the basic apparatus,
plus underwater cameras, DVDs and books, and
organises monthly soirées on photography, film and
everything aquatic.

© Bal du Moulin Rouge 2003/2005 – Moulin Rouge®

Kris Gunlar

Discover the Show of the Most Famous Cabaret in the World !
Dinner & Show at 7pm from €140 • Show at 9pm : €97, at 11pm : €87

Montmartre - 82, boulevard de Clichy - 75018 Paris
Reservations : 01 53 09 82 82 - www.moulin-rouge.com

Prices valid from 01.04.06 to 31.03.07

Arts & Entertainment

Ménagerie du Jardin des Plantes.
See p284.

Festivals & Events

Never a dull moment.

Paris is a good-time city par excellence. Along with a panoply of cultural events throughout the year, there are anniversaries (*see p273* **2006 and all that**) and religious festivals aplenty. Indeed, Paris has a propensity to turn every commemoration into a serious, state-funded, event – and the pro-active reign of Mayor Delanoë has done much to refresh the capital's diary. **Paris-Plage**, an urban beach set up by the Seine for the summer, and **Nuit Blanche**, an autumnal, all-night culture fest, have brought high-profile successes.

In terms of cultural seasons, Paris starts up in October, keeping busy until the beginning of summer, when companies heads south. Many summer events are free, such as Paris-Plage, the **Fête de la Musique** and **Bastille Day**.

PUBLIC HOLIDAYS

On *jours feriés*, banks, many museums, most businesses and a number of restaurants close; public transport runs a Sunday service. New Year, May Day, Bastille Day and Christmas Day are the most piously observed holidays.

The complete bank holiday calendar runs as follows: New Year's Day (*Jour de l'An*); Easter Monday (*Pâques*); May Day (*Fête du Travail*); VE Day (*Victoire 1945*) 8 May; Ascension Day (*Jour de l'Ascension*); Whit Monday (*Lundi de Pentecôte*); Bastille Day (*Quatorze Juillet*) 14 July; Feast of the Assumption (*Fête de l'Assomption*) 15 Aug; All Saints' Day (*Toussaint*) 1 Nov; Remembrance Day (*L'Armistice 1918*) 11 Nov; Christmas Day (*Noël*).

Spring

Six Nations

Stade de France, 93210 St-Denis (08.92.70.09.00/ www.stadedefrance.fr). RER B La Plaine Stade de France or RER D Stade de France St-Denis. **Admission** varies. **Date** Feb-Mar.
Paris is invaded by Brits and Celts for three big rugby weekends in winter. Tickets are hard to come by – log on to www.6nations.co.uk at least three months in advance.

Salon des Grands Vins

Le Carrousel du Louvre, 99 rue de Rivoli, 1st (www.salondesgrandsvins.com). M° Palais Royal Musée du Louvre. **Admission** €15. **Date** Mar.
Tastings, workshops, world experts – and, of course, wine, the focus of this annual oenophile celebration.

Fashion Week

Various venues (www.modeaparis.com). **Date** Mar & Oct.
Paris presents its haute couture and prêt-à porter collections to invited guests only. The better hotels fill up and the trendier bistros, too.

Le Printemps des Poètes

Various venues (www.printempsdespoetes.com). **Date** 4-12 Mar.
'Le Chant Des Villes' ('the Song of the Cities') is the theme for the eighth, 2006 edition of this popular national poetry festival, set up by Jack Lang in 1999.

Printemps du Cinéma

Various venues (www.printempsducinema.com). **Date** Mar.
Film tickets all across the city are cut to a bargain €3.50 for this popular three-day film event.

Banlieues Bleues

Various venues in Seine St-Denis (01.40.03.75.01/ www.banlieuesbleues.org). **Admission** €11-€15. **Date** Mar-Apr.
Five weeks of quality French and international jazz, blues, R&B, soul, funk, flamenco and world music.

Le Chemin de la Croix

Square Willette, 18th (01.53.41.89.00). M° Anvers or Abbesses. **Date** Good Friday.
Mini-pilgrimage as crowds follow the Archbishop of Paris from the bottom of Montmartre up to Sacré-Coeur as he performs the Stations of the Cross.

Foire du Trône

Pelouse de Reuilly, 12th (01.46.27.52.29). M° Porte Dorée. **Admission** free; rides €1.50-€4. **Date** early Apr-end May.
France's biggest funfair: stomach-churning rides, bungee jumping and *barbe à papa* (candyfloss).

Marathon de Paris

av des Champs-Elysées, 8th, to av Foch, 16th (01.41.33.15.68/www.parismarathon.com). **Date** Apr.
From the Champs-Elysées all along the Right Bank to the Bois de Vincennes and back again to the Bois de Boulogne, 35,000 marathon runners take in the city's sights for the 30th staging of this event in 2006.

Festival Paris Ile-de-France

Various venues (www.festivaldeparisidf.com). **Admission** €6-€7. **Date** Apr.
Paris' own film festival. Public previews of international films, plus star-spotting opportunities.

Fête du Travail

Date 1 May.

May Day is strictly observed. Key sights (the Eiffel Tower aside) close; unions march in eastern Paris via Bastille. Vendors sell lilies of the valley (*muguet*).

Printemps des Musées

Various venues (http://printempsdesmusees. culture.fr). **Date** May.

The Ministry of Culture's annual treat sees selected museums across France open their doors for free.

Foire de Paris

Paris-Expo, pl de la Porte de Versailles (01.49.09.60.00/www.foiredeparis.fr). M° Porte de Versailles. **Admission** €12. **Date** 28 Apr-8 May.

This enormous lifestyle salon includes world crafts and foods, plus the latest health and house gizmos.

Les Puces du design

Passage du Grand-Cerf, pl Goldoni, 2nd (01.53.40.78.77/www.pucesdudesign.com). M° Etienne Marcel. **Admission** free. **Date** May.

Set in the bustling, cobbled pedestrian streets of the shabby-but-chic Montorgueil district, this popular bi-annual (also staged in October), 20th-century design flea-market draws 20 specialist retailers from all over France.

La Nuit des Musées

All over France (www.culture.gouv.fr). **Admission** free. **Date** mid May.

For one night, landmark museums across Paris keep their doors open late and organise a number of special entertainments.

Festival de St-Denis

Various venues in St-Denis (01.48.13.12.10/ www.festival-saint-denis.fr). M° St-Denis Basilique. **Admission** €9-€55. **Date** end May-end June.

The Gothic St-Denis Basilica and other historic buildings in the neighbourhood host four weeks of quality classical concerts through the month of June.

2006 and all that

The French love to celebrate great names and events. These anniversaries will bring a slew of exhibitions, retrospectives, TV tributes, books, DVDs and theatre productions. See listings publications (*see p376*) for details.

Josephine Baker

With her high-voltage sass, barely-there costumes and sexy dance routines, Baker (born 1906) stormed Paris in the 1920s.

Jacques Becker

Director of classic films *Falbalas*, *Casque d'Or* and *Touchez pas au grisbi*, born in 1906.

Samuel Beckett

The Nobel Prize-winning novelist and playwright was born in Dublin in 1906, but spent most of his adult life in France.

Marcel Carné

Another of cinema's leading lights, born (like Becker) in 1906. His poetic realist genius produced such masterpieces as *Le Jour se lève* and *Le Quai des brumes*.

Pierre Curie

Curie and his wife Marie discovered elements radium and polonium, and set the foundations for subsequent radioactivity research. He died in 1906.

Dreyfus rehabilitated

Eleven long years after Zola's *J'Accuse!*, the French army's most talked-about soldier was rehabilitated in 1906. *See p142* **Scandale!**.

First edition of the *Petit Larousse* dictionary

The famous dictionary – the one whose cover shows a winsome woman blowing on a dandelion head – has been an annual best-seller since edition one, which went on sale in 1906.

Jean Gabin

The debonair French star of nearly 100 films – including Carné's *Le Jour se lève* – passed away in 1976. Expect special events to be organised at the museum (www.musee-gabin.com) in his home village of Mériel, in the Val d'Oise outside Paris.

Independence for Morocco and Tunisia

The two French protectorates were awarded full sovereignty in 1956.

André Malraux

Malraux, one of the 20th century's greatest novelists, man of action and France's first culture minister, died in 1976.

Motorised buses for Paris

The first buses not to leave horse dung in their wake started chugging along the St-Germain-des-Prés to Montmartre route as long ago as 1906.

Pont Neuf

The only time the 'new bridge' lived up to its name was at its completion in 1606 – though some historians aver this happened in 1607.

Arts & Entertainment

Le Cinéma en Plein Air. *See p275.*

Summer

French Tennis Open

Stade Roland Garros, 2 av Gordon-Bennett, 16th (01.47.43.52.52/www.frenchopen.org). M° Porte d'Auteuil. **Admission** €21-€53. **Date** 29 May-11 June.

The glitzy Grand Slam tennis tournament is always well attended by showbiz stars.

Quinzaine des Réalisateurs

Forum des Images, Porte St-Eustache, Forum des Halles, 1st (01.44.76.62.00/www.quinzaine-realisateurs.com). M° Les Halles. **Admission** €5.50. **Date** May-June.

As soon as the dust has settled at Cannes, the Directors' Fortnight programme comes to Paris.

Le Printemps des rues

01.47.97.36.06/www.leprintempsdesrues.com. **Admission** free. **Date** 3, 4 June.

Despite financial worries, this annual street-theatre fest is all set to continue in 2006.

Foire St-Germain

pl St-Sulpice and venues in St-Germain-des-Prés, 6th (01.43.29.61.04/www.foiresaintgermain.org). M° St-Sulpice. **Admission** free. **Date** June-July.

St-Germain-des-Prés lets its hair down for a month-long event of concerts, theatre and workshops.

Paris Jazz Festival

Parc Floral de Paris, Bois de Vincennes (39.75/ www.parcfloraldeparis.com/www.paris.fr). M° Château de Vincennes. **Admission** Park €3. **Date** June-July.

Free jazz weekends at the lovely Parc Floral.

Prix de Diane Hermès

Hippodrome de Chantilly, 16 av du Général-Leclerc, 90209 Chantilly (03.44.62.41.00/www.france-galop.com). **Date** June.

The French Derby draws high society in silly hats.

Festival Chopin à Paris

Orangerie de Bagatelle, Parc de Bagatelle, Bois de Boulogne, 16th (01.45.00.22.19/www.frederic-chopin.com). M° Porte Maillot, then bus 244. **Admission** €16-€31. **Date** June-July.

Candlelit evening recitals in the Bagatelle gardens.

Fête de la Musique

All over France (01.40.03.94.70/www.fetedela musique.fr). **Admission** free. **Date** 21 June.

Concerts all over the city for this free music festival.

Gay Pride March

Information: Centre Gai et Lesbien (01.43.57.21.47/ www.fiertes-lgbt.org). **Date** late June.

Outrageous floats and costumes parade towards Bastille, followed by an official fête and club events.

La Goutte d'Or en Fête

square Léon, 18th (01.46.07.61.64/www.gouttedor enfete.org). M° Barbès Rochechouart. **Admission** free. **Date** late June-early July.

Established and local artists play raï, rap and reggae in this Arab and African neighbourhood.

Paris Cinéma

Various venues (www.pariscinema.org). **Admission** varies. **Date** early July.

Premieres, tributes and restored films make up the programme of Paris' summer film-going initiative.

Solidays

Longchamp Hippodrome (01.53.10.22.22/ www.solidays.com). M° Porte d'Auteuil. **Admission** Day €20. Weekend €35. **Date** early July.

Three-day music bash with a mix of French, World and new talent, in the name of AIDS charities.

Le Cinéma en Plein Air

Parc de La Villette, 19th (01.40.03.75.75/www. villette.com). M° Porte de Pantin. **Admission** free. **Date** mid July-end Aug.

Settle back on the lawn at this summer fixture – a themed season of films screened under the stars on Europe's largest inflatable screen. **Photos** *left.*

Le Quatorze Juillet (Bastille Day)

Date 14 July.

France's national holiday commemorates the events of 1789. On the eve, Parisians dance at place de la Bastille. At 10am on the 14th, crowds line up down the Champs-Elysées as the President reviews a full military parade. By night, the Champ de Mars fills for the firework display.

Miss Guinguette

38 quai Victor Hugo, Ile du Martin-Pêcheur, Champigny sur Marne (information 01.49.83.03.02). RER Champigny sur Marne. **Admission** €7. **Date** 14 July.

A quest to find the light-footed queen of the open-air dance hall scene at this river island venue.

Paris, Quartier d'été

Various venues (01.44.94.98.00/www.quartierdete. com). **Admission** free-€15. **Date** mid July-mid Aug.

A series of classical and jazz concerts, dance and theatre performances in outdoor venues. **Photo** *p276.*

Paris-Plage

Pont des Arts to Pont de Sully (08.20.00.75.75/ www.paris.fr). M° Sully Morland, Louvre Rivoli, Châtelet, Hôtel de Ville, Pont Marie. **Admission** free. **Date** mid July-mid Aug.

Over the course of a month, for the fifth consecutive year in 2006, palm trees, huts, hammocks and 2,000 tonnes of fine sand bring a seaside vibe spread to a busy two-mile stretch of the Right Bank. There's a pool and holiday-reading lending library, too

Le Tour de France

Av des Champs-Elysées, 8th (01.41.33.15.00/ www.letour.fr). **Date** July.

The ultimate endurance test climaxes after 3,350km of calf-busting action. Blink and you'll miss the winner as the event concludes on the Champs-Elysées in a blur of pedals and yellow Lycra. **Photo** *p277.*

Arts & Entertainment

Fête de l'Assomption

Cathédrale Notre-Dame de Paris, pl du Parvis Notre-Dame, 4th (01.42.34.56.10). M° Cité/RER St Michel Notre-Dame. **Admission** free. **Date** 15 Aug.
A national holiday. Notre-Dame again becomes a place of religious pilgrimage for Assumption Day.

Rock en Seine

Domaine National de St-Cloud (08.92.68.08.92/ www.rockenseine.com). M° Porte de Sainte Cloud. **Admission** *Day* €39. *2 days* €65. **Date** end Aug.
Two days, two stages, one world-class rock line-up.

Autumn

Jazz à la Villette

Parc de la Villette, 211 av Jean-Jaurès, 19th (01.40.03.75.75/01.44.84.44.84/www.villette.com or www.jazzalavillette.com). M° Porte de Pantin. **Admission** €12-€22. **Date** early Sept.
One of the best local jazz fests, with varied acts.

Techno Parade

01.42.47.84.75/www.technopol.net. **Date** mid Sept.
This parade (finishing at Bastille) marks the start of electronic music festival Rendez-vous Electroniques.

Journées du Patrimoine

All over France (08.20.20.25.02/www.jp. culture.fr). **Date** Sept.
Embassies, ministries, scientific establishments and corporate headquarters open their doors. The festive Soirée du Patrimoine takes place on the first Journée. Get *Le Monde* or *Le Parisien* for a full programme.

Festival d'automne

Various venues. Information: 156 rue de Rivoli, 1st (01.53.45.17.00/www.festival-automne.com). **Admission** €9-€30. **Date** mid Sept-mid Dec.

Major annual festival of challenging contemporary theatre, dance and modern opera, intent on bringing non-Western culture into the French consciousness. 'Autumn Festival' is a bit of a misnomer, as some exhibitions run over the new year into January.

Nuit Blanche

Various venues (39.75/www.paris.fr). **Admission** free. **Date** early Oct.
Culture by moonlight: galleries and museums host one-off installations, and swimming pools, bars and clubs stay open till very late.

Prix de l'Arc de Triomphe

Hippodrome de Longchamp, Bois de Boulogne, 16th (01.49.10.20.30/www.france-galop.com). M° Porte d'Auteuil, then free shuttle bus. **Admission** free-€12. **Date** early Oct.
France's richest flat race attracts the elite of horse racing amid much pomp and ceremony.

FIAC

Paris-Expo, Porte de Versailles, 15th (01.41.90.47.80/www.fiac-online.com). M° Porte de Versailles. **Admission** €17. **Date** 26-30 Oct.
This respected international art fair gives France a chance to strut its contemporary stuff.

Fête des Vendanges à Montmartre

rue des Saules, 18th (01.46.06.00.32/www.fetedes vendanges demontmartre.com). M° Lamarck Caulaincourt. **Date** 2nd weekend in Oct.
Folk music, speeches, locals in costume and a parade celebrate the 800-bottle Montmartre grape harvest. Chansons accompany the village fête atmosphere, with produce stands in Montmartre all weekend.

Festival Inrockuptibles

Various venues (01.42.44.16.16/www.lesinrocks.com). **Admission** varies. **Date** early Nov.

Paris, Quartier d'été.
See p275.

A blur of pedals and yellow Lycra – **Le Tour de France**. *See p275.*

Once indie-centred, this festival curated by popular rock magazine *Les Inrockuptibles* today champions trance, techno and trip hop – but that could all change by autumn 2006.

Armistice Day

Arc de Triomphe, 8th. M^o Charles de Gaulle Etoile.
Date 11 Nov.
To commemorate French combattants who served in the World Wars, the President lays wreaths at the Tomb of the Unknown Soldier under the Arc de Triomphe. The *bleuet* (a cornflower) is worn.

Fête du Beaujolais Nouveau

Date mid Nov.
The third Thursday in November sees cafés and wine bars throng as patrons assess the new vintage.

Winter

Paris sur glace

pl de l'Hôtel de Ville, 4th; M^o Hôtel de Ville. pl Raoul Dautry, 15th; M^o Montparnasse Bienvenue. pl de la Bataille de Stalingrad, 19th; M^o Stalingrad. Information: 08.20.00.75.75/www. paris.fr.
Admission free (skate hire €6). **Date** Dec-Mar.
Totter around the edges of these outdoor rinks while fearless five-year-olds zoom past.

Africolor

Various venues in St-Denis (01.47.97.69.99/ www.africolor.com). M^o Basilique de St-Denis.
Admission €13 approx. **Date** mid Dec.
African music festival with a spirited wrap party.

Patinoire de Noël

Eiffel Tower, Champ de Mars, 7th (01.44.11.23.45/ recorded info 01.44.11.23.23/www.tour-eiffel.fr). M^o Bir-Hakeim/RER Champ de Mars Tour Eiffel.
Admission €2.30-€4.10. **Dates** mid Dec-late Jan.

Hire a pair of free skates (you don't have to bring your own!) and experience the city's snazziest winter wonderland as the first floor of the glittering tower gets a seasonal icy make-over.

Noël (Christmas)

Date 24-25 Dec.
Christmas is a family affair in France, with a dinner on Christmas Eve (*le Réveillon*), normally after mass. Notre-Dame cathedral fills for the 11pm service. Usually the only bars and restaurants open are the ones in the city's main hotels.

New Year's Eve/New Year's Day

Date 31 Dec-1 Jan.
Crowds running into the tens of thousands swarm along the Champs-Elysées and let off bangers. Nightclubs and restaurants hold expensive soirées. On New Year's Day the Grande Parade de Paris brings floats, bands and dancers.

Fête des Rois (Epiphany)

Date 6 Jan.
Pâtisseries sell *galettes des rois*, cakes with frangipan filling in which a *fève*, or tiny charm, is hidden.

Mass for Louis XVI

Chapelle Expiatoire, 29 rue Pasquier, 8th (01.42.65.35.80). M^o St-Augustin. **Date** Jan.
On the Sunday closest to 21 Jan, anniversary of the beheading of Louis XVI in 1793, royalists and right-wing crackpots mourn the end of the monarchy.

Nouvel An Chinois

Around av d'Ivry & av de Choisy, 13th. M^o Porte de Choisy or Porte d'Ivry. Also av des Champs Elysées, 8th. **Date** Jan.
Lion and dragon dances, and lively martial arts demonstrations, celebrate the Chinese new year.

Arts & Entertainment

Cabaret, Circus & Comedy

C'est showtime!

Glam girls dancing in a provocative way may be an age-old stereotype, but it's one that shows no sign of disappearing in Paris; there are still more boobs and boas in the city's traditional cabarets than anywhere else in the world. Beyond these coach-tour magnets, satire thrives in good old-fashioned *café-théâtres*, where songs and sketches come with supper and a bottle of plonk. Away from the glitz, venues range from cellars to converted cinemas.

On the comedy front, the **Bowler Pub** competes for laughs with veteran anglo venue **Laughing Matters**, drawing acts from across the Channel, the US and Australia.

Cabaret & café-théâtre

Glitzy cabaret

La Belle Epoque
36 rue des Petits-Champs, 2nd (01.42.96.33.33). M° Opéra or Quatre Septembre. **Dinner** 9pm daily. **Shows** 10pm daily. **Admission** *Show* (incl champagne) €52. *Dinner & show* €70-€100. **Credit** AmEx, DC, MC, V. **Map** p403 H4.
See p280 **Girls! Girls! Girls!** *Photo* right.

Crazy Horse Saloon
12 av George V, 8th (01.47.23.32.32/www. crazyhorse.fr). M° Alma Marceau or George V. **Shows** 8.30pm, 11pm Tue-Fri, Sun; 7.30pm, 9.45pm, 10.50pm Sat. **Admission** *Show* (incl 2 drinks) €69-€90. **Credit** AmEx, DC, MC, V. **Map** p402 D4.
See p280 **Girls! Girls! Girls!**

Le Lido
116bis av des Champs-Elysées, 8th (01.40.76.56.10/ www.lido.fr). M° George V or Franklin D.Roosevelt. **Dinner** 7pm. **Shows** 9.30pm, 11.30pm Mon-Thur, Sun; 9.30pm, midnight Sat. **Admission** *Show* (incl champagne) €80-€100; €25 under-12s. *Dinner & show* €140-€200; €30 under-12s. **Credit** AmEx, DC, MC, V. **Map** p402 D4.
See p280 **Girls! Girls! Girls!**

Moulin Rouge
82 bd de Clichy, 18th (01.53.09.82.82/www.moulin- rouge.com). M° Blanche. **Dinner** 7pm. **Shows** 9pm, 11pm daily. **Admission** *Show* (incl champagne) €85- €95. *Dinner & show* €135-€165. **Credit** AmEx, DC, MC, V. **Map** p403 G2.
See p280 **Girls! Girls! Girls!**

Café-théâtre

L'Ane Rouge
3 rue Laugier, 17th (01.47.64.45.77). M° Ternes. **Shows** 8pm-2am daily. **Admission** *Show* (incl 1 drink) €30. *Dinner & show* €50-€85. **Credit** MC, V. **Map** p402 C2.
The 'Red Donkey' is a glittery *café-théâtre* happy to combine good comic cabaret with a great atmosphere. Dine on unusual regional dishes, then watch the comedians do their stuff.

Au Bec Fin
6bis rue Thérèse, 1st (01.42.96.29.35). M° Pyramides. **Shows** 7pm, 8.15pm, 9.45pm Mon- Sat. *Matinées for children* 2.30pm, 4.30pm Wed, Sat. Closed Aug. **Admission** *Show* €14; €9-€12 concessions. *Dinner & show* €30-€36. **Credit** AmEx, MC, V. **Map** p403 H5.
This tiny *café-théâtre* claims a 300-year-old pedigree and provides wholesome family entertainment. Dine downstairs on traditional cuisine, then head up the rickety staircase to see anything from Oscar Wilde in French to a modern-day *Cendrillon* for the kids.

Les Blancs Manteaux
15 rue des Blancs-Manteaux, 4th (01.48.87.15.84/ www.blancsmanteaux.fr). M° Hôtel de Ville. **Shows** daily from 7pm (phone for details). **Admission** *Show* €14; €11 concessions. *Double show* €22. *Dinner & show* €25. **No credit cards. Map** p411 K6.
This Marais institution has kept the *café-théâtre* flame burning for over 30 years with its two theatres and multiple weekly performances. With a dinner- and-show ticket, punters can eat around the corner at the Epices et Délices, and there's new stand-up on the first Wednesday of the month.

Chez Michou
80 rue des Martyrs, 18th (01.46.06.16.04/www. michou.com). M° Pigalle or Abbesses. **Dinner** 9pm daily. **Shows** 11pm approx. **Admission** *Show* (incl 1 drink) €35. *Dinner & show* €95. **Credit** MC, V. **Map** p404 H2.
Drag, sparkling costumes, good food and wine: come to Michou's if you're looking for larger-than-life impersonations of Brigitte Bardot and Tina Turner.

Au Lapin Agile
22 rue des Saules, 18th (01.46.06.85.87). M° Lamarck Caulaincourt. **Shows** 9pm-2am Tue-Sun. **Admission** *Show* (incl 1 drink) €24. **No credit cards. Map** p404 H1.

La Belle Epoque. *See p278.*

The prices have gone up, but that's all that seems to have changed since this quaint, pink bar first opened in 1860. Tourists now outnumber the locals, but the Lapin harbours an echo of old Montmartre.

Comedy & fringe theatre

Le Bout

6 rue Frochot, 9th (01.42.85.11.88/www.bout.com). Mº Pigalle. **Shows** daily. **Admission** €14; €9 concessions. *Two shows* €18. **No credit cards.** **Map** p404 H2.

In the heart of Pigalle, this ex-*café-théâtre* school has been cramming them into its 40-seater venue since 1999. The emphasis is on newcomers, but that does not mean amateurs. Annual comedy festival, too.

Café de la Gare

41 rue du Temple, 4th (01.42.78.52.51/www.cafe-de-la-gare.fr.st). Mº Hôtel de Ville or Rambuteau. **Shows** 7.30pm, 9pm Mon, Tue, Sun; 8pm, 10pm Wed-Sat. **Admission** €10-€20. **Credit** MC, V. **Map** p408 K6.

From a cobbled courtyard, customers are led to one of the 300 stage-hugging seats in this atmospheric venue. House specialities include French stand-up and raucous, irreverent comedies.

Caveau de la République

1 bd St-Martin, 3rd (01.42.78.44.45/www.caveau.fr). Mº République. **Shows** 8.30pm Tue-Sat; 3.30pm Sun. **Admission** €27.50 Tue-Thur; €34.50 Fri-Sun; €10 under-26s (except Sat); €17.50 concessions (except Sat). Closed Aug. **Credit** MC, V. **Map** p404 L4.

Open since 1901, this is one of the last *chansonniers* on the block, where artists spurt out golden oldies before presenting their own sardonic compositions. The humour is of a political-satirical bent, so it helps if you're up on current affairs. Occasional matinées on Thursdays and Saturdays, too.

Le Point Virgule

7 rue Ste-Croix-de-la-Bretonnerie, 4th (01.42.78.67.03/www.netkiri.fr). Mº Hôtel de Ville. **Shows** 8pm, 9.15pm, 10.30pm daily. **Admission** €15; €12 concs. **No credit cards. Map** p411 K6.

This small Marais theatre is an ideal launch pad for up-and-coming comedians. The crowds tend to be

animated and the acts well polished: the most popular always appear at its annual comedy festival through the month of November, Top In Humour.

Le Zèbre

63 bd de Belleville, 20th (01.43.55.55.55). Mº Père Lachaise. **Shows** days vary. **Admission** varies. **Credit** MC, V. **Map** p405 N4.

Impresario Francis Schoeller rescued the art deco Zèbre cinema in 2002. After forays in all kinds of directions, the Z has stuck to satirical cabaret and chirruping *chanson* in true vaudeville style.

Comedy in English

The Bowler Pub

13 rue d'Artois, 8th (01.45.61.16.60). Mº St-Philippe-du-Roule. **Shows** days vary. **Admission** (incl 1 pint of beer) €10. **Credit** AmEx, MC, V. **Map** p403 E3.

Pints, chips and belly laughs are doled out in large portions in this British beer temple, where on-the-up comedians off the Eurostar test their new material.

Laughing Matters

La Java, 105 rue du Fbg-du-Temple, 10th (01.53.19.98.88/www.anythingmatters.com). Mº Goncourt or Belleville. **Shows** days vary. **Admission** €20; €17 students. **No credit cards. Map** p405 M4.

This anglophone comedy spot no longer has a monopoly in Paris, but promoter Karel Beer seems to be the only guy UK and US comedians will cross the water for. In 2006, look out for the likes of Greg Proops, Ardal O'Hanlon and Tommy Tiernan.

Circus

Circus – traditional big tops and avant-garde acts – is a year-round fixture. See *Cirque* in the children's section of *Pariscope* for listings and also *pp281-286* **Children.**

Cabaret Sauvage

Parc de La Villette, 19th (01.42.09.01.09/ www.cabaretsauvage.com). Mº Porte de la Villette. **Shows** days vary. **Admission** €12-€20. **Credit** MC, V. **Map** p405 inset.

Housed in an old circus venue, this mixture of tent, saloon and hall of mirrors provides a platform for contemporary jugglers and acrobats.

Cirque d'Hiver Bouglione
110 rue Amelot, 11th (01.47.00.28.81/www.cirque dhiver.com). M° Filles du Calvaire. **Shows** *Late Oct-late Feb days vary.* **Admission** €10-€39. **Credit** AmEx, MC, V. **Map** p411 L5.
This endearingly traditional circus, inaugurated in 1852, has been in the same family for seven decades. There's a new theme each year, but always in the classic circus fashion.

Cirque Pinder
Pelouse de Reuilly, Bois de Vincennes, 12th (01.45.90.21.25/www.cirquepinder.com). M° Porte Dorée or Porte de Charenton. **Shows** *Mid Nov-early Jan days vary.* **Admission** €12-€35; free under-2s. **Credit** AmEx, DC, MC, V.

With horses, lions, elephants and monkeys, Pinder is the oldest and most traditional travelling circus in France. The final leg of its annual tour is the Christmas show at the Pelouse de Reuilly.

Espace Chapiteaux
Parc de La Villette, 19th (01.42.09.01.09/www. villette.com). M° Porte de la Villette. **Shows** *vary.* **Admission** *varies.* **Credit** MC, V. **Map** p405 inset.
This big top hosts companies such as Cirque Plume, Cirque Vent d'Autan and aerialists Les Arts Saut.

Grand Céleste Cirque
13 av de la Porte-des-Lilas, 19th (01.53.19.99.13/ www.grandceleste.com). M° Porte des Lilas. **Open** *Oct-Apr.* **Shows** *8.45pm Fri, Sun. Matinées Wed, Fri, Sat, Sun (times vary).* **Admission** €10-€26. **No credit cards.**
Three blue tents host this circus of traditional acts. Also *guinguette*-style bar and circus courses.

Girls! Girls! Girls!

A century after cancan was born, busty babes are still slinking across the cabaret stages of Paris. The **Moulin Rouge** (*see p278*) created the concept in 1889 with skirt-raising called *Quadrille Réaliste* (later coined the cancan). Since then, the addition of two glitzy venues, **Le Lido** and the **Crazy Horse Saloon** (for both, *see p278*), institutionalised garter-pinging forever. The tacky, modern **Belle Epoque** (*see p278*) completes the quartet.

Today's cabaret, an all-evening, €100, smart-dress extravaganza, is served with a pre-show gourmet meal and champers. Male dancers, acrobats and magicians refreshingly complement the foxy foxtrots; the dancing is synchronised, the costumes beautiful, and the whole caboodle unreservedly respectable.

True to form, the Moulin Rouge is the most traditional glamour revue and the only place with cancan. Toulouse-Lautrec posters, glittery lamp-posts and fake trees lend tacky charm, while 60 Doriss dancers cover every inch of the stage with faultless synchronisation. Costumes are flamboyant, the entr'acte acts funny and the sets are solid: one daring number even takes place inside a giant tank of underwater boa constrictors. Sadly, elbow room is nil, with hundreds of tables packed in like sardines. But if you can bear intimacy with international businessmen, the Moulin Rouge, the cheapest of the food-serving cabarets, won't disappoint.

For space go to Le Lido. With 1,000 seats, this classy venue is the largest, priciest cabaret of the lot: the art nouveau hall's

high-tech touches (descending balcony and disappearing lamps) optimise visibility, and star chef Paul Bocuse has revolutionised the menu. The slightly tame show, with 60 Bluebell Girls, has boob-shaking, wacky costumes and numerous oddities: courtesan cats meeting Charlie Chaplin for example.

For a cheaper, more risqué show, see *Taboo* at the Crazy Horse. The Horse's *art du nu* was invented in 1951 by Alain Bernadin; since then, this ode to feminine beauty has entertained punters with 11 lookalike dancers whose names (Nooka Caramel and Misty Flashback) are as real as their wigs. Clad only in rainbow light and strategic squares of black tape, the girls put on such tantalising numbers as their signature piece *Va Va Voom*.

Children

Paris is easy and entertaining for *les enfants.*

Paris is a remarkably child-friendly city, a place where kids are fêted and culturally sated. If you come here with youngsters, any notion that Parisians are stand-offish will soon disappear under a barrage of praise and advice. For the most part, the famous sights on every child's wish list can be ticked off without undue stress, and a boat trip down the Seine makes for an ideal family outing. Kids are made welcome at most cafés and restaurants, and set mini-menus (€5-€8) of *saucisses-frites* plus dessert and drink are the order of the day at many bistros.

There's no shortage of venues for unscripted playtime, either. The many parks, an essential part of every Paris childhood, do duty as gardens for flat-dwelling nippers: generations of children have grown up among the sandpits, swings, puppet shows, pony rides and boating ponds of the **Luxembourg** and **Tuileries** gardens. Nearly all public parks have some kind of playground. What's more, in recent years the city has become much more cycle- and skate-friendly (*see p333*), so family cycle outings are feasible along newly created lanes by the Seine and the Canal St-Martin. The **Bois de Vincennes** in the east and **Bois de Boulogne** in the west offer woodland, picnic areas, boating lakes and cycle rental.

Gaps in the academic schedule – Wednesday afternoons, weekends and the holidays – are filled by all kinds of workshops, film seasons and theatre productions; parents will find lots of activities to keep their offspring occupied and switched on. Listings weeklies such as *Pariscope, L'Officiel des Spectacles, Zurban* and *Télérama*'s *Sortir* supplement have children's sections; daily paper *Libération* also publishes a bi-monthly supplement for parents, *Paris-Mômes.* For museums, the **Carte Musées et Monuments** (*see p67*), valid for up to 70 museums for between one and five days, allows access at members' entrances, saving time and tempers – notably at the **Louvre** (*see pp80-87*).

GETTING AROUND

Only cross the street at a zebra crossing and stay alert even then. Turning traffic should give priority to pedestrians, but often doesn't. Look out for skaters, scooter-riders and motorcyclists whizzing down narrow pavements.

Turnstiles, numerous stairs and crowded carriages make travelling by métro tricky with a pushchair. Try to make your journey between 10.30am and 4pm, or use the easier, driverless line 14 (Gare St-Lazare to Bibliothèque François Mitterrand); kids love to sit at the front and look down the tunnel as the train advances. The mostly overground lines 6 (Nation to Charles de Gaulle Etoile) and 2 (Nation to Porte Dauphine) offer attractive city views, and a number of RER stations have lifts.

It's often better to take the bus, some of which (Nos.24, 63) are mini sightseeing tours (www.ratp.fr), and dozens of which are accessible with a pushchair. These latter have four priority seats near the front of each bus, designed to be used if you're travelling with under-fours, who go free on public transport. Four- to ten-year-olds qualify for a half-price *carnet* (ten tickets) for all transport, including the Balabus, the Montmartrobus minibus and the Montmartre funicular.

Taxi drivers will generally take a family of four, as under-tens count as half; they charge €2 for a folding pushchair. If you're stuck miles from anywhere, try G7 taxis (01.41.27.66.99), which has an English-speaking booking line.

The waterborne Batobus links eight prime sights along the Seine, including the Eiffel Tower, Louvre, Notre-Dame, Orsay Museum and Jardin des Plantes (*see p76* **Boat tours**).

HELP AND INFORMATION

English-speaking, volunteer support group Message (01.58.60.00.53, www.message paris.org, annual membership €39) aims to provide a social network for mothers and mothers-to-be, and publishes the handy *ABCs of Motherhood in Paris* (€22 for non-members, €16 for members).

Babies & toddlers

If you're off out, make sure you pack a portable changing mat – facilities are not so common. A spot worth remembering is the WC chalet in the **Jardin du Luxembourg**, where 40¢ gives you access to loos with a padded changing table; **Galeries Lafayette** and **Printemps** (for both, *see p234*) department stores have clean, well-equipped change rooms.

When it comes to breastfeeding, the French are quite fussy. This usually means you'll have to feed *en plein air*, or in a quiet corner of a museum or restaurant. Take a scarf for places where modesty is essential.

Arts & Entertainment

Ménagerie du Jardin des Plantes.
See p284.

A city break with tots in tow doesn't have to mean spending every waking hour at the park; nearly all the main attractions have child-friendly activities nearby – handy as a reward for good behaviour or if you're prepared to split into two groups. In the Tuileries gardens, near the Louvre, a funfair runs from mid June to the end of August. And if the **Eiffel Tower** (*see p160*) is too daunting an experience for the smaller ones, lead a party to the go-kart track, duck pond, play areas and pony rides at the adjacent Champ de Mars – or march to the carousel opposite the tower, at the foot of the **Trocadéro** gardens (*see p119*). Other carousels are dotted about the city – there's a good one at the Jardin des Plantes (*see p285*) called the Dodo Manège, which features extinct animals for mounts. Even the **Musée Rodin** (*see p157*) has its distractions, with sandboxes, shade and wide open spaces.

Babysitting

The American Church in Paris

65 quai d'Orsay, 7th (01.40.62.05.00/www.acparis. org). Mº Invalides or Pont de l'Alma. **Open** 9am-10.30pm Mon-Sat; 1-10.30pm Sun. **Map** p407 E5.
The free noticeboard tucked inside the main entrance of this long-established church bristles with 'situations wanted' advertisements from recommended English-speaking babysitters and au pairs, as well as others for rooms to rent and a variety of useful services.

Baby Sitting Services

01.46.21.33.16/www.babysittingservices.com. **Open** 24hrs daily. *Office* 7am-9pm Mon-Fri; 7am-8pm Sat. **Rates** *Mon-Sat* 8am-10pm €6.80/hr; 10pm-8am €7.50/hr. *Sun* €8/hr + €11.90 fee. *Bank hols* €15.90/hr. €1/hr/child supplement for 3 or more children. **Credit** MC, V.
Babysitting can be organised at two hours' notice. School pickup, outings, children's parties and long-term babysitting can also be arranged.

Activity museums

Egyptian mummies at the **Louvre**, dinosaur skeletons at the Galeries de Paléontologie et d'Anatomie Comparée at the **Muséum National d'Histoire Naturelle**, flying machines at the **Musée de l'Air et de l'Espace** at Le Bourget, the Planetarium at the **Palais de la Découverte**, the Argonaut submarine at the **Cité des Sciences et de l'Industrie**… There's plenty for a child's imagination, and under-18s can usually get in free, or almost. Many places provide activity sheets (ask at the *accueil*) and offer children's activities (in French) on Wednesdays, at weekends and in the holidays. Most museums close on Mondays or Tuesdays.

At the Louvre, the programme for kids is led by artists, architects and filmmakers. Next door, the **Musée des Arts Décoratifs** (*see p93*) offers hands-on art workshops for ages four to 12. The **Palais de Tokyo** (*see p122*)

Cité des Enfants

Niveau 0, Cité des Sciences et de l'Industrie, 30 av Corentin-Cariou, 19th (01.40.05.80.00/www.cite-sciences.fr). M° Porte de la Villette. **Open** (90min visits) 10.30am, 12.30pm, 2.30pm, 4.30pm Tue-Sun. **Admission** €5 per session. **Credit** AmEx, MC, V. **Map** p405 inset.

Two vast hands-on discovery zones cater for under-fives and fives to 12s. Highlights for tots include the water cascades (switch the points and watch the wheels spin) and a building site with foam blocks, wheelbarrows, cranes and pulleys for aspiring *bricoleurs*. Older kids can try the working TV studio or the walk-in anthill.

Musée de la Magie

11 rue St-Paul, 4th (01.42.72.13.26/www.musee delamagie.com). M° St-Paul or Sully Morland. **Open** 2-7pm Wed, Sat, Sun; 2-7pm daily in half-term, Christmas & Easter hols. **Admission** €7; €5 3s-12s; free under-3s. **No credit cards. Map** p408 L7.

Kids will enjoy even the queue for this wonderful museum of magic and illusion: a magician is on hand to pull scarves out of ears. There's more conjuring inside and a hands-on approach to optical illusions.

Musée de la Poupée

impasse Berthaud, 3rd (01.42.72.73.11/www. museedelapoupeeparis.com). M° Rambuteau. **Open** 10am-6pm Tue-Sun. Closed bank hols. **Admission** €6; €3 3s-18s; free under-3s. **No credit cards. Map** p408 L7.

A stone's throw from the Centre Pompidou, this manageable and non-academic operation displays some 300 dolls (mostly French) and accompanying pets in thematic tableaux. Temporary exhibits, covering topics such as Barbie or the kit a doll needs for the kitchen, are presented in the last three rooms. A shop and doll's hospital share the premises.

Musée Grévin

10 bd Montmartre, 9th (01.47.70.85.05/www.musee-grevin.com). M° Grands Boulevards. **Open** 10am-6.30pm (last admission 5.30pm) Mon-Fri; 10am-7pm (last admission 6pm) Sat, Sun & hols. **Admission** €17; €14.50 concessions; €10 6s-14s; free under-6s. **Credit** AmEx, DC, MC, V. **Map** p404 H4.

Some 300 wax figures of entertainers, artists, writers and historical figures, from Einstein to Arnold Schwarznegger, Mahatma Gandhi to Britney Spears and Elton John to Zinédine Zidane. Here you can see a re-creation of Louis XIV's lavish wedding, Neil Armstrong's first step on the moon and more.

Muséum National d'Histoire Naturelle

36 rue Geoffroy-St-Hilaire, 2 rue Bouffon, 57 rue Cuvier, pl Valhubert, 5th (01.40.79.30.00/ www.mnhn.fr). M° Gare d'Austerlitz or Jussieu. **Open** 10am-6pm (last admission 5.15pm) Mon, Wed-Sun. **Admission** *Grande Galerie de l'Evolution* €8; €7 4s-18s; free under-4s. *Galeries de Paléontologie et Anatomie Comparée or Galerie de Minéralogie et de Géologie* €6; €4 4s-18s; free under-4s. **No credit cards. Map** p408 K9.

has Tok Tok workshops frequently led by contemporary artists, and the **Musée Rodin** (*see p157*) sets up children's clay-modelling workshops in August. The **Musée National Picasso** (*see p111*) offers family visits on Sundays, with children's workshops on Wednesdays in term-time, exploring animal sculptures and pictures by Pablo himself. **Paris Walks** (01.48.09.21.40, www.paris-walks.com) organises a series of child-friendly city strolls during the school holidays.

Centre Pompidou – Galerie des Enfants

rue St-Martin, 4th (01.44.78.49.13/www.centre pompidou.fr). M° Rambuteau/RER Châtelet Les Halles. **Open** 11am-10pm Mon, Wed-Sun. *Workshops* most Wed & Sat afternoons. **Admission** *Museum* €7; €5 concessions; free under-18s (accompanied by an adult). *Workshops* €9 Wed & Sat (children only); €4.50 Sun (children & parents). **Credit** MC, V. **Map** p404 K5.

Beautifully thought-out exhibitions by top artists and designers introduce children to modern art, design and architecture, with hands-on workshops for sixes to 12s, and family workshops one Sunday afternoon a month. Outside, look for the colourful and animated Stravinsky fountain on the south side, designed by Niki de Saint-Phalle and Jean Tinguely, and the animated clock in the Quartier de l'Horloge on the piazza's north side: every hour, its man-size automaton *Le Défenseur du Temps* ('Defender of Time') fights off a crab, a dragon or a cockerel (and all three at midday and 5pm). *See also p107*.

Arts & Entertainment

Of the three museums in the Jardin des Plantes, the most popular is the Grande Galerie de l'Evolution. Imaginative displays of its large collection of stuffed creatures create a Noah's Ark-like stream of animals (including Louis XV's pet rhino); the small Espace Découverte has microscopes and interactive games. Hunks of meteorites and crystals occupy the Galerie de Minéralogie et de Géologie, and the Galeries de Paléontologie et d'Anatomie Comparée includes skeletons of birds, monkeys, dinosaurs and humans.

Aquaria, safari parks & zoos

Ménagerie du Jardin des Plantes
57 rue Cuvier, 5th (01.40.79.37.94). M° Gare d'Austerlitz or Jussieu. **Open** 9am-5.30pm daily. **Admission** €7; €5 4s-18s; free under-4s. **Credit** AmEx, MC, V. **Map** p408 K8.
This small zoo was founded in 1794. Animals include vultures, monkeys, orang-utans, reptiles, a century-old turtle and a lovely red panda. **Photos** *pp282-283.*

Palais de la Porte Dorée Aquarium Tropical
293 av Daumesnil, 12th (01.44.74.84.80/www.palais-portedoree.org). M° Porte Dorée. **Open** 10am-5.15pm Mon, Wed-Sun. **Admission** €4; €2.60 concessions & under-12s; €7 families; free under-4s. **Credit** *Shop* MC, V.

This art deco palace houses the city aquarium and its colonial crocodiles, brought from Dakar in 1948; other watery residents include cuttlefish, clownfish and sharks. Though the Palais' collections of art from Africa and Oceania have been moved to the Musée du Quai Branly (*see p152* **Chirac's grand projet**), you can still visit several of its main rooms. *See also p117.*

Parc de Thoiry
78770 Thoiry-en-Yvelines (01.34.87.53.76/ www.thoiry.tm.fr). 45km west of Paris; by car A13, A12, then N12 direction Dreux until Thoiry, then follow signs. **Open** *Summer* 10am-5pm daily. *Winter* 11am-5pm daily. **Admission** (free under-3s) *Safari park* €21; €14.50 3-12s. *Château* €6; €5 3-12s. *Park & château* €26; €18.50 3-12s. **Credit** AmEx, MC, V.
The Parc de Thoiry includes not just a magnificent château but also one of Europe's first and best safari parks. Zebras rub their noses over your windscreen, lions laze and bears amble down a forest track. Zoo rarities include Siberian lynx and Tonkean macaques. The park is only accessible by car; the ticket is valid for the zoo, maze and gardens.

Parc Zoologique de Paris
53 av de St-Maurice, 12th (01.44.75.20.00/www.mnhn. fr). M° Porte Dorée. **Open** *Summer* 9am-6pm Mon-Sat; 9am-6.30pm Sun & bank hols. *Winter* 9am-5pm daily. **Admission** €5; free under-4s. **Credit** MC, V.

The *goûter* food guide

In France, the solution to the afternoon munchies is known as *le goûter*, a scheduled snack break that's a key entry in the catalogue of French childhood rituals when coming home from school. For the young visitor, it's the perfect excuse (as if one were needed) to make like a native and explore the delectable world of French pastries.

Standard examples include *pain au chocolat* (a pillow-shaped, chocolate-filled croissant) or *Viennois chocolat* (a soft loaf in the shape of a mini-baguette and chock-full of chocolate chips). Chocophobes might prefer a *pain aux raisins* (a bun stuffed with raisins), or a *chausson aux pommes* (from the same pastry family as the croissant, but stuffed with baked apples or, more often, apple jam). Rounding out the dental profession's bêtes noires are wonderfully spongy *madeleines* (perhaps with just a hint of orange) and *chouquettes* (small puff pastries sprinkled with sugar pieces – the French equivalent of mini doughnuts).

One of the above will go down a treat after a trawl through the zoo and museums of the Jardin des Plantes: drop into the nearby

Boulanger de Monge (*see p260*) for its mini or regular-sized *escargots* in chocolate, lemon, cinnamon or pistachio varieties; or cross the street to the organic *boulangerie* **Moisan** (*see p260*), for unparalleled *chouquettes* and cheesy *gougères*.

Sweeter tooths might demand crunchy *macarons*, made from egg whites, ground almonds and icing sugar. Available in plain, chocolate and coffee flavours in most *boulangeries*, they've reached a level of perfection, with heavenly and unexpected flavours, at **Pierre Hermé** (*see p263*) and **Ladurée** (*see p218*).

Though the daily *goûter* is a boon for *boulangeries* situated near schools, many favourite French treats are bought in grocery stores. When it comes to store-bought *goûter* biscuits, the leader of the pack is Lu, maker of the incomparable Petit Ecolier (extra-dark chocolate cookies stamped with the image of a schoolboy), Mikados (thin bread sticks dipped in dark chocolate) and some excellent chocolate-chip cookies.

● For reviews of more bakeries, *chocolatiers* and pâtisseries, *see pp260-264.*

Gibbons leap around the trees, baboons slide on the rocks, and human over-sevens can ascend the 65m Grand Rocher (by lift). More than 600 species in total can be seen at this spacious zoo in the heart of the Bois de Vincennes. Check the notice at the entrance for newborns and that day's feeding times, especially for seals. A mini train tours the zoo.

Parks, gardens & views

It's now possible to sit on the grass and picnic in most Paris parks. Two particularly pretty ones are **Parc Monceau** and **Parc Montsouris**. Most public gardens offer playgrounds, sandpits, concrete ping-pong tables and the like: there's a handy garden beside **Notre-Dame**, the **Tuileries** has trampolines and at posh **place des Vosges** there are wooden slides and rocking horses. Many parks have their own Guignol (Punch and Judy) puppet theatre, with shows at weekends and on most Wednesday afternoons. The language might be hard to follow, but the audience participation is contagious.

Kids love panoramic views, but if the queue at the Eiffel Tower is too much, there's always the view from the pushchair-friendly **Tour Montparnasse** (*see p167*) – take the lift to the 56th floor, then walk up to the terrace on the 59th. The ninth-floor terrace at the **Musée de l'Institut du Monde Arabe** (*see p145*) also has great views, as well as sticky treats served on mosaic-topped tables. You can rise to giddy heights at the **Arc de Triomphe** (*see p119*) and **Notre-Dame** (*see p74*).

Jardin de l'Acclimatation
Bois de Boulogne, 16th (01.40.67.90.82/www.jardin dacclimatation.fr). Mº Les Sablons. **Open** *June-Sept* 10am-7pm daily. *Oct-May* 10am-6pm daily. **Admission** €2.70; €1.35 concessions; free under-3s. **Credit** (€15 minimum) MC, V.
A much-loved feature since the 19th century, this amusement park has bears, a Normandy-style farm and an aviary, to say nothing of enchanted boat rides, a Chinese dragon rollercoaster and the Enchanted House for children aged two to four. Older kids can try the interactive gadgetry at the Explor@dome, mini racetrack and minigolf. Many attractions cost €2.50 each (€30 for 15); others are free. A mini train (Wednesdays and weekends; €5.20 including entrance fee) runs from Porte Maillot through the Bois de Boulogne to the park entrance. **Photos** *p286*.

Jardin des Plantes
57 rue Cuvier or pl Valhubert, 5th (01.42.34.20.00/www.paris.fr). Mº Gare d'Austerlitz or Jussieu. **Open** *Summer* 7.30am-dusk daily. *Winter* 8am-dusk daily. **Map** p408 K9.
A botanical garden surrounded by a small zoo (the Ménagerie) and the three museums of the Museum National d'Histoire Naturelle (*see p283*). There are

playgrounds, stalls and a constantly changing universe of plant life, including hundreds of varieties of flowers, grasses, alpine plants and what not, most of them labelled with their Latin names.

Jardin du Luxembourg
pl Edmond-Rostand, pl Auguste-Comte or rue de Vaugirard, 6th (01.42.34.23.89/www.paris.fr). Mº Odéon or St-Sulpice/RER Luxembourg. **Open** *Summer* 8am-dusk daily. *Winter* 9am-dusk daily. **Map** p407 H8.
The biggest and best play area on the Left Bank, thanks to the imaginative playground (€2), merry-go-round, pony rides, puppet shows, tennis courts and, in summer, a toy boating pond.

Parc des Buttes-Chaumont
rue Botzaris, rue Manin or rue de Crimée, 19th. Mº Buttes Chaumont. **Open** *Jan-Apr, Oct-Dec* 7am-8.15pm daily. *May, mid Aug-Sept* 7am-9.15pm daily. *June-mid Aug* 7am-10.15pm daily. **Map** p405 N2.
From its heights, the views here are arguably better than those from Sacré-Coeur, and there are picturesque grottos and waterfalls for kids to play among. A playground, puppet shows and donkey rides provide further entertainment in summer.

Parc Floral
Bois de Vincennes, 12th (www.parcfloraldeparis.com). Mº Château de Vincennes, then 10min walk or bus 112. **Open** 9.30am-dusk daily. **Admission** €1; 50c 7-26s; free under-7s. *During concerts/exhibitions* €4; €2.50 7s-16s. **No credit cards**.
The miniature train (€1.50) is just one outstanding feature of this verdant park, one of the city's best play areas for all ages. There's a nature resource centre and butterfly garden, plus a huge adventure playground with any number of slides, swings and climbing frames. Older kids will enjoy the minigolf course laid out like Paris or the racetrack with its pedal-powered horses. Wednesday afternoons bring free theatre shows, suitable for threes to tens.

Parc de la Villette
211 av Jean-Jaurès, 19th (01.40.03.75.03/www.villette.com). Mº Porte de Pantin or Porte de la Villette. **Open** 6am-1am daily. **Map** p405 inset.
Part of the redeveloped Villette canal basin, this series of themed parks includes Le Jardin des Miroirs – where you can walk through a bizarre landscape of mirrors – and the even more strange Jardin des Frayeurs Enfantines ('Garden of Childish Fears'), with accompanying spooky music to recreate a fairytale forest.

Sport & entertainment

A perennial pleasure is the funfair, the best being La Fête à Neu-Neu (Bois de Boulogne, autumn) and the Foire du Trône (Bois de Vincennes, spring); La Fête des Tuileries in summer offers dizzying views from the big wheel and other thrill rides. Other family-friendly events include the Chinese New Year

Arts & Entertainment

Fables, fairytales and folk stories from all over francophone Africa are regular favourites at children's shows at theatres and *café-théâtres* in Paris on Wednesday afternoons, at weekends and in the school holidays. **Théâtre Dunois** (7 rue Louise-Weiss, 13th, 01.45.84.72.00, www.theatredunois.org) is one place to try for theatre, dance and musical creations. Look for listings in *Pariscope* and in the last page of *Télérama*'s *Sortir* supplement.

Traditional **circuses** come to Paris every winter (*see p280*); there are funfairs at the Bois de Vincennes (spring), the Tuileries (summer) and the Bois de Boulogne (autumn).

Children's films are mostly dubbed into French, but you can see VO (*version originale*, or original version) screenings of the latest Hollywood hits at dozens of cinemas across town (*see pp291-296* **Film**). Also keep a look out for children's showings on Wednesdays at the Forum des Images (01.44.76.62.00, www.forumdesimages.net) and in the new Cinémathèque Française (*see p294* **'thèque five**). The IMAX cinema in La Villette's **Géode** (01.39.17.00.00, www.lageode.fr) will keep kids goggle-eyed; for more of the same, plus amazing 3D computer animations-cum-rides, head for **Futuroscope** (www.futuroscope.com), a thrilling futuristic park near Poitiers, an 80-minute TGV ride from Gare Montparnasse.

Paris is good for watery entertainment, too. As well as 35 public pools (www.paris.fr) and the opening of a floating one on the Seine in summer 2006 (*see p336* **One cool pool**), the indoor Aquaboulevard (44 rue Louis-Armand, 15th, 01.40.60.15.15, www.aquaboulevard.com) gives the over-threes the chance to splash down slides and ride the waves. In summer, **Paris-Plage** sees a plunge pool installed beside the Seine along with 2,000 tonnes of sand – enough for the most ambitious sandcastle. For sports activities, *see pp329-336* **Sport & Fitness**.

La Mer de Sable

60950 Ermenonville (03.44.54.18.44/www.merde sable.fr). RER Aéroport Charles de Gaulle 1, then shuttle (01.48.62.38.33). By car A1, exit 7. **Open** *9 Apr-25 Sept* 10am-6.30pm Mon-Fri; 10.30am-7pm Sat, Sun. **Admission** €16.50; €14 3-11s. **Credit** AmEx, MC, V.
This Wild West theme park in the 'sea of sand' of the Ermenonville forest offers shoot-outs and equestrian acrobatics, the Colorado Canyon rollercoaster and Cheyenne river ride. Opening hours can be quite erratic, especially in September, so phone ahead.

> ► *See pp354-355* for **Disneyland Paris**, **Walt Disney Studios Park** and the **Parc Astérix**.

Sweet **Jardin de l'Acclimatation**. *See p285.*

parade down the Champs-Elysées in February, the impromptu outdoor gigs of Fête de la Musique (21 June) and, from mid July to mid August, Quartier d'Eté, when parks form the backdrop for music and dance concerts (www.quartierdete.com). Bastille Day (14 July) comes with a parade, flypast and firework display, and Christmas brings marvellous window displays at the major department stores, free carousels and outdoor ice rinks at Hôtel de Ville, Montparnasse and La Défense. *See also pp272-277* **Festivals & Events**.

Dance

Tutus and tradition in step with exciting experimentation.

Now that Paris has a prestigious **National Dance Centre**, it need no longer rest on its laurels. Twelve years in the making, the Centre National de la Danse (*see p289* **All the right moves**) opened in June 2004 as the flagship of the nation's 600-plus dance companies. Located just outside Paris city centre in Pantin – near the Cité de la Musique – the CND not only serves as a major performance and rehearsal centre, but also as an archive of the city's stellar dance heritage.

Although Paris is revered for its sumptuous Opéra productions and groundbreaking avant-garde performances of a century ago, it also has an impressive contemporary scene: local punters are hungry for cutting-edge dance. Talent is constantly shuttling between Paris and Brussels; Anne Teresa de Keersmaeker and her company Rosas are among the commuters. Superstars Pina Bausch and William Forsythe also visit regularly, drawing healthy crowds.

For would-be performers, there are masses of dance classes – ballet and hip hop being the most popular – and there's also no letting up of the Buena Vista-inspired Latin phenomenon.

INFORMATION AND RESOURCES

For listings, see *Pariscope* and *L'Officiel des Spectacles*, and the *Aden* supplement in *Le Monde*. For events coverage, look out for two monthlies: *La Terrasse* (distributed free at major dance venues) and the glossy *Danser*. The Centre National de la Danse publishes the bi-annual in-depth review *Kinem* (subscription only, 01.41.83.98.98).

For shoes and equipment, **Repetto** (22 rue de la Paix, 2nd, 01.44.71.83.12) supplies the Opéra with pointes and slippers; the main department stores (*see p233*) also stock dance items.

Festivals

Every season sees some kind of contemporary dance festival in or near Paris. The year starts with **Faits d'Hiver** (www.faitsdhiver.com) in January; May/June welcomes the **Rencontres Chorégraphiques de Seine-St-Denis** (www.rencontreschoregraphiques.com) and the **IRCAM Agora festival** (www.ircam.fr). **Onze Bouge** (www.festivalonze.org) in June is followed by the street-dance **Rencontres de la Villette** (www.rencontresvillette.com)

at various surburban locations in October. There are smaller festivals at the **Maison des Arts de Créteil**, and the **Ménagerie de Verre** in the 11th. *See also pp272-277* **Festivals & Events**.

Paris quartier d'été

01.44.94.98.00/www.quartierdete.com.
Dates *July-Aug.*
This festival features eclectic programmes and free outdoor performances. Public rehearsals and talks give the audience the chance to meet prestigious international choreographers.

Festival d'Automne

01.53.45.17.00/www.festival-automne.com.
Dates *Sept-Dec.*
For 34 years, the Festival d'Automne has shown the way forward in the performing arts. Performances are highbrow and experimental, with works by big-name choreographers as well as newcomers.

Major dance venues

Centre National de la Danse

1 rue Victor-Hugo, 93507 Pantin (01.41.83.27.27/ box office 01.41.83.98.98/www.cnd.fr). Mº Hoche/ RER Pantin. **Open** *Box office* 10am-7pm Mon-Fri.
Admission €5-€15. **Credit** AmEx, MC, V.
France's impressive new centre for dance. *See p289* **All the right moves. Photos** *p288 and p290.*

Maison des Arts de Créteil

pl Salvador Allende, 94000 Créteil (01.45.13.19.19/ www.maccreteil.com). Mº Créteil-Préfecture. **Open** *Box office* 1-7pm Tue-Sat. Closed July & Aug.
Admission €8-€20. **Credit** MC, V.
This arts centre brings international acts to the Paris suburbs. In 2006, these include the Montalvo-Hervieu and Cré-Ange companies. Don't miss the Festival International Exit in the spring.

Palais Garnier

pl de l'Opéra, 9th (08.92.89.90.90/www.opera-de-paris.fr). Mº Opéra. **Open** *Box office* 11am-6pm Mon-Sat. *Telephone bookings* 9am-6pm Mon-Sat. Closed 15 July-end Aug. **Admission** €7-€160. Concessions 1hr before show. **Credit** AmEx, MC, V.
Map p403 G4.
The Ballet de l'Opéra National de Paris manages to tread successfully between tutu classics and new productions, between the Opéra Bastille (*see p312*) and lavish Palais Garnier, where the renovated grand foyer is a must-see. Maurice Béjart brings Bartok's *Miraculous Mandarin* and Ravel's *Bolero* to the Bastille in June and July, at the same time as

The **Centre National de la Danse**.
See p287.

All the right moves

Parisian cultural institutions and audiences abide by a long-standing principle: beyond the city ring road, there be dragons. With real estate prices soaring in the city centre and politicians determined to perk up the suburbs, the long-running saga of siting France's prestigious National Dance Centre saw it eventually end up by the Canal de l'Ourcq at Pantin, on the city's northeastern edge. In the pipeline since 1991, too frequently sidelined for want of consistent political and artistic decision, the **Centre National de la Danse** (*see p287*) was opened with grand ceremony in June 2004.

Oddly enough, in a country with a prestigious ballet tradition and some 600 active companies, dance is not a cultural policy priority. The CND has had to make do with a 1972 concrete-and-glass building that hosted the local offices, jail and courtroom. Key architects Antoinette Robain and Claire Guieysse redesigned the dreary, grey edifice, transforming it into a hi-tech and spacious structure. The angular lines are softened by bold red panels, Michelangelo Pistoletto's pop furniture, and Hervé Audibert's colourful yet dramatic lights.

As a cultural resource, in any case, the CND is second to none. Intended to provide professionals with pedagogical, technical and financial support, it features 11 rehearsal studios, classrooms, an exhibition hall, film-viewing rooms, audition posting boards, and a multimedia-library stacked with books, videos, archives and periodicals. Several studios can accommodate an audience of up to 135, but there is no actual performance hall. As if to accentuate the venue's previous function, Robain and Guieysse have laid out the café-restaurant in the form of a prison canteen.

Most shows, lectures and seminars are open to all. With guests such as Jochen Roller and the Ballet de Lorraine, and the Hip Hop Tanz festival set for June, the 2006 season definitely sounds attractive enough for any dance or architecture aficionado to head for Pantin – only a single métro stop away from the Cité de la Musique, the Conservatoire and the Parc de La Villette.

John Neumeier's take on Chopin's *La Dame aux Camélias* appears across town.

Théâtre National de Chaillot
1 pl du Trocadéro, 16th (01.53.65.30.00/www. theatre-chaillot.fr). M° Trocadéro. **Open** *Box office* 11am-7pm Mon-Fri. *Telephone bookings* 11am-7pm Mon-Sat. Closed July & Aug. **Admission** €19.50-€39; €10.50-€32 concessions. **Credit** MC, V. **Map** p402 C5.
Chaillot features big names and home-grown talents. The 2006 season is typically eclectic, with tango and flamenco evenings, contemporary dance from Catherine Diverrès and Merlin Nyakam's La Calebasse, plus Ballet Biarritz's Paris debut with an adaptation of Beethoven's only ballet, *Les Créatures*.

Théâtre de la Ville – Les Abbesses
2 pl du Châtelet, 4th (01.42.74.22.77/www.theatre delaville-paris.com). M° Châtelet. **Open** *Box office* 11am-7pm Mon; 11am-8pm Tue-Sat. *Telephone bookings* 11am-7pm Mon-Sat. Closed July & Aug. **Admission** €11.50-€23. **Credit** MC, V. **Map** p406 J6.
This leading contemporary dance venue has become a showcase for established choreographers; in 2006 Marie Chouinard and Anne Teresa de Keersmaeker will visit, as will Angelin Preljocaj. Book early: most shows sell out well before opening night. Sister venue Théâtre des Abbesses showcases classical Indian performers.

Other locations: Théâtre des Abbesses, 31 rue des Abbesses, 18th (same phone).

Other dance venues

L'Etoile du Nord
16 rue Georgette-Agutte, 18th (01.42.26.47.47). M° Guy Môquet. **Open** *Box office* 1-6pm Mon-Fri. Closed July & Aug. **Admission** €19; €8-€13 concessions. **Credit** MC, V.
Provides a welcome platform for the contemporary multimedia dance scene.

Ménagerie de Verre
12-14 rue Léchevin, 11th (01.43.38.33.44/www. menagerie-de-verre.org). M° Parmentier. **Open** *Box office* 1-7pm Mon-Fri. Closed July & Aug. **Admission** €13; €10 concessions. **No credit cards. Map** p405 N5.
This multidisciplinary hothouse is rooted in the avant-garde, with contemporary dance and classes. It also hosts bi-annual festival Les Inaccoutumés.

Regard du Cygne
210 rue de Belleville, 20th (01.43.58.55.93/redcygne. free.fr). M° Télégraphe. **Open** *Box office* 1hr before show. Closed Aug. **Admission** €5-€15. **No credit cards. Map** p405 Q3.
This picturesque studio is one of the few alternative spaces in Paris. Its Spectacles Sauvages allow unknowns to show a ten-minute piece to the public.

Arts & Entertainment

A blockish exterior for a dance blockbuster: the **Centre National de la Danse**. *See p287.*

Théâtre de la Bastille

76 rue de la Roquette, 11th (01.43.57.42.14/www. theatre-bastille.com). M° Bastille or Voltaire. **Open** *Box office* 10am-6pm Mon-Fri; 2-6pm Sat. Closed July & Aug. **Admission** €12.50-€19. **Credit** MC, V. **Map** p409 M6.
Small theatre showcasing ribald dance and drama.

Théâtre du Châtelet

1 pl du Châtelet, 1st (01.40.28.28.00/www.chatelet-theatre.com). M° Châtelet. **Open** *Box office* 1hr before show. Closed July-Sept. **Admission** from €10. **Credit** AmEx, MC, V. **Map** p404 J5.
A classical music institution across the square from the Théâtre de la Ville (*see p340*), Châtelet indulges dance audiences every year with international acts such as Les Ballets Trockadero de Monte-Carlo and the Zurich Ballet (performing *In den Windem im Nichts* in March 2006). French regional ballets also receive regular invites.

Théâtre de la Cité Internationale

21 bd Jourdan, 14th (01.43.13.50.50). RER Cité Universitaire. **Open** *Box office* 2-7pm Mon-Fri. *Telephone bookings* 2-7pm Mon-Sat. Closed July & Aug. **Admission** €23; €7.50-€12.50 concessions. **Credit** MC, V.
This well established contemporary dance venue at the Cité Universitaire hosts shows, workshops and other festive events.

Dance classes

Centre de Danse du Marais

41 rue du Temple, 4th (01.42.72.15.42/ 08.92.68.68.70/www.parisdanse.com). M° Rambuteau. **Open** 9am-9pm Mon-Fri; 9am-8pm Sat; 9am-7pm Sun. **Map** p404 K5.
This Marais venue has big-name teachers such as *danse orientale* star Leila Haddad and ballet's Casati-Lazzarelli team, and offers a huge choice of classes at amateur and professional level. Look out for the five-class 'sampler' pass, a good deal at €68.

Centre Momboye

25 rue Boyer, 20th (01.43.58.85.01/www.ladanse. com/centremomboye). M° Gambetta. **Open** 9am-10.30pm daily. **Map** p405 P4.
This is the only centre devoted entirely to African dance, taught to live drumming. There's hip hop, too.

Studio Harmonic

5 passage des Taillandiers, 11th (01.48.07.13.39/ www.studioharmonic.fr). M° Bastille. **Open** *Office* 10am-5pm Mon-Fri. *Classes* 9.30am-10pm Mon-Fri; 9am-7.30pm Sat. Closed 3wks Aug. **Map** p409 M7.
The rising star among Paris dance schools, its claim to fame is teacher Laure Courtellemont and her trademark raggajam, a blend of hip hop and Afro-Caribbean dance.

Film

Because France is the birthplace of cinema, after all.

Gorgeous **La Pagode**.
See p295.

Paris belongs to the movies – or is it the other way around? Consider: 88 cinemas mustering 388 screens, 150 of them independently owned – and of those, 89 showing nothing but arthouse. 700 crews, local and international, shooting in the city every year. More tickets per capita bought in Paris than anywhere else in Europe. And, in any given week, a choice of around 230 movies – not counting festivals (*see p295*). You like cinema? You'll love Paris.

Even if you're only in town for a couple of days, it would be a real shame not to visit at least one of the city's many and varied picture palaces. As well as retrospectives and cut-price promotions, there are many Q&A events: if you are lucky, your trip may coincide with a visit from a major international director or thespian.

Local interest is large enough to sustain a small avalanche of monthly movie magazines (*see p376* **Media**) – there's even a whole book fair, the **Salon du Livre de Cinéma et du DVD**, devoted to writing on film (*see p296*). French DVD labels produce some of the most expertly curated discs in the world. Take a look at the film sections of **Fnac** or **Virgin Megastore** (for both, *see p244*) and you're more than likely to find American and British titles unavailable in the US or UK.

INFORMATION AND TICKETS

New releases, sometimes 15 or more, hit the screens on Wednesdays. Hollywood is well represented, of course, but Paris audiences have a balanced diet that includes an insatiable appetite for international product and for non-standard formats like shorts or documentaries; then there are the 150-plus annual releases funded or part-funded with French money (the French film industry is still the world's third largest, after the US and India).

For venues, times and prices, consult one of the city's three main weekly listings mags: *L'Officiel des Spectacles*, *Pariscope* or *Zurban*. *Films nouveaux* are the week's new releases, *Exclusivités* are the also-showing titles, and *Reprises* means rep. For non-francophone flicks, take note of the two letters printed somewhere near the title: VO (*version originale*) means a screening in the original language with French subtitles; VF (*version française*) means that it's dubbed into French.

Tickets can be bought in the usual way at cinemas themselves (for new blockbusters, especially at multiplexes, it pays to buy tickets at least one screening in advance); by phone on **AlloCiné** (08.92.89.28.92, www.allocine.fr); or, in some cases, online – although this often entails a booking fee. Seats are often discounted by 20 to 30 per cent at Monday or Wednesday screenings, and the Mairie sponsors a number of cut-price promotions throughout the year. All the multiplex chains offer *cartes illimitées*, season tickets that allow unlimited access.

Cinemas

Giant screens & multiplexes

Gaumont Grand Ecran Italie

30 pl d'Italie, 13th (08.92.69.66.96/www.pathe.fr/cinema). M° Place d'Italie. **Admission** *Big screen* €9.50; €7 students. *Other screens* €8.40; €6.80 students. *All screens* €5.70 under-12s; €19.80 monthly pass. **Credit** MC, V. **Map** p408 J10.
This impressive three-screen complex, designed by Japanese architect Kenzo Tange, opened in 1992. Come here to see your favourite star emblazoned across its vast 24m screen – the biggest in Paris. Gaumont's unlimited entry card is called Le Pass, and is also valid in MK2 and Pathé cinemas, plus selected independents like La Pagode (*see p295*).

La Géode

26 av Corentin-Cariou, 19th (08.92.68.45.40/www.lageode.fr). M° Porte de la Villette. **Admission** €9; €7 under-25s. **Credit** MC, V. **Map** p405 inset.
The IMAX cinema at the Cité des Sciences (*see p134*) occupies a huge, shiny geodesic sphere. The massive 1,000m² hemispheric screen lets you experience 3D plunges through natural scenery, as well as animated adventures where the characters zoom out to grab you. **Photo** *p296*.

Le Grand Rex

1 bd Poissonnière, 2nd (08.36.68.05.96/www.legrandrex.com). M° Bonne Nouvelle. **Admission** €9; €7 students, over-60s; €5.95 under-12s. *Les Etoiles du Rex tour* €7.50; €6.50 under-12s; €5.50 for all 5-7pm. **Credit** MC, V. **Map** p404 J4.
With its wedding-cake exterior, fairy-tale interior, plush carpets and the largest auditorium in Europe (2,750 seats), Le Grand Rex is one of the few cinemas to upstage whatever it screens: no wonder it's a listed historic monument. Its blockbuster programming (usually in VF) is well suited to its vast, roll-down screen; it also hosts concerts and rowdy all-night compilation events. There are six smaller screens, too. The Etoiles du Rex tour provides a 50-minute, SFX-laden taste of movie magic.

Max Linder Panorama

24 bd Poissonnière, 9th (08.92.68.00.31/www.maxlinder.com). M° Grands Boulevards. **Admission** €8.50; €6.50 Mon, Wed, Fri, students (except weekends), under-12s. **Credit** MC, V. **Map** p404 J3.
This state-of-the-art cinema (THX sound and an 18m screen) is named after the dapper French silent comedian who owned it between 1914 and 1925. The walls and 700 seats are all black, to prevent even the tiniest twinkle of reflected light distracting the

audience from what's happening on the screen. Look out for all-nighters and one-offs such as rare vintage films or piano-accompanied silents.

MK2 Bibliothèque

128-162 av de France, 13th (08.92.69.84.84/www.mk2.com). M° Bibliothèque François Mitterrand or Quai de la Gare. **Admission** €9-€9.20; €6.70 (Mon-Fri before 6pm) students, 12s-18s; €5.50 under-12s; €5.10 before noon; €19.80 monthly pass. **Credit** MC, V. **Map** p409 M10.
The MK2 chain's flagship offers an all-in-one night out: 14 screens, three restaurants, a bar that opens until 5am at weekends and two-person 'love seats'. MK2 is a paragon of imaginative programming, and growing all the time; in 2005 it opened a new venue on the Canal de l'Ourcq. For €19.80 a month, its Le Pass card offers unlimited screenings at any MK2, Pathé or Gaumont venue, and at some independents.

UGC Ciné Cité Bercy

2 cour St-Emilion, 12th (08.36.68.68.58/www.ugc.fr). M° Cour St-Emilion. **Admission** €9.20; €6.50 students, over-60s; €5.50 under-12s; €18 monthly pass. **Credit** MC, V. **Map** p409 N10.
This ambitious 18-screen development screens art movies and mainstream fodder, and hosts regular meet-the-director events. The 19-screen UGC Ciné Cité Les Halles original (7 pl de la Rotonde, Nouveau Forum des Halles, 1st, 08.92.70.00.00) serves the same mix. The UGC Illimitée card provides all-you-can-watch access for €18 per month; there is a non-refundable €30 handling fee for new applicants.

Showcases

Auditorium du Louvre

Musée du Louvre, 99 rue de Rivoli, 1st (01.40.20.55.55/www.louvre.fr). M° Palais Royal Musée du Louvre. **Admission** €5; €3.50 under-26s. **Credit** MC, V. **Map** p404 H5.
This 420-seat auditorium was designed by IM Pei. Film screenings are often related to the exhibitions; silent movies with live music are regulars.

Centre Pompidou

rue St-Martin, 4th (01.44.78.12.33/www.centrepompidou.fr). M° Hôtel de Ville or Rambuteau. **Admission** €5; €3 students. **Credit** MC, V. **Map** p408 K6.
The programme here features themed series, experimental and artists' films, and a weekly documentary session. This is also the venue for the Cinéma du Réel festival in March, which, for 27 years, has championed the cause of documentary film.

Le Cinéma des Cinéastes

7 av de Clichy, 17th (01.53.42.40.20). M° Place de Clichy. **Admission** €7.65; €6 Wed, students, under-12s, over-60s. **Credit** MC, V. **Map** p403 G2.
Done out to evoke the film studios of old, this three-screen showcase of world cinema holds meet-the-director sessions and festivals of classic, foreign, gay and documentary films. Also offers a monthly pass.

La Cinémathèque Française

51 rue de Bercy, 12th (01.71.19.33.33/www. cinematheque.fr) M° Bercy. **Admission** *Permanent exhibitions* €2.50-€3. *Temporary exhibitions* €7-€9; €6 under-12s. *Films* €6; €5 students, 13s-18s; €3 under-12s; free for members. *Membership* €10/month. **Credit** MC, V. **Map** p409 N9. *See p294* 'thèque five.

Forum des Images

2 Grande Galerie, Porte St-Eustache, Forum des Halles, 1st (01.44.76.62.00/www.forumdesimages. net). M° Les Halles. **Open** 1-9pm Tue-Sun. Closed 2wks Aug. **Admission** (per day) €5.50; €4.50 students, under-26s. Membership available. **Credit** AmEx, MC, V. **Map** p404 J5.

The hyperactive four-screen Forum des Images is both a film archive dedicated to Paris on celluloid and a thought-provoking, entertaining programmer of films grouped around themes such as 'Gangsters' or 'Death'. It hosts the Rencontres Internationales du Cinéma (*see p295*), as well as the trash treats of L'Etrange Festival (*see p296*) and films from the critics' selection at Cannes.

Arthouses

Accattone

20 rue Cujas, 5th (01.46.33.86.86). M° Cluny La Sorbonne/RER Luxembourg. **Admission** €7; €6 Wed, students, under-20s (except Fri nights and weekends). **No credit cards. Map** p410 J8.

Named after Pasolini's first film, this tiny Latin Quarter cinema naturally enough has a clear preference for old Italian arthouse. That said, there's still plenty of room on the rolling weekly programme of around 30 films for the likes of Buñuel, Oshima, Roeg and Ken Russell. In the 1960s it was managed by no other than François Truffaut.

Action

Action Christine *4 rue Christine, 6th (01.43.29.11.30). M° Odéon or St-Michel.* **Admission** €7; €5.50 students, under-20s. **No credit cards. Map** p410 J7.
Action Ecoles *23 rue des Ecoles, 5th (01.43.29.79.89). M° Maubert Mutualité.* **Admission** €7; €5.50 students, under-20s. **No credit cards. Map** p410 J8.
Grand Action *5 rue des Ecoles, 5th (01.43.29.44.40). M° Cardinal Lemoine.* **Admission** €8; €6.50 students, under-20s. **No credit cards. Map** p408 K8.

A Left Bank stalwart since the early 1980s, the Action group is renowned for screening new prints of old movies. It's celluloid heaven for anyone who's nostalgic for 1940s and '50s Tinseltown classics and quality US independents.

Le Balzac

1 rue Balzac, 8th (01.45.61.10.60/www.cinema balzac.com). M° George V. **Admission** €8; €6 Mon, Wed, students, under-18s, over-60s. **No credit cards. Map** p402 D4.

Built in 1935 and boasting a mock ocean-liner foyer, Le Balzac scores highly for both its design and its programming. Jean-Jacques Schpoliansky, the ever-genial manager, often welcomes punters in person at the start of each screening. The Balzac recently acquired a digital projector, and awards prizes according to audience votes.

Le Cinéma du Panthéon

13 rue Victor-Cousin, 5th (01.40.46.01.21). RER Luxembourg. **Admission** €7; €5.50 Mon, Wed, students, 13s-18s; €4 under-13s. **Credit** MC, V. **Map** p410 J8.

The capital's oldest surviving movie house (founded in 1907) is one of the few to have retained its balcony. It still screens new, often quite obscure international films; meet-the-director evenings and discussions are regular events.

Le Champo

51 rue des Ecoles, 5th (01.43.54.51.60). M° Cluny La Sorbonne or Odéon. **Admission** €7; €5.50 Wed, last screening Sun, lunchtime matinées, students, under-20s. **No credit cards. Map** p410 J7.

The two-screen Champo has been in operation for nearly seven decades, a venerable past recognised in 2000 by the awarding of historic monument status. In the 1960s it was a favourite haunt of *nouvelle vague* directors such as Claude Chabrol.

Le Denfert

24 pl Denfert-Rochereau, 14th (01.43.21.41.01). M° Denfert Rochereau. **Admission** €6.50; €5 Mon, Wed, students, over-60s; €4.60 under-15s. **No credit cards. Map** p407 H10.

This friendly little cinema offers an eclectic repertory selection that ranges from François Ozon and Hayao Miyazaki to shorts and new animation, as well as new foreign films.

The best Screens

La Cinémathèque Française

New address, new tricks, new era: a cinematheque for the 21st century. *See above and p294* 'thèque five.

Forum des Images

Something for everyone. *See above.*

Le Grand Rex

An auditorium of heroic, even majestic proportions. *See p292.*

MK2 Bibliothèque

What a multiplex *should* look like. *See p292.*

La Pagode

Eastern promise – fulfilled. *See p295.*

Arts & Entertainment

'thèque five

The cubist building – sweetly compared by its architect Frank Gehry to 'a dancer lifting her tutu' – was put up in 1994 for another customer altogether; it stood empty for years, as the high-ups havered and intrigued and havered again; plans for the new occupancy were angrily contested. In September 2005 the place opened to a largely joyful public with a screening of Renoir's *The River*, and only a few voices in the local press have dared to wonder what the point of it all might be. What a very typical French success story.

Re-bonjour, then, to **La Cinémathèque Française** (*see p293*), most famous of the world's cinematheques and back in business, after a seven-month hiatus, at its fifth Paris address in 69 years. At the opening, the prevailing mood in the sometime American Center's airy labyrinth was one of Christmas morning excitement. Unwrap this: twice as many screens – four – as before, a proper bookshop, a restaurant, a return to public view of the Musée du Cinéma's multivarious artefacts (as permanent exhibition Passion Cinéma, watched over by the robot from 'Metropolis'), a second major exhibition space for temporary shows, the incorporation at the same address of the huge BiFi 'papers archive', and a programme stuffed with bold ways to pull in cinephiles and willing converts. To think that the whole enterprise began with one man storing film stock in his bath...

Henri Langlois (for it was he) founded the Cinémathèque with three friends, one of them Georges Franju, in 1936. Langlois was a man of private means who bought every piece of nitrate film he could find: the silent era was over, and *films muets* were only good for fairgrounds or the scrap heap. During the Occupation he saved his ever-growing collection from Nazi censors by scattering it across France's southern Free Zone (a tactic noted by Cocteau when he called Langlois 'the dragon who guards our treasures'). After the war he organised retrospectives that had enormous influence on the coming generation's film-makers. No Cinémathèque, no New Wave.

So what now? Gehry's building may have landmark looks, but the CF no longer has such a unique status. The new venue's Bercy neighbourhood alone has an 18-screen UGC multiplex, and MK2's 14-screen counterpart is just across the river. There are other Paris 'cinematheques', too: the **Forum des Images** (*see p293*) remains an important player, and the **Centre Pompidou** (*see p107*) and **Musée d'Orsay** (*see p159*) have started mounting major retrospectives – Scorsese, for instance, or Russian silents. But if anyone's feeling competitive, it's not the CF director, Serge Toubiana, who has Langlois' handwritten flowchart showing the functions of the 'ideal Cinémathèque' framed on his office wall. 'A modern Cinémathèque must combine two fundamental aspects: cinephilia as a private passion, and cinema as a public mission,' he says, alluding to the founding CF mission of conservation, restoration and education – and if the institution could also bring in a reasonable income, all to the good.

Money-spinning wheezes include the recent launch of the CF's own DVD collection (the 12-disc *Jean Renoir, L'Essentiel* box was its first release), and programming won't be exclusively about 'la politique des auteurs', either. And though the 'permanent history of cinema' strand will continue as in the Chaillot days, there's to be digital screenings and contemporary cinema, shorts, talks, cine-club nights, events for children and families, experimental cinema... A new era indeed.

L'Entrepôt

7-9 rue Francis-de-Pressensé, 14th (01.45.40.07.50/
www.lentrepot.fr). Mᵒ Pernéty. **Admission** €7; €5.60
students, over-60s; €4 under-12s. **No credit cards.**
Map p407 F10.
A diverse array of documentaries, shorts, gay
cinema, and productions from developing nations
are more common here than mainstream stuff. A
debate or a chance to meet the director often
accompanies the film.

Images d'Ailleurs

21 rue de la Clef, 5th (01.45.87.18.09). Mᵒ Censier
Daubenton. **Admission** €5.80; €5.10 Mon; €4.70
under-12s. **No credit cards. Map** 408 K9.
Opened in 1990, this cinema focuses on films from
Africa and offers other rare movie treats.

Le Latina

20 rue du Temple, 4th (01.42.78.47.86/www.
lelatina.com). Mᵒ Hôtel de Ville. **Admission** €7.50;
€6 Mon, Tue, students, under-20s. **No credit cards.**
Map p408 K6.
The programming at this flag-bearer for Latin cultures runs from Argentinian to Romanian films.
There's salsa or tango with the €16 film-dinner-
dancing deals on Monday and Wednesday evenings.

Le Mac Mahon

5 av Mac-Mahon, 17th (01.43.80.24.81/www.
cinemamacmahon.com). Mᵒ Charles de Gaulle Etoile.
Admission €6.50; €4.50 students. **No credit**
cards. Map p402 C3.
This single-screen, 1930s-era cinema has changed
little since its 1960s heyday (tickets are still, delightfully, of the tear-off type), when its all-American
programming fostered the label *'mac-mahonisme'*
among the gang of buffs who haunted the place.
Americana of the '30s to '60s is still the bulk of what
lights up the screen.

La Pagode

57bis rue de Babylone, 7th (01.45.55.48.48).
Mᵒ St-François-Xavier. **Admission** €8; €6.50
Mon, Wed, students, under-21s. **No credit cards.**
Map p407 F7.
This glorious edifice is not, as local legend might
have it, a block-by-block import, but is instead a
19th-century replica of a pagoda by a French architect (although there are authentic Japanese elements
present, including the carved beams). Renovated in
the late 1990s, this historic venue is one of the
world's loveliest cinemas. **Photo** *p291.*

Studio 28

10 rue Tholozé, 18th (01.46.06.36.07/www.
cinemastudio28.com). Mᵒ Abbesses or Blanche.
Admission €7.50; €6.30 students, under-18s.
No credit cards. Map p403 H1.
Montmartre's historic Studio 28 was the venue for
Buñuel's scandalous *L'Age d'Or,* and features in the
more heartwarming *Amélie.* It offers a decent repertory mix of classics and recent movies, complete
with Dolby sound and the rather civilised option of
having a drink before or after screenings.

Studio Galande

42 rue Galande, 5th (01.43.26.94.08). Mᵒ St-Michel
or Cluny La Sorbonne. **Admission** €7; €5.50 Wed,
students. **No credit cards. Map** p410 J7.
Some 20 different films are screened in VO at this
cheerful Latin Quarter venue every week – expect
international arthouse with the occasional *Matrix.*
Every Friday, fans of *The Rocky Horror Picture*
Show turn up with drag, rice and water pistols.

Festivals & special events

Festival International de Films de Femmes

Maison des Arts, pl Salvador-Allende, 94040 Créteil
(01.49.80.38.98/www.filmsdefemmes.com).
Mᵒ Créteil – Préfecture. **Date** Mar.
A selection of retrospectives and new international
films by women directors.

Printemps du Cinéma

Various venues (www.printempsducinema.com).
Date Mar.
Three days of €3.50-entry films across Paris.

Festival du Film de Paris

Gaumont Marignan, 27 av des Champs-Elysées,
8th (www.festivaldeparisidf.com). Mᵒ Franklin
D Roosevelt. **Date** Mar-Apr. **Map** p403 E4.
Given the city's love of the cinema, it's odd that its
own generalist film festival makes such a relatively
minor splash. Never mind: it's a chance to see some
80 French and foreign films and catch a few stars.
2006 will see the festival's 21st edition.

Côté Court

Ciné 104, 104 av Jean-Lolive, 93500 Pantin
(01.48.46.95.08/www.cotecourt.org). Mᵒ Eglise de
Pantin. **Date** June.
A great selection of new and old short films at Ciné
104 and a handful of neighbouring venues.

Paris Cinéma

Various venues (01.55.25.55.25/www.paris
cinema.org). **Date** July.
The Mairie sponsors this programme of shorts, documentaries, and experimental and animated films,
along with a slew of retrospectives, as well as *avant-*
premières and a handful or two of stars.

Rencontres Internationales de Cinéma

Forum des Images (see p293). **Date** July.
Map p406 J5.
A global choice of new independent features, and
documentary and short films, usually screened in
the presence of their directors.

Cinéma au Clair du Lune

Various venues (01.44.76.62.18/www.forumdes
images.net). **Date** Aug.
Films are screened under the stars on giant open-air
screens set up in squares and public gardens around
town: party atmosphere guaranteed.

Arts & Entertainment

La Géode. See p292.

3 Jours/3 Euros
All cinemas throughout Paris (www.paris.fr/fr/ culture/missioncinema). **Date** Aug.
This Mairie-sponsored promotion is timed to start getting kids into cinemas before the schools go back. For three days, every screening costs just €3.

L'Etrange Festival
Forum des Images (see p293/www.etrangefestival. com). **Date** Sept. **Map** p406 J5.
Explicit sex, gore and weirdness in the screenings and 'happenings' at this annual feast of all things unconventional draw large crowds.

Salon du Livre de Cinéma et du DVD
Espace des Blancs-Manteaux, 48 rue Vieille-du-Temple, 4th (www.cinemathequefrançaise.com). *Mº Hôtel de Ville.* **Date** Oct. **Map** p411 K6.
Some 150 European publishers of cinema books sell their wares; there are also round-table discussions and the chance to meet and question filmmakers. After a one-year hiatus, this (usually) annual event is set to return in 2006, probably at the Ecole Nationale Supérieure des Beaux-Arts (*see p149*).

Bookshops

Unsurprisingly, Paris is generously supplied with specialist film bookshops. **Virgin Megastore** (*see p244*) also stocks a decent range of English-language movie books.

Ciné Reflet
14 rue Serpente, 6th (01.40.46.02.72). *Mº Cluny La Sorbonne.* **Open** 1-8pm Mon-Sat; 3-7pm Sun. **Credit** MC, V. **Map** p410 J7.
An old projector stands in a corner of this sprawling shop, well stocked with old photos, posters, and new and second-hand books. Subjects covered range from Lithuanian formalism to Laurel and Hardy.

The strong English-language selection includes the *Time Out Film Guide* and mags like *Sight & Sound*. Current and back issues of *Les Cahiers du Cinéma* and *Première* fill shelf after shelf, as do fanzines and old press dossiers.

Cinédoc
45-53 passage Jouffroy, 9th (01.48.24.71.36). *Mº Grands Boulevards.* **Open** 10am-7pm Mon-Sat. **Credit** MC, V. **Map** p404 J4.
This long, narrow, tobacco-scented bookshop has so much in its dusty old cabinets and drawers, it can be hard to find what you're looking for. Ask the helpful staff or take pot luck among the old photos, even older US film mags and fanzines, disquisitions on the *nouvelle vague* and books about special effects in *Star Wars*.

Contacts
24 rue du Colisée, 8th (01.43.59.17.71/www. medialibrairie.com). *Mº St-Philippe-du-Roule.* **Open** 10am-7pm Mon-Fri; 2-7pm Sat. **Credit** DC, MC, V. **Map** p403 E4.
Truffaut's favourite *librairie* has been selling books on film for 40 years. The stock is well organised and boasts a large and up-to-date selection of English-language titles. You'll also find *Film Comment* and *American Cinematographer*, plus a few videos. They operate a mail-order service on their website.

Scaramouche
161 rue St-Martin, 3rd (01.48.87.78.58). *Mº Rambuteau.* **Open** 11am-1pm, 2-8pm Mon-Sat. **Credit** MC, V. **Map** p404 K5.
This large-ish shop covers cinema and *gestuelle* (mime and puppetry). The film section includes a wide range of new and second-hand titles in English, plus a huge collection of publicity photos and portraits filed in manilla envelopes under film title or actor's or director's name. Wim Wenders and Alain Renais have been known to pop in.

Galleries

Forget Old Masters – meet the up-and-coming names on the Paris art scene.

More than ever, the northern Marais is the focus of the Paris gallery scene: its historic *hôtels particuliers* are havens for the latest trends in painting, video and installation art. That said, young galleries and alternative spaces such as **Café au Lit** continue to set up in peripheral areas: in the 13th arrondissement – where the galleries around rue Louise-Weiss reveal a more hit-and-miss selection but an equally eclectic range of media – or in the north-east. Galleries in St-Germain-des-Prés, home of the post-war avant garde, largely confine themselves to tamer, traditional sculpture and painting.

Contemporary art galleries in Paris work closely with the city's public institutions – hardly surprising when the state is often the main customer, given the oft-bemoaned lack of support from French collectors. So keep a look out for shows at the **Centre Pompidou** (where the Espace 315 focuses on under-40s artists; *see p107*), **Palais de Tokyo** (*see p122*), **Jeu de Paume** (*see p93*), **Plateau** (*see p136*) and **ARC** (Musée d'Art Moderne de la Ville de Paris; *see p120*).

France's secretive private collectors are now surfacing, thanks to the annual Prix Duchamp – an attempt by collectors' association ADIAF to emulate the UK's Turner Prize; the reward is a solo show at the Centre Pompidou. There are also shows at the **Maison Rouge** (*see p114*) and out of town at the **Fondation d'Art Contemporain Daniel et Florence Guerlain** in Les Mesnuls (01.34.86.19.19).

October's **FIAC** (www.fiacparis.com) contemporary art fair at Paris-Expo gives a quick fix on the gallery scene, both French and global; **Art-Paris** (www.artparis.fr), held in March and due to move to the restored Grand Palais in 2006, has a more mainstream range; November's **Paris-Photo** (www.parisphoto.fr) draws specialists in classic and contemporary photography. The biennial **Mois de la Photo** (next in November 2006), a multitude of historic and contemporary exhibitions in galleries, museums and cultural centres across Paris.

To find out what's on, pick up bi-monthly booklet *paris-art* (www.paris-art.com), or the *Galeries Mode d'Emploi* and *Association des Galeries* listings foldouts, which can be found in galleries. The **Navette de l'Art** ('art bus'; 01.47.00.90.85/www.art-process.com) gives an insider's tour of selected new galleries, private collections and alternative spaces once a month. The outfit behind it also holds 'Dining with…' art dinners at **Point Ephémère** (*see p327* **Ephemeral art-ery**), and tailor-made tours.

Arts & Entertainment

Air de Paris. *See p301.*

Patrons wanted

France's older-generation artists Sophie Calle, Bernard Frize, Daniel Buren, Christian Boltanski and Annette Messager, and the often film-based trio of Dominique Gonzalez-Foerster, Philippe Parreno and Pierre Huyghe, are all familiar on the international stage. But what of a local scene often accused of navel-gazing? Here are the names of ten younger artists to keep an eye out for.

Boris Achour
Cartoons, urban signs and advertising are the inspiration for Achour, who works in a typically varied range of media – including drawing, painting, installation, video and digital imagery. He won the 2002 Prix Ricard for young artists.

Virginie Barré
Often posed sprawled in a pool of blood, Barré's lifesize figurines appear to act out murder mysteries redolent of old B-movies. She is also known for her stylised black-and-white drawings.

Valérie Bélin
From bodybuilders to gigantic crisp packets, Belin's distinctive black-and-white photos, made using no artificial lighting, take on a grotesque, almost pornographic aspect. She was shortlisted for the 2004 Prix Duchamp, France's equivalent of the Turner Prize.

Elina Brotherus
Ironic photos by the young Paris-based Finn depict her own life – from loneliness to love – and alternate with explorations of more formal themes, such as landscape and portraiture. She won one of France's top photography prizes, the Prix Niépce, in 2005.

Stéphane Calais
Calais began as a cartoonist and it shows in a fluent graphic style evident in both paintings and sculptural work, infused with references to art history.

Delphine Coindet
Coindet takes objects or signs – a water lily, a question mark – remodels them by computer, and makes 3D versions that play subtle games with architecture and scale.

Loris Gréaud
His collaborations with physicists, biologists, architects and other types of experts result in deliberately mysterious and elusive installations, videos, light- or sound-works, somewhere between art and science fiction.

Clarisse Hahn
Hahn's painstakingly made documentary-style films interweave different threads to look at voyeurism, religion, sex or family ties.

Anri Sala
Sala's brilliant videos encompass both investigations of time, light and suspense, and explorations of her Armenian roots. She scooped a young artist award at the 2001 Venice Biennale.

Bruno Serralongue
His glossy colour photos investigate news topics – football fans, illegal immigrants, demonstrations – from a socio-political perspective that questions official reportage.

OPENING TIMES
Most galleries close on Sundays, Mondays, from mid-July to the end of August, and at Christmas. Admission is free.

Beaubourg & the Marais

g module
15 rue Debelleyme, 3rd (01.42.71.14.75/www.g-module.com). M° St-Sébastien Froissart.
Open 2-8pm Wed-Sat. **Map** p411 L5.
American Jeff Gleich left SoHo for the Marais in 2000, on a mission to introduce American artists not previously seen in Europe. Artists such as fellow New Yorkers Gordon Terry and Peggy Preheim exemplify his dual tastes for psychedelia and intricate draughtsmanship.

Galerie Anne de Villepoix
43 rue de Montmorency, 3rd (01.42.78.32.24/www.annedevillepoix.com). M° Rambuteau.
Open 10am-7pm Tue-Sat. **Map** p404 K5.
Along with pieces by established names such as Chris Burden and Suzanne Lafont, you're likely to find virtuoso monochrome paintings by Ming and the varied conceptual work of Franck Scurti, as well as videos by Sara Rossi.

Galerie Cent 8
108 rue Vieille-du-Temple, 3rd (01.42.74.53.57/www.cent8.com). M° Filles du Calvaire.
Open 10.30am-7pm Tue-Fri, 10.30am-7pm Sat. **Map** p411 L5.
Stimulating, varied shows take in all media, from paintings by Rémy Zaugg and Jugnet & Clairet, to photography by Esko Männikki.

Galerie Chantal Crousel

10 rue Charlot, 3rd (01.42.77.38.87/www.crousel. com). M° Filles du Calvaire. **Open** 11am-1pm, 2-7pm Tue-Sat. **Map** p411 L5.

Crousel celebrated the 25th anniversary of her gallery in 2005 with a move to a new shopfront space in rue Charlot's burgeoning design and fashion scene. She was the first in France to show work by Mona Hatoum and Sophie Calle, and continues to pick out hot younger talents such as Gabriel Orozco and Rikrit Tiravanija, as well as rising local stars like Anri Sala (*see p298* **Patrons wanted**).

Galerie Chez Valentin

9 rue St-Gilles, 3rd (01.48.87.42.55/www.galerie chezvalentin.com). **Open** 2-7pm Tue-Fri; 11am-1pm, 2-7pm Sat. **Map** p411 L6.

A specialist in interesting if intellectual themes that mirror today's urban concerns. Look for photos by Nicolas Moulin, pseudo-documentaries by video-maker Laurent Grasso, videos and creeping detritus installations by Véronique Boudier, and projects by 2003 Prix Duchamp winner Mathieu Mercier.

Galerie Emmanuel Perrotin

76 rue de Turenne, 3rd (01.42.16.79.79/www. galerieperrotin.com). M° St-Sébastien Froissart. **Open** 11am-7pm Tue-Sat. **Map** p411 L5.

One of the more astute of the city's younger gallerists, Perrotin has moved out of the 13th and back to the Marais, settling in the palatial former home (complete with garden) of the short-lived Cosmic Galerie. As well as the funky Japanese set of Takashi Murakami, Moriko Mori et al, and big French names like Sophie Calle and Bernard Frize, he promises several artists' first solo outings for the 2006 season.

Galerie Karsten Greve

5 rue Debelleyme, 3rd (01.42.77.19.37/www.galerie-karsten-greve.com). M° Filles du Calvaire. **Open** 11am-7pm Tue-Sat. **Map** p411 L5.

The Cologne gallery's smart Paris outpost is the venue for retrospective displays of top-ranking artists. Jannis Kounellis, Louise Bourgeois, Pierre Soulages and Jean Dubuffet have all featured.

Galerie Marian Goodman

79 rue du Temple, 3rd (01.48.04.70.52/www.marian goodman.com). M° Rambuteau. **Open** 11am-7pm Tue-Sat. **Map** p411 K6.

The New York gallerist has an impressive Paris outpost in a beautiful 17th-century mansion. Look out in March for video artists Pierre Huyghe, Steve McQueen and Eija-Liisa Ahtila.

Galerie Michel Rein

42 rue de Turenne, 3rd (01.42.72.68.13/www. michelrein.com). M° Chemin Vert. **Open** 11am-7pm Tue-Sat. **Map** p411 L6.

Shows here are a bit hit-or-miss, but Rein presents some interesting, hard-to-classify individuals such as Didier Marcel and Jean-Pierre Bertrand, and up-and-comers Delphine Coindet (*see p298* **Patrons wanted**) and Stefan Nikolaev.

Galerie Nathalie Obadia

3 rue du Cloître-St-Merri, 4th (01.42.74.67.68/ www.galerie-obadia.com). M° Rambuteau. **Open** 11am-7pm Mon-Sat. **Map** p408 K6.

Nathalie Obadia recently moved to these spacious new premises. You'll find all media (with a predilection for painting): Manuel Ocampo, Fiona Rae, Carole Benzaken and Jessica Stockholder are regulars.

Galerie Nelson

59 rue Quincampoix, 4th (01.42.71.74.56/www. galerie-nelson.com). M° Hôtel de Ville or Rambuteau. **Open** 11am-1pm, 2-7pm Tue-Sat. **Map** p408 J6.

Nelson was the first gallery in France to show Thomas Ruff and Rodney Graham. It also features rising French artists such as Stéphane Calais (*see p298* **Patrons wanted**), and represents the late Fluxus maverick Robert Filliou.

Galerie Daniel Templon

30 rue Beaubourg, 3rd (01.42.72.14.10/www. galerietemplon). M° Rambuteau. **Open** 10am-7pm Mon-Sat. **Map** p404 K5.

Daniel Templon opened his first gallery in the early 1970s. Now an institution, Galerie T is a favourite with the French art establishment. It mainly shows painters – in other words, items private collectors might want to put on their walls. David Salle, Claude Viallat and Vincent Corpet are regulars, along with Raymond Hains and young German artists.

Galerie Thaddaeus Ropac

7 rue Debelleyme, 3rd (01.42.72.99.00/www.ropac. net). M° Filles du Calvaire. **Open** 10am-7pm Tue-Sat. **Map** p411 L5.

Ropac's main base is in Salzburg but he also has this attractive Paris gallery, featuring American Pop and neo-Pop by Warhol, Tom Sachs and Alex Katz, along with European artists such as Ilya Kabakov and Gilbert & George.

Galerie Yvon Lambert

108 rue Vieille-du-Temple, 3rd (01.42.71.09.33/ www.yvon-lambert.com). M° Filles du Calvaire. **Open** 10am-1pm, 2.30-7pm Tue-Fri; 10am-7pm Sat. **Map** p411 L5.

A powerhouse of the French scene, with a New York offshoot and Lambert's own personal collection on show in Avignon. The gallery has been restructured to include a dedicated video space. While the main gallery shows leading international names – US bigwigs Sol LeWitt, Nan Goldin and Jenny Holzer, plus next-generation Douglas Gordon and Jonathan Monk – the streetfront art bookshop has a window showcase and basement gallery for younger artists.

Galerie Zurcher

56 rue Chapon, 3rd (01.42.72.82.20/www.galerie zurcher.com). M° Arts et Métiers. **Open** 11am-7pm Tue-Sat. **Map** p404 K5.

Amid the Chinese wholesalers north of Beaubourg, Zurcher shows 'emerging artists' with a new take on painting and video: Camille Vivier, Gwen Ravillous, Marc Desgrandchamps and Elisa Sighicelli.

Arts & Entertainment

Warm and fuzzy: art by Charlemagne Palestine at the **Galerie Lara Vincy**. *See p301.*

Schleicher + Lange

12 rue de Picardie, 3rd (01.42.77.02.77/www. schleicherlange.com). Mº Filles du Calvaire. **Open** 2-7pm Tue-Sat. **Map** p411 L5.

First shows at this new gallery (opened in September 2004) have been promising. They focus on artists yet to exhibit in Paris, alternating between young London-based talents and discoveries from eastern Europe. They also host Vidéo Surveillance, an occasional programme of video screenings.

Bastille & north-east Paris

Galerie Alain Gutharc

47 rue de Lappe, 11th (01.47.00.32.10/www.alain gutharc.com). Mº Bastille. **Open** 2-7pm Tue-Fri; 11am-1pm, 2-7pm Sat. **Map** p409 M7.

Gutharc talent-spots young French artists. Check out Delphine Kreuter's fetishistic, colour-saturated slice-of-life photos, quirky text pieces by Antoinette Ohanassian and videos by Joël Bartolomméo and former fashion stylist François-Xavier Courrèges.

Galerie Maisonneuve

24-32 rue des Amandiers, 20th (01.43.66.23.99/ www.galerie-maisonneuve.com). Mº Père Lachaise. **Open** 2-7pm Tue-Sat. **Map** p405 P5.

On the fifth floor of a modern block, the unusual location of the Galerie Maisonneuve gives the gallery an out-of-the-ordinary atmosphere. It tends to feature installations and happenings courtesy of artists such as Claudia Triozzi and Jan Kopp.

Champs-Elysées

Galerie Jérôme de Noirmont

38 av Matignon, 8th (01.42.89.89.00/www. denoirmont.com). Mº Miromesnil. **Open** 11am-7pm Mon-Sat. **Map** p403 E4.

Its location at this glitzy end of town could arouse suspicions that Jérôme de Noirmont sells purely business art. Not so. Noirmont puts on eye-catching shows of, among others, AR Penck, Jeff Koons, Shirin Neshat, Bettina Rheims and Fabrice Hyber,

along with the glossily kitsch duo Pierre et Gilles, and art-world personalities Eva and Adèle.

Galerie Lelong

13 rue de Téhéran, 8th (01.45.63.13.19/www.galerie- lelong.com). Mº Miromesnil. **Open** 10.30am-6pm Tue-Fri; 2-6.30pm Sat. **Map** p403 E3.

Lelong presents bankable, post-war international names like Alechinsky, Hockney, Kounellis and Bacon. There are branches in New York and Zurich.

St-Germain-des-Prés

Galerie Denise René

196 bd St-Germain, 7th (01.42.22.77.57/www.denise rene.com). Mº St-Germain-des-Prés or Rue du Bac. **Open** 10am-1pm, 2-7pm Tue-Sat. **Map** p408 G6.

Denise René is a major name, and has remained committed to kinetic art, Op art and geometrical abstraction by Soto et al, ever since Tinguely first presented his machines here in the 1950s. **Other locations:** *22 rue Charlot, 3rd (01.48.87.73.94).*

Galerie G-P et N Vallois

36 rue de Seine, 6th (01.46.34.61.07/www.galerie- vallois.com). Mº Mabillon or Odéon. **Open** 10.30am- 1pm, 2-7pm Mon-Sat. **Map** p410 H7.

Vallois is a rarity: a truly contemporary gallery in St-Germain-des-Prés. It's worth the detour for *nou-veau réaliste* Jacques Villeglé, American provocateur Paul McCarthy, Turner Prize-winner Keith Tyson and a clutch of French thirty- and fortysomethings.

Galerie Kamel Mennour

60 & 72 rue Mazarine, 6th (01.56.24.03.63/www. galeriemennour.com). Mº Odéon. **Open** 10.30am- 7.30pm Mon-Sat. **Map** p410 H7.

Mennour runs one of the newest and most dynamic galleries in St-Germain. Expect fashionable, often provocative guests: mainly photographers such as David LaChapelle, Ellen von Unwerth and Nobuyoshi Araki, plus filmmaker Larry Clark. He also represents painter Djamel Tatah and the Franco-Peruvian activist Jota Castro.

Galerie Lara Vincy

47 rue de Seine, 6th (01.43.26.72.51/www.lara-vincy.com). M° Mabillon or St-Germain-des-Prés. **Open** 2.30-7pm Mon; 11am-1pm, 2.30-7pm Tue-Sat. **Map** p410 H7.

Liliane Vincy, daughter of the founder, is one of the few characters to retain something of the old St-Germain spirit and a sense of 1970s Fluxus-style happenings. Interesting theme and solo shows include master of the epigram Ben, and artists' text-, music- and performance-related pieces. **Photo** *left.*

Galerie Loevenbruck

40 rue de Seine, 6th (01.53.10.85.68/www.loevenbruck.com). M° Mabillon. **Open** 2-7pm Tue-Sat. **Map** p410 H6.

Funky Loevenbruck injected a dose of humour into St-Germain with a bunch of young artists – Virginie Barré (*see p298* **Patrons wanted**), Bruno Peinado and Olivier Blankart – who treat conceptual concerns with a light touch.

13th arrondissement

Air de Paris

32 rue Louise-Weiss, 13th (01.44.23.02.77/www.airdeparis.com). M° Chevaleret. **Open** 11am-7pm Tue-Sat. **Map** p409 M10.

This gallery, named after Duchamp's famous bottle of air, shows experimental, neo-conceptual and often somewhat chaotic material. A hip international stable includes Liam Gillick, Carsten Höller, Bruno Serralongue (*see p298* **Patrons wanted**), muralist Lily van der Stokker and fashionista Inez van Lamsweerde. Don't miss the 'Random Gallery', the displays in the shop window between Air de Paris and neighbour Praz-Delavallade. **Photo** *p297.*

Art:Concept

16 rue Duchefdelaville, 13th (01.53.60.90.30/www.galerieartconcept.com). M° Chevaleret or Bibliothèque François Mitterrand. **Open** 11am-7pm Tue-Sat. **Map** p409 M10.

This offers an eclectic list: installations by artists Michel Blazy and Martine Aballéa, the photoworks or happenings of Roman Signer and the intricate cartoon-style drawings by Philippe Perrot.

Galerie Almine Rech

127 rue du Chevaleret, 13th (01.45.83.71.90/www.galeriealminerech.com). M° Bibliothèque François Mitterrand or Chevaleret. **Open** 11am-7pm Tue-Sat. **Map** p409 M10.

A varied but classy agenda includes works by light maestro James Turrell, installations by Ugo Rondinone, films by Ange Leccia, and Philip Lorca DiCorcia's disconcertingly perfect glossy photos.

Galerie Kréo

22 rue Duchefdelaville, 13th (01.53.60.18.42/www.galeriekreo.com). M° Chevaleret. **Open** 2-7pm Tue-Fri; 11am-7pm Sat. **Map** p409 M10.

Occupying the ambiguous area between design as function and design as art, Kréo commissions

limited-edition pieces by leading contemporary designers. Look for Marc Newson, Jasper Conran, Ron Arad, young Dutch superstar Hella Jongerius, and native talent like the Bouroullec brothers.

gb agency

20 rue Louise-Weiss, 13th (01.53.79.07.13/www.gbagency.fr). M° Chevaleret. **Open** 11am-7pm Tue-Sat. **Map** p409 M10.

The gb agency revealed young artists Loris Gréaud and Elina Brotherus (*see p298* **Patrons wanted**), and rediscovered the likes of Robert Breer. Shows group several artists together in an exploration of temporality and the exhibition concept itself.

Jousse Entreprise

24 & 34 rue Louise-Weiss, 13th (01.53.82.10.18/www.jousse-entreprise.com). M° Chevaleret. **Open** 11am-1pm, 2-7pm Tue-Sat. **Map** p409 M10.

Philippe Jousse shows contemporary artists – such as Matthieu Laurette and challenging young video artist Clarisse Hahn (*see p298* **Patrons wanted**) – alongside 1950s avant-garde furniture by Jean Prouvé and ceramics by Georges Jouve. **Other locations:** 18 rue de Seine, 6th (01.53.82.13.60).

Alternative spaces

Café au Lit

16 rue de la Liberté, 19th (01.46.36.18.85/www.cafeaulit.com). M° Danube. **Open** selected dates or by rental.

Experience living with – and in – art in this experimental apartment-cum-installation rehabilitated by Franco-Portuguese architect-artist Didier Faustino. Exhibitions, curated by 'Weiswald' (a pair of German critics and journalists), last around three months and are open to those who rent the flat (three nights minimum), as well as for selected events.

Glassbox

113bis rue Oberkampf, 11th (01.43.38.02.82/www.glassbox.be). M° St-Maur or Ménilmontant. **Open** 3-7pm Fri-Sun (and by appointment). **Map** p405 N5.

Artist-run space up on the Oberkampf bar drag that puts on varied shows, often networking with like-minded organisations such as the Modern Institute in Glasgow and Filed in Zurich.

Immanence

21 av du Maine, 15th (01.42.22.05.68/www.art-immanence.org). M° Montparnasse Bienvenüe. **Open** 2-7pm Thur-Sat. **Map** p407 F8.

Set up by two artists in an alley of old studios, Immanence hosts installations and photo shows.

Public

4 impasse Beaubourg, 3rd (01.42.71.49.51). M° Rambuteau. **Open** varies. **Map** p404 K5.

This venue has an experimental programme of three-day features: installations, sculptures and short video projects, as well as debates and some interesting art-literature crossovers.

Gay & Lesbian

They don't call it gay Paree for nothing.

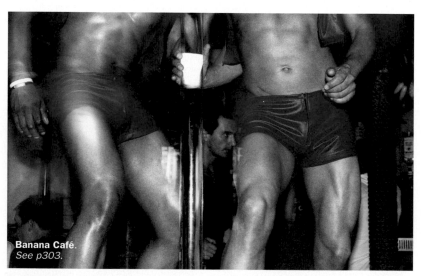

Banana Café.
See p303.

Paris Match charts the love life of tennis player Amélie Mauresmo beneath the headline 'J'ai trouvé la femme de ma vie'; the fate of landmark gay club **Queen** (*see p328*) hogs headlines; and Vincent McDoom queens it up with other French C-listers on reality show *Celebrity Farm*. Yup, French gay culture continues to move into the mainstream.

Doubts about the renewal of the lease on the Queen nightclub on the Champs-Elysées sent shivers across the landscape of gay Paris – but, thankfully, the plans for a fatal rent hike by a UK property speculator were nixed by the French courts. Also in the gay news, the continuing battle to overturn the appeal court's decision to invalidate France's first gay marriage (in the Bordeaux satellite town of Bègles); and, of course, there's the capital's gay mayor, Bertrand Delanoë, still a big player in the fight for the soul of the French Socialist Party. Though much saddened by the loss of the 2012 Olympics to London, he can console himself with the news that Paris, at the time of this guide going to press, was on the shortlist to host the 2010 Gay Games.

Although the pink euro is still strong in the Marais, the axis began shifting north-west with the rebranding in 2004 of the Scorp as Le Vogue (25 bd Poissonnière, 9th, 01.40.26.28.30) and the high-profile opening of the American-style sauna Westside (43 rue du Fbg-Montmartre, 9th, 01.47.70.57.89). However, the team behind Marais sex club **Le Dépôt** stayed closer to home when it branched out with its multi-storey sauna and sex club, **Sun City**.

On top of that, there's the return of a treasured Paris institution, the Sunday tea dance. The knees-up at **Club Mix** in Montparnasse (*see p326*) has gays of a certain age claiming it as a return to the tea dance glory days of the 1980s; and not to be left out, the Queen team is hosting a monthly tea dance at its swanky straight venue, **Le Cab** (*see p326*), in the environs of the Palais-Royal.

Nearby, trunk-wearing boys and old queens in corsets step out in force in summer along the quai des Tuileries, renamed quai François Mitterrand – and referred to as Tata Beach by the strutting or sunbathing riverbank cruisers. At night, the Bois de Boulogne comes gaily alive, but be warned: it can be dangerous, even for the most experienced cruiser.

The local sapphic scene is getting more and more lively, and you're guaranteed of a good time at **Pulp** and even, on certain occasions, at Le Dépôt.

Information & resources

The two must-have mags are fortnightly freebie
e.m@le, which hits the streets every other
Thursday, and glossy monthly mag *Têtu*,
on sale at most outlets. Fréquence Gay, on the
airwaves for more than a decade, has shortened
its name to Radio FG; found on 98.2FM, it also
has a nightlife resource at www.radiofg.com.
France's first gay TV channel launched on
cable and satellite in October 2004; half the
audience of the subscription-only Pink TV
lives in the Paris region.

ARCL

*Maison des Femmes, 163 rue de Charenton,
12th (01.46.28.54.94/01.43.43.41.13/arcl.free.fr).
M° Reuilly-Diderot.* **Open** 7-9.30pm Tue. Closed
Aug. **Map** p409 N8.
ARCL (Archives, Recherches, Cultures Lesbiennes)
deals with audio-visual documentation and bulletins
on lesbian and women's activities.

Centre Gai et Lesbien

*3 rue Keller, 11th (01.43.57.21.47/www.cglparis.org).
M° Ledru-Rollin.* **Open** 4-8pm Mon-Sat. **Map** p409 M7.
A cherished community meeting space, information
centre and gay-press resource.

Le Gay Village

*236 rue St-Martin, 3rd (01.42.78.03.50/
01.44.54.97.00/www.legayvillage.com). M° Arts et
Métiers or Réaumur Sébastopol.* **Open** 10am-8pm
Mon-Fri. **Map** p404 K4.
Information on accommodation, events and nightlife
for gay and lesbian visitors, in premises combining
a café/juice bar, free internet terminals, the Gay
Travel France agency and Absolu Living short-term
flat-letting service (*see p307*).

SNEG

*59 rue Beaubourg, 3rd (01.44.59.81.01/www.
sneg.org). M° Rambuteau.* **Open** 1-7pm Mon-Fri.
Map p411 K5.
SNEG (Syndicat National des Entreprises Gaies) is
a nationwide gay and lesbian business group, with
a membership of over 1,000 companies.

Gay Paris

Bars & cafés

Amnesia Café

*42 rue Vieille-du-Temple, 4th (01.42.72.16.94).
M° Hôtel de Ville or St-Paul.* **Open** 10am-2am daily.
Credit MC, V. **Map** p411 K6.
The height of cosiness: there are stools at the bar for
a quiet drink, mirrored walls, and nice leather arm-
chairs in secluded corners for relaxing with mates.
In the sweaty basement, camp French classics get
the crowd roaring.

Banana Café

*13 rue de la Ferronnerie, 1st (01.42.33.35.31/www.
bananacafeparis.com). M° Châtelet.* **Open** 5.30pm-
7am daily. **Credit** AmEx, DC, MC, V. **Map** p404 J5.
One of the only all-night gay bars in Paris – which
guarantees a steady throng of cruisers craning to
watch the go-go boys gyrating on the counter. The
worse-for-wear head downstairs for singalong show
tunes around the piano. **Photo** *left*.

Le Central

*33 rue Vieille-du-Temple, 4th (01.48.87.99.33).
M° Hôtel de Ville.* **Open** 4pm-2am Mon-
Fri; 2pm-2am Sat, Sun. **Credit** MC, V. **Map** p411 K6.
One of the oldest gay bars in Paris (30-plus years),
and feeling its age, Le Central has seen the bright
young things move on to sprucer joints. Handy for
a quick *pression* in the Marais – but on a slow night
you'll rattle around in it.

Le Cox

*15 rue des Archives, 4th (01.42.72.08.00). M° Hôtel
de Ville.* **Open** 12.30pm-2am Mon-Thur; 1pm-2am
Fri-Sun. **No credit cards. Map** p411 K6.
Despite the kitsch baroque style – what were they
thinking with that animal mural? – this is one of the
hot spots in the Marais, a gay zoo that packs them
in. Sedate afternoons precede the nighthawks and
in summer the crowd is spilling outside by 8pm.

Le Duplex

*25 rue Michel-le-Comte, 3rd (01.42.72.80.86).
M° Rambuteau.* **Open** 8pm-2am daily. **Credit** MC,
V. **Map** p411 K5.
Despite all the trappings of a *philo-café* – art on the
walls (changed every month), an educated crowd of
students, professors and saloon politicos, the near
permanent smoky fug – this small split-level bar
doubles up as a championship cruising ground. Pull
up a chair and get, er, philosophical.

Le Masque Rouge

*49 rue des Blancs-Manteaux, 4th (01.40.27.97.42).
M° Rambuteau.* **Open** 10pm-6am daily. **Credit** MC,
V. **Map** p411 K6.
What used to be the Piano Zinc has been reborn as
Le Masque Rouge, a three-floor space that's big on
piano-accompanied singalongs. A popular weekend
attraction is the Dalida impersonator – Dalida being
the tragic icon no French gay party can do without.

Okawa

*40 rue Vieille-du-Temple, 4th (01.48.04.30.69).
M° Hôtel de Ville or St-Paul.* **Open** 10am-2am daily.
Credit MC, V. **Map** p411 L6.
This undressy, straight-friendly corner bar with an
easy gay-lesbian split is done out in lumberjack chic.
There are always a few high-backed stools and soft
pouffes free, except during fortune-telling sessions.

Open Café

*17 rue des Archives, 4th (01.42.72.26.18). M° Hôtel
de Ville or Rambuteau.* **Open** 11am-2am Mon-Thur,
Sun; 11am-4am Fri, Sat. **Credit** AmEx, DC, MC, V.
Map p411 K6.

Read all about it at **Agora Press**. *See p306.*

A magnetic corner bar where many gay boys meet up before a night out; the spectacular, gender-free WCs are a talking point. The same management also runs Le Raidd (*see p305*).

Quetzal

10 rue de la Verrerie, 4th (01.48.87.99.07/www. quetzalbar.com). M° *Hôtel de Ville.* **Open** 5pm-5am daily. **Credit** MC, V. **Map** p411 K6.
The cruisiest bar in the Marais, with a posey front bar popular with *beur* (North African) boys, and a dancier back area full of muscle men. The terrace, at a strategic crossroads, is a vantage point for gay men of a certain age.

Le Thermik

7 rue de la Verrerie, 4th (01.44.78.08.18). M° *Hôtel de Ville.* **Open** 5pm-2am daily. **Credit** MC, V. **Map** p411 K6.
Technicolour signage belies the fact that this is a real spit-and-sawdust kind of place. Downstairs at weekends it has a village-disco-meets-rugby-club feel, the DJ spinning CDs worthy of the finest – or worst – wedding do.

Le Tropic Café

66 rue des Lombards, 1st (01.40.13.92.62). M° *Châtelet.* **Open** noon-5am daily. **Credit** AmEx, MC, V. **Map** p408 J6.
This bright, upbeat café-bar sees young clubbers fuel up around midnight on filling Frenchified tapas in between cocktails and shots: plates of goat's cheese in breadcrumbs and the like from €3.50, served up by bare-legged staff. The noisy techno terrace is heated in winter. Ample happy hours, too.

Restaurants

Le Curieux

14 rue St-Merri, 4th (01.42.72.75.97). M° *Hôtel de Ville.* **Open** 11.30am-2am daily; last orders taken at midnight. **Credit** MC, V. **Map** p411 K6.
Brightly lit by chandeliers that draw in crowds like moths, the long bar room has wallpaper and pine-block decor. The menu is stripped down (pasta with toppings), the atmosphere hot Latin.

Pig'z

5 rue Marie-Stuart, 2nd (01.42.33.05.89/www. pigz.fr). M° *Etienne Marcel.* **Open** 8pm-midnight Tue-Sat. **Credit** AmEx, DC, MC, V. **Map** p404 J5.
Where gay gourmets pig out on classic fusion food such as Scottish salmon with lemon vinaigrette, oriental-influenced chicken, and ravioli stuffed with button mushrooms.

Le Trésor

5-7 rue du Trésor, 4th (01.42.71.35.17). M° *Hôtel de Ville.* **Open** noon-3pm, 7pm-midnight Mon-Fri; noon-2am Sat, Sun. **Credit** AmEx, MC, V. **Map** p411 K6.
Rocco de Rubiens' VIP lounge-cum-Marais restaurant is a red-and-white wonderland. And the food? How about the tuna in sesame crust, or cold-cut brunch at weekends? Ace.

Aux Trois Petits Cochons

31 rue Tiquetonne, 2nd (01.42.33.39.69/www.aux troispetitscochons.com). M° *Etienne Marcel.* **Open** 8pm-midnight daily. Closed Aug. **Credit** AmEx, DC, MC, V. **Map** p404 J5.
'Three Little Pigs' eschews international boystown cuisine in favour of a tasty, daily changing menu spontaneously influenced by what's fresh and interesting at the market that day. It's high quality, so admission by reservation only.

Clubs

Le Dépôt

10 rue aux Ours, 3rd (01.44.54.96.96/www. ledepot.com). M° *Rambuteau.* **Open** 2pm-7am daily. **Admission** (incl 1 drink) €6-€12. **Credit** AmEx, MC, V. **Map** p404 J5.
Your basic sex disco, cutely positioned next to a police station. The decor is jungle netting and exposed air ducts, the dancefloor surrounded by video screens for idle cruising. Most of the action goes on in the never-ending network of backrooms.

Full Metal

40 rue des Blancs-Manteaux, 4th (01.42.72.30.05/ www.fullmetal.fr). M° Rambuteau. **Open** 5pm-4am Mon-Thur, Sun; 5pm-6am Fri, Sat. **Admission** free. **Credit** MC, V. **Map** p411 K6.

At this basement drinking den, against a backdrop of brickwork decorated with netting and handcuffs, the cute staff wear black armbands and open-ended chaps. Grab your condoms at the bar and take your drinks to the cabins (each with a lube dispenser), and wait. Home to regular theme events, including the capital's only night for skins. Older, hardcore crowd.

Next

87 rue St-Honoré, 1st (no phone/www.nextclubparis. com). M° Les Halles or Louvre Rivoli. **Open** noon-5am Mon, Wed; 7pm-2am Tue; 8pm-5am Thur; 11pm-6am Fri; noon-noon Sat; 2-10pm Sun. **Admission** €4.50-€8. **Credit** MC, V. **Map** p404 J5.

This cavernous recent addition to the sex-club circuit stays open until early morning. The basement area has all the latest accoutrements for the sex seeker. Theme nights range from underwear-only to totally starkers.

QG

12 rue Simon-le-Franc, 4th (01.48.87.74.18/www. qgbar.com). M° Rambuteau. **Open** 4pm-8am daily. **Admission** free. **Credit** MC, V. **Map** p411 K6.

There's no entry fee but QG has a strict dress code: only the hardest set (doormen favour military gear) get in. Those who make it past the chaps on the door earn a drink and can join the other lucky ones in the backroom, playing in the slings, cabins and the bath. Get naked on Saturday nights and Sunday afternoons; wear only your underwear on Sunday nights.

Le Raidd

23 rue du Temple, 4th (01.42.77.04.88/www. raiddbar.com). M° Hotel de Ville. **Open** 6.30pm-5am daily. **Admission** free. **Credit** (€10 minimum) MC, V. **Map** p411 K6.

Very much a Paris take on Fire Island, this brash new kid on the Marais block packs in the pecs at the weekend. Hollering and whooping greet the arrival of the showering go-go boys in the plexiglass shower cabinets. On Friday and Saturday nights you can expect to queue but this just lets you start the chat-up alfresco, before entering the hothouse.

That way inclined

After a very 'establishment' launch at the Théâtre de Chaillot, in the shadow of the Eiffel Tower, gay channel Pink TV quickly became a familiar feature of the French cable line-up. This all-new homovision pulls in top talent, such as news anchor Claire Chazal, France's answer to Barbara Walters. Meanwhile, on prime-time TV, gay drama is now a staple of the schedules. Macho France is having a diet of homosexuality fed into living rooms countrywide, no doubt helped by the fact that the recent boss of the two main public channels was Marc Tessier. Yes, this previous head of French cinema's most powerful body (the CNC – Centre National de Cinématographie), and now an *éminence grise*, is very comfortable with his pink status.

Also on the small screen, the serious-minded producer-presenter Marc-Olivier Fogiel is collecting scalps every week. The pint-sized inquisitor outraged national treasure Brigitte Bardot by grilling her on the non-PC aspects of her bestselling autobiography, *BB*. Bardot promptly threw a hissy fit and her reaction became almost an *affaire d'état*. Fogiel is now happily preparing to steal the crown of current-affairs king from older, wiser – and straighter – heads.

The movies are also tackling queer themes in a more adult way. *Grande Ecole* lifted the lid on same-sex inclinations in the eponymous

bastion of the French establishment, which has turned out the French ruling class since the 19th century. A far cry from *La Cage aux Folles*, it has sexy shower scenes and bed-hopping. As a further sign of how attitudes are changing, camp commercial fare has fared badly. The heavy-handed nudge-nudge-wink-wink of the French movie remake of *Absolutely Fabulous* failed to make a dent at the box office. Worse was to befall the follow-up to the crossover hit *Pédale Douce*: while the original pulled in an audience in excess of four million in 1996, its lame 2004 sequel, *Pédale Dure*, barely scraped the 400,000 mark. French audiences, gay and straight, were making a very clear (decimal) point to the producers.

On the stage, too, the representation of gay culture in the mainstream is largely breaking away from the *Cage aux Folles* stereotype. Queer theatrics have burst into the populist world of the Grands Boulevards – the Paris answer to the West End – with the opening of *Love! Valour! Compassion!*, Terence McNally's intelligent play dealing with a variety of well-drawn relationships between friends and lovers (and which also has a fair bit of male nudity). It even featured a housemate from France's version of *Big Brother* making his theatrical debut, a first career step unthinkable a few years ago.

Le Transfert

*3 rue de La Sourdière, 1st (01.42.60.48.42/www.
letransfert.com). Mº Tuileries or Pyramides.* **Open**
midnight-7am Mon-Fri; 4-10pm, midnight-7am Sat,
Sun. Also open 6-10pm 1st & 3rd Thur of mth.
Admission free (drink obligatory). **Credit** AmEx,
MC, V. **Map** p403 G5.

Small leather and S&M bar used by regulars, though
trainers fetishists also get their kicks at a special
Sunday nighter. At other times, it gets going late.

Saunas

IDM

*4 rue du Fbg-Montmartre, 9th (01.45.23.10.03).
Mº Grands Boulevards.* **Open** noon-1am Mon-Thur;
noon-2am Fri, Sat; 6am-midnight Sun. **No credit
cards. Map** p404 J4.

The city's largest gay sauna is modern, split over
four floors, and has a small gym and plenty of cabins and corridors to prowl.

Key West

*141 rue La Fayette, 10th (01.45.26.31.74). Mº Gare
du Nord.* **Open** noon-1am Mon-Thur, Sun; noon-2am
Fri, Sat. **No credit cards. Map** p404 K2.

This clean, modern and cruisy four-floor sauna has
a small pool, jacuzzi and – alongside the cabins –
cages for bad boys. It's used by off-scene Parisians
and Eurostar passengers making the most of its
proximity to Gare du Nord. Bring your sports kit
and you can even work out in the three-room gym.

Sun City

*62 bd Sébastopol, 3rd (01.42.74.31.41/www.ledepot.
com/sauna.html). Mº Etienne Marcel.* **Open** noon-
2am daily. **Admission** €11-€17; €9 under-26s.
Credit MC, V. **Map** p404 J5.

This new sauna is a sister to legendary Le Dépôt sex
club (*see p304*). The decor is suitably decadent: faux-
Roman pillars abound on its three levels. In the rest
area, the latest films play as men lounge, either cruising or recovering from the action in the steam rooms
and sauna or from a rigorous swim in the pool. Such
is its instant hit status, the queue is out of the doors
at peak hours, such as Sunday afternoon.

Univers Gym

*20-22 rue des Bons-Enfants, 1st (01.42.61.24.83).
Mº Palais Royal Musée du Louvre.* **Open** noon-1am
Mon-Thur, Sun; noon-2am Fri, Sat. **Credit** AmEx,
DC, MC, V. **Map** p404 H5.

More sauna than gym – despite the serious-minded,
buff guys working out – this is the busiest in Paris,
attracting some of the best-looking Frenchmen you
won't ever see in the clubs. Lubes on tap.

Shops & services

Agora Press

*19 rue des Archives, 4th (01.41.74.47.24). Mº Hôtel
de Ville or Rambuteau.* **Open** 8am-8.20pm Mon-Sat.
Credit AmEx, DC, MC, V. **Map** p411 K6.

This newsagent, temptingly pitched opposite Open
Café (*see p303*), stocks plenty of international newspapers, with a window display of the latest gay magazines. Browse and cruise in one spot. **Photo** *p304*.

Boy'z Bazaar

*5 rue Ste-Croix-de-la-Bretonnerie, 4th
(01.42.71.94.00). Mº Hôtel de Ville.* **Open** noon-
8.30pm Mon-Thur; noon-9pm Fri, Sat; 1-8pm Sun.
Credit AmEx, DC, MC, V. **Map** p411 K6.

A one-stop shop for your basic tight Ts, sportswear
and other classics, plus a wing devoted to Vivienne
Westwood, Bikkenberg and Evisu.

Eric Filliat

*24 rue Vieille-du-Temple, 4th (01.42.74.72.79).
Mº Hôtel de Ville or St-Paul.* **Open** 11am-2pm,
2.30-7.30pm daily. **Credit** MC, V. **Map** p411 K6.

A tiny but terrific boutique with tight racks of chic
sportswear, tops and trousers for gay clubbing, and
a window full of funky pumps. Boys on a budget
will appreciate the fact that its prices are somewhat
cheaper than at other Marais boutiques.

Legay Choc

*45 rue Ste-Croix-de-la-Bretonnerie, 4th
(01.48.87.56.88). Mº Hôtel de Ville.* **Open** 8am-8pm
Mon-Tue, Thur-Fri; 8am-10pm Sat, Sun. **No credit
cards. Map** p411 K6.

The first 'out' *boulangerie* in France. By a happy
coincidence, the brothers – one gay, one straight –
who set up this Marais bakery glory in the surname
Legay. While Richard (the gay one) does front of
house, brother Didier pounds the dough. This is not
gimmick baking: Legay Choc's baguettes have won
plaudits in the neighbourhood. That said, Richard
will happily fashion a penis-shaped loaf to order.

IEM

*208 rue St-Maur, 10th (01.40.18.51.51/www.iem.fr).
Mº Goncourt.* **Open** 10.30am-7.30pm Mon-Sat.
Credit AmEx, MC, V. **Map** p405 M4.

This sex hypermarket has its emphasis on the harder side of gay life. Videos, clothes and gadgets are
all stocked, with leather and rubber upstairs. Check
the website for branches.

Les Mots à la Bouche

*6 rue Ste-Croix-de-la-Bretonnerie, 4th
(01.42.78.88.30/www.motsbouche.com). Mº Hôtel de
Ville or St-Paul.* **Open** 11am-11pm Mon-Sat; 1-9pm
Sun. **Credit** AmEx, MC, V. **Map** p411 K6.

Well into its third decade of serving the local gay
community, this shop carries gay-interest literature
from all over the world; there's even an excellent
English-language section.

Space Hair

*10 rue Rambuteau, 3rd (01.48.87.28.51). Mº
Rambuteau.* **Open** noon-10pm Mon; 11am-11pm Tue-
Fri; 9am-10pm Sat. **Credit** MC, V. **Map** p411 K6.

This flamboyant barber, with its house music and
starry decor, is an institution on the gay scene. It is
split into two salons, Cosmic and Classic. The staff
are friendly and talkative.

Where to Stay

Absolu Living

236 rue St-Martin, 3rd (01.44.54.97.00/
www.absoluliving.com). M° Arts et Métiers or
Réaumur Sébastopol. **Open** 10am-8pm Mon-Fri.
Map p404 K5.
Short-term rentals in central Paris for a mainly gay
and lesbian clientele, from around €90 per night for
a studio; apartments and lofts for two to six people
are also available – and there are discounts for stays
of a week or longer.

Hôtel Central Marais

33 rue Vieille-du-Temple, 4th (01.48.87.56.08/
www.hotelcentralmarais.com). M° Hôtel de Ville
or St-Paul. **Rates** €87 double; €7 breakfast.
Credit MC, V. **Map** p411 K6.
This is the city's only strictly gay hotel (above Le
Central; *see p303*) and has been in operation for a
quarter of a century at least. It has seven rooms, with
nothing by way of a private bathroom to spoil the
fun. English spoken.

Hôtel Saintonge

16 rue de Saintonge, 3rd (01.42.77.91.13). M° Filles
du Calvaire. **Rates** €105 single; €115 double.
Credit AmEx, MC, V. **Map** p411 L5.
Although this hotel is open to everyone, its owners
cultivate a gay clientele. All rooms have a shower,
hairdryer, minibar, safe and TV.

Lesbian Paris

With female sexuality ever more upfront,
lesbian Paris is likewise more visible – risqué
fashion ads and mainstream films are spicing
the viewing diet with sapphic seasoning.

Groovy **Pulp** is still the local lesbian club of
choice, though on Wednesdays all the girls take
their turn at the glory holes in jungle-themed
Le Dépôt (*see p304*).

Bliss Kfé

30 rue du Roi-de-Sicile, 4th (01.42.78.49.36/
www.bliss-kfe.com). M° St-Paul. **Open** 5.30pm-2am
daily. **Credit** MC, V. **Map** p411 K6.
Leisurely lezza lounge that recreates (wo)Manhattan
inside an old pâtisserie, serving cocktails and
apéros, and weekend dancing, too. Male friends of
this lively crowd are also bar fixtures.

La Champmeslé

4 rue Chabanais, 2nd (01.42.96.85.20). M° Bourse
or Pyramides. **Open** 3pm-dawn Mon-Sat. **Credit**
MC, V. **Map** p403 H4.
The oldest girl bar in the city (it opened way back
in 1979), this pillar of the local lesbian community
is a welcoming neighbourhood retreat for out-of-
towners. There are imported beers on draught, and
regular cabaret (the Fetish Fantasm night is a highlight) and art shows. It's also an unofficial part of

the Lady Di tour – it was here that her driver Henri
Paul was allegedly drinking before he got behind the
wheel of her car.

Le Mixer

23 rue Ste-Croix-de-la-Bretonnerie, 4th
(01.48.87.55.44). M° Hôtel de Ville or St-Paul. **Open**
5pm-2am daily. **Credit** MC, V. **Map** p411 K6.
In this clubbiest of the main Marais bars, music is
taken very seriously and open-decks events pull in
serious amateur DJs. As the name suggests, it draws
a mixed crowd, where lesbians can hang easy.
There's a happy hour from 6pm to 8pm.

Pulp

25 bd Poissonnière, 2nd (01.40.26.01.93/www.pulp-
paris.com). M° Grands Boulevards. **Open** midnight-
5am Mon-Sat. **Admission** free-€10. **Drinks** €5-€9.
Credit MC, V. **Map** p404 J4.
The leading lesbian disco in Paris – and certainly
the grooviest – Pulp has also opened its doors to a
mixed midweek crowd (*see p325*). But it's gay girls
only at weekends, when bigger-name DJs come to
play. Visit the website for hip, animated flyers.

Unity Bar

176-178 rue St-Martin, 3rd (01.42.72.70.59).
M° Rambuteau. **Open** 4pm-2am daily. **No credit**
cards. Map p404 K5.
This raucous pool bar by the Centre Pompidou (look
for the spray-painted graffiti sign and huge windows) attracts a cruisy female crowd: hard-drinking,
militant but non-threatening. Chalk up a cue or try
cards or board games on Sundays. **Photo** *below.*

Time for a break at the **Unity Bar**.

Arts & Entertainment

Music

Magic moments for *mélomanes*.

Palais Garnier. *See p312.*

Classical & Opera

If Gérard Mortier's first season as director of the **Opéra National de Paris** had predictable moments of controversy, including a universally despised take on Mozart's *Magic Flute*, at least his efforts to introduce the public to unfamiliar work generally made a welcome change from the conservative approach of his predecessor, Hugues Gall. Mortier also takes the trouble to give personal pre-show talks, which appeal to an audience not always entirely free of intellectual pretension. Elsewhere, the newly elected director of the **Châtelet**, Jean-Luc Choplin (*see p310* **Choplin at the Châtelet**), should provide an interesting antidote to Mortier's elitist sensibilities.

France's rigorously applied retirement age means that René Koering, the former director of music at **Radio France**, has been put out to pasture and his place taken by Jacques Taddei. Koering is a fine composer and was nobody's man when it came to his choice of contemporary composers or adventurous, occasionally eccentric programming. Taddei,

though, is a more conservative figure, and this great church organist won't share Koering's fascination with techno music.

Musically, Radio France is responsible for two of the capital's main orchestras: the **Orchestre Philharmonique de Radio France**, whose musical director is Myung-Whun Chung, and the **Orchestre National de France**, led by Kurt Masur. Both these venerable organisations are being outpaced by the **Orchestre de Paris** and its dynamic conductor Christoph Eschenbach, who seems to be over the shock of the cancellation of plans for a new concert hall.

This year's most important world première is Kaija Saariaho's opera *Adriana Mater*, at the **Opéra National de Paris, Bastille**, conducted by Esa-Pekka Salonen and produced by Peter Sellars. Indeed, contemporary creation remains a strong suit in the capital's musical makeup, thanks to the work of the **IRCAM**, the **Ensemble Intercontemporain** and the active presence of Pierre Boulez. It's matched only by the Early Music scene, led by William Christie's **Les Arts Florissants**, with French conductor Emmanuelle Haïm joining other native specialists such as Christophe Rousset and Jean-Claude Malgoire.

There's plenty going on in churches and other venues, too. The **Festival d'Art Sacré** (01.44.70.64.10, www.festivaldartsacre.new.fr) presents church music in authentic settings in the run-up to Christmas; **Les Grands Concerts Sacrés** (01.48.24.16.97) and **Musique et Patrimoine** (01.42.50.96.18) also offer concerts at various churches, while music in Notre-Dame cathedral is taken care of by **Musique Sacrée Notre-Dame** (01.44.41.49.99, tickets 01.42.34.56.10). The main music in summer is the **Paris Quartier d'Eté** festival (www.quartierdete.com), with concerts in gardens across the city. *See also p272-277* **Festivals & Events**.

INFORMATION AND TICKETS

For listings, see *L'Officiel des Spectacles*, *Pariscope* or *Zurban*. Monthly magazines *Le Monde de la Musique* and *Diapason* also list classical concerts, while *Opéra International* provides good coverage of all things vocal, but at the time of writing is in serious financial trouble. *Cadences* and *La Terrasse*, two free monthlies, are distributed outside concerts. Another useful source of information is www.concertclassic.com.

Many venues and orchestras offer cut-rate tickets to students (under 26) an hour before curtain-up. Be wary of smooth-talking ticket touts around the Opéra and at big-name concerts. On **La Fête de la Musique** (21 June), all events are free, and year-round freebies crop up at the **Maison de Radio France** and the **Conservatoire de Paris**, as well as at certain churches.

Orchestras & ensembles

Les Arts Florissants

01.43.87.98.88/www.arts-florissants.com.
William Christie's 'Arts Flo' is France's most regarded Early Music group, and has been honoured by invitations from the Opéra National and the Comédie Française. The standards of the ensemble in Rameau and Lully have become benchmarks in authentic European performance. Arts Flo has also formed the 'Jardin des voix' to promote young baroque talent and participates in educational work to help children know their viols from their theorbos.

Ensemble Intercontemporain

01.44.84.44.50/www.ensembleinter.com.
Finnish conductor Susanna Mälkki has recently been named musical director of this prestigious bastion of contemporary music, founded by Pierre Boulez (who still occasionally conducts the ensemble). The standard of the 31 soloists is beyond

reproach, and the ensemble regularly commissions new work as well as participating in the thematic programming of the Cité de la Musique.

Ensemble Orchestral de Paris

08.00.42.67.57/www.ensemble-orchestral-paris.com.
John Nelson remains one of the finest conductors in France, and if his orchestra does not have the best players in the world, it nonetheless provides a stimulating addition to the city's musical life. In June 2006 it's in the pit at the Opéra Comique for Rossini's *Barber of Seville*, an interesting new venture for both opera house and orchestra, which normally performs at the Théâtre des Champs-Elysées.

Orchestre Colonne

01.42.33.72.89/www.orchestrecolonne.fr.
This venerable but underachieving orchestra now seems in better form with a new musical director, composer Laurent Petitgirard, joining principal guest conductor Paul Connelly. Commendably, each of this season's ten concerts features a contemporary work alongside more popular pieces.

Orchestre Lamoureux

01.58.39.30.30/www.orchestrelamoureux.com.
Saved from death by the government at the eleventh hour, this worthy orchestra suffers from insufficient funding, and its usually adventurous programming is very restrained this season. But its excellent musical director, Yutaka Sado, is a fine conductor – and his results may yet inspire more substantial financial investment in seasons to come.

Orchestre National de France

01.56.40.15.16/www.radiofrance.fr.
The firm hands of Kurt Masur have changed the profile of this prestigious orchestra, based at the Maison de Radio France, for the better: its performances of the German symphonic repertoire now rank with the best in the world. Look forward this year as the maestro turns his attention to Wagner; his bleeding chunks of *Tristan* in June/July 2006 with soprano Deborah Voigt should be splendid.

Orchestre de Paris

01.56.35.12.12/www.orchestredeparis.com.
Christoph Eschenbach and his orchestra go from strength to strength. This season is dominated by their presence in the pit for Wagner's *Ring* cycle at the Châtelet, but they still find time to celebrate two big musical birthdays, Shostakovitch's centenary and Mozart's 250th, at home base Théâtre Mogador. Guest conductors include Pierre Boulez, Frans Brüggen, Rafael Frühbeck de Burgos and Paavo Järvi.

Orchestre Pasdeloup

01.42.78.10.00/www.concertspasdeloup.com.
The Pasdeloup is the oldest orchestra in Paris, but the time when it premiered works by the likes of Ravel and Bizet has long gone. Now Saturday concerts at the Théâtre Mogador are given titles such as 'Songe' and 'Joie céleste' in an effort to attract and comfort a new public with soothing classics.

Arts & Entertainment

Choplin at the Châtelet

In January 2004 mayor Bertrand Delanoë named Jean-Luc Choplin as the new director of the **Théâtre du Châtelet** (*see below*). Choplin's work begins on 1 July 2006, when he officially takes over from Jean-Pierre Brossmann, but his plans for the theatre have already provoked enthusiasm and outrage in equal measure.

Brossmann's directorship of the theatre should climax in suitably epic fashion with the final opera in Wagner's *Ring* cycle, aptly entitled *Twilight of the Gods*. Paris music lovers will miss his powder-blue-jacket-clad figure greeting the great and the good to his temple of high art. His eclectic programming found space for both the classic repertoire as well as imaginative contemporary premières, which frequently left the Opéra National and the city's other concert halls in the shade.

Choplin is a very different figure, having trained not only as a musician but also as an economist. This acute business sense worries artistic purists and, one suspects, reassures the mayor. After working in music administration, Choplin moved on to the corporate sector (the Walt Disney Company, France's Lafayette Group); his final posting, which he left to take up his appointment at the Châtelet, was as the chief executive of Sadler's Wells, London, where his aggressive management style ruffled some feathers. More importantly, he also revealed his corporate artistic colours: 'There was not one corporate sponsor (when I arrived). And why is this? Because contemporary dance doesn't bring in corporate sponsorship.' He then cited the Disney musical *The Lion King* as an example of what he wanted to achieve.

His plans for the Châtelet are very different from Brossmann's highbrow programming. His opening season will celebrate French grand opera in a way not seen in the capital for decades. Not only will there be a crowd-pleasing *Carmen* conducted by Sir John Eliot Gardiner, but also a dusted-down *Samson et Dalila* with Olga Borodina and Ben Heppner, not to mention Massenet's *Le Cid* and *Thaïs* with Renée Fleming and Thomas Hampson, and a revival of Meyerbeer's *Les Huguenots*. A Meyerbeer revival has been the dream of many a musicologist and opera buff, but the French have been notoriously reluctant to appreciate their indigenous repertoire, especially Romantic opera with its embarrassingly sentimental texts.

Does all this home-grown music not smack of a fundamental lack of *sérieux*? Where are the challenging contemporary premières? And what about any rediscovered baroque masterpieces? The Châtelet looks set to return to its origins as a genuinely popular theatre with glitzy grand-scale shows. There are even plans to revive *Le Chanteur de Mexico*: a musically thin but undeniably popular operetta by Francis Lopez, it was one of the great successes of the 1950s, when the theatre was under the directorship of the great producer and populist Maurice Lehmann. Lehmann's benevolent statue looks down over the public from the first-floor foyer – with, one can imagine, the beginnings of a smile at this new turn of events.

Orchestre Philharmonique de Radio France

www.radiofrance.fr.
The highly respected musical director Myung-Whun Chung and his orchestra still play to a high standard, but programming this season lacks any thematic cohesion, and the repertoire is beginning to look too safe and conservative.

Venues

Auditorium du Louvre

Entrance through Pyramid, Cour Napoléon, Musée du Louvre, rue de Rivoli, 1st (01.40.20.55.55/ reservations 01.40.20.55.00/www.louvre.fr). M° Palais Royal Musée du Louvre. **Box office** 9am-7pm Mon, Wed-Fri. Closed July, Aug. **Admission** €20-€25. **Credit** MC, V. **Map** p403 H5.

A fine series of concerts is proposed at the Louvre, with a full season of chamber music as well as lunchtime concerts. In 2006 the concentration is on the figures of Mozart and Wagner, with an impressive line-up of artists and some interesting archival film material for dedicated Wagnerians.

Châtelet – Théâtre Musical de Paris

1 pl du Châtelet, 1st (01.40.28.28.40/www.chatelet-theatre.com). M° Châtelet. **Box office** 11am-7pm daily. *By phone* 10am-7pm Mon-Sat. Closed July, Aug. **Admission** €8-€106. **Credit** AmEx, DC, MC, V. **Map** p410 J6.

Jean-Pierre Brossmann's reign as director ends in monumental style with Wagner's *Ring* cycle, produced by Robert Wilson, and a series of Jessye Norman concerts in which the veteran soprano takes on Britten's Phaedra, Purcell's Dido and Bartok's Judith. New director Jean-Luc Choplin looks set to bring in more French music in 2006-07, with strongly cast revivals of *Samson et Dalila*, *Thaïs*, *Le Cid* and *Les Huguenots* (*see p310* **Choplin at the Châtelet**). Besides opera, the theatre also holds fine series of chamber music and symphonic concerts.

Cité de la Musique

221 av Jean-Jaurès, 19th (recorded information 01.44.84.45.45/reservations 01.44.84.44.84/ www.cite-musique.fr). M° *Porte de Pantin.* **Box office** noon-5.30pm Tue-Sun. *By phone* 11am-7pm Mon-Sat; 10am-6pm Sun. **Admission** €5.60-€33. **Credit** MC, V. **Map** p405 inset.
The energetic programming here tends to focus on contemporary and baroque music, but there's also a vast non-classical repertoire, including ethnic music and jazz. In this vein, June 2006 sees a series of concerts dedicated to all things Japanese, ranging from electronic music to Buddhist monks, via jazz pianist Yosuke Yamashita. The museum has a smaller concert space, the Conservatoire (01.40.40.45.45), host to world-class performers and professors, and which features many free concerts.

IRCAM

1 pl Igor-Stravinsky, 4th (01.44.78.48.16/www. ircam.fr). M° *Hôtel de Ville.* **Box office** 9.30-7pm Mon-Fri. **Admission** €9.50-€14. **Credit** AmEx, DC, MC, V. **Map** p408 K6.
The bunker set up to create electronic microtonal music for the new century is looking rather less redundant nowadays, thanks largely to its full programme of conferences and courses, and the showcase Agora festival. Particularly interesting is the Concerts Cursus, a series that presents new work by ten young composers who come from different cultural backgrounds. Ircam's concerts are performed both here and in the main hall of the neighbouring Centre Pompidou.

Maison de Radio France

116 av du Président-Kennedy, 16th (01.56.40.15.16/ information 01.42.30.15.16/www.radiofrance.fr). M° *Passy/RER Avenue du Pdt Kennedy.* **Box office** 11am-6pm Mon-Sat. **Admission** free-€55. **Credit** AmEx, DC, MC, V. **Map** p406 A7.
State-owned radio station France Musique broadcasts a superb range of classical concerts, operas and ethnic music from here. The main stage in the cylindrical building is the charmless Salle Olivier Messiaen, but the quality of music-making from the Orchestre National de France and the Orchestre Philharmonique de Radio France makes up for it. The Passe Musique offers under-26s admission to any four concerts for €18. Occasional free events are spread over themed weekends. **Photo** *right*.

Musée National du Moyen Age

6 pl Paul-Painlevé, 5th (01.53.73.78.16/www.musee-moyenage.fr). M° *Cluny La Sorbonne.* **Admission** €5.50. **Credit** AmEx, MC, V. **Map** p410 J7.
The museum presents a worthy programme of medieval concerts in which troubadours and the use of polyphony reflect the museum's collection.

All-rounder **Maison de Radio France**.

Musée d'Orsay

62 rue de Lille, 7th (01.40.49.47.57/www.musee-orsay.fr). M° *Solférino/RER Musée d'Orsay.* **Admission** €11-€30. **Credit** MC, V. **Map** p407 G6.
The museum runs a full and enterprising series of concerts at lunchtime and in the evening. These are usually divided thematically; notable in 2006 is a fascinating series of concerts commemorating the deaths of Clara and Robert Schumann.

Opéra Comique – Théâtre National

pl Boieldieu, 2nd (01.42.44.45.40/reservations 01.42.44.45.46/www.opera-comique.com). M° *Richelieu Drouot.* **Box office** 9am-9pm Mon-Sat. *By phone* 11am-6pm Mon-Sat. **Admission** €7-€90. **Credit** AmEx, DC, MC, V. **Map** p404 H4.
Jérôme Savary has done a fine job of promoting this bijou theatre, which saw the premières of so many great operas. Its new status as a Théâtre National has sadly not been matched by the budget needed to fully explore the planned repertoire. Savary is financing the house with his own revue-style shows, while hinting at a possible future with concert performances of *Le Calife de Bagdad* by Boieldieu and Offenbach's *Les Bavards*, as well as staged performances of Scarlatti's *Télémaque*. **Photo** *p312*.

The **Opéra Comique** has a glorious history of lavish premières. *See p311.*

Opéra National de Paris, Bastille

pl de la Bastille, 12th (08.36.69.78.68/www.opera-de-paris.fr). M° Bastille. **Box office** (130 rue de Lyon, 12th) 10.30am-6.30pm Mon-Sat. *By phone* 9am-6pm Mon-Fri; 9am-1pm Sat. **Admission** *Opera* €7-€300. *Concerts* €5-€44. **Credit** AmEx, MC, V. **Map** p411 M7.

The modern building everyone (other than the skateboarders outside) loves to hate. If you want to make the administration feel uncomfortable, be certain to mention the unfinished *salle modulable* or the unflattering acoustics of the theatre. Gérard Mortier's first season as the director of the Opéra National was adventurous and presented with a high level of dramatic intensity, which managed to survive the voices of dissent. Lovers of the Italian repertoire are rewarded this year with the return of Puccini's *Madame Butterfly* and new productions of Donizetti's *L'Elisir d'Amore* and Verdi's *Simon Boccanegra*, while hip opera buffs will be pleased to see Hindemith's *Cardillac* and the world première of Kaija Saariaho's *Adriana Mater*.

Opéra National de Paris, Palais Garnier

pl de l'Opéra, 9th (08.36.69.78.68/www.opera-de-paris.fr). M° Opéra. **Box office** 10.30am-6.30pm Mon-Sat. *By phone* 9am-6pm Mon-Sat. **Admission** €7-€130. **Credit** AmEx, MC, V. **Map** p403 G4.

The restored Palais Garnier is the jewel in the crown of Paris music-making, though the Opéra National favours the high-tech Bastille for most new productions. A notable exception to look for in June 2006 is the new production of Gluck's *Iphigénie en Tauride* by French star of stage and screen Isabelle Huppert, which stars the great American mezzo soprano Susan Graham and is conducted by Marc Minkowski.

Péniche Opéra

Facing 46 quai de la Loire, 19th (01.53.35.07.76/ reservations 01.53.35.07.77/www.penicheopera.com). M° Jaurès or Laumière. **Box office** 10am-7pm Mon-Fri; 2-7pm Sat. **Admission** €11-€23. **Credit** MC, V. **Map** p405 M1.

The Péniche Opéra is an enterprising, boat-based company that produces a programme of chamber-scale shows. It's directed by the indefatigable Mireille Larroche, whose shows sometimes wash ashore at the Opéra Comique.

Salle Cortot

78 rue Cardinet, 17th (01.47.63.85.72). M° Malesherbes. **No box office. Admission** phone for details. **Map** p403 E2.

This intimate concert hall in the Ecole Normale de Musique has an excellent acoustic for chamber music events and masterclasses, and offers a free chance to hear the stars of tomorrow.

Salle Gaveau

45 rue La Boétie, 8th (01.49.53.05.07/www.salle gaveau.com). M° Miromesnil. **Box office** 10am-7pm Mon-Fri. **Admission** €10-€80. **Credit** AmEx, V. **Map** p403 E3.

In addition to chamber music, the Salle Gaveau can now accommodate full orchestras without losing its intimacy. Conductors Brüggen and Tate grace the podium this season, but there is a worrying lack of the quality chamber music that used to be the hall's core repertoire.

La Sorbonne

Amphitheatre Richelieu, 17 rue de la Sorbonne, 5th (01.42.62.71.71/www.musique-en-sorbonne.org). M° Cluny La Sorbonne. **Box office** by phone or at the door. **Admission** €10-€25. **Credit** MC, V. **Map** p410 J7.
The lecture theatres of the great university make a glamorous setting for a seriously presented series of concerts featuring the orchestra and chorus of Paris Sorbonne, as well as more intimate chamber music.

Théâtre des Champs-Elysées

15 av Montaigne, 8th (01.49.52.50.50/www.theatre champselysees.fr). M° Alma Marceau. **Box office** 1-7pm Mon-Sat. By phone 10am-noon, 2-6pm Mon-Fri. **Admission** €5-€110. **Credit** AmEx, MC, V. **Map** p402 D5.
This beautiful theatre, with bas-reliefs by Bourdelle, hosted the scandalous première of Stravinsky's *Le Sacre du Printemps* in 1913. Director Dominique Meyer is rightly proud of the theatre's unsubsidised status, and maintains its tradition of quality programming. The agenda for 2006 features a new production of Mozart's *Don Giovanni* by André Engel in June, visits from the Vienna Philharmonic (conducted by Haitink and Prêtre), as well as a full programme of symphonic and chamber music.

Théâtre Mogador

25 rue de Mogador, 9th (01.53.32.32.00/www. mogador.net). M° Trinité or St-Lazare. **Box office** 10am-6pm Mon-Fri. **Admission** phone for details. **Credit** MC, V. **Map** p403 G3.
With the Salle Pleyel's closure for renovation, the Théâtre Mogador is filling in as a serious classical music venue. Built as a music hall to celebrate the Entente Cordiale, the Mogador stages large-scale, American-style musicals. Still, even with 'enhanced' acoustics, it does not make an ideal concert hall.

Théâtre du Tambour-Royal

94 rue du Fbg-du-Temple, 11th (01.48.06.72.34/ tambour.royal.monsite.wanadoo.fr). M° Belleville or Goncourt. **Box office** 6.30-8pm Tue-Fri; 3-8pm Sat, Sun. *By phone* 10am-8pm Mon-Sat. **Admission** €16-€20. **Credit** MC, V. **Map** p405 M4.
The charming and intimate venue where Maurice Chevalier launched his career. It puts on occasional chamber music concerts, and revue-style shows.

Théâtre de la Ville

2 pl du Châtelet, 4th (01.42.74.22.77/www.theatre delaville-paris.com). M° Châtelet. **Box office** 11am-7pm Mon-Sat. **Admission** €11.50-23. **Credit** MC, V. **Map** p410 J6.
Programming in this vertiginous concrete amphitheatre features hip chamber music outfits like the Kronos Quartet, the Takács Quartet and Fabio Biondi, as well as soloists like superstar violinist Midori. The musical season also extends to performances at Les Abbesses (31 rue des Abbesses, 18th), which shares the same box office. *See also p318.*

Rock, Roots & Jazz

Want to groove until dawn to the last word in cool? Think again. Trendsetters may flock here to meet, plan and jam (*see p314* **The next big sing?**), but many punters complain that the powers-that-be – the people who dreamed up the *lutte contre le bruit*, or noise clampdown – are spoiling the party. Playing live often means a 10.30pm finish or the cops pulling the plug if things rise above 75 decibels. Venues like **Triptyque**, **Nouveau Casino** and the newly opened **Point Ephemère**, all with a varied showcase of contemporary sounds, are fighting an ongoing battle to persuade the authorities that increased sound-levels will not bring social meltdown.

But it's not all bad. The *banlieue* raps on, currently to the strains of TTC, La Rumeur and Le Remède; and should you like your Francophonia delivered by husky-voiced ladies in smoky bars, you'll be glad to know *la chanson française* continues to thrive. The latest take on the genre comes courtesy of Camille, who croons 'new wave' musings with charm, wit and – *bien sûr* – good looks. On similarly solid foundations is the city's rep as an international hotspot for jazz and blues. Established venues like **New Morning** have been hosting big names for years, and few arrondissements are without a similarly hip cellar. Then again, Paris has a lively world music scene – often Arabic and African – and the inevitable US and UK indie acts and rocktagenarians dropping by on tour.

INFORMATION AND RESOURCES

For gig info, turn on the radio. There's **Nova** (101.5FM) for electronica; **TSF** (89.9FM) and **FIP** (105.1FM) for jazz; and **Le Mouv'** (92.1FM) and **OuiFM** (102.3FM) for rock. Listings can be had in the weekly *Zurban* and *Les Inrockuptibles*, whose online database at www.lesinrocks.com has all that's hot in town. Bi-monthly *Lylo* is distributed free at **Fnac** (*see p244*) and in bars such as **La Fourmi** (*see p219*) and **La Flèche d'Or** (*see p316*). **Virgin Megastore** (*see p244*) and Fnac each operate a ticket office. None of the venues listed below has a daytime box office unless otherwise stated. Get to the gig at the time stated on the ticket; owing to stringent curfews, concerts usually start on time – not an hour after the doors open. For standard rock and *chanson* venues, entry fees are nominal.

Paris

Rock en Seine

Parc de St-Cloud, 16th (www.rockenseine.com).
M° Pont de St-Cloud. **Date** late Aug.
Riverside, guitar-heavy antics from home and abroad. The hit 2005 edition starred the Foo Fighters, Franz Ferdinand and Robert Plant.

Solidays

Hippodrome de Longchamp, 16th (www.solidarite-sida.org/solidays). M° La Muette. **Date** mid July.
Anyone who's anyone in French rock – and international headliners, like Garbage in 2005 – does their bit for this festival, raising money for AIDS charities.

Further afield

Les Eurockéennes

www.eurockeennes.com. Gare de Lyon or Gare de l'Est to Belfort (4hrs). **Date** early July.
As close as France gets to a rock-festival experience, with tents, three stages and big names from the world of alternative guitar, with acts as varied as the Chemical Brothers and Nine Inch Nails in 2005.

La Route du Rock

www.laroutedurock.com. Gare Montparnasse to St-Malo (3hrs 30mins). **Date** mid Aug.
Indie newcomers and oldies alike (in 2005 that meant the Cure, Mercury Rev and Maximo Park) gather at this pretty port to rock out and scare unsuspecting families on caravan holidays.

The next big sing?

Arts & Entertainment

'Enoooooooorme!' (rough translation: 'Awwwwesome!') was the typical weblog verdict on a concert by new Paris rock group the Naast at **Le Triptyque** (*see p317*) in April of last year. The Naast are still in their teens, and this was the first time they had aired their year-zero punk racket in public. Just four months earlier, the fresh-faced adolescents had made a pilgrimage to the launch night in St-Ouen of a compilation

called *Le Nouveau Rock'n'Roll Français*. Eagerly clutching a demo, and chaperoned by their parents, they weren't alone in finding themselves galvanised by the idea that some new and unexpected avenues were opening up for French music.

Le Nouveau Rock'n'Roll Français was conceived by music-mad Frenchmen Ludovic Merle and Jean-Baptiste Guillot, together with London promoter Sean McClusky, as

Les Transmusicales

02.99.31.12.10/www.lestrans.com. Gare Montparnasse to Rennes (2hrs 30mins). **Date** early Dec.

A hive of musical activity at this Breton backwater, spread over every venue in town (tickets sold for each concert separately), showcasing veterans and unsigned sprogs yearning for a break. Great stuff.

Stadium venues

Palais Omnisports de Paris-Bercy

8 bd de Bercy, 12th (08.92.69.23.00/www.bercy.fr). M° Bercy. **Open** *Box office* 11am-6pm Mon-Sat. **Tickets** varies. **Credit** AmEx, DC, MC, V. **Map** p409 N9.

This vast sports arena hosts rock and pop megaliths à la Radiohead and Jamiroquai. Not really the place for the connoisseur, among 19,999 other punters.

Zénith

211 av Jean-Jaurès, 19th (www.le-zenith.com). M° Porte de Pantin. **Tickets** varies. **No credit cards. Map** p405 inset.

Ignore the skating-rink atmosphere and the logistical headache of 2,000-plus people heading back to Paris via one métro stop and a few taxis – here the amps go up to the max and the line-up (Carl Cox, the White Stripes) wows throughout the year.

Rock venues

Le Bataclan

50 bd Voltaire, 11th (01.43.14.00.30). M° Oberkampf. **Open** *Gigs* varies. **No credit cards. Map** p405 M5.

Rock legends and stars of *chanson* and world music play this former theatre. Salsa club at weekends.

a showcase for 22 largely new and unsigned French acts. Its release was primarily aimed at the UK, in the hope that any buzz that was generated there would boomerang back across the Channel and alert French record labels to the talent right under their noses. As unusual a tactic as this may seem, its logic becomes near unassailable when you consider that a) unlike the British hype machine, which pumps out Next Big Things at a rate of roughly one every five minutes, the French record industry is notoriously slow on the uptake, and b) it has worked before. The 1990s boom in electronic music, dubbed 'French Touch', was only acknowledged on its home turf once key players had started signing to UK labels and garnering rave reviews abroad.

It still remains to be seen whether the right people will sit up and take notice – and whether the music-buying public can accept that there is life for French rock beyond the ever-enduring Johnny Hallyday. As far as unlocking the domestic market goes, it's unlikely there'll be any decisive 'storming of the Bastille' moments. Press in the UK and France has been enthusiastic, but obstacles to major success are deeply ingrained in France's politics and institutions. Laws protecting French culture, such as the infamous French-language quotas for French radio (rock groups prefer to sing in English) are just part of the picture. And how exactly do you tackle powerful radio station Skyrock's policy of testing 30-second bites of new singles on selected listeners and junking those that don't find favour?

The good news is that the compilation has proved to be the catalyst for some pretty exciting activity. Inevitably, fortunes for the original *Le Nouveau Rock'n'Roll Français* alumni have been mixed. In the 'Where are they now?' file, there's at least one group that has officially thrown in the towel, while DVLagadam Smack the Tarmack was never a name likely to trip off lips. But acts like the Film and Prototypes have produced albums brim-full of hooky, inventive pop-rock, and Steeple Remove and Mono Taxi (*pictured*) are becoming familiar faces on the London live circuit. Fancy's glam-y amalgam of *Dirty Mind*-era Prince, Gang of Four and Van Halen should make them genuine contenders, too.

As for the next wave, hopefuls have been busily uploading recordings on to the NRRF website or, like the Naast, delivering their demos directly into the hands of Merle and co. They join Second Sex, Hush Puppies and Dorian Pimpernel as candidates for a likely sequel compilation. If you're itching to get into the action right now, Paris has a select few decent venues sympathetic to small rock acts, such as **Mains d'Oeuvres**, **Nouveau Casino** and **Point Ephemère** (for all, *see p316*), as well as **Bar Three** (3 rue de l'Ancienne-Comédie, 6th, 01.43.25.78.01). And there's even an unofficial HQ of sorts in the shape of **Planète Mars** (21 rue Keller, 11th, 01.43.14.24.44), where you can grab a drink with band members and gauge the temperature of this new movement.

● For more information, see the official *Le Nouveau Rock'n'Roll Français* website at www.nouveaurocknroll.com.

Arts & Entertainment

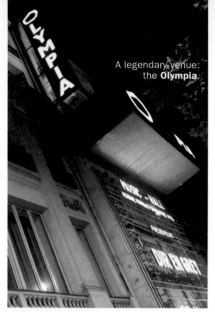
A legendary venue: the **Olympia**.

indie staples such as Sigur Rós and Royksöpp rub shoulders with wrinkly axe-men like Marillion.

La Flèche d'Or
102bis rue de Bagnolet, 20th (01.44.64.01.02/www.flechedor.com). M° Alexandre Dumas. **Open** 8pm-2am Mon, Sun; 8pm-5am Wed-Sat. *Gigs* times vary. **Tickets** free. **Credit** MC, V. **Map** p405 Q5.
Closed by the Mairie in December 2002, this impressive converted métro station has reopened under new management. It has free rock and *variété française* concerts nightly at 9pm. *See also p323.*

Mains d'Oeuvres
1 rue Charles-Garnier, 93400 St-Ouen (01.40.11.25.25/www.mainsdoeuvres.org). M° Porte de Clignancourt or Garibaldi. **Open** *Bar* 9.30am-midnight daily. *Gigs* 8.30pm, days vary. **Admission** €10. **Credit** *Bar* MC, V.
This music hive offers rehearsal and recording space to new acts, plus a 350-capacity venue in which to headline or support an Aphex Twin or John Spencer Blues Explosion. At occasional festivals, DJs spin in the staff canteen.

La Maroquinerie
23 rue Boyer, 20th (01.40.33.35.05/www.lamaroquinerie.fr). M° Gambetta. **Open** Box office (in person only) 2.30-6.30pm Mon-Fri. *Gigs* 8pm Mon-Fri. **Credit** MC, V. **Map** p405 P4.
Previously a world-music venue, La Maroquinerie now hosts a foray into indie, as with Editors and, er, Chumbawumba. There's an adjoining literary café in case you feel like a bit of posing.

Nouveau Casino
109 rue Oberkampf, 11th (01.43.57.57.40/www.nouveaucasino.net). M° Parmentier, Ménilmontant or St-Maur. **Open** *Gigs* times vary. **Credit** *Bar* MC, V. **Map** p405 N5.
A gem of a venue, run by the adjacent Café Charbon (*see p226*): fab acoustics, a leftfield line-up (post-rock, dub, garage) and reasonable drinks prices. The upstairs chill-out area gives a great view of the action.

Olympia
28 bd des Capucines, 9th (01.55.27.10.00/www.olympiahall.com). M° Opéra. **Open** *Box office* 10am-9pm Mon-Sat; 10am-7pm Sun. *Gigs* times vary. **Credit** AmEx, DC, MC, V. **Map** p403 G4.
Back in the day, this legendary venue was graced by the Beatles, Stones and top French names in the Charles Aznavour line. Now it's mainly a nostalgia circuit stopping-off point, though Coldplay did kick off their first 2005 world tour here. **Photo** *above.*

Point Ephémère
200 quai de Valmy, 10th (01.40.34.02.48/www.pointephemere.org). M° Jaurès or Louis Blanc. **Open** 10am-2am daily. *Gigs* 8.30pm daily. **Credit** AmEx, DC, MC, V. **Map** p405 Q5.
Brought to you by the people behind Mains d'Oeuvres (*see above*), this newly converted warehouse hosts up-and-coming rock, jazz and world music, and electro weekenders. *See also p327* **Ephemeral art-ery.**

Café de la Danse
5 passage Louis-Phillipe, 11th (01.47.00.57.59/www.cafedeladanse.com). M° Bastille. **Open** *Gigs* times vary. Closed July & Aug. **No credit cards.** **Map** p409 M7.
If it's folky, frail, expansive beauty you're after, this utterly lovely venue, with its high ceiling and cheery acoustics, is the place in which to find it. Mercury Rev and Granddaddy have graced the stage.

La Cigale/La Boule Noire
120 bd de Rochechouart, 18th (01.49.25.89.99/www.lacigale.fr). M° Anvers or Barbès Rochechouart. **Open** *Gigs* times vary. **Credit** MC, V. **Map** p404 J2.
Upstairs (La Cig) hosts the likes of Supergrass, the Tears and Goldfrapp, while downstairs in La Boule lithe young things on the rise get their piece of the action in an old-fashioned rock cellar.

Le Divan du Monde
75 rue des Martyrs, 18th (01.42.52.02.46/www.divandumonde.com). M° Anvers or Pigalle. **Open** *Gigs* times vary. **Credit** MC, V. **Map** p404 H2.
It's been done up since the days when Toulouse-Lautrec used to come in for his absinthe hit, but the decadent spirit of this old Montmartre haunt is still alive. Indie, hip hop and electro-dance get showcased for labels (Rephlex, NinjaTune) to gawp at.

Elysée Montmartre
72 bd de Rochechouart, 18th (08.92.69.23.92/www.elyseemontmartre.com). M° Anvers. **Open** *Bar* 11am-midnight daily. *Gigs* times vary. **Credit** *Bar* MC, V. **Map** p404 J2.
One of the many Montmartre venues to start life as a showcase for girls in various states of undress, this is now a top city venue. Large yet cosy, it's run by Garance, the biggest promoter in France, and sees

La Scène Bastille

*2bis rue des Taillandiers, 11th (01.48.06.50.70/www.
la-scene.com). M° Bastille.* **Open** *Gigs* midnight-6am
Wed-Sun. Closed Aug. **Credit** MC, V. **Map** p409 M7.
Watch from the chill-out alcoves overlooking the
dancefloor as the kids strut and smooch to hip hop,
funk and jazz. There are club nights here, too.

Le Trabendo

*211 av Jean-Jaurès, 19th (01.42.01.12.12/www.
trabendo.fr). M° Porte de Pantin.* **Open** *Gigs* times
vary. **Credit** MC, V. **Map** p405 inset.
Part minimal-futurist utopia, part wacky Ikea, this
spot in the Cité de la Musique complex cuts its niche
in all things alternative, from post-rock to drum 'n'
bass, avant-garde hip hop to modern jazz.

Le Triptyque

*142 rue Montmartre, 2nd (01.40.28.05.55/www.
letriptyque.com). M° Bourse or Grands Boulevards.*
Open 9.30pm-4am Mon-Wed; 9pm-6am Thur-Sat;
8pm-2am Sun. *Gigs* times vary. **Credit** AmEx, MC,
V. **Map** p404 J4.
Le Triptyque is one of the hippest places in town. It
has eclectic programming (Luke Vibert, the Zutons)
and the sweatiest moshpit-cum-dancehall in town;
freshen up on a sofa in the chill-out area. Alan
McGee brings his Poptones club here on Tuesdays.

Rock in bars

The Cavern

21 rue Dauphine, 6th (01.43.54.53.82). M° Odéon.
Open 7pm-3am Mon-Thur, Sun; 7pm-5am Fri, Sat.
Gigs Wed-Sat (times vary). **Admission** free. **Credit**
MC, V. **Map** p410 H6.
Deep in St-Germain, this lively, atmospheric cellar
is the perfect place at which to check out new acts.

Le Gambetta

*104 rue de Bagnolet, 20th (01.43.70.52.01).
M° Gambetta.* **Open** 10am-2am daily. *Gigs* 9pm.
Admission free-€5. **Credit** AmEx, DC, MC, V.
Map p409 Q6.
Here's the deal: you slump on a dilapidated sofa until
stirred rudely by local lads power-chording away
for all they're worth. Deserves a gander, all said.

O'Sullivans by the Mill

92 bd de Clichy, 18th (01.42.52.24.94). M° Blanche.
Open noon-5am Mon-Thur, Sun; noon-6am Fri, Sat.
Gigs times vary. **Credit** MC, V. **Map** p403 G2.
The basement of this drinking emporium is home to
anglophone radio station Paris Live – but it has no
say in the playlist, which sees all sorts of bands
strumming and thrashing in the big back room.

Le Réservoir

*16 rue de la Forge-Royal, 11th (01.43.56.39.60/
www.reservoirclub.com). M° Faidherbe Chaligny or
Ledru-Rollin.* **Open** 8pm-2am Mon-Thur; 8pm-5am
Fri, Sat; noon-2am Sun. *Gigs* 10.30pm Mon-Thur;
11pm Fri, Sat; 1pm, 3pm, 10.30pm Sun. **Credit**
AmEx, DC, MC, V. **Map** p409 N7.

As well as club nights and stand-up comedy, this
spot stages live *chanson* and indie acts. Jazzsters
musically accompany Sunday brunch.

Chanson

Roll up to one of these places and you could
find anything from Piaf covers to slam poetry,
from experimental theatre to a new *chansonnier*
clutching at the frail dream of stardom.

Chez Adel

*10 rue de la Grange-aux-Belles, 10th
(01.42.08.24.61). M° Jacques Bonsergent.*
Open noon-midnight Tue-Sun. *Gigs* 5pm Tue-Sun.
Tickets free. **Credit** MC, V. **Map** p404 L3.
The repertoire spans *chanson*, world music (often
Eastern European) and anything unclassifiable.
Atmosphere comes courtesy of the house sangria
and *patron* Adel himself, a man deserving of (and
receiving) cult status.

Le Limonaire

*18 cité Bergère, 9th (01.45.23.33.33/limonaire.
free.fr). M° Grands Boulevards.* **Open** *Gigs* 10pm
Mon-Sat; 7pm Sun. **Credit** MC, V. **Map** p404 J4.
A *bistro à vins* where serious *chanson* takes the limelight. Performances vary from acoustic, piano-led
chansonniers to cabarets.

Le Magique

*42 rue de Gergovie, 14th (01.45.43.21.32/www.
aumagique.com). M° Pernéty.* **Open** *Gigs* 9.30pm
Wed, Thur; 10.30pm Fri, Sat. **No credit cards**.
Map p407 F10.
Artiste-in-residence Marc Havet serenades punters
with politically incorrect *chanson*, plus a monthly
diet of songs inspired by Baudelaire and Aragon.

Sentier des Halles

*50 rue d'Aboukir, 2nd (01.42.61.89.96/www.sentier
deshalles.fr). M° Sentier.* **Open** *Gigs* 8pm, 10pm Mon-
Sat. **No credit cards**. **Map** p404 J4.
A concert venue rather than a bar with music, Le
Sentier des Halles is where celebrated and new
artists entertain a seated, sentient crowd.

Le Vieux Belleville

*12 rue des Envierges, 20th (01.44.62.92.66/www.le-
vieux-belleville.com). M° Pyrénées.* **Open** *Gigs* 9pm
Tue-Sat. **Credit** MC, V. **Map** p405 N4.
From the terrace, you're treated to a superb view of
Paris; inside, you get accordions, 20-a-day voices
and the eerie feeling that you have just walked on
to a film set, circa 1959.

Floating venues

Batofar

*Opposite 11 quai François-Mauriac, 13th
(01.53.60.17.30/www.batofar.org). M° Bibliothèque
François Mitterand or Quai de la Gare.* **Open** 9pm-
late Wed-Sat. **Admission** €5-€20. **Credit** MC, V.
Map p409 N10.

Arts & Entertainment

Into orbit at the **Satellit' Café**.

As good as it gets, with live acts from hip hoppers to underground noise merchants all enjoyed by an up-for-it crowd. Terrace open from 7pm in summer.

Guinguette Pirate

Opposite 11 quai François-Mauriac, 13th (01.43.49.68.68/www.guinguettepirate.com). M° Bibliothèque François Mitterrand or Quai de la Gare. **Open** 8.30pm-late Wed-Sat. **Admission** €5-€12. **Credit** MC, V. **Map** p409 N10.
Not the sturdiest vessel to have braved the seas, and, as the speakers have a propensity to cut out, rock gigs can be sober affairs. Stick to *chanson* nights.

World & traditional music

On any given night you can see anyone from Youssou N'Dour (a regular) to musicians from tiny Afghan villages. If ethnic music is your drop, you've come to the right place.

Cité de la Musique

221 av Jean-Jaurès, 19th (01.44.84.44.84/www.cite-musique.fr). M° Porte de Pantin. **Open** *Gigs* Tue-Sat (times can vary). **Tickets** €17-€37. **Credit** MC, V. **Map** p405 inset.
This Villette venue welcomes some of the best musicians from all four corners of the world. On top of that, it also does a fine line in contemporary classical, avant-jazz and electronica.

Institut du Monde Arabe

1 rue des Fossés-St-Bernard, 5th (01.40.51.38.38/www.imarabe.org). M° Jussieu. **Open** *Gigs* 8.30pm Fri, Sat. **Tickets** varies. **Credit** MC, V. **Map** p411 K7.
This huge, plush auditorium attracts some of the leading performers from the Arab world.

Kibélé

12 rue de l'Echiquier, 10th (01.48.24.57.74). M° Bonne Nouvelle. **Concerts** 9pm Mon-Sat. **Admission** free-€5. **Credit** AmEx, DC, MC, V. **Map** p404 K4.
Music from across the Mediterranean and beyond. Turkish restaurant in the same building.

Satellit' Café

44 rue de la Folie-Méricourt, 11th (01.47.00.48.87/www.satellit-cafe.com). M° Oberkampf, Parmentier or St-Ambroise. **Open** *Bar* 8pm-3am Tue-Thur. *Club* 10pm-6am Fri, Sat. *Gigs* 9pm Tue-Thur. **Admission** €10; €8 students. **Credit** *Bar* MC, V. **Map** p405 M5.
This spacious bar lends its sound system to all things global, but the focus is on traditional African music. Great late-night bar, too. **Photo** *left.*

Théâtre de la Ville

2 pl du Châtelet, 4th (01.42.74.22.77/www.theatre delaville-paris.com). M° Châtelet. **Open** *Box office* 11am-7pm Mon-Sat. **Tickets** 8.30pm Mon-Fri; 5pm, 8.30pm Sat. **Admission** €16; €11.50 students. **Credit** MC, V. **Map** p410 J6.
Bringing in musicians and dancers of the highest calibre to both its sites, the venue is homing in on the Middle East and Central Asia for 2006.
Other locations: 31 rue des Abbesses, 18th.

La Vieille Grille

1 rue du Puits-de-l'Ermite, 5th (01.47.07.22.11/vieille.grille.free.fr). M° Place Monge. **Open** *Gigs* 8.30pm Mon-Sat; 3pm, 5pm Sun. **Admission** varies. **No credit cards.** **Map** p408 K8.
From Kurt Weill to tango, Offenbach to klezmer (plus theatre, book readings and children's shows), this artist-run venue in the heart of the Mouffetard area offers fun for all the family.

Jazz & blues

Jazz and Paris go way back. The city is dotted with medieval cellars where you can get your fill of quality live jazz and blues, and big names from around the world stop off as often as they can – and not just for old time's sake. Younger French musicians, bringing in electronic and ethnic influences (Magic Malik Orchestra or Eric Truffaz) make sure the Paris jazz scene isn't a 'heritage' feature, but a living culture.

Baiser Salé

58 rue des Lombards, 1st (01.42.33.37.71/www.le baisersale.com). M° Châtelet. **Open** *Chanson gigs* 7pm daily. *Jazz gigs* 10pm daily. **Tickets** *Chanson* €13; €8 in advance. *Jazz* €15-18. **Credit** AmEx, DC, MC, V. **Map** p408 J6.
The 'salty kiss' provides a platform for passing *chansonniers* and jazzmen of every stripe.

Le Bilboquet

13 rue St-Benoît, 6th (01.45.48.81.84). M° St-Germain-des-Prés. **Open** *Gigs* 9pm daily. **Admission** (incl 1 drink) €18. **Credit** AmEx, DC, MC, V. **Map** p410 H6.

This was the joint where Miles changed modern music forever. In recent years it slid inexorably down the quality slope, but new ownership in 2005 might (we hope) bring improvements.

Caveau de la Huchette

5 rue de la Huchette, 5th (01.43.26.65.05/ www.caveaudelahuchette.fr). M° St-Michel. **Open** *Gigs* 9.30pm daily. **Tickets** €10.50 Sun-Thur; €13 Fri, Sat; €9 students daily. **Credit** MC, V. **Map** p410 J7.
Tourists boogie away in this medieval cellar, a Left Bank mainstay. The acts are usually good.

Caveau des Oubliettes

52 rue Galande, 5th (01.46.34.23.09). M° St-Michel. **Open** *Gigs* 10pm daily. **Admission** free (but drink compulsory). **Credit** MC, V. **Map** p410 J7.
A foot-tapping frenzy thrives in this medieval dungeon, complete with instruments of torture. Jam sessions in the week. Upstairs bar, too.

Au Duc des Lombards

42 rue des Lombards, 1st (01.42.33.22.88). M° Châtelet. **Open** *Gigs* 9.30pm Mon-Sat. **Tickets** €19-€25. **Credit** MC, V. **Map** p408 J6.
One of a number of musically inclined venues along rue des Lombards, this one is intimate (to say the least) and has a varied programme.

Jawad K-Fé

114 rue de Bagnolet, 20th (01.43.67.73.35/www. jawadkfe.com). M° Porte de Bagnolet or Alexandre Dumas. **Open** *Gigs* 9pm Tue-Sat. **Tickets** varies. **Credit** MC, V. **Map** p409 Q6.
Miles from the haunts of the Left Bank, this place serves up jazzy beats for a nominal fee.

Lionel Hampton Jazz Club

Hôtel Méridien Etoile, 81 bd Gouvion-St-Cyr, 17th (01.40.68.30.42/www.jazzclub-paris.com). M° Porte Maillot. **Open** *Gigs* 10.30pm, 12.30am Mon-Sat; 10pm Sun. **Admission** (incl 1 drink) €23; €25 Fri, Sat. **Credit** AmEx, DC, MC, V. **Map** p402 B2.
This classy hotel venue invites top American names to perform blues, jazz and gospel.

New Morning

7-9 rue des Petites-Ecuries, 10th (01.45.23.51.41/ www.newmorning.com). M° Château d'Eau. **Open** *Box office* 4-7.30pm Mon-Fri. *Gigs* 9pm daily. **Admission** €15-€21. **Credit** MC, V. **Map** p404 K3.
This prestigious and reliably exciting venue is host to some of the best in electronic jazz (but blues and hip hop also get a look-in). 2005 saw Ravi Coltrane and the James Taylor Quartet, among others.

Parc Floral de Paris

Route de la Pyramide, Bois de Vincennes, 12th (01.49.57.42.84/www.parcfloraldeparis.com). M° Château de Vincennes. **Open** *Gigs* (May-July) 4.30pm Sat, Sun. **Admission** €1.50-€3. **No credit cards.**
Well-known names serenade a chilled-out crowd at this open-air venue every summer.

Petit Journal Montparnasse

13 rue du Commandant-René-Mouchotte, 14th (01.43.21.56.70/www.petitjournal-montparnasse. com). M° Gaité or Montparnasse-Bienvenüe. **Open** *Gigs* 10pm Mon-Sat. **Admission** (incl 1 drink) €20. **Credit** MC, V. **Map** p407 F9.
A two-level jazz brasserie with Latin sounds, R&B and soul-gospel. Dinner (€50) starts at 8pm.

Quai du Blues

17 bd Vital-Bouhot, Ile de la Jatte, 92200 Neuilly-sur-Seine (01.46.24.22.00/www.quaidublues.com). M° Pont de Levallois. **Open** *Gigs* 10.30pm Fri, Sat. **Admission** €20. **Credit** MC, V.
Exclusively African-American music from the likes of the Carter Brothers and Lil' Joe Burton.

Le Sabot

6 rue du Sabot, 6th (01.42.22.21.56). M° St-Germain-des-Prés or St-Sulpice. **Open** noon-3pm, 6pm-2am Mon-Sat. *Gigs* 9pm. **Admission** free (but drink compulsory). **Credit** MC, V. **Map** p407 G7.
Jazz, blues and *chanson* with your *gigot d'agneau*? No problem. Intellectuals (at least they look like they must be) munch away as the multi-talented owner helps out on piano and sax.

Les 7 Lézards

10 rue des Rosiers, 4th (01.48.87.08.97/www. 7lezards.com). M° St-Paul. **Open** *Gigs* 10pm daily. **Tickets** €11-€18; free jam sessions on Sun. **No credit cards.**
From fusion to bop, *chanson* to improv, and one of the best jam sessions around (on Sunday evenings), this cellar hosts the hottest sounds. The only real drawback is that there's no pre-booking.

Le Slow Club

130 rue de Rivoli, 1st (01.42.33.84.30). M° Châtelet. **Open** *Gigs* 10pm Fri, Sat. **Admission** €9-€13. **Credit** MC, V. **Map** p408 J6.
The medieval cellar may be tiny but compensates with boogie-woogie big bands and dance-friendly R&B. One of the most famous jazz joints in Europe.

Le Sunset/Le Sunside

60 rue des Lombards, 1st (Sunside 01.40.26.21.25/ Sunset 01.40.26.46.60/www.sunset-sunside.com). M° Châtelet. **Open** *Gigs* 9pm daily. **Tickets** €8-€25. **Credit** MC, V. **Map** p408 J6.
With Sunset dabbling in the electric, Sunside the acoustic, and a reputation that pulls big names from both sides of the Atlantic, this duo of venues is one of the main ports of call on any Paris jazz pilgrimage. Its small, smoky rooms lend authenticity.

Théâtre du Châtelet

1 pl du Châtelet (information 01.40.28.28.00/ booking 01.40.28.28.41/www.chatelet-theatre.com). M° Châtelet. **Tickets** €16-€69. **Credit** AmEx, DC, MC, V. **Map** p408 J6.
When this theatre and classical music hall dabbles in jazz, it does it properly. Its annual Bleu sur Scène Festival (June) is the excuse for biggies like Herbie Hancock and Ornette Coleman to come out to play.

Nightlife

Good things come to those who stay up late.

Paris after-dark strengths are cinemas, bars and restaurants: it isn't really a clubbing city. That said, its nightclubs are a reliable source of surprises, and the locals are good fun – once they let their hair down and stop playing it cool.

Those who'd rather dance with a partner than trip out with BPMs, sweaty strangers and strobes have plenty of old-style discos to choose from. There are nightly sessions at **Le Saint** (7 rue St-Séverin, 5th, 01.43.25.50.04); Friday-nighters at **Le Globo** (8 bd de Strasbourg, 10th, 01.42.41.55.70); swing, be-bop and rock 'n' roll after the jazz concerts at **Le Slow Club** (*see p319*); and a stream of school-disco-type nights where the DJ is no superstar but a humble spinner of tunes: check out the monthly Bal at **Elysée Montmartre** and Le Gala des Ringards at **Le Divan du Monde** and **Le Glaz'art**. Salsa and world-music events are plentiful, too, with regular nights at **La Java**, **Cabaret Sauvage** and Le Divan du Monde.

Hardcore clubbers need not go hungry, either. Dance music of every stripe gets an outing at the Paris version of Berlin's Love Parade, the **Techno Parade** (*see p276*), which takes place in mid September and draws thousands into the street to dance. Then there are big clubs such as **Queen**, **Club Pure** and **Red Light**, which serve up more commercial mixes of house music, lasers and podium dancers to mainstream crowds. On the other hand, smaller venues like **Pulp**, **Nouveau Casino**, **Batofar** and **Triptyque** tend to opt for a combination of house, techno and electro – often with a live music element to kick off.

It's with the 'after' parties that things really get going; indeed, there are as many Sunday morning events as there are Saturday-nighters. For standard house there are **Folies Pigalle**, **Red Light**, **Vinyl** and **Club 287**; for deep, progressive or minimal sounds, make tracks for **Batofar**, **Nouveau Casino** and **Next One**. This said, hip hop and R&B fans will be surprised to see how under-represented is their favoured clubbing scene in comparison to the high record sales and radio play of said genres. Straightforward hip hop nights are held during the week at Triptyque and Batofar; R&B is played on Wednesdays at Queen's Break'n, and on Thursdays at **La Scène**. For drum 'n' bass the main nights are monthly Massive at **Rex** and I Love Jungle in a succession of

hired venues. Trance and hardcore tend to stay outside Paris, with outdoor events organised by local collectives and sound systems – though **Le Gibus** runs events on Tuesday and Thursday nights and Batofar runs the occasional trance event.

ADVICE AND INFORMATION

Paris clubs don't really get going until 2am, and people often hit a DJ bar beforehand. Many visit several clubs in one night and finish their evening at an 'after' party on Sunday morning. This can be a costly way to go, but you can find quality DJing at free nights in certain clubs during the week. And free passes can be found on various flyers; flyer information is available at www.flyersweb.com. Other useful sites are www.novaplanet.com, www.radiofg.com and www.lemonsound.com, for house and techno events. Radio stations FG (98.2FM) and Nova (101.5FM) provide regular listings.

Note that the last métro leaves at around 12.45am, and the first only gets rolling at 5.45am; in between those times you'll have to get home by night bus or taxi. *See also p325* **Clubbing commandments**.

Club bars

Café Chéri(e)

44 bd de la Villette, 19th (01.42.02.02.05). Mº Belleville. **Open** 11am-2am daily. **Admission** free. **Drinks** €2.80-€6.50. **Credit** MC, V. **Map** p405 M3.
A popular DJ bar, not least for its terrace. Expect anything from banging house to '80s classics. It's used as a daytime bar, too (*see p226*). **Photo** *right*.

La Fabrique

53 rue du Fbg-St-Antoine, 11th (01.43.07.67.07/ www.fabrique.fr). Mº Bastille. **Open** 6pm-5am Tue-Sat. **Admission** free Tue-Fri; €10 Sat. **Drinks** €2.50-€11. **Credit** MC, V. **Map** p409 M7.
A buzzy DJ bar-club-restaurant where local house DJs spin the wheels of steel to the appreciation of a trendy Bastille crowd. Formidable bouncers, though.

L'Ile Enchantée

65 bd de la Villette, 10th (01.42.01.67.99). Mº Colonel Fabien. **Open** 8am-2am Mon-Fri; 5pm-2am Sat, Sun. **Admission** free. **Drinks** €2.50-€6.50. **Credit** MC, V. **Map** p405 M3.
Not as popular lately, due to the closure of the mini-club upstairs, this space still has an up-to-date music policy and makes for a good pre-club drink.

Arts & Entertainment

Café Cheri(e).
See p320.

The **Bateau Concorde Atlantique**. *See p323*.

London's weekly listings bible

Le Man Ray

*34 rue Marbeuf, 8th (01.56.88.36.36). M° Franklin
D Roosevelt.* **Open** 7pm-2am Mon-Thur; 6pm-5am
Fri-Sun. **Admission** free (€25 after 11pm Fri, Sat).
Drinks €10-€15. **Credit** MC, V. **Map** p402 D4.
This see-and-be-seen bar-restaurant attracts glitzy
folk who gleefully make use of the dancefloor. DJs
spin house at weekends. *See also p193.*

La Mezzanine de l'Alcazar

*62 rue Mazarine, 6th (01.53.10.19.99/www.
alcazar.fr). M° Odéon.* **Open** 7pm-2am daily.
Admission free. **Drinks** €9-€11. **Credit** AmEx,
DC, MC, V. **Map** p408 H7.
The impressive DJ line-up at this stylish, Conran-
owned mezzanine bar draws mainly local yuppies;
the music really gets pumping past midnight. *See
also p207 and p229.*

Project 101

*44 rue de La Rochefoucauld, 9th (01.49.95.95.85/
www.project-101.com). M° Pigalle.* **Open** 9pm-1am
Fri. **Admission** free-€5. **Drinks** €2-€4. **No credit
cards. Map** p403 H2.
This underground venue with a shop on the ground
floor has been going solid for three years, hosting
regular experimental music concerts, as well as
film projections, and DJs and VJs in an intimate
home-from-home space. Concert dates vary, so call
or check the website first.

Le Troisième Lieu

*62 rue Quincampoix, 4th (01.48.04.85.64/www.
letroisiemelieu.com). M° Rambuteau.* **Open** 6pm-2am
Mon-Sat. **Admission** free. **Drinks** €2.50-€5. **Credit**
MC, V. **Map** p404 J5.
This vast venue was created by les Ginettes Armées,
famous for their Sunday lesbian and mixed events.
The ground floor hosts DJs mixing eclectic sounds
for chatting and relaxing to, while the clubbier basement is strictly dancefloor. *See also p223.*

Cool clubs

Bateau Concorde Atlantique

*Opposite 25 quai Anatole-France, 7th
(01.47.05.71.03/www.concorde-atlantique.com).
M° Assemblée Nationale.* **Open** *Mid June-mid Sept*
11pm-5am Mon-Fri; 5pm-5am Sat; 6pm-5am Sun.
Admission free-€10. **Drinks** €5-€8. **Credit** MC, V.
Map p403 F5.
With its terrace and voluminous dancefloor, this
two-level boat is the clubbers' spot of choice during
the summer. From July to September, the Respect
team holds a popular Wednesday night bash (free
before 10pm). Sunday's Terassa is as near as Paris
gets to a St-Tropez vibe. **Photo** *p321.*

Batofar

*Opposite 11 quai François-Mauriac, 13th (recorded
information 01.53.60.17.30/www.batofar.org).
M° Quai de la Gare.* **Open** 11pm-6am Mon-Sat;
6am-noon 1st Sun of mth. **Admission** €5-€12.
Drinks €3.50-€8. **Credit** MC, V. **Map** p409 N10.

Some clubbers jumped ship after a new management crew boarded this popular lighthouse boat.
The change means more eclectic, less experimental
programming, straight club nights at weekends and
an impressive live-music programme. In summer
clubbers chill on the quayside while DJs play on
deck. It's a rock venue, too (*see p317*).

Club 287

*33 av de la Porte d'Aubervilliers, 18th
(01.48.34.00.00). M° Porte de la Chapelle.* **Open**
11pm-5am Sat. **Admission** €18. **Drinks** €8-€16.
Credit AmEx, MC, V.
When it opened, the 287 was *the* place to be. But its
trendy followers have since moved on and the club
is populated by a non-Parisian crowd who have just
discovered house music. It's a fair distance (a good
15 minutes on foot) from any métro stop – and
under new management – so phone ahead.

Le Divan du Monde

*75 rue des Martyrs, 18th (01.40.05.06.99/
www.divandumonde.com). M° Pigalle or Anvers.*
Open 11pm-6am Wed-Sat. **Admission** free-€15.
Drinks €4-€8. **Credit** MC, V. **Map** p404 J2.
The Divan Japonais area upstairs specialises in VJ
events, while downstairs holds concerts (*see p316*)
and funk, rock and world-music club nights with
local DJs on the weekends.

Elysée Montmartre

*72 bd de Rochechouart, 18th (01.44.92.45.38/www.
elyseemontmartre.com). M° Anvers.* **Open** midnight-
6am Fri, Sat. **Admission** €10-€15. **Drinks** €4-€10.
Credit *Bar* MC, V. **Map** p404 J2.
Although this is more of a concert venue (*see p316*)
than a club, promoters hire it for big nights such as
the monthly Open House and Panic nights, which
attract a thousand clubbers at weekends.

La Flèche d'Or

*102bis rue de Bagnolet, 20th (01.44.64.01.02/www.
flechedor.com). M° Alexandre Dumas.* **Open** 8pm-
2am Mon, Sun; 8pm-5am Wed-Sat. **Admission** free.
Drinks €3-€10. **Credit** MC, V. **Map** p405 Q5.
Closed by the city council in December 2002, this
impressive converted métro station has returned
with new management and a new vibe. Gone is the
hardcore and world music of yore; now free rock and
variété française concerts at 9pm every night hint at
a slightly older, more chilled-out crowd. Having said
that, come 11pm DJs take to the stage to spin everything from classic funk to electro until well into the
early hours. *See also p316.*

Folies Pigalle

*11 pl Pigalle, 9th (01.48.78.25.26/www.folies-
pigalle.com). M° Pigalle.* **Open** midnight-dawn
Mon-Thur; midnight-noon Fri, Sat; 6pm-midnight,
midnight-dawn Sun. **Admission** €20; €7 Sun
evening. **Drinks** €10. **Credit** AmEx, MC, V.
Map p404 G2.
Pigalle types, *banlieue* bad boys and tourists squelch
to pumping and percussive house by resident DJs.

Le Triptyque. *See p326.*

Clubbing commandments

Clubbing has become a pretty global affair, with similar content from one country to another. But customs and etiquette vary enormously, so absorb these handy hints before venturing into Paris *nocturne*.

● **Do** check flyers, which can be found in bars and record shops, before going out: you can often get free passes or reduced entrance with a flyer (*see p320*).

● **Don't** arrive at a club before 1am unless you're purely out to save money (entrance might be free or reduced before a given hour). Paris clubs don't really get going until 2am, as most people eat out or go to a bar first.

● **Do** order a bottle of spirits at the door in more glitzy or mainstream clubs: it can work out cheaper than a round of drinks. What's more, this can often get you free entrance, a table for you and your friends, VIP treatment and lots of new pals for the evening.

● **Don't** wear a baseball cap, tracksuit bottoms or trainers to mainstream or glitzy clubs unless your name's Justin Timberlake or Paris Hilton. Trainers are fine at most other clubs, though be warned – bouncers may use them as a pretext to refuse entrance.

● **Do** talk loudly in English in the queue, as Paris clubs like to draw an international crowd. Anglophones are seen to be more likely to pay the entrance fee and spend money at the bar.

● **Don't** arrive in a big group unless you're all women (in which case you may get in for free).

● **Do** find someone tall and attractive to accompany you: Paris clubs are notorious worshippers of good looks.

● **Don't** try to strike up a conversation with the bouncers: they're trained to say nothing but 'Go ahead' and 'No, not possible tonight'.

● **Do** walk into a club as though you own the place or are the headlining DJ's manager.

● **Don't** get legless! Drunk and disorderly behaviour is frowned on and can lead to trouble (which may ruin your holiday).

● **Do** say goodbye and thank you as you leave: the *physionomiste* on the door may even remember your face and let you jump the queue next time you visit.

Le Gibus

18 rue du Fbg-du-Temple, 11th (01.47.00.78.88/ www.gibus.fr). M° République. **Open** midnight-dawn Tue-Fri; 11pm-dawn Sat; 6pm-2am Sun. *Concerts* 8-11.30pm Fri. **Admission** €5-€20. **Drinks** €5-€8. **Credit** *Bar* AmEx, DC, MC, V. **Map** p404 L4.

This '80s punk hotspot has gone through plenty of different styles, and does so now on a daily basis, kicking off with hard techno of a Tuesday. Reggae, psychedelic trance, '80s tunes and hip hop round out the week, with pumping house on Sundays. The mainly non-Parisian crowd is remarkably mellow.

Le Glaz'art

7-15 av de la Porte-de-la-Villette, 19th (01.40.36.55.65). M° Porte de la Villette. **Open** 8.30pm-2am Thur (sometimes Wed); 11pm-5am Fri, Sat. **Admission** €10. **Drinks** €4-€7. **Credit** AmEx, MC, V. **Map** p405 inset.

The converted Eurolines station is a bit far-flung, but its strong live acts and theme nights attract a loyal crowd. Regular dub, techno and drum 'n' bass nights.

Nouveau Casino

109 rue Oberkampf, 11th (01.43.57.57.40). M° Parmentier. **Open** midnight-5am Thur-Sat. **Admission** €5-€10. **Drinks** €5.50-€9. **Credit** *Bar* MC, V. **Map** p405 M5.

This Café Charbon annexe (*see p226*) is a prime rock concert venue, and hosts club nights from Wednesday to Saturday. Local collectives and international names play dub, techno and more. *See also p316.*

Pulp

25 bd Poissonnière, 2nd (01.40.26.01.93/www.pulp-paris.com). M° Grands Boulevards. **Open** midnight-5am Wed-Sat. **Admission** free Wed, Thur; €10 Fri, Sat. **Drinks** €5-€9. **Credit** MC, V. **Map** p404 J4.

Essentially a lesbian club (*see p307*), Pulp draws a mixed crowd on Wednesdays and Thursdays for an atmosphere midway between a late-hours bar and a club. Watch out for top international DJs and a regular spot from local Ivan Smagghe.

Red Light

34 rue du Départ, 15th (01.42.79.94.53). M° Edgar Quinet or Montparnasse Bienvenüe. **Open** 11pm-6am Fri, Sat. **Admission** €20. **Drinks** from €10. **Credit** AmEx, MC, V. **Map** p407 F9.

A house mecca with local and global DJs spinning harder house music. Monthly BPM and Strictly House nights take place on Fridays; Saturdays attract a well-groomed gay clientele for events with a strong Ibiza connection.

Rex

5 bd Poissonnière, 2nd (01.42.36.10.96/www.rex club.com). M° Bonne Nouvelle. **Open** 11.30pm-dawn Wed-Sat. **Admission** free Wed, Thur; €13 Fri, Sat. **Drinks** €5-€12. **Credit** *Bar* MC, V. **Map** p404 J4.

The Rex has held its reputation as a prime venue for electronic music for a decade or more. After more than ten years at the helm, Laurent Garnier has moved elsewhere; the new management promises more live entertainment on the newly built stage.

Arts & Entertainment

Spinning for a stylish crowd at **Le Triptyque**.

La Scène Bastille

2bis rue des Taillandiers, 11th (01.48.06.50.70/
www.la-scene.com). M° Bastille. **Open** midnight-
6am Wed-Sun. Closed Aug. **Admission** €10-€12.
Drinks €4-€9. **Credit** MC, V. **Map** p409 M7.
This restaurant-bar-club complex holds regular
concerts as well as club events from Thursday to
Saturday. There's an alternative gay emphasis on
Fridays, when popular nights such as Eyes Need
Sugar attract a fashionable crowd. *See also p317.*

Le Triptyque

142 rue Montmartre, 2nd (01.40.28.05.55/
www.letriptyque.com). M° Grands Boulevards.
Open 10.30pm-3am Wed; 11pm-6am Thur-Sun.
Admission free-€12. **Drinks** €4-€9. **Credit**
AmEx, MC, V. **Map** p404 J4.
Eclectic programming has allowed this prime club
and concert venue to attract a very stylish local and
international crowd. It has a pretty good live agenda,
too (*see p317*). **Photo** *above and p324.*

Wagg

62 rue Mazarine, 6th (01.55.42.22.00/
www.wagg.fr). M° Odéon. **Open** 11.30pm-6am Fri,
Sat; 3pm-midnight Sun. **Admission** €15 Fri, Sat;
€10 Sun. **Drinks** €7-€10. **Credit** AmEx, DC, MC,
V. **Map** p408 H7.
This old Jim Morrison hangout attracts a Left Bank-
ish crowd with house and disco at weekends, and a
salsa session on Sunday afternoons.

Glitzy clubs

Les Bains

7 rue du Bourg-l'Abbé, 3rd (01.48.87.01.80).
M° Etienne Marcel. **Open** 11pm-6am Wed-Sun.
Admission €10-€20. **Drinks** €6-€12. **Credit**
AmEx, MC, V. **Map** p404 J5.
This club has lost its kudos with the in-crowd, and
is now frequented by tourists and out-of-towners.

Le Cab

2 pl du Palais-Royal, 1st (01.58.62.56.25/
www.cabaret.fr). M° Palais Royal Musée du Louvre.
Open 11.30pm-5am Tue (bar only), Wed-Sat.
Admission free Tue-Thur; €20 Fri, Sat. **Drinks**
€13. **Credit** AmEx, MC, V. **Map** p404 H5.
The Cabaret, now 'Cab', has had an interior facelift
by Franco-Japanese designer Ora Ito – but the music
is dated: revival nights, R&B and commercial house.

Club Mix

24 rue de l'Arrivée, 15th (01.56.80.37.37/
www.mixclub.fr). M° Montparnasse Bienvenüe.
Open 11pm-6am Wed-Sat; 5pm-1am Sun.
Admission €12-€20. **Drinks** €8. **Credit** MC,
V. **Map** p407 F9.
This enormous venue formerly known as Amnesia
(and, very briefly, Club Pure) has been bought up by
the owner of Queen and Bus Palladium. Music is
strictly house; the most popular event is the gay tea
dance on Sundays.

Ephemeral art-ery

For ages and ages, the building on the lower banks of the Canal St-Martin was occupied by construction suppliers Point P: its open garages were full of cement and breeze blocks. Then Point P moved out to larger premises, and the place stood empty and abandoned for several years.

It turned out the buildings were owned by the city council, and when the team behind the city's two biggest legal squats – the Hôpital Ephémère (an old hospital in the 18th transformed into artists' studios and fashion designers' workshops, complete with bar and club) and Les Mains d'Oeuvres (an old factory remade as a concert venue, music studios and cinema) – got wind of this, they jumped at the chance. With a fun-loving chap in the mayoral chair, the timing couldn't have been better. Their proposal to turn the building into a concert venue, music studios, gallery, bar and restaurant was duly given the thumbs up.

The result was **Point Ephémère** (*see also p316*), which opened in the summer of 2004, initially as a small concert venue and bar. It's a fab set-up: a vast building with high ceilings, waterfront terrace in summer and a location handy enough for central Paris but not too close to residential areas. Perfect.

The place grew progressively over the following year, and is now one of the most exciting venues in Paris. The waterside restaurant and bar have been drawing large crowds, serving good and reasonably priced food in an atmosphere almost reminiscent of a pub garden. Culturally speaking, the emphasis has been on both the visual and performing arts, with regular contemporary dance performances and exhibitions. Point Ephémère has also become one of the few places to regularly programme experimental electronic music, as well as bands from the underground rock and hip hop scene and local DJs spinning hybrids of dance music rarely featured anywhere else in the city.

Bigger names like LCD soundsystem, Mike Ladd, Krikor, Kid 606 have played alongside lesser-known characters such as Turzi, Puyo Puyo, Takashi Wada and Stuntman 5. Interestingly (and promoters and managers from other clubs would do well to take note), the concerts and club events that would elsewhere be considered too 'experimental' are always packed. Of course, other clubs would argue that Point Ephémère is heavily subsidised by the council, and so can afford to take risks – but the public's presence and enthusiasm are undeniable. Paris clubland just got a welcome dose of energy and hope.

Point Ephémère
200 quai de Valmy, 10th (01.40.34.02.48/ www.pointephemere.org). Mº Jaurès or Louis Blanc. **Open** 10am-2am daily. **Credit** AmEx, DC, MC, V. **Map** p404 M2.

L'Etoile

*12 rue de Presbourg, 16th (01.45.00.78.70).
M° Charles de Gaulle Etoile.* **Open** 11pm-5am Mon-Sat. **Admission** €20 (free Tue for women). **Drinks** €16-€20. **Credit** AmEx, DC, MC, V. **Map** p402 C3.
Don't bother if you're not wearing Armani, as the door policy is strict. And have a model in tow.

Nirvana

3 av Matignon, 8th (01.53.89.18 91/www.le-nirvana.com). M° Franklin D Roosevelt. **Open** 11.30pm-6am daily. **Admission** €15 (free for women before 1am). **Drinks** €10-€12. **Credit** AmEx, DC, MC, V. **Map** p403 E4.
Opened by Buddha Bar disc-compiler Claude Challe, Nirvana has a vaguely Eastern theme, with music varying from lounge to Ibiza house.

La Suite

40 av George V, 8th (01.53.57.49.49). M° George V. **Open** midnight-4.30am Thur-Sat (often closed for private parties). **Admission** free. **Drinks** €20. **Credit** AmEx, MC, V. **Map** p402 D4.
Cathy and David Guetta, who made their name at Les Bains, are behind this venture; its lounge area attracts models and their walking wallets.

VIP Room

76-78 av des Champs-Elysées, 8th (01.56.69.16.66/www.viproom.fr). M° Franklin D Roosevelt. **Open** midnight-5am daily. **Admission** free. **Drinks** €20. **Credit** AmEx, DC, MC, V. **Map** p402 D4.
Run by celebrity Jean Roch, this club has become the place for launch parties and celebrity birthdays.

Mainstream clubs

Club Med World

39 cour St-Emilion, 12th (08.10.81.04.10). M° Cour St-Emilion. **Open** 11pm-2am Tue-Thur; 11.30pm-6am Fri, Sat. **Admission** €15 (free for women) Tue-Thur; €20 Fri, Sat. **Drinks** €9. **Credit** AmEx, MC, V. **Map** p409 N10.
This huge venue in the Bercy Village hosts popular disco and '80s nights at weekends for people who don't really like nightclubs but like to dance.

La Loco

90 bd de Clichy, 18th (01.53.41.88.89/www.laloco.com). M° Blanche. **Open** 11pm-5am daily. **Admission** €5-€14. **Drinks** €4-€7. **Credit** AmEx, MC, V. **Map** p403 G2.
After trying to pull in trendy and gay clubbers, La Loco has returned to the mainstream, and has a big teenage and *banlieue* following. The three dancefloors offer house, dance and chart hits on weekends, and metal and gothic concerts during the week.

Queen

102 av des Champs-Elysées, 8th (08.92.70.73.30/www.queen.fr). M° George V. **Open** midnight-dawn daily. **Admission** €15 Mon-Thur, Sun; €20 Fri, Sat. **Drinks** €10. **Credit** *Bar* AmEx, MC, V. **Map** p402 D4.
Queen was once a top-notch gay club, but in recent years the place has become rather commercial and

unimaginative (apart from those nights when an international DJ is invited to play). The crowd is a mix of unhip tourists, gym queens and business-school students except on Wednesday nights, when a hipper bunch grinds to maximum R&B.

La Scala

188bis rue de Rivoli, 1st (01.42.60.45.64/www.lascalaparis.fr). M° Palais Royal Musée du Louvre. **Open** 10.30pm-6am Tue-Sun. **Admission** €12 (free for women) Tue-Thur, Sun; €15 Fri, Sat. **Drinks** €9. **Credit** MC, V. **Map** p403 H5.
This huge central club has plenty of potential, but a chart-oriented, commercial soundtrack attracts a wet-behind-the-ears clientele.

World & rock 'n' roll venues

Le Cabaret Sauvage

59 bd Macdonald, 19th (01.42.09.03.09/www.cabaretsauvage.com). M° Porte de la Villette. **Open** 11pm-dawn, days vary. **Admission** €10-€20. **Drinks** €4-€8. **Credit** AmEx, MC, V. **Map** p405 inset.
This cabaret venue (*see p280*) is hired out for a mix of nights, the best of which are those dedicated to North African music.

Caveau de la Huchette

5 rue de la Huchette, 5th (01.43.26.65.05). M° St-Michel. **Open** 9.30pm-2.30am Mon-Thur; 9.30pm-3.30am Fri, Sat. **Admission** €10.50 Mon-Thur; €13 Fri, Sat; €9 students Mon-Sat. **Drinks** from €4.50. **Credit** MC, V. **Map** p408 J7.
A popular haunt for thirtysomethings and veterans not ready to settle down quite yet. Music varies from funky jazz to rock 'n' roll classics.

La Chapelle des Lombards

19 rue de Lappe, 11th (01.43.57.24.24/www.chapelledeslombards.com). M° Bastille. **Open** 11pm-7am Tue-Sun. **Admission** free Tue, Wed, Sun; €19 Thur-Sat (free for women Thur). **Drinks** €6-€12. **Credit** MC, V. **Map** p409 M7.
Latinos and Africans sweat it out in this friendly venue specialising in world music – zouk, salsa, soukous and raï. Occasional concerts, too.

Les Etoiles

61 rue du Château d'Eau, 10th (01.47.70.60.56). M° Château d'Eau. **Open** 9pm-3am Thur-Sat. **Admission** €10. **Drinks** €4-€6. **Credit** MC, V. **Map** p404 K3.
A quality salsa band electrifies the dancefloor every weekend. Anyone looking a little uncertain will be swept into a frenzy of footwork with free advice dished out to the less adept.

La Java

105 rue du Fbg-du-Temple, 10th (01.42.02.20.52). M° Goncourt. **Open** 11pm-5am Fri, Sat; 2-7pm Sun. **Admission** €5-€10. **Drinks** €8-€12. **Credit** MC, V. **Map** p405 M4.
Hidden away in a disused Belleville market, La Java is a mecca for the salsa-loving community, with bands featured at weekends.

Sport & Fitness

Healthy obsessions.

Boules: c'est cool. *See p331.*

Paris has been instrumental in setting up the world's major sports bodies and events. The modern Olympic Games, and football's FIFA, World Cup and European Cup were all planned and developed in the boardrooms of the French capital. In 2005 Paris was widely tipped to win its bid to host the 2012 Olympic Games. So it came as a painful shock when London inched ahead shortly before the finish and claimed the prize (and, undoubtedly, an enormous bill).

Never mind: Paris is still a world-class setting for games of all kinds. Much is owed to a dynamic, outward-looking sports press, particularly the daily newspaper *L'Equipe* and biweekly *France Football*. Their fin-de-siècle forebear, *L'Auto*, under Henri Desgrange, introduced the world's biggest annual cycling event into the calendar; the **Tour de France** (www.letour.fr). Although beset in recent years by doping scandals, the three-week summer Tour is still a national festival. Indeed, many in cycling circles believe France now to be a 'cleaner' ground for the sport, thanks to stricter local drug controls. Though locals despair of a home rider emulating Bernard Hinault's 1985 triumph, millions still flock to the avenue des Champs-Elysées in July to welcome the winner. (For details of other major sports events, *see pp272-277* **Festivals & Events**.)

Spectator sports

The national stadium is the **Stade de France** (93210 St-Denis, 08.92.70.09.00, www.stadede france.fr). Indoor events take place at the **Palais Omnisports de Paris-Bercy** (8 bd de Bercy, 12th, 08.92.39.04.90, www.popb.fr). The **Stade Roland Garros** (Porte des Mousquetaires, 2 av Gordon-Bennett, 16th, 01.47.43.48.00, www.fft.fr/rolandgarros) stages the French tennis open; the **Parc des Princes**, home of flagship football club Paris St-Germain (*see below*), also hosts other sports events.

Tickets are sold at branches of **Fnac** and **Virgin Megastore** (for both, *see p244*).

Basketball

Paris Basket Racing

Stade Coubertin, 82 av Georges-Lafont, 16th (01.46.10.93.60/www.parisbasket.com). M° Porte de St-Cloud. **Tickets** from €8. **No credit cards.**
After leading the San Antonio Spurs to the top of the NBA, Bruges-born Tony Parker has bought Pro A division Paris Basket Racing, where he began his career. Could it be a glorious homecoming?

Football

Paris St-Germain

Stadium *Parc des Princes, av du Parc-des-Princes, 16th (01.47.43.71.71/tickets & information 32.75/ www.psg.fr). M° Porte de St-Cloud.* **Tickets** from €14. **Credit** MC, V.
Shop *27 av des Champs-Elysées, 8th (01.56.69.22.22). M° Franklin D Roosevelt.*
Open 10am-8pm Mon-Fri, Sun; 10am-10pm Sat. **Credit** AmEx, MC, V. **Map** p403 E4.
If PSG didn't exist, it would have been necessary to invent them. Starved of top-class soccer in the capital since the demise of the famous Racing (now in the French third division), a group of donors set up PSG by amalgamating local clubs 30 years ago. Backed by TV channel Canal+, PSG bought top

stars to win silverware in the 1980s and '90s, much to the chagrin of poorer, traditional clubs from the provinces (like Olympique Marseille). PSG's raucous *banlieue* following hardly endears them, either. PSG had a promising start to the 2005-06 season, but the club is still light years away from the Champions League standard set by the likes of the new football superpower in France, Olympique Lyon.

Horse racing

There are seven courses in and around Paris. The full schedule, the *Calendrier des Courses*, is published by *France Galop* (08.21.21.32.13, www.france-galop.com). For information on trotting, consult www.cheval-francais.com. Tickets are €1.50-€8 (free for under-18s), with free babysitting and pony rides for under-tens.

Hippodrome d'Auteuil
route des Lacs, 16th (01.40.71.47.47).
M° Porte d'Auteuil.
Steeplechasing in the Bois de Boulogne. The biggest event is the Gras Savoye Grand Steeplechase de Paris on the last Sunday in May.

Hippodrome de Chantilly
16 av du Général-Leclerc, 90209 Chantilly
(03.44.62.41.00). Train from Gare du Nord.
Flat racing 40km (25 miles) from Paris. The fashion parade turns out in force for the Prix de Diane Hermès in June; the full length of the course, with its adrenalin-generating climb at the end, is used for the Prix du Jockey Club the weekend before.

Hippodrome d'Enghien
pl André-Foulon, 95230 Soissy-sous-Montmorency
(01.34.17.87.00). Train from Gare du Nord.
Steeplechase and trotting 18km (11 miles) from Paris.

Hippodrome de Longchamp
route des Tribunes, 16th (01.44.30.75.00).
M° Porte d'Auteuil then free bus.
Flat racing in the Bois de Boulogne. This course is host to the racing season's most fashionable social event, the Prix de l'Arc de Triomphe Lucien Barrière. Women in wild hats get in for free.

Hippodrome de Maisons-Laffitte
1 av de la Pelouse, 78602 Maisons-Laffitte
(01.39.12.81.70). RER Maisons-Laffitte then bus.
Flat racing.

Hippodrome de Paris-Vincennes
2 route de la Ferme, 12th (01.49.77.17.17/
www.cheval-francais.com). M° Château de
Vincennes/RER Joinville-le-Pont then free bus.
Trotting in the Bois de Vincennes. Floodlights on winter evenings add to the atmosphere.

Hippodrome de St-Cloud
1 rue du Camp Canadien, 92210 St-Cloud
(01.47.71.69.26). RER Rueil-Malmaison.
Flat racing.

Rugby

Stade Français Paris
Stade Jean-Bouin, 26 av du Général-Sarrail, 16th
(08.92.69.21.92/www.stade.fr). M° Porte d'Auteuil.
Tickets €8-€40. **Credit** AmEx, MC, V.
Le Stade Français Paris (the name of the team, not the stadium) were French rugby champions in 2003 and 2004, but lost out in the final (and also in the Heineken Cup final) in 2005. Already on a roll for 2006, the team will probably pose for another *Dieux du Stade* calendar – naked except for strategically placed rugby balls.

Activities & team sports

Some venues require proof of health insurance, ID and passport-sized photos for membership.

All-round sports clubs

The **Standard Athletic Club** (route Forestière du Pavé de Meudon, 92360 Meudon-la-Forêt, 01.46.26.16.09, www.standac.com) is a private sports and social club aimed at local English speakers. Full membership costs €700 per year, plus a joining fee. As well as football, cricket and hockey teams, there are tennis and squash courts, a heated outdoor pool, billiards table and a workout room with fitness classes.

Local top-level multi-sports clubs include **Racing Club de France** (01.45.67.55.86, www.racingclubdefrance.com), **ASPTT de Paris** (01.45.69.01.01, www.aspttparis.com), **Paris Université Club** (01.44.16.62.62, www.puc.asso.fr) and **Le Stade Français** (01.40.71.33.33, www.stadefrancais.com).

American football

There are about 15 teams in the suburbs, for all ages. There are also 'no-tackle' flag football teams open to both men and women – and even cheerleader squads. Contact the **Fédération Française de Football Américain** (01.43.11.14.70, www.fffa.org) for details.

Athletics & running

Paris has many municipal tracks (including eight indoor ones) of a good standard, open to individual runners for a monthly subscription

▶ The Mairie de Paris manages a wide range of facilities across the capital for a variety of participatory sports. For details, consult its free annual *Parisports: Guide du Sport à Paris*, or view the online version at www.sport.paris.fr.

Academy Billard Beaugrenelle.

of about €4. Details can be found in the *Guide du Sport* (*see p330*). Joggers use the banks of the Seine and the parks (Jardin du Luxembourg, Tuileries and Parc de la Villette). Note that the Bois de Boulogne and Bois de Vincennes are also gay cruising spots. The Paris Marathon takes place in April (*see pp272-277* **Festivals & Events**). The **Hash House Harriers** organises weekly runs through its four clubs located in the Paris region. Log on to parishhh. free.fr or the **Sans Clue HHH** at schhh.free.fr.

Baseball, softball & cricket

Most Paris teams practise in the Bois de Vincennes. Contact the Fédération Française de Baseball, Softball et Cricket (01.44.68.89.30, www.ffbsc.org). An English expat runs the **Château de Thoiry Cricket Club** (78770 Thoiry, 01.34.87.55.70, www.thoirycricket.com), 40km (25 miles) from Paris. **Paris University Club** (01.44.16.62.62, www.pucbaseball.com) has baseball teams for all ages.

Basketball

Almost every municipal sports centre has a court and club. The Fédération Française de Basketball (01.53.94.25.00, www.basketfrance. com) has details. Public spots include courts under the Métro tracks near M° Glacière in the 13th, and the Jardin du Luxembourg in the 6th.

Boules, pool & bowling

For boules or *pétanque*, try square des Arènes de Lutèce (5th) or the *boulodrome* at the Jardin du Luxembourg (6th). The Fédération Française de Pétanque (www.petanque.fr) has details. Some pool venues require your ID or passport. Paris has 25 ten-pin bowling centres; those listed below rent shoes and stay open late.

Academy Billard Beaugrenelle
28 rue Linois, 15th (01.45.79.67.23/www.aka-billard.com). M° Charles Michels. **Open** noon-2am Mon-Fri; noon-4am Sat, Sun. **Admission** €10.50-€13.50/hr. **Credit** MC, V. **Map** p406 B8.

Arts & Entertainment

Mur Mur.

The city's largest pool hall has 22 US, five French and four UK tables, plus a DJ. Photo *p331*.

Bowling-Mouffetard
73 rue Mouffetard, 5th (01.43.31.09.35/www.bowling-mouffetard.fr). M° Place Monge. **Open** 3pm-2am Mon-Fri; 10am-2am Sat, Sun. **Admission** from €2.70-€5.90 per set. *Shoe hire* €1.80. **Credit** MC, V. **Map** p408 J9.
Centrally located venue with eight bowling lanes.

Cercle Clichy Montmartre
84 rue de Clichy, 9th (01.48.78.32.85/www.academie-billard.com). M° Place de Clichy. **Open** 11am-6am daily. **Admission** *Pool* from €6/hr. *Billiards* from €5/hr. **Credit** (€30 minimum) MC, V. **Map** p403 G2.
Historic venue decorated in frescoes, with a huge bar and pool tables a-plenty. No under-18s.

Climbing

To use any municipal climbing wall, you will need to obtain a personal ID card. Take a photo, your passport, proof of valid insurance and

the fee (€4 per month) to the centre you want to use. Those who prefer the real thing can find superb boulder formations at the Forêt de Fontainebleau, 45 minutes south of Paris; **Grimporama** (www.grimporama.com) has full details, including maps, on their website. The **Club Alpin Français de Fontainebleau** (01.53.72.87.00, caf77.free.fr) organises group climbs and weekend outings.

Centre Sportif Poissonnier
2 rue Jean-Cocteau, 18th (01.42.51.24.68). M° Porte de Clignancourt. **Open** 7am-10pm Mon-Sat; 8am-6pm Sun. **Admission** free. **No credit cards.**
The largest of the six municipal walls in Paris.

Mur Mur
55 rue Cartier-Bresson, 93500 Pantin (01.48.46.11.00/www.mur.mur.online.fr). M° Aubervilliers – Pantin Quatre Chemins. **Open** noon-11pm Mon-Fri; 9.30am-6.30pm Sat, Sun. **Admission** €12-€14; €6-€7 under-12s. **Credit** AmEx, MC, V.

One of the best climbing walls in Europe, with 1,500sq m (16,000sq ft) of wall, 10,000 holds and ice-climbing. The joining fee is €23; €12 for under-12s. Hire kit and tuition are available. **Photo** *p332*.

Cycling

Cycling has improved with Mayor Delanoë's expansion of bike lanes. Ideal spots on Sundays and holidays, when local roads are traffic-free, are the Seine's embankments, Canal St-Martin and the Bois de Vincennes (reached via the Promenade Plantée, along the Viaduc des Arts).

The Fédération Française de Cyclisme (01.56.20.88.88, www.ffc.fr) has details of the many local cycle clubs. The **Stade Vélodrome Jacques-Anquetil** (Bois de Vincennes, 12th, 01.43.68.01.27) is regularly open to amateur cyclists, and the track at **Longchamp** (*see p330*) is open to speed cyclists when there are no horse races. **Mieux se Déplacer à Bicyclette** (01.43.20.26.02, www.mdb-idf.org) organises free rides for members (€30 per year). *See also p70* **Guided tours**.

Gepetto & Vélos

59 rue du Cardinal-Lemoine, 5th (01.43.54.19.95/ www.gepetto-et-velos.com). M° Cardinal Lemoine. **Open** 9am-7.30pm Tue-Sat; 9.30am-7pm Sun. **Credit** MC, V. **Map** p408 K8.
Rents, sells and repairs all types of bicycles.

Vélo Bastille

21 rue Alphonse Baudin, 11th (01.48.87.60.01/ www.parisvelosympa.com). M° Richard Lenoir. **Open** 9.30am-1pm, 2-6pm Mon, Wed-Fri; 9am-7pm Sat, Sun. **No credit cards. Map** p408 L7.
Repairs, rental and guided cycling tours of the city.

Diving

Courses for the French diving licence are offered at the **Club de Plongée du 5ème** (01.43.36.07.67), which uses the Piscine Jean-Taris (*see p336*) and runs trips to the Med. **Surplouf** (06.75.03.51.00, www.surplouf.com) offers courses in English. **Bleu Passion** (94 bd Poniatowski, 12th, 01.43.45.26.12, www.bleu-passion.fr) runs a diving school and sells all kinds of equipment.

Rolling, rolling, rolling...

As night falls on a Friday night, the neon-lit square between Montparnasse station and the Tour fills with skaters. Most are in their twenties and look like they were born on wheels, zipping easily between pedestrians. Some wear the four-wheel, in-line skates that sparkle; others sport '70s-style roller-skates with a toe-brake. This is where communal sport and fashion combine: **Friday Night Fever**, a high-speed, three-hour night tour organised by Pari-Roller (01.43.36.89.81, www.pari-roller.com). By 10pm, there are thousands of them, plus roller-mounted cops – to prevent traffic chaos – waiting for the bright Pari-Roller staff to give the word. Then they're off, like a swarm of bees. Cars have no choice but to wait until the pack – numbering anywhere from a thousand to a record 40,000 – passes by. It's the biggest weekly sporting fixture in Paris.

Friday Night Fever is free and open to whoever can keep up. Skaters must stick with a fast-moving crowd for three hours of cobbled streets, steep climbs and even steeper descents. Those who aren't quite up to speed can join the more sedate 'family' skate run by **Roller et Coquillage** (www.rollers-coquillages.org), on Sundays at 2.30pm from the **Nomades** shop (37 bd Bourdon, 4th, 01.44.54.94.42); it also rents out skates.

Roller Squad Institute (01.42.74.70.00, www.rsi.asso.fr) organises lessons for all ages. For real rollerblading and skateboarding acrobatics, head for vast **Rollerparc Avenue** (100 rue Léon Geffroy, 01.47.18.19.19, www.rollerparc.com) in Vitry-sur-Seine.

Fencing

For a list of clubs, consult www.escrime-ffe.fr. The fencing section at the **Racing Club de France** (5 rue Eblé, 7th, 01.45.67.55.86, www.racingclubdefrance.org) is suitable for leisure or competition, with 12 fencing masters and 18 pistes. All levels and ages are welcome.

Fitness clubs

The **Club Med** gyms (www.clubmedgym.fr) dominate the health-club scene, with 22 branches in Paris and the western suburbs, including five Waou Clubs with spa facilities. The gyms have state-of-the-art machines and pools, plus a solarium and even a piano room (at Montparnasse), and offer everything from dance classes to in-line skating outings. Single visits cost €25, annual memberships from €675.

The non-profit **La Gym Suédoise** (01.45.00.18.22, www.gymsuedoise.com) is an association that holds one-hour gym sessions in ten locations across Paris. Its method mixes stretching, cardio exercises and running to music. Membership is €75-€100 per term, or €10 per session. Unlike most gyms, there are free trials at specified locations.

There are free weekly 'Sport Nature' sessions of outdoor stretching, aerobics and running, set up by the Mairie at 13 locations around town. Check the annual *Guide du Sport* (*see p330*) or visit www.sport.paris.fr.

Club Quartier Latin

18 rue de Pontoise, 5th (01.55.42.77.88/www.club quartierlatin.com). M° Maubert Mutualité. **Open** 9am-midnight Mon-Fri; 9.30am-7pm Sat, Sun. **Admission** €18. **Credit** MC, V. **Map** p408 K7.
Home to the Pontoise pool (*see p336*), this venerable centre off boulevard St-Germain houses no-frills fitness facilities, and has a room for step, aerobics, stretching and yoga classes. There's a sauna, too.

Espace Vit'Halles

48 rue Rambuteau, 3rd (01.42.77.21.71/www.vit halles.com). M° Rambuteau. **Open** 8am-10.30pm Mon-Fri; 10am-7pm Sat, Sun. **Admission** €25/day. **Credit** AmEx, MC, V. **Map** p408 K5.
This sunken-level health club behind the Centre Pompidou has some of the best classes in Paris, step and spinning especially; payment is extra for each. There are Technogym fitness machines and a sauna.

Football

For information on the local amateur leagues, contact the **Ligue Ile de France de Football** (01.42.44.12.12). To join a weekend kickabout, try the Bois de Boulogne near Bagatelle, the Bois de Vincennes or the Champ de Mars.

Golf

The suburbs are full of top-rated courses suitable for all levels and all budgets. Contact the **Fédération Française de Golf** (68 rue Anatole-France, 92309 Levallois-Perret, 01.41.49.77.00, www.ffg.org).

Golf du Bois de Boulogne

Hippodrome d'Auteuil, 16th (01.44.30.70.00/ www.golfduboisdeboulogne.fr). M° Porte d'Auteuil. **Open** 8am-8pm daily. **Admission** €4-€5. **Credit** AmEx, MC, V.
The municipal green has one main course, putting greens and crazy golf. It's closed on horse-racing days, so check before you head out.

Golf National

78280 Guyancourt (01.30.43.36.00/www.golf-national.com). RER St-Quentin-en-Yvelines then taxi. **Open** 7.45am-7.15pm Mon-Fri; 7.30am-7.45pm Sat, Sun. **Admission** (annual membership €43) €34-€89. **Credit** MC, V.
The home of the French Open, this has two 18-hole courses and one nine-hole course.

Horse riding

To enjoy the lovely horse-riding trails in the Bois de Boulogne or the Bois de Vincennes, you need to join a riding club such as **La Société d'Equitation de Paris** (Centre Hippique du Bois de Boulogne, 16th, 01.45.01.20.06, www.equitation-paris.com), the **Centre Hippique du Touring** (Bois de Boulogne, 16th, 01.45.01.20.88) or the **Cercle Hippique du Bois de Vincennes** (8 rue de Fontenay, 94130 Nogent-sur-Marne, 01.48.73.01.28). Beginners can learn at the **Club Bayard Equitation** in the Bois de Vincennes (Centre Bayard, UCPA Vincennes, 12th, 01.43.65.46.87, www.clubbayard.com). Membership runs for one year (€83), or you can take a five-day course in July or August for €265. Out near Versailles, the **Haras de Jardy** (bd de Jardy, 92430 Marnes-la-Coquette, 01.47.01.35.30, www.haras-de-jardy.com) offers lessons by the hour for all ages, with no membership fee.

Leisurely rides at all levels in the forests of Fontainebleau are run by **La Bleausière** (06.82.01.21.18, la.bleausiere.free.fr).

Ice skating

The most popular open-air skating rink is the free one in front of the **Hôtel de Ville**, which runs from December to February (skate rental €5). There's another rink set up at the Tour de Montparnasse. When it's frozen, people skate on **Lac Supérieur** in the Bois de Boulogne. *See also pp272-277* **Festivals & Events.**

Patinoire de Boulogne

1 rue Victor-Griffuelhes, 92100 Boulogne-Billancourt (01.46.08.09.09). M° Marcel Sembat.
Open 4-6pm Mon; 3-6pm Wed; 3.45-5pm Fri; 10.30am-1pm, 3-6pm, 9pm-midnight Sat; 10am-1pm, 3-6pm Sun. **Admission** €5.10; €4.20 concessions. **No credit cards.**
Year-round indoor rink with free skate rental.

Patinoire Sonja Henie

Palais Omnisports de Paris-Bercy (01.40.02.60.60/ www.bercy.fr). M° Bercy. **Open** Sept-mid June 3-6pm Wed; 9.30pm-12.30am Fri; 3-6pm, 9.30pm-12.30am Sat; 10am-noon, 3-6pm Sun. **Admission** €3-€6. **No credit cards. Map** p409 N9.
Protection, helmets and skates for hire (€3).

Rowing & watersports

Paris residents can row, canoe and kayak for free on Saturdays at the **Base Nautique de la Villette** (41bis quai de la Loire, 19th, 01.42.40.29.90). Reserve a week in advance and bring along proof of residence and two photos. You can go waterskiing and wakeboarding at the **Club Nautique du 19ème** (Bassin de Vitesse de Saint Cloud, 92100 Boulogne-Billancourt, 01.42.03.25.24) and the **Ski Nautique Club de Paris** (01.46.02.72.50) between Pont de St-Cloud and Pont de Suresnes in the 16th. Serious rowers can join the annual **Traversée de Paris**, part of the Randon' Aviron EDF outings open to the public. Contact the **Ligue Ile-de-France d'Aviron** (94736 Nogent-sur-Marne, 01.48.75.79.17, lifa.chez.tiscali.fr). For a leisurely paddle, hire a boat at **Lac Daumesnil** or **Lac des Minimes** in the Bois de Vincennes, or at **Lac Supérieur** in the Bois de Boulogne.

Rugby

For a good standard of play, try the **Athletic Club de Boulogne** (Stade du Saut du Loup, av de la Butte-Mortemart, 16th, 01.46.51.11.91), which fields two teams. The **British Rugby Club of Paris** (58-60 av de la Grande-Armée, 17th, 01.40.55.15.15, www.brfcparis.com) fields two teams in the corporate league.

Skateboarding

Every five years or so the Mairie tries to clamp down on skateboarders, but the capital city's skateboard scene continues to thrive. With its infamous double-set, the riverfront courtyard at the **Palais de Tokyo** (*see p121*), colloquially known as 'Le Dôme', is popular as ever – as are the ledges and steps at **Trocadéro** (16th). **La Défense** (*see p177*) tends to be full of security guards, but is still worth exploring for smooth

marble, ledges and rails; **Palais Omnisports de Paris-Bercy** (*see p329*) has vast ledges and some almighty gaps.

A more relaxed scene is to be found at the **Place des Innocents** (by the Forum des Halles, 1st), which has low ledges and smooth ground, and at the **Opéra Bastille** (11th), which has some small steps. For more spots, check out www.paris-skate-culture.org or ask at shop **Street Machine** (6 rue Bailleul, 1st, 01.40.31.15.20, www.streetmachine.fr). For details about in-line skating in Paris, *see p333* **Rolling, rolling, rolling.**

Cosanostra Skatepark

18 rue du Tir, 77500 Chelles (01.64.72.14.04/ www.cosanostraskatepark.net). RER Gare de Chelles. **Open** 2-8pm Mon, Wed, Thur, Sat; 4-11pm Tue, Fri; 2-7pm Sun. **Admission** €6. **No credit cards.**
A huge indoor street course and micro-ramp, which hosts international competitions.

Squash

No membership is necessary to play squash at the **Club Quartier Latin** (*see p334*), which charges €17-€25 per game (racket rental from €2.50). The **Standard Athletic Club** (*see p330*) has squash courts for members or on payment of a €185 seasonal fee.

Squash Montmartre

14 rue Achille-Martinet, 18th (01.42.55.38.30/www. squash-montmartre.com). M° Lamarck Caulaincourt. **Open** 10am-11pm Mon-Fri; 10am-7pm Sat, Sun. **Admission** from €10. **Credit** V.
Period memberships available, plus equipment hire.

Swimming

Pools are plentiful and cheap, some with fine views or historical architecture; there's even one that floats on water (*see p336* **One cool pool**). Most require a swimming cap (available on site) and ban Bermudas; many open late – and swimming to music is integral to Nuit Blanche in October (*see pp272-277* **Festivals & Events**). The opening times given below, correct at the time of going to press, are nevertheless likely to change during school breaks and national holidays.

Aquaboulevard

4 rue Louis-Armand, 15th (01.40.60.15.15/ www.aquaboulevard.com). M° Balard. **Open** 9am-11pm Mon-Thur; 9am-midnight Fri; 8am-midnight Sat; 8am-11pm Sun. **Admission** 6hrs €25; €10 concessions. **Credit** AmEx, MC, V. **Map** p406 A10.
With year-round summer temperatures, this tropical water park under a giant atrium is great fun for kids. An extra charge gets you a steam bath and three saunas of varying intensity.

One cool pool

As unkept political pledges go, its ripples travel no great distance – but you can understand why Parisians might feel cheated. For it's now highly unlikely they'll ever see Jacques Chirac ease himself into the Seine for a dip. As Paris mayor in 1977, adding a flourish to a boast that his river clean-up programme held water, Chirac promised to do just that; yet, sadly, there's been no sign of the big Gaullist doing the front crawl under Pont Charles-de-Gaulle. Little wonder: the Seine may be cleaner than it was in 1977, but it's still not a river you'd willingly splash around in.

Wait, though – Chirac might yet get a chance to keep his promise. A swish new floating pool, costing €15 million, is set to open in the summer of 2006 – and its water, prior to treatment, will be pumped straight from the Seine. At 93 metres (305 feet) in length, with a 25-metre (82-foot) main pool, kiddies' paddling pool, café, large sundeck and sliding glass roof that will let it stay in business all year round, the pool-barge will be moored below the Bibliothèque Nationale. It's a project heartily endorsed by the current Paris mayor, Bertrand Delanoë – another big splash from the fun-seeking socialist.

Piscine Seine-Est

quai François-Mauriac, 13th (39.75/www. sport.paris.fr). M° Bibliothèque François Mitterrand. **Open** phone for details.

Piscine Butte-aux-Cailles

5 pl Paul-Verlaine, 13th (01.45.89.60.05). M° Place d'Italie. **Open** 7-8am, 11.30am-1pm, 4.30-6.30pm Tue; 7am-6.30pm Wed; 7-8am, 11.30am-6pm Thur, Fri; 7-8am, 10am-6pm Sat; 8am-5.30pm Sun. **Admission** €2.60; €1.50 concessions. **Credit** AmEx, MC, V.
This listed complex, built in the 1920s, has one main indoor pool and two outdoor pools. The water is a warm 28°C, thanks to the natural sulphurous spring.

Piscine Georges-Vallery

148 av Gambetta, 20th (01.40.31.15.20). M° Porte des Lilas. **Open** 10am-5pm Mon, Wed, Fri; 10am-10pm Tue, Thur; 9am-5pm Sat, Sun. **Admission** €2.60; €1.50 concessions. **Credit** (€15 minimum) MC, V.
Built for the 1924 Olympics, this complex features a retractable Plexiglas roof, a 50m pool and one for kids. It reopened in 2005 after renovation.

Piscine Jean-Taris

16 rue Thouin, 5th (01.55.42.81.90). M° Cardinal Lemoine. **Open** 7-8am, 11.30am-1pm Tue, Thur;

7-8am, 11.30am-5.15pm Wed; 7-8am, 11.30am-1pm, 5-7.45pm Fri; 7am-5.15pm Sat; 8am-5.15pm Sun. **Admission** €2.60; €1.50 concessions. **Credit** V. **Map** p408 J8.
This 25m pool has huge bay windows overlooking a sloping garden, with the Panthéon visible just above the trees. Mixed showers and locker area.

Piscine Pontoise Quartier Latin

18 rue de Pontoise, 5th (01.55.42.77.88/www. clubquartierlatin.com). M° Maubert Mutualité. **Open** 7-8.30am, 12.15-1.30pm, 4.30-8pm, 8.15-11.45pm Mon, Tue; 7-8.30am, 11.30am-7.30pm, 8.15-11.45pm Wed; 7-8.30am, 12.15-1.30pm, 4.30-7.15pm, 9-11.45pm Thur; 7-8.45am, noon-1.30pm, 4.30-8pm, 9-11.45pm Fri; 10am-7pm Sat; 8am-7pm Sun. **Admission** €3.80; €3.35 concessions; €9 for all 9-11.45pm. **No credit cards**. **Map** p408 K7.
A beautiful art deco pool with two mezzanine levels. It has private locker rooms, plus night swimming to underwater music. Small fee for lockers.

Piscine Suzanne-Berlioux

Forum des Halles, 10 pl de la Rotonde, 1st (01.42.36.98.44). M° Les Halles. **Open** 11.30am-10pm Mon, Tue, Thur, Fri; 10am-10pm Wed; 10am-7pm Sat, Sun. **Admission** €3.80; €3 under-16s. **Credit** (€8 minimum) MC, V. **Map** p404 J5.
This 50m pool with its own tropical greenhouse is good for lap swimming – but there are no lockers (check in your belongings with the attendants).

Tennis & table tennis

It used to be impossible to reserve a city-run court unless you had a special card. But thanks to the new Paris Tennis system, you can register a password and reserve a court online (www.tennis.paris.fr) or by phone on 01.71.71.70.70. Fees are €6.50 per hour; €12.50 for indoor courts. Among the 41 municipal courts, the six at the **Jardin du Luxembourg** (01.43.25.79.18) are good, but there's a better selection at the **Centre Sportif La Faluère** (route de la Pyramide, 12th, 01.43.74.40.93) in the Bois de Vincennes, with 19 courts.

To find public table-tennis tables in parks around town, consult the *Guide du Sport* (*see p330*). Club information is available online at www.paristt.com.

Club Forest Hill

4 rue Louis-Armand, 15th (01.40.60.10.00/www. aquaboulevard.com). M° Balard/RER Bd Victor. **Open** 9am-11pm daily. **Admission** varies. **No credit cards**. **Map** p406 A10.
Tennis, table-tennis and other racquet sports at most of the dozen branches in and around Paris.

Centre Sportif Suzanne-Lenglen

2 rue Louis-Armand, 15th (01.44.26.26.50). M° Balard. **Open** 7am-10pm Mon-Fri; 7am-7pm Sat, Sun. **Admission** from €3. **No credit cards**.
14 courts, two of which are covered.

Theatre

Racine, check; Molière, check; and there's plenty of political material, too.

Paris is rich in dramatic history. From moody medieval plays to revolutionary street theatre in 1968, French drama has always mirrored, shaped and commented on French society. Paris has led the pack in the development of new acting styles, popular dramatic movements and landmark theatre buildings.

Two stalwarts of theatrical tradition, the **Comédie Française** on the Right Bank and the **Théâtre de la Huchette** on the Left, have repertoires that have defined French drama, from the neo-classicists to the Theatre of the Absurd. Beyond these, nearly-native Peter Brook still reigns as an influential director at **Les Bouffes du Nord**, featuring smart programming with global flair. To the east, in the Bois de Vincennes, the **Cartoucherie** is a factory remade as a theatre commune that's home to five resident companies, accessible by a theatre bus.

Just south of Bastille is the petite **Théâtre de l'Opprimé**, a pocket-sized theatre with lofty productions. There are often more actors on stage than there are people in the audience, but the company tackles important issues, and demonstrates directorial and comedic prowess. (For more experimental theatres, such as the legendary **Café de la Gare**, *see pp278-280* **Cabaret, Circus & Comedy**.)

Outside the centre, the **Théâtre Gérard-Philipe** (55 bd Jules Guesde, 93207 St-Denis, 01.48.13.70.00, www.theatregerardphilipe.com), housed in a century-old building, offers quality fare for the 2006 spring season, ranging from Brecht to the Et Mois Alors? festival for youngsters. In the north-east, the **MC93 Bobigny** (1 bd Lénine, 93000 Bobigny, 01.41.60.72.72, www.mc93.com) is a slick institution dedicated to promoting global cross-cultural exchange.

Productions in English, German and Spanish come to the **Odéon**, Bouffes du Nord, **Théâtre de la Cité Internationale** and the stage at the **Centre Georges Pompidou** (www.cnac-gp.com), and **Sudden Théâtre** (14bis rue Ste-Isaure, 18th, 01.42.62.35.00, www.suddentheatre.fr) usually includes a couple of works in English each season. Numbers of local English-language troupes, though, have dwindled. **Dear Conjunction Theatre Company** (6 rue Arthur-Rozier, 19th, 01.42.41.69.65) is the main source of anglophone

theatre. Shakespeare in English is performed in June at the Bois de Boulogne's **Théâtre de Verdure du Jardin Shakespeare** (08.20.00.75.75) by London's Tower Theatre Company (www.towertheatre.org.uk).

TICKETS AND INFORMATION

For details of scheduling and programming, look in the Theatre section of the weekly *L'Officiel des Spectacles*. Further information can be found at www.parisvoice.com. Tickets can be bought at the theatres directly, at **Fnac** or the **Virgin Megastore** (for both, *see p244*) and at www.theatreonline.com. Check www.theatresprives.com for half-price tickets to performances at many of the private theatres during the first week of a new show. Two agencies that sell same-day tickets at half price are **Kiosque de la Madeleine** (15 pl de la Madeleine, 8th, closed Mon); and **Kiosque Montparnasse** (parvis de la Gare Montparnasse, 15th, closed Mon). These agency tickets, however, tend to be for commercial offerings. Queues can be long, and there's no way to contact the kiosks by phone or internet. For students, special subscriptions are available at many theatres, and almost all offer same-day rates with significant reductions.

Right Bank

Les Bouffes du Nord

37bis bd de la Chapelle, 10th (01.46.07.34.50/ www.bouffesdunord.com). M° La Chapelle. **Box office** 11am-6pm Mon-Sat. Closed until Sept 2006. **Admission** €8-€24.50. **Credit** MC, V. **Map** p404 K2. Theatre worshippers cannot come to Paris without paying tribute to director Peter Brook, whose experimental company CICT returns to a revamped venue from September 2006 onwards. Stéphane Lissner's co-direction has added classical music and opera.

Cartoucherie de Vincennes

route du Champ de Manoeuvre, bois de Vincennes, 12th. M° Château de Vincennes then shuttle bus or bus 112. Five independent theatres in old munitions warehouses. *See p338* **If you go down to the woods.**

Comédie Française

www.comedie-francaise.fr. **Salle Richelieu** *2 rue Richelieu, 1st (08.25.10.16.80/01.44.58.15.15). M° Palais Royal Musée du Louvre.* **Box office** 11am-6.30pm daily.

Admission €10-€35. *1hr before show* €5 for all (cheapest seats only); €10 under-27s. **Credit** AmEx, MC, V. **Map** p403 H5.

Studio Theatre *galerie du Carrousel du Louvre, 99 rue de Rivoli, 1st (01.44.58.98.54/ 01.44.58.98.58). Mº Palais Royal Musée du Louvre.* **Box office** 2-5pm on day. **Admission** €10-€35. **Credit** MC, V. **Map** p403 H5.

Théâtre du Vieux Colombier *21 rue du Vieux Colombier, 6th (01.44.39.87.00/01.44.39.87.01). Mº St-Sulpice.* **Box office** 1-6pm Mon, Sun; 11am-7pm Tue-Sat. **Admission** €14-€35. *1hr before show* €10 under-27s. **Credit** MC, V. **Map** p407 G7.

The gilded mother of all French theatres, the Comédie Française turns out season after season of classics, as well as lofty new productions. The red velvet and gold-flecked Salle Richelieu is located right by the Palais-Royal; under the same umbrella are the Studio, a black box inside the Carrousel du Louvre, and the Théâtre du Vieux Colombier. The line-up for 2006 includes *L'Amour Médecin* and *Le Sicilien ou l'Amour Peintre*; their author Molière suffered a fatal coughing fit while performing the latter here 333 years ago. **Photo** *right*.

Théâtre de l'Athénée-Louis Jouvet

7 rue Boudreau, square de l'Opéra Louis Jouvet, 9th (01.53.05.19.19/www.athenee-theatre.com). Mº Opéra. **Box office** 1-7pm Mon-Sat. **Admission** €6-€30. **Credit** MC, V. **Map** p403 G4.

This theatre is among the most beautiful in France, its Italianate decor like the interior of a jewellery box. The Athénée's mission is to stage new spins on clas-

If you go down to the woods

Past the Château and the Parc Floral, hidden deep in the Bois de Vincennes, is a drama-lover's paradise, an idyllic gathering of five theatres which provides performance space for relentlessly new, exciting spectacles: the **Cartoucherie**. This ex-army munitions warehouse (note the stone guard's hut as you enter the grounds) could not be better located; there are bucolic meadows all around, a rope swing and stables.

The best known of the quintet is the **Théâtre du Soleil** (01.43.74.87.63, www.theatre-du-soleil.fr), home to a troupe that was born in the political strife of the mid-1960s. Since then, the group has been producing unabashedly political, technically decadent spectacles at the rate of one every three or four years. The rehearsal process is long and thorough, and includes extensive international research done by the whole team. The Soleil runs as a collective (everyone is included in all aspects of production, from set-building to music-making), but the productions are largely shaped by de facto leader Ariane Mnouchkine, daughter of a Russian film producer; not only does she serve as director, she even dishes up food during intermissions.

The Théâtre du Soleil's work is generally Brechtian in nature, a true example of epic theatre; using puppets, masks and onstage musicians to distance the spectators, the troupe creates an arena of reflection. The stories they tell focus on such topics as ancient Chinese myths, contemporary refugee crises and more. When the company is in Paris (as opposed to being on tour) they are a must-see; but even if your visit doesn't coincide with one of theirs, Soleil's bravura 2003 puppet work *Tambours sur la Digue* is available as a DVD on the Arte label and is well worth picking up.

The four other residents are equally inspiring. The **Théâtre de l'Aquarium** (01.43.74.99.61, www.theatredelaquarium. com) was started in 1963 by students at the Ecole Normale Supérieure. From that upper-crust background they delved into the realm of radical street theatre. The **Théâtre de la Tempête** (01.43.28.36.36, www.la-tempete.fr) derives its name from Aimé Césaire's adaptation of Shakespeare's play *The Tempest*. Founded in 1970, today it is led by director/playwright Philippe Adrien. In their two performance spaces, the Tempête produce new plays from around the globe as well as contemporary French works. Finally, the **Théâtre de l'Epée de Bois** (01.48.08.39.74) and the **Théâtre du Chaudron** (01.43.28.97.04) complete the Cartoucherie quintet. June 2006 sees the Rencontres à la Cartoucherie, a gathering of more than 150 actors, writers and directors meeting to discuss the state of performance and theatre's role in society.

Performing in sheds, old warehouses and factories on the outskirts of town, these five troupes have revised not only the purpose of theatre but the definition of dramatic spaces. For spectators, the results of this are a free bus through the woods to a beautiful forest setting, home-made soup and bread in the lobby, a starlit backdrop – and some challenging, politically committed, first-class theatre.

The **Comédie Française**, seen from Jean-Michel Othoniel's métro entrance. *See p337*.

Arts & Entertainment

Lovely **Théâtre de l'Athénée**. *See p338.*

sic works; the 2006 season wraps up with Genet's *Le Bagne* and Bizet's *La Carmencita*. **Photo** *above.*

Théâtre de la Bastille

76 rue de la Roquette, 11th (01.43.57.42.14/ www.theatre-bastille.com). M° Voltaire. **Box office** 10am-6pm Mon-Fri; 2-6pm Sat. **Admission** €12.50-€19. **Credit** MC, V. **Map** p409 N6.
Effervescent, exotic productions are emblematic of the kind of spirit found here; the Bastille is a little smaller, a little edgier, and a little funkier than many of the more grand Parisian theatres.

Théâtre National de Chaillot

1 pl du Trocadéro, 16th (01.53.65.30.00/www. theatre-chaillot.fr). M° Trocadéro. **Box office** 11am-7pm Mon-Sat. **Admission** €9-€39. **Credit** MC, V. **Map** p402 B4.
Get here early and grab a cocktail; the lobby has a huge window with an Eiffel Tower view. Highlights for 2006 include director Jean-François Peyret's *Le Cas de Sophie K* from late April to late May, alternating with a pair of Bernard Noël monologues, *Anna et Gramsci*. The three auditoria range from an intimate, experimental space to a 2,800-seater.

Théâtre de l'Opprimé

78 rue du Charolais, 12th (01.43.40.44.44). M° Dugommier. **Box office** 1hr before show. **Admission** €10-€15. **No credit cards. Map** p409 P9.
This small theatre with great vision borrows its name – and vision – from Brazil's Augusto Boal,

who believed that theatre can change the world. The repertory is largely contemporary, the methods are inspired by Boal, and the troupe offers workshops in his technique and teachings.

Théâtre de la Ville

2 pl du Châtelet, 4th (01.42.74.22.77/www.theatre delaville-paris.com). M° Châtelet. **Box office** 11am-7pm Mon; 11am-8pm Tue-Sat. **Admission** €11.50-€30. **Credit** MC, V. **Map** p408 J6.
The 'city theatre' turns out the most consistently innovative and stimulating programming in Paris. Instead of running a standard rep company, the house imports music, dance and theatre productions, ranging from the classics to the avant-garde.

Left Bank

Odéon, Théâtre de L'Europe

pl de l'Odéon, 6th (01.44.85.40.00/bookings 01.44.85.40.40/www.theatre-odeon.fr). M° Porte de Clichy. **Box office** *By phone* 11am-6.30pm Mon-Sat. *On site* 2hrs before show. **Admission** €13-€26. **Credit** MC, V. **Map** p410 H7.
In May 1968 the Odéon was occupied by striking students and workers, a black anarchist flag was flown from the roof, and a banner declaring 'L'Odéon est ouvert' was draped over its sculpted façade. For the last three years, the Odéon has again been sheathed, but is all set to re-open after its €30 million renovation in late April 2006 with *Un Songe* by Georges Lavaudant (after Shakespeare). Until then, the company lives on, producing consistently smart, well-executed productions at the Ateliers Berthier, the space where the Paris Opéra rehearse.

Théâtre de la Cité Internationale

21 bd Jourdan, 14th (01.43.13.50.50/www.theatrede lacite.com). RER Cité Universitaire. **Box office** 2-7pm Mon-Fri. **Admission** €12.50-€21. **Credit** MC, V.
A polished professional theatre on the campus of the Cité Universitaire, the Théâtre de la Cité displays an international flair worthy of its setting. The 2006 season includes Strindberg's *Le Songe* (*A Dream Play*) and Rodrigo Garcia's monologues on *Borges & Goya*. In addition to the main theatre and dance season, the prestigious Ecole du Théâtre National de Strasbourg occupies the stage for a short stint each summer.

Théâtre de la Huchette

23 rue de la Huchette, 5th (01.43.26.38.99). M° St-Michel or Cluny La Sorbonne. **Box office** 5-9pm Mon-Sat. **Admission** €20; €15 concessions. **Credit** MC, V. **Map** p410 J7.
Eugene Ionesco's absurdist classic *La Cantatrice Chauve* ('The Bald Soprano') premiered in Paris in 1950; Nicolas Bataille first staged the play at this tiny theatre in 1957. Although the actors have changed, the same production plays, on a double bill (€28/ €20) with another of Ionesco's plays, *La Leçon*. Each play runs just short of an hour. A reasonable level of French should get you through the evening.

Trips Out of Town

Honfleur. *See p361*.

Trips Out of Town

Châteaux, cathedrals and country retreats – to say nothing of the wine.

In this chapter we've listed the local tourist information centres, which can provide further information about specific areas and their attractions. For the main entries – for the cathedrals, châteaux and other sightseeing attractions – we have included details of opening times, admission and transport, but be aware that these can change without notice: always phone to check.

For a list of main line railway stations in Paris and their destinations, *see p367.*

Day Trips

Auvers-sur-Oise

This charming rural retreat was where Vincent Van Gogh spent his last weeks, painting frantically. Many of his most well-known works, of crows over wheatfields, or the local church, were completed here and are now displayed on illustrated panels around the village, letting you compare his artistic vision to the locations today.

The tiny attic room at the **Auberge Ravoux**, that Van Gogh rented in May 1890 for 3.50 francs, is open to the public and gives an evocative sense of the artist's time here. Previous Auvers residents had included fellow artists Camille Pissarro, Paul Cézanne and Charles-François Daubigny, whose widow was still living in the village when Van Gogh arrived – he painted their garden. Today you can explore **Daubigny's museum** (Manoir des Colombières, 01.30.36.80.20) and his studio (61 rue Daubigny, 01.34.48.03.03), which is still decorated with his murals.

A further attraction here, linked with the artistic community of the day, is the **Absinthe Museum** (44 rue Callé, 01.30.36.83.26), a rather modest collection of art and artefacts related to the notorious drink. Banned in France since 1915, the green concoction is not available at the replica café-bar upstairs.

Local artistic legacy has not been overlooked by Auvers' main historical attraction, either. The 17th-century **Château d'Auvers** (rue de Léry, 01.34.48.48.45, www.chateau-auvers.fr) features a walk-through tour (for which visitors must wear a special helmet) themed around the Impressionists and their surroundings.

Auberge Ravoux

52 rue du Général-de-Gaulle, 95430 Auvers-sur-Oise (01.30.36.60.60). **Open** 10am-6pm Tue-Sun. **Admission** €5. **No credit cards**.

Where to eat & stay

You can always do as Van Gogh might have done, and dine at the **Auberge Ravoux** (*see above*) – these days they serve two traditional courses for €26, three for €33. Otherwise, try **La Guinguette** (Château d'Auvers, rue de Léry, 01.34.48.43.29), which does lunch for €15. The **Hostellerie du Nord** (6 rue Général-de-Gaulle, 01.30.36.70.74, www.hostelleriedunord.fr, closed dinner Sun, lunch €43, dinner €55) has master chef Joël Boilleaut running the kitchen; upstairs are eight comfy rooms (€95-€185).

Getting there

By car
35km (22 miles) north from Paris by A15, exit 7, then N184, exit Méry-sur-Oise for Auvers.

By train
From Gare du Nord, changing at St Ouen L'Aumone (whole journey takes about 1hr).

Tourist information

Office de Tourisme
Manoir des Colombières, rue de la Sansonne, 95430 Auvers-sur-Oise (01.30.36.10.06/www.auvers-sur-oise.com). **Open** 9.30am-12.30pm, 2-5pm (Apr-Oct until 6pm) Tue-Sun.

Chantilly & Senlis

From the 14th century until 1897, the town of **Chantilly** was the domain of the Princes of Condé, the cousins of the French kings. As well as its impressive **château**, Chantilly has a rich equestrian history, with its hunting forests and prestigious horse-racing centres.

The cream-coloured château stands as a fine example of the French Renaissance, its domes and turrets set high above the surrounding lake. In reality, much of the original palace was destroyed during the Revolution, leaving the main wing to be reconstructed in the 19th century by Henri d'Orléans, Duc d'Aumale, to house his collection of paintings and rare books.

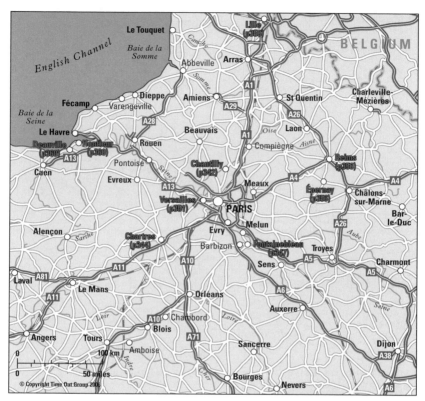

When the duke died in 1897, he bequeathed the Domaine de Chantilly – including the Grand Stables, the Hippodrome and the 15,000-acre forest – to the Institute de France on the condition that the château be opened to the public as the Musée Condé, and that none of the artworks would be moved or loaned to other museums. His remarkable collection is complemented by the surrounding **park**, beautifully landscaped by André Le Nôtre (of Versailles fame).

Thanks to the duke's foresight, the unique character of Chantilly and its forest have been preserved. It's still an important equestrian centre, known for the prestigious Prix de Diane Hermès at the Hippodrome in June.

The Grandes Ecuries ('great stables') at the château were commissioned in 1719 by Prince Louis-Henri de Bourbon (who believed that he would be reincarnated as a horse), and once housed 240 horses, 500 hunting dogs and a hundred palfreys and hunting birds. It was only lightly battered during the Revolution, and then became one of Napoléon's equestrian

training grounds. In 1982 the great horseman Yves Bienaimé restored the stables and turned them into the **Musée Vivant du Cheval**. The Bienaimé family has also restored and reopened the **Potager des Princes**, the princes' old vegetable garden.

The **Forêt de Chantilly** is full of hiking and cycling trails. A pleasant walk of around seven kilometres (4.5 miles) circles the four small lakes, the Etangs de Commelles, and passes the Château de la Reine Blanche, a mill converted in the 1820s into a pseudo-medieval hunting lodge. Steer clear of the sand alleys that criss-cross the forest by the hippodrome; they're used each morning to train the racehorses. For trail details, ask at the Office National des Forêts (1 av de Sylvie, 03.44.57.03.88, www.onf.fr).

Senlis, nine kilometres (5.5 miles) east of Chantilly, is known as the birthplace of the French monarchy – though little else has happened since the tenth century. Its historic centre has half-timbered houses, fine mansions, a Gothic cathedral and the remains of Gallo-Roman city walls and amphitheatre.

Château de Chantilly

Musée Condé, Chantilly (03.44.62.62.62/ www.chateaudechantilly.com). **Open** *mid Mar-Apr, Sept-Nov* 10am-12.45pm, 2-6pm Mon, Wed-Fri; 10am-6pm Sat, Sun. *May-Aug* 10am-6pm Mon, Wed-Sun. *Nov-mid Mar* 10.30am-12.45pm, 2-5pm Mon, Wed-Fri; 10.30am-5pm Sat, Sun. **Admission** €8; €7 12-17s; €3.50 4-12s; free under-4s. **Credit** MC, V.
Set in beautiful surroundings, the château's main attraction is the remarkable collection of paintings and drawings at the Musée Condé. It includes three paintings by Raphael, Filippo Lippi's *Esther and Assuarus*, and the *Très Riches Heures du Duc de Berry*, a medieval Book of Hours. Usually it'll be a facsimile on show.

Château park

Open *mid Mar-Oct* 10am-8pm Mon, Wed-Sun; 10am-12.45pm, 2-8pm Tue. *Nov-mid Mar* 10.30am-6pm Mon, Wed-Sun. **Admission** *Park only* €4; €3.50 12-17s; €2.50 4-11s; free under-4s. *Combined ticket* (boat tour, carriage ride, mini-train rides) from €9. **Credit** MC, V.
The main section of the château's sprawling park, designed by royal landscape architect Le Nôtre, features traditional French formal parterres and an extensive canal system, where visitors can see the park from electric-powered boats. (You can also tour around by horse-drawn carriage or aboard a mini-train.) Get off the beaten path to explore the English Garden, the Temple of Venus, the Island of Love, the kangaroo zoo and the original hamlet that inspired Marie-Antoinette to build her own version at Versailles.

Musée Vivant du Cheval

Les Grandes Écuries, Chantilly (03.44.57.40.40/ www.musee-vivant-du-cheval.fr). **Open** *Apr, July-Oct* 10.30am-6.30pm Mon, Wed-Fri; 10.30am-7pm Sat, Sun. *May, June* 10.30am-6.30pm Mon, Wed-Fri; 10.30am-5.30pm Tue; 10.30am-7pm Sat, Sun. *Nov-Mar* 2-6pm Mon, Wed-Fri; 10.30am-6.30pm Sat, Sun. **Admission** €8.50; €7.50 students; €7 13-17s; €6 4-12s; free under-4s. **Credit** MC, V.
More than 40 breeds live at these historic stables, a real treat for horse-mad youngsters. As opposed to the formal showmanship displayed at Versailles, this museum is an interactive affair where kids can pet the ponies and everyone gets to learn how the horses are trained to perform in the ring. There are demonstrations every day at 11.30am, 3.30pm and, in summer, also at 5.15pm.

Potager des Princes

Parc de la Faisanderie, 17 rue de la Faisanderie, Chantilly (03.44.57.40.40/www.potagerdesprinces. com). **Open** *Apr-mid Oct* 2-5pm Mon, Wed-Fri; 11am-12.30pm, 2-5.30pm Sat, Sun. **Admission** €7; €5.50 4-12s; free under-4s. **Credit** MC, V.
The restored princes' kitchen garden is today a 19th-century English garden with vegetable plots, trained fruit trees, a small farmyard, and an open-air theatre next to the lake. It plays host to musical performances all summer.

Where to eat & stay

Try the home-style cooking at **Le Goutillon** (61 rue du Connétable, 03.44.58.01.00, main courses €20, lunch €11-€19), a cosy wine bistro on the high street. **La Capitainerie** (03.44.67.40.00, lunch €22, dinner €55-€77) offers good French food in the old château kitchens. To sample Chantilly whipped cream, invented by one of the princes in the late 1700s, stop by for afternoon tea at **Aux Goûters Champêtres** (03.44.57.46.21, closed mid Nov-mid Mar) in the *hameau* at the château.
One of the only hotels in the town centre is the **Hotel du Parc Best Western** (36 av du Maréchal Joffre, 03.44.58.20.00, www.hotel-parc-chantilly.com, doubles €100), somewhat lacking in charm but equipped with the essentials for a good night's rest.

Getting there

By car
40km (25 miles) from Paris by N16 (direct) or A1 (Chantilly exit).

By train
SNCF Chantilly-Gouvieux from Gare du Nord (30 mins), then 5min walk to town, 20mins to château. Some trains stop at Creil, then loop back to Chantilly.

Tourist information

Office de Tourisme
60 av Maréchal Joffre, 60500 Chantilly (03.44.67.37.37/www.chantilly-tourisme.com). **Open** 9.30am-12.30pm, 1.30-5.30pm Mon-Sat.

Office de Tourisme
pl du parvis Notre-Dame, 60302 Senlis (03.44.53.06.40/www.ville-senlis.fr). **Open** 10am-12.30pm, 2-6.15pm Mon-Sat; 10.30am-1pm, 2-6.15pm Sun. From 1st Nov to end of Feb closes at 5pm.

Chartres

Seen from afar, the mismatched spires and brilliant silhouette of **Chartres cathedral** burst up out of the Beauce cornfields and dominate the skyline of this otherwise modest town located some 90 kilometres (56 miles) south-west of Paris.

One of the finest examples of Gothic architecture impresses millions of tourists today – and makes you wonder: what would it have been like to have walked here as a fervent believer and seen it 800 years ago?

Chartres was a pilgrimage site long before the cathedral was even built, ever since the Sacra Camisia (said to be the Virgin Mary's birthing garment) was donated in 876 by the

**Cathédrale
Notre-Dame**
at Chartres.
See p346.

king. The sublime stained glass of the cathedral, and its doorways bristling with sculpture, embody a complete medieval world view, in which earthly society and civic life reflect the divine order.

The town of Chartres is an attractive tangle of narrow, medieval streets on the banks of the river Eure that makes for a pleasant post-cathedral walk. Two sights merit mentioning: the **Musée des Beaux-Arts** (29 Cloître Notre-Dame, 02.37.90.45.80), tucked inside the former bishop's palace, housing a collection of 18th-century French paintings by Watteau and others; and the **Memorial to Jean Moulin**, the legendary figure of the Resistance, a war-time prefect of Chartres until dismissed by the Vichy government due to his refusal to cooperate with the Nazi authorities. He became de Gaulle's right-hand man on the ground, and died under torture in Lyon in 1943. Moulin's memorial stands a ten-minute walk west of the cathedral, at the corner of rue Collin d'Arleville and boulevard de la Résistance.

Cathédrale Notre-Dame

pl de la Cathédrale (02.37.21.59.08). **Open** *Cathedral* Jan-Apr, Nov, Dec 8am-7pm daily; May-Oct 8am-8pm daily. *Tower* May-Aug 9am-12.30pm, 2-5.30pm Mon-Sat; 2-5.30pm Sun; Sept-Apr 9am-12.30pm, 2-4.30pm Mon-Sat; 2-4.30pm Sun. **Admission** free. *Tower* €5. **No credit cards**.

The west front, or 'Royal Portal', of this High Gothic cathedral modelled in part on St-Denis (*see p173*) has three richly sculpted doorways. Inside, there's another era of sculpture, represented in the lively 16th-century scenes of the life of Christ that surround the choir. Note the circular labyrinth of black and white stones in the floor – such mazes used to exist in many cathedrals, but most have been destroyed. The cathedral is, above all, famed for its stained-glass windows depicting biblical scenes, saints and medieval trades in brilliant 'Chartres blue', punctuated by rich reds. Climb the tower for a fantastic view.

English-language tours, some of which are still given by lecturer Malcolm Miller – one of the world's most knowledgeable and entertaining experts on Chartres cathedral – are available from April to November (noon & 2.45pm Mon-Sat, €10). **Photo** *p345*.

Where to eat & stay

Tourists flock to the **Café Serpent** (2 cloître Notre-Dame, 02.37.21.68.81), in the shadow of the cathedral – if the café's full, there are plenty of other easy options nearby that you can try. For restaurant cuisine with a riverside view, **L'Estocade** (1 rue de la Porte Guillaume, 02.37.34.27.17, closed Mon and lunch daily, set menus €24-€40) is a decent option. For fireside treats, **La Vieille Maison** (5 rue au Lait, 02.37.34.10.67, closed Mon & Sun, set menu €29 & €46) serves up modern and traditional French fare in its warm and cosy 14th-century dining room.

Two chain hotels on the ring road, not far from the town centre, are **Grand Monarque** (22 pl des Epars, 02.37.18.15.15, www.bw-grand-monarque.com, doubles €115-€128) and the more basic **Ibis Centre** (pl Drouaise, 02.37.36.06.36, doubles €62-€71), which also has regular weekend rates of €46.

Château de Fontainebleau.

Getting there

By car
90km (56 miles) from Paris by A10, then A11.

By train
Direct from Gare Montparnasse (1hr).

Tourist information

Office de Tourisme
pl de la Cathédrale, 28000 Chartres (02.37.18.26.26/ www.chartres-tourisme.com). **Open** *Apr-Sept* 9am-7pm Mon-Sat; 9.30am-5.30pm Sun. *Oct-Mar* 10am-6pm Mon-Sat; 10am-1pm, 2.30-4.30pm Sun.

Fontainebleau

Home to 14 French kings since François I, Fontainebleau ('Fon-ten-blow') was once a sort of aristocratic club where gentlemen of the day came to hunt and learn the art of chivalry. The town grew up around the **château** in the 19th century, and today is a pleasant and lively place to visit, dominated by three major elements: the sumptuous royal palace that dominates the town centre; the hunting forest and its rock formations; and the INSEAD business school (the 'European Harvard') on the forest edge, which adds a cosmopolitan touch.

The château is bite-sized compared to the sprawling grandeur of Versailles, but has been completely furnished since its restoration. The style adopted by the Italian artists brought in by François I is still visible, as are the additions put in by later rulers – Napoléon redecorated

much in Empire style before leaving for exile on Elba from the front courtyard, the Cour des Adieux. The château gardens, park and grand canal, all free to enter, are also worth exploring.

The 42,000-acre **Forêt de Fontainebleau** is part of the Gâtinas regional nature park, which has bizarre geological formations and diverse wildlife. Its ravines, rocky outcrops and mix of forest and sandy heath where François I liked to hunt is the wildest slice of nature to be found near Paris and is very popular with weekenders for walking, cycling, riding and rock climbing. There are a number of well-marked trails, such as the GR1 from Bois-le-Roi train station, but more serious yompers would be better off with an official map such as the TOP25 IGN series 2417-OT, which covers the entire forest, highlighting climbing sites, campsites and picnic areas.

Trail maps are on sale at the Fontainebleau tourist office (*see p348*), which rents out bicycles (€20 per day) and has details on the nearby villages of Barbizon and Moret-sur-Loing. Bikes can also be rented from La Petite Reine (32 rue Sablons, 01.60.74.57.57, www.la-petite-reine.fr), plus baby seats, at around €16 per day – passport or €300 deposit required. **La Bleausière** riding school (06.82.01.21.18, la.bleausiere.free.fr), in Barbizon, on the edge of the Fontainebleau forest, offers year-round short and long guided tours for adults and children of all levels.

Château de Fontainebleau
pl Général de Gaulle (01.60.71.50.70/www.musee-chateau-fontainebleau.fr). **Open** *Château* June-Sept 9.30am-6pm Mon, Wed-Sun; Oct-May 9.30am-5pm

Mon, Wed-Sun. *Park & gardens* Mar, Apr, Oct 9am-6pm daily; May-Sept 9am-7pm daily; Nov-Feb 9am-5pm daily. **Admission** *Château* €5.50; €4 18-25s; free under-18s, CM. *Park & gardens* free. **Credit** MC, V.

This former hunting lodge is fascinating for the mish-mash of styles left by centuries of additions and changes. In 1528, François I brought in Italian artists and craftsmen to help architect Gilles le Breton transform a neglected lodge into the finest Italian Mannerist palace in France. This style, noted for its grotesqueries, contorted figures and crazy fireplaces, is still visible in the Ballroom and Long Gallery. Henri IV then added a tennis court, Louis XIII built a double-horseshoe entrance staircase, and Louis XIV and XV added some classical trimmings. Napoléon and Louis-Philippe also spent a fortune on redecoration.

The château gardens include Le Nôtre's formal Grand Parterre, the Jardin de Diane and a carp pond in the Jardin Anglais. There is also an informal château park just outside, with green lawns and a canal where locals fish and visitors stop to picnic. Other activities on the site include dinghy paddling on the lake and horse-drawn carriage rides. **Photos** *p346 and p347.*

Where to eat & stay

Rue Grande is lined with restaurants such as the inventive, stylish **Au Délice Impérial** (No.1, 01.64.22.20.70, main courses €17), and **Au Bureau** (No.12, 01.60.39.00.01, main courses €12), which has Tex-Mex specialities and global beers in a pub setting. DJs and bands comprise the evening agenda here. At No.92, picnickers can find excellent local cheese at **Fromagerie Barthélémy** (01.64.22.21.64).

For a blow-out meal, head for **Le Caveau des Ducs** (24 rue Ferrare, 01.64.22.05.05, lunch €19-€30, dinner €22-€39), with traditional French cuisine in a 17th-century interior of heavy oak tables and tapestries.

The charming **Hôtel de Londres** (1 pl Général-de-Gaulle, 01.64.22.20.21, www.hotel delondres.com, doubles €90-€150) is centrally located and has free, private parking. Some of the dozen rooms have balconies overlooking the château. Set in a 19th-century post house, the elegant **Hôtel Napoléon** (9 rue Grande, 01.60.39.50.50, www.hotelnapoleon-fontainebleau.com, doubles €125-€190) overlooks an interior garden, and provides decent meals at its restaurant, **La Table des Maréchaux** (set menu €28-€45).

Getting there

By car

60km (37 miles) from Paris by A6, then N7 (about 75mins). Beware of the likelihood of traffic jams when heading back to Paris on Sundays.

By train

Gare de Lyon to Fontainebleau-Avon (35mins), then bus AB (marked 'Château'). Ask for a Forfait Château de Fontainebleau (€20; €16 10-17s; €8 4-9s) at the Gare de Lyon; it includes train fare, bus connection, château entrance and audio guide.

Tourist information

Office de Tourisme

4 rue Royale, 77300 Fontainebleau (01.60.74.99.99/ www.fontainebleau-tourisme.com). **Open** *May-Oct* 10am-6pm Mon-Sat; 10am-12.30pm, 3-7pm Sun. *Nov-Apr* 10am-6pm Mon-Sat; 10am-1pm Sun.

Giverny

In 1883 Claude Monet moved his mistress and their eight children into a quaint pink-brick house in bucolic Giverny, and concentrated as much time on cultivating a beautiful garden here as painting the water lilies in it.

Monet was fascinated by light. The leader of the Impressionist movement – his *Impression: Sunrise* gave rise to the group's name in 1874 – thrived on outdoor scenes, whether along the Seine near Argenteuil or by the Thames in London. Having once seen the tiny village of Giverny from the window of a train, he was smitten. By 1890 he had bought his dream home and soon had a pond dug, bridges built and a tableau of greenery created. As Monet's eyesight began to fail, he produced endless impressions of his man-made paradise, each trying to capture how the leaves and water refracted light. He died here in 1926.

Of the hundreds of tourists who visit here on any given day, not all are art-lovers – there are no original Monets in the large studio and two-storey house, though there are the 32 Japanese woodblock prints collected by the artist. Most visitors are simply here for the lilies, and to have their picture taken beside them. (Giverny is overrun with visitors snapping each other.)

The garden, it must be said, is a masterpiece, its famous water-lily pond, weeping willows and Japanese bridge remarkably intact; and the charming house, the **Fondation Claude Monet**, is dotted with touching mementos. But once you're back in the village, be prepared for heated arguments over finding a table at one of the scarce eating places and long queues of impatient tourists almost everywhere you turn. Get here early or, alternatively, book ahead for dinner at the famous **Hôtel Baudy** museum-restaurant (81 rue Claude Monet, 02.32.21.10.03, set menu €18.50, closed 1 Nov-31 Mar), where Monet's American disciples (such as Willard Metcalf and Dawson-Watson) set up their easels for several decadent years, expanding the old

Flemish influences in Vieux-Lille – the **Nouvelle Bourse**. *See p350.*

hotel into an art-atelier extraordinaire, complete with ballroom, rose garden and tennis courts – Cézanne even stayed in one of the attic rooms for a month. After dinner, stay overnight in Giverny (booking essential; *see below*) and get to the Monet museum first thing in the morning. Up the road, the **Musée d'Art Américain de Giverny** (99 rue Claude-Monet, 02.32.51.94.65, www.maag.org) has a collection of works by the American Impressionist colony.

Fondation Claude Monet

84 rue Claude-Monet (02.32.51.28.21/www.fondation-monet.com). **Open** *Apr-Oct* 9.30am-6pm Tue-Sun. **Admission** *House & garden* €5.50; €4 students; €3 7s-13s; free under-7s. **Credit** AmEx, MC, V.

Where to stay

Les Rouges Gorges B&B (6 rue aux Juifs, 02.32.51.02.96, doubles €60), run by Eric and Christelle Carrière, has pretty country lodgings available. **Le Coin des Artistes** (65 rue Claude Monet, 02.32.21.36.77, doubles €58) is a comfortable B&B that doubles as an art gallery. For further suggestions, www.giverny.org provides links to hotels and B&Bs in the area.

Getting there

By car

80km (50 miles) west of Paris by A13 to Bonnières, then D201.

By train

Gare St-Lazare to Vernon (45mins), then 5km (3 miles) taxi ride or bus from the station.

Tourist information

Comité Départemental du Tourisme de l'Eure

3 rue du Commandant-Letellier, BP 367, 27003 Evreux cedex (02.32.62.04.27/www.cdt-eure.fr). **Open** 9am-12.30pm, 1.30-6pm Mon-Thur; 9am-1pm, 1.30-6pm Fri.

Closer to Brussels than it is to Paris and only 90 minutes from London on the Eurostar, the old Flemish city of Lille has been transformed from a grimy, northern industrial town with an identity crisis to a well-located cultural stronghold of cosmopolitan character. Key to this transformation was Lille's stint as a European Capital of Culture in 2004, which saw the renovation of landmark buildings in the restored old quarter of **Vieux Lille**. The separate development of a modern international train station, a new urban centre by top European architects (including Rem Koolhaas and Jean Nouvel) and a new métro system also point towards a dynamic city that's light years away from the one local hero Charles de Gaulle would have recognised.

Although part of France for 350 years, Lille (Rijsel in Flemish) is still redolent of a classic Flanders wool town. Stroll around cobbled streets amid the grand architecture of its lovely medieval centre and you could be in Ghent, not one of the biggest cities in France. An enjoyably confusing complex of main squares is the centrepiece of Vieux Lille: the interlinked Grand' Place (otherwise known as place du Général de Gaulle), place Rihour and place du Théâtre (*pictured p349*). City buses trundle incongruously over the worn cobblestones, temporarily stopping the flow of shoppers feeding in from the bright, commercial tributaries of rue Nationale, rue Esquermoise, rue de Béthune and rue Faidherbe. On and around these squares are Lille's main sights: the neo-Gothic cathedral **Notre-Dame-de-la-Treille** (rue de la Monnaie); pretty Gothic **Eglise St-Maurice** (rue de Paris) and, most attractive of all, the **Hospice Comtesse**. This former hospital, founded in the 12th century and rebuilt in the 18th, houses a museum of Flemish art, furniture and ceramics (32 rue de la Monnaie, 03.28.36.84.00, closed Tue), a lovely garden, chapel and concert venue.

The Flemish influence doesn't end there. The best Belgian beers are standard in most bars; mussels, oysters and rich sauces are the main features of an attractive local cuisine; and interesting shops purveying obscure collectables – a typical Belgian trait – dot a varied horizon of shopfronts. Said beers – perhaps a Kriek or Trappist variety – are poured into their own logoed glass and served with a 'S'il vous plaît' from the waiter, just as would be done in Belgium.

The infrastructure, though, is proudly French: a modern, two-line métro system links with a swish tramway and city bus network, connecting to the brash Euralille Eurostar/TGV station. Just over the bridge from the original 19th-century station of Gare Lille-Flanders, Euralille contains one of the biggest shopping malls in France, with 140 establishments spread over two levels.

French icons also provide the most interesting attractions outside the centre. The house where de Gaulle grew up, at 9 rue Princesse, just in from the Canal de la Deule, is a museum in his name, located in a distinctly Flemish neighbourhood. The French military architect Vauban was responsible for the star-shaped **Citadelle** (accessible by guided tour only – ask at the tourist office) across the canal.

One of the finest art collections in France is held at the **Palais des Beaux-Arts** (pl de la République, 03.20.06.78.00, closed Mon morning, all Tue), south of the city centre, with works by Rubens, El Greco, Goya and Delacroix. Unfortunately, the **Musée d'Art Moderne** (1 allée du Musée, 03.20.19.68.68, www.nordnet.fr/mam) is closed until late 2007.

One of the best times to visit the city is for La Braderie, thought to be Europe's second-biggest event (after Munich's Oktoberfest). For one weekend in early September, Lille becomes a huge flea market, with almost every central street lined with stalls and beer vendors offering *moules-frites*. The tradition dates back centuries, and as you try and make your way through the anarchic bartering, you feel you could almost be back in medieval times.

Where to eat, drink & stay

Flemish taverns typify the local dining scene: you can get attractive lunchtime deals on standard Belgian dishes. For something that's a little more adventurous, the landmark restaurant **A L'Huitrière** (3 rue Chats Bossus, 03.20.55.43.41, closed dinner Sun and 22 July-24 Aug, main courses €36, set menu Mon-Fri €43) is the gourmet choice in town; oysters and fish are the speciality. In a similar vein, the cheaper **L'Ecume des Mers** (10 rue de Pas, 03.20.54.95.40, main courses €45) provides quality seafood without skimping on style. For location and ambience, **L'Houblonnière** (42 pl du Général-de-Gaulle, 03.20.74.54.34, lunch €18, dinner €24) has a cosy upstairs dining room. Set back from the old town, **Le Sébastopol** (1 pl Sébastopol, 03.20.57.05.05, www.restaurant-sebastopol.fr, closed lunch Mon & Sat, dinner Sun, lunch €28, dinner €61) specialises in top-flight classic cuisine. Friendly and central **Alcide** (5 rue Debris St-Etienne, 03.20.12.06.95, closed dinner Sun, set menu €15-€33) does a fine job of whatever's on the set menu.

Most bars offer full menus twice a day. Venues can be wacky and arty, such as the

Maison du Moulin d'Or (31-33 pl du Théâtre, 03.20.55.00.10) and **L'Illustration** (18 rue Royale, 03.20.12.00.90), or more unpretentiously local, such as the downmarket but delightful **Le Vinci** (70 rue de l'Hôpital Militaire, 03.20.57.36.60).

As far as accommodation goes, for luxury and convenience you could do worse than stay at the **Crowne Plaza Lille** (335 bd de Leeds, 03.20.42.46.46, www.lille-crowneplaza.com, doubles €175-€235) by the Euralille station, with well-equipped rooms and a sauna. Mid-range, the **Hôtel de la Treille** (7-9 pl Louise de Bettignies, 03.20.55.45.46, doubles €86-€95) is comfortable and modern; **Hôtel Brueghel** (3-5 parvis St- Maurice, 03.20.06.06.69, www.hotel-brueghel.com, doubles €73-€86) is surprisingly attractive for the price. For budget lodgings head to place de la Gare's **Hôtel Faidherbe** (No.42, 03.20.06.27.93, doubles €30-€45) or **Hôtel Le Coq Hardi** (No.34, 03.20.06.05.89, doubles €32-€37).

Getting there

By car
210km (130 miles) north from Paris by A1.

By train
The TGV from Gare du Nord takes 1hr. The Eurostar from London takes 1hr 40mins.

The Fun King

The easiest, although not the cheapest, way to see Versailles is to get a **Passeport Versailles**. It allows quick access via Porte C to the main section of the château, the audio-guided tour of the Chambre du Roi, the Grand and Petit Trianon, the gardens and their displays. Buy the Passeport in advance from Fnac stores (*see p244*), tourist offices or any RER station (price of journey added to the ticket); or go directly to Porte C2 or D before 2pm. Those who hold a Carte Musées et Monuments (*see pXXX*) can enter via Porte B2. Those just wanting a day ticket must queue with the masses at Porte A. Any number of guided tours are available from Porte D; it's essential to book early that morning, and then meet by Porte F.

Passeport Versailles

Admission *Apr-Oct* €20; €6 10s-17s; free under-10s. *Nov-Mar* €15.50; €4 10s-17s; free under-10s.

Tourist information

Office du Tourisme de Lille
pl Rihour, 59800 Lille (03.59.57.94.00/www. lilletourism.com). **Open** 9.30am-6.30pm Mon-Sat; 10am-noon, 2-5pm Sun.

Versailles

Centuries of makeovers have made Versailles the most sumptuously clad **château** in the world – a veritable bouquet of over-the-top brilliance, and an absolute must-see. Architect Louis Le Vau first embellished the original building – a hunting lodge built in the centre of marshlands during Louis XIII's reign – after Louis XIV saw Vaux-le-Vicomte, the impressive residence of his finance minister, Nicolas Fouquet. The Sun King had the unlucky minister jailed and stole away not only his architect, but also his painter, Charles Le Brun, and his landscaper, André Le Nôtre, who turned the boggy marshland into terraces, parterres, fountains and lush groves.

After Le Vau's death in 1670, Jules Hardouin-Mansart took over as principle architect, transforming Versailles into the château we know today, dedicating the last 30 years of his life to adding the two main wings, the Cour des Ministres and the Chapelle Royale. In 1682 Louis moved himself and his court in – thereafter he rarely set foot in Paris. In the 1770s, Louis XV had Jacques-Ange Gabriel add the sumptuous Opéra Royal, used for concerts by the Centre de Musique Baroque (01.39.20.78.10). It still has the original spy holes Louis' bodyguards used to keep an eye on him. The expense of building and running Versailles cost France dear. With the fall of the monarchy in 1792, most of the furniture was lost but the château was saved from demolition after 1830 by Louis-Philippe.

Versailles has hosted the official signings of many historic treaties – European recognition of the United States, the unification of Germany in 1871, the division of Europe after 1918 – and is still used by the French government for major summits. In the gardens, the **Grand Trianon** accommodates heads of state.

The **gardens** are works of art in themselves, their ponds and statues once again embellished by a fully working fountain system. On summer weekends, the spectacular jets of water are set to music, a prelude to the occasional firework displays of the Fêtes de Nuit.

Beyond the gardens is the Grand Canal, where visitors can laze around in small boats, and the wooded parkland and sheep-filled pastures of the estate's park. Hidden here are the Grand Trianon, the **Petit Trianon** – and

Fit for a sun king: **Château de Versailles**. *See p353*.

Marie Antoinette's replica village, Hameau. Outside the château gates are the recently restored **Potager du Roi** (the Sun King's vegetable garden), and stables, now housing the **Académie du Spectacle Equestre**.

Versailles is currently undergoing a complete overhaul, notably in its entrance and ticketing area. The first phase won't be ready until 2010, so expect a little chaos for the next few years.

In the town of Versailles, grab a *Historical Places* brochure free from the tourist office (*see p356*) and explore. The Quartier St-Louis opposite the Potager was developed by Louis XV around the Cathédrale St-Louis. Just off rue d'Anjou are the Carrés St-Louis, four market squares surrounded by 18th-century boutiques housing galleries and antique shops. North-east of the château is the Quartier Notre-Dame, part of the 'new town' designed by the Sun King himself. Eglise Notre-Dame is where members of the royal family were baptised and married. Around the corner is the Marché Notre-Dame, a market square dating back to 1671 and restored in 1841, surrounded by restaurants and cafés. The covered market is closed on Mondays.

Bicycles can be rented from outside RER Versailles-Chantiers (pl Raymond Poincaré, 01.39.20.16.60) for €5 an hour or €12 a day.

Académie du Spectacle Equestre

Grandes Ecuries, Château de Versailles (01.39.02.07.14/www.acadequestre.fr).
Les Matinales des Ecuyers *(practice & visit)* **Open** *Mar-Dec* 9am-noon Tue-Fri; 11am-2pm Sat, Sun. **Admission** €8; €3 5-18s, students. **Credit** MC, V.
Reprise Musicale *(performance & visit)* **Open** *Mar-Dec* 2-3.30pm Sat, Sun. **Admission** €16; €7 under-18s, students. **Credit** MC, V.
Across from the château entrance is the Sun King's magnificent stables, restored in 2003. They house the Académie du Spectacle Equestre, which is responsible for the elaborate shows of tightly choreographed theatrics on horseback run by famous horse trainer Bartabas. Visitors can catch a show either on the weekends or at special evening performances (see website for details), or attend training sessions to see how the white horses and their young riders learn their tricks.

Château de Versailles

78000 Versailles (01.30.83.76.20/advance tickets 08.92.68.46.94/www.chateauversailles.fr). **Open** *Apr-Oct* 9am-6.30pm Tue-Sun. *Nov-Mar* 9am-5.30pm Tue-Sun. **Admission** €7.50; €5.30 after 3.30pm; free under-18s, CM, Passeport Versailles. **Credit** AmEx, DC, MC, V.
Versailles is a masterpiece – and it's almost always packed with visitors. Allow yourself a whole day to appreciate the sumptuous State Apartments, and the Hall of Mirrors, the highlights of any visit – and mainly accessible with just a day ticket (*see p351*

The Fun King). The Grand Appartement, where Louis XIV held court, consists of six gilded salons (Venus, Mercury, Apollo and so on), all opulent examples of baroque craftsmanship. No less luxurious, the Queen's Apartment includes the Queen's Bedroom, where royal births took place in full view of the court. Hardouin-Mansart's 75m-long (246ft) showpiece, the Hall of Mirrors, where a united Germany was proclaimed in 1871 and the Treaty of Versailles signed in 1919, is flooded with natural light from its 17 spacious windows. Designed to catch the last of the day's rays, it was here that the Sun King would hold extravagant receptions. A host of other private apartments can only be seen as part of a guided tour. **Photo** *left.*

Grand Trianon/Petit Trianon

Open *Apr-Oct* noon-6pm daily. *Nov-Mar* noon-5pm daily. **Admission** €5; €3 after 3.30pm; free under-18s, CM, Passeport Versailles. **Credit** AmEx, DC, MC, V.
In 1687 Louis XIV had Hardouin-Mansart build the pink marble Grand Trianon in the north of the park, away from the protocol of the court. Here Louis and his children's governess, and his secret second wife, Madame de Maintenon, could admire the intimate gardens from the lovely colonnaded portico. It still retains the Empire decor of Napoléon, who stayed here with his second Empress, Marie-Louise.

The Petit Trianon, built for Louis XV's mistress Madame de Pompadour, is a wonderful example of neo-classicism. Marie-Antoinette took this as her main residence, and had the gardens completely changed to include an open-air theatre and her fairy-tale farm and dairy known as the Hameau de la Reine, built for her by Mique in 1783. Here, the queen escaped from the discontent of her subjects and the Revolutionary fervour of Paris by pretending to be a humble milkmaid.

Domaine de Versailles

Gardens Open *Apr-Oct* 7am-dusk daily. *Nov-Mar* 8am-dusk daily. **Admission** *Winter* free (statues covered over). *Summer* €3; €1.50 10s-17s; free under-10s, Passeport Versailles.
Grandes Eaux (01.30.83.78.88). **Open** *Apr-Oct* Sun. *July-Sept* Sat, Sun. **Admission** €5; €3.50 10s-17s; free under-10s, Passeport Versailles. **Credit** AmEx, DC, MC, V.
Park Open dawn-dusk daily. **Admission** free.
Sprawling across 815 hectares, the meticulously planned gardens consist of formal parterres, ponds, elaborate statues – many commissioned by Colbert in 1674 – and a spectacular series of fountains served by an ingenious hydraulic system only recently restored to working order. On weekend afternoons from spring to autumn, these great fountains are set in action to music for the 'Grandes Eaux Musicales' – and also serve as a backdrop, seven times a year, for the extravagant Fêtes de Nuit, capturing the regal splendour of the Sun King's celebrations with fireworks, music and theatre.

The Mouse and the Gaul

Mickey and Astérix are slugging it out for your euros. The figureheads of two huge theme parks outside Paris – **Disneyland Paris** 32km south-east and **Parc Astérix** (pictured) 36km north – attract millions of families here every year. Astérix is cheaper, but Disneyland Paris also boasts the Walt Disney Studios Park and white-knuckle rides of Adventureland and Frontierland. Parc Astérix has hit back with Goudurix and Le Grand Splatch. Astérix scores higher for its educational benefits, Disneyland Paris turns out thousands of satisfied customers every week, all the year round – Parc Astérix closes for the winter. And it is Disneyland Paris which attracts families over from the UK by the bucketload – Astérix scores heavily with the domestic and European market.

Split into neat historical sections (Ancient Greece, the Roman Empire, the Middle Ages and 19th Century Paris), Parc Astérix is packed with varietyand easy to get around. Thrill seekers can defy gravity on Goudurix, Europe's largest roller coaster with seven stomach-churning loop-the-loops, while younger kiddies will squirm to get wet on Le Grand Splatch log-flume. Astérix, Obélix and their fellow Roman bashers hang out in the

spanking new Gaul Village (an exact replica of the one in Albert Uderzo's original comic book) that adjoins the Druid's Forest adventure playground and nearby magic school (Ecole des Druides), where evil Romans have been turned into real pigmy goats. A jamboree of live acts also pump up the pace, with quality shows from dancing dolphins in the Théâtre de Poséidon to awe inspiring acrobatics and synchronised swimming inside the Roman Circus. The food in the park is reassuringly French with an attractive huge choice of eateries including the Rélais Gaullois canteen, where three courses run at €11.

Despite rumours, Disneyland Paris was not built in the shape of Mickey's ears – but that doesn't detract from the frivolous fun on offer in this huge resort (one-fifth the size of Paris) with its main Disneyland park and adjacent film studio complex. Enter the Walt Disney Studios via the Front Lot and head into Animation courtyard for a lesson in cartoon production at Animagique, a 'black light' show based on cult moments from Disney classics. From there, the special effects Studio Tram Tour in Production Courtyard takes you onto an imitation film set with real fireballs and cascading torrents of water. Daredevils should try the Rock 'n' Roller Coaster in the Back Lot which rips off at mega speed before hurtling round hairpin turns and loops to the sounds of Aerosmith. In the main park, little ones can enjoy Fantasyland with Sleeping Beauty's pink fairy-tale castle, while white-knuckle seekers will prefer Adventureland and Frontierland with bone-shaking rides like Indiana Jones et le Temple du Péril which tears around backwards. If you've not much time, get to the park early for a free Fastpass so you can jump the queues on most big rides. Disneyland Paris comes into its own at Hallowe'en and Christmas when there are parades and performances. A golf course and seven Disney-themed hotels make up the resort. For both Disneyland Paris and Parc Astérix certain rides have height restrictions.

Disneyland Paris/ Walt Disney Studios Park

Marne-la-Vallée (01.60.30.60.30/UK 0870 503 0303/www.disneylandparis.com). RER A or TGV Marne-la-Vallée-Chessy. By car A4 Metz-Nancy exit 14. **Open** *Sept-mid July* 10am-8pm Mon-Fri; 9am-8pm Sat-Sun. *Mid July-Aug* 9am-11pm daily.
Studios Park *Winter* 10am-6pm Mon-Fri; 9am-6pm Sat, Sun. *Summer* 9am-6pm daily. All times may vary for public hols. **Admission** *Disneyland Park or Walt Disney Studio Park* €41; €33 3s-11s. Free under-3s. *One-day Hopper for both parks* €49; €39 3s-11s. Free under-3s. *Three-day Hopper* €109; €89 3s-11s. Free under-3s. **Credit** AmEx, MC, V. One-day tickets are valid for the main Park *or* the Studio Park; and for both only after 6pm in summer and 5pm in winter. They are also sold at UK Disney stores, and in Paris at Fnac, Virgin Megastore (*see p246*) and at tourist offices. All-in one-day RER-Disneyland Paris tickets are sold at major stations. Hoppers for both parks are sold at the venue.

Parc Astérix

60128 Plailly (08.26.30.10.40/www. parcasterix.fr). RER B Roissy-Charles de Gaulle 1, then shuttle bus (9.30am-1.30pm, 4.30pm-closing time). By car A1 exit Parc Astérix. **Open** *Apr-Jun* 10am-6pm daily. *July-Aug* 9.30am-7pm daily. *Sep-Oct* 10am-6pm Wed, Sat-Sun. Closed Nov-Mar. Call ahead for extra closure dates. **Admission** €32; €23 3s-11s; under-3s free. **Credit** MC, V.

Potager du Roi

10 rue Maréchal Joffre (01.39.24.62.62/www.
potager-du-roi.fr). **Open** *Apr-Oct* 10am-6pm
Mon-Fri; (by guided tour only) times vary Sat, Sun.
Admission *Mon-Fri* €4.50; €3 concessions; free
under-6s. *Sat, Sun* €6.50; €3 students; free under-6s.
Credit AmEx, DC, MC, V.
The Potager du Roi, the restored king's vegetable
garden, features 16 small squares surrounded by
5,000 fruit trees espaliered into fabulous shapes.

Where to eat & stay

Set in a building dating back to the construction
of the château, **Le Chapeau Gris** (7 rue Hoche,
01.39.50.10.81, www.auchapeaugris.com, closed
dinner Tue, all Wed, lunch €17, dinner €26)
is the oldest restaurant in Versailles and offers
French country cuisine served under wooden
beams. **Boeuf à la Mode** (4 rue au Pain,
Marché Notre-Dame, 01.39.50.31.99, lunch
€16-€26, dinner €21-€26) is an authentic 1930s
brasserie serving steak and seafood specialities.
For a proper splurge, consider sampling the
Michelin-starred haute cuisine of **Les Trois
Marches** (Hôtel Trianon Palace, 1 bd de
la Reine, 01.39.50.13.21, closed Mon & Sun,
lunch €58, dinner €160). You'll find plenty
of bars that stay open late in the area around
the Marché Notre-Dame.

The centre of town also has several
reasonably-priced hotels under €100. One
of the more historic is the **Hôtel du Cheval
Rouge** (18 rue André-Chénier, 01.39.50.03.03,
www.chevalrouge.fr.st, doubles €69), built in
Louis XIV's former livery, overlooking the
Marché Notre-Dame. Located in an 18th-century
townhouse across from the château, the **Hôtel
de France** (5 rue Colbert, 01.30.83.92.23,
www.hotelfrance-versailles.com, doubles from
€141) is a classic hotel with period furnishings;
triples and suites also available.

Getting there

By car

20km (12.5 miles) from Paris by A13 or D10.

By train

For the station nearest the château, take the RER C5
(VICK or VERO trains) to Versailles-Rive Gauche.
Alternatively, take a Transilien SNCF train from
Gare St-Lazare to Versailles-Rive Droit (10mins on
foot to the château).

Tourist information

Office de Tourisme

2bis av de Paris, 78000 Versailles (01.39.24.88.88/
www.versailles-tourisme.com). **Open** 11am-5pm Mon,
Sun; 9am-6pm Tue-Sat.

Epernay & Reims

Named after the region in which it's produced,
champagne – nearly all 300 million bottles a
year of it – comes from the towns of **Reims**
(nasally pronounced 'Rrance') and **Epernay**,
some 25 kilometres (16 miles) apart. At less
than two hours by train from Paris, both are
ideal destinations for a day trip or a weekend
break, with historical sites and champagne
houses to visit. Most champagne cellars give
detailed explanations of how the drink is
produced – from the grape varieties (Pinot
Noir, Chardonnay and Pinot Meunier), to strict
name and quality controls – and tours finish
with a sample. Don't forget your woollies as
the cellars are chilly and damp.

Epernay developed in the 19th century as
expanding champagne houses moved out from
Reims to acquire more space. Today, the aptly
named avenue de Champagne is home to most
major brands – but the best tours are at **Moët
& Chandon** and **Champagne Mercier**.

In Reims, nearly all the major champagne
houses are open by appointment only:
Krug (03.26.84.44.20); Lanson (03.26.78.50.50);
Louis Roederer (by appointment *and*
recommendation only, 03.26.40.42.11) and
Veuve Clicquot (03.26.89.53.90, www.veuve-
clicquot.com). **Champagne Pommery** is
set in an intriguing Elizabethan building.

Home of the coronation church of most
French monarchs dating back to Clovis in 496,
Reims was an important city since Roman
times. The present **Cathédrale Notre-Dame**
(03.26.47.55.34, www.cathedrale-reims.com),
begun in 1211, has rich Gothic decoration that
includes thousands of well-preserved figures on
the portals. Look out, too, for the stained-glass
windows designed by Chagall, in the axial
chapel. The statues damaged during heavy
shelling in World War I can be seen next door
in the former archbishop's palace, the Palais de
Tau (2 pl du Cardinal-Luçon, 03.26.47.81.79).

L'Ancien Collège des Jésuites
(1 pl Museux, 03.26.85.51.50, closed all Tue
and Sat & Sun mornings) is a classic example
of 17th-century baroque architecture, housing
a panelled library decorated with religious
carving and paintings by Jean Hélart. The
college has also given over a considerable
space to modern art.

Mercier

68 av de Champagne, 51200 Epernay
(03.26.51.22.22/www.champagne-mercier.fr).
Open *mid Mar-mid Nov* 9.30-11.30am, 2-4.30pm

daily. *Mid Nov-mid Mar* 9.30-11.30am, 2-4.30pm
Mon, Thur-Sun. **Admission** (incl 1 glass) €6.50; €3
12-15s; free under-12s. **Credit** MC, V.
Some 7,000 tonnes of chalk were extracted to create
the 18km (11 miles) of cellars at Mercier, opened in
1858. Note the 20-tonne champagne barrel at the
entrance: it took 24 bulls and 18 horses to drag it all
the way from Epernay to Paris for the 1889
Universal Exposition. The 45-minute underground
tour takes place on a little train and covers a stretch
of tunnel that was used for mini-car races in the 1950s.

Moët & Chandon

*20 av de Champagne, 51200 Epernay
(03.26.51.20.00/www.moet.com).* **Open** *mid Mar-
mid Nov* 9.30-11.30am, 2-4.30pm daily. *Mid Nov-mid
Mar* 9.30-11.30am, 2-4.30pm Mon-Fri. **Admission**
(incl 1 glass) €7.50; €4.50 12-16s; free under-12s.
Credit AmEx, DC, MC, V.
Moët & Chandon started life in 1743 as champagne
supplier to Madame de Pompadour, Napoléon and
Alexander I of Russia. Since then, they have kept
pole position with the largest domaine and more
than 250 global outlets. In the hour-long tour, visitors are led through a section (under the grand
house) of the 28km (17 miles) of chalk tunnels.

Champagne Pommery

*5 pl du Général Gouraud, 51100 Reims
(03.26.61.62.63/www.pommery.com).* **Open** *mid
Apr-mid Nov* 9.30am-7pm daily. *Mid Nov-mid Apr*
(by appointment only) 10am-6pm daily. **Admission**
(incl 1 glass) €7.50; (incl 2 glasses) €10. **Credit** MC, V.
Built in 1868, this unusual château was modelled on
Elizabethan architecture so that it would stand out
from the surrounding competitors. The visit takes
place some 30m (98ft) underground, in 18km-long
(11-mile) tunnels, which link 120 chalk mines from
the Gallo-Roman period.

Where to eat & stay

In Reims, countless cafés and brasseries line
lively **place Drouet d'Erlon**, as do many
hotels. If you fancy staying at a working
champagne domaine, contact **Ariston Fils
Champagne** (4-8 Grande-Rue, Brouillet,
03.26.97.43.46, www.champagne-aristonfils.
com, doubles €45-€48), who offer three rooms
and pamper their guests. To sleep like a king,
book one of the luxuriously extravagant rooms
at the **Château les Crayères** (64 bd Henry
Vasnier, 03.26.82.80.80, www.chateaules
crayeres.com, doubles €275-€475), a grand
country-house hotel set in lush grounds.
In Epernay, **La Cave à Champagne**
(16 rue Gambetta, 03.26.55.50.70, set menus
€15-€29) does good traditional French food,
as does the charming **Théâtre** (8 pl Pierre
Mendès-France, 03.26.58.88.19, closed dinner
Tue & Sun, all Wed and 15 Feb-2 Mar, 15 July-
2 Aug & 22-28 Dec, lunch €23, dinner €45).

Known for its selection of champagnes, **Les
Cépages** (16 rue Fauvette, 03.26.55.16.93,
closed Wed & Sun and July & Christmas,
lunch €18, dinner €67) serves homely food.
Occupying a recently renovated 19th-century
red-brick mansion, the family-run **Le Clos
Raymi** (3 rue Joseph de Venoge, 03.26.51.00.58,
www.closraymi-hotel.com, doubles €90-€115),
is a cosy mix of traditional and modern. Part
of the international Best Western chain, the
Hôtel de Champagne (30 rue Eugène
Mercier, 03.26.53.10.60, www.bw-hotel-
champagne.com, doubles €75-€115) is a
comfortable place to stay, and the **Hôtel
Kyriad** (3bis rue de Lorraine, 03.26.54.17.39,
doubles from €57) has basic, clean rooms.

Getting there

By car

150km (93 miles) from Paris by the A4. For Epernay,
exit at Château Thierry and take the N3.

By train

From Gare de l'Est, trains take about 90mins for
Reims and Epernay.

Tourist information

Office de Tourisme

*7 av de Champagne, 51200 Epernay
(03.26.53.33.00/www.ot-epernay.fr).* **Open** *mid
Apr-mid Oct* 9.30am-12.30pm, 1.30-7pm Mon-Sat;
11am-4pm Sun. *Mid Oct-mid Apr* 9.30am-12.30pm,
1.30-5.30pm Mon-Sat.

Office de Tourisme

*2 rue Guillaume de Machault, 51100 Reims
(03.26.77.45.00/www.reims-tourisme.com).* **Open**
Jan-Easter 10am-7pm Mon-Sat; 11am-7pm Sun.
Easter-mid Oct 9am-7pm Mon-Sat; 10am-6pm Sun.
Mid Oct-Dec 10am-7pm Mon-Sat; 11am-4pm Sun.

The Loire Valley

Renowned for its sumptuous Renaissance
châteaux – the relics of the Valois kings who
preferred ruling from Amboise and Blois rather
than overcrowded Paris – the stunning Loire
Valley brims with historical splendour and
intrigue. Throughout the lavish countryside
bordering the Loire river, you'll find awe-
inspiring châteaux dating from medieval times
to the 19th century, excellent food and some of
the best wines in the world.
A railway line serves the valley, with Tours
as the hub – most of the château towns are less
than an hour's journey away. Buses also run,
but less frequently. The TGV between Paris
and Tours takes one hour. There are also a
couple of car-hire offices at Tours station (Avis,

02.47.20.53.27; Budget, 02.47.46.22.21), plus desks at Tours airport, served by Ryanair from London Stansted. The Loire Valley is also perfect cycling country – there are cycle-hire offices at and near Tours station.

The lively town of **Amboise** arose at a strategic crossing point on the Loire. The **Château Royal d'Amboise** (02.47.57.00.98, www.chateau-amboise.com), built within the walls of a medieval stronghold, was the first royal Renaissance residence in the Val de Loire. Although only a small part of Charles VIII and Louis XII's complex remains today, the château's interior spans several styles, from vaulted Gothic to Empire. The exquisite late St-Hubert chapel holds the tomb of Leonardo Da Vinci, who died at Amboise in 1519. It's a short walk up the hill, past several cave dwellings, to reach the **Château du Clos Lucé** (02.47.57.00.73, www.vinci-closluce.com), the Renaissance manor where Leonardo lived at the invitation of François I for the three years before his death. On place Michel Debré, beneath the Château Royal, the Caveau des Vignerons (02.47.57.23.69) has plenty of local wine to sample, including the region's speciality – Crémant de Loire – a light sparkling wine made from Pineau and Chardonnay grapes.

The last Renaissance château to be built on the Loire was **Villandry** (02.47.50.02.09), famed for its spectacular Renaissance knot gardens by Jacques Androuet du Cerceau. The castle, whose interior was refitted in the 18th century, has a fine Hispanic-Moresque ceiling and shelters a collection of Spanish paintings. The main draw, though, is its three-tiered gardens, the most unusual of which is the colourful and appetisingly aromatic *jardin potager*, where patterns have been created with ornamental artichokes, cabbages and pumpkins.

Rising from an island in the river Indre west of Tours, **Château Azay-le-Rideau** (02.47.45.42.04) is the quintessential fairy-tale castle, especially when viewed during the nocturnal garden openings in summer. Built in 1518-27 by the treasurer to François I, Gilles Berthelot (although he died in hiding before it was finished), it combines period features (high roofs, narrow pepper-pot turrets) with the imposing symmetry of the Italian Renaissance style. The château's interior is mostly Gothic and Renaissance, with intricate tapestries, paintings and 16th-century furniture.

At the far end of Louis-Philippe's Pont de Langeais (built in 1849), the **Château de Langeais** (02.47.96.72.60), where Charles VIII married Anne de Bretagne in 1491, stands as a stern, archetypal medieval fortress. The castle, dating from 1465, retains its moat, wooden drawbridge and the vestiges of the oldest

medieval stone donjon in France. Amid the lovely furnishings inside, be sure not to miss the 16th-century Flanders tapestries.

The genuine *Sleeping Beauty* castle is **Rigny-Ussé** (02.47.95.54.05), Charles Perrault's inspiration for writing the classic fairy story. The pivotal spinning-wheel scene is even reconstituted at the top of one of the turrets. The north wing was knocked down by the Marquis de Valentinay in the 17th century to provide a view onto his beautiful terraces, designed by Le Nôtre. The interior dates mostly from this period, and has striking tapestries.

High on a cliff, looming over the picturesque town of Chinon (famous for its wine), are the ghostly ruins of the **Château de Chinon** (02.47.93.13.45). You can admire the scale of this huge medieval fortress from the south bank of the Vienne. Split into three distinct forts, separated by deep moats, the castle was the property of the counts of Blois in the tenth century, before the Plantagenets took it for the English crown in the 1200s. The Fort St-Georges cannot be visited, but the Château du Milieu (the entrance to the castle) and the 13th-century Tour de l'Horloge, with its museum on Jeanne d'Arc (who met with Charles VII here in 1429), provide compensation. Down in the medieval town, **Au Vieux Marché**, by the river (2 route de Tours, 02.47.93.04.10), offers daily wine-tasting, with a tour around the wine cellar on request.

The **Château de Brézé** (02.41.51.60.15) fancies itself as being one-of-a-kind – and not without reason. For under the château itself (an amalgam of Renaissance and Empire styles) exists a Medieval subterranean village complete with its own working bakery. Don't miss the magnificent Cathédrale d'Images, where strange lights are projected onto the cave walls to produce eerie art. After your unusual upstairs-downstairs visit, you can taste the estate's own Saumur wine (considered one of the best vintages in the Anjou region).

Chocolate-box **Saumur** – as known for its wine as for its striking **Château de Saumur** (02.41.40.24.40) – was a stronghold for the Anjou dynasty. In the 16th century, governor Philippe Dupleiss-Mornay decided to fortify the castle, then turn it into a jail. The Marquis de Sade was imprisoned here in 1768. The château is an example of 14th-century architecture, with a collection of decorative pieces and a horse-riding museum; although the museum is closed until 2007, the gardens and panoramic lookout remain open. Behind the castle, 12 metres (40 feet) underground, the Caves Louis de Grenelle (20 rue Marceau, 02.41.50.17.63) gives a tasting tour through their stone cellars, including sparkling varieties from Château de Brézé.

The charming old port of **Honfleur**. *See p361.*

If you're driving back to Paris, the **Château de Chambord** (02.54.50.40.00), **Château de Chaumont** (02.54.51.26.26) and **Château de Chenonceaux** (08.20.20.90.90) are Renaissance castles near Amboise well worth a detour.

Where to stay

Amboise is a pleasant, centrally located stop-off point for exploring the Loire. In town, try the **Manoir de la Maison Blanche** (18 rue de l'Epinetterie, 02.47.23.16.14, doubles €80, incl breakfast) near the centre. Situated in a wood on the edge of town, the ivy-fronted former stronghold of **Château de Pray** (Route de Chargé, 02.47.57.23.67, praycastel.online.fr, doubles €98-€175) offers opulent rooms, and has a swimming pool in grounds that date back to the 13th century. In Azay-le-Rideau, **Le Biencourt** (7 rue Balzac, 02.47.45.20.75, www.hotelbiencourt.com, doubles €47-€53) offers basic rooms for two to four people.

For a taste of the high life at low prices, the **Château de la Vrillaye** (02.47.58.24.40, www.chateaudelavrillaye.com, doubles €85-€100), in Chaveignes, 18 kilometres (11 miles) from Chinon and 23 kilometres (14 miles) from Azay-le-Rideau, offers stunning rooms, wine-tasting, tennis courts and a swimming pool. The **Château des Réaux** (02.47.95.14.40, doubles €80-€160), at Chouzé-sur-Loire, is another comfortable option.

In Saumur, the **St-Pierre** (8 rue Haute-St-Pierre, 02.41.50.33.00, www.saintpierresaumur. com, doubles €114-€130) is set between the church of the same name and the château. For details of the town's other options, the tourist office provides a helpful service.

Getting there

By car
Take A10 to Blois (174km/108 miles), then follow the Loire along N152 to Saumur via Amboise and Tours. Sights should be signposted along this road.

By train
TGV from Gare de Montparnasse takes 1hr 50mins to Saumur, and as little as 1hr 30mins to Langeais and 2hrs to Chinon (for both, TGV may be to Tours or St-Pierre-des-Corps). From Gare d'Austerlitz to Amboise takes 2hrs.

Tourist information

Comité Régional du Tourisme Centre
www.visaloire.com.
Regional tourist body whose coverage includes the eastern part of the Loire Valley.

Comité Régional du Tourisme des Pays de la Loire
www.enpaysdelaloire.com/www.westernloire.com.
Regional tourist body for the Western Loire.

Office de Tourisme
7 pl Kennedy, 49051 Angers cedex 02, (02.41.23.50.00/www.angers-tourisme.com). **Open** May-Sept 9am-7pm Mon-Sat; 10am-6pm Sun. Oct-Apr 2-6pm Mon; 9am-6pm Tue-Sat; 10am-1pm Sun.

Office de Tourisme
pl de la Bilange, 49400 Saumur (02.41.40.20.60/ www.saumur-tourisme.com). **Open** 9.15am-12.30pm, 2-6pm Mon, Wed-Sat; 10am-12.30pm, 2-6pm Tue.

Office de Tourisme
78-82 rue Bernard Palissy, 37042 Tours cedex 1 (02.47.70.37.37/www.ligeris.com). **Open** 8.30am-12.30pm, 1.30-6pm Mon-Sat; 10am-1pm Sun.

The Norman Riviera

Fabulous, glamorous **Deauville** – just a two-hour train journey from Paris – knows how to look after its guests. Whether you come here to inhale sea air, spot celebrities or deepen your all-over tan, you'll find a town that is primed and equipped to rejuvenate, satiate and titillate – it can't help it, it was designed that way.

Deauville was born in the mid 19th century when the Duc de Morny, Napoléon III's half-brother, recognised an opportunity to attract fashionable tourists and built a racecourse on an empty patch of the Côte Fleurie, just across a narrow stretch of water from Trouville-sur-Mer. Later he added grandiose hotels and a casino, and by the 1910s the town had been established as the prime holiday destination for Paris jet-setters and British aristocracy. This early growth period has indelibly left its mark on the town's personality: the bright bathing huts and the famous beach-side promenade, designed to protect ladies' flowing dresses, are a reminder of more genteel days, while the local spa centres and gourmet food market (place du Marché, Tue, Fri and Sat mornings) attend to today's seekers of *bien-vivre*.

Like the French Riviera, Deauville caters to old-style leisure and wealth: there are two marinas, three golf courses, including the only floodlit course in Europe (02.31.14.42.00), and a yachting school (02.31.88.38.19). The occasions to drop coin are endless: serious designer boutiques, top-dollar restaurants and Paris-style cafés (with prices to match) line the streets. Then there's the **casino**, just behind the seafront. This massive belle-époque edifice stands like a bastion of decadence and cannot be missed (ID is required and, for some rooms, formal attire). *Faites vos jeux* at the roulette tables graced by Coco Chanel.

Deauville is no museum piece. Its population swells from 4,500 to around 75,000 in season, when the sweeping expanse of beach fills with a multicoloured festival of parasols; watersports and sand-surfing keep the restless occupied. An energetic calendar also brings in the crowds; there are international polo and racing events all year, and two big film festivals – the Asia Film Festival (www.deauvilleasia.com) in March, and the American Film Festival in September (www.festival-deauville.com), when Harrison Ford usually turns up to crease a grin.

Just a dice tumble away, the 17th-century port town of **Trouville-sur-Mer** shares the same railway station. Family-owned shops, narrow backstreets and a daily fish market lend Trouville an authenticity that its flashier sister lacks. Check out the beach, casino (with one room decorated as a Louisiana paddle steamer) and Napoléon's summer residence, Villa Montebello (64 rue du Maréchal-Leclerc, 02.31.88.16.26), which regularly hosts art exhibitions.

A short drive or bus journey further east is **Honfleur**, a small, very pretty fishing town at the mouth of the Seine. Honfleur has none of Deauville's glitz, but plenty of charm. The old port (*pictured p359*) and the narrow and winding streets leading off it are perfect for lazy exploration on foot; there are two sandy beaches nearby; and the town has a long list of associations with major artistic figures. Baudelaire spent time at his mother's house here, and the Impressionists were frequent visitors – the 'Honfleur School' included Monet and Courbet. The Musée Eugène Boudin (pl Erik-Satie, 02.31.89.54.00, closed 1 Jan-10 Feb) contains paintings by Monet, Boudin, Jongkind and others, as well as sculptures and folk artefacts from the local area. Also worth a look is the wooden, 15th-century Eglise Ste-Cathérine (rue des Capucins, 02.31.89.11.83), with its roof built using boat-construction methods and detached belfry.

Casino Barrière de Deauville
rue Edmond Blanc, Deauville (02.31.14.31.14). **Open** 11am-2am Mon-Thur; 11am-3am Fri; 10am-4am Sat; 10am-3am Sun. **Admission** (over-18s only, formal dress) €14. **Credit** AmEx, MC, V.

Where to eat & stay

In Deauville, tuck in to oysters at **Le Ciro's** (2 rue-Edmond Blanc, 02.31.14.31.31, main courses €30, set menu €39 Mon-Fri except July & Aug) on the seafront or tackle a roast lobster and rich Normandy treats at **Le Spinnaker** (52 rue Mirabeau, 02.31.88.24.40, €29-€44). The twin peaks of Deauville's hotel selection are the palatial **Royal Barrière** (bd Cornuché,

02.31.98.66.33, doubles €270-390) and the half-timbered **Normandy Barrière** (38 rue Jean Mermoz, 02.31.98.66.22, doubles from €288), linked by a tunnel to the casino.

Those looking to stay on a budget should head in from the seafront – or find somewhere in Trouville-sur-Mer. A comfortable and quite cheap option – though you'll pay the higher rate for a sea view – is the **Flaubert Hôtel** in Trouville (rue Gustave Flaubert, 02.31.88.37.23, www.flaubert.fr, doubles €85-€120).

In Honfleur you'll find **La Ferme Saint Siméon** (rue Adolphe-Marais, 02.31.81.78.00, www.fermesaintsimeon.fr, doubles €220-€450, closed Mon & lunch Tue, set menu €120), a luxury inn set in landscaped gardens, with a spa and gastronomic restaurant. In the town centre, **Les Maisons de Léa** (02.31.14.49.49, www.lesmaisonsdelea.com, doubles €95-€220) occupies four characterful houses on place Ste-Catherine, next to the church, and a cottage for four to six people (€260). Centuries-old stonework adds atmosphere to the harbour views from the hotel and restaurant **L'Absinthe** (10 quai de la Quarantaine, 02.31.89.39.00, www.absinthe.fr, doubles €135, closed mid Nov-mid Dec, set menus €30-€60), where the focus is on fish and seafood; the same outfit runs the cheaper **La Grenouille Brasserie** nearby (No.16, 02.31.89.04.24, closed mid Nov-mid Dec, main courses €20).

Getting there

By car
195km (121 miles) west from Paris by A13.

By train
From Gare St-Lazare to Deauville-Trouville (2hrs).

Tourist information

Office de Tourisme
pl de la Bastille, 14800 Deauville (02.32.14.40.60/ www.deauville.org). **Open** 9am-12pm, 2-6pm (Apr-Oct until 7pm) daily.

Office de Tourisme
quai Lepaulmier 14600 Honfleur (02.31.89.23.30/ www.ot-honfleur.fr). **Open** *Easter-June, Sept* 10am-12.30pm, 2-6.30pm Mon-Sat; 10am-5pm Sun. *July, Aug* 10am-7pm Mon-Sat; 10am-5pm Sun. *Oct-Easter* 10am-12.30pm, 2-6pm Mon-Sat; 10am-5pm Sun (during school hols only).

Office de Tourisme
32 quai Fernand-Moureaux, 14360 Trouville-sur-Mer (02.31.14.60.70/www.trouvillesurmer.org). **Open** *Apr-June, Sept & Oct* 9.30am-noon, 2-6.30pm Mon-Sat; 10am-1pm Sun. *July & Aug* 9.30am-7pm Mon-Sat; 10am-1pm Sun. *Nov-Mar* 9.30am-noon, 1.30-6pm Mon-Sat; 10am-1pm Sun.

GET IT OFF YOUR CHEST

Let us know what you think about Time Out guides and you could win ten guides of your choice. We know you've got an opinion – and we want to hear it.

Go to www.timeout/guidesfeedback.com
Every month another reader will win ten city guides of their choice.

Directory

Features

Musée National des Arts Asiatiques – Guimet. *See p121.*

Directory

Getting Around

By air

Roissy-Charles-de-Gaulle airport

Most international flights arrive at Roissy-Charles-de-Gaulle airport (www.paris-cdg.com), 30km north-east of Paris. Its two main terminals are some way apart, so check which one you need for your return flight; for information in English, call 01.48.62.22.80 or see www.aeroportsdeparis.fr. The **RER B** (SNCF helpline, 08.91.36.20.20) is the quickest and most reliable way to central Paris (about 40min to Gare du Nord; 45min to RER Châtelet-Les Halles; €7.75 single). A new station gives direct access from Terminal 2; from Terminal 1 you take the free shuttle bus. RER trains run every 15min, 5.24am-11.56pm daily. **Air France buses** (08.92.35.08.20, www.cars.airfrance.fr; €12 single, €18 return) leave every 15min, 5.45am-11pm daily, from both terminals, and stop at Porte Maillot and place Charles-de-Gaulle (35-50min trip). Air France buses also run to Gare Montparnasse and Gare de Lyon (€12 single, €18 return) every 30min (45-60min trip), 7am-9pm daily; there's a bus between Roissy and Orly (€16) every 30min, 6am-10.30pm Mon-Fri, 7am-10.30pm Sat, Sun. The RATP **Roissybus** (08.92.68.77.14; €8.40) runs every 15min, 5.45am-11pm daily, between the airport and the corner of rue Scribe/rue Auber (at least 45min); buy tickets on the bus. **Paris Airports Service** is a

door-to-door minibus service between airports and hotels, 24/7. It works on the 'more passengers the less each one pays' system. Roissy prices go from €24 for one person to €12.40 each for eight people, 6am-8pm (minimum €34, 5-6am, 8-10pm); Orly from €22 for one to €9 each for eight; book on 01.55.98.10.80, www.parisairportservice.com. **Airport Connection** (01.43.65.55.55, www.airport-connection.com; reservations 7am-7.30pm) runs a similar service, 4am-10.30pm. Prices for Roissy are €26 per person, €39 for two, then €15 per extra person; for Orly, €22 per person, €30 for two, then €14 per extra person. **A taxi** to central Paris can take 30-60mins depending on traffic and your point of arrival. Expect to pay €30-€50, plus €1 per item of luggage.

Orly airport

French domestic and several international flights use Orly airport (English-speaking information service on 01.49.75.15.15, 6am-midnight daily, www.paris-ory.com), 18km south of the city. It has two terminals: Orly-Sud (mainly international flights) and Orly-Ouest (mainly domestic flights). **Air France buses** (08.92.35.08.20, www.cars. airfrance.fr; €8 single, €12 return) leave both terminals every 15min, 6am-11pm daily, and stop at Invalides and Montparnasse (30-45min). The RATP **Orlybus** (08.92.68.77.18; €5.80) runs between the airport and Denfert-Rochereau every 15min, 5.35am-11.05pm daily (30min trip); buy tickets

on the bus. The high-speed **Orlyval** shuttle train runs every 7min (6am-11pm daily) to RER B station Antony (Orlyval and RER together cost €9.05); getting to central Paris takes about 35min. You could also catch the **Orlyrail** (€5.65) to Pont de Rungis, where you can take the RER C into central Paris. Trains run every 15min, 6am-11pm daily; 50min trip. **A taxi** into town takes 20-40min and costs €16-€26, plus €1 per piece of luggage. The minibus services listed above also run to and from Orly.

Paris Beauvais airport

Beauvais (08.92.68.20.66, www.aeroportbeauvais.com), 70km from Paris, is served by budget airlines such as **Ryanair** (03.44.11.41.41, www.ryanair.com), which flies from Dublin, Shannon and Glasgow. Buses (€13) to Porte Maillot leave the airport 20min after each arrival; buses going the other way leave 3hr 15min before each departure. Tickets can be bought at the arrival lounge or from the Beauvais shop at 1 bd Pershing, 17th (01.58.05.08.45).

Airline contacts

Aer Lingus 01.70.20.00.72, www.aerlingus.com
Air France 08.20.82.08.20, www.airfrance.fr
American Airlines 08.10.87.28.72, www.aa.com, www.americanairlines.fr
bmibaby 08.90.71.00.81, www.bmibaby.com
British Airways 08.25.82.54.00, www.britishairways.fr
British Midland 01.41.91.87.04, www.flybmi.com
Continental 01.71.23.03.35, www.continental.com

Easyjet 08.25.08.25.08,
www.easyjet.com
KLM & NorthWest
08.91.71.12.31, www.klm.com
United 08.10.72.72.72,
www.united.fr

By car

For car travel between France
and the UK, there's tunnel
Le Shuttle (Folkstone-Calais
35mins) (08.10.63.03.04,
www.eurotunnel.com); fast
service **Hoverspeed** (Dover-
Calais, Newhaven-Dieppe)
(03.21.46.14.00, www.hover
speed.com); or ferries **Brittany
Ferries** (08.25.82.88.28, www.
brittanyferries.com), **P&O
Stena Line** (01.55.69.82.28,
www.poferries.com) and
SeaFrance (08.25.04.40.45,
www.seafrance.com).

Shared journeys
Allô-Stop *1 rue Condorcet, 9th
(01.53.20.42.42/08.25.80.36.66,
www.allostop.net; M° Poissonière).*
Open 10am-1pm, 2-6.30pm Mon-Fri;
10am-1pm, 2-5pm Sat. **Credit** MC, V.
Call several days ahead to be put in
touch with drivers. There's a fee

(€4.50 under 200km; up to €10 over
500km), plus €0.50 per km to the
driver. Most-served destinations:
Cologne, Lyon, Marseille, Nantes,
Rennes, Toulouse.

By coach

International coach services
arrive at the Gare Routière
Internationale Paris-Galliéni
at Porte de Bagnolet, 20th. For
reservations (in English) call
Eurolines on 08.92.69.52.52
(€0.34/min), or in the UK 01582
404511, www.eurolines.fr.

By rail

The **Eurostar** service between
London and Paris takes 2hrs
25min direct; allow slightly
longer for trains stopping at
Ashford and Lille. You must
check in at least 30min before
the train is due to leave, and
passports must be carried.
Eurostar trains from London
Waterloo (01233 617575,
www.eurostar.com) arrive at
Gare du Nord (08.92.35.35.39,
www.sncf.fr), with easy access

to public transport and taxi
ranks (the long queues do
move fairly quickly). **Bicycles**
can be transported as hand
luggage if they are dismantled
and carried in a bike bag. You
can also check them in at the
Eurodispatch depot at Waterloo
(Esprit Parcel Service, 08705
850850) or Sernam depot at
Gare du Nord (01.55.31.54.54).
Check-in must be done 24hr
in advance, a Eurostar ticket
must be shown and the service
costs £20/€45.39.

Travel agencies

Nouvelles Frontières *13 av de
l'Opéra, 1st (08.25.00.07.77/www.
nouvelles-frontieres.fr). M° Pyramides.*
Open 9am-7pm Mon-Sat. **Credit** MC,
V. Agent with 16 branches in Paris.
Thomas Cook *17 rue du Colisée,
8th (01.58.36.49.25/www.
thomascook.fr). M° Opéra.* **Open**
10am-7pm Mon-Sat. **Credit** AmEx,
DC, MC, V. General travel agent with
more than 33 branches in Paris.

Maps

Free maps of the métro, bus
and RER systems are available
at airports and métro stations.
Other brochures from métro
stations are *Paris Visite – Le
Guide*, with details of transport
tickets and a small map, and
Plan de Paris, a fold-out map
that shows *Noctambus* night
bus lines. Maps sponsored
by Galeries Lafayette and
Printemps can be picked up
at most hotels. A Paris street
map (called *Plan de Paris*) can
be bought from newsagents
or stationers (*papeteries*). The
blue-covered *Paris Pratique*
is nicely clear and compact.

Public transport

Almost all of the Paris public
transport system is run by
the **RATP** (Régie Autonome
des Transports Parisiens;
08.92.68.77.14, in English
08.92.68.41.14, www.ratp.fr):
the bus, métro (underground)
and suburban tram routes, as
well as lines A and B of the

Navigo lucky

The Carte Orange is no longer orange, and staffed
kiosks are to disappear from some stations. Yes, it's all
change on the Paris métro, with the introduction of the
electronic **Navigo** card: simply swiping this chip-carrying
smart card over a scanner opens the turnstile. The system
has been in place since 2001 for annual subscribers,
but now monthly and weekly Carte Orange holders have
also gone electronic – and purple (the colour of Navigo).
Carrying encrypted information about the holder – digital
photo and personal details – the Navigo card can be
charged with credit on the internet or at portals in métro
stations. While its main use is for regular travel in Paris,
the card can also be charged for one-off journeys to
anywhere on the RER network – to Versailles, say. In
the future, Navigo could theoretically let users connect
with other forms of transport, and there are plans to
give it an extra role: that of electronic purse for low-value
purchases in *boulangeries*, newsagents, and *tabacs*.
Technophobes needn't panic, though: the traditional
magnetic-strip cards are still around – as Paris Visite,
carnets, and single tickets. But in a few years, these
too will be phased out and replaced by disposable,
contactless tickets. For more details, see www.ratp.fr.

RER (Réseau Express Régional) suburban express railway, which connects with the métro inside Paris. State rail operator **SNCF** (08.92.35.35.35, www.sncf.com) runs RER lines C, D and E, and serves the Paris suburbs (*Banlieue*), and French regions and abroad (*Grandes Lignes*).

Fares & tickets

Paris and its suburbs are divided into eight travel zones; zones 1 and 2 cover the city centre. RATP **tickets** and passes are valid on the métro, bus and RER. Tickets and *carnets* can be bought at métro stations, tourist offices and *tabacs* (tobacconists); single tickets can be bought on buses. Hold on to your ticket in case of spot checks; you'll also need it to exit from RER stations.
● A standard ticket costs €1.40, but it's often more economical to buy a *carnet* of ten tickets for €10.50.
● A one-day *Mobilis* pass costs from €5.40 for zones 1 and 2 to €18.40 for zones 1-8 (not including airports).
● A three-day *Paris Visite* pass for zones 1-3 is €18.25; a five-day pass is €26.65, with discounts on some tourist attractions.
● One-week or one-month *Carte Orange* passes (passport photo needed) offer unlimited travel in the relevant zones; if bought in zones 1 or 2, each is delivered as a Navigo swipe card (*see p365* **Navigo lucky**). A *forfait mensuel* (monthly *Carte Orange* valid from the first day of the month) for zones 1 and 2 costs €51.50; a weekly *forfait hebdomadaire* (weekly *Carte Orange* valid Mon-Sun inclusive) for zones 1 and 2 costs €15.90 and is better value than *Paris Visite* passes.

Métro & RER

The Paris **métro** is at most times the fastest and cheapest means of getting around. Trains run daily 5.30am-12.40am. Individual lines are numbered, with each direction named after the last stop. Follow the orange *Correspondance* signs to change lines. Some interchanges, such as Châtelet, Montparnasse Bienvenüe and République, involve long walks. The exit (*Sortie*) is indicated in blue. The driverless line 14, also known as the Météor, runs from Gare St-Lazare to the new Bibliothèque Nationale. Pickpockets and bag-snatchers are rife on the métro – pay special attention as the doors are closing. The five **RER** lines (A, B, C, D and E) run 5.30am-1am daily across Paris and into commuterland. Within Paris, the RER is useful for making faster journeys – for example, Châtelet Les Halles to Charles de Gaulle Etoile in only two stops on the RER, compared with eight on métro line 1. Métro tickets are valid for RER journeys within zones 1-2.

Buses

Buses run 6.30am-8.30pm, with some routes continuing until 12.30am, Mon-Sat; more limited services operate on selected lines Sun and public holidays. You can use a métro ticket, a ticket bought from the driver (€1.40) or a travel pass. Tickets should be punched in the machine next to the driver; passes should be shown to the driver. When you want to get off, press the red request button, and the *arrêt demandé* (stop requested) sign lights up.

Night buses

After the métro and normal buses stop running, the only public transport – apart from taxis – are the 18 **Noctambus** lines, between place du Châtelet and the suburbs (hourly 1.30am-5.35am Mon-Thur; half-hourly 1am-5.35am Fri, Sat); look out for the owl logo on bus stops. Routes A to H, P, T and V serve the Right Bank and northern suburbs; I to M, R and S serve the Left Bank and southern suburbs. A ticket costs €2.70 and allows one change; travel passes are valid.

River transport

Batobus (*08.25.05.01.01/ www.batobus.com*). River buses stop every 15-25mins at: Eiffel Tower, Musée d'Orsay, St-Germain-des-Prés (Quai Malaquais), Notre-Dame, Jardin des Plantes, Hôtel de Ville, Louvre, Champs-Elysées (Pont Alexandre III). They run Feb-Mar & Oct-Dec 10am-7pm; Apr-Sept 10am-10pm. A one-day pass costs €11 (€5, €7); two-day pass €13 (€6, €8); five-day pass €16 (€7, €10); one-month pass €22 (€12 children); season-ticket €50 (€30 children). Tickets can be bought at Batobus stops, RATP ticket offices and the Office de Tourisme.

Trams

Two modern tramlines operate in the suburbs, running from La Défense to Issy-Val de Seine and from Bobigny Pablo Picasso to St-Denis. They connect with the métro and RER; fares are the same as for buses.

Rail travel

Several suburban attractions, Versailles and Disneyland Paris in particular, are served by the RER. Most locations farther from the city are served by the SNCF railway; the TGV high-speed train has slashed journey times and is steadily being extended to all the main regions. There are few long-distance bus services.

Tickets can be bought at any SNCF station (not just the one from which you'll travel), SNCF shops and travel agents. If you reserve online or by phone, you can pay and pick up your tickets from the station or have them sent to your home. SNCF automatic machines (*billeterie automatique*) only work with French credit/debit cards. Regular trains have full-rate White (peak) and cheaper Blue (off-peak) periods. You

Wi-Fi, where find?

What with all its history, grand architecture and carefully observed traditions, you could forget that Paris is – yes – a modern metropolis. One item of proof is the dramatic increase in the last few years of wireless internet access, or Wi-Fi. Suitably equipped commuters and travellers can now whip out their laptops and check emails in any mainline railway station, the lounges at Roissy-Charles-de-Gaulle airport – and, of course, in a growing number of cafés, bars and hotel lobbies.

Peripatetic internet addicts will soon have further cause to celebrate, as Mayor Delanoë's plans to install public wireless internet access right across the city nudge closer to fruition. The year-long pilot scheme, entitled WIXOS, began as far back as 1 April 2003, brainchild of Cisco Systems and the RATP, which runs the métro. The Paris métro is one of the densest transport networks in the world, and with nearly 400 stations and an average distance of only 550 metres between each one, its tunnels are ideal conduits for the fibre-optic cables a pan-city Wi-Fi network will need.

So, for the WIXOS wheeze, the necessary transmitters were placed in métro signs and advertisement housings outside métro stations, roughly following the north-south route of bus 38 between Gare du Nord and Porte d'Orléans. Anyone within a 100 metre radius of one of the transmitter hotspots – provided he or she had already registered online for the privilege – was able to get online for free.

More than two years on, with the pilot scheme a tolerable success, more transmitters are being installed and rented out to the likes of Orange and Bouygues Télécom, who in turn provide a wireless service for their paying customers. Not exactly the mayor's dream of free Wi-Fi for all, then, but a good step closer to it.

can save on TGV fares by buying special cards. The *Carte 12/25* gives under-26s a 25%-50% reduction; even without it, under-26s are entitled to 25% off. Buy tickets in advance to secure the cheaper fare. Pensioners over 60 benefit from similar terms with a *Carte Senior*. Before you board any train, stamp your ticket in the orange *composteur* machines located on the platforms, or you might have to pay a hefty fine.

SNCF reservations & tickets
(national reservations and information 08.92.35.35.35 (€0.34 per min)/www.sncf.com). **Open** 7am-10pm daily. The line can also be reached by dialling 3635 and saying 'billet' at the prompt.

SNCF information *(in Ile-de-France, no reservations 08.91.36.20.20).* **Open** 7am-10pm daily.

Paris mainline stations

Gare d'Austerlitz: Central and SW France and Spain.

Gare de l'Est: Alsace, Champagne and southern Germany.

Gare de Lyon: Burgundy, the Alps, Provence, Italy.

Gare Montparnasse: West France, Brittany, Bordeaux, the Southwest.

Gare du Nord: Northeast France, Channel ports, Eurostar, Belgium and the Netherlands.

Gare St-Lazare: Normandy.

Taxis

Paris taxi drivers are not known for their charm, nor for their flawless knowledge of the Paris street plan; if you have a preferred route, say so. Taxis can also be hard to find, especially at rush hour or early in the morning. Your best bet is to find a taxi rank (*station de taxis*, marked with a blue sign) on major roads, crossroads and at stations. A white light on a taxi's roof indicates the car is free; an orange light means the cab is busy. Taxi charges are based on zone and time of day: **A** (10am-5pm Mon-Sat central Paris, €0.62 per km); **B** (5pm-10am Mon-Fri, 5pm-midnight Sat, all day Sun central Paris; 7am-7pm Mon-Sat inner suburbs and airports, €1.06 per km); **C** (midnight-7am Sun central Paris; 7pm-7am Mon-Sat, all day Sun inner suburbs and airports; all times outer suburbs, €1.24 per km). Most journeys in central Paris cost €6-€12; there's a minimum charge of €5.10, plus €0.90 for each piece of luggage over 5kg or bulky objects, and a €0.70 surcharge from mainline stations. Most drivers will not take more than three people, although they should take a couple and two children. Don't feel obliged to tip, although rounding up by €0.30-€0.70 is polite. Taxis are not allowed to refuse rides because they are too short and can only refuse to take you in a particular direction during their last half-hour of service (though both rules are blatantly ignored). If you want a receipt, ask for *un reçu* or *la note*. Complaints should be made in writing to the **Bureau de la réglementation publique de Paris**, 36 rue des Morillons, 75732 Paris Cedex 15.

Phone cabs

The following accept phone bookings around the clock; you also pay for the time it takes your radioed taxi to get to where you are (assuming it does indeed turn up). If you wish to pay by credit card (€15 minimum), mention this when you order.
Airportaxis *to and from Paris airports, 01.48.40.17.17/www. airportaxis.com.*
Alpha *01.45.85.85.85/www. alphataxis.fr.*
G7 *01.47.39.47.39/in English 01.41.27.66.99/www.taxis-g7.fr.*
Taxis Bleus *01.49.36.10.10/ 08.25.16.24.24/www.taxis-bleus.com.*

Driving

If you bring your car to France, you must bring its registration and insurance documents – an insurance green card, available from insurance companies and the AA and RAC in the UK, is not compulsory but is useful. As you come into Paris, you will meet the Périphérique, the giant ring road that carries traffic in, out and around the city. Intersections, which lead onto other main roads, are called *portes* (gates). Driving on the Périphérique is not as hair-raising as it might look, though it's often congested, especially at rush hour and peak holiday times. If you've come to Paris by car, it may be a good idea to park at the edge of the city and use public transport. Some hotels have parking spaces which can be paid for by the hour, day or by various types of season tickets. In peak holiday periods, the organisation Bison Futé hands out brochures at motorway *péages* (toll gates), suggesting less-crowded routes. French roads are categorised as *Autoroutes* (motorways, with an 'A' in front of the number), *Routes Nationales* (national 'N' roads), *Routes Départementales* (local, 'D' roads) and rural *Routes Communales* ('C' roads).

Autoroutes are toll roads, though some sections, including most of the area immediately around Paris, are free. *Autoroutes* have a speed limit of 130km/h (80mph); this is not adhered to with any degree of zeal by French motorists. The limit on most *Routes Nationales* is 90km/h (56mph); within urban areas the limit is 50km/h (30mph), and 30km/h (20mph) in selected residential zones.
Traffic information for Ile-de-France
08.26.02.20.22/www.securite routiere.gouv.fr.

Breakdown services

The AA or RAC do not have reciprocal arrangements with an equivalent organisation in France, so it's advisable to take out additional breakdown insurance cover, for example with **Europ Assistance** (01.41.85.85.41/www.europ assistance.co.uk). If you don't have insurance, you can use its service (01.41.85.85.85), but it will charge you the full cost. Other 24-hour breakdown services in Paris include: **Action Auto Assistance** (01.45.58.49.58); **Dan Dépann Auto** (01.40.06.06.53).

Driving tips

● At junctions where no signposts indicate right of way, the car coming from the right has priority. Many roundabouts now give priority to those on the roundabout. If this is not indicated (by road markings or a sign with the message *Vous n'avez pas la priorité*), priority is for those coming from the right.
● Drivers and all passengers must wear seat belts.
● Children under ten are not allowed to travel in the front of a car, except in baby seats facing backwards.
● You should not stop on an open road; pull off to the side.

● When drivers flash their lights at you, this often means they will not slow down and are warning you to move out of their path or keep out of the way. But friendly drivers also flash their lights to warn you when there are *gendarmes* lurking in the vicinity.
● Try to carry plenty of change, as it's quicker – and less stressful – to make for the exact-money line on *péages*. If you are caught short, cashiers do give change and *péages* accept credit cards.

Parking

There are still a few free on-street parking areas in Paris, but they're often full. If you park illegally, you risk getting your car clamped or towed away (*see below*). It's forbidden to park in zones marked for deliveries (*livraisons*) or taxis. Parking meters have now been replaced by *horodateurs*, pay-and-display machines, which take a special card (*carte de stationnement* at €15 or €30, available from *tabacs*). Parking is often free at weekends, after 7pm and in August. There are plenty of underground car parks in the city centre. Most cost €2.50 per hour, €20 for 24 hours; some have lower rates after 6pm, and many offer various season tickets – a week at €80 or, much more common, a month at around €150.
Parking information for Paris *www.parkingsdeparis.com.*

Clamps & car pounds

If your car is clamped, contact the nearest police station. There are eight car pounds (*préfourrières*) in Paris. You'll have to pay a €136 removal fee plus €10 storage charge per day, and a parking fine of €35 for parking in a no-parking zone. Bring your driving licence and insurance papers. But before you can pay, you need to find your vehicle – no small task. Here goes. Once clamped, your car will first be sent to the *préfourrière* nearest to where it was snatched, then moved on to a different pound after 72hrs. To find out where it might be, call 01.53.71.53.53 or 08.91.01.22.22. Information: www.prefecture-police-paris. interieur.gouv.fr.

Car hire

To hire a car you must be 25 or over and have held a licence for at least a year. Some agencies accept drivers aged 21-24, but a supplement of €20-€25 per day is usual. Take your licence and passport with you. There are often good weekend offers (Fri evening to Mon morning). Week-long deals are better at the bigger companies: with Avis or Budget, for example, it's around €300 a week for a small car with insurance and 1,750km included. Costlier hire companies allow the return of a car in other French cities and abroad. Bargain companies may have an extremely high charge for damage: read the small print before signing.

Hire companies

Ada 08.25.16.91.69/www.ada.fr.
Avis 08.20.05.05.05/www.avis.fr.
Budget 08.25.00.35.64/
www.budget.fr.
Calandres 01.43.06.35.50/
www.calandres.com. Its *flotte prestige* of luxury cars is for those who've held a licence for at least five years.
EasyRentacar www.easycar.com.
Europcar 08.25.82.55.13/
www.europcar.fr.
Hertz 01.41.91.95.25/www.hertz.fr.
Rent-a-Car 08.91.70.02.00/
www.rentacar.fr.

Chauffeur-driven cars

Carey (01.41.40.84.84/www.carey-first.com). **Open** 24hr daily. **Prices** from €145 airport transfer; €240 for 4 hours. **Credit** AmEx, DC, MC, V.

Cycling

Since 1996, the Mairie de Paris has been promoting cycling in the city. There are now 353km of bike lanes and there are even plans for a bicycle 'Périphérique' circling Paris. Mayor Delanoë has continued with predecessor Jean Tiberi's enthusiasm, though his decision to close 3km of the Right Bank beside Paris-Plage for cyclists, rollerbladers and pedestrians was aimed at leisure cyclists rather than commuters. The Itinéraires Paris-Piétons-Vélos-Rollers – scenic strips of the city that are closed to cars on Sundays and holidays – have been consistently multiplied; the city website (www.paris.fr) can provide an up-to-date list of routes and a downloadable map of cycle lanes. A free *Paris à Vélo* map can also be picked up at any Mairie or from bike shops. Cycle lanes (*pistes cyclables*) run mostly N-S and E-W. N-S routes include rue de Rennes, av d'Italie, bd Sébastopol and av Marceau. E-W routes take in the rue de Rivoli, bd St-Germain, bd St-Jacques and av Daumesnil. You could be fined (€22) if you don't use them, which is a bit rich considering the lanes are often blocked by delivery vans and the €135 fine for obstructing a cycle lane is barely enforced. Cyclists are also entitled to use certain bus lanes (especially the new ones, which are set off by a strip of kerb stones): look out for traffic signs with a bike symbol. The Bois de Boulogne and Bois de Vincennes offer paths away from traffic although they are still criss-crossed by roads bearing menacing motor vehicles.

Don't let the Parisians' blasé attitude to helmets and lights convince you it's not worth using them. Be confident, make your intentions clear and keep moving – and look out for scooter-mounted bag-snatchers. If the thought of pedaling around alone in a city known for the verve of its drivers fazes you, consider joining a guided bike tour (*see p67*, **Guided tours**).

Cycles & scooters for hire

Note that bike insurance may not cover theft: be sure to check before you sign up.

Atelier de la Compagnie 57 bd de Grenelle, 15th (01.45.79.77.24/www.atelier-de-la-compagnie.com). *M° Dupleix*. **Open** 9am-6pm Mon; 9am-7pm Tue-Sat. **Credit** MC, V. A scooter for €19 per day or €95 per week. Deposit of €1,200, plus passport and photocopy of credit card, required.

Freescoot 63 quai de la Tournelle, 5th (01.44.07.06.72/www.freescoot. com). *M° St-Michel or Maubert Mutualité*. **Open** 9am-7pm daily; closed Sun from Oct to mid-Apr. **Credit** AmEx, MC, V. Scooter for €30 per day, €40 per weekend, €145 per week. Deposit of €1,300/€1,600, plus passport, required. **Other locations**: 144 bd Voltaire, 11th (01.44.93.04.03).

Maison Roue Libre 1 passage Mondétour, 1st (08.10.44.15.34). *M° Châtelet*. **Plus** (Mar-Oct) four RATP cyclobuses at Stalingrad, pl du Châtelet, porte d'Auteuil and parc Floral in the Bois de Vincennes (01.48.15.28.88/www.rouelibre.com). **Open** 9am-7pm daily. **Credit** MC, V (for weekend hire only). Bike hire costs €3 an hour, €9 a day, €14 a weekend. Helmets come free. Passport and €150 deposit required. **Other locations**: 37 bd Bourdon, 4th (01.44.54.19.29).

Paris-Vélo 2 rue du Fer-à-Moulin, 5th (01.43.37.59.22/www.paris-velo-rent-a-bike.fr). *M° Censier-Daubenton*. **Open** 10am-7pm daily. **Credit** MC, V. Good selection of mountain bikes (VTT) and 21-speed models for hire. Five hours costs €12, a weekend €30, a month €116. Passport and €300 deposit required.

Walking

Walking is the best way to explore Paris; just remember to remain vigilant at all times. Crossing Paris streets can be perilous, as the 3,000 or so pedestrians who end up in hospital – or worse – each year can tell you. Brits must realise that traffic will be coming from the 'wrong' direction and that zebra crossings mean little. By law, drivers are only obliged to stop at a red traffic light – and even then, many will take a calculated risk.

Resources A-Z

Addresses

Paris arrondissements are indicated by the last two digits of the postal code: 75002 denotes the 2nd, 75015 the 15th. The 16th arrondissement is divided into two sectors, 75016 and 75116. Some business addresses have a more detailed postcode, followed by a Cedex number which indicates the arrondissement; *bis* or *ter* is the equivalent of 'b' or 'c' after a building number.

Age restrictions

You must be 18 or over to drive, and 18 in order to consume alcohol in a public place. There is no age limit for buying cigarettes. The age of consent for heterosexuals and homosexuals is 15.

Attitude & etiquette

Parisians take manners seriously and are generally more courteous than their reputation may lead you to believe. If someone brushes you accidentally they will more often than not say '*pardon*'; you can do likewise, or say '*c'est pas grave*' (don't worry). In shops it is normal to greet the assistant with a '*bonjour madame*' or '*bonjour monsieur*' when you enter and say '*au revoir*' when you leave. The business of '*tu*' and '*vous*' can be tricky for English speakers. Strangers, people significantly older than you and professional contacts should be addressed with the respectful '*vous*'; friends, relatives, children and pets as '*tu*'. Among themselves, young people often launch straight in with '*tu*'.

Business

The best first stop in Paris for initiating business is the CCIP (*see below* **Useful Organisations**). Banks can refer you to lawyers, accountants and tax consultants. Other US and British banks provide expatriate services.

Conventions & conferences

The world's leading centre for trade fairs, Paris hosts over 500 exhibitions a year.

CNIT *2 pl de la Défense, BP 321, 92053 Paris La Défense (01.72.72.17.00/www.parisexpo.fr). M°/RER Grande Arche de La Défense.* Mainly computer fairs.

Palais des Congrès *2 pl de la Porte-Maillot, 17th (01.40.68.22.22/www.palais-congres-paris.fr). M° Porte-Maillot.*

Paris-Expo *Porte de Versailles 15th (01.72.72.17.00/www.parisexpo.fr). M° Porte de Versailles.* Paris' biggest expo centre, from fashion to pharmaceuticals.

Parc des Expositions de Paris-Nord Villepinte *SEPENV 60004, 95970 Roissy-Charles-de-Gaulle (01.48.63.30.30/www.expoparisnord.com). RER Parc des Expositions.* Trade fair centre near Roissy airport.

Courier services

ATV *(01.41.72.13.63/www.atoutevitesse.com).* **Open** 24-hr daily. **Credit** MC, V. 24-hr bike or van messengers. Higher rates after 8pm and at weekends.

Chronopost *(Customer service: 08.25.80.18.01/www.chronopost.com).* **Open** 8am-8pm Mon-Fri; 9am-3pm Sat. **Credit** MC, V. This overnight delivery offshoot of the state-run post office is the most widely used service for parcels of up to 30kg.

UPS *34 bd Malesherbes, 8th (08.00.87.78.77/www.ups.com). M° St-Augustin.* **Open** 8am-7pm Mon-Fri; 8am-1pm Sat. **Credit** AmEx, MC, V. International courier services.

Secretarial services

ADECCO International *14 pl de la Défense, 92974 Paris La Défense (01.49.01.45.25/www.adecco.fr). M° Grande Arche de La Défense.* **Open** 8.30am-12.30pm, 2-6.30pm Mon-Fri. Large international employment agency specialising in bilingual secretaries and office staff – permanent or temporary.

Translators & interpreters

Certain documents, from birth certificates to loan applications, must be translated by certified legal translators, listed at the CCIP (*see p371*) or embassies. For business translations

---

Travel advice

For up-to-date information on travel to a specific country – including the latest news on safety and security, health issues, local laws and customs – contact your home country government's department of foreign affairs. Most have websites packed with useful advice for would-be travellers.

Australia
www.smartraveller.gov.au

Canada
www.voyage.gc.ca

New Zealand
www.mft.govt.nz/travel

Republic of Ireland
foreignaffairs.gov.ie

UK
www.fco.gov.uk/travel

USA
www.state.gov/travel

there are dozens of reliable independents.

Association des Anciens Elèves de l'Esit *(01.44.05.41.46)*. **Open** by phone only, 8am-8pm Mon-Fri; 8am-6pm Sat. A translation and interpreting co-operative whose 1,000 members are graduates of the Ecole Supérieure d'Interprètes et de Traducteurs.

International Corporate Communication *3 rue des Batignolles, 17th (01.43.87.29.29). Mº Place de Clichy*. **Open** 9am-1pm, 2-6pm Mon-Fri. Translators of financial and corporate documents plus simultaneous translation.

Useful organisations

American Chamber of Commerce *262 rue du Fbg-St-Honoré, 8th (01.53.89.11.00/www.faccparisfrance.com). Mº Ternes*. (Closed to the public, calls only.)
British Embassy Commercial Library *35 rue du Fbg-St-Honoré, 8th (01.44.51.34.56/www.amb-grandebretagne.fr). Mº Concorde*. **Open** by appointment. Stocks trade directories, and assists British companies that wish to develop or set up in France.
CCIP (Chambre de Commerce et d'Industrie de Paris) *27 av de Friedland, 8th (01.55.65.55.65/ www.ccip.fr). Mº Charles de Gaulle Etoile*. **Open** 9am-5pm Mon-Fri. This huge organisation provides a variety of services for people doing business in France and is very useful for small businesses. Pick up free booklet *Discovering the Chamber of Commerce* from its head office (*above*). There's also a legal advice line (08.92.70.51.00, 9am-4.30pm Mon-Thur, 9am-1pm Fri). **Other locations**: Bourse du Commerce, 2 rue de Viarmes, 1st (has a free library and bookshop). 2 rue Adolf Jullien, 1st (support for businesses wishing to export goods and services to France).
Chambre de Commerce et d'Industrie Franco-Britannique *31 rue Boissy d'Anglas, 8th (01.53.30.81.30/fax 01.53.30.81.35/ www.francobritishchambers.com). Mº Madeleine*. **Open** 2-5pm Mon-Fri; by phone 9am-6pm. This organisation promotes contacts through conferences and social/cultural events. It publishes its own trade directory, as well as *Cross-Channel*, a trade magazine.
INSEE (Institut National de la Statistique et des Etudes Economiques) *Salle de consultation, 195 rue de Bercy, Tour Gamma A, 12th (01.41.17.50.50/ 08.25.88.94.52/www.insee.fr). Mº Bercy*. **Open** 9.30am-12:30pm,

2-5pm Mon-Thu, 9.30-12.30pm, 2-4pm Fri. Source of seemingly every statistic to do with French economy and society. Visit the reading room or search the website for free stats.
US Commercial Service *US Embassy, 2 av Gabriel, 8th (01.43.12.28.14/fax 01.43.12.21.72/ csfrance.amb-usa.fr). Mº Concorde*. **Open** by appointment 9am-6pm Mon-Fri. Helps US companies looking to export to France. Advice by fax and e-mail.

Consumer

The customer is always right? If only. Shop staff surliness is an everyday occurrence, and it's by no means only foreigners who may be treated with disdain or even pointedly ignored. That said, in the event of a more serious misdemeanour, try one of the following.

Direction Régionale de la Concurrence, de la Consommation et de la Répression des Fraudes *8 rue Froissart, 3rd (01.40.27.16.00). Mº St-Sébastien Froissart*. 9am-noon, 2-5pm Mon-Fri. Come here to make a consumer complaint concerning Paris-based businesses.

Institut National de la Consommation *80 rue Lecourbe, 15th (08.92.70.75.92/www.conso. net). Mº Sèvres Lecourbe*. **Open** by phone 9am-12.30pm Mon-Fri; recorded information at other times. Queries on consumer, regulatory, housing and administrative matters

Customs

There are no customs on goods for personal use between EU countries, provided tax has been paid in the country of origin. Quantities accepted as being for personal use are:
● 800 cigarettes or 400 small cigars or 200 cigars or 1kg loose tobacco.
● 10 litres of spirits (over 22% alcohol), 90 litres of wine (under 22% alcohol) or 110 litres of beer.
For goods from outside the EU:
● 200 cigarettes or 100 small cigars or 50 cigars or 250g loose tobacco.
● 1 litre of spirits (over 22% alcohol) or 2 litres of wine and beer
● 50g perfume
● 500g coffee

Size charts

Women's clothes			Women's shoes		
British	French	US	British	French	US
4	32	2	3	36	5
6	34	4	4	37	6
8	36	6	5	38	7
10	38	8	6	39	8
12	40	10	7	40	9
14	42	12	8	41	10
16	44	14	9	42	11
18	46	16			
20	48	18			

Men's clothes			Men's shoes		
British	French	US	British	French	US
34	44	34	6	39	7
36	46	36	7.5	40	7.5
38	48	38	8	41	8
40	50	40	8	42	8.5
42	52	42	9	43	9.5
44	54	44	10	44	10.5
46	56	46	11	45	11
48	58	48	12	46	11.5

Directory

Tax refunds

Non-EU residents can claim a refund or *détaxe* (around 12%) on VAT if they spend over €175 in any one day and if they live outside the EU for more than six months in the year. At the shop ask for a *bordereau de vente à l'exportation*, and when you leave France have it stamped by customs. Then send the stamped form back to the shop. *Détaxe* does not cover food, drink, antiques, services or works of art.

Disabled travellers

It's always wise to check up on a site's accessibility and provision for disabled access before you visit. General information (in French) is available on the Secrétaire d'Etat aux Personnes Handicapées website: www.handicap.gouv.fr.

Association des Paralysés de France *13 pl de Rungis, 13th (01.53.80.92.97/www.apf.asso.fr). M° Place d'Italie.* **Open** 9am-12.30pm, 2-6pm Mon-Fri. Publishes *Guide 98 Musées, Cinémas* (€3.81) listing cinemas and museums accessible to those with limited mobility, and a guide to restaurants and sights.

Fédération APAJH (Association pour Adultes et Jeunes Handicapés) *185 Bureaux de la Colline, 92213 St-Cloud Cedex (01.55.39.56.00/www.apajh.org). M° Marcel Sembat.* Advice for disabled people living in France.

Plateforme d'Accueil et d'Information des Personnes Handicapées de la Marie de Paris *(08.00.03.37.48).* Advice in French to disabled persons living in or visiting Paris. The Office de Tourisme website www.paris bienvenue.com also gives useful information for disabled visitors.

Getting around

Neither the métro nor buses are wheelchair-accessible, with the exception of métro line 14 (Méteor), bus lines 20, PC (Petite Ceinture) and some 91s. Forward seats on buses are intended for people with poor mobility. RER lines A and B and some SNCF trains are wheelchair-accessible in parts. All Paris taxis are obliged by law to take passengers in wheelchairs.

Aihrop *3 av Paul-Doumer, 92508 Rueil-Malmaison Cedex (01.41.29.01.29/www.aihrop.com).* **Open** 9.30am-12.30pm, 1.30-5.30pm Mon-Fri. Closed Aug. Transport for the disabled, anywhere in Paris and Ile-de-France; book 48 hours in advance.

Drugs

French police have the power to stop and search anyone. It's wise to keep prescription drugs in their original containers and, if possible, to carry copies of the original prescriptions. If you're caught in possession of illegal drugs you can expect a prison sentence and/or a fine. *See also* **Health**, **Helplines**.

Electricity & gas

Electricity in France runs on 220V. Visitors with British 240V appliances can change the plug or use an adapter (*adaptateur*). For US 110V appliances, you'll need to use a transformer (*transformateur*), available at BHV or branches of Fnac and Darty. Gas and electricity are supplied by state-owned Electricité de France-Gaz de France. Contact EDF-GDF (01.45.44.64.64/www.edf.fr/www.gazdefrance. com) about supply, bills, power failures or gas leaks.

Embassies & consulates

For a full list of embassies and consulates, see the Pages Jaunes (www.pagesjaunes.fr) under 'Ambassades et Consulats'. Consular services are for citizens of that country (passports, etc) only.

Australian Embassy *4 rue Jean-Rey, 15th (01.40.59.33.00/www.austgov.fr). M° Bir-Hakeim.* **Open** *Consular services* 9.15am-noon, 2-4.30pm Mon-Fri; *Visas* 10am-12am Mon-Fri.

British Embassy *35 rue du Fbg-St-Honoré, 8th (01.44.51.31.00/www.amb-grandebretagne.fr). M° Concorde. Consular services 18bis rue d'Anjou, 8th. M° Concorde.* **Open** 9.30am-12.30pm, 2.30-5pm Mon, Wed-Fri; 9.30am-4.30pm Tue. *Visas 16 rue d'Anjou, 8th (01.44.51.33.01/03/recorded info 01.44.51.33.02/emergency consular services 01.44.51.31.00).* **Open** 9am-noon Mon-Fri; by phone 2.30-5pm Mon-Fri. British citizens wanting consular services (new passports etc) should ignore the long queue along rue d'Anjou for the visa department, and walk straight in at No 18bis.

Canadian Embassy *35 av Montaigne, 8th (01.44.43.29.00/www.amb-canada.fr). M° Franklin D Roosevelt. Consular services (01.44.43.29.02).* **Open** 9am-noon, 2-4.30pm Mon-Fri. *Visas 37 av Montaigne (01.44.43.29.16).* **Open** 8.30-11am Mon-Fri.

Irish Embassy *12 av Foch, 16th. Consulate 4 rue Rude, 16th (01.44.17.67.00). M° Charles de Gaulle Etoile.* **Open** (consular/visas) 9.30am-noon Mon-Fri; by phone 9.30am-1pm, 2.30-5.30pm Mon-Fri.

New Zealand Embassy *7ter rue Léonard-de-Vinci, 16th (01.45.01.43.43/www.nzembassy.com/france). M° Victor Hugo.* **Open** 9am-1pm, 2pm-5.30pm Mon-Fri (closes 4pm Fri). July, Aug 9am-1pm, 2-4.30pm Mon-Thur; 9am-2pm Fri. *Visas* 9am-12.30pm Mon-Fri. Visas for travel to New Zealand can be applied for using the website www.immigration.govt.nz.

South African Embassy *59 quai d'Orsay, 7th (01.53.59.23.23/www.afriquesud.net). M° Invalides.* **Open** by appointment; by phone 8.30am-5.15pm Mon-Fri. Consulate and visas 9am-noon.

US Embassy *2 av Gabriel, 8th (01.43.12.22.22/www.amb-usa.fr). M° Concorde. Consulate and visas 2 rue St-Florentin, 1st (01.43.12.22.22). M° Concorde.* **Open** (consular services) 9am-12.30pm, 1-3pm Mon-Fri. For visas, phone 08.99.70.37.00 or check website for non-immigration visas.

Emergencies

Most of the following services operate 24 hours a day. In a medical emergency, such as a road accident, call the Sapeurs-Pompiers, who have trained paramedics. *See also* **Health**: **Accident & Emergency, Doctors; Helplines**.

Ambulance (SAMU)	**15**
Police	**17**
Fire (Sapeurs-Pompiers)	**18**
Emergency (from a mobile phone)	**112**
GDF (gas leaks) 08.10.43.32.75/www.gazdefrance.fr	
EDF (electricity) 08.10.33.39 + number of arrondissement (01-20)	
Centre anti-poison 01.40.05.48.48	

Gay & lesbian

For information on HIV and AIDS, *see* **Health**. *See also pp302-307* **Gay & Lesbian**.

Health

Nationals of non-EU countries should take out insurance before leaving home. EU nationals staying in France are entitled to use of the French Social Security system, which refunds up to 70% of medical expenses. British nationals should obtain form E111 from a post office before leaving the UK (or E112 for those already in treatment). If you're staying for longer than three months, or working in France but still paying NI contributions in Britain, you'll need form E128 filled in by your employer and stamped by the NI contributions office in order to get a French medical number. Consultations and prescriptions have to be paid for in full on the spot, and are reimbursed on receipt of a completed *fiche*. If you undergo treatment the doctor will give you a prescription and a *feuille de soins* (bill of treatment). Stick the small stickers from the medication boxes on to the *feuille de soins*. Send this, the prescription and form E111 to the local **Caisse Primaire d'Assurance Maladie** for a refund. For those resident in France, more and more doctors (especially in Paris) now accept the **Carte Vitale**, which lets them produce a virtual *feuille de soins* and for you to pay only

the non-reimbursable part of the bill. Information on the health-insurance system can be found at www.ameli.fr. You can track refunds with Allosecu (08.20.90.09.00). For general information, visit the ministry of health's website: www.sante.gouv.fr.

Accident & emergency

Note that many hospitals specialise in one type of medical emergency or illness. Consult the Assistance Publique's web site (www.aphp.fr) for details. In a medical emergency, call the Sapeurs-Pompiers or SAMU (*see* **Emergencies**). The following (in order of arrondissement) are Paris hospitals with 24-hr accident and emergency services:

Adults

Hôpital Hôtel Dieu *1 pl du Parvis Notre-Dame, 4th (01.42.34.82.34).*

Hôpital St-Louis *1 av Claude Vellefaux, 10th (01.42.49.49.49).*

Hôpital St-Antoine *184 rue du Fbg-St-Antoine, 12th (01.49.28.20.00).*

Hôpital de la Pitié-Salpêtrière *47-83 bd de l'Hôpital, 13th (01.42.16.00.00).*

Hôpital Cochin *27 rue du Fbg-St-Jacques, 14th (01.58.41.41.41).*

Hôpital Européen Georges Pompidou *20 rue Leblanc, 15th (01.56.09.20.00).*

Hôpital Bichat-Claude Bernard *46 rue Henri Huchard, 18th (01.40.25.80.80).*

Hôpital Tenon *4 rue de la Chine, 20th (01.56.01.70.00).*

Children

Hôpital Armand Trousseau *26 av du Dr Arnold Netter, 12th (01.44.73.74.75).*

Hôpital St-Vincent de Paul *74-82 av Denfert Rochereau, 14th (01.40.48.81.11).*

Hôpital Necker *149 rue de Sèvres, 15th (01.44.49.40.00).*

Hôpital Robert Debré *48 bd Sérurier, 19th (01.40.03.20.00).*

Private Hospitals

American Hospital in Paris *63 bd Victor-Hugo, 92200 Neuilly (01.46.41.25.25/www.american-*

hospital.org). M° Porte Maillot, then bus 82. **Open** 24hrs daily. English-speaking hospital. French Social Security refunds only a small percentage of treatment costs.

Hertford British Hospital (Hôpital Franco-Britannique) *3 rue Barbès, 92300 Levallois-Perret (01.46.39.22.22/www.british-hospital.org). M° Anatole-France.* **Open** 24hrs daily. Most of the medical staff speak English.

Complementary medicine

Académie d'Homéopathie et des Médecines Douces *2 rue d'Isly, 8th (01.43.87.60.33). M° St-Lazare.* **Open** 11am-8pm Mon-Fri. Health services include acupuncture, aromatherapy and homeopathy.

Contraception & abortion

To get the pill (*la pilule*) or coil (*stérilet*), you need a prescription, available on appointment from the first two places below, from a *médecin généraliste* (GP) or from a gynaecologist. The morning-after pill (*la pilule du lendemain*) can be had from pharmacies without prescription but is not reimbursed. Condoms (*préservatifs*) and spermicides and are sold in pharmacies and supermarkets, and there are condom machines in most métro stations, club lavatories and on some street corners. If you're considering an abortion (IVG – *interruption volontaire de grossesse*) but want to discuss options in detail, you may get better information and counselling from the *orthogénie* (family planning) department of a hospital than from the two organisations below (see www.aphp.fr for IVG services). While abortion rights are strongly grounded in France, some doctors remain opposed. Ultrasound examinations to ascertain the exact stage of pregnancy are obligatory.

Centre de Planification et d'Education Familiales *27 rue Curnonsky, 17th (01.48.88.07.28). M° Porte de Champerret.* **Open** 9am-

5pm Mon-Fri. Free consultations on family planning and abortion. Abortion counselling on demand; otherwise phone for an appointment.

MFPF (Mouvement Français pour le Planning Familial) *10 rue Vivienne, 2nd (08.00.80.38.03/01.42.60.93.20/ www.planning-familial.org). M° Bourse.* **Open** 9.30am-5.30pm Mon, Tue, Thur, Fri; 9.30am-7.30am Wed. Phone for an appointment for prescriptions and contraception advice. For abortion advice, turn up at the centre at one of the designated time slots. The approach here, however, is brusque. **Other locations:** 94 bd Masséna, 13th (01.45.84.28.25).

Dentists

Dentists are found in the *Pages Jaunes* under *Dentistes*. For emergencies contact:

Urgences Dentaires de Paris *(01.42.61.12.00/01.43.37.51.00).* **Open** 8am-10pm Sun, holidays.

SOS Dentaire *87 bd Port-Royal, 13th (01.43.37.51.00). M° Les Gobelins/RER Port-Royal.* **Open** *phone* 9am-midnight. Phone service for emergency dental care.

Hôpital de la Pitié-Salpêtrière *(see above,* **Accident & Emergency***)* also offers 24hr emergency dental care.

Doctors

You'll find a complete list of GPs is in the *Pages Jaunes* under *Médecins: Médecine générale*. To get a social security refund, choose a doctor or dentist who is *conventionné* (state registered). Consultations cost €20 or more, of which a proportion can be reimbursed. Seeing a specialist costs still more.

Centre Médical Europe *44 rue d'Amsterdam, 9th (01.42.81.93.33/ dentists 01.42.81.80.00). M° St-Lazare.* **Open** 8am-7pm Mon-Fri; 8am-6pm Sat. Practitioners in all fields, charging minimal consultation fees.

House calls

SOS Infirmiers (Nurses) (01.47.07.00.73). House calls 24hrs. Costs vary, and are higher after 8pm and at weekends.

SOS Médecins (01.43.37.77.77 or 08.20.33.24.24). House calls cost €35 before 7pm; from €50 after and on holidays; prices are higher if you don't have French social security.

Urgences Médicales de Paris (01.53.94.94.94). Doctors make house calls for €35 daytimes (€60 if you don't have French social security); €50/€80 until midnight; €63.50/€90 after midnight. Some speak English.

Opticians

Branches of **Alain Afflelou** (www.alainafflelou.com) and **Lissac** (www.lissac.com) stock hundreds of frames and can make prescription glasses within the hour. For an eye test you'll need to go to an *ophtalmologiste* – ask the optician for a list. Contact lenses can be bought over the counter if you have your prescription details.

Hôpital des Quinze-Vingts *28 rue de Charenton, 12th (01.40.02.15.20).* Specialist eye hospital offers on-the-spot consultations for eye problems.

SOS Optique *(01.48.07.22.00/ www.sosoptique.com).* 24hr repair service for glasses.

Pharmacies

All French *pharmacies* sport a green neon cross. Paris has a rota system of *pharmacies de garde* during the night and on Sunday. If closed, a pharmacy will have a sign indicating the nearest one open. Staff can provide basic medical services like disinfecting and bandaging wounds (for a small fee) and will indicate the nearest doctor on duty. *Parapharmacies* sell almost everything pharmacies do but cannot dispense prescription medication. Toiletries, sanitary products and cosmetics are often cheaper in supermarkets.

Night pharmacies

Pharma Presto *(01.61.04.04.04/ www.pharma-presto.com).* **Open** 24hrs daily. Delivery charge €40 8am-6pm; €55 6pm-8am & weekends. Delivers prescription medication (may make non-prescription exceptions). Will also chauffeur your ailing pet to the vet.

Pharmacie des Halles *10 bd de Sébastopol, 4th (01.42.72.03.23). M° Châtelet.* Open 9am-midnight Mon-Sat; 9am-10pm Sun.

Dérhy/Pharmacie des Champs-Elysées *84 av des Champs-Elysées, 8th (01.45.62.02.41). M° George V.* Open 24hrs daily.

Matignon *2 rue Jean-Mermoz, 8th (01.43.59.86.55). M° Franklin D Roosevelt.* **Open** 8.30am-2am daily.

Pharmacie Européenne de la Place de Clichy *6 pl de Clichy, 9th (01.48.74.65.18). M° Place de Clichy.* **Open** 24hrs daily.

Pharmacie de la Place de la Nation *13 pl de la Nation, 11th (01.43.73.24.03). M° Nation.* Open 8am-11pm daily.

Pharmacie d'Italie *61 av d'Italie, 13th (01.44.24.19.72). M° Tolbiac.* **Open** 8am-2am daily.

STDs, HIV & AIDS

Centre Medico-Sociale (Mairie de Paris) *2 rue Figuier, 4th (01.49.96.62.70). M° Pont-Marie.* Open 9am-5.30pm Mon, Tue, Thur; noon-5.30pm Wed; 1.30-5.30pm Fri; 9.30-10.30am Sat. Free, anonymous tests (*dépistages*) for HIV, Hepatitis B and C and syphillis (wait one week for results). Good counselling service, too.

Le Kiosque Infos Sida-Toxicomanie *36 rue Geoffroy l'Asnier, 4th (01.44.78.00.00). M° St-Paul.* Open 10am-7pm Mon-Fri; 2-7pm Sat. Youth association that offers information on AIDS and sexuality, as well as drug addiction and abuse. Face-to-face counselling service.

SIDA Info Service *(08.00.84.08.00/www.sida-info-service.org).* **Open** 24hrs daily. Confidential AIDS information in French. English-speaking counsellors 2-7pm Mon, Wed, Fri.

Helplines

Alcoholics Anonymous in English *(01.46.34.59.65/www. aaparis.org).* 24-hr recorded message gives details of AA meetings at the American Cathedral (*see p380*) or American Church (*see p381*).

Allô Service Public *(39.39/www.service-public.fr).* Open 8am-7pm Mon-Fri; 9am-2pm Sat. An efficient source of information and contacts for all aspects of officialdom, tax, work and administrative matters. They even claim to be able to help if you have problems with neighbours. The catch: you can only dial from inside France, and operators speak only French.

The Counseling Center *(01.47.23.61.13).* English-language counselling service, based at the American Cathedral.

Drogues Alcool Tabac Info Service *(08.00.23.13.13/www.drogues.gouv.fr)*. Phone service, in French, for help with drug, alcohol and tobacco problems.

Narcotics Anonymous
(01.43.72.12.72/www.nafrance.org). Meetings in English three times a week.

SOS Dépression *(01.40.47.95.95)*. Open 24hrs daily. People listen and/or give advice. Can send a counsellor or psychiatrist to your home in case of a crisis.

SOS Help *(01.46.21.46.46)*. Open 3-11pm daily. English-language helpline.

ID

French law requires that some form of identification be carried at all times. Be ready to produce a passport or *carte de séjour* in response to that old police refrain, 'Papiers, s'il vous plaît'.

Insurance

See p373 **Health.**

Internet

ISPs

America Online
(08.26.02.60.00/www.aol.fr).
Club-Internet
(08.00.97.01.58/www.club-internet.fr).
Free *(08.92.13.51.51/www.free.fr)*.
Noosnet *(08.26.20.03.80/www.noos.com)*.
Neuf *(08.92.22.21.09/www.neuf.fr)*.
Wanadoo (France Télécom) *(08.10.63.34.34/www.wanadoo.fr)*.

Internet access

Many hotels offer Internet access, some from your own room – and an increasing number of public spaces are setting themselves up as Wi-Fi hotspots (*see p367* **Wi-Fi, where find?**). For websites *see p389*.

Access Academy *60-62 rue St-André des Arts, 6th (www.accessacademy.com). M° Odéon.* Open 8am-2am daily.

Cyber Cube *12 rue Daval, 11th (01.49.29.67.67/www.cybercube.fr). M° Bastille.* Open 10am-10pm daily.

Language

See p387 **Essential vocabulary**; for food terms, *see p206* **Menu lexicon.**

Left luggage

Gare du Nord

There are self-locking luggage lockers (6.15am-11.15pm daily) on Level -1 under the main station concourse: small (€3.50), medium (€7) and large (€9.50) for 48 hours. SNCF luggage service on 01.55.31.54.54 can give basic details.

Roissy-Charles-de-Gaulle airport

Bagages du Monde
(01.48.16.84.90/www.bagagesdumonde.com). **Terminal 1** *Niveau Arrivée, Porte 14 (01.48.16.34.90)*. Open 8am-2pm daily. **Terminal 2** *Niveau Départ, Porte 3 (01.48.16.20.61)*. Open 8am-8pm daily. **Terminal 2F** *Niveau Arrivée, Porte 4 (01.48.16.20.64)*. Open 7am-7pm daily. Company with counters in CDG terminals and an office in Paris (102 rue de Chemin-Vert, 11th, 01.43.57.30.90, 10am-2pm Sat only by appointment) that can ship excess baggage anywhere in the world, or store luggage.

Legal help

Mairies can answer some legal enquiries; phone for timetables of their free *consultations juridiques*.

Direction Départementale de la Concurrence, de la Consommation, et de la Répression des Fraudes *8 rue Froissart, 3rd (01.40.27.16.00). M° St-Sébastien Froissart.* Open 9am-noon, 2-5pm Mon-Fri. Part of the Ministry of Finance; deals with consumer complaints.

Palais de Justice Galerie de Harlay *Escalier S, 4 bd du Palais, 4th (01.44.32.48.48). M° Cité.* Open 9am-noon Mon-Fri. Free legal consultation. Arrive early and obtain a numbered ticket for the queue.

SOS Avocats (08.25.39.33.00). Open 7-11.30pm Mon-Fri. Closed July, Aug. Free legal advice by phone.

Libraries

Every arrondissement has its free public library. To get hold of a library card, you need ID and evidence of a fixed address in Paris.

American Library *10 rue du Général-Camou, 7th (01.53.59.12.60/www.americanlibraryinparis.org). M° Ecole-Militaire or RER Pont de l'Alma.* Open 10am-7pm Tue-Sat (shorter hours in Aug). Admission day pass €11; annual €96; discount for students. A useful resource: this is the largest English-language lending library on the Continent. It receives 400 periodicals, as well as popular magazines and newspapers (mainly American).

Bibliothèque Historique de la Ville de Paris *Hôtel Lamoignon, 24 rue Pavée, 4th (01.44.59.29.40). M° St-Paul.* Open 9.30am-6pm Mon-Sat. Closed first 2 weeks in Aug. Admission free (bring passport photo and ID). Books and documents on Paris history in a Marais mansion.

Bibliothèque Marguerite Durand *79 rue Nationale, 13th (01.53.82.76.77). M° Tolbiac or Place d'Italie.* Open 2-6pm Tue-Sat. Closed 3 weeks in Sept. Admission free. 40,000 books and 120 periodicals on women's history and feminism. Collection includes letters of Colette and Louise Michel. The library is closed until summer 2006.

Bibliothèque Nationale de France François Mitterrand *quai François-Mauriac, 13th (01.53.79.59.59/www.bnf.fr). M° Bibliothèque.* Open 10am-8pm Tue-Sat; noon-7pm Sun. Closed 2wks in Sept & bank holidays. Admission day pass €3; annual €30. Books, papers and periodicals, plus titles in English. An audio-visual room lets you browse photo, film and sound archives.

Bibliothèque Publique d'Information (BPI) *Centre Pompidou, 4th (01.44.78.12.71/www.bpi.fr). M° Hôtel de Ville/RER Châtelet Les Halles.* Open 12am-10pm Mon, Wed-Fri; 11am-10pm Sat, Sun. Closed 1 May. Admission free. Now on three levels, the Centre Pompidou's vast library has a huge international press section, reference books and language-learning facilities.

BIFI (Bibliothèque du Film) *51 rue de Bercy, 12th (01.71.19.32.32/www.bifi.fr). M° Bercy.* Open 10am-7pm Mon-Fri. Closed 2 weeks in Aug. Admission €3.50 day pass; €34 annual; €15 students annual. Housed in the same building as the Cinémathèque Française (*see p294* **'thèque five**), this world-class researchers' and film buffs' library offers books, magazines film stills and posters, as well as films on video and DVD.

Directory

Documentation Française
29-31 quai Voltaire, 7th
(01.40.15.72.72/www.ladocument
ationfrancaise.fr). Mº Rue du Bac.
Open 9am-6pm Mon-Fri. Closed
Aug & first week in Sept. The
official government archive and
central reference library has
information on French politics
and economy since 1945.

Locksmiths

Numerous round-the-clock
repair services handle locks,
plumbing and, sometimes,
car repairs. Most charge a
minimum €18-€20 call-out
(*déplacement*) and €30 per
hour, plus parts. Charges are
higher on Sunday and at night.

Allô Assistance Dépannage
(08.00.00.00.18). No car repairs.

SOS Dépannage
(01.47.07.99.99/www.okservice.fr).
Double the price of most, but claims
to be twice as reliable.

Lost property

Bureau des Objets Trouvés
36 rue des Morillons, 15th
(08.21.00.25.25/01.55.76.20.20/
www.prefecture-police-paris.interieur.
gouv.fr). Mº Convention. **Open**
8.30am-5pm Mon-Thur; 8.30am-
4.30pm Fri. Visit in person to fill in
a form specifying details of the loss.
This may have been the first lost
property office in the world, but it
is far from the most efficient. Huge
delays in processing claims mean
that if your trip to Paris is short you
may need to nominate a proxy to
collect found objects after you leave,
although small items can be posted.
If your passport was among the
items lost you'll need to go to your
consulate to get a single-entry
temporary passport in order to
leave the country.

SNCF lost property Some
mainline SNCF stations have their
own lost property offices.

Media

See also **Websites** *p389.*

Magazines

Arts & listings

Three smallish publications
compete for consumers of
basic Wednesday-to-Tuesday
listings details: handbag-sized
L'Officiel des Spectacles

(€0.35) and **Pariscope** (€0.40),
and the larger, more magazine-
like **Zurban** (€0.80). Affiliated
to Radio Nova, monthly **Nova**
gives multi-ethnic information
on where to drink, dance and
hang out. **Technikart** tries –
not entirely successfully –
to mix clubbing with the arts.
Highbrow TV guide
Télérama has superb arts
coverage and comes with
Sortir, a Paris listings insert.
Les Inrockuptibles (fondly
known as *Les Inrocks*) is
strong on contemporary
music scenes at home and
abroad; strong coverage of
film and books, too.

Then there are the specialist
arts magazines, at least one for
every interest. The choice of
film-related titles, in particular,
is wide, and includes long-
established intellectual
heavyweights **Les Cahiers
du Cinéma**, **Positif** and
Trafic, fluffy **Studio** and
celebrity-heavy **Première**.

Business

Capital, its sister magazine
Management and weightier
L'Expansion are notable
monthlies. **Défis** has tips for
the entrepreneur; **Initiatives**
is for the self-employed.

English

The springtime **Time Out
Paris Free Guide** is widely
distributed in visitor venues
such as hotels, and the **Time
Out Paris Visitors' Guide**
is on sale in newsagents across
the city. Free monthly **GoGo**,
available at bookshops and
bars, has cultural listings and
features in English. **FUSAC**
(France-USA Contacts) is a
small-ads magazine that lists
flat rentals, job ads and
appliances for sale.

Gossip

The French love gossip.
Public gives weekly celebrity
updates; **Oh Là!** (sister of
Spain's *Hola!* and UK's *Hello!*)
showcases celebs. **Voici** is
the juiciest scandal sheet;

Gala tells the same stories
without the sleaze. **Paris
Match** is a French institution
founded in 1948, packed
with society gossip, celeb
interviews and regular photo
scoops. **Point de Vue**
specialises in royalty (no
showbiz fluff). Monthly
Entrevue aims to titillate
and tends toward features
on nonconformist sex.

News

Weekly news magazines are
an important sector in France,
offering news, cultural sections
as well as in-depth reports;
they range from serious
L'Express, **Le Point** and
Le Nouvel Observateur
and sardonic, chaotically
arranged **Marianne**. Weekly
Courrier International
publishes a fascinating
selection of articles, translated
into French, from newspapers
all over the world.

Women, men & fashion

Elle was a pioneer among
women's mags and has
editions across the globe. In
France it's a weekly, and spot-
on for interviews and fashion.
Monthly **Marie-Claire** takes
a more feminist, campaigning
line. Both have design spin-
offs (**Elle Décoration**,
Marie-Claire Maison) and
Elle has spawned foodie **Elle
à Table**. **DS** has lots to read
and coverage of social issues.
Vogue, bought for its fashion
coverage and big-name guests,
is rivalled during fashion week
by **L'Officiel de la Mode**.
The underground buys more
radical publications **Purple**
(six-monthly art, literature and
fashion tome), **Crash**, and the
new wave of fashion/lifestyle
mags: **WAD** (stands for We
Are Different), **Citizen K**,
Jalouse and **Numéro**. Men's
mags include the naughty-
bizarre **Echo des Savanes**
and French versions of lad
bibles **FHM**, **Maximal** and
Men's Health.

The anglo frequency

One commercial radio station in Paris broadcasts entirely in English. Launched in May 2004, **Paris Live Radio** mixes Paris-centric content with the best of back home, making it a complete aural accompaniment for the capital's estimated 200,000 anglophone residents. But there's one catch: for the moment you can only tune in via cable, satellite, the internet, and DAB Digital Radio. Technology barrier notwithstanding, the station still reckons to attract some 30,000 listeners daily – and technology duffers shouldn't have to wait long; plans are under way to apply for an AM and eventually an FM licence, perhaps in 2006.

Targeted at anglophiles as well as anglophones, Paris Live Radio has assembled a fittingly cosmopolitan broadcasting team – meaning you're as likely to tune in to an American accent as an Aussie, Welsh, English, or even Swedish one. The formula is classic enough: news, music and 'what's on' articles, but the blend of French and Anglo is what sets the station apart.

If you've not yet acquired a taste for French music, you may prefer to retune your digital dial, as French law obliges DJs to play at least 40 per cent home-grown artists. On the whole, though, the music is likely to appeal to the twenty- to thirtysomething crowd (which also happens to be the biggest demographic group among the capital's anglo ex-pats). During the daytime, think Coldplay, Red Hot Chilli Peppers, Air and the occasional classic from Pink Floyd or Bowie; weekend and evening sessions are given over to more eclectic tastes, such as jazz, hip-hop or classical. The station's niche, though, is its focus on Paris. Local news is delivered on the hour, and there are regular previews and reviews of the latest concerts, plays, shows, and art exhibitions in town. Self-proclaimed ex-pat cultural guerrilla David Applefield also hosts a weekly chat show for the more intellectually inclined.

You can sample the full anglo aural experience at **www.parislive.fm**.

Paris Live Radio

01.53.09.26.20/www.parislive.fm.

Newspapers

National dailies have relatively high prices and low print runs. Only 20% of France reads a national paper; regional dailies dominate outside Paris. Serious, centre-left **Le Monde** is must-read material for business types, politicians and intellectuals; despite its lofty reputation, subject matter is eclectic. Founded in the aftershocks of 1968 by a group that included Sartre and de Beauvoir, snappier **Libération**, affectionately known as *Libé*, is now centre-left but still the preferred read of the *gauche caviar* (champagne socialists) and worth buying for wide news and arts coverage. Conservative upper and middle classes go for daily broadsheet **Le Figaro**, which has a devotion to politics, shopping, food and sport. Its sales are boosted by lots of property and job ads and Wednesday's **Figaroscope** Paris listings. The Saturday edition has three magazines. For business and financial news, the French dailies **La Tribune**, **Les Echos** and the weekly **Investir** are the tried and trusted sources. The easy-read tabloid **Le Parisien** is strong on consumer affairs, social issues, local news, events and vox pops. Downmarket **France Soir** has gone tabloid. **La Croix** is a Catholic, right-wing daily. The Communist Party **L'Humanité** (shortened to *L'Huma*) struggles on. Sunday broadsheet **Le Journal du Dimanche** comes with **Fémina** mag and a Paris section. **L'Equipe** is the doyen of European sports dailies, its sister bi-weekly magazine **France Football** the bible of world soccer. Each was instrumental in setting up the game's top competitions during the golden age of French sports journalism after the war. **Paris-Turf** is for horse fans.

English-language papers

Paris-based **International Herald Tribune** is on sale throughout the city; British dailies, Sundays and **USA Today** are widely available on the day of issue at larger kiosks in the centre, though often without their supplements. The most popular (and many esoteric) English and US newspapers and magazines can be had in central bookshops (*see p242*).

Satirical papers

Wednesday institution **Le Canard Enchaîné** is the Gallic *Private Eye* – in fact it was the inspiration for the *Eye*. It's a broadly left-wing satirical weekly broadsheet that's full of in-jokes and breaks political scandals. **Charlie Hebdo** is mainly bought for its cartoons.

Radio

For a complete list of all Paris radio frequencies, go to www.bric-a-brac.org/radio/ville/paris; for up-to-date info on TV and radio see www.csa.fr. Many of the following can be heard online at their respective websites. A mandatory state-defined minimum of 40% French music has led to overplay of Gallic pop oldies and to the creation of dubious hybrids by local groups that mix words in French with a refrain in English. Trashy phone-in shows also proliferate. Wavelengths are in MHz.

87.8 France Inter Highbrow, state-run; jazz, international news and discussion slots aplenty. Good cultural coverage.

90.4 Nostalgie As you'd expect.

90.9 Chante France 100% French chanson.

91.3 Chérie FM Lots of oldies.

91.7 France Musiques State classical music channel: highbrow concerts and top jazz.

92.1 Le Mouv' New public station aimed at luring the young with pop and rock music.

93.1 Aligre From local Paris news to literary chat.

93.5/93.9 France Culture Talky state culture station.

94.8 RCJ/Radio J/Judaïque FM/Radio Shalom Shared wavelength for Jewish stations.

95.2 Ici et Maintenant/Neo New stations hoping to stir local public debate about current events.

96.0 Skyrock Pop station with loudmouth presenters. Lots of rap.

96.4 BFM Business and economics.

96.9 Voltage FM Dance music.

97.4 Rire et Chansons A non-stop diet of jokes and pop oldies.

97.8 Ado Music for teenagers.

98.2 Radio FG Beloved of clubbers for its on-the-pulse tips, this station ditched its all-gay remit in 1999.

99.0 Radio Latina Great Latin and salsa music.

100.3 NRJ 'Energy' – geddit? National leader with the under-30s.

101.1 Radio Classique Top-notch, state-run classical music station.

101.5 Radio Nova Hip hop, trip hop, world, jazz.

101.9 Fun Radio Now embracing techno alongside Anglo pop hits.

102.3 Ouï FM Ouï will rock you.

103.9 RFM Easy listening.

104.3 RTL The most popular French station nationwide mixes music and talk programmes.

104.7 Europe 1 News, press reviews, sports, business, entertainment. Much the best weekday breakfast news broadcast, with politicians interviewed live.

105.1 FIP Traffic and weather info, what's on in Paris and a mix of jazz, classical, world and pop. 'Fipettes', female continuity announcers employed for their come-to-bed voices, are a much-loved feature.

105.5 France Info 24-hr news, weather, economic updates and sports bulletins. Reports get repeated every 15 minutes: good if you're learning French.

106.7 Beur FM North African music and discussion.

English

You can receive the **BBC World Service** (648 KHz AM), with its English-language international news, current events, pop and drama; also on 198KHz LW, from midnight to 5.30am daily. At other times 198KHz LW carries **BBC Radio 4**, with British news, talk and *The Archers*. **RFI** (738 KHz AM; www.rfi.fr) has an English-language programme of news and music from 7-8am, 2.30-3.30pm and 4.30-5pm daily. There's also the French capital's first all-English radio station, **Paris Live** (www.parislive.net).

Television

In March 2005, the choice of free TV channels available in France more than doubled. Under the explosive acronym TNT (Télévision Numérique Terrestre, or terrestrial digital television), seven new channels – available via the traditional rooftop aerial with a decoder that costs about €100, or automatically to cable and satellite customers – began

broadcasting. For details, go to www.tdf.fr or pick up a copy of weekly mag *Télérama*. The channels listed below are the six 'core' stations available on an unenhanced TV set.

TF1 *(www.tf1.fr)*. The country's biggest channel, first to be privatised (in 1987). Reality shows, dubbed soaps and football are staples.

France 2 *(www.france2.fr)*. This state-owned station mixes game shows, chat, documentaries, and the usual cop series and films.

France 3 *(www.france3.fr)*. This, the more heavyweight of the two state channels offers wildlife and sports coverage, debates, *Cinéma de Minuit* – classic films in V.O. (*version originale*, or original language) – and endearing cookery show *Bon Appétit Bien Sûr*, fronted by superchef Joël Robuchon.

Canal+ *(www.canalplus.fr)*. Subscription channel shows recent films, exclusive sport and late-night porn. A week's worth of the satirical puppets show *Les Guignols* is broadcast unscrambled on Sunday at 1.40pm.

Arte/France 5 *(www.arte-tv.com)*. Intellectual Franco-German hybrid Arte shares its wavelength with educational channel France 5 (3am-7pm).

M6 *(www.m6.fr)*. Dubbed US sci-fi series and made for TV movies, plus investigative reportage, popular science and kids' shows.

Cable TV & satellite

France offers a decent range of cable and satellite channels but content in English is still limited. CNN and BBC World offer round-the-clock news coverage. BBC Prime keeps you up to date on *EastEnders* (omnibus Sun 2pm), while Teva supplies comedy such as *Sex and the City*.

Noostv *(08.26.20.03.80/www.noos.fr)*. The first cable provider to offer an interactive video service via Internet.

Money

Visitors can carry a maximum of €7,600 in currency (www.finances.gouv.fr).

The euro

Non-French debit and credit cards can be used to withdraw

and pay in euros, and currency withdrawn in France can be used subsequently all over the euro zone. Daylight robbery occurs, however, if you try to deposit a euro cheque from any country other than France in a French bank: they are currently charging around €15 for this service, and the European parliament has backed down on its original decision that cross-border payments should be in line with domestic ones across the euro zone. Good news for Brits, though – if you transfer money from the UK to France in euros you'll pay the same charges as if Britain were within the euro zone (but watch the exchange rate carefully). For useful euro information online, *see p389*.

ATMs

Withdrawals in euros can be made from bank and post office automatic cash machines. The specific cards accepted are marked on each machine, and most can give instructions in English. Credit card companies charge a fee for cash advances, but their rates are often better than bank rates.

Banks

French banks usually open 9am-5pm Mon-Fri (some close at lunch); some banks also open on Sat. All are closed on public holidays, and from noon on the previous day. Note that not all banks have foreign exchange counters. Commission rates vary between banks; the state-owned Banque de France usually offers good rates. Most banks accept travellers' cheques, but may be reluctant to accept personal cheques even with the Eurocheque guarantee card, which is not widely used in France.

Bank accounts

To open an account (*ouvrir un compte*), French banks require proof of identity, address and your income (if any). You'll probably be required to show your passport, *carte de séjour*, an electricity/gas or phone bill in your name and a payslip/letter from your employer. Students need a student card and may need a letter from their parents. Of the major banks (BNP, Crédit Lyonnais, Société Générale, Banque Populaire, Crédit Agricole), Société Générale tends to be most foreigner-friendly. Most banks don't hand out a Carte Bleue/Visa until several weeks after you've opened an account. A chequebook (*chéquier*) is usually issued in about a week. Payments made with a Carte Bleue are debited directly from your current account, but you can choose for purchases to be debited at the end of every month. French banks are tough on overdrafts, so try to anticipate any cash crisis in advance and work out a deal for an authorised overdraft (*découvert autorisé*) or you risk being blacklisted as 'interdit bancaire' – forbidden from having a current account – for up to ten years. Depositing foreign currency cheques is slow, so use wire transfer or a bank draft in euros to receive funds from abroad.

Bureaux de change

If you arive in Paris very early or late, you can change money at the **American Express** bureaux de change in terminals 1 (01.48.16.13.26), 2A, 2B, 2C and 2D (01.48.16.48.40) and 2E (01.48.16.63.81) at Roissy, and at Orly Sud (01.49.75.77.37); all are open 6.30am-11pm daily. **Travelex** has bureaux de change at the following train stations – though opening hours can vary.

Gare Montparnasse *01.42.79.03.88.* **Open** 8am-8pm daily. **Gare du Nord** *01.42.80.11.50.* **Open** 6.30am-11.25pm daily.

Credit cards

Major international credit cards are widely used in France; Visa (more commonly known in France as *Carte Bleue*) is the most readily accepted. French-issued credit cards have a security microchip (*puce*) in each card. The card is slotted into a reader, and the holder keys in a PIN to authorise the transaction. Non-French cards also work, but generate a credit slip to sign. In case of credit card loss or theft, call one of the following 24hr services that have English-speaking staff.

American Express 01.47.77.70.00
Diners Club 01.49.06.17.50
MasterCard/Visa 08.36.69.08.80.

Foreign affairs

American Express *11 rue Scribe, 9th (01.47.77.79.28/www.american express.com). M° Opéra.* **Open** 9am-6.30pm Mon-Sat.
Travel agency, bureau de change, poste restante (you can also leave messages here for other card holders Euro-travelling), card replacement, travellers' cheque refund service, international money transfers and a cash machine for AmEx cardholders.
Other locations: Galeries Lafayette, 40 bd Hausmann, 9th (01.45.26.78.68).

Barclays *6 rond point des Champs-Elysées, 8th (01.44.95.13.80/www. barclays.fr). M° Franklin D Roosevelt.* **Open** 9.15am-4.30pm Mon-Fri.
Barclays' international Expat Service handles direct debits, international transfer of funds, etc.

Citibank *125 av des Champs-Elysées, 8th (01.49.05.49.05/www. citibank.fr). M° Charles de Gaulle Etoile.* **Open** 10am-5.30pm Mon-Fri.
Existing clients get good rates for international money transfers, preferential exchange rates and no commission on travellers cheques.

Global Change *150 av des Champs-Elysées, 8th (01.45.61.05.62) M° Charles de Gaulle Etoile.* **Open** 8am-11.30pm daily. Seven other branches, which have variable hours.

Travelex *52 av des Champs-Elysées, 8th (01.42.89.80.33/www. travelex.fr). M° Franklin D Roosevelt.*

Directory

Open 9am-10.30pm daily. Hours of other branches (over 20 in Paris) vary. Issues travellers' cheques and insurance; deals with bank transfers.
Western Union Money Transfer *(08.25.82.58.42/www.westernunion. com)*. Numerous post offices in Paris (*see below*) provide Western Union services. Money transfers from abroad should arrive within 15 minutes; charges are paid by the sender.

Tax

French VAT (*taxe sur la valeur ajoutée* or *TVA*) is arranged in three bands: 2.1% for items of medication and newspapers; 5.5% for food, books, CDs and DVDs; and 19.6% for all other types of goods and services.

Natural hazards

Paris has no natural hazards as such, though in recent years the town hall has produced evacuation plans to cover flooding. The deadly heatwave of 2003 led to *anti-canicule* measures for 2004, though these were widely ridiculed in the press. *See also* **Walking**.

Opening hours

Standard opening hours for shops are 9am/10am-7pm/8pm Mon-Sat. Some shops close on Mon. Shops and businesses often close at lunch, usually 12.30-2pm; many shops close in August. While Paris doesn't have the 24hr consumer culture beloved of some capitals, some branches of Monoprix stay open until 10pm. Also most areas have a local grocer that stays open until around 10pm and will often open on Sundays and public holidays, too – although you do pay for the convenience.
24-hr florist Elyfleur *82 av de Wagram, 17th (01.47.66.87.19). M° Wagram.* **Credit** MC, V.
24-hr newsagents include: *33 av des Champs-Elysées, 8th, M° Franklin D Roosevelt. 2 bd Montmartre, 9th, M° Grands Boulevards.*

24-hr garage Select Shell *6 bd Raspail, 7th (01.45.48.43.12). M° Rue du Bac.* This round-the-clock garage has a large if pricey array of supermarket standards from the Casino chain. No alcohol sold 10pm-6am.
Late-night *tabacs*
Le Brazza *86 bd du Montparnasse, 14th (01.43.35.42.65). M° Montparnasse-Bienvenüe.*
Open 6am-2am daily.
La Favorite *3 bd St-Michel, 5th (01.43.54.08.02). M° St-Michel.*
Open 7am-2am daily.

Photo labs

Photo developing can often be more expensive than in the UK or USA (although developing slide films can often be cheaper). **Fnac Service**, **Photo Station** (www.photostation.fr) and **Photo Service** (www.photoservice.com) have numerous branches.

Police stations

The French equivalent of 999/911 is **17** and **112** from a mobile, but don't expect a speedy response. That said, the Préfécture de Police has no fewer than 94 outposts in the city. If you're assaulted or robbed, report the incident as soon as possible. You'll need to make a statement (*procès verbal*) at the *point d'accueil* closest to the site of the crime. To find the nearest, call the Préfecture Centrale (08.91.01.22.22) day or night, or go to www.prefecture-police.paris.interieur.gouv.fr. Stolen goods are unlikely to be recovered, but you'll need a police statement for insurance purposes.

Postal services

Post offices (*bureaux de poste*) are open 8am-7pm Mon-Fri; 8am-noon Sat. All are listed in the phone book: under Administration des PTT in the *Pages Jaunes*; under Poste in the *Pages Blanches*. Most post offices have automatic

machines (in French and English) that weigh your letter, print out a stamp and give change, saving you from wasting time in an enormous queue. You can usually buy stamps and often envelopes at a tobacconist (*tabac*). For info see www.laposte.fr.
Main Post Office *52 rue du Louvre, 1st (01.40.28.76.00). M° Les Halles or Louvre Rivoli.* **Open** 24hrs daily for Poste Restante, telephones, stamps, fax, photocopying and some banking operations. This is the best place to get your mail sent to if you haven't got a fixed address in Paris. Mail should be addressed to you in block capitals, followed by Poste Restante, then the post office's address. There's a charge of €0.50 for each letter received.

Recycling & rubbish

The city has a recently-established system of colour-coded domestic recycling bins. A yellow-lidded bin can take paper, cardboard cartons, tins and small electrical items; a white-lidded bin takes glass. All other rubbish goes in the green-lidded bins except for used batteries (all shops that sell batteries should accept them), medication (take it back to a pharmacy), toxic products (call 08.20.00.75.75 to have them picked up) or car batteries (take them to an official tip or return to garages exhibiting the 'relais verts auto' sign). Green, hive-shaped bottle banks can be found on street corners. Information: www.environnement.paris.fr.

Religion

Churches and religious centres are listed in the *Pages Jaunes* under 'Eglises' and 'Cultes'. Paris has several English-speaking churches. The *International Herald Tribune*'s Saturday edition lists Sunday church services in English.
American Cathedral *23 av George V, 8th (01.53.23.84.00/www. americancathedral.org). M° George V.*

American Church in Paris
*65 quai d'Orsay, 7th (01.40.62.05.00/
www.acparis.org). M° Invalides.*

**Emmanuel Baptist Church of
Paris** *56 rue des Bons Raisins,
92500 Rueil-Malmaison
(01.47.51.29.63/www.ebcparis.org).
RER Reuil-Malmaison, then bus 244.*

Kehilat Gesher *10 rue de
Pologne, 78100 St-Germain-en-Laye
(01.39.21.97.19/www.kehilatgesher.
org). RER St-Germain-en-Laye.* The
Liberal English-speaking Jewish
community has rotating services in
Paris and the western suburbs.

La Mosquée de Paris
*2 pl du Puits de l'Ermite, 5th
(01.45.35.97.33/www.mosquee-de-
paris.org). M° Place Monge.*

St George's Anglican Church
*7 rue Auguste-Vacquerie, 16th
(01.47.20.22.51/www.stgeorgesparis.
com). M° Charles de Gaulle Etoile.*

**St Joseph's Roman Catholic
Church** *50 av Hoche, 8th
(01.42.27.28.56/www.stjoeparis.org).
M° Charles de Gaulle Etoile.*

St Michael's Church of England
*5 rue d'Aguesseau, 8th
(01.47.42.70.88/www.saintmichaels
paris.org). M° Madeleine.*

Renting a flat

Flats are generally cheapest
in northern, eastern and
southeastern Paris. Expect to
pay roughly €20 per month/m²
(so, say, €700 per month for a
35m² flat). Studios and one-
bedroom flats fetch the
highest prices proportionally;
the provision of lifts and
cellars will also boost the rent.

Flat hunting

Given the scarcity of housing
in Paris, it's a landlord's world;
you'll need to search actively,
or even frenetically, in order
to find an apartment. The
internet is a decent place to
start: www.explorimmo.fr
lists rental ads from *Le Figaro*
and specialist real estate
magazines; you can place a
classified ad or check lettings
on www.avendrealouer.fr.
Thursday morning's *De
Particulier à Particulier*
(www.pap.fr) is a must for
those who want to rent directly
from the owner, but be warned
– most flats go within hours.
Fortnightly *Se Loger*

(www.seloger.com) is also
worth getting, though most of
its ads are placed by agencies.
Landlords keen to let to
foreigners advertise in the
International Herald Tribune
and English-language *FUSAC*
(www.fusac.fr); rents tend to
be higher than in the French
press. There are also assorted
free ad brochures that can be
picked up from agencies.
Private landlords often set a
visiting time; prepare to meet
hordes of other flat-seekers
and have your documents
and cheque book to hand.

There's also the option of
flat-sharing – one that's been
growing in popularity in recent
years. To look for housemates,
pick up a copy of *FUSAC* (*see
p376*) or browse the 3,000-odd
weekly announcements at
www.colocation.fr – which
also organises monthly soirée
Le Jeudi de la Colocation,
a chance to meet potential
roomies in the flesh.

Rental laws

The minimum lease (*bail de
location*) on an unfurnished flat
is three years (though the tenant
can give notice and leave before
this period is up); furnished
flats are generally let on one-
year leases. During this period
the landlord can only raise the
rent by the official construction
inflation index. At the end of the
lease, the rent can be adjusted,
but tenants can object before
a rent board. Tenants can be
evicted for non-payment, or if
the landlord wishes to sell the
property or use it as his own
residence. It is illegal to throw
people out in winter. Landlords
will probably insist you
present a dossier with pay
slips (*fiches de paie/bulletins
de salaire*) showing income
equivalent to three to four
times the monthly rent, and,
for foreigners in particular, to
provide a financial guarantor
(someone who will sign a
document promising to pay
the rent if you abscond). When

taking out a lease, payments
usually include the first month's
rent, a deposit (*une caution*)
equal to two month's rent, and
an agency fee, if applicable. It's
customary for an inspection of
the premises (*état des lieux*) at
the start and end of the rental,
the cost of which (around
€150) is shared by landlord
and tenant. Landlords may try
to rent their flats *non-declaré* –
without a written lease – and
get rent in cash. This can make
it hard for tenants to establish
their rights – one reason why
landlords do it.

**Centre d'information et de
défense des locataires** *9 rue
Severo, 14th (01.45.41.47.76).
M° Pernety.* **Open** *by appointment*
10am-12.30pm, 2.30-3.30pm Mon-
Thur. Helps sort out problems with
landlords, rent hikes, etc.

Safety & security

Beware pickpockets, especially
in crowded tourist hotspots.
See also **Métro & RER**.

Shipping services

Hedley's Humpers *6 bd de la
Libération, 93284 St-Denis
(01.48.13.01.02/www.hedleyshumper
s.com). M° Carrefour Pleyel.* **Open**
9am-1pm, 2-6pm Mon-Fri. Closed 2
wks in Aug. **Other locations:** *102
rue des Rosiers, 93400 St-Ouen
(01.40.10.94.00). M° Porte de
Clignancourt.* **Open** 9am-5pm Mon,
Fri-Sun. Specialist in transport of
furniture and antiques. **In UK:** 3 St
Leonards Rd, London NW10 6SX, UK
(020 8965 8733). **In USA:** 21-41 45th
Road, Long Island City, New York
NY 11101, USA (1-718-433-4005).

Smoking

Although smoking seems to be
an essential part of French life
(and death), the French state
and public health groups have
recently waged war against
the cigarette on several fronts.
Smoking is now banned in
most public spaces, such as
theatres, cinemas and public
transport, and there are
increasingly strident anti-
smoking campaigns. Health
warnings on cigarette packets

Directory

are now unignorable, and prices have soared. Restaurants are obliged to have a non-smoking area (*espace non-fumeurs*) – though it will often be the worst corner in the house, and there's no guarantee other people seated in the section won't light up anyway. For information about stopping smoking, contact the Tabac Info Service (08.25.30.93.10/ www.tabac-info.net). If you're a dedicated smoker, you'll soon learn that most *tabacs* close at 8pm (for a few that don't, *see p380* **Opening hours**). Some bars sell cigarettes behind the counter, generally only to people who stay for a drink.

Study

Language

Most large multinational language schools, such as **Berlitz** (www.berlitz.com) have at least one branch in Paris. **Konversando** (01.47.70.21.64/www. konversando.fr) specialises in exchanges and talk.

Alliance Française *101 bd Raspail, 6th (01.42.84.90.00/ ww.alliancefr.org). M° St-Placide.* Non-profit French-language school. Beginner and specialist courses start every month. Film club and lectures.

Ecole Eiffel *3 rue Crocé-Spinelli, 14th (01.45.38.57.41/www.ecole-eiffel.fr). M° Pernéty.* Intensive classes, business French, and phonetics.

Eurocentres *13 passage Dauphine, 6th (01.40.46.72.00/www.eurocentres. com). M° Odéon.* Intensive classes with emphasis on communication. Also has a *médiathèque*.

Institut Catholique de Paris *12 rue Cassette, 6th (01.44.39.52.68/ www.icp.fr/ilcf). M° St-Sulpice.* Courses in French culture and language. You must hold a *baccalauréat*-level qualification and be 18 or over (but don't have to be Catholic).

Institut Parisien *87 bd de Grenelle, 15th (01.40.56.09.53). M° La Motte Picquet-Grenelle.* Dynamic private school offers courses in language and French civilisation, business French.

La Sorbonne – Cours de Langue et Civilisation *47 rue des Ecoles, 5th (01.40.46.22.11/www.ccfs-sorbonne.fr). M° Cluny-La Sorbonne/*

RER Luxembourg. Classes for foreigners ride on the name of this eminent institution. Teaching is grammar-based. Courses are open to anyone over 18 and fill up quickly.

University of London Institute in Paris *11 rue Constantine, 7th (01.44.11.73.83/www.ulip.lon.ac.uk). M° Invalides.* Linked to the University of London, the 4,000-student Institute offers English courses for Parisians, and French courses at university level. Also offers a degree course and MAs.

Specialised

Many of the prestigious Ecoles Nationales Supérieures (including film schools La FEMIS and ENS Louis Lumière) offer summer courses in addition to their full-time degree courses – ask for formation continue.

Adult education courses
Information: www.paris.fr or from your local mairie. A huge range of inexpensive adult education classes is run by the City of Paris, including French as a foreign language, computer skills and applied arts.

American University of Paris *31 av Bosquet, 7th (01.40.62.07.20/ www.aup.edu). M° Ecole-Militaire/ RER Pont de l'Alma.* International college awarding four-year American liberal arts degrees (BA/BSc).

Christie's Education Paris *4 av Bertie-Albrecht, 8th (01.42.25.10.90/www.christies.com/ education). M° Ternes.* The international auction house offers a one-year diploma, ten-week intensive courses and specialisations. They have a five-day art-history tour/ class in English in September.

Cordon Bleu *8 rue Léon-Delhomme, 15th (01.53.68.22.50/ www.cordonbleu.edu). M° Vaugirard.* Courses range from three-hour sessions on classical and regional cuisine to a nine-month diploma for those starting a culinary career.

Ritz-Escoffier Ecole de Gastronomie Française *38 rue Cambon, 1st (01.43.16.30.50/www. ritzparis.com). M° Madeleine.* Everything from afternoon demos in the Ritz kitchens to diplomas, but at a price. Courses are in French with English translation.

Ecole du Louvre *Porte Jaugard, Aile de Flore, Palais du Louvre. quai du Louvre, 1st (01.55.35.17.35/ www.ecoledulouvre.fr). M° Palais Royal Musée du Louvre.* Art history and archaeology courses. Foreign students not wanting to take a degree can attend lectures.

INSEAD *bd de Constance, 77305 Fontainebleau (01.60.72.40.00/ www.insead.edu).* Highly regarded international business school offers a ten-month MBA in English, and PhDs in business subjects.

Parsons School of Design *14 rue Letellier, 15th (01.45.77.39.66/ www.parsons-paris.com). M° La Motte-Picquet-Grenelle.* Subsidiary of New York art college offers BFA programmes in fine art, photography, fashion, marketing and interior design.

Spéos – Paris Photographic Institute *7 rue Jules-Vallès, 11th (01.40.09.18.58/www.speos.fr). M° Charonne.* Full-, part-time and summer programmes. Exchange programmes with four art schools, including the Rhode Island School of Design.

Student life

Cartes de séjour and housing benefit

Take a deep breath before you read the following. Foreign students wishing to qualify for housing benefit or to work legally during their course in Paris must get a *carte de séjour* (*see p385*). You may then (note the 'may') be eligible for the ALS (*allocation de logement à caractère social*), which is handled by four CAFs (*caisses d'allocations familiales*). The '*calculez votre aide au logement*' feature of their website (www.caf.fr) lets you see how much you'll receive; enter your address on the site to find which office to contact. Website www.droitsdesjeunes. gouv.fr gives information on your rights.

Accommodation

The simplest budget accommodation for medium-to-long stays can be found at the **Cité Universitaire** or *foyers* (student hostels). Another option is a *chambre contre travail* – free board in exchange for childcare, housework or English lessons; for this, look out for ads at language schools and the American Church. For cheap hotels and youth hostels, *see chapter* **Where to Stay**. As students often cannot provide proof of income, a *porte-garant* (guarantor) is required who will guarantee payment of rent and bills.

Cité Universitaire *19 bd Jourdan, 14th (01.44.16.64.00/www.ciup.fr). RER Cité Universitaire.* **Open** *Offices* 8am-6pm Mon-Fri. Foreign students enrolled on a university course, or interns who are also studying, can apply for a place at this campus of halls of residence (but be forewarned: only about 10% of the students that apply get in). Rooms can be booked for a week or for an entire academic year. Rents are around €300-€400/month single, €200-€300 per person double. UK citizens must apply to the Collège Franco-Britannique, and Americans to the Fondation des Etats-Unis.

CROUS (Centre Régional des Oeuvres Universitaires et Scolaires) *39 av Georges-Bernanos, 5th (01.40.51.36.00/08.92.25.75.75/www.crous-paris.fr). Service du Logement: (01.40.51.55.55). RER Port-Royal.* **Open** 9am-5pm Mon-Fri. Manages all University of Paris student residences, posts ads for rooms and has a list of hostels. Requests for rooms must be made by 1 April for the next academic year. CROUS also runs cheap canteens (listed on website) and is the clearing house for all *bourses* (grants) issued to foreign students. Call the Service des Bourses on 01.40.51.55.55.

UCRIF (Union des Centres de Rencontres Internationales de France) *27 rue de Turbigo, 2nd (01.40.26.57.64/www.ucrif.asso.fr). M° Etienne Marcel.* **Open** 9am-6pm Mon-Fri. Operates cheap, short-stay hostels from four help centres: 5th (01.43.29.34.80); 12th (01.44.75.60.06); 13th (01.43.36.00.63); 14th (01.43.13.17.00); 20th (01.40.31.45.45).

Student & youth discounts

To claim a *tarif étudiant* (around €1.50 off cinema seats, up to 50% off museums and standby theatre tickets), you must have a French student card or International Student Identity Card (ISIC), available from CROUS, student travel agents and the Cité Universitaire. ISIC cards are only valid in France if you are under 26. Under-26s can get up to 50% off rail travel on some trains with the SNCF's Carte

12/25 and the same reduction on the RATP network with the 'Imagine R' card.

Working

Foreign students can legally work up to 20 hours per week. Non-EU members studying in Paris must apply for an *autorisation provisoire de travail* from the DDTEFT. The job service at the CROUS (01.40.51.37.52 through 57) finds part-time jobs for students. For pointers to vacancies, consult www.crous-paris.fr/emploi.

DDTEFT (Direction Départementale du Travail, d'Emploi et du Formation Professionelle) *109 rue Montmartre, 2nd (01.44.84.41.00/www.travail.gouv.fr). M° Bourse.*

Useful organisations

CIDJ (Centre d'Information et de Documentation Jeunesse) *101 quai Branly, 15th (01.44.49.12.00/www.cidj.com). M° Bir-Hakeim/RER Champ de Mars.* **Open** 10am-6pm Mon-Wed, Fri; 1-6pm Thur; 9.30am-1pm Sat. Library gives students advice on courses and careers; youth bureau of ANPE (Agence Nationale pour l'Emploi/www.anpe.fr) helps with job applications.

Edu France *173 bd St-Germain, 6th (01.53.63.35.00/www.edufrance.fr). M° St-Germain-des-Prés.* **Open** 9am-6pm Mon-Fri (call as hours vary). Fees €200-€500. Government-run organisation promotes the French university system abroad and assists foreign students in France. The website has some useful free information.

Maison des Initiatives Etudiantes (MIE) *50 rue des Tournelles, 3rd (01.49.96.65.30/www.paris.fr).* **Open** 10am-10pm Mon-Fri; 2-9pm Sat. Provides student associations with logistical assistance and Paris-based resources like meeting rooms, grants and on-line computers. From September 2004, Radio Campus Paris, a radio station for students, will be broadcast.

Socrates-Erasmus Programme
Britain: *UK Socrates-Erasmus Council, Rothford, Giles Lane, Canterbury, Kent CT2 7LR (01227 762712/www.erasmus.ac.uk).*
France: *Agence Socrates-Leonardo Da Vinci, 25 quai des Chartrons, 33080 Bordeaux Cedex (05.56.00.94.00/www.socrates-*

leonardo.fr). The Socrates-Erasmus scheme lets EU students with reasonable written and spoken French spend a year of their degree in the French university system. Applications must be made via the Erasmus co-ordinator at your home university. Non-EU students should find out from their university whether it has an agreement with the French university system. US students can find out more from the following:

MICEFA *(26 rue du Fbg-St-Jacques, 14th, 01.40.51.76.96/www.micefa.org).*
Relais d'accueil *(Foreign students helpdesk) Cité Universitaire, 19 bd Jourdan, 14th. RER Cité Universitaire. CROUS de Paris, 39 av Georges-Bernanos, 5th (01.43.13.66.46/www.eduparis.net). RER Port-Royal.* **Open** *Sept-Nov* 8.30am-4pm Mon-Fri (Cité); 9am-4.30pm Mon-Fri (CROUS). Advice on housing, getting a bank account, a Carte de Séjour, social security and university registration is available (by appointment) to foreign students at the two addresses above.

Telephones

Mobile phones

A subscription (*abonnement*) will normally get you a free phone if you sign up for at least one year. Two hours' calling time a month costs about €35/month. International calls are normally charged extra – a lot extra. The three companies that rule the cell phone market in France are:

Bouyges Télécom *(08.10.63.01.00/www.bouygues telecom.fr).*
France Télécom/Orange *(08.25.00.57.00/www.orange.fr).*
SFR *(08.05.80.08.05/www.sfr.fr).*

Dialing & codes

All French phone numbers have ten digits. Paris and Ile-de-France numbers begin with 01; the rest of France is divided into four zones (02-05). Mobile phone numbers start with 06. 08 indicates a special rate (*see below*); numbers beginning with 08 can only be reached from inside France. If you are calling France from abroad leave off the 0 at the start of the ten-digit number. The country code is 33. To call abroad from France dial 00, then country code, then the number. Since 1998 other phone companies have been allowed to enter the market, but France Télécom still has the monopoly on basic service. It has a useful website with information on rates, contracts and the like: www.agence.france telecom.com.

France Télécom English-Speaking Customer Service *(08.00.36.47.75/from abroad +33 1.55.78.60.56)*. **Open** 9am-5.30pm Mon-Fri. Freephone information line in English on phone services, bills, payment, Internet.

Public phones

Most public phones in Paris, of which almost all are maintained by France Télécom, use *télécartes* (phonecards). Sold at post offices, *tabacs*, airports and train and métro stations, they cost €7.50 for 50 units and €15 for 120 units. For cheap international calls you can also buy a *télécarte à puce* (card with a microchip) or a *télécarte pré-payée* that features a numerical code you dial before making a call; these can be used on domestic phones, too. Travelex's International Telephone Card can be used in more than 80 countries (from Travelex agencies, *see p379*). Cafés have coin phones, while post offices usually have card phones. In a phone box, the display screen will read 'Décrochez'. Pick up the phone. When 'Introduisez votre carte' appears, put your card into the slot; the screen should then read 'Patientez SVP'. 'Numérotez' is your signal to dial. 'Crédit épuisé' means you have no more units left. Hang up ('Raccrochez') – and don't forget your card. Some public phones take credit cards. If you're using a credit card, insert the card, enter your PIN number and 'Patientez SVP' will appear.

Operator services

Operator assistance, French directory enquiries
(renseignements) 12. To make a reverse-charge call within France, ask to make a call *en PCV*.

Airparif (01.44.59.47.64). 2-5.30pm Mon-Fri. Information about pollution levels and air quality in Paris and Ile-de-France: invaluable for asthmatics.

International directory enquiries 32.12, then country code. €3 per call.

International news (France Inter recorded message, in French), 08.92.68.10.33 (€0.34 per min).

Telegram *all languages, international* 08.00.33.44.11; *within France* 36.55.

Telephone engineer 10.13.

Time 36.99.

Traffic news 08.26.02.20.22.

Weather (08.99.70.12.34 (€1.39 then €0.34 per min) for enquiries on weather in France and abroad, in French or English; dial 08.92.68.02.75 (€0.34 per min) for a recorded weather announcement for Paris and region.

Telephone directories

Phone books can be found in all post offices and most cafés. The *Pages Blanches* (White Pages) list people and businesses alphabetically; *Pages Jaunes* (Yellow Pages) list businesses and services by category. Online versions can be had at www.pagesjaunes.fr.

Telephone charges

All local calls in Paris and Ile-de-France (to numbers beginning with 01) cost €0.11 for three minutes, standard rate, €0.04/min thereafter and only apply to calls towards other land phones. Calls beyond a 100km radius (*province*) are charged at €0.11 for the first 39 seconds, then €0.24/min. International destinations are divided into 16 zones. Reduced-rate periods for calls within France and Europe: 7pm-8am during the week; all day Sat, Sun. Reduced-rate periods for the US and Canada: 7pm through to 1pm Mon-Fri; all day Sat, Sun.

Cheap providers

Getting wise to market demand, smaller telephone providers are becoming increasingly prolific and popular, as rates from giant France Télécom are not exactly bargain-basement. The following can offer alternative rates for calls (you'll still need to rent your telephone line from France Télécom):

AT&T Direct (local access) 08.00.99.00.11.

Free *www.free.fr*. With the Freebox (Free's modem for ASDL connection) €29.99 per month gets you ten hours of free calls to land lines (additional calls: €0.01 per minute), €0.19 per minute to mobiles and €0.03 per minute for most international calls.

IC Télécom *www.ictelecom.fr.*

9 Télécom *08.00.95.99.59/ www.neuf.fr.*

Onetel *www.onetel.fr.*

Télé 2 *08.05.04.44.44/www.tele2.fr.*

3U Télécom *08.05.10.16.45/ www.3utelecom.fr.*

Special-rate numbers

0800 Numéro Vert Freephone.

0810 Numéro Azur €0.11 under three min, then €0.04/min.

0820 Numéro Indigo I €0.118/min.

0825 Numéro Indigo II €0.15/min.

0836.64/0890.64/0890.70 €0.112/min.

0890.71 €0.15/min.

0891.67/0891.70 €0.225/min.

0836/0892 €0.337/min. This rate is for the likes of ticket agencies, cinema and transport information lines.

10.14 France Télécom information; free (except from mobile phones).

Minitel

France Télécom's Minitel, launched in the 1980s, is an enduring dinosaur: a videotext service available to any telephone subscriber. The Internet has made it virtually redundant. If you come across one of these beige plastic boxes, type in 3611 for Minitel directory in English, wait for the beep, press 'Connexion', type MGS, then hit 'Envoi'. Then type 'Minitel en anglais' for the English service.

Ticket agencies

The easiest way to reserve and buy tickets for concerts, plays and matches is from a **Fnac** store. You can also reserve on www.fnac.com or by phone (08.92.68.36.22; 9am-8pm Mon-Sat) and pick them up at one of their *points de vente* (see site for full list) – or pay with your credit card and have them sent to your home. **Virgin** has teamed up with **Ticketnet** to create an online ticket office (www.virginmega.fr). Tickets can also be purchased by phone (08.25.12.91.39) and sent to your home for a €5.50 fee.

Fnac Forum *Forum des Halles, Porte Lescot, 1st (01.40.41.40.00/ www.fnac.com). Mº Les Halles/RER Châtelet-Les Halles.* **Open** 10am-7.30pm Mon-Sat. **Credit** AmEx, MC, V.

Virgin Megastore
52-60 av des Champs-Elysées, 8th (01.49.53.50.00). Mº Franklin D Roosevelt. **Open** 10am-midnight Mon-Sat; noon-midnight Sun. **Credit** AmEx, MC, V.

Time & seasons

France is one hour ahead of Greenwich Mean Time (GMT). France uses the 24-hr system (eg. 18h for 6pm).

Tipping

A service charge of ten to 15% is legally included in your bill at all restaurants, cafés and bars. However, it's polite to either round up the final amount for drinks, and to leave a cash tip of €1-€2 or more for a meal, depending on the restaurant and, of course, on the quality of the service.

Toilets

The city's automatic street toilets are not as terrifying as they look. You put your coin in the slot, and open sesame. Each loo is completely washed down and disinfected after use, so don't try to avoid paying by sneaking in as someone is leaving: you'll get covered in bleach). Once inside, you have 15 minutes. If a space-age-style lavatory experience doesn't appeal, you can always nip in to the loos of a café; although theoretically reserved for customers' use, a polite request should win sympathy with the waiter – and you may find you have to put a 20¢ coin into a slot in the door-handle mechanism, customer or not. Fast food chain toilets often have a code on their toilet doors which is made known to paying customers only.

Tourist information

Espace du Tourisme d'Île de France *Carrousel du Louvre, 99 rue de Rivoli, 1st (08.26.16.66.66/ www.paris-ile-de-france.com). Mº Pyramides.* **Open** 8.30am-7pm Mon-Fri. Information showcase for Paris and the Ile-de-France.

Maison de la France *20 av de l'Opéra, 1st (01.42.96.70.00/www. franceguide.com). Mº Opéra.* **Open** 10am-6pm Mon-Fri; 10am-5pm Sat. The state organisation for tourism in France: information galore.

Office de Tourisme et des Congrès de Paris *Carrousel du Louvre, 99 rue de Rivoli, 1st (08.92.68.30.00 recorded information in English & French/ www.parisinfo.com). Mº Palais Royal Musée du Louvre.* **Open** 9am-7pm daily. Information on Paris and the suburbs, shop, bureau de change, hotel reservations, phonecards, museum cards, travel passes and tickets. Multilingal staff. **Other locations:** *Gare de Lyon* 20 bd Diderot, 12th, Mº Gare de Lyon. Open 8am-6pm, Mon-Sat. Closed Sun, 1 May. *Gare du Nord* 18 rue de Dunkerque, 10th, Mº Gare du Nord. Open 8am-6pm daily. Closed 1 May, 25 Dec. *Montmartre* 21 pl du Tertre, 18th, Mº Abbesses. Open 10am-7pm daily. *Opéra* 11 rue Scribe, 9th, Mº Opera. Open 9am-6.30pm Mon-Sat. Closed Sun, 1 May. *Pyramides* 25 rue des Pyramides, 1st, Mº Pyramides. Open 9am-7pm daily. *Tour Eiffel* Champ de Mars, 7th, Mº Bir-Hakeim. Open late Mar-Oct 11am-6.40pm daily. Closed 1 May.

Visas

European Union nationals do not need a visa to enter France, nor do US, Canadian, Australian or New Zealand citizens for stays of up to three months. Nationals of other countries should enquire at the nearest French Consulate before leaving home. If they are travelling to France from one of the countries included in the Schengen agreement (most of the EU, but not Britain or Ireland), the visa from that country should be sufficient.

Cartes de séjour

Officially, all foreigners – EU citizens and non-Europeans – who stay in France for more than three months must apply at the Préfecture de Police for a *carte de séjour*, valid for one year. Those who have had a *carte de séjour* for at least three years, have been paying French income tax, can show proof of income and/or are married to a French national can apply for a *carte de résident*, valid for ten years. Students arriving from England wishing to make a first application for a student's carte de séjour should go directly (no appointments) to 13 rue Miollis, 15th, Mº Ségur or Cambronne, 8.35am-4.30pm Mon-Thur, 8.35am-4.15pm Fri. Applicants must bring ID, three recent photos, plus proof of studies, of an address in Paris and of sufficient funds.

CIRA (Centre Interministeriel de Renseignements Administratifs) *(0821.08.09.10 0.12€/min/www.service-public.fr).* **Open** 8am-7pm Mon-Fri; 8am-noon Sat. Advice on French admin procedures.

Préfecture de Police de Paris Service Etrangers *7-9 bd du Palais, 4th (01.53.71.51.68/www. prefecture-police-paris.interieur. gouv.fr). Mº Cité.* Open 9am-4pm Mon-Fri. Information on residency and work permits for foreigners.

Weights & measures

France uses only the metric system; remember that all

speed limits are in kilometres per hour. One kilometre is equivalent to 0.62 mile (1 mile = 1.6km). Petrol, like other liquids, is measured in litres; one UK gallon = 4.54 litres; 1 US gallon = 3.79 litres).

What to take

Binoculars or opera-glasses for studying high-altitude details of monuments, a pocket knife with corkscrew (the better to improvise picnics with food bought in markets) and – vital – comfortable shoes.

When to go

In July and August, when there are good deals on hotels and a good range of fun summer events: the city seems empty but is more relaxed than usual. Avoid October, with its glut of fashion weeks and trade shows.

Women in Paris

Though Paris is not especially threatening for women, the precautions you would take in any major city apply: be careful at night in areas like Pigalle, the rue St-Denis, Stalingrad, La Chapelle, Château Rouge, Gare de l'Est, Gare du Nord, the Bois de Boulogne and Bois de Vincennes. If you receive unwanted attention a politely

scathing *N'insistez pas!* (Don't push it!) makes your feelings clear. If things get too heavy, go into the nearest shop or café and ask for help.

CIDFF (Centre d'Information et des Droits des Femmes et de la Famille) *7 rue du Jura, 13th (01.42.17.12.00). Mº Gobelins.* **Open** visits by appointment only.The CIDFF offers health, legal and professional advice for women.

Violence Conjugale: Femmes Info Service *(01.40.33.80.60).* **Open** 7.30am-11.30pm Mon-Sat. Telephone hotline for battered women, directing them towards medical aid or shelters.

Viols Femmes Informations *(08.00.05.95.95).* **Open** 10am-7pm Mon-Fri. Freephone service. Help and advice, in French, to rape victims.

Working in Paris

All EU nationals can work legally in France, but should apply for a French social security number and *carte de séjour*. Some job ads can be found at branches of the French national employment bureau, the **Agence Nationale pour l'Emploi** (ANPE), or on its website, www.anpe.fr. Branches are also where to go to sign up as a *demandeur d'emploi*, to be placed on file as available for work and possibly to qualify for French unemployment benefits. Britons can only

claim French unemployment benefit if they were already signed on before leaving the UK. Non-EU nationals need a work permit and cannot use the ANPE network without valid work papers.

Club des Quatre Vents *1 rue Gozlin, 6th (01.40.51.11.81). Mº St-Germain-des-Prés.* **Open** 9am-6pm Mon-Fri. Provides three-month work permits for US citizens at or recently graduated from university.

Espace Emploi International (OMI et ANPE) *48 bd de la Bastille, 12th (01.53.02.25.50/www.emploi-international.org). Mº Bastille.* **Open** 9am-5pm Mon, Wed-Fri; Tue 9am-noon. Provides work permits of up to 18 months for Americans aged 18-35 and has a job placement service.

The Language Network *(01.44.64.82.23).* Helps to orient native English speakers who wish to teach.

Job ads

Help wanted ads sometimes appear in the *International Herald Tribune*, in *FUSAC* and on noticeboards at language schools and the American Church. Bilingual secretarial/PA work is available for those with good written French. If you're looking for professional work, have your CV translated, including French equivalents for any qualifications. Most job applications require a photo and a handwritten letter (employers often use graphological analysis).

Average monthly climate

Month	High temp (C°/F°)	Low temp (C°/F°)	Rainfall
Jan	7/45	2/36	53cm
Feb	10/50	2/36	43cm
Mar	13/55	4/39	49cm
Apr	17/63	6/43	53cm
May	20/68	9/48	65cm
June	23/73	12/54	54cm
July	25/77	15/59	62cm
Aug	26/79	16/29	42cm
Sept	23/73	12/54	54cm
Oct	20/68	8/46	60cm
Nov	14/57	4/39	51cm
Dec	7/44	3/37	59cm

Essential Vocabulary

In French the second person singular (you) has two forms. Phrases here are given in the more polite *vous* form. The *tu* form is used with family, friends, children and pets; you should be careful not to use it with people you do not know sufficiently well. Courtesies such as *monsieur, madame* and *mademoiselle* are used more than their English equivalents.

General expressions

good morning/afternoon, hello bonjour; **good evening** bonsoir; **goodbye** au revoir; **hi** (familiar) salut; **OK** d'accord; **yes** oui; **no** non; **how are you?** comment allez vous?/vous allez bien?; **how's it going?** comment ça va?/ça va? (familiar); **sir/Mr** monsieur (Mr); **madam/Mrs** madame (Mme); **miss** mademoiselle (Mlle); **please** s'il vous plaît; **thank you** merci; **thank you very much** merci beaucoup; **sorry** pardon; **excuse me** excusez-moi; **do you speak English?** parlez-vous anglais?; **I don't speak French** je ne parle pas français; **I don't understand** je ne comprends pas; **speak more slowly, please** parlez plus lentement, s'il vous plaît; **I am going** je vais; **I am going to pay** je vais payer; **it is** c'est; **it isn't** ce n'est pas; **good** bon/bonne; **bad** mauvais/mauvaise **small** petit/petite; **big** grand/grande; **beautiful** beau/belle; **well** bien; **badly** mal; **a bit** un peu; **a lot** beaucoup; **very** très; **with** avec; **without** sans; **and** et; **or** ou; **because** parce que **who?** qui?; **when?** quand?; **what?** quoi?; **which?** quel?; **where?** où?; **why?** pourquoi?; **how?** comment?; **at what time/when?** à quelle heure?; **forbidden** interdit/défendu; **out of order** hors service (HS)/en panne; **daily** tous les jours (tlj)

On the phone

hello allô; **who's calling?** c'est de la part de qui?/qui est à l'appareil?; **this is... speaking** c'est... à l'appareil; **I'd like to speak to...** j'aurais voulu parler avec...; **hold the line** ne quittez pas; **please call back later** rappelez plus tard s'il vous plaît; **you must have the wrong number** vous avez du composer un mauvais numéro

Getting around

where is the (nearest) métro? où est le métro (le plus proche)?; **when is the next train for... ?** c'est quand le prochain train pour... ?; **ticket** un billet; **station** la gare; **platform** le quai; **entrance** entrée; **exit** sortie; **left** gauche; **right** droite; **straight on** tout droit; **near** pas loin/près d'ici; **far** loin; **street map** le plan; **road map** la carte; **bank** la banque; **is there a bank near here?** est-ce qu'il y a une banque près d'ici?

Sightseeing

museum un musée; **church** une église; **exhibition** une exposition; **ticket** (*for museum*) un billet; (*for theatre, concert*) une place; **open** ouvert; **closed** fermé; **free** gratuit; **reduced price** un tarif réduit

Accommodation

do you have a room (for this evening/for two people)? avez-vous une chambre (pour ce soir/pour deux personnes)?; **full** complet; **room** une chambre; **bed** un lit; **double bed** un grand lit; **(a room with) twin beds** (une chambre à) deux lits; **with bath(room)/shower** avec (salle de) bain/douche; **breakfast** le petit déjeuner; **included** compris

At the café or restaurant

I'd like to book a table (for three/at 8pm) je voudrais réserver une table (pour trois personnes/à vingt heures); **lunch** le déjeuner; **dinner** le dîner; **coffee** (espresso) un café; **white coffee** un café au lait/café crème; **tea** le thé; **wine** le vin; **beer** la bière; **mineral water** eau minérale; **fizzy** gazeuse; **still** plate; **tap water** eau du robinet/une carafe d'eau; **the bill, please** l'addition, s'il vous plaît

Shopping

cheap pas cher; **expensive** cher; **how much?/how many?** combien?; **have you got change?** avez-vous de la monnaie? **I would like...** je voudrais...; **may I try this on?** est-ce que je pourrais essayer cet article?; **do you have a smaller/larger size?** auriez-vous la taille en-dessous/au dessus?; **I'm a size 38** je fais du 38; **I'll**

take it je le prends; **could you gift wrap it for me?** pourriez-vous me faire un paquet cadeau?

Behind the wheel

no parking stationnement interdit/gênant; **toll** péage; **speed limit 40** rappel 40; **petrol** essence; **speed** vitesse; **traffic moving freely** traffic fluide

The come-on

do you have a light? avez-vous du feu?; **what's your name?** comment vous vous appellez?; **would you like a drink?** vous voulez boire un verre?; **you have lovely eyes, you know** tu as de beaux yeux, tu sais?; **your place or mine?** chez toi ou chez moi?

The brush-off

leave me alone laissez-moi tranquille; **get lost, you cretin** casse-toi, imbécile

Staying alive

be cool restez calme; **I don't want any trouble** je ne veux pas d'ennuis; **I only do safe sex** je ne pratique que le safe sex

Numbers

0 zéro; **1** un, une; **2** deux; **3** trois; **4** quatre; **5** cinq; **6** six; **7** sept; **8** huit; **9** neuf; **10** dix; **11** onze; **12** douze; **13** treize; **14** quatorze; **15** quinze; **16** seize; **17** dix-sept; **18** dix-huit; **19** dix-neuf; **20** vingt; **21** vingt-et-un; **22** vingt-deux; **30** trente; **40** quarante; **50** cinquante; **60** soixante; **70** soixante-dix; **80** quatre-vingts; **90** quatre-vingt-dix; **100** cent; **1000** mille; **10,000** dix mille; **1,000,000** un million

Days, months & seasons

Monday lundi; **Tuesday** mardi; **Wednesday** mercredi; **Thursday** jeudi; **Friday** vendredi; **Saturday** samedi; **Sunday** dimanche; **January** janvier; **February** février; **March** mars; **April** avril; **May** mai; **June** juin; **July** juillet; **August** août; **September** septembre; **October** octobre; **November** novembre; **December** décembre; **spring** le printemps; **summer** l'été; **autumn** l'automne; **winter** l'hiver

Further Reference

Books

Non-fiction

Petrus Abaelardus & Heloïse *Letters* The full details of Paris' first great romantic drama.

Robert Baldick *The Siege of Paris* The bloodshed, the hunger, the rats for supper: a gripping account of the Paris Commune of 1871.

Antony Beevor & Artemis Cooper *Paris after the Liberation* Rationing, freedom and Existentialism.

NT Binh *Paris au cinéma* Gorgeous coffee-table round-up of Paris sights on film.

Henri Cartier-Bresson *A propos de Paris* Classic black and white shots by a giant among snappers.

Danielle Chadych, Dominique Leborgne *Atlas de Paris* Lavishly appointed survey of Paris bricks and blocks and their movements through the centuries.

Rupert Christiansen *Tales of the New Babylon* Blood and sleaze in Napoléon III's Paris.

Vincent Cronin *Napoleon* A fine biography of France's most famous megalomaniac.

Christian Dupavillon *Paris Côté Seine* Nicely illustrated history of riverside Paris.

Julien Green *Paris* Short, sweet, personal account of Green's favourite city.

Alastair Horne *The Fall of Paris* Detailed chronicle of the Siege and Commune 1870-71.

J-K Huysmans *Croquis Parisiens* The world that Toulouse-Lautrec painted.

Douglas Johnson & Madeleine Johnson *Age of Illusion: Art & Politics in France 1918-1940* French culture in a Paris at the forefront of modernity.

Marc Lemonier, Jacques Lebar *Fascinating Paris* All the photos – in colour – you wish you could take yourself.

Ian Littlewood *Paris: Architecture, History, Art* Paris' history and its treasures.

Colin MacCabe *Godard* Ostensibly a biography of one man, but also an accessible introduction to intellectual life in late 20th-century France.

Patrick Marnham *Crime & the Académie Française* Scandals in Mitterrand-era Paris.

François Maspero *Roissy Express: Journey Through the Paris Suburbs* Take the train: Maspero examines day-to-day life mid-1990s Paris with photographer in tow.

Nancy Mitford *The Sun King; Madame de Pompadour* Great gossipy accounts of the courts of the *ancien régime*.

Noel Riley Fitch *Literary Cafés of Paris* Who drank what, where and when.

Virginia Rounding *Les Grandes Horizantales* Racy, entertaining lives of four 19th-century courtesans.

Renzo Salvadori *Architect's Guide to Paris* Plans, maps and a guide to Paris' growth.

Simon Schama *Citizens* Epic, wonderfully readable account of the Revolution.

William Shirer *The Collapse of the Third Republic*. Forensic account of the reasons for France's humiliating 1940 defeat.

Fiction & poetry

Louis Aragon *Le Paysan de Paris* A great Surrealist view of the city.

Honoré de Balzac *Illusions perdues*; *La Peau de chagrin*; *Le Père Goriot*; *Splendeurs et misères des courtisanes* Many of the best-known novels in the 'Comédie Humaine' cycle are set in Paris.

Charles Baudelaire *Le Spleen de Paris* Prose poems with Paris settings.

Simone de Beauvoir *Les Mandarins* Paris intellectuals and idealists just after the Liberation.

Louis-Ferdinand Céline *Mort à crédit* Vivid, splenetic account of an impoverished Paris childhood.

Victor Hugo *Notre Dame de Paris* Romantic vision of medieval Paris. Quasimodo! Esmerelda! The bells!

Guy de Maupassant *Bel-Ami* Gambling and dissipation.

Patrick Modiano *Honeymoon* Evocative story of two lives that cross in Paris.

Gérard de Nerval *Les Nuits d'octobre* Late-night Les Halles and environs, mid 19th-century.

Georges Perec *La Vie, mode d'emploi* Cheek-by-jowl life in a Haussmannian apartment building.

Raymond Queneau *Zazie dans le Métro* Paris in the 1950s: bright and very *nouvelle vague.*

Nicolas Restif de la Bretonne *Les Nuits de Paris* The sexual underworld of Louis XV's Paris, by one of France's most famous defrocked priests.

Jean-Paul Sartre *Les Carnets de la drôle de guerre* Existential angst as the German army takes over Paris.

Georges Simenon The Maigret books. Many of Simenon's novels featuring his laconic detective provide vivid pictures of Paris and its underworld. See also *L'Homme qui regardait passer les trains.*

Emile Zola *L'Assommoir*; *Nana*; *Le Ventre de Paris* Vivid accounts of the underside of the Second Empire from the master Realist.

The ex-pat angle

Adam Gopnik *From Paris to the Moon* A 'New Yorker' raises a family in this alien city.

Ernest Hemingway *A Moveable Feast* Big Ern chronicles 1920s Paris.

Henry Miller *Tropic of Cancer* Love, lust, lice and low-life: bawdy, yes. Funny, too.

Anaïs Nin *Henry & June* More lust in Montparnasse with Henry Miller and his wife.

George Orwell *Down and Out in Paris and London* Work in a Paris restaurant (it's hardly changed), hunger in a Paris hovel, suffering in a Paris hospital.

Edmund White *The Flaneur: a Stroll through the Paradoxes of Paris* US ex-pat maps out some of the hidden nooks of the city's history.

Film

Olivier Assayas *Irma Vep* Jean-Pierre Léaud and Maggie Cheung endeavour to remake Feuillade's vampire classic in 1990s Paris. And fail.

Luc Besson *Subway* Christophe Lambert goes underground. Hokum, but easy on the eye.

Marcel Carné *Hôtel du Nord* *Atmosphère!* Arletty's finest hour.

Jean-Luc Godard *A Bout de Souffle* Belmondo, Seberg, Godard, the Champs-Elysées, the attitude, the famous ending. Essential.

Jean-Luc Godard *Une Femme est une femme* Belmondo, Karina, Godard, the Grands Boulevards, the attitude, the riffing on musical tropes.

Edouard Molinaro *Un Témoin dans la ville* Lino Ventura on the run in 1950s nocturnal Paris. Superb *noir*.

Bertrand Tavernier *L.627* The drugs war in the 1990s, as seen from the cops' side. Gritty and polemic-making.

François Truffaut *Les 400 Coups* The first of the Antoine Doinel cycle.

Agnès Varda *Cléo de 5 à 7* The *nouvelle vague* heroine spends an anxious afternoon drifting around Paris.

Claude Zidi *Les Ripoux (Le Cop)* Cops Philippe Noiret and Thierry Lhermitte scam the whole of the Goutte d'Or.

Music

Air *Moon Safari* Relaxing, ambient beeps and sonics from that rara avis, a credible French pop group.

Serge Gainsbourg *Le Poinçonneur des Lilas* Classic early Gainsbourg: jazzy, elegant, mordant.

Thelonius Monk *The Paris Concert* A blend of the experimental and the romantically gentle.

Pink Martini *Sympathique* 'Je ne veux pas travailler' and other dinner-party starters by some French singing Americans.

Websites

paris.webcity.fr Compendious cultural calendar, plus small ads and information on shops, hotels, restaurants, traffic conditions and more.

www.culture.fr Current and forthcoming cultural events of all kinds, in Paris and other big French cities.

www.edible-paris.com Customised gastronomic itineraries in Paris – you send your requirements before you arrive – by the editor of Time Out's *Eating & Drinking in Paris* guide.

www.eduparis.net Lots of practical advice for anyone thinking of studying in Paris.

www.euro.gouv.fr Official euro website: information, updates and online currency converter.

www.fnac.com Browse and buy the multidisciplinary Fnac's books, CDs, DVDs and electronics – and reserve tickets for all sorts of events.

www.fusac.org Online version of the free fortnightly small ads mag: jobs, removals, personals, classes and more.

www.gogoparis.com Online version of free monthly anglo listings mag.

www.mappy.fr Maps of Paris and France.

www.meteo.fr Weather forecasts and stats from the state meteorology office.

www.pagesjaunes.fr The Paris yellow pages, with maps and multi-angle photos of every address in the city. Also has a link to the Pages Blanches phone directory.

www.paris-anglo.com An abundance of nuts-and-bolts information, in English, on living in Paris.

www.paris-art.com Contemporary art exhibitions and galleries.

www.parisdigest.com Paris listings, shopping tips and general information in English.

www.parissi.com Films, concerts and a strong calendar of clubbing events.

www.paris-touristoffice.com Official site of the Office de Tourisme et des Congrès de Paris.

www.pidf.com Official site of the Paris regional tourist board: a goldmine of info on museums, events, transport, shopping et al.

www.quidonc.fr The phone book in reverse: type in a number, it tells you the owner. Can only be used in France.

www.ratp.com Everything you'll need to know about using the buses, métro, RER and trams.

www.timeout.com/paris A pick of current events and good hotels, eateries and shops.

Index

Index

Index

Index

Advertisers' Index

Please refer to the relevant pages for contact details

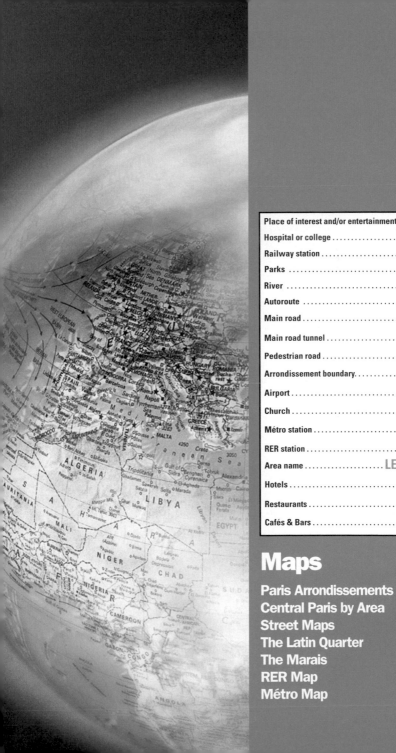

Place of interest and/or entertainment	
Hospital or college	
Railway station	
Parks	
River	
Autoroute	
Main road	
Main road tunnel	
Pedestrian road	
Arrondissement boundary.	—
Airport	✈
Church	✚
Métro station	Ⓜ
RER station	Ⓡ
Area name	LES HALLES
Hotels	❶
Restaurants	❶
Cafés & Bars	❶

Maps

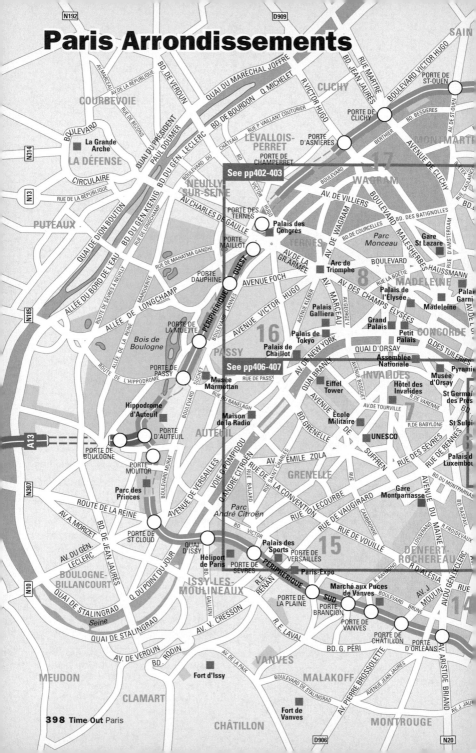

Paris Arrondissements

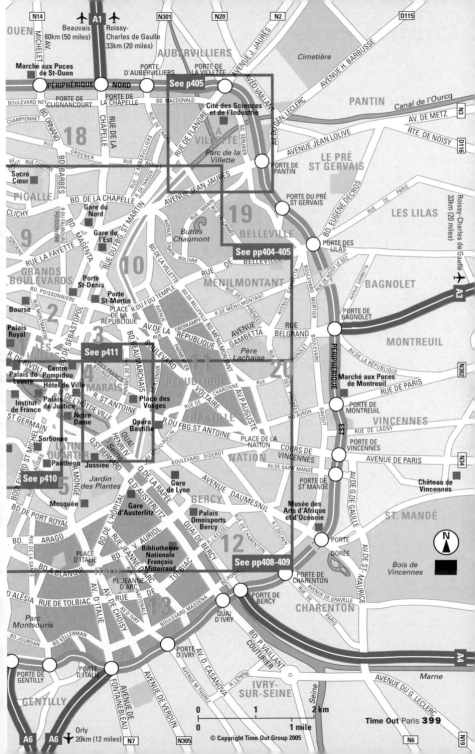

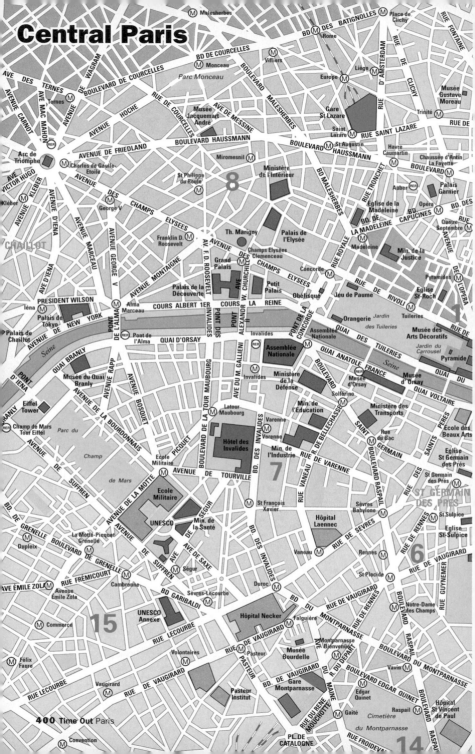

Central Paris

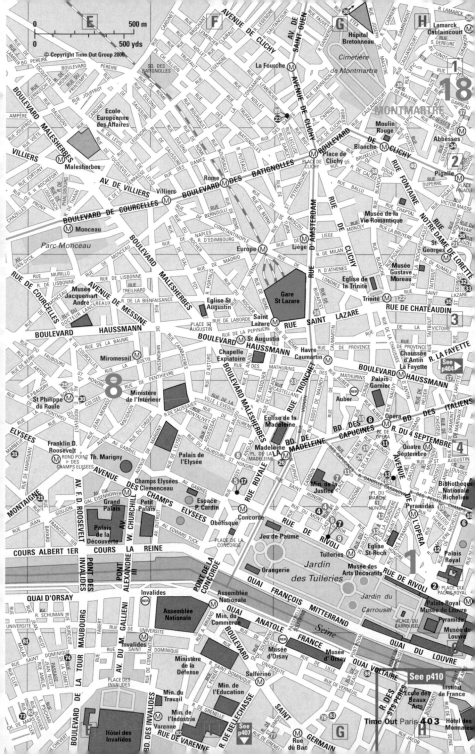

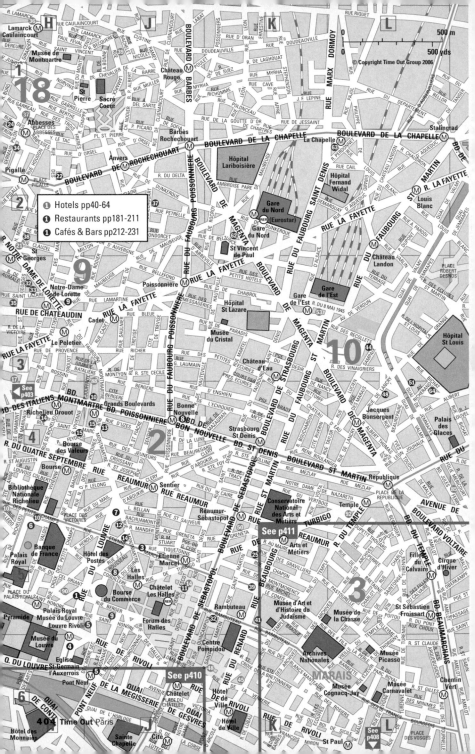

Hotel

New Years Eve
la petite cour

New Years Day
Apollo

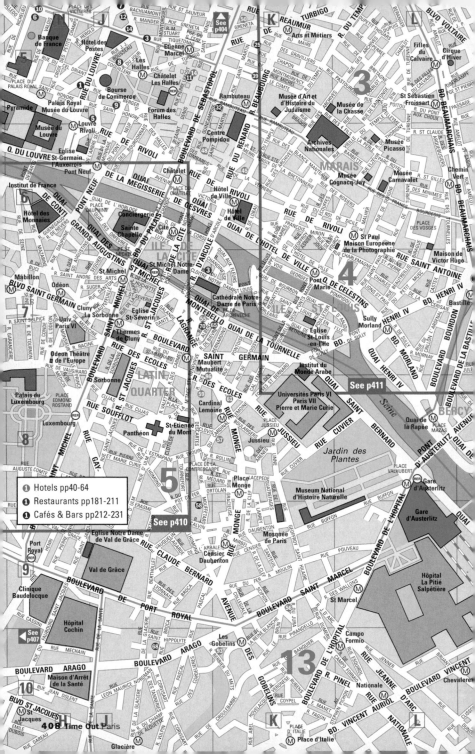

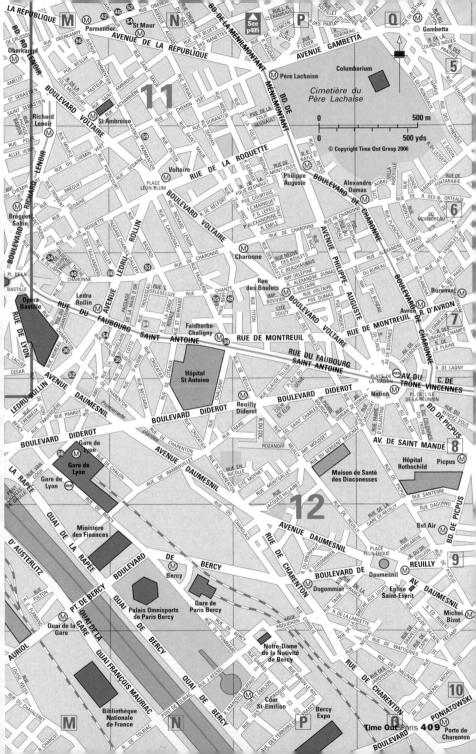

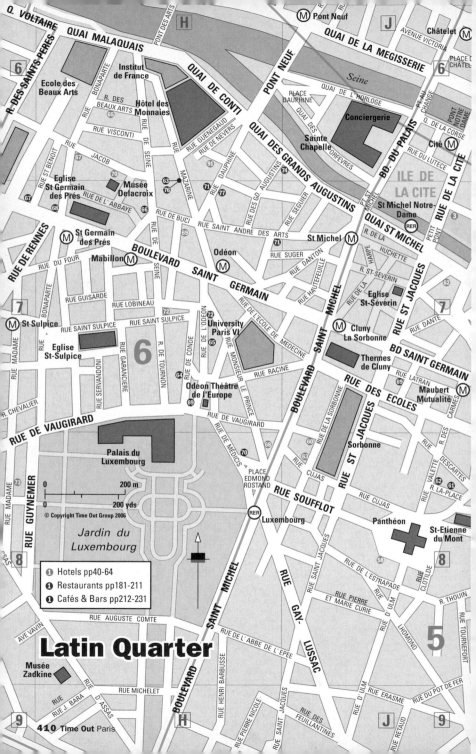

Latin Quarter

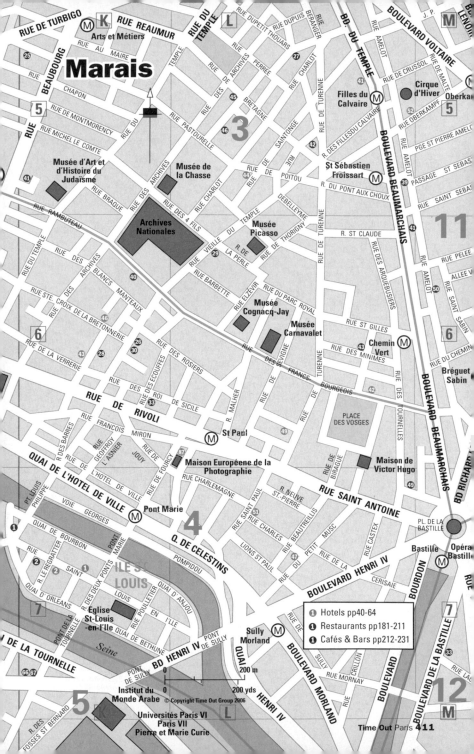

Marais

RUE DE TURBIGO

K Arts et Métiers

RUE REAUMUR

L

BOULEVARD VOLTAIRE

M

BD DU TEMPLE

3

Musée d'Art et d'Histoire du Judaïsme

Musée de la Chasse

Archives Nationales

Musée Picasso

11

Cirque d'Hiver

Filles du Calvaire

St Sébastien Froissart

5

Oberka

RUE RAMBUTEAU

5

Musée Cognacq-Jay

Musée Carnavalet

6

Chemin Vert

6

Bréguet Sabin

RUE DE RIVOLI

St Paul

PLACE DES VOSGES

Maison de Victor Hugo

4

Maison Européene de la Photographie

Pont Marie

QUAI DE L'HOTEL DE VILLE

RUE SAINT ANTOINE

Bastille

Opéra Bastille

M

Q. DE CELESTINS

ILE ST LOUIS

7

Eglise St-Louis -en-l'Île

BD HENRI IV

Sully Morland

7

12

M

Institut du Monde Arabe

Universités Paris VI Paris VII Pierre et Marie Curie

L

Seine

1 Hotels pp40-64
1 Restaurants pp181-211
1 Cafés & Bars pp212-231

200 m

200 yds

© Copyright Time Out Group 2006

Street Index

Paris RER

Paris Métro

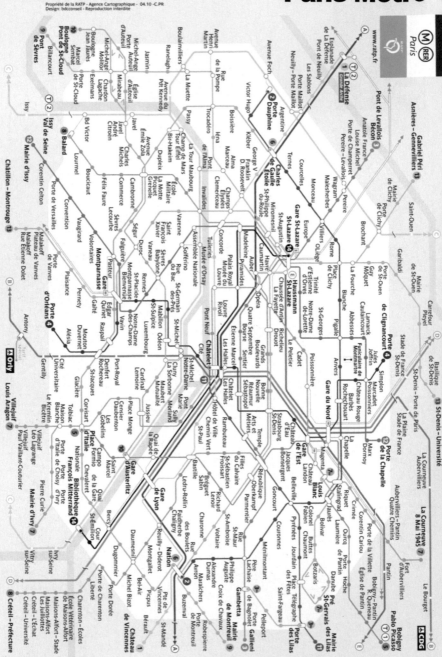

www.ratp.fr